Presented to

_____

By

_____

SOMETHING *to* THINK ABOUT

IN REVERATION

DANIEL YORK

Unless otherwise noted, all Scripture quotations are taken from the Holman Christian Standard Bible ®, Copyright © 1999, 2000, 2002, 2003, 2005 by Holman Bible Publishers. Used by permission. Holman Christian Standard Bible®, Holman CSB® and HCSB® are federally registered trademarks of Holman Bible Publishers. Other Scripture references are from the following sources. The New Testament in Modern English Translated by J.B. Phillips Copyright ©J.B. Phillips 1958, 1960, 1972, 1986, and 1988. The Contemporary English Version (CEV) © 1991, 1992, 1995 by the American Bible Society. Used by permission. The Living Bible (TLB) copyright ©1971 by Tyndale House Publishers, Inc. Wheaton, Illinois 60189. Used by permission; The New International Version (NIV) copyright © 1973, 1978, 1984 by the International Bible Society. Used by permission of Zondervan Publishing House; and the New Living Translation (NLT) copyright 1996. Used by permission of Tyndale House Publishers, Inc. Wheaton, Illinois 60189. All rights reserved.

Photos on pages 178,426 and 434 contributed by Bryan D. York. Copyright © Bryan York. All rights reserved.

Cover photo by Devin Tuning (Devinchy Productions). Cover Design by Will Robertson

York, Daniel L., 1958-
    Something to think about . . . in Reveration/Daniel York
    ISBN : 978-1484981986
    Library of Congress Control Number: 2013919960

    1. Devotional   2. Spiritual Growth   3. Christianity   4. Inspiration

Dedication † † †

This book is dedicated to God. He is the inspiration. He alone deserves all glory. He is worthy to be praised. My life is in His hands.

Thoughts from Reveration readers
the past 13 years . . .

- AMEN!—wow, stoke the fire HOT!—Tom Gillihan, Oregon, president of Sterling Communications Inc.

- I find **Reveration** relevant to the African Culture which has a tradition of teaching truths in parables and stories. I always look forward to receiving it.—Pastor David Joel, Jos, Nigeria

- Keep the **reverations** coming. I get probably 50-100 emails a day, but stop when I see yours, open it immediately, and have a sort of "quiet time" right then and there.—Randal Lovell, businessman, Texas

- **REVERATION** thoughts have always contributed encouragements, guidance, teachings and been a spot-light into my Christian living and the rest of the readers here in Uganda.—Apostle Daniel Mugeni, Uganda

- **Reveration** helped me on several occasions to think in a nonconventional way. I had used several times the devotions for my messages in cell churches.—Pastor Arun Ramakridhnan, Kochi, India

- Your writing is certainly blessed by the Holy Spirit.—Greg Hiebert, professional business coach, Georgia

Ecclesiastes 12:10—The Teacher sought to find delightful sayings and to accurately write words of truth.

Topical Index

Title	Topic	Scripture	Date
Jesus Increased	Goals	Luke 2:52	Jan 1
Cling to the Vine!	Loyalty	1 Ch 29:17,18	2
In the Beginning	Creation	Gen 1:1,27	3
Grandpa's Winnebago	Innocence	Gen 3:2-6	4
Shoddy Gifts	Disfavor	Gen 4:7	5
Heart Grief	Pain	Gen 6:5,6	6
How Do We Gain It?	God's Favor	Gen 6:8	7
The Tower of Babylon	Communication	Gen 11:1,4-9	8
Sarah's Remedy	Compromise	Gen 16:1,2	9
A Heavy One Indeed	Self-Pity	Gen 16:13	10
Be Like Joseph	God's Plan	Gen 37:5-11	11
Two Kinds of Ground	Holy vs Unholy	Exo 3:5	12
Send Someone Else	Inadequacy	Exo 3:11 . . .	13
Walk on Dry Land	Faith	Exo 14:19,20	14
How Numb we Become	Respect for God	Exo 20:7	15
Worship	Worship	Exo 9:13	16
Wearing Patches	Alteration	Lev 16:4	17
Junior Holy Spirits	Meddling	Lev 19:15	18
Green Moss on Gray Shingles	Grudges	Lev 19:18	19
Flying Over Oregon	Land Stewardship	Lev 25:4	20
Fifty	Milestone	Num 8:24-26	21
Never Say to God	Insubordination	Num 16:12-14	22
Our Name	Heritage	Num 27:4	23
Followers	Following God	Deu 1:35,36	24
Teach Them to Your Children	Educating Children	Deu 4:9,10	25
The Secret	Loving God	Deu 6:5	26
The Medal of Honor	Commitment	Deu 30:19,20	27
I Can No Longer Act as Your Leader	Resignation	Deu 31:1,2	28
Their Rifles Barely Worked	Maintenance	Jos 1:8	29
Mel Was Run Over	Assumptions	Jos 9:14,15	30
Readiness	Readiness	Jud 7:5-7	31
Samsonite Baggage	Decision Making	Jud 16:17	Feb 1
Segadores	Ownership	Ruth 2:12	2
Orpah Goes Home	Rationalism	Ruth 4:13-17b	3
Frozen Rain	Hard Hearts	1 Sa 6:6	4
Helpless Rejoicing	Trust through trials	Eph 6:12	5
Holy Cows	Testing God	1 Sa 6:7-9	6
Fatal Attraction	Self-absorption	1 Sa 13:13,14	7

Title	Topic	Scripture	Date
Taking the Easy Way	Expedience	1 Sa 26:8	8
Obed-edom the Gittite	Gaining God's favor	2 Sa 6:11,12	9
Intoxicated with God	Enthusiasm	2 Sa 6:14,15	10
Don't Blame God When Things Go Bad	Attitude	2 Sa 10:12	11
Lagom	Enough	2 Sa 22:31-33	12
Bread and Meat	God the Provider	1 Ki 17:14	13
You can Learn a Lot from a U-Haul	God the Lifter	1 Ki 19:4	14
Lost Reception	Hearing God	1 Ki 22:13	15
Kimmy Caught a Brook Trout	Trusting God	2 Ki 6:5-7	16
Nehushtan	Idols	2 Ki 18:4-6	17
Thanksliving	Gratitude	1 Ch 16:8	18
Honor	Honor	1 Ch 29:12	19
Virtue	Virtue	1 Ch 29:17	20
Matsa	God's Blessing	2 Ch 15:2	21
Defects	Character	2 Ch 20:32,33	22
Joash Goes Bad	Evil Persuasion	2 Ch 24:2	23
Leakage	Pride	2 Ch 26:5	24
Lessons on Timing	Timing	Ezra 1:2,3	25
Joy	Joy	Ezra 6:22	26
Opposition	Overcoming persecution	Neh 4:7,8	27
He Wanted to Help	Conscientious	Neh 5:16,19	28
Obstinate	Stubbornness	Neh 9:29,30	Mar 1
No Funds Arrived	Nothing	Est 6:1-3	2
Premonitions	Worry	Job 3:25,26	3
Three Truths about Plans	Plans	Job 17:11	4
Aber Strays	Obedience	Job 23:11	5
The Power of Knowing	Knowing God	Psa 4:3	6
Make a Poster for God	Expectancy	Psa 5:3	7
By Your Great Mercy	Mercy	Psa 5:7	8
A Song For God's Name	God's Name	Psa 7:17	9
Questions	Asking God	Psa 10:1	10
Life is Full of Rings	God's Presence	Psa 16:11	11
The Rain	Nature's declaration	Psa 19:1-3	12
Cleanse Me	Examination	Psa 19:12-14	13
Shannon	Lost without Christ	Psa 25:14-17	14
Meaning	Life's Value	Psa 27:4	15
Changing My Focus	Prayer	Psa 28:2	16
2.47 a.m.	Protection	Psa 31:1,2	17

Title	Topic	Scripture	Date
Time with the Kids	Delighting in God	Psa 37:4	18
Depressed	Dealing with Depression	Psa 42,43	19
Some Distinctive Shape	Essentials	Psa 45:4	20
In the Midst of Lions	Dealing with Problems	Psa 57:4	21
This Time I Will Praise	Praising God	Psa 57:9,10	22
Finding Balance	Rest	Psa 62:1,2	23
Billy Was Run Over	Dependence	Psa 62:5-8	24
Two Firs and a Cherry	Satisfaction	Psa 63:4,5	25
King of the Hill	Jesus' Death	John 19:17,18	26
Not in Service	Service	Mark 10:45	27
When Darkness Reigns	Good Friday	Luke 23:44-46	28
Cincinnati Connection	Providence	Pro 20:24	29
Peace to You	Peace	John 20:19	30
The Day of Pentecost	Gospel Proclaimed	Acts 2:5,6	31
Mega Memory	Memory	Psa 77:11-13	Apr 1
By Faith or By Reason	Faith over Reason	Psa 94:11	2
I Crashed the Minivan	Sufficiency in Christ	Psa 106:1,2	3
Can I Trust God?	Trust	Psa 112:1,7	4
Benefits of God's Laws	God's Laws	Psa 119	5
Without Bearing	God's Word	Psa. 119:105	6
Eyes Toward the Mountains	God's Help	Psa 121	7
"They Lit Me Up . . ."	Glory to God	1 Co 10:31	8
One Horse Laugh	Laughter	Psa 126:1,2	9
God's Celestial Nurse	Sleep	Psa 127:2	10
No Discard Pile	Individual Worth	Psa 139:14	11
Divine Inspiration	Inspiration	Psa 143:8	12
Using Only His Hands	Victory	Pro 2:7,8	13
Philosophy	Man's Reasoning	Pro 9:10	14
Command	God's Authority	Pro 13:13	15
Imbality	Wrong Priorities	Pro. 13:23	16
Motives	Our Motives	Pro 16:2	17
In the Middle of Nowhere	Trusting God	Pro 16:9	18
Standing in the Immigration Line	Friendship	Pro 17:17	19
The Killing Song	Murder	Eze 7:7	20
The Best Advice	God's Counsel	Pro 19:20	21
Uncaring	Heart for People	Pro 21:13	22
Raiders	Proliferation of Evil	Pro 24:15,16	23
What If	Living for God	Ecc 3:1,4,10-14	24

Title	Topic	Scripture	Date
Cancelled Orders	God's Sovereignty	Ecc 7:13	25
Are People Good?	Reality of Sin	Ecc 7:20	26
Trapped in an Elevator	Hope in Christ	Ecc 9:12	27
Unextinguished Love	Love	SOS 8:6,7	28
Lying	Lying	Isa 5:20	29
Agony	Agony	Isa 13:7,8	30
Confusion and Doubt	Problems with Self	Isa 26:3	May 1
Beyond the Chest	Recognition	Isa 26:12,13	2
Yaga	Burnout	Isa 40:27-31	3
I, the LORD, Speak Truthfully	Truth	Isa 45:18-19	4
Canine Purgatory	Handling Injustice	Isa 53:7	5
Unwind	Rest	Isa 57:2	6
Losing My Agenda	Prayer	Jer 10:23	7
Coram Deo	Living for God	Jer 17:16	8
The Veneer of Tyranny	Poor Leadership	Jer 30:21	9
Worried About . . .	Worry	Jer 38:17-20	10
911 Calls	Scrutiny	Lam 3:40	11
Heartless	Unloving	Lam 4:3,4	12
Awakening	Spiritual Awareness	Dan 2:1	13
Verdict	Truth Assurance	Dan 4:17	14
A Man to Emulate	Role Model	Dan 6:10	15
Precious	God's Preciousness	Dan 9:23	16
Rafting the Deschutes	Safety	Hos 2:18	17
Sowing	Outcomes	Hos 10:12	18
Unrecognized	Neglecting God	Hos 11:3,4	19
Dreams	God-Given Vision	Joel 2:28,32a	20
Marriage—Conflict Resolution	Unity in Marriage	Amos 3:3	21
Misunderstanding God	Judging God	Oba 15	22
Don't Run Away	Disobeying God	Jon 3:1,2	23
Concerns about Earnestness	Proper Priorities	Jon 3:8	24
Pop Can Tabs	Longsuffering	Jer 15:15	25
The Ultimate Business Card	God's Credentials	Nah 1:7	26
Idolatry	Idolatry	Hab 2:18,19	27
Silence	Silence	Zep 3:17	28
Gentleness	Gentleness	Zec 9:9	29
Nepes	Soul	Zec 12:1	30
Stagnation	Spiritual Lethargy	Mal 1:10	31
Loving the Wrong Thing	Misplaced Values	Mal 2:1,2	Jun 1

Title	Topic	Scripture	Date
Ten Principles for Effective Training	Training	Mat 4:19	2
Affinity is not Easy	Loving People	Mat 5:43,44	3
Rock or Sand	Kingdom of Heaven	Mat 7:21	4
Be Made Clean	Healing	Mat 8:2,3	5
Partnership and the Trinity	Triune Partnership	Mat 9:37,38	6
Accessible	Finding God	Mat 11:28	7
Parables	Communicating Truth	Mat 13:34,35	8
Life Saver	Jesus the Savior	Mat 14:29,30	9
The Value Pipe	Values	Mat 16:26	10
Personal Values	Values	1 Ti 4:7,8	11
The Power of Agreement	Agreement	Mat 18:19	12
Our Cause or His Cause	Christ First	Mat 19:13,14	13
Cheap Thrills	Misplaced Priorities	Mat 21:8,9	14
Beware of Posing	Appearance	Mat 23:1-6,12	15
Rule-Obsessed	Legalism	Mat 23:13	16
Broken Neck	Rescue	2 Co 4:7,16,17	17
Ironman	Jesus	Mat 26:67-68	18
Let's Take Our Shoes Off	Not Defensive	Mat 27:12-14	19
Fatherhood	Fathers	1 Th 2:11,12	20
Rising Ire	Anger	Mark 3:4,5	21
Don't You Ever . . . !	Controllers	Mark 10:42-45	22
His Name is John	Obedience	Luke 1:59-63	23
Otherworldly	Witnesses	Luke 2:13,14	24
Be quiet and come out of him	Christ's Authority	Luke 4:36	25
Authenticate	Verifying Legitimacy	Luke 5:18,19	26
Choosing Your Team	Selection	Luke 6:13	27
When it is Appropriate	Judging	Luke 6:36,37	28
Lordship	Headship of Christ	Luke 6:46	29
Centurion	Role Model	Luke 7:1-10	30
She's a Sinner!	Callousness	Luke 7:39	Jul 1
We're Going to Die!	Trust	Luke 8:24,25	2
Plowing	Obedience	Luke 9:61,62	3
Independence	Righteous Nation	Psa 33:12,22	4
Valuable	God's Love for Us	Luke 12:24	5
Paganism	Truth	Luke 12:29-31	6
Surrender	Christians	Luke 14:33	7
Blind Spots	Awareness	Luke 18:41	8

Title	Topic	Scripture	Date
Nirvana	Salvation	John 1:4,5	9
Wilderness and Civilization	Rejuvenated	John 1:11	10
Truth	Truth	John 1:14	11
More Truth	Truth	2 John 1-4	12
New Birth	Salvation	John 3:3,4	13
Misplaced Principles	Principles	John 3:17	14
Assimilation	Absorbing Truth	John 4:34	15
"You Give Them Something to Eat"	Responsibility	John 6:5-7	16
If God Chooses	Election	John 6:37,44	17
Emancipated	Parable	John 8:36	18
Offended	Rejecting Christ	John 9:32-34	19
Labels	False Assumptions	John 10:4,14	20
Branches of the Vine	Connected to Christ	John 15:5	21
Tundra	Valley Life	John 18:1	22
How to Share Your Testimony	Evangelism	John 19:35	23
Empowered	Evangelism	Acts 1:8	24
Obscurity	Obscurity	Acts 1:26	25
The Greatest Gift	Baptism of the Holy Spirit	Acts 2:38	26
Lillian	Fellowship	Acts 2:46,47	27
Christianity	Authenticity	Acts 3:6	28
Uneducated Men	Ordinary	Acts 4:13	29
We Need a Lift!	Help from God	Acts 4:31	30
Two Types of Martyrs	Martyrs	Acts 7:55,56	31
Baptism	Baptism	Acts 8:36	Aug 1
Noticed	Recognition	Acts 10:4	2
Listening	Listening to God	Acts 10:33	3
Faith Is	Importance of Faith	Acts 11:21	4
Commissioned	Missionary Call	Acts 13:2,3	5
Fatwood	Evangelism	Acts 13:48	6
The Labor of Thinking	Thinking	Acts 17:2,3	7
If I Grow My Hair Long	Relevance	Acts 17:23	8
17 Months of Double House Payments	Uncertainty	Acts 18:9-11	9
Digging Deeper	Bible Study	Acts 18:24-28	10
Pastors	Pastors	Acts 20:28	11
Playing the One Stringed Violin	Persevering	Acts 27:34	12
Potholes	Persevering	Acts 28:19,20	13

Title	Topic	Scripture	Date
Finely Evolved Creatures?	Design	Rom 1:20	14
No Plaque or Ceremony	Ingratitude	Rom 1:21,22	15
Justification	Justification	Rom 3:21-24	16
Craig is Blind	Dignity	Rom 5:1,2	17
Fruit Trees	Living in the Son	Rom 5:3-5	18
Messy Desk	Intentions	Rom 7:15,18	19
The Deity of Jesus	Jesus' Deity	Rom 8:9	20
Predestination	Predestination	Rom 8:29,30	21
When Pain Seems Intolerable	Anguish	Rom 9:1,2	22
The Antidote to Busyness	Availability	Rom 12:1	23
We Have Different Gifts	Spiritual Gifts	Rom 12:6	24
They Stood Up	Respect	Rom 13:7	25
Bimbo	Infidelity	Rom 13:13,14	26
A Ship Called *Me*	Lordship	Rom 14:8	27
Strength As One	Accountability	Rom 14:11,12	28
Nemesis	Satan	Rom 16:20	29
Signs and Wisdom	Focus	1 Co 1:22,23	30
Take Off the Training Wheels	Reliance	1 Co 2:1,2	31
Labor Day	Work	1 Co 3:12-15	Sep 1
Preoccupation	Thought Life	1 Co 3:16,17	2
None of These Rights	Letting Go of Our Rights	1 Co 9:15	3
Watch Out for Sneaker Waves	Warnings	1 Co 10:6-12	4
Example is Leadership	Our Example	1 Co 11:1	5
Each of You are a Part	Body of Christ	1 Co 12:25-27	6
Orderly	Orderly	1 Co 14:40	7
Broken Fellowship	Leaving Fellowship	2 Co 1:3-5	8
A System of Moral Principles	Ethics	2 Co 1:12	9
Mashach	Anointing	2 Co 1:21,22	10
Getting the Boot	Competence	2 Co 2:15,16	11
On the Day After	Introspection	Rom 8:35	12
Mud, Mud, Mud	Spiritual Growth	2 Co 4:16,17	13
Kooley's Awakening	Spiritual Newness	2 Co 5:17	14
Ministry of Reconciliation	Reconciliation	2 Co 5:18	15
We Are Ambassadors	Ambassadors	2 Co 5:20	16
The Battle of Antietam	Indecisiveness	Hag 1:7	17

Title	Topic	Scripture	Date
Convent Tunnels	Reputation	2 Co 6:3	18
Unequal	Unequally Yoked	2 Co 6:14-	19
Heartmissing	Longing	2 Co 7:6,7	20
He Made Me Hit Him	Repentance	2 Co 7:10	21
Don't Put Ashes in Cardboard Boxes	Battles	2 Co 10:4b,5	22
Unashamed Tears	Brokenness	2 Co 11:26-30	23
Bryan the Lion	Weakness	2 Co 12:9	24
Pretermit	Abandonment	2 Co 12:15	25
By God's Power	Relinquishing Control	2 Co 13:4	26
Jerry Shares on Restoration	Restoration	2 Co 13:11	27
Understanding Truth	What is Genuine	Gal 1:8,9	28
I No Longer Live	Beyond Temperament	Gal 2:19,20	29
God's Promises	Covenants	Gal 3:14	30
How Can I Know For Sure?	Assurance of Salvation	Gal 5:4,5	Oct 1
Noticed or Unnoticed	Modeling Christ	Gal 6:7-10	2
She Carries Julie	God's Love for Us	Eph 1:4,5	3
Fulfillment	Finding God's Plan	Eph 1:9,10	4
God's Power	Divine Power	Eph 1:18-21	5
Identity Crisis	The Church	Eph 1:22,23	6
Children Under Wrath	God's Anger	Eph 2:3	7
Circulation	Fellowship	Eph 2:19-21	8
Capacity	Underestimating God	Eph 3:20,21	9
Call of God	Calling—Jerry	Eph 4:1-3	10
The Lost Art of Training	Spiritual Training	Eph 4:11-13	11
Mote Doesn't Care	Callous	Eph 4:17-19	12
Cynics	Cynicism	Eph 4:20-24	13
Build Them Up	Affirmation	Eph 4:29	14
Imitation	God-like	Eph 5:1,2	15
Light	Testimonies	Eph 5:8-10	16
Making Music to the Lord	Relationship	Eph 5:19	17
Full Canteens	True Christians	Php 1:9-11	18
Persecuted Saints	Suffering Saints	Php 1:29-2:4	19
Perspective	Spiritual Eyes	Php 3:8,9	20
Memories	Living in the Past	Php 3:12-14	21
Heaven	Heaven	Php 3:20,21	22

Title	Topic	Scripture	Date
The Message of Hope	Gospel	Col 1:5b,6	23
The Cross	The Cross	Col 1:19,20	24
Spiritual Filters	Discernment	Col. 1:28,29	25
Continue to Live in Him	Continuing in Christ	Col 2:6,7	26
Succulents	Indwelt	Col 2:9,10	27
Distractions	Christ-Centered	Col 3:1,2	28
Fundamentals	Essential Priorities	Col 3:17	29
Devoted to Prayer	Prayer	Col 4:2	30
Teaming Up in Cameroon	Teamwork	Col 4:7-14	31
Gentle Among You	Nurturing	1 Th 2:6,7,11	Nov 1
Two Miles Just to Get Water	Persecution	1 Th 3:4	2
Hank Acephalous	Sanctification	1 Th 4:3,7	3
Bettis Hates God	Free Will	2 Th 2:`10b	4
Down the Mountain	Belief in Christ	2 Th 2:13	5
Tell a Man He is Brave	Encouragement	2 Th 2:16,7	6
Understanding God's Love	God's Love	2 Th 3:5	7
Deep Inside I Knew	Conscience	1 Ti.1:5	8
God's Godness	God's Attributes	1 Ti.1:17	9
Discharged in Disgrace	Reputation	1 Ti 3:13; 4:12	10
Reaching the Next Generation	Youth	1 Ti 4:12	11
Progress	Spiritual Growth	1 Ti 4:14,15	12
Wine	Health	1 Ti 5:23	13
Apprenticeship	Training	1 Ti 6:11,12	14
Build Me a Son!	Prayer	2 Ti 1:3	15
This Morning	Gratitude	2 Ti 1:8-10	16
Preserving Context	Truth in Context	2 Ti 2:15	17
Robbed of Gold	Judging	2 Ti 4:8	18
They Deny Him	Self-centeredness	Tit 1:16	19
Avoiding Frostbite	Discipline	Tit 2:11-13	20
Consider God	Leadership	Phi 8-10	21
Drifting	Spiritual Drift	Heb 2:1	22
Miracles	Supernatural Work	Heb 2:4	23
Like Her Mother	Hardness	Heb 3:7,8a,12	24
The Right Food	Scripture Feeding	Heb 5:13,14	25
Vigilant	Spiritual Awareness	Amos 6:1	26
After Waiting Patiently	Patience	Heb 6:11,12,15	27
Stuck on the Tarmac	Assurance	Heb 10:21-23	28
Tenacity	Tenacity	Heb 10:34,35	29
Living with PTSD	Faith	Heb 11:37-40	30

Scripture Abbreviations

Books of the Bible

Genesis	Gen	Matthew	Mat
Exodus	Exo	Romans	Rom
Leviticus	Lev	1 Corinthians	1 Co
Numbers	Num	2 Corinthians	2 Co
Deuteronomy	Deu	Galatians	Gal
Joshua	Jos	Ephesians	Eph
Judges	Jud	Philippians	Php
1 Samuel	1 Sa	Colossians	Col
2 Samuel	2 Sa	1 Thessalonians	1 Th
1 Kings	1 Ki	2 Thessalonians	2 Th
2 Kings	2 Ki	1 Timothy	1 Ti
1 Chronicles	1 Ch	2 Timothy	2 Ti
2 Chronicles	2 Ch	Titus	Tit
Nehemiah	Neh	Philemon	Phi
Esther	Est	Hebrews	Heb
Psalms	Psa	James	Jam
Proverbs	Pro	1 Peter	1 Pe
Ecclesiastes	Ecc	2 Peter	2 Pe
Song of Songs	SoS	1 John	1 Jn
Isaiah	Isa	2 John	2 Jn
Jeremiah	Jer	3 John	3 Jn
Ezekiel	Eze	Revelation	Rev
Daniel	Dan		
Hosea	Hos		
Obadiah	Oba		
Jonah	Jon		
Micah	Mic		
Nahum	Nah		
Habakkuk	Hab		
Zephaniah	Zep		
Haggai	Hag		
Zechariah	Zec		
Malachi	Mal		

Translations of the Bible

Holman CSB	
Contemporary English Version	(CEV)
Living Bible	(TLB)
New International Version	(NIV)
New Living Translation	(NLT)
Phillips Translation	(PT)

Before You Begin . . .

Many years ago at sunset, I stood on a hill in remote Fort Hunter Liggett, California. My friend Mark Armstrong knows this place well. Often growing up, he hunted here with his father.   The sky was a hue of deep blue I had never seen before, with swashes of red and orange blazoned across wispy clouds that feathered the heavens. I literally stood transfixed. *God, You are an awesome Painter*!

This book is meant to take you to some distant hill where you can read in silence and find your heart and mind motivated to know more deeply the Painter. It is not meant to be read quickly but rather savored. Too much of life is cheapened by mindless rush.

During the 1990's I read *My Utmost For His Highest* by Oswald Chambers.[1] So profoundly did he exercise my mind and heart that I began to capture quotes from all his works and type them into my computer. In 1997, I started writing topically about things that touched my spirit. Focusing on Scripture meditations and pulling quotes from Chambers (and later other authors and friends) to accent my own writing, I emailed friends devotionals called *Reverations*. *Reveration* is a word I coined that means *reverent adoration* and ties in with my life theme—reverence for God.   I mostly utilize the *Holman Christian Standard Bible* (CSB) because I appreciate the accuracy of this translation and the fact that pronouns referring to God are capitalized (something I believe every translation ought to do).

My *writing guidelines* are simple. I don't write unless I feel inspired so as not to type shallow messages. I typically spend hours on each new piece carefully constructing the words and content so as to be fresh and creative. I try to avoid idioms so the meaning is clear in any place where English is spoken.   Finally, so as to protect myself from a personal agenda, I will not write a devotional targeted to a particular person.

Before I hit the send button, launching a new *reveration* across the internet, I reread the content, sometimes sending it to wise friends to further validate accuracy. Then I pray that it will be used by the Lord for His glory in the lives of His children just as He used Chamber's works to help me in my own life.

Every book of the Bible is represented, mostly in order, so that you can work through reading the Bible.   Occasionally, I interrupted the order for holidays, to maintain a theme, or to commemorate certain days as mentioned in the content of the devotional. Page 477 provides my own Bible-marking code. Finally, a web version will be posted on our web site, www.firstcause.org so that anyone can access and read a daily devotional if the book is not accessible. If you would like to learn more about our First Cause ministry, see page 475.

As you read this devotional, my prayer is that Paul's words to the Ephesians in chapter one, verses 16-19 will be true for you.

I thank God continually for you and I never give up praying for you; and this is my prayer. That God, the God of our Lord Jesus Christ and the all-glorious Father, will give you spiritual wisdom and the insight to know more of Him: that you may receive that inner illumination of the spirit which will make you realise how great is the hope to which He is calling you—the magnificence and splendour of the inheritance promised to Christians—and how tremendous is the power available to us who believe in God. (Phillips Translation)

Jesus Increased

Luke 2:52—And Jesus increased in wisdom and stature, and in favor with God and with people.

Matthew 4:23 clearly depicts Jesus' three-fold ministry on earth:
1. *"Jesus was going all over Galilee, teaching in their synagogues,"*
2. *"preaching the good news of the kingdom,"*
3. *"healing every disease and sickness among the people."*

Jesus taught us, *"All things have been entrusted to Me by My Father"* (Mat. 11:27). Even when Pharisees came to Jesus warning Him to leave because King Herod wanted to kill Him, He replied in Luke 13:32: *"Go tell that fox, 'Look! I'm driving out demons and performing healings today and tomorrow, and on the third day I will complete My work"* (reach my goal—NIV). Facing a gruesome death, He still submitted His life under His Father's authority. *"Going a little farther, He fell facedown and prayed, 'My Father! If it is possible, let this cup pass from Me. Yet not as I will, but as You will'"* (Mat. 26:39).

I admire people that are goal-oriented. Those who act as if goal setting is some presumptuous folly perplex me. Those who are too lazy to even make the effort to formulate goals sadden me. Clearly, Jesus went about heaven's business with goals in mind. As Randy Alcorn writes in *Heaven*, "To be Heaven-oriented is to be goal-oriented in the best sense."

When the saints wake up to the task of denying self (Luke 9:23) so as to be wholly committed to fulfilling God's plan, the earth will glow from the magnificent wattage! Lest we think we are anywhere close to this happening now, read what George Barna's team discovered and reported in his book *Growing True Disciples*:

. . . most born-again adults are limited in their ability to grow spiritually because they have failed to set any goals for their spiritual development, failed to develop standards against which to measure their growth, or failed to establish procedures for being held accountable for their growth.

Not one of the adults we interviewed said that their goal in life was to be a committed follower of Jesus Christ or to make disciples.

. . . six out of ten believers have no sense of what they want to achieve or become, and roughly two out of ten have only the vaguest idea . . . That leaves only two out of ten believers who are serious about their spiritual development and have defined rather specific goals.[2]

When I was a senior in high school, my dad taught me how to set short, medium and long-range goals. We prayed over those goals while he helped me understand key principles in setting objectives. Today we continue to refine the process.
1. Goals must be realistic, measurable and attainable.

2.   I may set goals but it is the Lord who determines my steps (Pro. 16:9).

3.   My heart and mind must submit to the leading of the Holy Spirit. *"For My thoughts are not your thoughts, and your ways are not My ways"* (Isa. 55:8).

4.   Luke 2:52 is a superb guide for setting goals. Every year I use this model to set goals in four areas. Amazingly, *every* goal I set at the age of eighteen, God fulfilled in my life! Today at the young age of 50, I select a key Bible passage for the year ahead. Next, I carefully review the past year. Finally, prayerfully, I set goals for the year ahead. Jesus set the example and calls us to follow after Him. So let's get after it! We find true meaning and value in life when we live so as to honor God! Great goals accomplished are rewarding! No goals are a sure formula for discouragement and defeated living. Let's make it our careful aim to please our Father by setting goals that honor Him! Let's aspire in His grace and thrive in His graciousness! Something to think about . . . in reveration!

Example of how I set goals according to the Luke 2:52 format:

WORSHIP (Favor with God)

1.   Read through the Bible this year in the Holman translation focusing on the theme of blessing.

2.   Increase time in prayer; (one prayer walk/week); 3 days praying with key friends.

WISDOM

3.   Write 12 songs; work on recording a Christmas CD

4.   Weekly write/send out one Reveration

SOCIAL (Favor with Man)

5.   Family: wisely lead and invest quality time with family (1 family vacation; 12 dates w/ Kathleen; help Bryan and Mark land jobs

6.   Conduct two international trips: Latin America and Nigeria/Kenya

PHYSICAL

7.   Physical Fitness: exercise min. of 3x/week, score 300 on both APFTs

8.   Rest: in bed by 11:00 p.m.

Inspiration   † † †

The greatest tragedy in life is not in failing to get what you go after. The greatest tragedy in life is getting it and finding out it wasn't worth the trouble.—Jeanette Cliff George, Author and founder and Artistic Director of the A.D. Players

Cling to the Vine!

The beginning of the year is a time when people in our society reflect. For many, new resolutions and goals are forged on the gold-embossed pages of a new journal. Yet as the past is closed for the door of tomorrow a timeless God is not concerned with another year. He asks a simple question—are we loyal to Him?

Beware of setting goals over the wrong things! If we would ask God what He sees as a hindrance to our loyalty, we might be surprised by His answer. The call of loyalty begins with Jesus' advice, *"I am the vine; you are the branches. The one who remains in Me and I in him produces much fruit, because you can do nothing without Me"* (John 15:5). What branches do we nourish that hamper our loyalty to our Father in heaven?

Reputation—meaningless if it trumps obeying the voice of the Holy Spirit.
Work—hazardous if God does not come first.
Marriage or *friendship*—misguided if it exceeds my love for my Savior.
Education—foolishness if God is disdained.
Pleasure—cancerous if it moves Christ away from the throne of my heart.
Possessions—a trap if they spoil my allegiance to the King of Kings.
Emotions—selfish and deceitful whenever they ignore the Lord.
Position—a stumbling block of pride if Almighty God is not honored.
Health—a disease if He is absent.

1 Chronicles 29:17, 18—I know, my God, that You test the heart and that You are pleased with uprightness. I have willingly given all these things with an upright heart, and now I have seen Your people who are present here giving joyfully and willingly to You. LORD God of Abraham, Isaac, and Israel, our ancestors, keep this desire forever in the thoughts of the hearts of Your people, and confirm their hearts toward You.

Oswald Chambers wrote in *My Utmost For His Highest*, "The greatest competitor of devotion to Jesus is service for Him." Do you want to know God? Then courageously pick up the axe of integrity and sever every competing branch that weighs down your heart and keeps you from being nourished by Jesus. Loyalty is not for the faint of heart. If it is too hard to swing the blade, cry out to your Father. Give Him permission to cut. Will it be painful? Absolutely. Will it seem unfair? Most likely. When does it *not* hurt to lose what we don't want to let go of to gain what we could never see? The foundation of loyalty is trust. What better way to begin a year than by believing that the God who made us, is worth following wholeheartedly!

In the Beginning

If someone offered you a house with no foundation, would you take it? I suppose if you lived somewhere where no storms or catastrophes occurred that would be okay. But, since no place on earth is trouble-proof, it is exceedingly wise to build upon a strong foundation. Now imagine sharing that Jesus is the Savior with someone who has never heard the gospel. Jesus' mission prophesied in Isaiah 42 was to fulfill God's promise to rescue people, to be a light to open blind eyes. Jesus told His disciples in Mark 16:15 that the whole creation should hear the good news about Him. Too often, this news only concerns Jesus coming to earth, living a sinless life and dying on the cross to save us. Left out is the incredible part of why He came in the first place. If we don't understand the whole reason for Jesus coming, we have a foundationless house! We need to take people back to the beginning . . .

Genesis 1:1,27—In the beginning God created the heavens and the earth . . . So God created man in His own image; He created him in the image of God; He created them male and female.

God made the earth to be inhabited (Isa. 45:18) but creation is more than an incredible formation chronicle. It is *our* love story! Yes, God made us in His image to have as friends for an eternal partnership. King David wrote in Psalm 139:13, *"For it was You who created my inward parts; You knit me together in my mother's womb."* God lovingly fashioned us—this is why we possess unique DNA, fingerprints, voices, eyes and souls. We are not products of chance we are people of choice! As Isaiah reveals, we are created for God's glory (Isa. 43:7)! Amos teaches us that God even reveals His thoughts to us (Amos 4:13). And as the Apostle Paul helps the Ephesians understand (2:10), we were created with a purpose! *"For we are His creation—created in Christ Jesus for good works, which God prepared ahead of time so that we should walk in them."*

The gospel begins in Genesis not in Matthew! Everything created by God is good (1 Ti. 4:4). Creation explains why we are here and establishes our worth. But the Bible's first book also reveals the shocking account of what went wrong. Adam and Eve disobeyed God and by so doing transmitted evil to every human descendant. Sin deems us unworthy. Jesus came because God created us for good not evil, to restore our worth! As we learn in Colossians 1:15,16, Jesus was engaged with us from our inception. By Him we exist! His love for us is revealed by the sacrifice He made to untaint and justify us before God (the *Encarta World English Dictionary* defines justify as "to free somebody from sinfulness through faith in Jesus Christ or by the grace of Jesus Christ").

The why of our salvation is answered in the beginning. Understanding creation is paramount as Paul demonstrated standing in the middle of the Areopagus before the Athenians:

From one man He has made every nation of men to live all over the earth and has determined their appointed times and the boundaries of where they live, so that they might seek God, and perhaps they might reach out and find Him, though he is not far from each one of us. For in Him we live and move and exist, as even some of your own poets have said, "For we are also His offspring" (Acts 17:26-28).

We are better disciples when we grasp the significance of our value before the Creator. You see it was in the very beginning that God gave us something to think about . . . in reveration!

Grandpa's Winnebago

My parents were missionaries which meant that we didn't often see members of our extended family. One year we took a trip to Washington and stayed with Grandma and Grandpa Erickson. My cousins were there and we spent great time playing together. Loren and I, as the oldest, got to stay in Grandpa's Winnebago parked just outside their home. One night Loren decided to teach me a game I'd never played—strip poker.

For every hand you lose in strip poker, you shed one item of clothing. Being a competitive child and certain that I would win, I agreed to Loren's terms. The loser had to run around the motor home in the buff. The game proceeded and my cards consistently were inferior to his. Loren assured me my luck would change. But as it turned out, he won several straight hands. I protested there was no way I was taking my underwear off—what if someone saw me! But a boy's word was a solemn thing. I ran my obligatory lap at impressive speed and pounced on the door to leap inside only to discover it was locked. While I viciously threatened I'm sure to kill him, Loren laughed in triumph at my predicament. I guess sympathy finally won over for he unlocked the door and I found refuge under the covers just as Grandma came out to investigate the commotion. Later I found out he was hiding aces and had cheated. Humiliation has a marvelous way of exposing naïve notions.

Genesis 3:2-6—The woman said to the serpent, "We may eat the fruit from the trees in the garden. But about the fruit of the tree in the middle of the garden, God said, 'You must not eat it or touch it, or you will die."

"No! You will not die," the serpent said to the woman. "In fact, God knows that when you eat it your eyes will be opened and you will be like God, knowing good and evil."

Then the woman saw that the tree was good for food and delightful to look at, and that it was desirable for obtaining wisdom. So she took some of its fruit and ate it; she also gave some to her husband, who was with her, and he ate it.

What caused Eve and Adam to sin was not some sophisticated plot to become godlike. They fell to a crafty devil because they took their eyes off God's word and fixed it upon a forbidden fruit. The danger of innocence is that we think we don't need God. Eve should have brought the serpent's slick line under the judgment of her Maker. We are always at risk if we trust our own reasoning and fashion an intended outcome oblivious to the power of evil. Perhaps true innocence should be thought of as in-no-sense. In no sense do we set aside God's Word for any reason.

The realization of nakedness is the understanding that I missed God's will because I let go of His wise words. It's not a good thing to be bare on the outside of a locked Winnebago; even worse to be outside of God's will!

Shoddy Gifts

How it started I don't know. Perhaps in the course of conversation, God gave the idea to Adam's family. Nothing is stated in Genesis 1-3 about God asking anyone to bring Him offerings. Yet, for some reason, Cain brought to the Lord some of the fruit of his land. His brother, Able, presented fat portions from the firstborn of his flock. *"God looked with favor on Abel and his offering, but on Cain and his offering he did not look with favor"* (Gen. 4:4b). Cain got angry. His face revealed his poor attitude. God asked him why he was upset and then gave him profound advice.

Genesis 4:7—If you do right, won't you be accepted? But if you do not do right, sin is crouching at the door. Its desire is for you, but you must master it.

Many wonder why God seems unfavorable towards them. They claim allegiance to Him yet His blessing falls on someone else. The implication is that He is fickle and resentment simmers. Cain brought God an offering. *Hmmm*—that seems like a nice thing to do. So, why was God unimpressed? Evidently, something was not right. Perhaps he grabbed fruit (any ol' fruit) from plants he tended and plopped them before the Lord—a simple action that took little time or effort. Something about his attitude or action did not please God. In contrast, his brother's offering required preparation and sacrifice. Able gave the best of what he had.

Is it possible that we do not have God's favor because we offer Him shoddy gifts? Do we give Him *our* time or resources only when it is convenient and even then grudgingly? Do we compare ourselves with others and work from a self-centered foundation? Just because we are not sinning does not mean we earn God's favor. One can live in compliance with the law and not hunger for God. One can be giving and yet possess a hard heart. We can be Christians in name but have little heart for Christ. If our motives are wrong is it any surprise that God's favor is absent! Cain couldn't find a satisfying relationship with his Father. He let bitterness and a jealous spirit lead to murder and lying. It all started with a substandard offering.

Brother Lawrence & Frank Laubach wrote in *Practicing His Presence*, "When the soul is at rest in God it does not follow its usual selfish behavior; its love is only for God."[3] The Apostle Paul wrote, *"Therefore, brothers, by the mercies of God, I urge you to present your bodies as a living sacrifice, holy and pleasing to God; this is your spiritual worship"* (Rom. 12:1). Do you long for God's favor? Then give Him your heart. Stop holding back—let go of convenience and embrace the cross. You'll find love waiting outside an empty tomb.

Heart Grief

Genesis 6:5,6—When the LORD saw that man's wickedness was widespread on the earth and that every scheme his mind thought of was nothing but evil all the time, the LORD regretted that He had made man on the earth, and He was grieved in His heart.

There is an old Hungarian proverb, "Adam ate the apple and our teeth still ache." When man corrupted God's plan the consequences were staggering. A fruitful planet became a fallen world where evil, disaster and death leave no one untouched.

The first one to experience pain was God. Lucifer rebelled in heaven and that must have hurt deeply. Man followed suit and we see the effect on God in the meditation above. Philip Yancey noted, "Suffering can never ultimately be meaningless, because God Himself has shared it."[4]

Until God establishes a new heaven and a new earth pain will continue to squeeze us to levels of hurt that even a pill-preoccupied culture cannot escape. So we must embrace and understand it. When an earthquake and a giant tsunami wave kill and destroy at staggering proportions there are key lessons we should remember that would help us and those more deeply suffering.

● *Do not run from pain.* John Powell noted, "When I enter into my pain rather than run from it, I will find at the center of my pain an amazing insight."[5] Grief is real and grieving is important. Let those who have lost linger and learn in deprivation. To hide and run is only to put off suffering that in later days will be more difficult to handle. What those suffering need is comfort not escape. Philip Yancey wrote in *Where Is God When It Hurts*, "If I ever wonder about the appropriate 'spiritual' response to pain and suffering, I can note how Jesus responded to His own: with fear and trembling, with loud cries and tears."

● *Pain is not abated by platitudes.* To push spiritual principles upon a hurting person, to say, "Cheer up things will get better" or, "God must have a plan in this" or "It *could* have been worse . . ." is like kicking a lame man. Those awash in hurting need a preserver not counsel. Silence and caring hands surpass a running mouth.

● *Pain doesn't just go away and there is nothing spiritual about pretending to ignore it.* It is over two decades since the death of my best friend and 248 fellow soldiers. I *still* feel the loss. Arthur Hallam once said, "Pain is the deepest thing we have in our nature." Ah, but is it? Does not love run deeper! However, pain abides and when we accept that we find the steps that lead to a greater love. And while pain on earth is enduring some day when God gives us new bodies the Bible promises, *"He will wipe away every tear from their eyes. Death will exist no longer; grief, crying, and pain will exist no longer, because the previous things have passed away"* (Revelation 21:4).

● *Pain is an opportunity to rouse those who are lost to a hope that is eternal.* C.S. Lewis, a philosopher acquainted with grief wrote, "God whispers to us in our pleasures, speaks in our conscience, but shouts in our pains: it is His megaphone to rouse a deaf world."[6] Nothing happens by accident before a sovereign Lord.

● *Pain leads to a choice.* The Gospel is meant to lift up! So, we carefully convey it under the leading of the Holy Spirit. In time the anguished woman may ask, "What is the meaning of life? Why did this disaster happen? How do I fill this empty void that gnaws at my soul and yearns to be filled?" If we have been faithful in compassion, good listeners and authentic lovers, God may give us the privilege of sharing with her and countless others the message of His love through Jesus. The question is, are we willing to go and be lights where darkness dwells? God does not hold us accountable for explaining tragedy but we will give account for what we did or did not do with our hope in Christ—herein is the paradox of the wave.

Inspiration † † †

When pain is to be borne, a little courage helps more than much knowledge, a little human sympathy more than much courage, and the least tincture of the love of God more than all.—C. S. Lewis, Irish writer and scholar, (1898-1963) in *The Problem With Pain*

Pleasures seldom awaken people to their need for God; pain often does.—Pastor John Piper in *In Our Joy*

How Do We Gain It?

Genesis 6:8—Noah, however, found favor in the eyes of the LORD.

Seeking favor is something we all understand. Those of us who work want to be well regarded by our boss or supervisor. Those of us who are children want the approval of our parents. Those of us with relationships want the support of our spouse, friends or peers. Everyone who cares desires favor. And the greatest favor we can obtain is from God. The question is how do we gain it?

What does God feel when He looks down on the world today? What thoughts run through His all-knowing mind? Is the condition of our world anything like what was described long ago in Gen. 6:5,6? *"When the LORD saw that man's wickedness was widespread on the earth and that every scheme his mind thought of was nothing but evil all the time, the LORD regretted that He had made man on the earth, and He was grieved in His heart."*

Sinful people grieve God's heart. Therefore, the way to find His approval must begin with personal examination—am I engaged in sin? If I am, there is no way I will please Him. *"These are the family records of Noah. Noah was a righteous man, blameless among his contemporaries; Noah walked with God."* In Gen. 6:9, we glean three qualities about Noah that set him apart from the people of his era. First, he was a moral man. Second, he was blameless among the people of his time. His reputation was intact; there was no fault to be found in his character, attitude or conduct. Third, he walked with God. Essentially, he made a conscious decision to regularly communicate with Him, to follow His laws and do what pleased Him. God was Noah's best friend.

The sons of Korah sang, *"For the LORD God is a sun and shield. The LORD gives grace and glory; He does not withhold the good from those who live with integrity"* (Psa. 84:11). Moses told God in Exodus 33:13, *"Now if I have indeed found favor in Your sight, please teach me Your ways, and I will know You and find favor in Your sight. Now consider that this nation is Your people."*

Like a cup of hot chocolate on a cold winter day, is the affirming favor of our heavenly Father. Like the cool refreshing taste of water in a parched desert is the love He gives to those who please Him. Live to make Him proud; be like Noah and savor His favor.

Inspiration † † †

May He who holds in His hands the destinies of nations, make you worthy of the favors He has bestowed, and enable you, with pure hearts and hands and sleepless vigilance, to guard and defend to the end of time the great charge He has committed to your keeping.—President Andrew Jackson, 7th president of the United States (1767-1845)

The Tower of Babylon

Genesis 11:1,4-9—At one time the whole earth had the same language and vocabulary . . . And they said, "Come, let us build ourselves a city and a tower with its top in the sky. Let us make a name for ourselves; otherwise, we will be scattered over the face of the whole earth." Then the LORD came down to look over the city and the tower that the men were building. The LORD said, "If, as one people all having the same language, they have begun to do this, then nothing they plan to do will be impossible for them. Come, let Us go down there and confuse their language so that they will not understand one another's speech." So the LORD scattered them from there over the face of the whole earth, and they stopped building the city. Therefore its name is called Babylon, for there the LORD confused the language of the whole earth, and from there the LORD scattered them over the face of the whole earth.

God's intervention with people at the Tower of Babel explains why people speak so many different languages. It is an account of man's rebellious spirit towards God. The Lord told Noah and his sons, after purging the earth of all people with a worldwide flood, to be fruitful, increase in number, and fill the earth (Gen. 9:1). But Noah's descendants disdained the notion of scattering across the planet. In truth, their desire to make a name for themselves came from a God-resistant spirit. So He confused their ability to unite by removing their universal language. Then He dispersed them in accordance with His divine plan.

In Acts 2:2-6, the Holy Spirit descended upon Jesus-followers. He filled each person, with the result that they were able to speak in a foreign language! For the first time, the disciples declared the wonders of God in the native tongues of Jews from other nations gathered in Jerusalem to celebrate Pentecost. The same Lord who once confused the tongues of people, miraculously brought linguistic understanding.

Ministering in Peru and Guatemala, I needed translators in order to communicate. Many times I thought how wonderful it would be to have no language barrier. Were it not for sin, we would speak one language and God would be the central focus of our conversation. That day will come when Jesus returns! No longer will we be stymied by the inability to communicate. Imagine how awesome it will be to stand together with people from every part of the world, sharing words all understand, in praise to the Lord of communication! The curse of Babylon lingers, the cure of Jesus beckons.

Inspiration   † † †

The limits of my language means the limits of my world.—Ludwig Wittgenstein, Austrian-British philosopher (1889-1951)

Sarah's Remedy

God promised Abram that He would make him into a great nation, bless him, and make his name (Abraham) great and that all peoples on earth would be blessed through him (Gen. 12:2,3). The promise implied that he and Sarai would have offspring. Years later when God spoke to him in a vision, he despairingly shared his childless situation and the reality that all he owned would go to his servant Eliezer. But God said Eliezer would not be his heir and that Abram's descendants would one day be like the stars—too many to count. Again, Abram believed God (15:1-6). But as the years continued to pile up, Sarai (Sarah) became an old woman.

Genesis 16:1,2—Abram's wife Sarai had not borne him children. She owned an Egyptian slave named Hagar. Sarai said to Abram, "Since the LORD has prevented me from bearing children, go to my slave; perhaps I can have children by her." And Abram agreed to what Sarai said.

As a result of consensual sex, Hagar bore her 86 year-old master a son, Ishmael. This was not the child God intended to carry out His promise. Consequently, when Sarah finally gave birth to Isaac, he arrived into a family seeded in conflict.

The English word *compromise* is not found in Scripture, but the concept exists throughout God's Word. When God gives us a promise or instruction, it is our responsibility and privilege to believe and obey Him. As Abraham and Sarah aged, they doubted God. So Sarah came up with her own remedy. Charles Swindoll said, "The swift wind of compromise is a lot more devastating than the sudden jolt of misfortune." Compromise focuses on the problem and is based upon doubt. It relies on human ingenuity instead of divine prescription. Had Abram asked God if his offspring would come through Hagar, the Lord would have told him no. Compromise offers an immediate remedy at the sacrifice of long-term implications. Twelve rulers would descend from Ishmael. Many scholars believe he is the Arab's progenitor (ancestor), a civilization at constant enmity with the Jews.

Compromise is all about making concessions. In essence, we sacrifice what is absolutely right for what is relatively convenient. We surrender what is best for what is good. Has God asked you to do something that seems too difficult? Don't give up! Trust Him. Has God allowed you to be uncomfortable without seeing His blessing? Be steadfast—don't relinquish what you know to be right to gain respite. God's promises are based on His power. To rely on our reasoning at the expense of trusting Him is like settling for a roman candle and missing the northern lights. As Robert E. Coleman wrote in *The Master Plan of Discipleship*, "One did not have to be smart or talented to enroll in Christ's mission, but one had to be faithful. The cross permitted no compromise."[7]

A Heavy One Indeed January 10

Have you ever felt sorry for yourself? I have! Whenever self-pity is at work it is because I do not have something *I* want. Self-pity is the logical result of a self preoccupied with expectations that may or may not be realistic or even right. I have also noticed that the solution to self-pity always comes from God reminding me that He is all I need. Usually His prompts are gentle. He speaks through His word, or His Spirit brings to mind the blessings He faithfully provides. I have never had an extended, self-pity party. God is too awesome and nothing good comes from sulking, brooding or moping. Even the sound of those words should make us want to avoid them!

Life does not always go the way we would like it. We don't always receive the treatment we think we deserve. Hagar thought she was doing pretty well. She was Sarah's maidservant and it had to feel good having her mistress give her to her powerful husband. When Hagar conceived a son, she must have felt like the favored woman in a tent of frustration. Unfortunately, her success was short-lived and she began to despise Sarai.

Sarai, instead of finding happiness vicariously, now had an uppity servant. She went into a funk and did the natural thing—blame her husband for her suffering. Realizing he was in a no-win situation, Abram threw the responsibility back on her. Angry and feeling sorry for herself, Sarai so badly mistreated Hagar that the maidservant fled. An angel of the Lord found her near a spring beside the road to Shur, (which should have been named Unshur). The angel told her to go back and submit to Sarai and he promised that God would make her descendants too numerous to count! Suddenly, life was not so bad anymore.

Genesis 16:13—So she named the LORD who spoke to her: The God Who Sees, for she said, "Have I really seen here the One who sees me?"

There's a great lesson in Hagar's words. No matter what you are going through, God sees you. He knows your circumstances and He cares. So instead of tripping over self-pity and focusing on what is wrong or perceived as *messed up*, why not praise the One who sees you and get back to serving Him! Oswald Chambers wrote in *My Utmost For His Highest*:

> No sin is worse than the sin of self-pity, because it obliterates God and puts self-interest upon the throne. It opens our mouths to spit out murmurings and our lives become craving spiritual sponges, there is nothing lovely or generous about them.

Inspiration †††

The wrong asceticism torments the self: the right kind kills the selfness. We must die daily: but it is better to love the self than to love nothing, and to pity the self than to pity no one.—C.S. Lewis in *The Joyful Christian*

Be Like Joseph

Genesis 37:9-11—Then he had another dream and told it to his brothers. "Look," he said, "I had another dream, and this time the sun, moon, and 11 stars were bowing down to me." He told his father and brothers, but his father rebuked him. "What kind of dream is this that you have had?" he said. "Are your mother and brothers and I going to bow down to the ground before you?" His brothers were jealous of him, but his father kept the matter in mind.

Joseph is one of my favorite Biblical characters. He is such a great example of what it means to trust God though times and circumstances may be trying. I believe there are three key lessons we can learn about God from Joseph that will help us in our daily living.

I. *God has a plan for your life.* God gave Joseph an amazing dream that revealed a key aspect of his destiny. Unfortunately, as a young man, he did not have the maturity to keep the dream to himself and he offended his brothers.

God wants to work His will in *your* life. Here are some points to consider.

● *Pray and ask God what His plan for your life is—start at an early age.* Here are some helpful passages to consider—Acts 22:10; Psa. 31:3,5; 32:8.

● *Don't be consumed with your plan.* Your dreams and ambitions may not fit God's will and purpose.

● *Don't worry what others think.* Joseph's family did not care for his dream.

Many people may criticize or oppose what you believe God is calling you to do or be. Be faithful to your calling at all costs. Remember who your Master is!

While following God's plan, count on facing adversity and temptation. Joseph was thrown into a pit and sold into slavery. He languished in prison for years after his employer's wife tried to seduce him and then falsely accused him of attacking her. When you experience trouble, ask God what He wants you to learn from it. Don't be so quick to pray for healing—it may be that God has a lesson for you in suffering. Trust that He will lead you through the dark valleys and don't worry about what others think. Anyone watching Job would have concluded he was a loser. But, they had no clue that God's permissive will orchestrated his misfortunes.

If you are tempted, ask God for the strength to resist the temptation and then ask for His deliverance. Run from evil and recognize that some lures may come from our own tendency to insert our will in place of God's plan.

II. *God's plan may not be fully understood.* Joseph had no idea for years what God was doing in his life. If your life seems purposeless and confusing, ask the Lord to help you be faithful in the little things. If He can use you in the prison, He can use you in the palace. When circumstances or people turn against you don't leave room for bitterness or seek revenge (Rom. 12:17-19). Joseph could easily have killed or ruined the lives of his evil brothers. Instead, he forgave them. How often we miss God's plan because we enforce our own misguided will. Even worse, we miss God because we were more in love with our reputation or "success."

III. God's plan brings reward when you follow His will and not your own. In Gen. 45:4-8 and 50:19,20 Joseph shares his realization that it was God's intention all along to bring him to Egypt so that he might rescue his family from famine. Joseph was faithful to God and upright in his conduct and character, so, his Father used him to bring blessing. Joseph did not get bitter because he was better knowing God was bigger. God wants to bless you and He wants to use you to bring blessing. You can opt to live like Joseph's older brothers—selfish and sorely acquainted with their Maker. Or, you can be sensitive and discerning to His voice and will, eager to please Him and obedient for His glory.

Inspiration † † †

Can God do with you whatever he likes? Can He change your plans, goals or ambitions? Can He veto your plans, without explaining to you? Can He move you from one situation to another without your protesting? Is your will so surrendered that God can ask of you whatever He will? If you can answer yes to those questions, then you are the Lord's property.— Wesley L. Duewel in *Mighty Prevailing Prayer: Experiencing the Power of Answered Prayer*

Until you have given up your self to Him, you will not have a real self. Sameness is to be found most among the most 'natural' men, not among those who surrender to Christ.—C.S. Lewis in *Mere Christianity*

Two Kinds of Ground

There are two kinds of ground in this world, holy and unholy ground. The former is found wherever God's presence abides. We clearly see this when Moses, seeing the burning bush, approached it to determine why it was not consumed only to be met by the voice of the Lord.

Exodus 3:5—"Do not come any closer," God said. "Take off your sandals, for the place where you are standing is holy ground."

When we walk with God, our steps are sure and we can say in confidence with King David, *"He lifted me out of the slimy pit, out of the mud and mire; He set my feet on a rock and gave me a firm place to stand"* (Psa. 40:2). Where God IS the Ground Maker humbles both believer and unbeliever. *"Saul got up from the ground, but when he opened his eyes he could see nothing. So they led him by the hand into Damascus"* (Acts 9:8). It was holy ground on which that persecutor Saul was blinded and holy ground where his sight returned (9:17,18).

I've found a place not far from my house that is ideal for prayer walking. It is an asphalt path behind two public schools that encompasses their sports fields. When Kevin and I (or others who join us), walk that circular path in prayer we often experience God's encouragement. We feel His presence on righteous ground.

The world defines walking in circles as a euphemism for confusion, a state of lostness or ineptitude. Those who walk apart from God in their own strength pace unholy, sinking sand. It opens and consumes them as happened to Dathan, Korah and his followers.

> *But if the LORD brings about something totally new, and the earth opens its mouth and swallows them, with everything that belongs to them, and they go down alive into the grave, then you will know that these men have treated the LORD with contempt." As soon as he finished saying all this, the ground under them split apart and the earth opened its mouth and swallowed them, with their households and all Korah's men and all their possessions. They went down alive into the grave, with everything they owned; the earth closed over them, and they perished and were gone from the community.* Numbers 16:30-33

The question we must ask ourselves is this, "What kind of ground am I walking upon? If we walk with God in faith and obedience, we are on His holy ground and we find His favor!

- *"You broaden the path beneath me, so that my ankles do not turn."*—2 Sa. 22:37
- *"You have made known to me the path of life; You will fill me with joy in Your presence, with eternal pleasures at Your right hand."*—Psa. 16:11
- *"He restores my soul. He guides me in paths of righteousness for His name's sake."*—Psa. 23:3

● *"In the way of righteousness there is life; along that path is immortality."*—Pro. 12:28

● *"The path of the righteous is level; O upright One, You make the way of the righteous smooth."*—Isa. 26:7

Conversely, those *"who leave the straight paths to walk in dark ways,"* (Pro. 2:13) will reap the pain that comes on unholy soil. *"In the paths of the wicked lie thorns and snares, but he who guards his soul stays far from them"* (Pro.22:5). Are you grounded in God's holiness or grounded in sin? One leads to glory the other to worms.

Inspiration   † † †

A man who professes an external law is like someone standing in the light of a lantern fixed to a post. It is light all round him, but there is nowhere further for him to walk. A man who professes the teaching of Christ is like a man carrying a lantern before him on a long, or not so long, pole: the light is in front of him, always lighting up fresh ground and always encouraging him to walk further.—Count Lev Nikolayevich Tolstoy, Russian novelist (1828–1910)

Send Someone Else

● *Exodus 3:11—But Moses asked God, "Who am I that I should go to Pharaoh and that I should bring the Israelites out of Egypt?"*

Moses fled Egypt after murdering an Egyptian. He married a Midianite priest's daughter and lived a simple life for decades, tending his father-in-law's sheep. One day God appeared to him out of a burning bush to appoint him as rescuer of his enslaved countrymen. God told Moses that He was sending him to Pharaoh to win the release of the Israelites from Egypt. What an assignment! One would think that Moses, raised in a royal family and gifted with a great education, would have leaped at the opportunity to be a hero! Alas, he had other ideas. Whenever, the first word uttered is *"But,"* grab an umbrella because it's about to rain excuses!

Excuse #1: *I'm the wrong person.* (God, don't forget I'm wanted on a felony in Egypt!) This job is too tough for me. I'm not worthy.

● *3:13—"Then Moses asked God, 'If I go to the Israelites and say to them: The God of your fathers has sent me to you, and they ask me, 'What is His name?' what should I tell them?'"*

Excuse #2: *I don't know You well enough to represent You.* What if they don't really know You either? We could have a credibility problem.

● *4:1—"Then Moses answered, 'What if they won't believe me and will not obey me but say, 'The LORD did not appear to you?'"*

Excuse #3: *I'm afraid to fail.* You're sending me to a hostile crowd. I don't want to be rejected. These people have problems and issues You don't understand.

● *4:10,13—"But Moses replied to the LORD, 'Please, Lord, I have never been eloquent—either in the past or recently or since You have been speaking to Your servant—because I am slow and hesitant in speech.' Moses said, 'Please, Lord, send someone else.'"*

Excuse #4: *I'm inadequate.* I have low self-esteem. I don't trust You because I know my own failings. I'm not capable of doing what You ask.

Fortunately, Moses ultimately obeyed God and returned to Egypt. God fortified him with strength, coached him, and worked through him to lead a rebellious nation forty tough years. Moses became one of Israel's greatest leaders.

God wants to accomplish His purposes through you as well. Relax! He won't ask you to lead Israel out of Egypt. However, He will ask you to do more than you think you can or should do. It is true that He loves you and uniquely made you to contribute to the expansion of His kingdom. He will give you all you need to succeed! You won't experience the joy of *really* knowing Him and the pleasure of fulfilling His will if you choose to hide behind excuses. Nip it in the *"but"* and listen to the Lord. Don't focus on yourself, others, or your circumstances. Trust in the One who is able!

Walk on Dry Land

At breakneck speed they moved across the desert, angry with revenge burning in their hearts. Six hundred bully chariots commanded by officers led a thundering army across the hard, rocky soil. Pharaoh knew his freedom-seeking slaves were trapped. Enraged by the death of his firstborn son and hardened against an omnipotent God who had ravaged his country, he would make Moses and his pathetic people pay. As the Egyptian warriors approached, the Israelites panicked. They turned on their reluctant leader and cried out, *"Isn't this what we told you in Egypt: Leave us alone so that we may serve the Egyptians? It would have been better for us to serve the Egyptians than to die in the wilderness"* (Exo. 14:12).

Moses watched as the dust of the approaching legions billowed. He looked into the eyes of fearful men and cried, *"Don't be afraid. Stand firm and see the LORD's salvation He will provide for you today; for the Egyptians you see today, you will never see again. The LORD will fight for you; you must be quiet"* (Exo.14:13,14).

Exodus 14:19,20—Then the Angel of God, who was going in front of the Israelite forces, moved and went behind them. The pillar of cloud moved from in front of them and stood behind them. It came between the Egyptian and Israelite forces. The cloud was there in the darkness, yet it lit up the night. So neither group came near the other all night long.

The Israelites did not see the angel of God nor understand at that time that the cloud leading them and buffering them from their enemy was the visible symbol of God's presence. Even the impact of supernatural power levied against Egypt could not lift their eyes from slavery to salvation. Instead of rejoicing in that great canopy of grace, they floundered as if it were fog.

No matter what you face today, can you trust that God is with you? He may lead you to a place where there is no escape. You may have to cross your sea of doubt on the path He creates in order to learn that His power is sufficient to meet your predicament. As a follower of Christ, you won't find God revealing Himself through a dense cloud because His Holy Spirit resides inside you. The glory of the Lord is your strength—with you to guide you. Be quiet in the turmoil, knowing that He will direct you where you need to go and protect you from that which seems bent on your demise. So go ahead! Walk on dry land!

Inspiration † † †

Living becomes an awesome business when you realize that you spend every moment of your life in the sight and company of an omniscient, omnipresent Creator.—J.I. Packer

How Numb We Become

He's just ten years old. From what little I've seen of his home life, I know he has a step-dad that struggles to get him to listen. The same holds true for his mother—she gets thoroughly exasperated trying to rein him in. So, I'm not surprised when Jimmy challenges my authority on the court. But I was caught off guard when he repeatedly said *"good God Almighty"* repeatedly as we practiced shooting hoops. He was looking for a reaction from me and I obliged.

"Jimmy, don't say that."

"Why not, coach."

"Because what you are doing is disrespectful to God."

He didn't say anything more. Why? Because, I suspect in his heart he knew his words were wrong and Someone far greater was at work in his conscience.

Exodus 20:7—Do not misuse the name of the LORD your God, because the LORD will punish anyone who misuses His name.

One of the reasons I enjoy being around children is their tenderness towards God that exists even in those with no spiritual background. That innocence seeps away in most as they gain increasing exposure to a society bent on mocking God at all costs. Sin-hardened lives resist a holy Judge and His absolute plan of salvation.

Sometimes I wonder if we realize how numb we become to the effects of our culture. As God's children, we ought to stay tender towards Him. The evidence of our softhearted love is a fierce desire to uphold His holy name. Does that sound contradictory? Adoring is not a sign of weakness. It is a courageous stand that zealously proclaims, "I'll lay down my life for You because You are worthy." Elizabeth Barrett Browning, an English poet, wrote,

> "Earth's crammed with Heaven,
> And every common bush aflame with God,
> But only he that sees takes off his shoes."

We wouldn't let our children address those in authority with a casual "hey dude!" So we shouldn't oblige people disrespecting God by shrugging as if it didn't really matter. One of the ways we reveal our love for the Lord is to take a stand for His name. I imagine it hurts Him even more when we are too ashamed to speak up. Don't be afraid to tell your co-workers or your unsaved family members that you would appreciate it if they would desist from swearing. They may mock you. They may not comply. But you may cause them to consider God. You'll identify yourself as an ambassador. You most certainly will be credited in heaven. As John Piper loves to teach, "God is most glorified in us when we are most satisfied in Him."

Worship

Exodus 9:13—Then the LORD said to Moses, "Get up early in the morning and present yourself to Pharaoh. Tell him: This is what the LORD, the God of the Hebrews says: Let My people go, so that they may worship Me."

All around the planet somewhere, someplace, someone is worshiping God—24/7! Heaven is the final destination of praise, prayers, confession, thanksgiving, songs, dance, shouting, offerings and communion before an adored Father. If you asked me to pick the single most important thing I could do in life I would unhesitatingly answer, *WORSHIP!*

Worship for me is the lifelong practice of glorifying God through reverent communication, righteous conduct, and moral character that affirms my love for Him. There are four primary reasons why I believe we should worship our awesome LORD.

1. *God wants us to worship Him and Him only! "Each of the four living creatures had six wings; they were covered with eyes around and inside. Day and night they never stop, saying: Holy, holy, holy, Lord God, the Almighty, who was, who is, and who is coming" (Rev. 4:8). "You are to never bow down to another god because the LORD, being jealous by nature, is a jealous God" (Exo. 34:14).* "Man's chief end is to glorify God and to enjoy Him forever"—Westminster Shorter Catechism (1647).

2. *We worship to glorify and therefore please Him. "I will praise God's name with song and exalt Him with thanksgiving. That will please the LORD more than an ox, more than a bull with horns and hooves"(Psa. 69:30,31).*

3. *It enables us to enjoy life by changing our attitude and setting our heart right with God. "But I will sing of Your strength and will joyfully proclaim Your faithful love in the morning. For You have been a stronghold for me, a refuge in my day of trouble" (Psa. 59:16).* Jack Hayford noted in *Worship His Majesty*, "You become like the god you worship."[8]

4. *We worship to testify to what God has done* (His love, faithfulness, justice, powerful acts, etc.) *"I will sing about the LORD's faithful love forever; with my mouth I will proclaim Your faithfulness to all generations" (Psa. 89:1). "I will praise You, LORD, among the peoples; I will sing praises to You among the nations" (Psa. 108:3).* Later in his book, Pastor Hayford notes, "I am totally persuaded that worship is the key to evangelism as well as to the edification of the Church."

May I encourage you to: (1) write your own personal definition of worship; (2) evaluate how you are doing in worshiping God; (3) stop whatever you are doing right now and tell God how much you love Him! A.W. Tozer taught, "Worship rises or falls with our concept of God . . . The world is perishing for lack of the knowledge of God and the church is famishing for want of His presence."

Wearing Patches

When a person joins the military, an amazing alteration takes place. Uniforms are issued and the new soldier's identity and look is changed. The Army has an effective way of signifying its own. Each soldier on his or her uniform wears a patch on the left shoulder marking the unit with which the soldier serves. On active duty, I wore a patch called "the Screaming Eagle" which identified me as a member of the 101st Airborne (Air Assault) Division.

Wouldn't it be novel if people wore patches identifying their religious belief? If we wore patches that signified we were Christians, wouldn't we be much more careful how we lived? Others would observe our behavior and form their opinion of Christianity accordingly.

Leviticus 16:4—He is to wear a holy linen tunic, and linen undergarments are to be on his body. He must tie a linen sash around him and wrap his head with a linen turban. These are holy garments; he must bathe his body with water before he wears them.

In the nation of Israel, Aaron and the priests who ministered in the tabernacle wore special clothing which identified them and the service they performed for God and the people. God altered their attire because He wanted to teach the Israelites about what it meant to fear and serve Him as their holy Lord and Leader. He wanted those in ministry to be reminded of the seriousness of their work. In putting on attire God designated, they were reminded visually of their responsibilities.

If I am living for Jesus, my life is being altered. People should see the changes Jesus brings about in my character, my actions and my disposition. The key to alteration is consciously working at taking off the depraved uniform of self with its "I" patch, to wear the uniform Jesus is making for me—a uniform whose distinctive patch is His name. Jesus never forces me to be altered. I must of my own free will follow Him.

Inspiration   † † †

But when Christ was nailed to the cross, He took off His robe of seamless perfection and assumed a different wardrobe, the wardrobe of indignity.—Pastor Max Lucado in *3:16*

If Jesus Christ cannot alter me now, so that the alteration shows externally in my home life, in my business life, when is He going to alter me?—Oswald Chambers in *God's Workmanship*

Junior Holy Spirits

Leviticus 19:15—You must not act unjustly when rendering judgment. Do not be partial to the poor or give preference to the rich; judge your neighbor fairly.

So what's wrong with trying to help someone else when their conduct or circumstances are questionable or, they don't know how to act? What if they seem clueless about key issues? Well for starters, we ought to think about our:

● *Motives*—perhaps I challenge what I perceive to be selfishness in the way you handle money when really what I would like is for you to be generous to me.

● *Methods*—Jesus creatively shared the gospel. Some people want to take the *Four Spiritual Laws* or *hottest* tract and train everyone to use them correctly so people will "get saved." This causes Christians to focus on the tool instead of the Holy Spirit. He may not want us turning pages but rather praying for discernment as to what is preventing a person from finding salvation. Our training becomes counterproductive to our spiritual growth if we rely on it more than on the Holy Spirit.

● *Presumption*—We do not like what we see in someone else's life so we jump in and push our solutions. The Bible teaches that God tests us and often allows us to suffer in order to build our character or teach us valuable lessons. Premature intervention on our part presupposes that we know what is best. Only God knows what is best.

● *Pride*—Before we judge others with capricious (impulsive) diagnosis we ought to carefully examine ourselves. A consistent habit of looking to "fix" others may actually cause us to miss hearing what God wants to do!

Don't be a junior holy spirit! The first thing to do before intervening is pray. The second thing we ought to do is pray some more!

Inspiration   † † †

One of our severest lessons comes from the stubborn refusal to see that we must not interfere in other people's lives. It takes a long time to realize the danger of being an amateur providence, that is, interfering with God's order for others.—Oswald Chambers in *My Utmost For His Highest*

Green Moss on Gray Shingles

Leviticus 19:18—Do not take revenge or bear a grudge against members of your community, but love your neighbor as yourself; I am the LORD.
Mark 11:25—But when you are praying, first forgive anyone you are holding a grudge against, so that your Father in heaven will forgive you your sins too. (TLB)

{Scene: Outside the tent on a hot day in the desert Miriam and Aaron are engaged in an intense discussion. I wonder if Numbers 12:1,2 sounded something like this.}
Miriam: "I've never liked his wife."
Aaron: "I know. She's not one of us. She's a *Cushite*. And God said we weren't to take foreign wives."
Miriam: "And how come *Moses* is always in charge? God speaks through us. Moses has too much authority . . ."

Evidently, two people who should have known better held a grudge against their own brother. At the end of Num. 12:2 four words ought to catch our attention—*"And the Lord heard."*

Grudges are like green moss on gray shingles. They feed on the moisture of resentment and slowly grow—jeopardizing a roof's ability to shed water. Grudging consists of four elements: *retention of negative thoughts, judging, complaining,* and *self-elevating.* To sustain a grudge costs us dearly. First, it violates God's law subjecting us to His judgment. Second, it hinders His will by harming fellowship and hampering ministry. Third, it taints our attitude, sapping us spiritually and physically.

You will not grow to be the person God wants you to be if you carry a grudge. Why let smoldering resentment keep you from the joy you can experience by adorning yourself with L-O-V-E! If God were a grudging God, we would not know Jesus. Our perfect Father was under no obligation to sacrifice His Son for sinners. Yet, because of His mercy:

He will not always accuse us or be angry forever. He has not dealt with us as our sins deserve or repaid us according to our offenses. For as high as the heavens are above the earth, so great is His faithful love toward those who fear Him. As far as the east is from the west, so far has He removed our transgressions from us. (Psa. 103:9-12)

If only we could learn from His example! The Lord hears us. What are we saying?

Inspiration   † † †

To carry a grudge is like being stung to death by one bee.—William H. Walton, author

The glory of Christianity is to conquer by forgiveness.—William Blake, English artist, (1757-1827)

Flying Over Oregon

Leviticus 25:4—But there will be a Sabbath of complete rest for the land in the seventh year, a Sabbath to the LORD: you are not to sow your field or prune your vineyard.

Flying over Oregon recently, I was moved by the vast beauty beneath our jet. Crater Lake, the second deepest lake in the nation, (according to our Alaska Airlines pilot), is incredible! Snow-adorned mountains, the vast array of timber and winding rivers directed my thoughts toward a Creator who has a phenomenal artistic touch.

Does it seem like conservationists often come under great scorn? The fear that our land is dangerously abused seems somehow absurd to many because of its sheer enormity. Tree-huggers and land-lovers take their share of knocks. Yet, we as Christians ought to be concerned about the land. It's an issue of stewardship. To be sure, there are those who worship the earth and call her mother. This passion, be it old or New Age, is nothing short of idolatry in the Father's sight. But the excesses of some in search of a savior do not legitimize the neglect of others who see earth as a temporary blimp surpassed by a heavenly home.

Do we think the same God who gave Adam instructions to tend Eden and taught the Israelites to care for their land and give it rest from constant use, drafted cosmic legislation relieving us of responsibility to nourish our surroundings! Do we focus solely on propagating the gospel message and miss that the land is a testifying voice to the reality of God! *"From the creation of the world His invisible attributes, that is, His eternal power and divine nature, have been clearly seen, being understood through what He has made. As a result, people are without excuse"* (Rom. 1:20).

Damaged land hardly glorifies God! How can the fields be jubilant, and everything in them and how can the trees of the forest sing for joy (Psa. 96:12), if they are polluted and trashed? What kind of spiritual example are we if we litter the land in apathy?

This land is our land. May we wisely treat it with honor so that those still searching see our good deeds and are led to our Savior-Designer.

Fifty

Numbers 8:24-26—In regard to the Levites: From 25 years old or more, a man enters the service in the work at the tent of meeting. But at 50 years old he is to retire from his service in the work and no longer serve. He may assist his brothers to fulfill responsibilities at the tent of meeting, but he must not do the work. This is how you are to deal with the Levites regarding their duties.

God gave Moses a work formula for His servants the Levites. At the age of fifty, they reached retirement. They could assist their younger brothers in the tent of meeting but they were not to do the work. Only once does this instruction appear in the Bible but we should not dismiss it as insignificant because God repeats His plan to Moses regarding the cessation of work. Why do you suppose God would mandate retirement for His servants at an age where they still possessed energy?

Perhaps the number 50 signified completion. Each fifty years, the Israelites celebrated the year of Jubilee and were required to rest their land. Maybe God was not concerned with energy but rather maturity. By retiring at 50, the Levites held at most 25 years of experience serving the Lord. That experience was invaluable to the younger adults they assisted. By God moving them into a season of mentoring, He also opened up service for the younger men. He set in place perpetual training. What would happen to ministries today if leaders at the age of 50 shifted into a new season of mentoring? I believe it would invigorate the church! I believe it would also be a difficult step for those servants who define their identity by what they do.

Chris and I were talking about this and he said, "What's the first question someone who doesn't know you asks?" I responded, "What do you do?" We live in a society obsessed with doing! Many men retire from their jobs and within a short period of time die. It's as if by not working they lose their purpose in life. But those whose lives are defined by a higher purpose, a spiritual relationship with God, find that "being" is every bit as significant as "doing." God made us to love us and to be loved by us. When we enjoy the course and are able to live in time instead of for time we discover a great secret—the meaning of eternity.

For 46 of my 50 years I've known Jesus, my best Friend and profoundly awesome Lord. I'm a blessed man looking forward to forever with my Father in heaven! Isn't it exciting to realize our future is in the hands of our Lord? That's something to think about . . . in reveration!

Inspiration † † †

Other men see only a hopeless end, but the Christian rejoices in an endless hope.— Reverend Gilbert Beenken (1926-2009)

Never Say to God . . .

Insubordination is the oldest recorded sin. Lucifer resisted God's authority. He then contaminated humanity through his seditious lies to Eve. Today the planet the Lord God made for His glory is pockmarked with contumacious, (obstinately disobedient), disregard for His rule.

Numbers 16:12-14—Moses sent for Dathan and Abiram, the sons of Eliab, but they said, "We will not come! Is it not enough that you brought us up from a land flowing with milk and honey to kill us in the wilderness? Do you also have to appoint yourself as ruler over us? Furthermore, you didn't bring us to a land flowing with milk and honey or give us an inheritance of fields and vineyards. Will you gouge out the eyes of these men? We will not come!"

In Numbers 14:2, the Israelite path to rebellion began with the words *"If only we had died in the land of Egypt!"* Insubordination sprang naturally from an unreal preoccupation with the past. They forgot how miserable they were as slaves in a land not their own (Exo. 3:7). They focused on creature comforts as opposed to believing that God would safely lead them into Canaan. When we utter the words, "if only" to heaven, we may as well just say, *"God we don't trust You."*

Lucifer couldn't wait to be in charge. The Israelites clamored to escape the desert. We insist circumstances be favorable to our aim and ambitions and grow angry when they are not. Insubordination is fueled by impatience.

Insubordination is blind to reality. Lucifer lost sight of God's glory. The Jews ignored the miracles God worked to free them from Pharaoh, feed them in sandy wastelands, and bring water from rock. When we focus on our agendas at the expense of God's will, mutiny is not far away.

Moses' countrymen were champion complainers. They were sick of following a divine cloud, festered over wasteland training, faulted Moses' leadership and routinely set aside godly fear for willful disobedience. In the end, the earth swallowed up Dathan and his grumbling followers, fire consumed Korah and his 250 Levite conspirators, and plague killed 14,700 renegades. Twice God threatened to destroy the entire assembly (16:20,45)! How would history read today had not Moses and Aaron fell on their faces and begged for God's mercy to prevail.

Never say to God, *No we will not come!* You cannot afford the cost of insubordination. Jonah saw the insides of a great fish for saying "No!" The Bible is replete with examples of what happens to the rebellious. *"But land that produces thorns and thistles is worthless and is in danger of being cursed. In the end it will be burned"* (Heb. 6:8 NIV). Do you know someone resisting God's authority? Warn him to submit! Do you see a life opposed to the Holy Spirit's gentle leading? Implore her to repent! Only God's way brings us to perfection and the fruit is everlasting joy!

Our Name

Numbers 27:4—Why should the name of our father be taken away from his clan? Since he had no son, give us property among our father's brothers.

The story goes that many years ago the Chinese government commissioned an author to write a biography of Hudson Taylor. He was asked to distort the facts of this incredible missionary so that Taylor's reputation would be smeared. Yet, as the author conducted his research, he was profoundly impressed by God's servant. Taylor's saintly character and godly life were above reproach. The writer realized he could not fulfill the mission he was assigned with a clear conscience. Instead, aware of the danger that he could lose his own life, he set aside his pen, renounced his atheism, and received Jesus as his personal Savior.

Our name is our heritage (the God of Abraham, Isaac and Jacob). In a land of immigrants, this is not so obvious. However, in other countries, a person can be saddled with the baggage of what happened ten generations earlier. The sin of Adam affects us all. The grace of Jesus likewise redeems those who run to Him. *"For everyone who calls on the name of the Lord will be saved"* (Rom. 10:13).

Our name is our reputation. If our character is unblemished, our name is like the clear running water of a bubbly mountain spring. If our label is tarnished, our reputation is like the Pasig river, a polluted Filipino waterway that changes colors according to the daily infusion of chemicals.

Our name is our future. By placing our trust and allegiance in Jesus, our names are recorded in God's Book of Life. We gain entrance through the blood of His Son to an eternal celebration with our Almighty Father! If we blow off God as the myth of crippled personalities and turn our prideful backs on Jesus, our names will not be found when the final accounting is taken. We will be exiled to a place of eternal torment where God's presence is forever removed (Rev. 20:15).

What's in a name? In short, everything! The reason we strive to be like Jesus is that we might be identified with the One given *"the name that is above every name, so that at the name of Jesus every knee should bow—of those who are in heaven and on earth and under the earth"* (Php. 2:9b,10).

Protect your name at all costs! Imagine standing in heaven conversing with someone who met the Jesus they saw in you, the Name by your name.

Inspiration   † † †

The beginning of wisdom is to call things by their right names.—Chinese proverb

Followers

Followers—what thoughts does this word conjure? Are they passive, wimpy, sheep-like figures too meek to do anything but comply with those leading? Are they mature loyalists? In actuality, we cannot rightly answer the question unless we know concrete evidence about who is leading.

Deuteronomy 1:35,36—None of these men in this evil generation will see the good land I swore to give your fathers, except Caleb the son of Jephunneh. He will see it, and I will give him and his descendants the land on which he has set foot, because he followed the LORD completely.

One of the world's most storied leaders—Moses, revealed that those who faithfully followed the Almighty would:

● *Show themselves to be wise and understanding people.* Is it better to be a follower of the Creator who is perfect, powerful and loving or to acquiesce to what is created, flawed and incapable of rendering on-going blessing? (Deu. 4:6,15-19)

● *Favorably impact other nations who would hear about His decrees and recognize with praise, people wise enough to follow them.* (4:6)

● *Carefully remember and guard the lessons learned from observing His handiwork.* (4:9, 32-35)

● *Teach their children and their grandchildren the importance of following Him.* (4:9,10)

● *Understand that He is a jealous Father who loves His people and will be provoked if they turn away from following Him.* (4:23,24)

● *Realize that turning away from Him would result in disaster.* (4:26)

● *Be able to return to obeying Him if they fell away because He is merciful.* (4:29-31)

If we are criticized simply for following God we ought to recognize that the criticism ultimately is towards God and not ourselves. And He, above all, is perfectly capable of handling criticism. If we are criticized for behavior which is at odds with what others know to be God's will, then we must stand the scrutiny and ask ourselves if we are unfaithful, thereby smearing the reputation of the One we follow. To be followers of God is a great and awesome responsibility. May we be found faithful in His sight!

Inspiration ✝✝✝

There are no neutral followers; we either scatter or gather.—John Piper in *In Our Joy*

Teach Them to Your Children

If love were a waterfall one would be thoroughly drenched spending time with the Ferraros. In a small town in Illinois, this family radiates what happens when God permeates a household. What strikes me most about them is their commitment to live simply to give as generously as possible to support Christians on the frontlines for their faith—men and women who serve in organizations like Gospel For Asia (GFA) or receive help through Voice of the Martyrs (VOM).

John and Beth eloquently teach their eight children the joy that comes from obediently following God. Their pure delight in seeking to be *living sacrifices* is both contagious and heart-warming for they have learned a secret most adults struggle to understand—all we have is God's and should be used for His glory!

Deuteronomy 4:9,10—Only be on your guard and diligently watch yourselves, so that you don't forget the things your eyes have seen and so that they don't slip from your mind as long as you live. Teach them to your children and your grandchildren. The day you stood before the LORD your God at Horeb, the LORD said to me, "Assemble the people before Me, and I will let them hear My words, so that they may learn to fear Me all the days they live on the earth and may instruct their children."

Do you suspect kids grasp far more conceptually than we often give them credit? What they understand is hinged upon what we do in our daily living. If we want our children to grow up loving God then we must love God. For example, parents who drop off their children at church while they go home to engage in leisurely activity on Sunday morning send a clear message—God is important until you become an adult.

Our example matters! I can explain to my children why it honors God to speak kindly, but they must see me, in the heat of emotion, control my tongue. I can pray in their presence for the homeless or sick but leave them ambivalent towards the plight of others by acting as though prayer absolves me of taking further action. And if I devote my time and money toward cable, videos, games and other pursuits what have I revealed about my heart?

Jesus called the children to Himself because they mattered, not so He could win some election. We dare not forsake our responsibility to teach our children! They are an investment in life. What excuse might we offer to our Heavenly Father as to why we passed off our children to others and neglected their spiritual growth for our own pursuits? I believe the Ferraro's have their priorities straight! Let's resolve to build a treasure chest of stories of what we learned through serving God! Let us raise up a generation of God-followers!

The Secret

Deuteronomy 6:5—Love the LORD your God with all your heart, with all your soul, and with all your strength.

Would you like to know the secret for living a successful life? The key is found in understanding and obeying the Bible's Greatest Commandment given by God to Moses in the verse above. Over 22 times in the Bible we are directly encouraged to love God. Loving God requires a wholehearted commitment in a half-hearted world. Aside from the obvious fact that God desires our love, I believe there are at least four benefits that come from loving Him.

1. *When our focus is on loving God, our eyes are on God and not on problems.* We make life complicated when we fixate on problems. Our Father wants us to focus on loving Him knowing that when we do so, what once seemed insurmountable becomes manageable. He retains His rightful place as Lord and we maintain joy.

2. *When our focus is on loving God, we obtain a godly perspective.* Proverbs 9:10 says, *"The fear of the LORD is the beginning of wisdom, and the knowledge of the Holy One is understanding."* Reverence, (love in the awe-mode), brings us to a much deeper understanding of God, which, in turn, helps us make wise decisions, set proper goals, and avoid becoming ensnarled in fleshly conflicts.

3. *When our focus is on loving God, we obtain a balanced lifestyle.* Our love for God and our ability to live in harmony with His will is measured by the way we spend our time. Busyness is not a disease! It generally is a statement that God is not our top priority. Balance is attained by those who remember God is on the Throne and live accordingly.

4. *When our focus is on loving God, we are able to love people.* We understand the importance of loving everyone and sharing Jesus with those who do not know Him. We help them understand that eternal life begins by obtaining God's favor, a condition predicated by confessing our sin and placing our faith in His Son.

If we believe these things, perhaps the question is, "How do we go about loving God?"

We have to make Him first in our life. God is a jealous God and He will not tolerate idolatry. *"Do not have other gods besides Me"* (Exo. 20:3).

We have to find out what pleases Him.

For you were once darkness, but now you are light in the Lord. Walk as children of light—for the fruit of the light results in all goodness, righteousness, and truth—discerning what is pleasing to the Lord. Don't participate in the fruitless works of darkness, but instead, expose them. (Eph. 5:8-11)

We have to obey His commands. *"For this is what love for God is: to keep His commands. Now His commands are not a burden"* (1 Jo. 5:3).

We have to accept His plan. *"A man's heart plans his way, but the LORD determines his steps"* (Pro. 16:9).

The proof of love is when I can live victoriously knowing that it does not matter that I get what I want, it matters that I accept what God gives and trust that He knows best. Something to think about . . . in reveration.

Inspiration †††

People who love God crave His companionship.—Randy Alcorn in *Heaven*

. . . it has not entered into the heart of man what God can do for those who love Him.—Andrew Murray, South African writer, teacher and pastor (1828-1917) in *The Believer's Prayer Life*

The Medal of Honor

He humbly sat at our head table in his Dress Greens. Around his neck, a blue ribbon held a precious five-pointed star that symbolizes the highest award for valor in combat action a soldier can earn. We admired this World War II veteran and he seemed genuinely touched that we made him an honorary member of our battalion.

Robert D. Maxwell, Technician Fifth Grade, displayed conspicuous gallantry and intrepidity at risk of life above and beyond the call of duty on 7 September 1944, near Besancon, France. Armed only with .45 caliber automatic pistols, Maxwell and three fellow soldiers defended their battalion observation post against an overwhelming attack by enemy infantrymen in approximately platoon strength, supported by 20mm. flak and machinegun fire at ranges as close as 10 yards. Despite a hail of fire from automatic weapons and grenade launchers, Maxwell aggressively fought off the advancing enemy and by his calmness, tenacity, and fortitude, inspired his fellows to continue the unequal struggle. When an enemy hand grenade was thrown in the midst of his squad, Maxwell unhesitatingly hurled himself squarely upon it, using his blanket and his unprotected body to absorb the full force of the explosion. This act of heroism permanently maimed him, but saved the lives of his comrades . . .[9]

Deuteronomy 30:19,20—I call heaven and earth as witnesses against you today that I have set before you life and death, blessing and curse. Choose life so that you and your descendants may live, love the LORD your God, obey Him, and remain faithful to Him. For He is your life, and He will prolong your life in the land the LORD swore to give to your fathers Abraham, Isaac, and Jacob.

True commitment is formed around the free will of choice. Robert Maxwell without coercion smothered a tiny bomb to save the lives of men he resolved to protect. Commitment gives us direction in how we should live (and die). A soldier swears to protect his country. A mother pledges to raise her children. A counselor promises to help her patients. An athlete determines to train hard so as to win.

When God asks us to choose life, He is asking for our commitment! We decide to love Him, to listen to His voice, and to obey His instruction. God is not honored by whim and fad. He searches for those who walk resolved to know Him, to serve Him, to set aside personal agendas, and to stand passionately against the very flak hell spews. Are you committed to the One who smothered the grenade of sin with the body of His own Son? As Robert Boardman, decorated WWII marine and author notes, "It is impossible to carry a cross with one hand."

I Can No Longer Act as Your Leader

Deuteronomy 31:1,2—Then Moses continued to speak these words to all Israel, saying, "I am now 120 years old; I can no longer act as your leader. The LORD has told me, 'You will not cross this Jordan.'"

Moses amazes me. He took well over a million people with countless animals out of Egypt for forty years wandering across harsh deserts where food and water were scarce. He had a phenomenal friendship with God which afforded him incredible power and the confidence to lead. Despite the heartaches of dealing with whining rebels, he passionately set out to accomplish a compelling mission he didn't want.

Moses was not perfect. In a fit of anger he disobeyed and dishonored his Lord (Num. 20:11-12). God's punishment was to remove his privilege of leading the Israelites into Canaan. Moses pled with Him for the right to take them in— it must have broken his heart to be barred from the ultimate privilege of crossing the Jordan River. Instead, God graciously allowed him to climb Mount Nebo to gain a panoramic view of the land. Then he died in the land of Moab. Just before his death, he spoke to his people the words in the meditation above. Moses then passed the mantle of leadership to Joshua.

The American Heritage Dictionary defines resignation as "Unresisting acceptance of something as inescapable; submission." Moses resigned in obedience to God's timing. *"Moses was 120 years old when he died; his eyes were not weak, and his vitality had not left him"* (Deu. 34:7). I believe that one of the true tests of a leader is knowing when to step down from a position of authority. There are at least nine reasons why Christian leaders fail to resign graciously and effectively.

1.   The position becomes more important than the people
2.   The people become more important than the Savior
3.   The Savior is subordinate to the mission
4.   Work (leading) becomes the primary source of satisfaction
5.   The need for adulation exceeds the giving of adoration
6.   Failure to identify, train and mentor a replacement
7.   Pride as evidenced by a sense of being "irreplaceable," or an unwillingness to admit ineffectiveness or the possibility that someone else is better suited to the position
8.   Fear of losing one's identity and purpose
9.   Inability to discern the Holy Spirit's leading

The wise leader knows when to say, *"I am no longer able to lead you."* His reward is to one day hear God say, *"Well done, you good and faithful servant!"*

Inspiration   † † †

For true leaders, failure will not destroy them but will, instead, further develop their character.—Henry & Richard Blackaby in *Spiritual Leadership*

Their Rifles Barely Worked

Do you remember the 507th Maintenance Company and its infamous soldier—PFC Jessica Lynch? While serving in Iraq, she was badly hurt, the sole survivor in her humvee which crashed into a disabled truck attempting to escape an ambush. Lynch did not fight the enemy as the U.S. media first reported, but a fellow soldier did—PFC Patrick Miller. He won the Silver Star for his valiant efforts and a Purple Heart. Miller was fortunate to have survived and later as a captive to be rescued by a marine patrol. Almost all of those who could fight experienced jammed weapons. Their rifles barely worked because they rarely cleaned and maintained them. Evidently, the soldiers of the 507th took their weapons for granted. They did not expect to be ambushed.

Joshua 1:8—Do not let this Book of the Law depart from your mouth; meditate on it day and night, so that you may be careful to do everything written in it. Then you will be prosperous and successful. (NIV)
Psalm 119:93—I will never forget Your precepts, for You have given me life through them.

Haplessness is fed by neglect. What things draw us away from spending time with the sword of the Spirit, the Word of God? We all know that sin contaminates and that the Bible was written to help us overcome sin. But covert sin may not be much of an issue for us. Life may seem fairly good—free of evil as we busy ourselves with relationships, our jobs and pleasures. Slowly, subtly we become disengaged from studying God's life-instruction manual. No, like the 507th, we don't plan on taking wrong turns. We forget that Satan, the roaring lion, is eagerly set to devour us (1 Peter 5:8). When trouble comes, if we are not competent and familiar with Scripture, we are in effect—defenseless.

Maintenance may seem humdrum and boring. But God does not offer a onetime spiritual crash course for overcoming evil or understanding Him. He expects us to regularly absorb and obey His Word because it is for our own good and protection! So, out of reverence for God, let's soberly make time for His holy manual—full of everlasting promises and powerful wisdom!

Inspiration † † †

The Bible is proved to be a revelation from God, by the reasonableness and holiness of its precepts; all its commands, exhortations, and promises having the most direct tendency to make men wise, holy, and happy in themselves, and useful to one another.—Adam Clarke, British theologian, (1760-1832)

Mel Was Run Over!

Kathleen called me on my cell phone. "Dan, I think Mel was run over . . ." Mel, short for Melbourne, is our Siamese-mix cat well beloved in the York household. So on my way home I deviated from the normal route and sure enough, found him lying beside the sidewalk close to our home. I walked down to where he lay and noticed the blood trail running from the center of the road. I was surprised because Mel is rather skittish and I'd never known him to cross the busy street.

Bryan and I placed him in a bag and then I buried him in our backyard. Later that evening, Kathleen called me into the cave, our windowless computer room, to look at a touching video eulogy Stephen put together. As our family watched the pictures of our cat against the backdrop of a sad song, in walked Mel! We all whooped and hollered and of course wondered how he could be alive. The cat I buried obviously was not Mel!

Joshua 9:14,15—So the Israelites examined their food, but they did not consult the Lord. Then Joshua made a peace treaty with them and guaranteed their safety, and the leaders of the community ratified their agreement with a binding oath. (NLT)

The Gibeonites lived in Canaan and were part of the wicked civilization God targeted for destruction. They heard what the Israelites did to Jericho and Ai and knew that God commanded Moses to destroy them. Their cities were in the path of imminent attack. Cleverly, they sent ambassadors to Joshua, wearing ragged clothes, patched sandals and carrying badly worn gear and dry, moldy bread. They deceived Israel into thinking they traveled from a land far away to sign a peace treaty.

Joshua and the elders assumed after inspecting the delegation and sampling their provisions, that they were telling the truth. They did not ask God for His wisdom. Consequently, they obligated themselves to assimilate and protect the Gibeonites contrary to His explicit instructions.

Sometimes making wrong assumptions can turn out positively as in the case of Mel (with apologies to the owners of the cat that died). But in matters that involve obeying God, we should be adept at seeking His wisdom. Whenever in doubt or faced with making an important decision don't cut God out of the equation. Ask Him for His advice. James 1:5 says, *"Now if any of you lacks wisdom, he should ask God, who gives to all generously and without criticizing, and it will be given to him."* The only condition that God places on this promise is that we must have faith! If we don't believe, James writes, we won't receive anything from the Lord. So don't make poor decisions or reach false conclusions on the basis of faulty assumptions—ask God for help and trust in the answer He gives you when He chooses to give it!

Readiness

Readiness means much more than having our bags packed. Quite frankly, there are many Christians who seem to have made the necessary requirements to obey God's call. They have the knowledge, the equipment, and the backing of others, yet God will not use them. They will never set foot outside their own encampment. He will leave them, not necessarily because they did not prepare, but because of the attitude they project.

Judges 7:5-7—So he brought the people down to the water, and the LORD said to Gideon, "Separate everyone who laps water with his tongue like a dog. Do the same with everyone who kneels to drink." The number of those who lapped with their hands to their mouths was 300 men, and all the rest of the people knelt to drink water. The LORD said to Gideon, "I will deliver you with the 300 men who lapped and hand the Midianites over to you. But everyone else is to go home."

God handpicked 300 men to fight for Gideon against an army that numbered over 135,000! He sent the rest of the Israelites home. The test of readiness God established was simple. Most of the soldiers got down on their knees and put their face in the water to drink. By drinking in this manner, they could not observe enemy approaching. If God had fought for these self-centered soldiers, they would have claimed their own prowess won the battle. The 300 who cupped the water in their hands were alert to their surroundings. They were the men God selected as fit for His fight (Jud. 7:4-7).

To be spiritually ready means:

● *We are physically prepared*! We are not constrained by the things of this world. If need be, we can quickly pack and go!

● *We are mentally alert!* We are aware that we have a spiritual enemy who would destroy us in an instant if he could. We remain watchful so as not to be surprised.

● *We have a godly attitude!* Our desire is to hear and obey God's call. We are not enslaved to pleasing our own flesh.

● *We go!* When the drum of God's will beats, we are marching in step with His rhythm.

Are you ready? Our Heavenly Jumpmaster says the light is green, the door is open, your chute is packed, and you're standing in the door. Now go—leap out the airplane! God will decide where you land; your responsibility is to jump! As Dietrich Bonhoeffer, German Lutheran pastor and theologian who helped the German Resistance movement against Nazism wrote, "Action springs not from thought, but from a readiness for responsibility."[10]

Samsonite Baggage

Judges 16:17—he told her the whole truth and said to her, "My hair has never been cut, because I am a Nazirite to God from birth. If I am shaved, my strength will leave me, and I will become weak and be like any other man."

Samson was a muscular warrior who typified the nation of Israel. He was specially chosen by God, and empowered with eye-popping strength. Yet, like his countrymen, he was more prone to chase women and feed his lusts. How did a guy with so much going for him end up so badly?

Samson's girlfriend Delilah was paid by Philistine rulers to lure from him the secret of his strength. She nagged him daily until the Bible says he was *"tired to death."* Then he revealed to her his spiritual source of power. He consistently made feeling-based decisions without considering or consulting God. His operative philosophy was "if it feels good, do it." Confiding in Delilah cost him his strength and eventually his life. Plus he gave his enemies reason to exult in their god Dagon.

Much of our life is determined by our decision-making. The Apostle Paul wrote, *"In the same way the Spirit also joins to help in our weakness, because we do not know what to pray for as we should, but the Spirit Himself intercedes for us with unspoken groanings"* (Rom. 8:26). If Paul, a spiritual giant, admitted the inability to know what to pray for, how critical is it that we depend on the Holy Spirit for help in decision-making!

Many times I make choices based on a gut feeling or because it is self-pleasing. I clearly recall key decisions made many years ago I wish I could do over. I should have relied on the Holy Spirit for direction. I also observe leaders who choose not to make decisions, put their trust in waiting and miss God-given opportunities because they fail to act. When it comes to decision making the spectrum for error is wide; there is a huge difference between Samsonite luggage and Samsonite baggage!

Before making important decisions, *we ought to pray and seek God's will.* Second, *we should examine our motives.* Whatever we decide must be in consonance with God's Word. *Time permitting, we should seek the opinion of those who have a track record for making God-honoring decisions* (it is often wise to consult people much different than we are). Finally, *we should trust God and recognize that the process of trusting may be more important than the result.* Often our worst decisions are those that come from our strength and abilities—we take God for granted and He grants what we take.

Are you about to make an important decision? Here's a great place to start. *O Heavenly Father, may Your Kingdom come, may Your will be done, here on earth as it is in heaven. I am not sure what to do, but You know. So guide me Lord, show me Your way and receive all the glory!* May God guide you and bless you because He delights in you and you depend upon Him.

Segadores

Ruth 2:12—May the LORD reward you for what you have done, and may you receive a full reward from the LORD God of Israel, under whose wings you have come for refuge.

Our taxi leaves paved highway for a potholed road. We meander across the brown desert surface towards the San Francisco barrio nestled among one of the treeless hills that ring the city of Lima. Patricia directs Carlos to the large blue gates that open to a compound owned by Segadores. Here for the next three days I will speak to men and women from the jungle, Peruvian cities, and distant nations whose hearts all beat with the desire to reach 16 unreached Peruvian tribes with the life-changing news of Jesus Christ.

We meet in an unfinished concrete building. Two stories stand in what Director Peter Hocking hopes will one day be a four-story structure equipped for lodging, a library, a training institute, and place for worship and fellowship. Already Segadores ministers to well-over a hundred children in the immediate neighborhood.

Arturo, from Venezuela, strums his guitar bringing us into the Lord's presence. Adina closes her eyes and adds her Spanish words of adoration. This professor fluent in four languages came from Romania to serve in the jungle. Around the room I glance at a myriad of faces each with its own story. If contact is made with an unreached tribe, there are Peruvians in this room prepared to leave everything in order to live among them. Their concept of evangelism takes sharing to a deeper level than most of us will ever experience. They are willing to lose their lives to bring the gospel to tribes who have never heard the name of Jesus. Just recently, God spared one of them from an unreleased arrow aimed at his back.

To own Jesus' command to go out and make disciples requires a willingness to live under His unseen protection. Ruth left Moab to accompany her mother-in-law to the foreign land of Israel. She made Naomi's God, her God. Because of her noble character and willingness to leave her homeland, the Lord made her part of the lineage from which Jesus would descend. God honors us when we make His will our own. His rewards are great. I am blessed to see His hand at work among His people and to know that same hand cares for me.

Inspiration   † † †

The instinct of ownership is a right one, though the disposition expressed through it may be wrong. In a saint the idea of ownership is that we have the power to glorify God by good works (see Matthew 5:16). What we own is the honour of Jesus Christ.—Oswald Chambers in *The Moral Foundations of Life*

Orpah Goes Home

Ruth 4:13-17b—Boaz took Ruth and she became his wife. When he was intimate with her, the LORD enabled her to conceive, and she gave birth to a son. Then the women said to Naomi, "Praise the LORD, who has not left you without a family redeemer today. May his name be famous in Israel. He will renew your life and sustain you in your old age. Indeed, your daughter-in-law, who loves you and is better to you than seven sons, has given birth to him." Naomi took the child, placed him on her lap, and took care of him. The neighbor women said, "A son has been born to Naomi," and they named him Obed. He was the father of Jesse, the father of David . . .

She said I should go back home to my mother. It seemed like the logical thing to do. I mean why travel to a place I've never been to live with people I don't know? My husband, Kilion died. Life was tough. It was like all my dreams just disintegrated into tiny, bitter ashes. I wanted to do the right thing but what was the right thing to do?

You know she complimented me for my kindness to Kilion and to her. It felt good. I knew she loved me—what a sweet, wonderful woman. She even asked God to give me another husband—one in whom I would find the answer to my anxiety and worry.

When she kissed me, I cried so hard. I told her I would stay with her but again she said I should go home. She asked why I would live with her when it was not as if she was going to have another son for me to marry or that I would even *want* to wait. Her logic seemed faultless.

She said it was more bitter for her even than for me. That was probably true because not only had she lost her husband and both her sons but it seemed like God had deserted her. That thought really got me to thinking. If God abandoned her what was the point of me worshiping Him. He pretty much abandoned me as well. So, I said my tearful goodbye and left her knowing in my heart I would never see her again. I returned to my own culture and people to worship my childhood god—Chemosh.

I've always wondered what happened to my mother-in-law, Naomi, as well as my sister-in-law, Ruth. She also lost her husband Mahlon. He was Kilion's older brother. Naomi tried to convince Ruth to go home to her mother as well. But she insisted on returning to Israel with her. Ruth was tough as nails. I was much more pragmatic.

I guess I should tell you my name is Orpah. Like Ruth, I'm from Moab. But you've probably never heard of me and my name will never amount to anything more than just an obscure footnote in history. But then I don't suppose anything significant happened for Ruth or Naomi either—poor things.

Frozen Rain

1 Samuel 6:6—Why harden your hearts as the Egyptians and Pharaoh hardened theirs? When He afflicted them, didn't they send Israel away, and Israel left?

In twelve years of living in Tigard, I do not ever recall a snowfall that lasted more than two days. This is day five and the yard is still covered! Roads are slushy and treacherous. Of course, our cousins in Minnesota and North Dakota laugh at our frailty. They live with such conditions for months at a time. In the newspaper, I read a woman's bewildered commentary. Her husband was cursed and mocked by many passersby for shoveling the driveway—a time honored tradition in the Midwest. Evidently, snow and ice bring out the best and worst in Oregonians.

There is a fine degree of separation between flakes and frozen rain but the difference is profound. Have you ever heard of a gentle ice storm? Over 1300 flights at Portland's airport were cancelled and many businesses are closed. People's lives are changed by lost revenue, canceled trips, accidents and shattered dreams. Ice brings us to our knees and in some cases, backs. Stuck in the confines of my home, I have time to reflect . . .

The Bible has many things to say about our heart. God gave us hearts meant to be soft and pliable like snow. He intended that we revere Him and live our lives in worship by honoring Him in our work, play, language and thought. The sheen of snow reminds me that we were created to be holy and that God's purity is whiter still! Wow—our eyes have yet to see what shine really means! Moral hearts please Him. Virtuous hearts experience blessing through trial or triumph because the focus is always on God and not on circumstances.

What makes a good heart turn hard? What subtle change in temperature freezes Savior-worship into idolatry? Why do we lose our childish glee for cynical glum? Turning from God to please ourselves is a vile storm. Pride smears our noesis (understanding) and leaves us obtuse. If ice is treacherous, imagine what trouble a hard heart brings. *Lord, please do not let me ever become callous towards You and slick.* I opt for grace. I'll drink the hot cup of mercy Jesus gives and keep my heart pointed towards heaven. I'll revere the One who somehow saw enough value in me to sacrifice His Son. Will you join me?

Inspiration   † † †

Watch spiritual hardness, if ever you have the tiniest trace of it, haul up everything else till you get back your softness to the Spirit of God.—Oswald Chambers in *Run Today's Race*

The soul would have no rainbow if the eyes had no tears.—Native American Proverb

Helpless Rejoicing

When Nancy was thirteen years old, she was diagnosed with a heart disease, osteoporosis, and the verdict that she would never bear children. She and her mother bargained with God. They would pray wherever they were every day for two months at six a.m. and six p.m. if He would heal her. At home, they had no food and life was miserable. One day several Costa Ricans came to her Nicaraguan church. While the visiting pastor spoke with Nancy's mom, his wife spoke with Nancy. On a Friday afternoon, she told her that she would receive everything back in double for her faithfulness. On Monday when the doctors examined her, she was completely healed. God in His mercy blessed the young girl.

Just three years later she fell in love with a nonChristian boy and after a year and a half became pregnant. On February 5, 2001, she left home so as not to embarrass her family. Two months later after being alone, her boyfriend joined her. In the pit of despair from abandoning her walk with God, she nearly had an abortion. Instead, she returned to her church. Seven months into her pregnancy her umbilical cord wrapped three times around the neck of her unborn child. Again, she pled with God and He answered so that she delivered a healthy boy. Nancy married the child's father and rededicated her life to the Lord. After three years, her pastor asked her to be the church secretary.

For three hours each day, Nancy prayed and asked God to shine through her. She read her Bible an additional two hours. Still she struggled. She dealt with the physical abuse her father heaped on her as a child by abusing her own son. Finally, at a Christian camp she found forgiveness for herself and her dad. She learned to love her family and to be a blessing in her church.

Ephesians 6:12—For our battle is not against flesh and blood, but against the rulers, against the authorities, against the world powers of this darkness, against the spiritual forces of evil in the heavens.

At a youth conference in Managua, Nicaragua, I observed Nancy and a group of about 15 young people preparing to return home. They had miscalculated and did not have enough money for their trip home to Leon. Nancy, like a mother hen, gathered the young people in a circle. She wept loudly to the Lord over their need and then fervently praised Him for what He would do. When helpless people come humbly before their helping Father with praise and faith I suspect heaven rejoices. God answered Nancy and provided the *Cordobas* she and her group needed.

Struggles are not our undoing, they are our time of opportunity. In a sin-soaked world, we will wrestle and grapple with evil, unfairness and our own unfitness. But victory is ours if we will take our eyes off our problems and fasten them on Jesus!

Holy Cows

1 Samuel 6:7-9—Now then, prepare one new cart and two milk cows that have never been yoked. Hitch the cows to the cart, but take their calves away and pen them up. Take the ark of the LORD, place it on the cart, and put the gold objects in a box beside it, which you're sending Him as a guilt offering. Send it off and let it go its way. Then watch: If it goes up the road to its homeland toward Beth-shemesh, it is the LORD who has made this terrible trouble for us. However, if it doesn't, we will know that it was not His hand that punished us— it was just something that happened to us by chance.

Incredible! The Philistines captured the Ark of God but in every city they took it, Ashdod, Gath and Ekron, people were afflicted with tumors and the surrounding areas were rat-ravaged. Finally, the priests and diviners hatched a plan. They told their rulers to make five gold tumors and five gold rats and present them as a guilt offering before God. Then they did something that defied logic. Rather than ask the Israelites to reclaim their sacred possession, they took two recently calved cows that had never been yoked, and hitched them to a cart. If the cows pulled the cart down the road towards Judah, they would know for sure God was responsible for their distress.

Hello! Mama cows do not leave their calves. Cows that have never been yoked to anything do not suddenly cooperate to pull a cart down a road away from their home. But you can guess what happened. Those bovine beauties traveled straight to Judah and miraculously stopped in Beth Shemesh (a town that belonged to priests) without ever wandering off course. You can imagine the joy of those townspeople at the return of the Ark. Americans like to say, "Don't have a cow!" In other words, stay calm. The slang in that village surely became "Have a cow!" (May good things come to you.)

Two issues provoke me in this story found in 1 Samuel 5 and 6. First, pagan religious leaders tested God with conditions that clearly required divine intervention. They *knew* God's hand was behind their afflictions yet they challenged Him to prove it was really His hand at work. We don't serve a wimpy Lord. So why are we so afraid to trust God to do the impossible? If we want people to believe in our God they ought to see the incredible work He does through us! We ought to expect Him to do great things. We must quit confining Him to the limits of our eyes and minds. Beware of shackling God according to your reasoning and incontrovertible evidence. The Philistines expected God to fulfill a test worthy of His press. Do we ask God to go beyond our reason or are we afraid He will somehow make us look bad?

Second, the Philistines saw their idol Dagon smashed in his own temple before the ark of the Lord. They experienced plagues and a rodent invasion they knew were orchestrated from heaven. They understood historically what God did to Pharaoh and the Egyptians when they opposed the Israelites. They watched two cows do the unthinkable. So why don't we read in 1 Sa. 7 about revival breaking out in their land? Why didn't they abscond a decapitated Dagon to follow Yahweh? Perhaps it's easier to fashion gold rats and send them off as appeasement than give up perversity to obey an unseen Father. Faithlessness coupled with a strong fascination for sin makes it impossible to follow God even after holy cows.

Inspiration † † †

But true worship is the consequence, the result, of seeing God as He is. It springs naturally from a soul purified by love; it rises like incense from a heart without idols.—Francis Frangipane in *Holiness, Truth and the Presence of God*

Fatal Attraction

1 Samuel 13:13,14—Samuel said to Saul, "You have been foolish. You have not kept the command which the LORD your God gave you. It was at this time that the LORD would have permanently established your reign over Israel, but now your reign will not endure. The LORD has found a man loyal to Him, and the LORD has appointed him as ruler over His people, because you have not done what the LORD commanded."

King Saul decided to offer up sacrifices without waiting for Samuel, the prophet and rightful priest, to arrive. He was more concerned about what his men thought of him than in obeying God's clear commands.

A great danger we face as people who serve God is the tendency to lose sight of who gets the glory. We say the Lord is worthy but we live to receive recognition. The lure of personal fame seduces us. There is an explanation for why so many prominent Christians fall into immorality. Whenever we begin to believe that our achievements are the stuff God needs so He can be glorified—look out.

A preoccupation with personal glory results in a mirror-based *meology*, a fatal attraction. Whenever a Christian says "I deserve to do this, look at all I've done for God," it is not because his or her eyes are on Christ.

The book of Revelation does not resound with the triumph of man and all his accomplishments. There are no galactic choirs that fill space with ethereal tributes to human moon-landings, breakthroughs in animal cloning or high-speed laser technology. Why? Revelation is not about man it is about God, more specifically, the triumph of His Son Jesus over Satan and sin. Revelation is all about a grandiose paying of dues to the awe-inspiring Lamb of God. Revelation 4:11 proclaims, *"Our Lord and God, You are worthy to receive glory and honor and power, because You have created all things, and because of Your will they exist and were created."*

God's radiance does not fade! God's glory does not flicker. His brilliance is not wired to our energized *look-at-me batteries*. What makes us attractive is the Light that shines in us not the gleam of well-scrubbed teeth. If you have ever been in the presence of someone in love with God, you know this to be true. There is a quality of humility that warms the entire room with the genuine workings of the Holy Spirit! Jesus was not implying by His statement *"In the same way, let your light shine before men, that they may see your good deeds and praise your Father in heaven"* (Mat. 5:16) that we are the source of attraction. Rather He was affirming the truth that there is a divine Oil inside us burning and our glass needs to be clean enough for all to see this holy Fire at work!

Taking the Easy Way

By June of 1997, our church was $11,000 in debt to a property owner who unfairly raised our maintenance costs outside of our lease agreement. Because of the need to pay our $3000 monthly property bill, I went six months without a salary as the pastor. God sustained my family through the generosity of a senior citizen who attended Horizon Community Church. An opportunity arose for us to merge with another church that served in a nearby community and, like ourselves, was about five years old. We prayed. We held several meetings. I championed the plan and was supported by many people who eagerly shared Scripture and a sense that the Holy Spirit was directing us. It seemed that God had given us a great opportunity. So we dissolved and were absorbed into a larger body of believers.

Looking back many years later, I believe our decision was a good one, but not the best one. I wish that instead of merging, the elders and I had called for a prolonged time of fasting and prayer and even with mounting debt relied upon the Lord for relief. We took the easy way out, the expedient path. In the process, we terminated the life of our vibrant church and missed the opportunity to experience a greater deliverance.

1 Samuel 26:8—Then Abishai said to David, "Today God has handed your enemy over to you. Let me thrust the spear through him into the ground just once. I won't have to strike him twice!"

Twice God provided David opportunities to end the life of King Saul, a leader bent on destroying him. The prophet Samuel, in obedience to God, had already anointed David and declared God's rejection of Saul as king. Yet, David refused to take Saul's life. Instead he said to Abishai:

> *Don't destroy him, for who can lift a hand against the LORD's anointed and be blameless?" David added, "As the LORD lives, the LORD will certainly strike him down: either his day will come and he will die, or he will go into battle and perish. (1 Sa. 26:9,10)*

The Philistines in battle later killed Saul. David waited over seven years before becoming Israel's king.

God created the conditions for David to take action. He literally put Saul and his men into a deep sleep (vs. 12). I believe He often works to give us what we want or need. But what is expedient and seems providential may be a test. What is good may not be what is best. We honor God when we do what *most* honors Him. Sometimes that means waiting instead of acting. Sometimes it means choosing the harder right instead of the easier right. Sometimes it means accepting prolonged suffering instead of opting for immediate relief. How do we know what to do? The first three phrases of the Lord's Prayer give us our clue.

Obed-edom the Gittite

Some day I look forward to talking to Obed-edom the Gittite. After God killed Uzzah for touching His ark, (he grabbed it when the oxen transporting it stumbled), King David was afraid to bring it to Jerusalem. Instead, he left it at Obed's house.

2 Samuel 6:11,12—The ark of the LORD remained in his house three months, and the LORD blessed Obed-edom and his whole family. It was reported to King David: "The Lord has blessed Obed-edom's family and all that belongs to him because of the ark of God."

The ark of the covenant containing the Ten Commandments preceded the Israelites as God led them through the desert to the Promised Land. It was sacred and symbolic of Yahweh's glory (see Jos. 3:3 and 1 Sa. 4:22). I am sure Obed's family for generations talked about the three special months they hosted this hallowed object.

Why did an ark in the center of a living room so profoundly change a family's situation? Could it be that they were reminded every day of the great God they worshiped as they looked at this resplendent container? Did reverence replace routine? In the process of savoring holiness, Obed's family became more holy and that of itself ignited blessing.

Do you realize that we who follow Jesus have something far greater than the ark in our homes? 1 Corinthians 3:16 asks, *"Don't you know that you are God's sanctuary and that the Spirit of God lives in you?"* If the Spirit that led a nation now lives in our hearts, the evidence of His presence should be unmistakable and with it should come the handiwork of divine favor in our homes.

By the grace of God, all of my children know Him. My hope is that they will not love Him because of their parent's love, but because they are inexorably drawn to His presence of their own accord. A completed, favored family always finds at its heart the Lord. When God is present, blessing is normative. Does this mean that troubles and trials vanish and sorrow and sin are extinct? No. What it means is that our hearts overflow with joy that is not situation-dependent but rather Savior-centric.

Most of us live like we need an ark to move forward spiritually. But what we need is to make worship normative in our midst for our unseen Savior. It is by faith that we please God and it is by obedience to His will that we as families experience His eternal blessing. May our families spawn such reports by the surpassing goodness of God's presence in our homes! For when we live for Him, we cannot help but experience His goodness. To Him we belong for a world to behold! He gave us birth, He calls us His bride and He adopted us into His family and that's something to think about . . . in reveration!

Intoxicated with God

2 Samuel 6:14,15—David was dancing with all his might before the LORD wearing a linen ephod He and the whole house of Israel were bringing up the ark of the LORD with shouts and the sound of the ram's horn.

The king was excited—no question about it. The prized Ark of the Lord was back in Jerusalem, freed from the hands of the dreaded Philistines. As he danced in the streets, David felt relief mingled with joy! But his wife watching from an upstairs window didn't share his enthusiasm. She despised him in her heart. When he came home she sarcastically said, *"How the king of Israel honored himself today! . . . He exposed himself today in the sight of the slave girls of his subjects like a vulgar person would expose himself"* (2 Sa. 6:20).

David wasn't about to let her icy words sleet on his celebration. He was unfrosted by her thoughts. Evidently, God agreed with him for we read in 2 Sa. 6:23 that Michal, daughter of Saul, bore no children.

When I think of enthusiasm, I can't help but remember the Black Hats of Airborne School. Now those sergeants had verve! They would yell at us, *"You soldiers are moving like pond water!"* *"Get up ladies! What 'cha wanna be girls!"* When it came to creative uses of the English language to motivate people—the Black Hats ruled! Of course, who wouldn't be enthusiastic being paid to drop people for push-ups?

There's something powerfully motivating about being around people full of joy. I didn't say unrestrained for some times enthusiasm is rightfully bottled. I'm speaking of those whose joy is in the Lord no matter what life throws at them.

When's the last time you cut loose with a powerful chortle? Are you guilty of walking in the clay trenches of humdrum? Have your eyes grown accustomed to forming critical crosshairs so everyone in your path is a target? *Ah, drop it!* Take a moment and grab a deep breath of air! In fact, get a life! Go find a linen ephod and pick a street to dance! After all, God loves you. He gave you the awesome privilege of life. He honors those who dance for His glory and God knows we need more dances!

Inspiration   † † †

I know what it means to be "God-intoxicated."—Brother Lawrence (Frenchman born Nicolas Herman 1614-1691) & Frank Laubach (American missionary 1884-1970) in *Practicing His Presence*

Enthusiasm means, to use the phrase of a German mystic, "intoxicated with God," filled to overflowing with God, no spasmodic spirituality about us but a perennial source of freshness making us a delight to our Lord and a channel of blessing to all with whom we come in contact.—Oswald Chambers in *God's Workmanship*

Don't Blame God When Things Go Bad

During a two-year period, I moved into four different offices within the same organization. As I got ready to move for the fifth time I eyed an office that best served the needs of my team and me. But to move into this office I had to displace a man highly resistant to change. I did not look forward to the conversation with him knowing that he would resist my directive. At first, this is exactly what he did. He cited injustices he experienced in the past. He said he would raise a ruckus. Then he said according to regulation he was entitled to a space of at least 120 square feet. All of his objections were raised before I even mentioned the office in which I planned to relocate him. Other members of the team measured the dimensions of that space and "gleefully" informed him that it was sufficiently large. They too had anticipated a defensive posture. Fortunately, the situation was resolved favorably.

2 Samuel 10:12—Be strong! We must prove ourselves strong for our people and for the cities of our God. May the LORD's will be done.

The Bible records that sometime around 1000 BC the Ammonite King Hanun elected to go to war with Israel. King David's general was Joab, a cunning and brave man. Joab deployed his army against a hired force of Arameans to his front and Ammonite forces to his rear. This forced Joab to divide his army putting one group under the leadership of his brother Abishai. Joab's final words of instruction to Abishai before going into battle are the words in the meditation above.

Joab's attitude in a position of vulnerability was excellent. He simply chose to trust in God and he communicated his faith to his warrior brother. He knew that ultimately victory was in God's hands. No surprise, the Israelites won in stunning fashion.

Our attitude is a profound indicator of our spiritual condition. It's nigh near impossible to trust in God and have a whining disposition. What comes out of our mouth reveals our operating philosophy. For this reason we ought to put a banner in whatever room we frequent the most with these words: THE LORD WILL DO WHAT IS GOOD IN HIS SIGHT!

As Epictetus, the Greek, stoic philosopher said, "It isn't your problems that are bothering you. It is the way you are looking at them." If our attitude is wrong, our hope is not in our Sovereign Lord. Our mind-set is indicative of trust or lack of trust. If we want people to see the power of Christ, they must see us rise above misfortune and inconvenience—confident in the power of YAHWEH! Don't blame God when things go bad. Don't praise yourself when things go well. Believe that He is in control and live accordingly. He gets the glory; we get the joy. He deserves our trust; we learn how to live.

Lagom

Silas took me to lunch at a Swedish restaurant in Gothenburg called Lagom. *Lagom* has no single English word that matches its meaning. Essentially, it translates *"enough, sufficient, not too much or too little—just right"*.

2 Samuel 22:31-33—God—His way is perfect; the word of the LORD is pure. He is a shield to all who take refuge in Him. For who is God besides the LORD? And who is a rock? Only our God. God is my strong refuge; He makes my way perfect.

God's grace is *lagom*. The Apostle Paul wrote in 2 Co. 12:7-9:
. . . Therefore, so that I would not exalt myself, a thorn in the flesh was given to me, a messenger of Satan to torment me so I would not exalt myself. Concerning this, I pleaded with the Lord three times to take it away from me. But He said to me, "My grace is sufficient for you, for power is perfected in weakness." Therefore, I will most gladly boast all the more about my weaknesses, so that Christ's power may reside in me.
In Jesus, we have the grace to be *just right*. But to understand this we must have eyes that see beyond our circumstances.

A good friend, Dave, dropped dead of a heart attack. Two weeks prior to dying he had a physical and was pronounced fit. While out jogging, his heart failed. Dave left behind a wife and four children. Another friend unexpectedly lost his job. A woman we know was diagnosed with cancer. How is grace *lagom* when a wife is widowed with a family to raise by herself and children are left without a father? What about those times when life is more like a landslide than a sturdy bridge?

King David sang the verses in the meditation above despite the fact that he had already lost three sons, was betrayed by those closest to him, and constantly endured criticism and the attack of enemies. Somehow, he recognized that God gave him strength and made his way *lagom*.

There is much about life and circumstances we cannot understand. Yet, I know with certainty that no matter how desperate my situation may be, if I trust in the Lord, He gives me the strength to proceed. He makes my way *lagom*. If we think that *just right* means everything is smooth and to our liking, we are mistaken. It does not mean we avoid suffering or repeatedly win. It means that God's will is always right. Because of who He is and what He promises, we can ride the worst storms and know that under His wings we are *lagom*. Oswald Chambers wrote in *If You Will Be Perfect*, "Beware of mental quibbling over the word perfect. Perfection does not mean the full maturity and consummation of one's powers, but perfect fitness for doing the will of God (compare Php. 3:12-15)."

Bread and Meat

1 Kings 17:14—For this is what the LORD, the God of Israel says: "The jar of flour will not be used up and the jug of oil will not run dry until the day the LORD gives rain on the land." (NIV)

The ravens brought him bread and meat every morning and he drank all his water from a brook. The sky was like a stone and the stream dried up before the prophet heard a word from the Lord. *"Go at once to Zarephath there's a widow in that town. I'll put it in her heart to make your meals"* (NIV). It's a little coastal village where idols abound but it'll be a safe place for him to stay.

He asked her for some water he implored her for some bread. He has a grumbling stomach in a drought. She's never met this man, he's a foreigner to her town, and what a time to show his gnarly face. She's astounded by his offer. She's floored by his boldness. She tells him that her flour's running out. The oil in her jar is down to the bottom and now he comes along making his request.

"Don't be afraid, go home and make a cake and make it so the three of us can dine." Her little son is helping her gather up the sticks to cook their final meal before they die.

He asked her for some water he implored her for some bread. He's hungry as a prophet in a drought. She has never met this man he is a foreigner to her town but there is something in his eyes she cannot explain. She's a good cooking woman with a heart made of gold. It's Elijah's bed and breakfast on the coast. The flour's never gone and the oil ever flows 'cause the Lord never fails to keep His word!

So the moral of the story is for every one with ears. The time will come when you will hear the Lord. When He asks for sacrifice and it seems impossible. He will make a way where none was there before. He's the mighty God of Israel, He's the Maker of your soul, He's the ever running River through the drought. He's the Father to the widow and the resurrecting power—the One in whom your faith should never doubt!

The same God who fed about 5,000 men plus women and children with two fish and five loaves of bread, can feed a few people 5,000 times with a handful of flour and a little oil! Our God is the Great Provider! Are we willing to trust that He is able to meet our needs when we, in our limited faith, can only see what we don't have?

Inspiration † † †
God feeds even the worm in the earth.—Yiddish Proverb
He who gives us teeth will give us bread.—Jewish Proverb

You can Learn a Lot from a U-Haul

Growing up we moved a lot. One of the fun challenges of moving was trying to figure out how to fit everything into the U-Haul truck. Watching my dad, I learned three important principles for packing a truck. First, evaluate what needs to be moved. Pack what is heaviest or large first and be willing to leave behind or give away some things. Second, to protect the back from injury, always lift from the legs when carrying heavy or awkward objects. Third, work as a team—don't try to carry something that is too heavy alone. I suspect those principles have spiritual applications.

1 Kings 19:4—But he went on a day's journey into the wilderness. He sat down under a broom tree and prayed that he might die. He said, "I have had enough! LORD, take my life, for I'm no better than my fathers."

Perhaps you carry the emotional luggage of an abusive past. You may struggle with marital or family problems. Maybe your health is constantly under attack. Could it be that you have a boss that is corrupt or unkind? The prophet Elijah knew what it was like to carry a burden. He fled an evil queen intent on taking his life. Exhausted from running, he prayed the words in the meditation above. Elijah was so depressed he lost the ability to have a clear perspective towards his problems. Can you relate?

All of us carry burdens. The question is, "Are we carrying loads God never meant us to lift?" King David wrote, *"Cast your burden on the LORD, and He will support you; He will never allow the righteous to be shaken"* (Psa. 55:22). David understood that there were troubles He could give over to the Lord. God would provide the relief he needed.

Lifting from the legs utilizes different muscle groups to evenly distribute the challenge of maneuvering weight. Instead of trying to carry his problems on his shoulder David noted, *"May the Lord be praised! Day after day He bears our burdens; God is our salvation. Selah"* (Psa. 68:19). David relied upon God to help him handle trouble. Burdens take on new meaning if I realize the Lord is with me every day to help me. This is why Jesus says to us in Mat. 11:28, *"Come to Me, all of you who are weary and burdened, and I will give you rest."* Note that Jesus did not promise that our burdens would go away but rather that He would give us rest. Just knowing that He cares can fortify us to deal with whatever we are bearing.

Finally, there are many times because of pride or insecurity we fail to let others help us overcome problems. The Apostle Paul counseled the Galatians to *"Carry one another's burdens; in this way you will fulfill the law of Christ"* (Gal. 6:2). It's a sign of wisdom, not weakness, to know when to ask for help! It's also a sign of maturity to comprehend the struggle someone else endures and bring relief.

Lost Reception

If the weather is good, I love driving Bell Road! This five-mile curvy route affords a clear view of Mount Hood, the town of Newberg, forestland and beautiful farm country. But along Bell are two spots where I lose cell phone reception. If I'm engaged in conversation with someone, I have to keep driving until I can regain the signal before redialing.

About 400 prophets prophesied to King Ahab of Israel and King Jehoshaphat of Judah that if they went to battle against the Aramean army they would be successful. But something about them caused King Jehoshaphat to doubt their authenticity. So he asked Ahab (1 Ki. 22:7), *"Isn't there a prophet of Yahweh here any more?"* Reluctantly, Ahab told him about Micaiah, who was prone to give unfavorable pronouncements to the king, and then he dispatched a messenger to get this unpopular exhorter.

1 Kings 22:13—The messenger who went to call Micaiah instructed him, "Look the words of the prophets are unanimously favorable for the king. So let your words be like theirs, and speak favorably.

Micaiah was a prophet with a clear connection with God. But what the people wanted was a recording. They wanted this man of God to parrot the religious establishment—"Go and you will succeed." But he knew that disaster awaited Ahab and he told him so. Scripture tells us Ahab died in battle exactly as Micaiah predicted.

People, who rely on their own wisdom, or whose relationship with God is a sham, speak words that may sound good spiritually but in truth are as disconnected from reality as a signal-less cell call. The best result of garble is confusion! Ahab's 400 prophets had a bad, or at best, weak connection with the Lord, and were easily deceived into broadcasting a false message. Just because they were religious didn't make them right.

So, how do we get a clear connection with the God we cannot see, so we can know His will? Certainly, we must leave any place or thing that causes sin and breaks our connection with Him. He will not abide where there is evil. Second, we must listen and obey His Spirit. Third, don't assume the religious crowd speaks for God. Finally, if we still cannot discern His voice, it may be that He is silent for His own purposes. If this is the case, we must patiently wait on Him and not take hasty action we may later regret.

How's your connection to your heavenly Father? Are you hearing from Him or do you feel like you are in some dead cell zone? Ask for His help in reconnecting, trusting that He has a word for you!

Kimmy Caught a Brook Trout

All of our family met together in northern Idaho to celebrate my parent's 40th wedding anniversary. One day a bunch of us drove to a remote lake to fish for rainbow and brook trout. The fishing pole one of the grandkids used broke and we could not fix it. But Sandy's daughter, Kimmy, asked if she could just take some fishing line and with her hook baited with worm toss it out to see what she could catch. She was bored watching an inactive bobber and her idea seemed much more fun.

Vicki and I asked her to walk further down the shoreline so as she thrashed through the water she would not scare away the fish near our lines. Vicki pointed to a good spot for her to throw her line out. We also hinted that it was unlikely she would catch anything because she was too noisy and too close to her bait. We didn't want her to be discouraged when nothing happened. But Kimmy was quite content to fish her way. Of course, you know what happened. Kimmy caught a brook trout!

2 Kings 6:5-7—As one of them was cutting down a tree, the iron ax head fell into the water, and he cried out: "Oh, my master, it was borrowed!" Then the man of God asked, "Where did it fall?" When he showed him the place, the man of God cut a stick, threw it there, and made the iron float. Then he said, "Pick it up." So he reached out and took it.

Picture this unfortunate man who has lost the valuable tool a friend lent him. Either he cannot swim and therefore does not jump in the Jordan River to find the ax head, or the current is too swift to even bother trying. I've stood by the bank of the Jordan River and it is far too murky to see anything. So, this son of a prophet does the smartest thing he can think of—he asks the prophet Elisha for help.

An iron ax head does not float. What do you suppose went through the minds of the apprentices when their master cut a stick and threw it into the water. Logically, Elisha's technique for ax head retrieval seemed ludicrous. But Elisha was not acting logically. He acted in faith. He saw a problem and trusted God to fix the issue assumingly by doing what the Spirit of God led. God *can* make metal float!

I agree with Richard Bach's statement, "Argue for your limitations, and sure enough, they're yours."[11] Isn't it easy to find fault with the techniques people choose that we think are ridiculous? Yet, before we pack ice on a hot, new method, perhaps we should remember that we serve a clever God who delights in being creative. The moral of the story is there are often many ways to reach solution and the greatest thing we can do when there seems to be no answer is to trust *The Answer*. He will provide. It may not be the way we expect, or according to our timetable, but then is that really the point?

Nehushtan

2 Kings 18:4-6—He removed the high places and shattered the sacred pillars and cut down the Asherah poles. He broke into pieces the bronze snake that Moses made, for the Israelites burned incense to it up to that time. He called it Nehushtan. Hezekiah trusted in the LORD God of Israel; not one of the kings of Judah was like him, either before him or after him. He held fast to the LORD and did not turn from following Him but kept the commandments the LORD had commanded Moses.

Did you know that God was once so displeased with the complaining Israelites that He sent venomous vipers to bite them during their trek through the desert? When they cried out to Him for help, He provided an unusual solution. Everyone bitten who looked upon the bronze snake He told Moses to make, recovered. You can read about this in Num. 21:4-9.

I don't know why God had Moses make a snake replica when He could have just answered the people's prayer by healing them. Perhaps He wanted them to look upon something disgusting to remind them of their sinful behavior. Or maybe He wanted to use it to test them. In 2 Ki. 18:4 we learn the rest of the story. Evidently, over 700 years after Moses made the bronze snake, it not only still existed, but the people in Judah were burning incense before it. King Hezekiah, disgusted by what had become an idol, named it *Nehushtan*, which means "a bronze thing." Then he broke it into pieces. The prophet Habakkuk wrote, *"What use is a carved idol after its craftsman carves it? It is only a cast image, a teacher of lies. For the one who crafts its shape trusts in it and makes idols that cannot speak"* (Hab. 2:18).

God created a one-time antidote that worked against snakebites. Man turned the antidote into a visual keepsake of God's deliverance. The image became a god, a trust-sucker. Lest we laugh at such nonsense and ignorance, perhaps we should let the Holy Spirit inspect our hearts! John Calvin, French Protestant theologian and author noted, "Every one of us is, even from his mother's womb, a master craftsman of idols." Is there something God worked through once that we hold onto expecting to be used again? Do we own some lucky charm that we dare not lose? Any object, habit or belief that absorbs our veneration as opposed to going straight to God, is a *Nehushtan*.

Hezekiah saw the danger. He didn't care about popular opinion, an authentic antique or the meetings at the pole. He got rid of the snake! His faith was in God—nothing else, just GOD! His path was straightforward—the way of obedience. Is it a surprise then that God blessed him mightily, saving his kingdom at a time when Judah should have been annihilated by Assyria! Friend, God wants to bless you mightily too, the question is, do you trust Him?

Thanksliving

1 Chronicles 16:8—Give thanks to the LORD; call on His name proclaim His deeds among the peoples.
Psalm 30:12b—LORD my God, I will praise You forever.
Philippians 4:4,11,12—Rejoice in the Lord always. I will say it again: Rejoice! . . . I don't say this out of need, for I have learned to be content in whatever circumstances I am. I know both how to have a little, and I know how to have a lot. In any and all circumstances I have learned the secret of being content—whether well-fed or hungry, whether in abundance or in need.
Colossians 2:6,7—Therefore as you have received Christ Jesus the Lord, walk in Him, rooted and built up in Him and established in the faith, just as you were taught, and overflowing with thankfulness.
1 Thessalonians 5:18—Give thanks in everything, for this is God's will for you in Christ Jesus.

Two men in the Bible particularly strike me as thankful—David and Paul. Both of them were well acquainted with suffering, tragedy and persecution yet both maintained a remarkable attitude of thanksgiving. They possessed and operated by a philosophy I call *thanksliving!*

Thanksliving is:

- An attitude rooted and anchored by faith in God.
- Contagious proclamation. One cannot help but tell people about God who is the true source of joy.
- Permanent. No circumstance or condition can defeat it—ever. Even in the midst of deep sorrow, pain and affliction *thanksliving* is both possible and appropriate.
- Centered, rooted, fed and focused on Christ Jesus. Without Him, it is impossible to attain.
- A mindset of contentment and peace regardless of external circumstances.
- An obedient response to the will of God that becomes a glory offering.
- Hopeful—one day we receive a kingdom that cannot be shaken!

Thanksgiving is a holiday set aside to remind us that we should be grateful for God's provisions. *Thanksliving* is a daily state that marks us as children of an awesome Father.

Inspiration † † †

Gratitude is not only the greatest of virtues, but the parent of all the others.—Cicero, Rome's greatest orator, politician, (106-43 B.C.)

Honor

1 Chronicles 29:12—Riches and honor come from You, and You are the ruler of everything. In Your hand are power and might, and it is in Your hand to make great and to give strength to all.

Honor seems to be a lost concept in these decaying days. As she declines, cynicism ascends to ravage our land. People watch their heroes fall to lust, haughtiness and hypocrisy to the point that scandal has become ho-hum. Of course, this makes sense for honor cannot be owned long by anything infected by sin. When people conclude it is hopeless to live a virtuous life they must find some means to justify their tainted tastes. Rather than fight an insatiable flesh some condone it as natural and reinvent virtue in defiled ways. *"They devise crimes and say, "We have perfected a secret plan." The inner man and the heart are mysterious"* (Psa. 64:6). Whenever evil is called good understand that honor is despised as intolerant. Thus, the mother who decries the neighborhood pedophile is labeled by sexual deviants as hateful.

True honor must come from Truth and only Jesus claimed this title (John 14:6). He backed up His claim by living perfectly. Therefore, we gain our honor by gaining Christ. We fellowship with His honorable Father through His merit and not our own. Jesus challenges us to deny ourselves so we can be free of our selfishness and set our eyes on God. He showed us how to live. He sent His Spirit to help us be like Him.

When we call ourselves Christians, we associate ourselves with Christ. To live dishonorably is to slander His holy name. To live through His power is to generate light that brings hope to those trapped in darkness. You don't have to be greatly gifted or famous to be honorable. God can use you in the humblest of settings and obscure places to further His kingdom if you will commit to doing your best wherever you are for His glory. This is honor.

Homage Lord we give to You who made us by Your perfect will.

Our dignity was bought by grace when all our sins Your blood erased.

Noble Light, Your love proclaimed; from our darkness we were saved!

Only You deserve the words, "King of kings and Lord of lords!"

Reverence woven rich by awe for You are worthy over all!

Inspiration † † †

When one seeks the honor that comes from God only, he will take the withholding of the honor that comes from men very quietly indeed.—George Macdonald, Scottish author, (1824-1905)

Who loses honor can lose nothing else.—Latin proverb

Virtue

1 Chronicles 29:17—I know, my God, that You test the heart and that You are pleased with uprightness. I have willingly given all these things with an upright heart, and now I have seen Your people who are present here giving joyfully and willingly to You.

Have you noticed how desperately our society yearns for moral role models? Yogi Berra, the master of chaotic one-liners once quipped, "If you can't imitate him, don't copy him."   Virtue doesn't come easily it takes effort. Just ask my good friend Cissy, who had to leave a job she desperately needed because her boss, a pastor, wanted her to mislead senior citizens on the capabilities of the beds they were selling. In every crumbling civilization, one has only to measure the absence of virtue to understand the reason for decay.

Often our virtue is measured by our words. Either we strive to be honest or we become masters of *spin*, altering the picture to our benefit. If we were born holy, virtue would come easily. Instead, we strive to overcome a nature that at its core is selfishly wired. Oswald Chambers in *My Utmost For His Highest*, noted, "Everything that does not partake of the nature of virtue is the enemy of virtue in me, and it depends on what moral caliber I have whether I overcome and produce virtue."

The secret to virtuous living is found in the Bible. God says in Lev. 11:44, *"For I am the LORD your God, so you must consecrate yourselves and be holy because I am holy."* God says, *"Be like Me."* He showed us how by sending Jesus, who lived a perfect life on earth amidst the watchful eyes of humanity. We cannot attain purity in our own effort, but by obeying God's instruction and allowing His Holy Spirit to lead us, we can become virtuous.

Inspiration   † † †

Without God, there is no virtue, because there's no prompting of the conscience. Without God, we're mired in the material, that flat world that tells us only what the senses perceive. Without God, there is a coarsening of the society. And without God, democracy will not and cannot long endure. If we ever forget that we're one nation under God, then we will be a nation gone under.—Ronald Reagan, 40th President of the United States, (1911-2004)

Recommend virtue to your children; it alone, not money, can make them happy. I speak from experience.—Ludwig van Beethoven, German composer, (1770-1827)

Matsa

Zerah the Cushite marched out against Judah with a humongous army. King Asa deployed 580,000 troops but they were still vastly outnumbered. Thirty years earlier, facing similar overwhelming odds, King Rehoboam capitulated before King Shishak of Egypt and his Libyan, Sukkite and Cushite hordes. Fortunately, Asa was not like Rehoboam. Instead of surrendering, this king prayed to the Lord asking for His help. His heavenly Protector responded by leading them to victory. It was after this battle that the prophet Azariah came and spoke the following words.

2 Chronicles 15:2—So he went out to meet Asa and said to him, "Asa and all Judah and Benjamin, hear me. The LORD is with you when you are with Him. If you seek Him, He will be found by you, but if you abandon Him, He will abandon you."

God promised to be with Asa and his countrymen so long as they sought Him and obeyed Him. The phrase *"The Lord is with you"* comes from the Hebrew word *matsa* and literally means, "His presence coming forth to enable, to bless." *Matsa* is illustrated in Mat. 18:20 where Jesus said, *"For where two or three are gathered together in My name, I am there among them."*

Sarah and Stephen talked us into bringing home two kittens. I said, "As long as you commit to responsibly caring for them, I'll agree." So a little female black bundle of fur and her Siamese-marked brother left our friends the Jacksons to join the York household. Bear, our overgrown Rottweiler-Lab, was quite excited. Unfortunately, because of his size and power, he is quite capable of inflicting harm, whether accidentally or intentionally. So long as the kittens stay close to us, they are safe from Bear. We provide *matsa*—the blessing of protection and an environment where two vulnerable kitties can eat, drink, play and sleep safely.

Sometimes I wonder if God sees us as wayward kittens. Despite His protective presence, we are prone to wander. Instead of confident living, we hide in terror behind the piano, hoping that big fearsome beast will leave us alone! Yet, every day at every hour, we have a Father in heaven who loves us and promises to be with us and protect us. No matter what the world may throw at us, God's arms are sufficient to protect and hold us. We are children of the Almighty who promises us His *matsa*!

Inspiration † † †

Participation in the blessings of the union with Christ comes when the faithful have all the things needed to live well and blessedly to God.—William Ames, English theologian, (1576-1633)

God's "whoever" policy has a "however" benefit.—Max Lucado in 3:16

Defects

John works at Gunderson, a manufacturing and assembly plant that makes cast steel parts. He shared how he and a team of workers travelled to China to investigate why the parts they were receiving from the foundry in China were breaking. What they discovered was profound.

When a mold is poured, it must be smooth and complete. Metal must be at the right temperature to flow in and fill all the cavities. Then it must set for the right period of time. The temperature must also be hot when the mold (made of volcanic black sand), is broken. The Chinese workers in their hurry to produce parts were breaking molds too soon by cooling them too rapidly. The products looked fine when they were shipped to the U.S. However, when the parts were fitted into machinery for use, they cracked because they were defective.

2 Chronicles 20:32,33—Jehoshaphat was a good king, following the ways of his father, Asa. He did what was pleasing in the Lord's sight. During his reign, however, he failed to remove all the pagan shrines, and the people never fully committed themselves to follow the God of their ancestors. (NLT)

King Jehoshaphat was a descendent of King David and a good king. But contrast his description with Jotham, his great, great, great, great grandson. *"King Jotham became powerful because he was careful to live in obedience to the Lord his God"* (2 Ch. 27:6—NLT).

Jehoshaphat took moral shortcuts. He didn't get rid of all the pagan shrines (impurities), thereby encouraging half-hearted commitment to God in his countrymen. Nor did he spend enough time mentoring (curing the mold), of his oldest son, Jehoram. After he died, Jehoram murdered all his brothers and many of Judah's moral leaders. Judah descended into decades of idol worship and conduct that angered God. Small problems in the father became huge problems in the son and the nation!

So, how's your mold? Are you following God wholeheartedly, allowing Him to develop you into His image? Or are you allowing character defects to mar your condition? Are you obedient or do you vitiate (impair) God's plan for your life? Let's pray that God will give us the courage to walk in holiness and the wisdom to do what is right all the time so when we are engaged in life's battles, we don't crack!

Inspiration † † †

Children are excellent observers, and will often perceive your slightest defects. In general, those who govern children, forgive nothing in them, but everything in themselves.—Francois Fenelon, French Roman Catholic theologian, poet and writer, (1651-1715)

Joash Goes Bad

2 Chronicles 24:2—Throughout the time of Jehoiada the priest, Joash did what was right in the LORD's sight.

It's the classic story of a good boy who turns out to be a rotten man. The wicked mother of King Ahaziah decided upon his death to become queen. She slaughtered the entire royal family except for Joash, a baby boy that Jehoiada the priest was able to hide from her. When Joash turned seven, Jehoiada made his move. With the help of five army commanders and the Levites, he placed the crown on King David's descendant. Then the commanders executed the treason-yelling Queen Athaliah.

Jehoiada the priest lived to be 130 years old. He served as the primary mentor and counselor to young King Joash. For most of the king's 40-year reign, he was a good man who honored God. But when Jehoiada died, everything changed. An influential group of evil leaders convinced Joash to ditch worshiping God. The people bowed down to fabricated idols and abandoned God's temple. The Lord sent many prophets in an attempt to turn the people back to Him. But they would not listen.

Then the Spirit of God came upon the prophet Zechariah. Boldly he stood before his countrymen and confronted them for disobeying God's commands. This infuriated Judah's vile leaders! So they persuaded Joash to kill Zechariah. In the courtyard of the Lord's Temple, they stoned him to death. *"King Joash didn't remember the kindness that Zechariah's father Jehoiada had extended to him, but killed his son. While he was dying, he said, 'May the LORD see and demand an account'"* (2 Ch. 24:22).

God swiftly executed judgment against Joash. He helped Aram's much smaller army attack and conquer Judah's troops, severely wounding King Joash in the process. Then, a few of his own officials disgusted by what he did to Zechariah, assassinated him as he lay in bed. A king who should have lived far beyond the age of 47, who could have enjoyed God's continuous blessings and left a legacy, died instead a failure.

What made this man who owed his very life to a kind priest, diabolically eliminate his righteous son? What made this sovereign whose heart thumped the beat of faith, turn to embrace wooden poles honoring Asherah the Canaanite goddess? A strong priest led an impressionable king to do what was right. Corrupt leaders persuaded that same monarch to commit unthinkable treachery.

Persuasion is a two-way street.
One way leads to glory for God defines its path,
The other leads to shame and disregards His wrath.
So who persuades you? And whom do you persuade?
Will you stand up for God or will you turn away?

Leakage

Sometimes for relaxation, I will sit down and watch the fish in our aquarium. Their territorial battles, peculiar habits, and beautiful coloring make for interesting (albeit slow) entertainment. We purchased our 60-gallon tank in San Diego and had it for over 12 years. Then one morning I awoke to find the water level had dropped. Horror of horrors, the glass zoo had sprung a leak.

2 Chronicles 26:5—He (King Uzziah) sought God throughout the lifetime of Zechariah, the teacher of the fear of God. During the time that he sought the LORD, God gave him success.

King Amaziah, a direct descendant of King David, was a good king who often did what was right in God's eyes but not wholeheartedly (see 2 Ch. 25:2). Unfortunately, he had a pride problem and turned away from God. This ultimately cost him his life. His son, Uzziah, was just 16 years old when the people of Judah made him their king. As the passage above teaches, Uzziah was successful so long as he sought the Lord. He defeated Judah's enemies in battle and fortified Jerusalem. He employed many people to plant vineyards and gardens because he loved the soil. Life was good in the land of Judah. *"But when he became strong, he grew arrogant and it led to his own destruction"* (2 Ch. 26:16a). God struck Uzziah with leprosy and he died a horrible death. Because of his disease, he was not even buried with his fathers.

It is not a complicated thing to follow God. So why is it that few follow the straight path without going crooked? Uzziah watched his dad turn from God and suffer the consequences. Yet, he too became victim to the same malady we know as pride.

I suspect it happens to all of us if we are not extremely careful. We begin with good intentions eager to please God. Spiritual growth is profitable and exciting. It feels good to *be* good. Then we get a little lazy. We stop spending as much time studying our Bibles. We frequently forget to pray. Over time, we assume more of the load of decision-making without consulting the Lord. Life goes on and we notice we are doing just fine. Cockiness subtly sets in as we grow increasingly confident in our own wisdom. Then *bang* we sin in a major way! We justify our errant behavior because we no longer fear God. We behold Him as caterer instead of as King.

The unattended glass badly needed caulking. Are you seeking God? If you're too busy for Him, you are already leaking. Do not take Him for granted! Humble yourself! Why suffer downfall when He offers uplift! May we seek Him wholeheartedly before we find our tanks are empty!

Lessons on Timing

Have you ever engaged on a mission convinced you were doing the Lord's will only to see your efforts defeated by some unforeseen event? Have you taken a job sure that it was God's choice for you only to discover the boss was mean-spirited or the co-workers were adept at making your life miserable? Have you lost a family member or experienced prolonged illness, convinced that God would bring healing and He didn't? If you answered "yes" to any of these questions you probably have sincere issues to discuss with God regarding His will and timing.

Ezra 1:2,3—This is what King Cyrus of Persia says: "The LORD, the God of heaven, has given me all the kingdoms of the earth and has appointed me to build Him a house at Jerusalem in Judah. Whoever is among His people, may his God be with him, and may he go to Jerusalem in Judah and build the house of the LORD, the God of Israel, the God who is in Jerusalem.

In the book of Ezra, homesick Jews left Babylon, their place of exile, journeying to Jerusalem. They returned to a land populated by relocated foreigners who worshiped heathen idols. King Cyrus issued an edict authorizing them to rebuild their temple. However, as soon as Zerubbabel, Jeshua, and the rest of the leaders began rebuilding they encountered opposition from Jew-hating inhabitants. Rehum, the area's commanding officer, and Shimshai, a secretary, wrote such a condemning letter that the successor to King Cyrus, Artaxerxes, ordered all temple building stopped. It was a serious, morale-deflating ruling. It would take long years and a new king before a counter-order came allowing the Jews to finish building God's temple. No doubt many died without seeing the temple restored, bewildered by baffling events that ran counter to God's promises. Why did God inspire two Persian kings to authorize the rebuilding of the temple yet permit another king to stand in opposition?

The Bible gives us helpful insight into the sovereign workings of God. Here are seven lessons to consider about timing and why He allows things to happen differently than what we might expect.

1. *The exercise of justice*: rather than wait, sometimes God punishes us for our willful sin, refrains from helping because of our disobedience and permits suffering as a natural consequence of our sin nature—Num. 14:21-23; Jud. 2:20-23; Gen. 3:16-19.

2. *The use of tolerance:* God allows people and Satan to oppose His work and will to accomplish His greater purpose—Ezra 4:4,5; Mat. 16:23; Luke 22:3; Acts 8:1,4.

3. *The testing of faith and reverence*: see Gen. 17:17, Ecc. 3:14

4. *The importance of testimony:* God may use circumstances to reveal world-wide His power and glory—Jos. 2:10,11; Ezra 7:27; Acts 2:5-11.

5. *The reality of timelessness:* God holds an eternal perspective—Ecc. 3:11,15; John 17:1-3.

6. *The need for priority:* our concern is not always God's concern nor does He weight things the same way we do—Acts 1:7.

7. *The promise of favor: God eventually works all things ". . . for the good of those who love God: those who are called according to His purpose"* (Rom. 8:28).

Don't be discouraged if things don't work out the way you planned. Trust in the Lord and believe that He loves you and has your best interests (the ones we can't always see or understand) at heart. Something to think about . . . in reveration.

Inspiration   † † †

Every day is a messenger of God.—Russian Proverb

God has said He will exalt you in due time, but remember, He is referring to His time and not yours! —A. W. Tozer, pastor, editor and author (1897-1963)

Joy

Stephen blew fiercely against the candles on his cake. But try as he may, those flames would not die. He was the victim of trickery and everyone howled with merriment. There was a wonderful lesson on top of all that delicious frosting.

So often as Christians, we wear our joy like normal candles. At the slightest breeze of adversity, we find our light snuffed. It is much easier to be critical and whine than it is to rest in the certainty of Christ. Joy is not defined by the absence of wind or rain or by the presence of paradise. It is not conceived under the banner of pleasure. True joy cannot be formed by what is already in essence tainted. For joy to be complete it must be centered in the only thing that is perfect—God!

Ezra 6:22—They observed the Festival of Unleavened Bread for seven days with joy, because the LORD had made them joyful, having changed the Assyrian king's attitude toward them, so that he supported them in the work on the house of the God of Israel.
1 Kings 1:40—All the people followed him (Solomon), playing flutes and rejoicing with such a great joy that the earth split open from the sound.

Imagine a seven-day joy festival! God made His people happy because He changed the attitude of King Darius the Persian king, so that he supported the rebuilding of the temple. Then imagine a coronation ceremony that rocked with such rejoicing that the earth actually split open! That is some seriously powerful joy—the kind I want to see operational in my life!

I have found that certain elements directly contribute to my ability to be joyful. First, I must have the habit of eating from God's Word. Without the nourishing wisdom the Bible gives, I lose God's perspective, embrace my own notion of life and reap the sour taste of a convoluted attitude. Second, I must be in prayer. For some profoundly simple reason, talking to God and listening to Him dynamically fortifies my spirit so that regardless of what happens I am at peace. Without prayer, I plunge into stress and find my body like a guitar string too tightly wound—sharp to the ear. Third, I need times of fellowship with other believers. It's hard to be encouraged, and to gain a healthy perspective if I am without the companionship of brothers and sisters in love with Jesus.

How's your joy quotient? "Joyful, Joyful we adore Thee . . ." Hmmmm. Those words have a polished ring. If the Lord is the subject of our adoration, joy is the operative expression!

Inspiration † † †

Joy produces energy. Joy makes us strong.—Richard J. Foster in *Celebration of Discipline*

Opposition

Angel started her job in July. She looked forward to the opportunity to share Christ with her new coworkers and in utilizing her cooking skills in the popular restaurant on the busy street of MG in Cochin, India. A month later, she fought back tears—work was not going as she had expected. When the other girls on her shift learned she was a Christian, many were curious and began to ask her questions, but not Varuni, a tall woman from Pune. She let Angel know clearly that she did not care for Jesus chatter.

Varuni complained to the manager that Angel was trying to convert them to Christianity. So he forbade her from discussing religion in the restaurant. One day Varuni accidentally knocked over a stack of plates near Angel. As the plates crashed to the floor and broke, Varuni blamed Angel. Angel did not defend herself; she knew it would just be her word against Varuni. Unfortunately, as the stress mounted she began to experience migraine headaches. It seemed like nothing was going right for the young woman from Cochin. Yet she knew she was where God wanted her to be and so she prayed and asked Him for help to be strong and effective as His witness.

Over the next year, Angel's coworkers admired her for her good work habits, her kind disposition and integrity. Even her Hindu manager could see that her presence was a blessing to the restaurant. She was given more responsibility as a cook and a slight pay raise. Meanwhile, Varuni did all she could to make her life miserable. Eventually she stole funds from the cash box and placed them in Angel's handbag. When an investigation was done and the rupees were found in Angel's possession, the manager was forced to fire her despite her protestations of innocence. Although he suspected Varuni, he had no choice but to let Angel go. Now she is out looking for another job.

Nehemiah 4:7-8—When Sanballat, Tobiah, and the Arabs, Ammonites, and Ashdodites heard that the repair to the walls of Jerusalem was progressing and that the gaps were being closed, they became furious. They all plotted together to come and fight against Jerusalem and throw it into confusion.

It's not easy to be a target. Sorrow grows when we are the victim of dirty tactics and constant badgering. Nehemiah came with God's blessings from Susa, a major city in Elam, to rebuild the Jerusalem wall and make the city safe for his fellow Jews. Immediately, Sanballat and his cadre of thugs did all they could to stop Nehemiah. So he and his countrymen *prayed to our God and stationed a guard because of them day and night"* (Neh. 4:9).

Followers of Jesus should expect opposition—we should not be surprised that hell opposes heaven. Like Angel, we may lose our job. Like Nehemiah, we may find that building walls is four times harder than it should be. Second, *no matter what we face our best course of action is to pray!* We need God's help—if we forget this, our problems are even deeper than we think.

Third, *we continue to run the race.* Never give up! If necessary, post the guard and stand the watch but don't quit!

You may lose your job, but God will not forsake you—He will provide. You may find your name unjustly smeared. Jesus was called "demon-possessed" (John 8:48). You may endure pain and emotional distress. Don't despair—Jesus left His blood on many stones stumbling to Golgotha. He proceeded with His eyes on His Father. So keep moving upward, the path is narrow but the payoff is indescribable! Opposition molds our character, tests our resolve, stretches our faith and reveals our convictions. So press on mighty child of God and be blessed by the King of Blessings.

Inspiration † † †

The essence of morality is a questioning about morality; and the decisive move of human life is to use ceaselessly all light to look for the origin of the opposition between good and evil.—Georges Bataille, French writer, (1897-1962)

He Wanted To Help

While Kathleen was talking to me in my office, Stephen came running in and said there was a man at the door. It was a deliveryman from UPS. He asked me to sign for a large box and then went back to his truck to pick up an even larger one. As he returned to his vehicle, I said to my wife, "I think I will put these in the garage." Almost to his truck, the deliveryman turned around and asked if he could carry them for me.

Nehemiah 5:16,19—Instead, I devoted myself to the construction of the wall, and all my subordinates were gathered there for the work. We didn't buy any land . . . Remember me favorably, my God, for all that I have done for this people.

He didn't have to turn back. He finished his job. He had purveyed the boxes and I'm sure he had plenty more to deliver. It was the sincerity in his voice that really got me. This young man *wanted* to help. I almost felt bad declining his offer.

It's so easy to just do our job. There never is an end to work. But to put an exclamation point on what we do is what defines conscientiousness. To be conscientious reveals humility, pride, and kindness. Humility because the one working strives to serve another superbly. Pride because the work rendered must be of the highest quality. Kindness because the receiver is blessed. As we discover from the root of the word, a conscientious person is acting in accordance with the dictates of the conscience. Traced further, we see the signature of God. He made man and woman in His image (Gen. 1:27). He has placed in our conscience a desire to do right.

Isn't the greatest example of conscientiousness the Son of Man hanging on a cross for an undeserving humanity? Humble—He gave up His power and glory to die mocked and abused. Matthew 17:5 records the voice of His proud Father: *"This is My beloved Son. I take delight in Him. Listen to Him!"* No mistakes marred His life. Kind—what greater love is there than to model holiness yet die for the unholy?

Do your actions tell a story? Do they glorify God?

Inspiration   † † †

Service that is duty-motivated breathes death. Service that flows out of our inward person is life, and joy and peace. The risen Christ beckons us to the ministry of the towel.—Richard J. Foster in *Celebration of Discipline*

The rarest asset to a godly life is to be practically conscientious in every situation.—Oswald Chambers in *Not Knowing Where*

Obstinate

Brian came over and sprayed Crossbow on the *Rubus fruticosus* on the field behind my house. About two thirds of the plants died. So I sprayed the remaining plants three weeks later, waited a few more weeks, and then rented a brush beater to cut the dried stalks at their base. Later, I raked the dead plants off the hill. Incredibly, there are new shoots growing. When will my work end? Because of their thorns, deep root system and amazing rate of growth, I have to destroy those blackberry plants or they will take over the hill.

If asked to determine the obstinate plant winner my vote would split between bamboo and blackberries. They both are extremely difficult to eradicate. My arms are cut by thorns, my hands pricked by splinters, my feet stabbed repeatedly *through my shoes* and I'm starting to get a clear understanding of what stubborn means!

Nehemiah 9:29,30—You warned them to turn back to Your law, but they acted arrogantly and would not obey Your commandments. They sinned against Your ordinances, by which a person will live if he does them. They stubbornly resisted, stiffened their necks, and would not obey. You were patient with them for many years, and Your Spirit warned them through Your prophets, but they would not listen. Therefore, You handed them over to the surrounding peoples.

The core of obstinacy is a will centered on pleasing the flesh. If tenacious roots characterize stubborn plants, stiff necks substitute nicely for humans. God makes His will clear but we don't want to give up our obsessions or habits. So we ignore His commands to our peril. George Barna wrote in *Growing True Disciples*, "The real obstacles to becoming fully devoted, zealous disciples of Christ are not money, time, methods, or knowledge. The major obstacle is the human heart."

Can you think of any blessing inherited by blowing off God's plan? If the law, prophets and the promptings of the Holy Spirit from a patient God are ignored, He does what we force Him to do. He hands us over to the surrounding people. In the Bible, surrounding people is synonymous with idol-worshiping, pagan-frenzied, evil-generating, pain-festering, God-hating villains led by Satan. It's a terrible thing to fall out of the hands of a loving God into the jaws of twisted demons. Henry Ward Beecher observed, "The difference between perseverance and obstinacy is that one comes from a strong will, and the other from a strong won't."[12]

No Funds Arrived

Raul lives in Chinandega, Nicaragua and served with our **First Cause** team by translating *reverations* into Spanish. Raul lost his job yet needed funds to help pay his school tuition and a training conference with Timothy Academy in Honduras. I wired Raul money based on the bank instructions he gave me. However, when he went to the bank, they said no funds had arrived. For three weeks this went on—each time Raul went to the bank, they reported no money. Yet on my end, I had a receipt showing $146 was wired. Raul believed me and I believed Dolex Dollar Express and we both trusted God but Raul had no funds.

Esther 6:1-3—That night sleep escaped the king, so he ordered the book recording daily events to be brought and read to the king. They found the written report of how Mordecai had informed on Bigthana and Teresh, two eunuchs who guarded the king's entrance, when they planned to assassinate King Ahasuerus. The king inquired, "What honor and special recognition have been given to Mordecai for this act?" The king's personal attendants replied, "Nothing has been done for him."

Mordecai was a humble man of integrity, a Jew who faithfully served the Persian King, Xerxes. Bigthana and Teresh hung on a gallows. But no reward came to Mordecai, the man who saved the king's life, until much later in God's perfect timing.

Often life does not take expected turns! We do not receive a raise at work despite stellar production. Recognition is passed out but we are left out. We expect an answer from God for an important prayer and receive silence. There is nothing encouraging about zilch. But the absence of anything is often the very substance that enables us to grow. We learn patience. We enlarge our faith on the evidence of what is unseen. Nothing happening makes us question what we don't have and perhaps really need. Nothing happening reminds us that when all is said and done we are truly dependant on God who is Everything.

Raul found the money. Somehow, we became confused and he was going to the wrong bank. The money was there the whole time! Isn't that so often the case! We ask and trust God for help and He provides—we just can't see it! We need the eyes of our heart to be enlightened. We need to trust that the Lord's timeless watch is perfect for our finite thinking. We need to take Ethel Barrymore's advice, "When life knocks you to your knees, and it will, why, get up! If it knocks you to your knees again, as it will, well, isn't that the best position from which to pray?"

Inspiration † † †

You may be deceived if you trust too much, but you will live in torment if you don't trust enough.—Frank Crane

Premonitions

Job 3:25, 26—For the thing I feared has overtaken me, and what I dreaded has happened to me. I cannot relax or be still; I have no rest, for trouble comes.

He was the picture of success, a blameless and upright man who feared God and shunned evil. He had ten children and was fabulously wealthy—the greatest man among all the people of the East. Job was so concerned about living a pleasing life to God that he insisted his children purify themselves after partying and he offered sacrifices on their behalf in case they might have sinned. So why was this mighty man fearful that something bad would happen to him?

I suspect there is not a person alive who does not have premonitions. Underneath our psyche is a resident fear that for most is well buried but for others is a real and constant companion. When sin entered the world through Adam and Eve, fear took up residence in our genes.

A significant part of premonition is an underlying sense that we deserve to be punished. In fact, as disasters occur around the world there are often preachers who tie the disaster to God's hand of judgment. But even Job, in his goodness, feared he would experience the unpleasant application of God's discipline. We may not understand tragedy but the important question is never whether we deserved what we got, or the conclusion of who got what they deserved. The reality is that God's desire is that we would fear Him. In the presence of God, Job concluded he was insufficient to understand His workings. Confronted with the awesomeness of his Creator, he shifted his pleas of innocence to confessions of repentance (42:6). *God may it be so for us.*

Premonitions are real but they don't have to be debilitating. Fearing God means giving Him our fears. David, God's beloved friend, courageously proclaimed, *"I will sing to the LORD all my life; I will sing praise to my God while I live"* (Psa. 104:33). These words came from a man who constantly faced foes intent on his destruction. *"Why am I so depressed? Why this turmoil within me? Put your hope in God, for I will still praise Him, my Savior and my God"* (Psa. 43:5).

James Russel Lowell, the Romantic poet, diplomat, and abolitionist, said, "Let us be of good cheer, remembering that the misfortunes hardest to bear are those which will never happen." In the valley of trust, the floods we face ultimately do not matter. God promises to love us and rescue us. While we may lose all we have on earth, He prepares for those whose faith is in Jesus, mansions in places where no tragedy may inflict harm. Don't let the fears of what might happen, or the pain of what did happen ever take your eyes off the One who understands all that happens. Praise Him!

Three Truths about Plans

Job 17:11—My days have slipped by; my plans have been ruined, even the things dear to my heart.

They built a dream-house overlooking the Columbia River. Their blueprint was excellent, their planning they thought complete. Unfortunately, they misunderstood and violated the zoning regulations Skamania county officials insisted be kept. Their structure was overly prominent in its profile, marring the scenic Columbia gorge with its natural beauty. Their unfinished home must move!

I wonder how many houses we build where God-never intended. What foundations have we laid on slopes that would later slide? If we believe in the value of planning then we best understand that for our plans to succeed at least three truths must be in place:

Truth #1. In order to walk on God's paths we must understand His ways (Mic. 4:2). God's thoughts and actions are different from ours (Isa. 55:8). The key to effective planning is to learn from Scripture how God works, discern through the Holy Spirit what He is doing around us and then get involved with Him. Without spiritual understanding, plans are bound to be presumptuous, self-centered and costly.

Truth #2. In order for plans to succeed, they must be committed to the Lord (Pro. 16:3). Committed to the Lord, means submitted to His authority and leadership (Pro. 3:5,6). Committed does not mean we design a course of action, inform God of our intentions and expect His blessing. The Lord God does not take second-place. If we operate outside His leading are we not headed for trouble?

Truth #3. Our relationship with God is more important than accomplishing our plans. What good does it do to serve God if our attitude or priorities are wrong? It is easy to be seduced or embittered by focusing on a plan and miss the all-important reality that knowing God is what counts most (Mal. 3:14)!

Whenever we venture outside God's clear leading it is only ticks in time before we experience the disappointment that comes from following faulty and non-fulfilling plans. God's plans and purposes *never* fail! (Psa. 33:11). If what we are doing is through Christ we can claim the "I Can Do" promise—Php. 4:13! Jesus always provides the resources, strength and wisdom necessary to carry out His work. Plan on Him!

Inspiration † † †

Your plans and purposes must be God's plans and purposes or you will not experience God working through you. God reveals His purposes so you will know what He plans to do. Then you can join Him.—Henry Blackaby in *Experiencing God: Knowing and Doing the Will of God*

Aber Strays

Aber and I sat at the table and dipped the addicting chips in delicious hot sauce. Aber was spiritually hungry, eager to learn more about God. After our usual chitchat, he shared about a vivacious gal at work on his team. She had recently moved to Oregon from Massachusetts. He noted her athleticism and that the two of them were working out three times a week during lunch. He was losing weight and felt great. Suddenly, the chips I'd been munching lost their flavor.

"Aber you're married. Do you think it is wise for you to be working out with this woman?" His answer was evasive. Red flags began flapping. I shared Pro. 16:17. *"The highway of the upright avoids evil; the one who guards his way protects his life."* We looked at Job 31:1. *"I made a covenant with my eyes not to look lustfully at a girl"* (NIV). But Aber laughed at my concern. He was mildly offended at the implication that any evil might be involved. He said I was overreacting—after all they were just friends and he loved his wife and wouldn't do anything stupid.

Eight weeks later Aber would not look me in the eyes. He'd decided to separate from his wife. He rented an apartment and in order to afford the cost talked his workout partner into moving in with him. He swept over every move with a tightly twined broom of rationalism. He rationalized his sin with the opportunity to share about Christ with his new live-in.

Job 23:11—My feet have followed in His tracks; I have kept to His way and not turned aside.

Moses taught his people that following God meant obeying the commands He made for their own betterment (see Deu. 28). Jesus said, *"Just as the Father commanded Me, so I do"* (John 14:31b). Do we understand through what the Bible teaches that in following God's commands there is no room for deviation? The moment we create our own path, aren't we in effect saying we know better than God does? The instant we rationalize aberrant behavior we cease to follow wholeheartedly our Father and we cut ourselves off from His blessing.

Follow is not a wishy-washy word. Nor is it hard to find out what God wants. He supplements His commands by equipping us with a built-in conscience. The Infantry says, "Lead, follow or get the hell out of the way." God says follow my lead and hell won't be in your way!

Inspiration † † †

Obedience is the most important factor in our whole relationship to God.—Andrew Murray in *The Believer's Prayer Life*

The Power of Knowing

The certainty of knowing is a medicine of incalculable worth. I breathe knowing unseen air is present in this room. I know (brake inspections help); my Subaru will slow down when I push my foot against the pedal. If I miss eating several meals, I am aware that I will easily get cold outside. After 25 years of marriage, I have a good sense of what my wife will or will not do. What I know shapes my behavior, reflects my beliefs and gives me a confidence that ignorance could not manufacture.

Psalm 4:3—Know that the LORD has set apart the faithful for Himself; the LORD will hear when I call to Him.

How does King David *know* that God sets the godly apart for Himself? How does he *know* the Lord will hear him when he prays? By reading through Samuel, the first book of Kings and Chronicles, and the Psalms, it is evident that David possesses knowledge of God that gives him the ability to make these declarations.

First, *David from his childhood learned to trust God.* At an age when contemporary youth are mastering video games, he was protecting sheep from lions and bears. He trusted God and was unafraid to take on creatures easily capable of killing him. If Goliath knew what David knew, he would never have taken the field to combat his little opponent. What David knew about God was fashioned by FAITH.

Second, *David compiled a mental record of EXPERIENCES that proved God's reliability.* Over time, he saw God do amazing things in his life and the lives of those around him.

Third, *David learned about God from his godly parents and from the prophet Samuel.* Much of what he knew about God came from EDUCATION.

Finally, *David invested a significant amount of time building a solid RELATIONSHIP with His Father in heaven.* He regularly sought God in prayer, sang to Him and sacrificially worshiped Him. God was pleased with his heart and often revealed His will to His loyal friend.

You know what encourages me about knowing this? We too can be certain that godly living endears us to God and predisposes Him to hear us when we pray. Faith, experience, education and relationship are all available to us! In time, the power of knowing reveals our manner of living!

Inspiration   † † †

The man who knows that God is at the end of the road will make all life a preparation to meet Him—William Barclay, Scottish pastor and theologian, (1907-1978)

Make a Poster For God

Growing up, Dad often had to travel. The day he would arrive home was always a special event. Often we would make cool posters and cards for him. Not only were we glad to see him safely returned, we also knew he would have a surprise for us. In my study today are many carvings, especially of elephants he brought home from different countries. They remind me of my father's love.

Now as an adult, I understand how much pleasure it gave Dad to see the look on our faces whenever he returned. Years ago, when I returned home from trips, my three kids excitedly greeted me and expectantly waited to see what little treasures I carried home for them. Often they decorated our walls with wonderful banners joyfully expressing their affection and recognition of my love for them.

If as a dad I long to be with my children and gain pleasure in demonstrating my love to them, imagine what my Heavenly Father feels like! How He must enjoy surprising His children with His perfect touch. What pleasure it must give God when we get up eager to be in His presence, to pour out our hearts to Him. Will He reveal a special truth from His Word? Will He bring someone into our lives today with just the right message of encouragement? Will He heal us of some malady or bring relief from much suffering? Will He send chills down our spine as we reach out our hands to embrace Him?

Psalm 5:3—At daybreak, LORD, You hear my voice; at daybreak I plead my case to You and watch expectantly.

When's the last time you made a poster for God? May I encourage you to eagerly seek Him this week with an enthusiastic heart and an anticipative mind! Share how much He means to you by devoting time to Him in meaningful worship. Bring Him your requests. Look forward to what special blessings He will unpack for you. Our creative Creator is profoundly incredible in surprising us with His love. So be expectant, like Moses who wrote, *"Satisfy us in the morning with Your faithful love so that we may shout with joy and be glad all our days"* (Psa. 90:14).

Inspiration † † †

There is no medicine like hope, no incentive so great, and no tonic so powerful as expectation of something tomorrow.—Orison Swett Marden, author, (1850-1924)

By Your Great Mercy

Have you ever had a day when you wished to be alone; when your heart felt crushed beyond repair and your dreams were smashed like a wooden boat against the jagged reefs of reality? Like the eye of a hurricane, misery has its own island of calm. Often it is in the center of pain where God reveals His warm will and tender truth.

The Apostle Paul discovered the priceless treasure of God's mercy and it forever changed his life. This man, who so zealously persecuted Jesus' followers, fell to the ground blinded by the piercing love extended by the One he hated. When Paul met Jesus, his sanity became insanity. Mercy met pride and humility was born. Later as a mature Christian, he wrote *"Therefore, since we have this ministry, as we have received mercy, we do not give up"* (2 Co. 4:1).

Paul realized it was not by education, noble pedigree, wealth, imperial decree, talent or the approval of people that one met and served God. He concluded that ministry was not sustained through deception, or secret and shameful ways. Wrapped in the blanket of God's mercy he could endure hunger, cold, and gnawing poverty yet model contentedness. Profoundly altered by the extension of God's grace to his sinful self, he endured being stoned, whipped, mocked and imprisoned to boldly proclaim, *"For me, living is Christ and dying is gain"* (Php. 1:21).

Psalm 5:7—But I, by your great mercy, will come into your house; in reverence will I bow down toward your holy temple. (NIV)

President Abraham Lincoln once said, "I have always found that mercy bears richer fruits than strict justice." In a nation that loves to franchise success it is easy to forget that it is because of God's mercy we are saved and equipped to serve. The Holy Spirit commits surgical kindness to open our hearts to our own depravity. He opens our eyes to the necessity of repentance and faith in God's extended Son, who alone gains us access to God and victory over sin!

Our spiritual fervor will not die if we understand why we have life and the privilege to serve. God's mercy keeps us from becoming cynical, critical, and harsh towards others. His mercy liberates trapped souls, transforming gloom into praise! Are you dying? His mercy promises you a new and incorruptible body. Are you discouraged? Drink from the well of God's love and be refreshed. Are you defeated? So was Christ on the cross and look what He won for you! Jeremiah, the weeping prophet, wrote in Lam. 3:22,23, *"Because of the LORD's faithful love we do not perish, for His mercies never end. They are new every morning; great is Your faithfulness!"*

A Song for God's Name

When I read my Bible, I have a code for marking it that helps make it easier to find things and to notice trends. (To see my Bible Marking code, go to Appendix A). For example, I underlined every reference to God's name. One day, while playing my guitar I discovered a melody that cried for words. Almost immediately, I believe the Holy Spirit prodded me to write a song about God's name. Therefore, I opened up the Psalms and begin examining the underlined phrases and from that search, a song emerged. I was unprepared and abundantly blessed by the wonder of the richness, power, majesty and provision (just in Psalms) of the name of our God. I hope you will meditate on the lines below and be as blessed. Now have a time of soaking in the glory of His Name! You can go to our website, www.firstcause.org and click on Name to hear the song.

There's a Name, a Name above all names, a Name of glory
    we call Him Yahweh!
A Name of power, a Name for living in; a Name that's sung to;
    a Name for lifting hands.
Magnificent, a Name that's trusted; a Name for pride in
    and lifting banners;
A Name proclaimed before the brothers; that brings forgiveness
    we'll praise forever!
We adore, we bow before, Your Name for Who You are.
We extol with hearts of praise Your mighty Name, O Lord!

There's a Name that leads and guides us, a Name that's holy,
    through Whom we conquer
A Name that stretches beyond the heavens; for placing hope in
    and never failing!
There's a name that's meant for fearing, a Name that's near and
    forever honored;
A Name that's called on, we shout for joy in; and awe-inspired,
    forever saving!

There's a Name that acts in kindness, that leads to blessing
    that's long remembered;
Endures forever and brings deliverance; His Name exalted
    and full of justice
There's a Name that all creation proudly sings of across the nations
Fully loved and fully loving, high in splendor, never changing!

Psalm 7:17—I will thank the LORD for His righteousness; I will sing about the name of the LORD, the Most High.

Questions

Psalm 10:1—LORD, why do You stand so far away? Why do You hide in times of trouble?
Ecclesiastes 7:10—Don't say, "Why were the former days better than these?" For it is not wise of you to ask this.
Jeremiah 12:1—. . . Why does the way of the wicked prosper? Why do the treacherous live at ease?
Matthew 13:10—. . . "Why do You speak to them in parables?"

There is that stage in a child's life when questions never seem to end. "Why Mommy?" can change from melodic cuteness to dripping rain. Yet, we must be careful not to let our impatience squelch curiosity. Jesus loved the children and admonished His disciples not to prevent them from coming to Him. I suspect He loved their questions, their innocence and uncontained affection.

Have you ever felt restricted from asking God questions that burn inside your heart? Is there a sense that Christians are supposed to have all the answers—that questioning is a sign of immaturity? I, for one, am skeptical of those who always have some pat solution. Sometimes even a *spiritual* bucket can contain hogwash.

The Bible illustrates a variety of questions that godly people felt free to send heavenward. It reveals that God is big enough to address apposite (relevant) dilemmas. It also indicates growth or immaturity (and the need for growth) in the lives of those who dialogue with Him. King David is a great example of this. He wrote psalms that began by questioning God. Yet in the end, we find him praising the Father He didn't understand.

Questions can be an excuse to avoid obeying the Lord, or a sign that we lack faith. But they can also be very appropriate. There are also those times when our hurt boils to the surface and we need to ask, "Why God?" assured that He is glad we ran to Him. Life is full of quandaries. Better to be honest about what we don't know than to give the appearance that we have all the answers. Who is omniscient, the Creator or the created?

Inspiration   † † †

It is better to ask some of the questions than to know all the answers.—James Thurber, humorist and cartoonist, (1894-1961)

Who questions much, shall learn much, and retain much.—Sir Francis Bacon, English philosopher, statesman, scientist, jurist, orator and author (1561-1626)

Life is Full of Rings

Psalm 16:11—You reveal the path of life to me; in Your presence is abundant joy; in Your right hand are eternal pleasures.

Have you ever watched a Sumo match? Two men of huge girth stand apart from each other in the middle of a large circle wearing only loincloths. Each warrior attempts to expel the other outside the ring by exerting clever technique combined with brute force. Sumo wrestling is the national sport and pastime of the Japanese. It is a more elegant, ancient and simplified version of pro-wrestling, without the scripting.

As a young man bound for West Point, I knew that I would be wrestling against a fierce opponent. His name was Calculus. He threw terror in my heart. If I failed to master him, I was at risk of being hurled from a ring that provided me a paid education—one I could not afford. But I did not have to face these foes alone. Before I entered the college ring, I memorized a Bible verse that seemed highly appropriate for my circumstances. *"I have set the LORD always before me; Because He is at my right hand I shall not be moved"* (Psa. 16:8 NKJV).

Life is full of rings we must enter and do battle in. When we wrestle in our own strength we get beat up! Our sinful desires cause us to lose. Evil overpowers us because we try to compete alone. God never intended for us to fight solo. Unlike the sumo wrestler who has no one to tag for help, we have the ability to call on our Heavenly Father. In His presence, under His leadership, we cannot be defeated.

Many Christians mistakenly believe that if they will just read their Bible once a day, spend a few moments in prayer and attend church once a week, they will be able to prosper and succeed. While those activities are vital, they are rendered puny if we do not understand how to maintain God's presence. We must bring God into the everyday activities of our thoughts, our work, and our relationships, if we are to stand fast in the ring of holiness. Christianity is not a formula! It is a relationship that calls us to know Christ and to set Him before us as Lord, moment-by-moment.

Inspiration †††

If a Christian is to truly practice the presence of his Lord, and do so properly, then the heart of that Christian must be empty of all else. *All.* Why? Because God wills to possess that heart, and He wills to be the only possessor of that heart, and the only possession in that heart. He cannot be the only possessor of your heart unless it is empty of all else. He cannot put what he desires into a heart unless that heart has been left vacant for Him alone to refill it.—Brother Lawrence & Frank Laubach in *Practicing His Presence*

The Rain

The rain pours in Oregon today—steady and persistent. It is a most fascinating messenger of nature. Rain promotes green vegetation and air that is clean to the taste. It gives the sun true reason to sparkle. It vanquishes the parch of drought. Conversely, rain is the mother of rust, the father of mold and the saturnine (gloomy) priest of depression. Its airborne invasion creates tabescent (wasting away) mountains as earth gives way to water. Houses lose their foundations; trees buckle under the roar of new mudslides. Floods wipe away the very dreams of those once nourished by peaceful rivers.

Psalm 19:1-3—The heavens declare the glory of God, and the sky proclaims the work of His hands. Day after day they pour out speech; night after night they communicate knowledge. There is no speech; there are no words; their voice is not heard.

Who is God? Is He the bubbling Spring of new life—the sweet mountain flow of Living Water? Is He the Brook who washes sins over rocks of repentance? Does He moisten chapped lips with the soothing balm of His liquid grace? Or is He the One whose powerful undertow flows around piers of self-reliance? Does His righteous steam rise off brittle consciences? Do His waves threaten pleasure palaces so carefully constructed? Is He the Sea of healing for those who pant for His water or the Lake of fire to those who disdain His mercy? The heavens give the answer—every day, in every language. Listen. You will know.

Inspiration   † † †

Anthropological evidence suggest that every culture has a God-given, innate sense of the eternal—that this world is not all there is.—Randy Alcorn in *Heaven*

If the whole universe has no meaning, we should never have found out that it has no meaning: just as, if there were no light in the universe and therefore no creatures with eyes, we should never know it was dark. Dark would be without meaning.—C.S. Lewis

Cleanse Me

What thoughts crisscrossed King David's mind when he penned Psalm 19? His language is deeply reflective. *"The heavens declare the glory of God"* (Psa. 19:1). Creation testifies to the whole world God's greatness (vs. 2-6). Moving on, he notes, *"The instruction of the LORD is perfect, reviving the soul"* (vs. 7). David lauds God's Word for its marvelous qualities (vs. 8-11), and concludes, *"In addition, Your servant is warned by them; there is great reward in keeping them"* (vs. 11).

Psalm 19:12-14—Who perceives his unintentional sins? Cleanse me from my hidden faults. Moreover, keep Your servant from willful sins; do not let them rule over me. Then I will be innocent, and cleansed from blatant rebellion. May the words of my mouth and the meditation of my heart be acceptable to You, LORD, my rock and my Redeemer.

As David meditated on the majesty of His Heavenly Father and the weight of His truth, he seems convicted by his own shortcomings. Did he feel like some soiled cloak that needed washing? Surely, the fact that he mentions sins ruling over him implies some wrong pattern of behavior or thinking. Or did he just know the proclivity of his heart and seek God's protection? I'm not sure, but I love his conclusion.

This year, as I daily spend time in Scripture I write down the key verses I've highlighted in my prayer journal. The passage of meditation above works over my soul like a tractor plowing soil. His words remind me that it is better to be proactive in seeking God's protective help than to try to live a holy life and avoid sin on my own effort.

I already know there are times I unintentionally break God's will. For those times, *God forgive me.* But what concerns me more is when I willfully do what I know to be wrong, feeding the flesh. David called it *"blatant rebellion."* Hmmm, that's pretty accurate isn't it! Unkind words, impure thoughts, time wasted doing things of questionable or even objectionable value, tending a selfish attitude, the list goes on . . .

Lord of the heavens, Giver of precious, perfect words, let my life be acceptable in Your sight. Let what I say, do and think inside be up to Your standards. I'm totally counting on You! I can't be what You want me to be without Your help! Yet, with You, I can do all things for Your glory! Amen.

Inspiration † † †

For the first time I examined myself with a seriously practical purpose. And there I found what appalled me; a zoo of lusts, a bedlam of ambitions, a nursery of fears, a harem of fondled hatreds. My name was legion.—C.S. Lewis in *Surprised By Joy*

Shannon

Shannon's desperate eyes spoke volumes. She told me she'd walked from Albany to Salem with her backpack and handbags to get away from her husband. She had had nothing to drink all day, was overheated and felt ill. Thirty years old, she described herself as a misfit mother whose own mother watched two of her children while despairing of her incompetent daughter.

I asked her who she turned to when her world fell apart. She didn't know. I asked if I could share what I do when life is brutal and help is desperately needed. She said, "Sure." So I shared with her my Champion, Jesus, and an amazing thing happened. She said she'd lied to me. She really had four children. One was a runaway 13-year old prostituting her body somewhere on the streets of Portland; the two youngest were on their way to a foster home in Idaho. The other son was in a foster home in Portland. The state was about to terminate her parental rights because of her oft-repeated drug use. She once believed in God but now struggled to think He could really exist.

Shannon listened closely as I shared about God and the richness of His love—a love that meant abandoning His own Son upon the cross to deal permanently with our sins. She heard about a Savior who doesn't expect us to be perfect to find Him. He calls us in our imperfection to admit our sins and trust Him as our Lord and Savior. She heard of the hope that comes in knowing a Father in heaven is there for us—always.

Psalm 25:14-17—The secret counsel of the LORD is for those who fear Him, and He reveals His covenant to them. My eyes are always on the LORD, for He will pull my feet out of the net. Turn to me and be gracious to me, for I am alone and afflicted. The distresses of my heart increase; bring me out of my sufferings.

Someone recently handed me a survey of how adults say they deal with the pressures of life: 37% overeat; 32% smoke; 21% bite their nails; 13% drink alcohol. How many of those same people are unaware there is a God clued in to their struggles? O Shannon, how many of you are out there? If only your eyes could see the reality that stress is not mitigated by methamphetamines. If only you could believe that your voice is heard by a Father who longs to embrace you forever. Your relief will come through pouring out your struggles and releasing your problems to Him. He's given you His book, the Bible, to point you to His grace and mercy. It teaches you how to find joy in the midst of pain. Find those who know and love Him. Let them help share your grief, listen and be there for you. Don't give up! Call on the One who loves you.

A broken woman listened as I prayed that Jesus might heal her and bring her to Himself. A broken society needs us to go where they are to share the antidote they are missing. Why isn't Jesus a listed solution on a survey? Have we become mute about our relevant Lord? Have we become so anxious to protect our rights that we have overlooked so many needs?

Twenty-four thousand people die in the world everyday from physical hunger. How many thousands die every day spiritually starved? What will it take for our hearts to be broken for those without Jesus?! Forgive us God for our apathy. Take us outside of our comfortable churches to where the world is—waiting, wondering, worrying. En*courage* us to proclaim Your name to a stressed out land of Shannons.

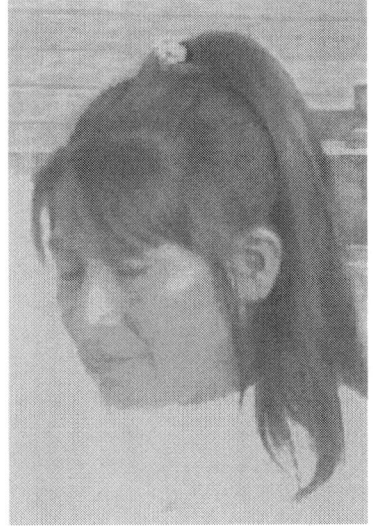

Inspiration † † †

Number of aspirin taken by Americans each year: 33,000,000,000.—*Reader's Digest Book of Facts.*

"I can't do it!" I cried to God. "I can't handle the housework, my work, the loneliness of a husband who works so much." Then I sensed the Holy Spirit saying, You are trying to do everything on your own strength. Just worship Me—and I'll do the rest. I said out loud, "I praise you, God, in the midst of my situation. Thank you that nothing is too hard for You." Slowly, the pressure left—my burden was now His. Praise isn't always my first reaction to frustration, so I have to remind myself to do it. But now, when my flesh can't go any further, I stop and worship God.—Stormie Omartian in "Heart to Heart," *Today's Christian Woman.*

Meaning

Psalm 27:4—I have asked one thing from the LORD; it is what I desire: to dwell in the house of the LORD all the days of my life, gazing on the beauty of the LORD and seeking Him in His temple.

There is a long stretch of freeway between Fayetteville, North Carolina and Atlanta, Georgia, that is mostly flat and lined by green pine trees. Most machines need tune-ups. I need occasional four-wheel journeys. There is something therapeutic about driving for me—as long as the highway is not jammed with motorists all rushing to get some place. Most of us spend too much time honking at our own taillights when we ought to be setting aside time to reflect on life's true meaning.

Once I drove my family down a mountain pass on icy roads. An accident ahead caused several vehicles to converge and nearly block the road. We were able to fit by the width of our car through the narrowing gap and escape injury. My heartbeat must have hit 200 bpm! You may have experienced your own harrowing incident where life wrestled death and there was a good chance death might win. Suddenly life becomes exceedingly precious.

It shouldn't take near tragedies to make us appreciate life. We need to ponder what it means to breathe, to think, to love, to hurt, to care. Is there anything better in life than to worship God? If we just go through the motions, our reward will be cramps. Why? Because perpetual, purposeless motion is as useful as a turtle trying to mate an ostrich.

Where is the meaning:
- in putting kids in day care to earn more money for stuff when what the children want is nothing more than to have time with dad and mom?
- in staring at a television programmed to scorch the conscience, numb the mind, glorify sex, model violence, mock God and devalue humanity?
- in slaving through life to gain a splendid retirement for a worn-out body?
- in speed? Why does everything have to be fast?

Are you feeling frazzled, over-starched, under-loved, burnt-out or emotionally bankrupt? Consider this! God painted unbelievable colors on tropical fish for our enjoyment. He made plants with medicinal properties for our health. He fashioned sunsets, songbirds, roses, huckleberries and feathers for our viewing, hearing, smelling, tasting and touching pleasure! Most of all He gave us His Son so that we might know Him. In Him there is *meaning . . .* something to think about in reveration.

Inspiration   † † †

The tragedy of modern man is not that he knows less and less about the meaning of his own life, but that it bothers him less and less.—Blaise Pascal

Changing My Focus

Psalm 28:2—Listen to the sound of my pleading when I cry to You for help, when I lift up my hands toward Your holy sanctuary.

Have you ever studied the Psalms? A most interesting phenomenon occurs with the poet David. He often begins his psalms by telling God of some distressing circumstance he is anxious about. Sometimes he frets over his wicked enemies. Other times his heart is convicted of personal sin or he longs for the taste of God's mercy and strong presence. Curiously, towards the end of these stress-permeated laments a shift takes place. The poet who is troubled becomes a troubadour extolling his love for his Lord. What began as an imbroglio (complicated mess) ends as praise!

I will never forget the week I received a letter from an attorney attempting to collect on a $58,000 bill over which I had no liability or obligation. It caused stress for my wife and tension in my spirit for part of the day—until I went to the Lord. On my knees, I shared the injustice with my Father who loves me. When I arose from prayer, the letter still existed and the situation had not changed, but I had.

If poor health, mental stress from a tough work environment, unruly children, financial debt, low self-esteem or any other distressing circumstances threaten to rob you of joy, run to the Heaven-Maker! When we come to Him in prayer, He is able to take our load and bear it.

Transformation is not about circumstances changing but rather the recreation that takes place in my own heart as I let go of what I should not hold on to and confidently announce with David: *"The LORD is my strength and my shield; my heart trusts in Him, and I am helped. Therefore my heart rejoices, and I praise Him with my song"* (Psa. 28:7). Go ahead set aside time to pray! Then as God massages your heart let loose with your own great song of praise!

Inspiration ✝ ✝ ✝

When prayer doesn't bring the answers, adding praise will lead to victory.—Friedrich von Hügel, Austrian Roman Catholic layman, religious writer and thinker, (1852-1925)

When you pray, things remain the same, but you begin to be different.—Oswald Chambers in *If You Will Ask*

Prayer is not merely coming to God to ask something from Him. It is above all fellowship with God, and being brought under the power of His holiness and love, till He takes possession of us, and stamps our entire nature with the lowliness of Christ, which is the secret of all true worship.—Andrew Murray in *The Believer's Prayer Life*

At 2:47 a.m., the house shuddered. I looked over at my sleeping wife and asked if she had noticed anything. Since the dogs were not barking and I felt no sense of urgency, I drifted back to sleep. About a half an hour later, the doorbell rang and our two canines erupted. I opened the door to two policemen, bright flashing lights and the reality that an abandoned car sat atop the berm in front of our home.

Strangely enough before I had gone to bed, I had asked the Lord to provide an illustration for my message the next morning on God's protection. There it was right in front of my sleepy eyes!

After we moved into our Tigard home, our neighbors informed us that the house had been hit several times by cars that failed to stop at the intersection. Not comfortable with the danger that a vehicle could crash into the room our boys occupied, I built a long berm. All the hard work paid off with the realization that it worked.

Psalm 31:1,2—In you, O LORD, I have taken refuge; let me never be put to shame; deliver me in your righteousness. Turn your ear to me, come quickly to my rescue; be my rock of refuge, a strong fortress to save me. (NIV)

Jesus knew we would face many trials and dangers in this life. He was well aware of Satan's capability to inflict harm and that people who hated Him would hate His disciples. Before He left His followers to return to glory, He prayed for their safety. *"Holy Father, protect them by Your name that You have given Me, so that they may be one as We are one"* (John 17:11b). We, who call Him Lord, are included in His prayer for safety.

An out-of-control car may not be the handiwork of a rapacious devil, but it is a good reminder of how important it is that we pray in the powerful name of our God for protection. Are you troubled? Does fear sit inside you like a bad cavity? Run to the One who is able, the One described as omnipotent. Have the mindset of the Psalmist who long ago wrote, *"But the LORD is my refuge; my God is the rock of my protection"* (Psa. 94:22).

If your confidence in the providential care of God is rock-steady, still persist in praying for His protection on others as well as yourself. Jesus set the example! We should thank our Heavenly Father for the angels He's assigned in our overwatch. Even a pile of dirt can be cause for praise!

Inspiration   † † †

I know not where His islands lift
Their fronded palms in air;
I only know I cannot drift
Beyond His love and care.
—John Greenleaf Whittier Quaker poet (1807-1892) in *The Eternal Gardens*

Time with the Kids

Some adults love to sit in airports and people-watch. I prefer a playground or a setting with lots of kids. Children greatly amuse me—mostly because they know how to live. Here's a brief sampling from a party.

● Stephen (6), figured out how to get to the second notch on the white climbing rope hanging from our huge maple—a momentous achievement.

● Little Matthew discovered that grass clippings are a neat addition to the inside of the goldfish tank. I wonder what the fish are thinking?

● Katie let me know that she is three but last year she was two and she knows how to pump on the swing set. Man, can she fly high.

● Honestly, what could be more fun than dropping an ice cube down your uncle's shirt? When Erin has a twinkle in her eyes look out!

● Who needs baseball scouts? If you ever want to assess future big leaguers give a boy a stick, blindfold him and watch him go after a piñata.

If your life is as bland as tofu maybe it's time to wake up with a new attitude. Start with a spiritual breakfast. Read God's Word as if He actually wrote it to you—which He did! Pray with Jesus in the same room and praise Him for the joy of life. Need a reminder? Are you wearing clothes? Is there a solid roof over your head? Does someone love you? Can you regain that child-like perspective that claps for the rainbow as opposed to groaning over thunderclouds? Thank God for . . . !

Let's get radical. When's the last time you really let the ol' belly rip with a deep chortle of pure delight? I double-dare you to just bust up laughing right now. Why? Because. Life became too somber when we chose to forget the Be Cause.

Psalm 37:4—Take delight in the LORD, and He will give you your heart's desires.

Are the words above, those of a sappy shepherd boy? Or does this verse give us insight as to why God called David a man after His own heart? Is David giving us a promise or a heavenly teaser? How you answer the question says much about how you live your life.

Inspiration † † †

Praise renews your strength . . . Praise clarifies your vision . . . Praise cleanses your soul . . . Praise empowers your prayer . . . Praise multiplies your faith . . . Praise unites you in spirit with the angels . . . Praise puts Satan on the run.—Wesley L. Duewel in *Touch the World through Prayer*

Praise is your pathway through the mired circumstances of the present world.—Jack Hayford in *Worship His Majesty*

Depressed

Psalm 42 and 43 belong together as one work and could aptly be titled "Depressed." Verses 1-3 of chapter 42 indicate the writer's distance from God in stark contrast with previous times of worship:

> As a deer longs for streams of water, so I long for You, God. I thirst for God, the living God. When can I come and appear before God? My tears have been my food day and night, while all day long people say to me, "Where is your God?"

Next, the writer seems unable to understand why he is depressed and in so much turmoil. Thrice he mentions, "Why am I so depressed? Why this turmoil within me?" He even states, "I am deeply depressed." God allowed him to be overwhelmed like one helpless beneath roaring water. Twice he agonizes, "I will say to God my Rock, 'Why have you forgotten me? Why must I go about in sorrow, because of the enemy's oppression?' My adversaries taunt me, as if crushing my bones, while all day long they say to me, 'Where is your God?'"

If you are prone to depression or periods of melancholy don't feel somehow unworthy in God's eyes. The Bible shares numerous accounts of depressed saints. Don't devalue your image because your feelings hurt. Rather, recognize the normalcy of sadness and despair in life. Solomon, the disheartened sage, penned:

> For with much wisdom is much sorrow; as knowledge increases, grief increases . . . For what does a man get with all his work and all his efforts that he labors with under the sun? For all his days are filled with grief, and his occupation is sorrowful; even at night, his mind does not rest. This too is futile. (Ecc. 1:18; 2:22,23)

So what do we do when we feel as cheery as a lost goose in a foggy cloud? "Put your hope in God [key antidote], for I will still praise him, my Savior and my God [praise applied 3x]. . . The LORD will send His faithful love by day; His song will be with me in the night—a prayer to the God of my life [faith applied] . . . Vindicate me, God, and defend my cause against an ungodly nation; rescue me from the deceitful and unjust man [focus on God the Deliverer]. Send Your light and Your truth; let them lead me. Let them bring me to Your holy mountain, to Your dwelling place [submission to God's way]. Then I will come to the altar of God, to God, my greatest joy. I will praise You with the lyre, God, my God" [worship applied].

When the psalmists couldn't sleep; lost interest in what they once enjoyed; felt restless, even despairing of life, there were no pills with venlafaxine, paroxetine, mirtazapine, bupropion or sertraline. They don't mention St. John's Wort, God's natural herb. No, they reached for hope and faith, submitted to God's authority and practiced praise and worship. Somehow, I think they felt better. When our eyes are on God, there is RELIEF!

Some Distinctive Shape

What in life truly matters? Imagine if God placed you in a huge glass pot in the middle of a giant plaza where hundreds of thousands of people walk by you. He turns a dial that sets in motion transforming heat from coils underneath the container on which you stand. All that you have and represent on earth, as a Christian, is about to be melted down into the pure essentials which define and determine your worth. What crystalline object will the world see? All you have lived for and what characterizes you is about to emerge in some distinctive shape.

Psalm 45:4—in your splendor ride triumphantly in the cause of truth, humility, and justice. May your right hand show your awe-inspiring deeds.

Psalm 45 is a wedding song composed by the Sons of Korah for a king on his wedding day. The words in the meditation above leaped from the pages of my Bible and grabbed my heart. They contain profound truth for us. The writer is telling us what the three champion causes are for a victorious, majestic king—truth, humility and righteousness. These are the essentials.

TRUTH—Those without truth crumble against the incessant rain of scrutiny. Truth protects us, allows us to sleep peacefully, builds confidence, and lights the path upon which we walk toward heaven. Truth is the breath of God and the mark of godly character.

HUMILITY—Jesus, the King of all Kings, humbled Himself and became a man. Humility is the fragrance of love and the mark of a godly attitude. It values the concerns of others and deftly dims the incessant, inner cry of "feed me!" Humility is attractive, refreshing and peace promoting.

RIGHTEOUSNESS—When we do the right thing we prosper. When sin is allowed to flourish, we flounder and fail. It is far wiser to engage in God-honoring conduct than to feed our lusts only to reap what will surely rot. Righteousness is the touch of Deity and the mark of godly conduct.

What are your essentials?

Inspiration †††

The revelation given by Jesus Christ of God is not the revelation of Almighty God, but of the essential nature of deity—unutterable humility and moral purity, utterly worthy in every detail of actual life. In the Incarnate God proves Himself worthy in the sphere in which we live, and this is the sphere of the revelation of the self-giving of God.—Oswald Chambers in *Baffled to Fight Better*

In the Midst of Lions

Psalm 57:4—I am in the midst of lions; I lie down with those who devour men. Their teeth are spears and arrows; their tongues are sharp swords.

He was treated like an outlaw, a condemned man with an entire army pursuing him. Despite the fact that he had committed no crime, the ruler of the land was determined to kill him. With a band of ragtag followers, he skillfully ran and hid, always remaining one-step ahead of his countrymen tracking his every move.

Consider what obstacles he faced. He had to survive in the En Gedi desert, a place with venomous snakes, scorpions and dangerous animals. A broiling sun, high desert winds and cold nights made just living painful. His emotions plummeted to depression and leaped to joy only to fall again as new obstacles replaced old triumphs. On top of his own needs, he carried the burden of leading and caring for his loyal friends and fellow warriors. Finding food and water was a major challenge. At night, they slept the fitful sleep of the hunted. Every noise could be the advance of an approaching enemy.

He found a cave to hide in. His enemies camped outside not knowing they literally had him trapped. Most astonishingly, the jealous king who sought his death came into the same cave to rest. Now the hunted became the hunter. With one quick thrust of a sword he would be the conqueror putting an end to the mad king obsessed with killing him.

Instead, David spared Saul's life. You can find this incredible story in 1 Sa. 24. Rather than act in his human strength to be rid of his pursuer he chose to trust in God Most High.

I call to God Most High, to God who fulfills His purpose for me. He reaches down from heaven and saves me, challenging the one who tramples me. Selah. God sends His faithful love and truth . . . God, be exalted above the heavens; let Your glory be above the whole earth. (Psa.57:2,3,5)

Yes, David had problems. He also had a steadfast heart capable of generating praise songs in dire occasions. Why? Because beneath the coat of unfair he was forced to wear was a heart that beat the indestructible theme—I trust God! How about you? Do you sometimes feel like a rusted VW Bug trying to avoid being run over by three lanes of SUVs and 18-wheeler trucks? Does life seem unfair? Excellent—now is the perfect time to praise God. That's right! The best way to understand problems begins with praise. God, who fulfilled His purpose in David's life, will fulfill His purpose in your life. Will you let Him? Will you let go of solving problems your way and trust in His way? I hope so—you won't regret it.

This Time I Will Praise

Psalm 57:9,10—I will praise You, Lord, among the peoples; I will sing praises to You among the nations. For Your faithful love is as high as the heavens; Your faithfulness reaches to the clouds.

She became his wife through the deceit of her father. It was poetic justice because the man she was marrying had himself deceived his own father. But her new husband did not fancy her and insisted on marrying her sister as well. Sound scandalous? Such is the story of Leah, the wife of Jacob, the grandson of Abraham.

In Gen. 29:31, we discover that the Lord saw Leah was not loved by Jacob. So He was compassionate to her and blessed her with children. She bore Jacob three sons—Reuben, Simeon, and Levi before conceiving her fourth son. When he was born, she said, *"This time I will praise the Lord"* (vs. 35). She gave him the name Judah, which sounds like the Hebrew word for praise. Later, she would have two more sons and a daughter.

Does God delight in being praised? Is it just coincidence that King David and later the Messiah—Jesus, were descended from the line of Judah, the son born to a grateful mother?

I read that in Africa there is a fruit called the "taste berry." This fruit supposedly affects a person's taste buds so that everything eaten after the berry is sweet and pleasant. Before you sit down and enjoy a birthday meal or open gifts, why not commit to first offer up praise to the awesome Father in heaven who made us and gave us the unceasing gift of life through His majestic Son! Be like the taste berry and fill God's senses with the indescribably delicious flavor of gratitude—no matter what your circumstances. The same Lord who looked down and blessed an obscure woman named Leah, might just do a mighty work in your life—all because you cared enough to praise Him.

Inspiration † † †

Praise is the honey of life which a devout heart extracts from every bloom of providence and grace.—Charles H. Spurgeon, British Reformed Baptist pastor and author, (1834-1892)

God wants to give everyone his or her own song of praise to Him.—Jack Hayford in *Worship His Majesty*

Finding Balance

Do you ever have times where the zoom and vroom of life flows so unrelentingly that to celebrate what should be sacred somehow seems more of an inconvenience? I was talking to a friend recently, and he commented on how people are so busy that there just seems to be little to no interest in preparing for Easter. I found myself nodding in agreement, for the same thoughts filled my mind. But I was the culprit! There was no escaping the fact that I'd rather just have a nice quiet day to myself than plan events that might minister to those coming to celebrate Christ's resurrection.

There comes a time when the pace of life is deceptively dangerous. It is easy to feel productive and somehow important when our calendar is filled to the brim with activity. But rest must balance a constant churning of meetings and work, of running from one scheduled appointment to the next. God, the indescribable Creator, did not have to stop creating. What if day seven was a continuation of days one through six? What if He simply continued to conceive and celebrate an endless progression of what was good! Instead He rested and He blessed the seventh day and made it holy (see Gen. 2:3).

King David strikes me as a type A personality. If he was not thumping enemies, pursuing innovative construction, or giving counsel he was plucking a harp and writing new songs to His first love. Yet, for all his endeavors, David was a man with great balance. I believe he understood a deep secret that won heaven's accolades. Listen to what he wrote in the Psalm below.

Psalm 62:1,2—I am at rest in God alone; my salvation comes from Him. He alone is my rock and my salvation, my stronghold; I will never be shaken.

There is only one place to find true rest and that is in God alone. With Him a bed of calm can be gained in the direst of circumstances. Jesus often left activity and people for solitude with God. We must intentionally put aside our flurry. We need to rest in God to remain healthy. If we find our emotions growing stale, our enthusiasm ebbing, our joy jaundiced, our mindset one of just getting through the calendar, then it is a sure sign that we have neglected respite!

Dr. Vincent Muli Wa Kituku wrote in *Overcoming Buffaloes:*
Wise leaders . . . want people with a balanced life; people with non-work related priorities that they have the same enthusiasm for play as they have for their jobs. They want double hitters—people who work hard and play hard.[13]

As Easter approaches, I am glad to leave for the coast to spend extended time with the Lord. He is my Rock and I look forward to resting in Him. Are you in need of a scheduled break? Will you set aside time to be with God and get your batteries recharged? Remember, Satan will never give you a speeding ticket.

Bill Was Run Over

Billy's dad kissed his wife goodbye and walked out into the cool dark of early morning to go hunting. As he backed up, he felt the vehicle go over a mysterious bump in his driveway. Concerned, he stopped opened the door and went back to examine the object. His two-year old son lay under the vehicle. He'd just run over his head.

They rushed Billy to the hospital, his skull badly cracked in three places. The doctor sent the stricken parents home and told them to come back the next day.

Psalm 62:5-8—Rest in God alone, my soul, for my hope comes from Him. He alone is my rock and my salvation, my stronghold; I will not be shaken. My salvation and glory depend on God; my strong rock, my refuge, is in God. Trust in Him at all times, you people; pour out your hearts before Him. God is our refuge. Selah

Often today, we hear cocky voices disparage Christians as weak because they trust in some fabricated Being. Never mind that agony brings our disputed God to the forefront in the minds of His harshest critics. I am quite happy to be *feeble* in my dependence on God. I am grateful to have fellow believers to turn to for help and consolation in times of distress. If dependence on God is a sign of weakness, let me be chief among His wimps. I'd rather fall in the hands of my invisible Lord and gain true solace than rage against heaven with an empty heart. I don't know any proud atheists or brilliant agnostics who have managed to undo the dust-to-dust process. I have yet to see abiding joy in Savior scoffers.

Billy's parents did not go home to wail and weep alone. They turned to their pastor and the families in their small new church. Together they all lifted their hearts to their Father in heaven and pled for the life of a precious child. I met Billy at a men's retreat in Washington where I had the privilege to speak about friendship with God. He shared with me how his parents returned to the hospital the next day to find him healed—no brain swelling or infection occurred. Billy, this well-known fifth generation logger, is unashamed of the gospel of Christ *"because it is the power of God for the salvation of everyone who believes"* (Rom. 1:16 NIV). He and his folks know all about the value of dependence. Dependence is an ingredient of faith not the affliction of the dysfunctional. It is the love song of God's children who look to Him, the mighty Rock, as their refuge and fortress in times of peace and times of battle.

Inspiration † † †

Faith is a living daring confidence in God's grace. It is so sure and certain that a man could stake his life on it a thousand times.—Martin Luther, German monk, theologian and church reformer, (1483-1546)

Two Firs and a Cherry

Psalm 63:4,5—So I will praise You as long as I live; at Your name, I will lift up my hands. You satisfy me as with rich food; my mouth will praise You with joyful lips.

Sometimes it's hard to really know how much you love something until you lose it. We knew today was coming and dreaded it.

I've scored the winning goal in the final minute of a close soccer game yet the euphoria faded. First place ribbons and medallions from cross-country and track cannot sustain joy. I've tasted the delicious double scoop daiquiri ice cream Baskin & Robbins makes but even it cannot overcome the bland onslaught of saliva. The New York Yankees have won the World Series. The Green Bay Packers have won the Super Bowl. My children have blessed my socks off; it's harder to pull my socks on! Even ecstatic bubbles of victory eventually burst and descend as tiny reality droplets to the valley where most of life is lived.

Poignant satisfaction must run deeper than framed achievements and Kodak memories or we will find ourselves adrift in a volcanic lake of meaninglessness! Promotions, passing the driving test, buying that first house, recovering from a severe illness, childbirth, sharing intimate moments on some fantastic island, giving to someone in dire need, receiving recognition for great work; the list is long of those things that please our spirits. Yet, I've never found *anything* that can bring long-lasting, spirit-nourishing satisfaction like loving Jesus.

By loving the Messiah, I find my heart is continuously satisfied. This morning chainsaws and the ruthless steel jaws of a tractor toppled two tall firs and a stately cherry. Our once wonderfully shaded home now sits naked before every passerby. Sidewalks and a sewer line will be better for the neighborhood but don't tell that to five sad tree fans. Under the gleaming sun, we already feel the heat. No, life on Tiedeman won't be the same, but life with Jesus will still be satisfying. I hope it's the same for you. Worse than losing trees is not knowing the abundant life that comes from an awesome Lord.

Inspiration   † † †

Those who seek for much are left in want of much. Happy is he to whom God has given, with sparing hand, as much as is enough.—Horace (Quintus Horatius Flaccus) in *Carmina (bk. III, 16, 42)*

We cannot possibly be satisfied with anything less than to walk with God—each day, each hour, each moment, in Christ, through the power of the Holy Spirit.—Handley Carr Glyn Moule, British Anglican Bishop of Durham, (1841-1920)

King of the Hill

King of the Hill is a great game if you are tough, athletic and big. It would seem that conquering mountains has always been an obsession for mankind. Even today on the radio, I heard about a blind man who climbed to the top of Mount Everest! The possessor of high ground occupies the strategic advantage and holds bragging rights.

John 19:17,18—Carrying His own cross, He went out to what is called Skull Place, which in Hebrew is called Golgotha. There they crucified Him and two others with Him, one on either side, with Jesus in the middle.

How fitting that the Romans led Jesus to high ground to crucify Him. Calvary provided a view of Jerusalem. It was a place where convicted criminals were displayed so all could see the folly of breaking the law. Nailed to wooden beams, Jesus, God's holy Son, was raised a spectacle before the jeering countrymen He came to save.

He didn't need to open His mouth. Just a thought would have sufficed. Instantly, legions of angels would have streaked to His defense. He could easily fry his adversaries with one laser look. Just a wave of the hand and Calvary might have blazed on fire instead of an agonized silence.

Satan laughed no doubt at the puny sight of a slain Creator. The religious leaders smirked at the pathetic manner in which the One they jealousy despised succumbed. But God never intended to take the hill. His plan was not to make Calvary a historical battleground on which His Boy would be King. Instead, Calvary became Paradox Hill. The One who was perfect took on all our sins. The One who possessed authority let others decide His fate. The One with miraculous powers would not turn spikes into spears. The One who came to save others died Himself.

One military man watched closely the battle on Calvary between good and evil. He reached a conclusion not shared by the masses. We read in Luke 23:47: *"When the centurion saw what happened, he began to glorify God, saying, 'This man really was righteous!'"*

God let a hill be taken to win the world. Lives are not changed today because of the authority of those who decided Jesus would hang on dead timber on a hilltop. Lives are changed because of an empty grave off the hill from which Jesus rose victorious to give us our only shot at salvation. The real King of the hill is not the one left standing at the top but the One who ascended into heaven and now sits at the right hand of God, the Maker of all hills. He is the Champion of Calvary!

Inspiration † † †

At the cross God wrapped his heart in flesh and blood and let it be nailed to the cross for our redemption.—E. Stanley Jones, theologian, (1894-1973)

"Not in Service"

I was driving behind a Metro bus on my way north on Interstate 5. On the back of it a neon sign flashed, *Not in Service*. The thought crossed my mind, "I wonder how many times I have communicated *Not in Service* to God or to people."

Mark 10:45—For even the Son of Man did not come to be served, but to serve, and to give His life—a ransom for many.

What if Jesus decided His Father's plan was overly horrific? What if on that heavy last Friday, He announced to His disciples, "Men, tonight, I'm taking the night off, I won't be in service." There would have been no betrayal in the garden, no arrest, and no hope for us..

What if Jesus tired of the endless crowds demanding His time, miracles and voice? In the process of resting, what if He'd decided to take an extended vacation—encouraging Andrew, Peter, James and John to fish—and the rest of the disciples to do whatever they wanted? What stories would disappear from the gospel accounts and might the disciples have interpreted Luke 9:23 as figurative language?

What if Jesus wearied of the disciples' pettiness, bickering, and failure to understand His teaching? What if He told them, "Guys, stop! I'm done serving—I've had it with trying to help you people, you just don't get it!"

Do we really understand that the Son of Man never quit! He perfectly followed heaven's script. He knew my sin and your sin before we sinned and *still* died for us. The Roman soldiers didn't crucify Him; He crucified Himself by refusing to wave the *Not in Service* sign.

I don't deserve such love. I think of the times I've copped an attitude, avoided helping someone else, or looked after my agenda, and I'm ashamed how easy it was to desert *Yahweh* for my way. There's nothing in my life that merits God's Son horrifically suffering for me or offering me the key to eternal fellowship.

The Son of Man came to serve to the extent of martyrdom. What a loving Savior and incredible role model! I feel challenged again to live honorably in His strength *in service*. What is good about this Friday before Easter is the greatness of our Servant, the One we worship as Lord and marvel at His sense of duty. Like Him, let's be in service!

Inspiration † † †

Only a life lived for others is a life worthwhile.—Albert Einstein, German-born theoretical physicist, (1879-1955)

The highest form of worship is the worship of unselfish Christian service. The greatest form of praise is the sound of consecrated feet seeking out the lost and helpless.—Billy Graham, evangelist

When Darkness Reigns

Luke 23:44-46—It was now about noon, and darkness came over the whole land until three, because the sun's light failed. The curtain of the sanctuary was split down the middle. And Jesus called out with a loud voice, "Father, into Your hands I entrust My spirit." Saying this, He breathed His last.

When darkness reigns, envy credits miracles as the work of the devil.
When darkness reigns, love is handed over for coins of silver.
When darkness reigns, those who should pray fall asleep.
When darkness reigns, man's depravity glows with burning intensity.
When darkness reigns, the high priest's house is hell's model home.
When darkness reigns, Jealousy is the cologne of choice.
When darkness reigns, a kiss only burns.
When darkness reigns, Truth receives a beating.
When darkness reigns, suicide is the betrayer's only recourse
When darkness reigns, belief disrobes to doubt and flees naked.
When darkness reigns, denial is the preferred action.
When darkness reigns, the state bird is a rooster.
When darkness reins, the corrupt lead the crowd in a symphony of hate.
When darkness reigns, the governor convicts thc Innocent and washes.
When darkness reigns, the crowd screams to pardon the murderer.
When darkness reigns, tears taste bitter.
When darkness reigns, the cross stands silhouetted against a stormy sky.
When darkness reigns, wine is replaced by vinegar.
When darkness reins, the Son stops shining.
When darkness reigns, fear melts peace into a pond of pain.
When darkness reigns, God turns His back on His own Son.
When darkness reigns, the forces of evil party.
When darkness reigns, the righteous mourn; women wail wordless songs.
When darkness reigns, questions replace answers.
When darkness reigns, the tomb is a place to gather and contemplate.
When darkness reigns, hope has no forum.
When darkness reigns, coldness wraps the globe in its miserable cloak.

And then came resurrection . . . something to think about, in reveration!

Inspiration † † †

The early Christians . . . vigorously preached the Resurrection of the crucified Christ as the core of their message . . . They wrote book after book to defend the Christian doctrine of the resurrection . . . The early church fathers paid more attention to the theme of resurrection than almost any other single subject.—James E. Leuschen in *Gospel of Victory: The Revolutionary Keys of the Early Church Gospel*

Cincinnati Connection

Proverbs 20:24—A man's steps are determined by the LORD, so how can anyone understand his own way?

On March 29, 2004, I clearly witnessed the Lord's providence. After giving two concerts and speaking in a friend's church in Atlanta, I was on my way home. I called my wife from the airport to coordinate picking me up in Portland when she informed me of the death of our friend Laurie. Laurie's husband, Dan, a West Point classmate of mine, was serving as a reservist in Afghanistan. After getting the pertinent information from Kathleen, I called Dan's reserve unit and asked for someone to call me with the flight information for Dan's arrival. At the time of my call, the unit did not know his arrival time, what airline he was on, etc.

As soon as I hung up I felt led to pray. I asked God to put me on Dan's flight. I then boarded my plane and flew to Cincinnati. As I waited in Ohio for my connecting flight, Delta announced that the flight was overbooked and asked for volunteers to give up their seats. Eager to get the free ticket and able to delay my return, I moved to the check-in counter to volunteer. While standing there, a voice called out "Hey Dano." I looked over to my right and there sat Dan! Amazed and gratified, I left the counter to join him. I was able to change my seat and sit next to him. God put us together on the last leg of his long journey.

The Heidelberg Catechism (1563) asks:

What is your only comfort in life and death?

Answer: That I, with body and soul, both in life and in death, am not my own, but belong to my faithful Savior Jesus Christ who . . . so preserves me that without the will of my Father in heaven not a hair can fall from my head; yea, that all things must work together for my salvation.

God sent me to Atlanta and planned my return so that I could be with my ranger buddy! I cannot even begin to calculate the odds of us meeting! What matters, is that God lovingly foreknew, answered prayer and illustrated His powerful providence. Our loving Father cares for us. Even in the midst of difficult times, we should trust Him! We can believe with Paul, *"We know that all things work together for the good of those who love God: those who are called according to His purpose"* (Rom. 8:28).

Inspiration † † †

. . . The longer I live, the more convincing proofs I see of this truth, that God governs in the affairs of men. And if a sparrow cannot fall to the ground without His notice, is it probable that an empire can rise without His aid?— Benjamin Franklin, U.S. founding father, author, politician, scientist, inventor, and diplomat, (1706-1790)

Peace to You

John 20:19—In the evening of that first day of the week, the disciples were gathered together with the doors locked because of their fear of the Jews. Then Jesus came, stood among them, and said to them, "Peace to you!"

Studying the Easter story gives us amazing insight into what it means to be human. Jesus, on many occasions, told His disciples that He was going to die, even hinting to how He would be killed (John 12:23-32). But His forewarning was unfathomable and when He was crucified, they were devastated. Imagine the men who watched Jesus raise Lazarus from the dead, calm an angry sea, feed thousands with a few pieces of bread and fish, and silence the brightest religious minds with pithy one-liners, reduced to hiding in a room—afraid for their lives. When Jesus appeared to them, His action gives us brilliant insight into the human need. He didn't recite previous warnings, or scold them for hiding. He simply shared with them three words. *"Peace to you!"* He filled their despondent hearts with joy and courage that eventually turned the world upside down.

If we cannot understand how vital peace is, then we cannot understand what it means to be human. God informs us through His Word but He transforms us by His presence. We live every day in a world at war. When trials He warned us about come, for some reason we fall apart. We wonder where God disappeared. We doubt the essence of our faith and question if God really could reign over such a twisted planet. We signed up for a triumphant Messiah and His promise to include us on the winning team. But, we didn't bargain on suffering, or forecast the fear that would grip us when people or circumstances viciously turn against us.

Easter is the paradox of peace. Jesus died to conquer death. He endured horrendous pain to bring an end to our suffering. He bore our burden of sin and yet is the only human to live a sinless life. He felt the rejection of His Father, to gain our acceptance. Each way He turns is illogical to our way of thinking. And maybe this is our problem. We do too much thinking. We fashion in our brains what life should be like but we are *not* the Creator of life. We have but a smidgen of understanding of God, and life, and life with God. And this is why we need peace. Peace puts an end to endless questions. In the same way children run for the arms of their mother, so ought we to run to the One who says, *"I will never leave you or forsake you"* (Heb. 13:5b).

No matter what our circumstances are at this moment—God *loves* us. There are two ways to spend Easter—huddled behind a door afraid of what's outside, or gathered in joy worshiping the redeemer King. Homeless? Jobless? Sick? Emotionally spent? Frustrated? Angry? Tired? Heartsick? Betrayed? In-debt? Lost? Bewildered? Alone? God has a word for you—P-E-A-C-E! Peace be with you.

The Day of Pentecost

Acts 2:5,6—At that time there were devout Jews from every nation living in Jerusalem. When they heard the loud noise, everyone came running, and they were bewildered to hear their own languages being spoken by the believers. (NLT)

On the day of Pentecost after Jesus' resurrection, there was a major gathering of devout Jews. They came to celebrate the Feast of Weeks, in obedience to God's directive through Moses. Pentecost was a time to give offerings proportionate to God's blessings in the past year. But this day's celebration was unlike any ever held! The Holy Spirit descended upon a group of Jesus-followers all assembled in a house centrally located near the Temple. As tongues of fire rested upon their heads, each believer began speaking in a different language. God, in one fell swoop, broadcast the truth about Jesus in a way sure to reach foreign Jews.

God dynamically fulfilled Jesus' promise made in Acts 1:8, *"But you will receive power when the Holy Spirit has come upon you, and you will be My witnesses in Jerusalem, in all Judea and Samaria, and to the ends of the earth."* Imagine how incredible it must have been to hear men who were Galileans— ordinary people from small towns each fluently speaking foreign languages to astonished listeners! The timing, location, language and message were all carefully orchestrated in heaven to coincide with a major religious gathering. While the Jews focused on thanksgiving offerings, God focused on igniting Jesus' disciples to tell the world about their Savior.

In the midst of rejoicing over Jesus' triumph from the grave don't lose sight of what He came to accomplish and commands us to do! God wants to speak through you! He placed His light in you to shine around all you know. So are you burning bright or is your light hidden beneath symbols and traditions? Easter is not about the bunny and it's not about dressing up nicely to attend a special service or mass. It's not about painting eggs and hanging banners or eating ham or filling baskets with chocolate. It's not simply about celebrating Jesus' resurrection. Religious trappings can easily turn into a Feast of *Weaks.* All around us are people who need to hear about Christ. Let's remember that Easter means:

> **E**agerly
> **A**ctively
> **S**haring
> **T**he
> **E**ternal
> **R**edeemer!

Mega Memory

Have you ever walked up to someone, introduced yourself, listened to the other person's name and then promptly forgotten it? I hate it when that happens! Kevin Trudeau has a course called *Mega Memory*. I listened to his tapes during my thirteen-hour drive to Fort Hunter Liggett, California. My intent was to improve my memory (especially for names), so I listened to the tapes I'd heard before but forgotten.

Psalm 77:11-13—I will remember the LORD's works; yes, I will remember Your ancient wonders. I will reflect on all You have done and meditate on Your actions God, Your way is holy. What god is great like God?

I'm glad that God gave us a memory. While I may not do well in recalling the names of new faces, let alone the techniques for improving memory, it is not hard to remember the incredible things God did to give my life meaning and purpose. I like what Jeduthun shares in Psalm 77. *"I will remember the LORD's works."* Memory focused on God:

● Reminds me that I serve One who ceaselessly works on the behalf of His children

● Makes the mundane pale as the reality of miracles past point towards a mouth-watering future

● Calls for a holy contemplation, a meditation in what God does, not what I do

● Defines greatness for what it really is—God loving His children with a love through actions that surpass understanding

A God-deficient memory:

● Leads to despair

● Cannot answer *"so what?"*

If we fail to remember God, we should not be surprised if the stress of daily living in a sin-infected world seems at times overwhelming. Don't let today's battles become bigger than your God. What He did for your yesterdays should fill you with hope for both today and tomorrow! Remember and believe! Recall His deeds and say, "He is able!"

Inspiration ✝ ✝ ✝

God gave us memory so that we might have roses in December.—Sir James Matthew Barrie, Scottish novelist and dramatist, creator of Peter Pan, (1860-1937)

The heart that truly loves never forgets.—Proverb

By Faith or By Reason

Psalm 94:11—The LORD knows man's thoughts; they are meaningless.

There are those who walk by faith and there are those who walk by reason. There are those who think they trust in God and those who trust they think. The lifestyle of holiness that Jesus modeled and called us to emulate usually places us directly in conflict with the world—the same world that crucified Him. The logical conclusion is the more godly we become the more we can expect to suffer. Our challenge is to agree with the Apostle Paul—*"For me, living is Christ and dying is gain"* (Php. 1:21).

The place of reason is to support, not replace faith. *"But set apart the Messiah as Lord in your hearts, and always be ready to give a defense to anyone who asks you for a reason for the hope that is in you"* (1 Pe. 3:15). May I suggest that the power of reason hinders our ability to trust and obey God more than we might believe? For example, there is nothing ambiguous about the Great Commission Jesus proclaimed in Mat. 28:19,20 to His disciples:

> Go, therefore, and make disciples of all nations, baptizing them in the name of the Father and of the Son and of the Holy Spirit, teaching them to observe everything I have commanded you. And remember, I am with you always, to the end of the age.

Jesus' command is an unpopular heavenly mandate which necessitates making personal sacrifices in order to accomplish it. So why are so few complying with Christ's order? Reason dictates setting aside these verses because they are not addressed to us but only to Jesus' disciples; unrealistic; offensive to many people; only written for ministers and missionaries; or, secondary to other more vital causes.

In a climate of rain, moss grows upon a roof. Moss builds upon itself and if it is not removed, hastens the decline of shingles until eventually the roof leaks. In a climate of fear, reason grows upon one's faith. Reasoning creates excuses and if left unchecked paralysis sets in and faith cannot overcome fear. Therefore, the pertinent question is, "Are you living more by faith or by reason?"

Inspiration † † †

The heart has its reasons, of which reason knows nothing . . . It is the heart which perceives God and not the reason. That is what faith is: God perceived by the heart, not by the reason.—Blaise Pascal, French mathematician, physicist, and religious philosopher, (1623-1662)

Whenever I say, "I want to reason this thing out before I can trust," I will never trust. The reasoning out and the perfection of knowledge come after the response to God has been made.—Oswald Chambers in *God's Workmanship*

I Crashed the Minivan

It's not hard to feel inadequate. In the middle of an intersection, I zeroed in on what John was asking me. I didn't see the silver Nissan approaching from the right. He couldn't swerve in time or stop to avoid me. Bang!!! In one unceremonious crunch, our Plymouth Voyager was totaled. With one lapse of attention I joined the other side—the team of drivers in accidents because they were talking on cell phones. The best intentions don't erase crumpled metal. Fortunately, no one was hurt and the other car suffered only minor damage.

Psalm 106:1,2—Hallelujah! Give thanks to the LORD, for He is good; His faithful love endures forever. Who can declare the LORD's mighty acts or proclaim all the praise due Him?

When the Bible says God is good, it's easy to gloss over that word *"good."* Yet, in reality, His goodness is indescribable. His love never ends! His works are so fantastic that no one can fully fathom, let alone give Him the glory He is truly due. God is so awesome that our inadequacy is rendered irrelevant by His sufficiency.

Without God, I would have spent days beating myself up for a careless accident. I would have sought ways to justify my negligence. I would have lain awake at night replaying the scene. With God, I could recognize my fault and minister to the other young man who suffered his first accident. I could sit in the parking lot of Home Depot and praise God for His love and thank Him that He is my sufficiency.

Without God, I would have despaired over the loss of our minivan. With God, I have no reason to worry because He is my faithful Provider. It is immensely satisfying to praise God when circumstances scream for cursing. Experiencing joy during times of adversity confirms what a huge difference God makes in our lives. This does not excuse what I did. I should not have talked on the cell phone while driving.

Contrary to what the world teaches, I don't need to be my own man. I need to be God's man. The former leads to pride and eventual hopelessness. The latter brings purpose and peace. *"Who can declare the LORD's mighty acts or proclaim all the praise due Him?"* I can't. I'm inadequate—flawed and incapable of knowing all God does. But, I can worship my Father who makes all the difference in the world. And, you can do the same. No matter what you are going through right now, God's goodness is sufficient for you. Believe it! Live, and if necessary, die in it. Either way, He will see you through if your trust is in Him.

Henry & Richard Blackaby wrote in *Spiritual Leadership*, "Character building takes time. There are no shortcuts. Two factors determine the length of time required for God to develop character worthy of spiritual leadership—trust in God and obedience to God."[4]

Can I Trust God?

Psalm 112:1,7—Hallelujah! Happy is the man who fears the LORD, taking great delight in His commandments . . . He will not fear bad news; his heart is confident, trusting in the LORD.

It started when my good friends Rob and Glenn realized they had to install a handicapped accessible restroom in their San Diego church. The molehill they faced turned into a mountain. At a cost of $50,000 a ramp had to be built, doors had to be widened, and handicap accessible doors with electronic openers installed. During the construction, the carpet was ruined. Beneath the tiles underneath the carpet, they found asbestos requiring them to call in a removal team. Finally, after much expense, the renovations were complete.

Two weeks later a plugged urinal flooded such that water streamed out the front and side doors. Pews were damaged and brand new carpet was ruined. At the same time, many people within the body were suffering. People's jobs didn't pay enough to meet their expenses; relationships were tearing apart. It seemed the more they pressed to serve God the more opposition they faced.

Rob began to paint his back room at home but the wallpaper came off in sheets. He discovered subterranean termites feasting on his home. All of the sheet rock had to come out. This led to the discovery that the electrical wiring was not up to code and was a fire hazard. His VCR and television stopped working. Repair costs climbed higher and higher. When the stress became too great, Rob experienced a massive pity party. While bemoaning his circumstances, he turned on his old TV and happened to catch a preacher by the name of Jesse Duplantis. God used his message on trust to cheer up his servant. Rob thought about all that went on in the church and his home and concluded:

> We don't love God enough to trust Him to meet all of our needs. *Our job is to believe that God can do His job.* (With the church) We could have responded in many different ways but when something this big happens—what can you do? We chose to believe God. We prayed over the Sanctuary and claimed God's provision for us His people and put the whole thing in His hands. God met our needs through the insurance company . . . The resources are His, the time is His, and we are His . . . The question for me became, 'Can I trust God or not?' I believe the answer is yes, that all He requires of me He has resourced me for. Can I let go of the hurts of my past and believe that He can bring something good out of the ashes? Yes!! I certainly can. All I need has been, is, and will be provided. Wherever you are in your life circumstances, He can do the same thing for you.

Benefits of God's Laws

A crumpled, gray Saturn blocks the intersection while scores of drivers stuck by the accident, sputter at the infuriating delay. Firemen extract the old woman from her car smashed by a young man in a big hurry. She saw a green light and preceded east on Canon Street. He was headed south on Anarchic Avenue. Irritated and in a hurry he ignored the red and sped through the intersection broadsiding the hapless woman.

Why is it that so many people disdain laws and take unbelievable steps to circumvent them? Why did the Lawgiver also build within us the freedom to obey or disobey Him? It is interesting to read in Psa. 119:97 the words *"How I love Your law! I meditate on it all day long"* (NIV). Can you remember anyone ever walking up to you and saying, "I just love God's laws!"? What we love says a lot about our character. *"Open my eyes so that I may see wonderful things in Your law"* (119:18).

Selfishness is a formidable enemy of the law. The Psalmist wrote, *"Turn my heart to Your decrees and not to material gain"* (119:36). Our desire to please our flesh results in our undoing. Because selfishness is often subtle and insidious a good prayer is, *"Give me understanding, and I will keep your law and obey it with all my heart"* (119:34 NIV).

We also need to avoid making excuses. Satan whispers, "You're already flawed and it's impossible to be holy so just do the best you can and don't worry about breaking a few laws." Oswald Chambers notes, "Because a thing is impossible in a man's present moral imperfection it does not mean he is exonerated from it. God's law has nothing to do with possibility or impossibility." When we set our desires first we find the result of our experiments to be chaos, pain and disrepute. When we put His kingdom and will first we die to self and profoundly experience the liberty contained in obedience.

Meditation on the Benefits of God's Laws

- *They provide us counsel and delight—"Your decrees are my delight and my counselors"* (119:24).
- *They provide us comfort—"LORD, I remember Your judgments from long ago and find comfort"* (119:52).
- *They give us peace and keep us from moral failure—"Abundant peace belongs to those who love Your instruction; nothing makes them stumble"* (119:165).
- *They preserve our lives—"I will never forget Your precepts, for You have given me life through them"* (119:93).
- *They make us wise and understanding—"I gain understanding from Your precepts; therefore I hate every false way"* (119:104).
- *Keeping them brings God's approval!—"You reject all who stray from Your statutes, for their deceit is a lie"* (119:118).

Without Bearing April 6

Pastor John Repsold wrote in a newsletter, *The Fourth Dimension*, the true story of a cook on a work crew at Lewis and Clark Caverns in Montana. This man became tired of his job and decided to quit. But before leaving, he determined to go deeper into the cave and break off stalactites he could later sell to rock collectors. Late on a Friday afternoon, he maneuvered away from his departing work detail. But, the flame of his lantern blew out! To his horror, he realized he had no matches. He would spend a weekend alone, trapped underground!

When this poor fellow was discovered, he was "delirious, disoriented and panic-stricken. Lying on the damp floor of the cavern, he thought he was actually standing." When they brought him to the surface, he experienced temporary blindness for several hours. Yes, living in darkness is a treacherous thing.

Years ago, my oldest son, Bryan, was encouraged by his AWANA teacher to ask God to reveal His truth to him through studying His Word. Bryan complied. In the course of his reading the Holy Spirit impressed on his young heart Pro. 16:3—*"Commit your activities to the LORD and your plans will be achieved."* Bryan shared with me his desire to get up each day and apply this verse to his life. He follows in the footsteps of his grandfather who still daily sets aside time to feed from the banquet table we know as the Bible.

Psalm 119:105—Your word is a lamp for my feet and a light on my path.

God's Word reveals truth! It is our light in a world where darkness reigns. When we neglect time meditating in the Bible, we lose our bearing and the path God would have us take becomes obscured by the fog of fleshly living. I am so thankful that the Lord loves us and provides us living, inspiring truth to guide us. I am even more blessed to see Bryan come of age with the same realization. Together we pray that you too, will find joy walking in the light of God's Word! It will be your glory for His GLORY!

Inspiration † † †

A thorough understanding of the Bible is better than a college education.—Theodore Roosevelt, 26th President of the United States, 1858-1919

The Bible is one of the greatest blessings bestowed by God on the children of men. It has God for its author; salvation for its end, and truth without any mixture for its matter. It is all pure.—John Locke, English philosopher, (1632–1704)

Eyes Toward the Mountains

Psalm 121—I raise my eyes toward the mountains. Where will my help come from? My help comes from the LORD, the Maker of heaven and earth. He will not allow your foot to slip; your Protector will not slumber. Indeed, the Protector of Israel does not slumber or sleep. The LORD protects you; the LORD is a shelter right by your side. The sun will not strike you by day, or the moon by night. The LORD will protect you from all harm; He will protect your life. The LORD will protect your coming and going both now and forever.

My knees are such that I don't enjoy hiking much anymore. It's not the going up that is difficult but rather the coming down! But the fact that descent is problematic in no way dampens my love for hills. *"I raise my eyes toward the mountains."* There's something majestic about towering peaks covered in white, descending like a beautiful wedding gown over verdant firs. Let me drive up mountain roads and my spirit rises and my head fills with inspired song!

Mountains force us to look up. Perhaps, in doing so, our eyes come away from the drab that dulls us. Mountains move us away from the smog of sin to the fragrance of pine that clears away frustration and fretting. Mountains remind us that a Creator far greater than we can imagine moved rock into grandiose formations. They form spiritual temples alive in worship, profound in testimony.

"Where will my help come from?" Mountains remind me. *"My help comes from the Lord."* Climbing to Him on the pathway home, He will not let my feet slip. People are fickle, easily distracted. God is vigilant. He does not sleep while we walk towards Him, so that His eyes cannot see to help when avalanches roar, or winds snap limbs, or rain sends floods across the trail of faith. *"The Lord protects you."* Thank You, Father. *You are the perfect shelter. When the sun blazes and the moon shines through frigid air, Your arms remain open to envelop us, Your blessed children.*

My life matters to my Maker. He who watches my every step, up and down, causes my faith to soar. The key to understanding His assistance is to look up with an eternal perspective. Nothing can harm us, not even death, for our future is secure in His will. When we know this, we walk differently remembering:

His

Eternal

Loving

Protection is something to think about . . . in reveration!

Inspiration   † † †

A log cannot move without the help of rollers.—Kenyan Proverb

"They Lit Me Up . . ."

In March of 1992, Captain David Knecht learned he was passed over for promotion to major. Despite the setback, he determined to press on with his career. Weeks later, on April 8th, he was out on a field exercise conducting a routine night live fire defense. When the exercise ended, he looked forward to traveling to Russia for a short gospel mission trip.

That night an M2 Bradley platoon was positioned about one kilometer to the right of the spot Dave selected for his Command M113 vehicle. Apparently, the platoon leader or his gunner was scanning for targets out of sector because when Dave's M113 showed up in their thermals sights, "they lit me up with eight 25mm rounds." One training round glanced off the hatch next to his head and penetrated the soft CVC helmet he was wearing, exploding fragments into his brain and right eye. Dave was flown by two helicopters, a UH-60 Blackhawk and later a CH-47 Chinook to a civilian medical center for emergency brain surgery.

After operating, Dave's surgeon prayed with Annette (Dave's wife) in the hospital chapel. Because his death was all but a foregone conclusion, a military lawyer with whom they attended chapel, rushed through a disability retirement so his survivors would receive maximum government benefits. But God had other plans.

1 Corinthians 10:31—Therefore, whether you eat or drink, or whatever you do, do everything for God's glory.

David's left side is mostly paralyzed, "so I walk with a limp," and his right eye is blind, but "it is well with my soul." The man who should be dead or bitter is instead a joyful testimony to the transformation that comes through serving God. Earthly wisdom renders tragedy as senseless. Godly trust discovers meaning even in suffering. Out of loss, God builds gain. Consider this. Residing in Florida, Dave and Annette have ten children. Sarah, the oldest, is one of three daughters already married. Their sixth son, Micah, (the first born after Dave's accident), at the age of seven was sharing Christ with children in a nearby park. He is a walking evangelist carrying tracts wherever he goes. Glory is the tribute, honor, and praise God receives and we experience when we allow His will to find His expression in our lives.

When I asked Annette to describe Dave she said, "He just glows God's glory!" In evaluating the last twelve years she shared, "The lower we are laid and emptied of ourselves the more God is able to work through us and gain glory." It's not easy to suffer, to go lower. But glory is not defined by what is easy or ordinary. You and I will undoubtedly never take a shot to the brain like my West Point classmate Dave did. But we will be tested. We will find days when life evokes pain or confusion and God seems distant. Perhaps for you that time is now. If so, Dave has a word he would love to share from Php. 1:6, *"I am sure of this, that He who started a good work in you will carry it on to completion until the day of Christ Jesus."* Glory! Something to think about . . . in reveration!

Inspiration ✝ ✝ ✝

Grace is but glory begun, and glory is but grace perfected.—Jonathan Edwards, preacher and theologian (1703-1758)

One Horse Laugh

Pity the stuffy religious leader who wears frowns as a badge of maturity and looks down upon those who laugh as frivolous contenders for God's eventual wrath. He has missed the divine engineering of our marvelous Creator, misused the ministry of role modeling and will most likely die the premature death of one repressed instead of blessed. The human capacity to laugh is a God-given gift and for good reason.

Laughter reduces levels of certain stress hormones . . . It provides a safety valve that shuts off the flow of stress hormones and the fight-or-flight compounds that swing into action in our bodies when we experience stress, anger or hostility. These stress hormones suppress the immune system, increase the number of blood platelets (which can cause obstructions in arteries) and raise blood pressure. When we're laughing, natural killer cells that destroy tumors and viruses increase, as do Gamma-interferon (a disease-fighting protein), T-cells, which are a major part of the immune response, and B-cells, which make disease-destroying antibodies. Laughter also increases the concentration of salivary immunoglobulin A, which defends against infectious organisms entering through the respiratory tract . . . researchers estimate that laughing 100 times is equal to 10 minutes on the rowing machine or 15 minutes on an exercise bike. Laughing can be a total body workout! Blood pressure is lowered, and there is an increase in vascular blood flow and in oxygenation of the blood, which further assists healing. Laughter also gives your diaphragm and abdominal, respiratory, facial, leg and back muscles a workout. That's why you often feel exhausted after a long bout of laughter— you've just had an aerobic workout![15]

Psalm 126:1,2—When the LORD restored the fortunes of Zion, we were like those who dream. Our mouths were filled with laughter then, and our tongues with shouts of joy. Then they said among the nations, "The LORD has done great things for them."

A Multnomah Seminary professor was asked to officiate a baptismal ceremony in a small church. A large tub served as the immersion tank. Behind it was a white curtain hung to provide privacy for changing clothes. The elderly professor baptized a businessman and proceeded on to a large woman. Unfortunately, as she went under the water he realized to his dismay that he was not strong enough to lift her up. The woman panicked and furiously began grasping for anything that would get her above the water. Her hands found the white curtain which in one desperate tear came down exposing the business-man naked before the incredulous congregation. The totally embarrassed man, seeing no place to hide, jumped in the tub with the woman.

By now, the professor realizing something had to be done asked the worship leader to lead the congregation in a final number. Can you guess what the last song was? *Just As I Am!*

Did the angels laugh at what can only be described as comical? Does God chuckle at the unintended mishaps of His children and join with us when we find humor in life? I imagine He does for laughter is the contagious remedy He created in us for our merriment and His glory.

Inspiration † † †

Nothing shows a man's character more than what he laughs at.— Johann Wolfgang Von Goethe, German writer, (1749-1832)

One horse-laugh is worth ten thousand syllogisms. It is not only more effective; it is also vastly more intelligent.—H L Mencken, journalist, magazine editor, satirist, (1880-1956)

God's Celestial Nurse

As a child, I suffered growing pains and often cried before finally drifting off. To this night, I still experience tight leg muscles or an overly active mind that makes it difficult to relax. Many times I have tossed and turned in frustration—unable to escape consciousness. Counting sheep never worked for me—I think it's a math thing. One night in this predictably unpredictable occurrence, I sensed there was an issue over which I needed to pray. Upon returning from the couch and time on my knees with God, something incredible happened—sleep came readily.

Psalm 127:2—It is useless to get up early and stay up late in order to earn a living. God takes care of His own, even while they sleep. (CEV)

Jesus said to His followers, *"Come to Me, all of you who are weary and burdened, and I will give you rest"* (Mat. 11:28). Often sleep is elusive because my mind is torqued over many concerns. I need to let go of what ails me and trust that God is sovereign over all circumstances. So, I go to God as His weary son, to dump my truck in His bottomless landfill. I return to a bed sweetened with an angelic aroma of heavenly rest!

Jesus also said to His key disciples, *"'Why are you sleeping?' He asked them. 'Get up and pray, so that you won't enter into temptation'"* (Luke 22:46). Do you ever have times you know God is calling you to pray? I'm beginning to believe my leg pains are God's means of alerting me to get up and intercede! There are nights I can't sleep and I need to get up and listen to the Lord regarding what I should pray. Afterwards, sleep comes.

Perhaps you're a member of the insomniac squad. Instead of popping pills or consuming midnight turkey sandwiches, consider spending time with the One who needs no bed, yet, who understands our needs.

Inspiration † † †

Sleep is one of life's great pleasures.—Randy Alcorn in *Heaven*

A good laugh and a long sleep are the best cures in the doctor's book.—Irish Proverb

No Discard Pile

Delnora sits before her canvas. Her eyes walk across the wild flowers that carpet the valley before her. They climb up the dark green firs higher and higher until only the magnificent face of a snow-capped mountain is left to kiss the clear blue sky. She gulps the fresh air and sighs—the exhalation of ecstasy an artist feels in the presence of grandeur. She mixes assorted paints to find the perfect color to match what she views. The painting begins . . .

Psalm 139:14—I will praise You, because I have been remarkably and wonderfully made. Your works are wonderful, and I know this very well.

High in the home we have not yet lived, a Master Artist creates from His divine knowledge another life. He draws unique fingerprints and invents a new voice. He knows every baby born from a man-woman joining. *"Because by Him everything was created, in heaven and on earth, the visible and the invisible, whether thrones or dominions or rulers or authorities—all things have been created through Him and for Him"* (Col. 1:16).

The One who drew the delicate brilliant colors across tropical fish; focused eagle eyes to see a rabbit a mile away; wrapped the alligator in armor; scented the rose and honeysuckle; honored a gray cliff with a singing waterfall; lent voice to a cheerful canary; made apatetic (camouflaged) fur to hide the leopard; coated the lamb in flocculent (soft, wooly) attire; gave simple cane the sweetness of sugar and hid milk in coconuts; never makes mistakes.

The Master Artist has no discard pile. Each life He forms is precious. We judge by the exterior and applaud the fittest. He sees what is inside and loves what is honest. Whether you get up bursting with energy or lie still in depression the truth still remains. Jesus lovingly made you. You are not the mistake of two misguided souls or the work of parents who carefully planned for your arrival. You are God's designed-child, meant to be His own. He calls you to Him as you are. Don't let the roar of a sin-soaked earth fool you. May you be the prize He intended, one that angels celebrate, in loving admiration for the Artist.

Inspiration ✝✝✝

The joy of an artist is not in the fame that his pictures bring him, but that his work is the creation of his personality. The work of Jesus is the creation of saints; He can take the worst, the most misshapen material, and make a saint.—Oswald Chambers in *Bringing Sons Into Glory*

Divine Inspiration

My two sons and I enjoyed watching *Star Trek Voyager*. We regularly followed the space adventures and mini-plots that revolved around the homesick Voyager crew desperately trying to reach the Alpha Quadrant. I remember sitting down to view a new episode when I felt a direct nudging by the Holy Spirit to go and pray.

"But Lord, do you really want me to go pray right now!" Immediately I recalled a lesson our home group learned from our *Experiencing God* study. When God speaks that is the time to act. I could make excuses not to pray until later and potentially miss God's leading, or be obedient and in accordance with His will. I got up to go pray.

"Okay Lord, what do You want me to pray about?" The Holy Spirit brought several things to mind. Later that evening, while reading John Maxwell's book, *The 21 Indispensable Qualities of a Leader,* I was inspired with an idea directly related to what I had been in prayer over earlier. It gave me hope about a course of action that seemed crucial to our ministry. It was exciting and encouraging for had I shirked praying, I would have missed what God wanted me to discern.

Psalm 143:8— Let me hear of your unfailing love each morning, for I am trusting you. Show me where to walk, for I give myself to you. (NLT)

Inspiration from the Holy Spirit when immediately acted upon in obedience, never fails to yield godly fruit. God speaks—the more pressing question is, *am I listening!* The key is not to live for inspiration, for then, we become weary and dissatisfied with our daily duties. We begin looking for the exceptional and miss what God is doing in the ordinary.

There are times when I know a song is inside me that God wants to breathe into life. Therefore, when I pick up my guitar I don't have to struggle to write—the song forms naturally. But if I tried to write a new song every day, I would quickly become a frustrated artist—prolific perhaps, but with a binder of mediocre music. Ultimately, the way I know if a song is from the Lord, is by the effect it has on people's hearts. That is the way it is with inspiration. God may take us when He is ready to the mountaintop to give us that fresh word, or blessing we need to serve Him, so long as we do not lose sight of Him and start worshiping the mountain!

Inspiration † † †

God will give us touches of inspiration when He sees we are not in danger of being led away by them. We must never make our moments of inspiration our standard: our standard is our duty.—Oswald Chambers in *My Utmost For His Highest*

Using Only His Hands

Bob Wieland lost his legs to a mortar round in the Vietnam War. But that didn't stop the 57 year-old veteran from finishing the Los Angeles Marathon. Using only his hands and with less than twelve hours of sleep, it took Bob *a week* to complete the 26.2 mile course. Surrounded at the finish by well-wishers and admirers, Wieland said, "This was not natural. This was supernatural. It was only done by the grace of God."

Proverbs 2:7,8— He holds victory in store for the upright, he is a shield to those whose walk is blameless, for he guards the course of the just and protects the way of his faithful ones. (NIV)

Had Bob Wieland focused on the loss of his legs he would never have entered or finished the L.A. Marathon. He could have wasted away a bitter man. The race was over for everyone else. The cheering crowds were gone. But one meter at a time, Bob plodded towards his destination. He moved with the firm awareness of God's grace.

If you are a follower of Jesus Christ, you don't have to live in defeat. No matter how bad things may seem to you, you already possess the ultimate triumph—eternal life with a loving Father who will banish all pain and sorrow and fill you with unspeakable ecstasy when He one day ushers you into His glorious presence. It is possible to live a life of joy no matter how terrible things seem if our focus is on our destination.

Can you let go of disturbing disappointments and vexing trials that scream like bulging blisters, to run with perseverance the race set before you? Have you fixed your eyes on Jesus (Heb. 12:1,2)? He ran with joy knowing He faced a cross. His eyes were on His Father. The Apostle Paul wrote the Corinthian church in 1 Co. 15:57, *"But thanks be to God, who gives us the victory through our Lord Jesus Christ!"* That's right! Jesus gives us V-I-C-T-O-R-Y! *Thank You, God!*

I'm running on a one-way path to heaven. I'm not going to let the enemy rob me of joy. I refuse to dwell on disappointments. Forget excuses that justify quitting! By grace, I will not indulge my selfish nature. I'm stoked to do God's will. I'm not ashamed to follow a Winner. I have victory in Jesus and so do you—so let's live like it! Hallelujah!

Inspiration † † †

Life brings sorrows and joys alike. It is what a man does with them— not what they do to him—that is the test of his mettle.—Theodore Roosevelt

Our real blessings often appear to us in the shape of pains, losses and disappointments; but let us have patience and we soon shall see them in their proper figures.—Joseph Addison, English writer, (1672-1719)

Philosophy

Proverbs 9:10—The fear of the LORD is the beginning of wisdom, and the knowledge of the Holy One is understanding.

Philosophy, a word that comes from the Greek (*philein, sophia*), literally means "the love of wisdom." Philosophy is cultivated by various means.

● *Pragmatism.* Pragmatism is a grouping of associated theories, originally developed by Charles S. Peirce and William James and is distinguished by the doctrine that "the meaning of an idea or a proposition lies in its observable practical consequences." Essentially, pragmatism approaches and assesses situations and solves problems in a matter-of-fact manner.

● *Rationalism.* A rationalist relies upon human reasoning as the best guide for belief and action. "The exercise of reason, rather than the acceptance of empiricism, authority, or spiritual revelation, provides the only valid basis for action or belief and that reason is the prime source of knowledge and of spiritual truth."[16] In 580 B.C., the Greek philosopher Thales, stated that the source of everything was water. He observed that earth floats on water and that water surrounded all matter therefore, water must be the source of everything.

● *Superstition.* Often the basis of wisdom can be traced to superstition. One adopts an irrational belief that "an object, an action, or a circumstance not logically related to a course of events influences its outcome."

The Apostle Paul wrote in 1 Co. 1:17-25:

> *For Christ did not send me to baptize, but to preach the gospel— not with clever words, so that the cross of Christ will not be emptied of its effect. For to those who are perishing the message of the cross is foolishness, but to us who are being saved it is God's power. For it is written: I will destroy the wisdom of the wise, and I will set aside the understanding of the experts. Where is the philosopher? Where is the scholar? Where is the debater of this age? Hasn't God made the world's wisdom foolish? For since, in God's wisdom, the world did not know God through wisdom, God was pleased to save those who believe through the foolishness of the message preached. For the Jews ask for signs and the Greeks seek wisdom, but we preach Christ crucified, a stumbling block to the Jews and foolishness to the Gentiles. Yet to those who are called, both Jews and Greeks, Christ is God's power and God's wisdom, because God's foolishness is wiser than human wisdom, and God's weakness is stronger than human strength.*

Wisdom based on pragmatism, rationalism or superstition, is self-centered. It exalts human reasoning as the primary means of determination and its final destination is an intellectual cul-de-sac. Perhaps in our quest to value understanding we ought to consider revering God. Could it be that worship is the vehicle God intended for us to discover the highway of wisdom that runs upward and wider as we come closer to Him? Something to think about . . . in reveration.

Inspiration   † † †

To cognize the Divine Essence—this is the highest purpose of soul, sent by the Creator to the Earth!—Pythagoras, Ionian Greek mathmatician and philosopher, (c.582 - 507 BC)

But it is the knowledge of necessary and eternal truths, which distinguishes us from mere animals, and gives us reason and the sciences, raising us to knowledge of God and ourselves. It is this in us which we call the rational soul or mind.—Gottfried Wilhelm Leibniz, German rationalist philosopher, (1646-1716)

Command

Before he came to our battalion, numerous stories circulated about his heroic accomplishments in battle. His chiseled face, refined manner, and unique oration invited respect. His heritage was Cherokee Indian. This only added to the luster of our unit the 1/506th Currahees—a Cherokee word for *"we stand alone."* When Johnnie Gilreath gave a command, we didn't question it. We didn't analyze his motives or disobey. We trusted him and knew he would look after our welfare.

Marcus Tullius Cicero said, "The man who commands efficiently must have obeyed others in the past, and the man who obeys dutifully is worthy of being some day a commander." Soldiers learn to follow orders because the good of the unit depends upon disciplined compliance. But it is not so easy to obey those in positions of authority who demand obedience because of the rank on their shoulders. Their power and decision-making are tainted by insecurity.

Proverbs 13:13—The one who has contempt for instruction will pay the penalty, but the one who respects a command will be rewarded.

Isn't it profound that God's Son, the Lord of lords, didn't say, "Do this, or I'll zap you!" He never cajoled, demeaned, or manipulated the allegiance of His disciples. He appealed to their hearts by stating—*"If you love me, you will keep My commandments"* (John 14:15).

Trust and a humble willingness to comply, are two major factors in whether or not we choose to submit to God's command. Yet without love, both are anemic. What commander finds joy in soldiers who do their duty only because of obligation! Jesus once said, *"I know that His command is eternal life. So the things that I speak, I speak just as the Father has told Me"* (John 12:50). Because His Son overcame the cross to become our heavenly Advocate, our souls should burst with the unquenchable holy fire of gratitude and loyalty. Our hearts should explode with love for Him. His command is our safety, refuge, heritage and eternal joy.

If evil is called good in the name of rationalism or enlightenment, a nation's foundations will crumble. God directs the way to acme (ne plus ultra)—who will choose to follow?

Inspiration † † †

The primary goal of spiritual leadership is not excellence, in the sense of doing things perfectly. Rather, it is taking people from where they are to where God wants them to be. —Henry & Richard Blackaby in *Spiritual Leadership*

He who is not a good servant will not be a good master.—Plato, Greek philosopher, (424/423–348/347 BC)

Imbality

As I was leaving my office late one afternoon, an amusing sight caught my eyes. Three workers and one supervisor were laboring over a small rhododendron carefully trimming its leaves. But while it was funny to see so many adults working on one bush, it was also poignant. Kim, one of our counselors, recently shared how much the farmers are impacted this year by the lack of migrant workers to pick their fields. A bumper crop of strawberries is poorly harvested because there are not enough laborers. When I asked Kim why this situation existed she explained that many migrant workers no longer picked fruit because they were able to find jobs that were much easier (i.e. fast-food establishments) with better pay. In addition, fewer workers came north because the government was more stringent in blocking illegal entries.

Proverbs 13:23—The field of the poor yields abundant food, but without justice, it is swept away.

I cannot find a word that communicates what I am thinking so I've coined a new word—*imbality*. It means an imbalance in priorities; *a deficient sense of what is important leading to a misutilization of assets.* When four people are working over one small bush, we have an imbality. Many of us are familiar with reports of money the government wastes on frivolous projects. Recently, the media reported on Federal Emergency Management Agency (FEMA) funds meant for disaster recovery for Katrina victims, spent instead, on luxurious vacation trips and pornography—clear imbality!

When a church can get thirty volunteers to organize a potluck but only two people willing to pray, we have spiritual imbality. Why is it that so many families have time for sporting events, concerts, television and movies but are too busy to spend time with their unsaved neighbors? Our investments should be in worshiping God, in sharing Jesus with those without Him, in training to be Christ-like so that we seek the fulfillment of God's will in our daily activities. We are to be Jesus to the Jesus-less.

Instead, we concede to drivel. We feed our self-centered needs and misappropriate the incredible resources God has given for the pursuit of fleeting pleasure. The logical end to imbality is futility. If we don't get out among the hurting, we will spiritually atrophy while they starve!

Inspiration † † †

I have found there are many effective ministry methods that also hold back multiplication.—Neil Cole in *Organic Church*

Simplicity is freedom. Duplicity is bondage.—Richard J. Foster in *Celebration of Discipline*

Motives

Proverbs 16:2—All a man's ways seem right in his own eyes, but the LORD weighs the motives.
Proverbs 20:27—The lamp of the Lord searches the spirit of a man; it searches out his inmost being. (NIV)

In the marketplace of life, it is a tempting thing to measure our spiritual worth by the applause of people. But an apple can look good on the outside and be rotten in the middle. A watermelon can be huge and yet be devoid of sweetness. What makes God so special is His ability to see beyond the external. He knows our thoughts. He sees what no one else can. There is no impressing God with a show of Christianity if inside there is no Christ.

God is not honored when we wave our verbal banners of praise if our inner character is selfish. The Bible is decisively clear on the fact that God is able to discern what our motives are no matter how well we think they are concealed. *". . . for the LORD searches every heart and understands the intention of every thought . . ."* (1 Ch. 28:9). *"Therefore don't judge anything prematurely, before the Lord comes, who will both bring to light what is hidden in darkness and reveal the intentions of the hearts. And then praise will come to each one from God"* (1 Co. 4:5). *"You ask and don't receive because you ask wrongly, so that you may spend it on your desires for pleasure"* (Jam. 4:3).

The American Heritage Dictionary defines a motive as "An emotion, desire, physiological need, or similar impulse that acts as an incitement to action." *Our action is predicated by motive.* For example, I may decide I need to spend more time in prayer. You may think that my motive is to grow closer to God. In reality, my desire may be to be known by others as a praying person. Or, I may want something from God and calculate that more time in prayer will earn His favor.

No one but God truly knows our motives. We can have the best behavior yet inside be contaminated with an ugly attitude. We can say all the right things while thinking all the wrong thoughts. This is why we continually need God to examine us. David wrote, *"Search me, God, and know my heart; test me and know my concerns. See if there is any offensive way in me; lead me in the everlasting way"* (Psa. 139:23,24). The Bible communicates that God loves us and desires to have a vibrant relationship with us. Unless He has a hidden motive disguised to us, our Creator made us for fellowship. He is the best suited to help us examine and make right our motives!

If I believe God loves me and wants to fellowship with me, then my supreme motivation in life ought to be to love Him and to reciprocate by seeking to know Him. Before I take action, I should ask myself the question, *Will what I am about to do glorify God and bring me closer to Him?* If it won't, then why do it! If it will, then why delay?

God gathered the dust to form the man (Gen. 2:7)
  He acted in love for that was His plan.
What saddens my Friend and hastens His hurt
  Is when I don't care and treat Him like dirt.

Alabado seas, Señor, por el hermano sol.

Inspiration † † †

Need-based visions not only allow unregenerate people to set the agenda for churches, but they also tempt churches to focus on symptoms rather than causes . . . Spiritual leadership is moving people on to God's agenda.—Henry & Richard Blackaby in *Spiritual Leadership*

In the Middle of Nowhere

Nate and I climbed out of his silver chariot and wondered, "what will we do if the car has died?" We stood along a beautifully forested highway at least 120 miles from Fairbanks with over 220 miles yet to travel. My plane from Anchorage would leave at midnight. Neither of us were mechanics so we could not fix whatever was wrong. We had no cell phone and there was no town anywhere near us. The trunk was full of caribou meat that we had to get to Wasila to freeze. Nate found a detached rubber hose. Unfortunately, connecting it did nothing.

After standing by the roadside, clueless as to what we should do, a man in a Ford Bronco saw us and stopped. His name was John. He saw and heard our plight and informed us that he was on his way to Anchorage. He agreed to load up our meat and my bags and take us. After securing Nate's car, we were back on the highway headed south.

It turned out that John was a Christian. He often picked up hitchhikers and would give them tracts about God. John took us to Wasila where we were able to get the meat in a freezer. We took him to dinner and then he dropped me off at the airport. He told Nate he would tow his car to the nearest town so it could be fixed. During our time together, he shared struggles going on in his life that were amazingly similar to things I was feeling.

Proverbs 16:9—A man's heart plans his way, but the LORD determines his steps.
Proverbs 19:21—Many plans are in a man's heart, but the LORD's decree will prevail.

Here's another true story. At approximately 3:30 a.m., the bright flashing lights of the police car in his rearview mirror meant pullover time. He stopped and started to get out of his car—not a good move! The stern voice of the policeman ordered him to keep his hands in sight and get back in his vehicle. He noticed with apprehension the lawman holding a flashlight in one hand while unlatching his holster with the other. The agitated officer moved forward checked his license and then searched the contents of his car. Fortunately, he was not charged or ticketed; one of his headlights was not working.

Later that day, he purchased the necessary lamp. When he opened the hood of the car to install the new bulb he discovered that three of the four bolts holding his engine block in place had come off. In essence, his car was in a precarious state. Had he not been pulled over how many miles more would he have traveled before his engine twisted loose potentially causing serious damage to his car and possible injury to himself or others? Instead of being angry at being stopped and therefore late to work, Alan recognized the providential hand of God and was thankful.

Have your ever been frustrated because circumstances worked against your well-designed plans? For sure! Yet, what we see as disastrous God may see as salvific! We may be groaning over His handiwork. Corrie Ten Boom, the famous holocaust survivor once said, "If God sends us on stony paths, he provides strong shoes." Maybe we should spend more time thanking Him for what's on our feet than complaining about the condition of a trail we would not have selected.

D. Martyn Lloyd Jones wrote, "Though you are one of the teeming millions in this world, and though the world would have you believe that you do not count and that you are but a speck in the mass, God says, 'I know you.'"[7] Not only does our God know us, He cares for us, often exercising His divine direction. Does this mean that when bad things occur God isn't around? Maybe it depends on how we define "bad."

Human perspective of an event, or series of events, is always snapped from a handicapped shutter speed. No matter how brilliant we may be, we are still fallible and incapable of truly seeing the BIG picture. Our eternal Lord sees all, knows all and directs accordingly. The fiber that makes up faith therefore is the trust that although I may not understand life, God knows what He is doing!

British Prime Minister Benjamin Disraeli, (1804-1881), noted, "It is circumstances (difficulties) which show what men are." Do I accept God's purposes for me? If the answer is yes, I can never be intimidated by my circumstances. Whether in the middle of nowhere, or under the beam of a policeman's flashlight, God can rescue and encourage us. Often we miss opportunities to be taught by what is inconvenient in our hurry to script our own life movie. How much greater it is to wait, trusting that God has a plan and will take care of us!

I look for the brush strokes of the Master Painter and He continues to amaze me in every circumstance. He is Lord.

Inspiration † † †

The longer I live, the more convincing proofs I see of this truth, that God governs in the affairs of man; and if a sparrow cannot fall to the ground without his notice, is it probable that an empire can rise without his aid?—Benjamin Franklin

Who sees with equal eye, as God of all, A hero perish, or a sparrow fall, Atoms or systems into ruin hurl'd, And now a bubble burst, and now a world.—Alexander Pope, English poet, according to the *Oxford Dictionary of Quotations,* he is the third most frequently quoted writer in the English language, after Shakespeare and Tennyson, (1688-1744)

Standing in the Immigration Line April 19

While standing in the immigration line in Narita airport near Tokyo, Japan, after a long flight from San Francisco, I heard my name called by a voice from the past. There ahead of me was my best friend and West Point roommate, whom I'd spent an additional five years in the Army with—Dave Mead. Wow! What are the odds of a guy from Oregon running into his friend from New York in one of the largest airports in the world?

Proverbs 17:17—A friend loves at all times, and a brother is born for a difficult time.
Proverbs 18:24—A man with many friends may be harmed, but there is a friend who stays closer than a brother.

There is a Spanish proverb that says, "Life without a friend is like death without a witness." Do you ever have times in your life when you need a reminder from God that He loves you? I did and do! At a phase in my ministry where I was searching for direction, God did not hand me a road map, He delivered a friend. He provided Dave—the loves-at-all-times, sticks-closer-than-a-brother type. What an awesome God!

Sometimes in life, what's most important is not knowing what comes next but rather who holds the future. Friendship with God is the most important thing we can have in life. Friendship with people who love God is a great extension of the same truth. Who's your friend? This might be a good time to let someone you know cares, hear from you how much you appreciate them. Go ahead, pick up the phone and call a friend you haven't talked to in years. Send an email to a special person you've thought about and meant to tell how much he or she ministered to you at a time when you greatly needed it! And while you're at it, thank God for being your always-loving, ever-caring, completely knowing Friend.

Inspiration   † † †

In poverty and other misfortunes of life, true friends are a sure refuge. The young they keep out of mischief; to the old they are a comfort and aid in their weakness, and those in the prime of life they incite to noble deeds.—Aristotle

The Killing Song

A young girl clings with tear-stained eyes
Amidst a sea of friends
They hug, and weep in disbelief
With nowhere left to run.
The brutal boys are silent now
Just mocking echoes ring . . .
Across the halls and through the rooms
The face of evil grins.

What voice of reason stills the crowd
To make the pain seem clear?
A million whys launched heavenward
As if the sun could hear
Who will explain what cannot be
And climb inside insane
There is no peace when panic comes
With terror follows blame.

"The guns" they cry, "those wicked tools,
They are the cause of grief.
Take all those wretched firearms
And wrong will soon recede."
"The parents are the culprits, yes!
They failed to stop the wrong
They're the ones who are at fault
And they must wear the shame."

"No, no, the school! Those utter fools!
So unprepared for crimes
Detectors weren't installed or used
To spot the homemade bombs."
"The media—the violence spewed
Infecting tender minds
This is the cause of those who laugh
While shooting those who cry."

"Culpable? The ones who fired
They bear the judgment gavel!"
The voices rise in bitterness
For lives that should have mattered.

Round and round the fingers point
While stomachs churn and gnaw
They cannot quell the rising fear
Or stop the killing song.
There is no peace in panic
There is no truth in terror
When man steps in to conquer sin
He only finds more error.

A young girl sings with tear-stained eyes
Amidst a sea of friends
They hug, and weep in disbelief
Yet call upon their King.
They raise their voices to the Lord
The One who lost His Son.
He knows Himself the killing song
He overcame with love.*

Ezekiel 7:7—Doom has come on you, inhabitants of the land. The time has come; the day is near. There will be panic on the mountains and not celebration.

Inspiration   † † †

Grieve is a love word. One can anger an enemy, but not grieve him. The words are mutually exclusive. Only one who loves can be grieved, and the deeper the love the greater the grief.—J. Oswald Sanders, New Zealand, Director of Overseas Missionary Fellowship (1902-1992) in *The Holy Spirit And His Gifts*

Anxiety is love's greatest killer. It makes others feel as you might when a drowning man holds on to you. You want to save him, but you know he will strangle you with his panic.—Anaïs Nin, Cuban-French author, (1903-1977)

*Written as a response to the Columbine school shootings April 20, 1999

The Best Advice

Proverbs 19:20—Listen to counsel and receive instruction so that you may be wise in later life.
Psalm 25:14—The secret counsel of the LORD is for those who fear Him, and He reveals His covenant to them.
Psalm 16:7-- I will praise the LORD who counsels me—even at night my conscience instructs me.

Are there times when we know either from God's Word or from the Holy Spirit's leading what we are to do, and do not proceed because of insecurity or a unwilling heart? If I sense the Lord directing me and choose instead to go after the advice of others, I may miss what God has for me.

Today I faced a decision. My wife knew what course I should take. I was not excited about proceeding. So I asked other good friends who also are spiritually wise. They agreed with my reasoning and affirmed my course of action. So why did I feel so unsettled? Finally, I called another friend and asked his counsel. He shared a different perspective. Then I realized what I had known from the beginning—I was attempting to avoid what God wanted me to do, by gathering counsel that fit my desire! As I shared with Kathleen what I felt God was saying (which lined up with her conviction), she elaborated more fully why she felt the way she did. Suddenly, my feelings no longer mattered. God's way is the right way—always!

President Abraham Lincoln wrote, "I have been driven many times to my knees by the overwhelming conviction that I had no where else to go. My own wisdom, and that of all about me, seemed insufficient for the day." Proverbs 12:15 says, *"The way of a fool seems right to him, but a wise man listens to advice"* (NIV). We are to be commended for seeking counsel. We are wise to seek direction. But when God speaks to us, woe unto us if we don't obey because we chose instead to follow the opinions of others. The best advice is to do what God says. *If* we are not sure of His leading then we seek help from those who love Him!

Inspiration † † †

He who will not answer to the rudder, must answer to the rocks.— Hervé, French writer, (1911-1996)

Uncaring

Uncaring is not a disease acquired overnight. No, I suspect this state is more akin to cholesterol. Its level in the bloodstream slowly creates the pathogenesis of certain conditions, like the development of atherosclerotic plaque and heart disease. Uncaring is simple hardening of the spiritual arteries. The ability to sympathize is slowly choked by a steady increase of annoyance, critical thinking, anger and a sense of self-righteousness.

I think of myself as a caring person. I believe most would agree with my assessment. But God has a knack for jarring my conscience with facts. My caring is a pathetic pittance to the love Jesus models. Too many mornings I read the words of jaded columnists and conniving journalists in our city newspaper. I'm disgusted by context distortion. It infuriates me that the pen and keyboard can be used to smear those the media dislike with no repercussion. It appalls me how fear is hyped while hope is belittled. I don't think to pray for them. It's much easier just to be mad.

Elected officials violate state law to sanction marriage between men, to make official the union of two women. I decry the incessant plot to bludgeon the time-honored tradition of marriage. I am angry with homosexuals who flagrantly work with schools to reprogram the minds of children to justify sin and flaunt evil. I don't hate them, I'm repulsed by what they do. I'm sick of their methods. Yet, in protecting values, have I lost sight that those who disobey God's laws are still valuable?

I pass the man with his cardboard sign (the one I've seen on multiple days at different spots) standing by the freeway off-ramp. He hopes I'll feel guilty and help him. I don't see him as a person, I see a plot behind a sign and wish he would quit the scam and go get a real job.

I'm afraid if an angel came disguised as a poor person needing help I'd ask how she got in such a mess. I'd think of whom I could refer her to, concerned she might become dependent upon me, wary of being duped, unwilling to be some "welfare agency." I've become hardened and I don't like it.

Proverbs 21:13—The one who shuts his ears to the cry of the poor will himself also call out and not be answered.

Oh God, I have not prayed for those I care little for because I'm too full of myself. They need Your love. I need Your love. In my zeal to be right, I've let judging replace mercy. I've put my intellect before Your still small voice. Why should You hear me when I exhibit little compassion for those whose values aren't like mine? I cannot be a cold light. Please forgive me and help me to be caring as You are caring. Show me how to act, how to listen and what to pray for Jesus' sake. Amen.

Raiders

For generations the Pokot of Western Kenya crossed into the land of the Karamonjong in Uganda and vice versa. These were not social gatherings or athletic competitions but rather cattle raiding. But unlike the past when both tribes attacked with bows and spears now the Pokot come at night armed with AK47s and pistols. When they raid, they slaughter whole villages and then take off with their cattle. Consequently, towns along the border live in fear of losing their lives or livelihood to these bands of ruthless fighters.

Across the world, there is no shortage of carnage and fear. How many neighborhoods in our own nation rest uneasily at night? The prospect of warring gangs and drug violence is all too common in many big cities. The demons of lawlessness and murder feast on the shedding of blood and dance to the sounds of wailing sirens.

Proverbs 24:15,16—Don't set an ambush, wicked man, at the camp of the righteous man; don't destroy his dwelling. Though a righteous man falls seven times, he will get up, but the wicked will stumble into ruin.

Jesus tells us in Matthew 24:12,13 that before He returns there will be a substantial increase of wickedness. *"Because lawlessness will multiply, the love of many will grow cold. But the one who endures to the end will be delivered."* Paul informed the Thessalonians, *"For the mystery of lawlessness is already at work . . ."* (2 Th. 2:7). Around the world, raiders are multiplying. Against the righteous, come those who reject God to make their own way. Some fight with weapons, some manipulate with laws, some use intimidation while others lie, steal and cheat. For the followers of Christ suffering will increase but we must not lose hope!

The answer to falling down (the righteous do get knocked down), is to rise again. The response to torture, torment and persecution is joy in the Lord. Even if we die, in Christ we rise again! Therefore, we ought not to spend so much time worried about what might go wrong. The wicked will succumb to cosmic calamity. Rather than worry about raiders we should pray for them. Instead of plotting revenge, we tell them about Jesus. Loaded guns and captured cows may give power and possession but neither creates joy—the core of what the righteous possess in Christ. The Lord who holds the future, transforms us to confound misguided ruffians and reach those sick of life on the dark side. Don't be afraid of evil. Be afraid of losing sight of the only One who is *GOOD*. As my Kenyan friends Ombima and Moses like to sing, "Hold on to Jesus!" Something to think about . . . in reveration!

What If?

Ecclesiastes 3:1,4, 10-14—There is an occasion for everything, and a time for every activity under heaven . . . a time to weep and a time to laugh; a time to mourn and a time to dance . . . I have seen the task that God has given people to keep them occupied. He has made everything appropriate in its time. He has also put eternity in their hearts, but man cannot discover the work God has done from beginning to end. I know that there is nothing better for them than to rejoice and enjoy the good life. It is also the gift of God whenever anyone eats, drinks, and enjoys all his efforts. I know that all God does will last forever; there is no adding to it or taking from it. God works so that people will be in awe of Him. Whatever is, has already been, and whatever will be, already is. God repeats what has passed.

Watching people could easily become a favorite hobby for me. Do you ever notice the faces of oncoming drivers while sitting at a traffic light? Try it sometime. There is a lot to be learned about life in the expressions of those we encounter each day.

A friend of mine concluded that if one were to attend a multilevel marketing meeting where Jesus' name was substituted for the product being hyped, people would swear they were at a revival. His thought pushes my *what if* button. *What if*:

● *Church were more celebratory*—would people conclude that cheering for Christ was far more meaningful than sitting on some plastic seat bellowing for the latest sports hero?

● *We truly took the time to weep with those in mourning?*

● *We dared to laugh in the face of adversity because we had the courage to share with others that we read the whole book and we win in the end.*

● *We quit criticizing those who lift up their hands, those who sit on their hands, those who dance to a different beat, or those who can't dance,*

● *We freely confessed our sin, fell on our knees before our Holy God and wept at the sorry state of our nation's moral condition.*

● *We were most concerned about God being glorified.*

● *We quit acting like giving God 1-2 hours of time each week on Sunday was somehow sufficient!*

We are created in God's image! Life ought to be appropriately lived for His glory. He's given us more than we deserve. Let's open up our hearts to Him so the world can see Jesus in our what ifs.

Inspiration   † † †

Never apologize for showing feeling. When you do so, you apologize for truth.—Benjamin Disraeli, politician, writer, aristocrat (1804-1881)

Cancelled Orders

I was supposed to go to Hawaii for two weeks of military duty. I've always wanted to visit that island paradise so I was pretty excited. Until I received a notice in the mail telling me my orders were rescinded. When I called the people responsible for issuing them, I discovered that another person with the last name of York was supposed to have his duty cancelled. It was too late to correct the mistake. Instead, the Army sent me to North Carolina. Because of that snafu, I ended up attending a Civil Affairs course. This in turn enabled me to join a civil affairs unit less than seven miles from our home—a great convenience and blessing. And from that assignment in 1997 God continues to give me fantastic opportunities to meet people and serve in challenging roles. Looking back, I see the hand of the Lord at work redirecting my steps.

Ecclesiastes 7:13—Notice the way God does things; then fall into line. Don't fight the ways of God, for who can straighten out what He has made crooked? (NLT)

Often life does not go the way we intended or hoped. Maybe this is why Jesus taught us to pray, *"Your kingdom come, Your will be done on earth as it is in heaven"* (Mat. 6:10). Opportunity is not the right to impose my will. *Opportunity is the ability to determine God's leading and follow it.* Instead of getting frustrated or angry when our plans go awry, we should heed the Apostle Paul's warning. *"Pay careful attention, then, to how you walk—not as unwise people but as wise—making the most of the time, because the days are evil. So don't be foolish, but understand what the Lord's will is"* (Eph. 5:15-17).

God wants to work through you to accomplish His will! You are surrounded every day with opportunities to serve Him! Don't be flustered if events and circumstances line up differently than you imagined. Rather ask the Lord to help you see what He is doing. There is no misfortune associated with His providence. This is why walking by faith is so glorious— what matters is not the condition of the road and its surroundings, or the direction it takes, but rather that we are in the company of our loving Father.

Inspiration †††

When one door closes, another one opens, but we often look so long and so regretfully upon the closed door that we do not see the one that has opened for us.—Alexander Graham Bell, scientist and inventor, (1847-1922)

God gives the nuts, but he does not crack them.—German proverb

Are People Good?

For two years, three days of each week I had the privilege of helping lead an emergency food ministry. When people came into our facility, they read a pre-intake form which told them that they were about to receive food but must first agree to meet with a counselor to discuss personal and spiritual issues.

Some found us through word-of-mouth, some walked-in as a result of seeing our signs, while others were referred to us by an organization called Love Inc. When we sat down with a person, after hearing their struggles (which necessitated their coming in for food), we asked them a simple question. "If you were to die today and stand before God, what would you say to Him if He were to ask you why He should let you into His heaven."

About 90% responded that God should let them in because they were good. I often asked them if they really thought He would accept that answer. About half hung their head and said "no." But even for those who persisted optimistically, we shared that God cannot let anyone into heaven based on their goodness for several reasons.

● What defines "good enough?" If we think God accepts us into heaven based on our goodness, then He must make a subjective call. Where does He draw the line as to who is acceptable and who is not for entrance?

● God cannot let good people into heaven. The fact is He is perfect. Perfection that admits imperfection is tainted. God's justice demands that evil be properly requited.

● The reality is that none of us is as "good" as we think we are. We've lied, stolen, lusted, envied, cheated, been selfish, said unkind things, thought mean thoughts, etc. Any honest person will readily admit to this. Those who won't are just adding to their sin!

Ecclesiastes 7:20—Not a single person on earth is always good and never sins. (NLT)

Why do so many people think God will let them into heaven based on their goodness? Ephesians 2:8,9 resoundingly trounces such thinking. *"For by grace you are saved through faith, and this is not from yourselves; it is God's gift—not from works, so that no one can boast."* Nowhere does Scripture say a person is admitted into heaven based on their goodness or accomplished deeds. Only when we repent of our badness and put our trust in Jesus Christ—making Him our Lord, does the Bible affirm that we can be assured that His Father will let us into heaven. (See Rom. 10:9-13). Jesus lived a perfect life and died to save us for our sins. He was resurrected to stand before God as an advocate for all who trust in Him! We saw over 75 people come to know Jesus as a result of sharing the gospel—an astonishing number of changed lives! How wonderful it is to see people admit what is bad to find what is GOOD!

Trapped in an Elevator

Eldon, an elderly couple, a widow and I chatted as we descended from the 14th floor on our way to the banquet. Suddenly the elevator lurched and we heard what sounded like slipping chains, or misaligned gears, and we came to a stop somewhere just below the 6th floor. If the cables holding us broke, I figured we had about a 7-story fall and who knows what injuries we might sustain. The notion of death crossed my mind and I thought how weird and unforeseen it would be to die with my great one-star-Lord-loving boss in a hotel elevator!

I think we both had the same idea to remain calm and reassure the other descenders. Since I stood next to the intercom, I buzzed the front desk and let them know of our plight. Repeatedly the receptionist spoke to us and asked if we were okay assuring us that help was just five minutes away. I thought, *Yeah right! Help never comes that fast.* For forty minutes, we were trapped. Finally, the cables pulled us up to the eleventh floor where we made a happy exit and walked into the adjacent compartment to ride back down.

Ecclesiastes 9:12—For man certainly does not know his time: like fish caught in a cruel net, or like birds caught in a trap, so people are trapped in an evil time, as it suddenly falls on them.

All of humanity is ensnared by sin. But unlike our container on cables built to rise and fall, when the elevator of life plummets, the result is always death. Most of us have no idea when or how we will die. But what matters is not so much the when, or the how, but the what. What are we dying into—eternal life with God or eternal separation from Him?

It felt good to stand in that elevator knowing that hope cannot be trapped. Faith is the awareness that a high-speed plunge is inconsequential when you know the Creator. Faith is the confidence that fear is mastered by life that matters. Faith is the calmness that confinement is no big deal.

I wonder what was going through the minds of the other three people. I wish now that I had shared my Savior while I had a captive audience. And the next time I push the lobby button, I'll be thinking to a certain tune as the doors close, *What a lift we have in Jesus!*

Inspiration † † †

Prayer is never answered due to the position of the person who prays but on the promise of the provision of God—Judson Cornwell, author

Man is the only kind of varmint who sets his own trap, baits it, then steps in it.—John Steinbeck, author of Grapes of Wrath, (1902-1968)

A blind man does not forget his walking stick.—Kenyan Proverb

Unextinguished Love

Song of Songs 8:6,7—Set me as a seal on your heart, as a seal on your arm. For love is as strong as death; ardent loves is as unrelenting as Sheol. Love's flames are fiery flames—the fiercest of all. Mighty waters cannot extinguish love; rivers cannot sweep it away. If a man were to give all his wealth for love, it would be utterly scorned.

Solomon composed 3000 proverbs and 1005 songs (1 Ki. 4:32). Perhaps his finest piece is the musical production Song of Songs, a work of Hebrew poetry utilizing parallelism and wonderfully descriptive language. Jewish religious leaders held this wee book of Scripture in high regard. Note the words of Rabbi Akiba (50-135 AD), who wrote in the Mishnah (Yadaim 3.5): "... the whole of the world is not worth the day on which the Song of Songs was given to Israel; all the Writings are holy, and the Song of Songs is the holy of holies . . ." [18]

Many commentators teach that this writing allegorically describes the love of Christ for His bride the Church. But let's simply focus on the central theme of this writing—love. Andy Bannister wrote, "The primary message of the book is this: that human love, marriage, and, dare I say it, sexual love, are a gift from God."

A beautiful Shulamite maiden, from the northern hill country of Lebanon, gains the attention of the world's most powerful king. From her mountainous home, she travels to Jerusalem wooed by a lovesick Solomon transfixed by her physical beauty. He flatters her. He tries masterfully to seduce her favor. If only she will marry him. But she will have none of it. Her thoughts remain with her true love, a shepherd boy from her own village.

The Shulamite teaches us that love is not about sexual conquest or the gaining of all the wealth and attention one could achieve from a handsome lord. She resists Solomon's advances because her heart belongs to another. Three times, she reminds the young women of Jerusalem, *"do not stir up or awaken love until the appropriate time."* True love is not to be manipulated or fondled by the fleeting passion of admirers! Her loyal and faithful adoration exquisitely ties memory and emotion to her shepherd friend. The thought of him consumes her dreams and sends tingles through her body. She will not compromise her convictions and feelings for the pleasure of Israel's potentate (ruler).

Love is a sacred gift of incalculable value. To unwrap it merely for physical thrill or temporary pleasure is to cheapen its deep meaning and damage the spiritual wick from which its oil burns strongly through the darkest nights. With relentless chatter, the world depicts love through beauty, costly adornment, power, fame, and attaining our desires. Beware, too often, this is love's sensual cousin lust. 1 Corinthians 13:4-7 and not *Glamour* magazine defines God's treasure:

> *Love is patient; love is kind. Love does not envy; is not boastful; is not conceited; does not act improperly; is not selfish; is not provoked; does not keep a record of wrongs; finds no joy in unrighteousness,*

but rejoices in the truth; bears all things, believes all things, hopes all things, endures all things. Love never ends.

Shunamite woman
Palace dreams for her shepherd
Heaven's love story

Inspiration † † †

You don't love a woman because she is beautiful, she is beautiful because you love her.—Author Unknown

Let your love be like the misty rains, coming softly, but flooding the river.—Malagasy Proverb

Lying

While browsing through a magazine at an X-ray clinic, an advertisement caught my eyes. The bold headlines proclaimed something to the effect of, "It is WRONG! . . . It is Nationally Televised." The ad promoted some upcoming cable channel roast of Playboy magazine's founder and owner, Hugh Hefner.

It used to be in our nation when something was labeled wrong the implication was that the activity should not occur. Now it seems that wrong is delightfully accepted. How is it that evil has become such a good thing?

Isaiah 5:20—Woe to those who call evil good and good evil, who substitute darkness for light and light for darkness, who substitute bitter for sweet and sweet for bitter.

The Apostle Paul wrote the church in Thessalonica that:
The coming of the lawless one is based on Satan's working, with all kinds of false miracles, signs, and wonders, and with every unrighteous deception among those who are perishing. They perish because they did not accept the love of the truth in order to be saved. For this reason God sends them a strong delusion so that they will believe what is false, so that all will be condemned—those who did not believe the truth but enjoyed unrighteousness. (2 Th. 2:9-12)
Why would anyone fall for blatant lies? Paul says it's because the truth is no longer loved. Standards of rightness are considered confining. What once was honorable is viewed as stilted. Consider that God, in His precious love, sent Jesus to rescue the world from sin. He provided clear guidance that by confessing our sin and obediently placing our faith in Christ, we could be saved. But instead of focusing on the gift of salvation and the truth behind grace, those who would rather live as they please, accuse God of being tyrannical, unfairly absolutist for His solitary solution to evil.

Oswald Chambers wrote in *Studies In The Sermon On The Mount*, that "A lie is not an inexactitude of speech, a lie is in the motive. I may be actually truthful and an incarnate liar. It is not the literal words that count but their influence on others." Lying reflects the desire of the heart. One cannot embrace a lie without first divorcing the truth.

When Satan works his miracles and spreads God-rejecting lies, those who march to a self-pleasing beat fall easy prey to his agenda. Doing right becomes distasteful. Clear boundaries for decent speech are steadily erased to feed vulgar appetites. The American Library Association refuses to filter pornography from library computers. Its line that the First Amendment would be violated, supports its underlying theme that there is nothing wrong with exposing children to nudity. The obvious truth that pornography hooks and depraves those who feast upon it, is denied for the freedom to sin—the true motive. Those who support safeguards are derided as puritanical which is also ironic since the Puritans were once considered noble and worthy of emulating.

154

What should we do in a society fixated on calling evil "good" and good "evil?" We should embrace Christ and cling tightly to His teaching. We should take inventory and determine just how much slippage has occurred in our lives. Finally, we should expose lies when they are uncovered but love and pray for those guilty of lying. Even in a land that grows darker, God's lights are needed—so shine!

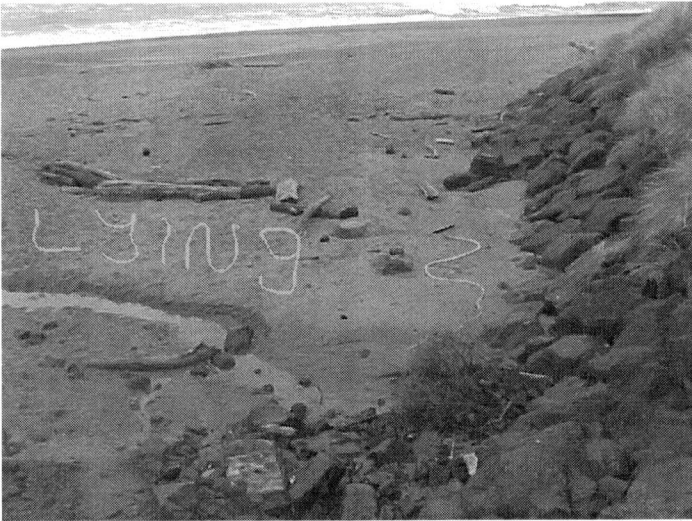

Inspiration † † †

He who lies once is never believed again.—Polish Proverb

He who says there is no such thing as an honest man, you may be sure is himself a knave.—Bishop George Berkeley, Irish philosopher, (1685-1753)

Agony

Isaiah 13:7,8—Therefore everyone's hands will become weak, and every man's heart will melt. They will be horrified; pain and agony will seize them; they will be in anguish like a woman in labor. They will look at each other, their faces flushed with fear.

Agony is the struggle that precedes death. We so often think of this state as prolonged, gruesome and slow—a patient fighting to beat some dreaded disease. Yet, agony may also be camouflaged beneath a happy exterior. While appearance suggests that life is good, underneath a desperate struggle to find meaning takes place.

Agony is the:

●   headlong flight to reach the top only to get there and be disappointed

●   canard (false report) of naturalism as the passionate explanation for life mixed with animus towards a Creator

●   unsatisfied pursuit of new and better toys, homes, cars, etc.

●   proliferation of green paper that cannot buy joy

●   reality of aging despite drugs, plastic surgery and super vitamins

●   fight for rights that result in guilt and endless rationalization

●   incomprehensible song whose scream is loud and penetrating

●   desperate desire to be loved yet repeated stiff-arming of the Lover

●   scorn for absolutes and pain experienced without their protection

●   result of calling good "evil" and evil "good"

A young boy of six guns down his classmate and a thousand attend her funeral asking, "Where did we go wrong?" Methyl Tertiary Butyl Ether (MTBE) dangerously pollutes our water nationwide as underground fuel tanks leak. Many who fight our nation's battles come back suffering Post Traumatic Stress Disorder (PTSD). The stock market plunges further and further downward and people in despair end their lives. No matter how fast we run, what we invent, how splendidly we live, sin and death still stalk, unimpressed by human effort.

Agony! It doesn't have to be so. Jesus solves agony.

Inspiration   † † †

When the pain comes from God, then God alone can take the pain away. The Lord often sends diseases to the body in order to cure the disease of the soul.—Brother Lawrence & Frank Laubach in *Practicing His Presence*

Confusion and Doubt

Isaiah 26:3—With perfect peace You will protect those whose minds cannot be changed because they trust You. (GWT)
Luke 1:13,18—But the angel said to him: Do not be afraid, Zechariah, because your prayer has been heard. Your wife Elizabeth will bear you a son, and you will name him John . . . "How can I know this?" Zechariah asked the angel. "For I am an old man, and my wife is well along in years."

Confusion is not the mind state God intends for His children. The cord of confusion is often plugged into the outlet of self and ungrounded in God. One is not confused by the maze of materialism, when focused on Christ who said in Mat. 6:19, *"Don't collect for yourselves treasures on earth . . ."* One does not chase power when listening to Christ who says, *"All authority is given unto me . . ."* (Mat. 28:18). One does not find love hopelessly compromised by lust, who agrees with Job *"I made a covenant with my eyes not to look lustfully at a girl"* (Job 31:1—NIV). One does not wallow in deceit who says, *"let God weigh me with an accurate balance, and He will recognize my integrity"* (Job 31:6).

We lack understanding when we seek destinations God did not call us to—when we do that which God never sanctioned. We promote ignorant pride when we attempt to go where the Lord would have us but disregard asking Him for directions. If you feel trapped by indecision or bewildered by life, stop! Go to the Author of Truth. He will give you the wisdom you need to walk and the peace that passes all understanding.

To be undecided or skeptical is not necessarily a path towards failure it may be the genesis for learning. The blind, deaf and very wise Helen Keller wrote:

> It need not discourage us if we are full of doubts. Healthy questions keep faith dynamic. Unless we start with doubts, we cannot have a deep-rooted faith. One who believes lightly and unthinkingly has not much of a belief. He who has a faith which is not to be shaken has won it through blood and tears-has worked his way from doubt to truth as one who reaches a clearing through a thicket of brambles and thorns. Most of us can relate to children whose frequent word is not *yes* but *why?*[19]

Henry Drummond wrote in *Listening to the Giants*, "Doubt is the prelude of knowledge."[20] H. W. Shaw said, "The less we know the more we suspect." There is such a thing as healthy doubt and good intentions may flood the questioning voice.

But what if Doubt daily embraces Unlikely, Fear and Distrust the tenebrific (dark producing) children of Gloom? The words of Archbishop Fulton J. Sheen reveal danger, ". . . man hid from God in the garden; now man hides within himself." The man who constantly feeds doubt may have a tiny God. The man who feeds his faith is unafraid of a tiny self.

Our propensity as humans is to doubt. There are at least three reasons why this is true:

1. *We focus on our limitations.* Zechariah did not believe Gabriel in the passage above. Nor did Sarah believe the angel who told her husband, Abraham, that she would bear a son (Gen. 18:10-15). They forgot that God is unfettered by the laws of nature, which restrict us. *"Is anything impossible for the Lord?"* (Gen. 18:14)

2. *We prefer our ways to God's ways.* Often the motive behind questioning is an unwillingness to budge. As my friend Todd explained, the passage in Psa. 95:7 that says *"Today, if you hear His voice"* in the Hebrew, can also mean *"O that you would obey."* The Israelites repeatedly experienced the supernatural leadership of God in rescuing them from Egypt and an unforgiving desert. Still, they questioned Him.

3. *We don't think that we really matter to God.* In the throes of heartbreak, defeat, sickness or what seems like a boring life, we forget that because of His great love and mercy, God miraculously made us alive in Christ even when we were dead in sin (Eph. 2:4,5). In the middle of the bog of uncertainty is a Rock upon which we are meant to stand! On that Rock called Jesus, a holy temple is being built. The caption on the Cornerstone says "I love you!" *"The whole building is being fitted together in Him and is growing into a holy sanctuary in the Lord, in whom you also are being built together for God's dwelling in the Spirit"* (Eph. 2:21,22). In Mark 9:22-24, a father says to Jesus about his demon-oppressed son:

> *"And many times it has thrown him into fire or water to destroy him. But if You can do anything, have compassion on us and help us." Then Jesus said to him, "If You can? Everything is possible to the one who believes." Immediately the father of the boy cried out, "I do believe! Help my unbelief."*

Oh Lord, please help us to believe!

Inspiration   †††

The devil's first and most common scheme, then, is to make you doubt your understanding of what God has said.—Stu Weber in *Spirit Warriors*

Our doubts are traitors, and make us lose the good we oft might win by fearing to attempt.—William Shakespeare, English author, poet, (1564-1616)

Beyond the Chest

I often notice when I meet people for the first time they look at my chest. Now that sounds weird doesn't it! What I mean is that when I am wearing a uniform I often feel like I am being sized up by the cloth patches sewn on my shirt. Whether it is the military, Girl Scouts, AWANA, varsity jackets, etc., patches, medals, ribbons and pins tell a story of what kind of training or accomplishments a person achieved.

Everyone needs recognition and desires it to some extent. You may be the kind of person who shies away from the spotlight and prefers not to be noticed publicly. Yet, still it is important to receive thanks and to know that your work or contribution in some way matters. Many spend their entire life trying to earn the praise of their parents. Others feel unfulfilled in their job because the boss is rarely satisfied with their work. It is a terrible thing to feel unworthy, unrecognized, and ultimately unwanted.

Isaiah 26:12,13—LORD, you will grant us peace; all we have accomplished is really from you. O LORD our God, others have ruled us, but you alone are the one we worship. (NLT)

The prophet Isaiah's observations in the verses above are important to us for several reasons. *First, remember that no matter what you and I do or accomplish, the glory should go to God.* Authentic humility occurs when we know why we have what we have. Continuous striving for recognition from people reveals an absence of peace in our hearts. When we quit straining for personal credit and rest in God's glory, that is when we obtain serenity.

Second, you and I don't have to live our lives trying to measure up before others. Our identity is not determined through the lips of people but rather in the affirmation of our Savior. Many lords rule over us but God's name alone is the one we honor. We give His name glory because He truly cares about us. He already recognizes our worth. The proof of this is the cross—a sacrificial measure we neither merit or understand. When I meditate on God's love for me, I have all the recognition I need. When I consider what He has done, I'm reminded that my quest is to honor Him for each success.

Inspiration   † † †

One must decide where he wants his ministry to count—in the momentary applause of popular recognition or in the reproduction of his life in a few chosen men who will carry on his work after he has gone. Really it is a question of which generation we are living for.—Robert Coleman in *The Master Plan of Evangelism*

Don't worry when you are not recognized, but strive to be worthy of recognition.—President Abraham Lincoln (1809-1865)

Yaga

Isaiah 40:27-31—Jacob, why do you say, and Israel, why do you assert: "My way is hidden from the LORD, and my claim is ignored by my God"? Do you not know? Have you not heard? Yahweh is the everlasting God, the Creator of the whole earth. He never grows faint or weary; there is no limit to His understanding. He gives strength to the weary and strengthens the powerless. Youths may faint and grow weary, and young men stumble and fall, but those who trust in the LORD will renew their strength; they will soar on wings like eagles; they will run and not grow weary; they will walk and not faint.

I believe the secret to maintaining spiritual strength is contained in the Bible. The Hebrew word, *yaga*, (yaw gah`) and variations thereof, appears 31 times in the Old Testament. *Yaga* means to be weary, worn out or exhausted. The prophet, Isaiah, gives us word pictures in the passage above of what it is like for those whose energy is replenished by their hope in God. From the context of the passage, is it possible that Isaiah is primarily referring to overcoming spiritual discouragement?

The author of Hebrews writes in 12:3, *"For consider Him who endured such hostility from sinners against Himself, so that you won't grow weary and lose heart."* If we want to maintain spiritual vitality, consider Jesus! The Greek translation for *consider* is the word, *analogizomai,* from which we get the word *analogy.* Essentially, we focus our eyes on Jesus (vs. 2), because He models perseverance. What did Christ consistently do during His life on earth? He looked to God for His strength and direction. All His hope was in His Father and that was enough to endure the cross!

Former Colorado governor Bill Owens said, "Leadership is an active role; 'lead' is a verb. But the leader who tries to do it all is headed for burnout, and in a powerful hurry." With the exception of sickness, if you are burnt out, could it be that your eyes have lost sight of Christ? If you are spiritually washed up, is your hope really in the Lord? Every Christian I have encountered that is worn out and unwilling to serve God is either:

● Unable to get over disappointment and hurt caused by a person(s).
● Bitter with God for failing to achieve results they expected in some venture (mission effort, job, etc.);
● Sidelined by depression.

Unless depression was caused by a chemical imbalance or physical malady, in each case notice that the cause of weariness was taking one's eyes off the Lord and fastening them on people, expectations or circumstances. Let's be honest! *People will fail us just as we have failed.* Second, *we don't always achieve our goals.* This does not give us license to sit on the bench and pout! Is God more concerned that we attain success or that we keep our hope in Him? Both Isaiah and Hebrews teach us that the key to overcoming weariness is to keep our eyes (trust) on God! So look to the Lord and be renewed! He's eager and able to strengthen you.

I, the LORD, Speak Truthfully

I needed to set up DSL over a phone line. When I called the phone company to set up the service, the line was answered by a voice-automated machine. The options I was presented did not help me so I repeatedly asked to speak with an operator. Finally, the emotionless computer relented and patched me to a real voice. I set up the service thinking I would receive the special discount the company offered. But the price quoted to me was different and much higher. The salesperson explained that we would receive a substantial rebate, but in fact, we would over time lose money because the contractual cost was too high.

Several days later, I cancelled the service. But before letting me go, the operator offered a discounted price in line with what initially attracted me to the company in the first place. It sounded good and I almost took the deal. However, when I inquired for how long that price would last I learned it would only be for 6 months. Growing weary of marketing gimmicks, I remained firm with the cancellation.

The reason most of us value honesty is because it offers protection—what we hear is what we get, what we are told is substantiated. Half-truths and deception may win companies business deals, but eventually when the truth is exposed, they will suffer. No one likes to be taken advantage of, or slickly manipulated. King Solomon wrote, *"Righteous lips are a king's delight, and he loves one who speaks honestly"*—Pro. 16:13.

Isaiah 45:18-19—For this is what the LORD says—God is the Creator of the heavens. He formed the earth and made it; He established it; He did not create it to be empty, but formed it to be inhabited—"I am the LORD, and there is no other. I have not spoken in secret, somewhere in a land of darkness. I did not say to the descendants of Jacob: Seek Me in a wasteland. I, the LORD, speak truthfully; I say what is right.

Isaiah 45 is a powerful treatise from God to King Cyrus. The Almighty lets this foreign emperor know who He is and what He will do. In the passage above, God affirms His practice of truth telling. Isn't it comforting and encouraging knowing that our Lord always tells the truth! He is not duplicitous (deceitful). What He promises He delivers. What He values is honesty. May it be so for us as well. Let us speak the truth and declare what is right for the glory of the One who is forever pure. Something to think about . . . in reveration!

Inspiration † † †

Nothing so completely baffles one who is full of trick and duplicity himself, than straightforward and simple integrity in another.—Charles Caleb Colton, English cleric, writer and collector, (1780-1832)

Canine Purgatory

Imagine you are a 42 year-old man and you are unemployed. Your boss wanted help pilfering the company's money and your integrity cost you your job. You cannot be hired because being a Christian proves you are an intolerant bigot. You had to step down from your position as the outreach leader in your church because the pastor's brother moved into town and liked the position you labored to create. Now your wife thinks you're a *wuss* because you let the bullies push you.

Have you had enough! Let's try entering another world. Dusty was the best dog I had ever owned. This yellow Labrador Retriever was the model of intelligence and good behavior. Aside from one upstart kitten, he ruled his domain with dignity and skill.

Meet Bear. This cuddly combination Rottweiler/Lab doesn't know the word fear. His favorite target is a yellow tail and two floppy ears and they aren't his own. He looks our hissing cat in the eye and absorbs jabs swung twice as fast as I remember Sugar Ray Leonard swinging. If Dusty is minding his own bone, Bear steals it. I have never heard my yellow champion bark so much or appear so flustered. It is as if this puppy has invaded his psyche and turned his castle into canine purgatory.

I fed Dusty his food and checked to see how he was holding up. While he was eating, Bear made his move. No subtlety to this pup—straight into the bowl he plunged his head. I expected instant decapitation. You never stick your head in a full-grown dog's bowl. That is like pulling a grenade pin and counting to seven before you throw it.

But Dusty showed no teeth. He did not growl or end Bear's charmed life. He quietly raised his head and let the whippersnapper eat. Wow! What consideration in the face of injustice. He modeled self-control when instinct must have raged "Attack!"

Isaiah 53:7—He was oppressed and afflicted, yet He did not open His mouth. Like a lamb led to the slaughter and like a sheep silent before her shearers, He did not open His mouth.
John 19:10—So Pilate said to Him, "You're not talking to me? Don't You know that I have the authority to release You and the authority to crucify You?"

When life seems unfair, how do you respond? When people smear your reputation with lies, do you get even? It is one thing for a dog to model decency. How exceedingly more incredible was the example of God's Son, who took abuse as if it was His due and refrained from turning His enemies into leprous zombies.

The reason we detest injustice is because it steals away our comfort. Thomas Jefferson said, "The mass of mankind has not been born with saddles on their backs, nor a favored few to ride them." The reason we hate tyranny is because it threatens our rights. However, Jesus did not die so we could be comfortable. He did not wave a placard demanding justice. He wore a crown of thorns that sent streams of blood flowing down His slandered head. He entrusted Himself to the care of His Father and got smoked. But if Satan thought He was a patsy, He did not understand the Holy Fire that would come.

Martin Luther King Jr. said, "Injustice anywhere is a threat to justice everywhere. We are caught in an inescapable network of mutuality, tied in a single garment of destiny. Whatever affects one directly, affects all indirectly." Are you weary of the bend-over-here-it-comes syndrome? Go all the way! That's right! Move from leaning over to the full kneeling position and pray, *"Lord, not my will but Your will be done!"* Oh friend, do not give up. Life may seem cruel. But in God's grace, you too can raise your head above the injustice of a sinful world that hates Jesus. In His strength, you can handle wrong treatment and not retaliate; face scorn and return love; endure mocking and deliver kindness. Always remember, the river of injustice will some day flow into the sea of Judgment and God's holiness will prevail. Drive on!

Inspiration † † †

Expecting the world to treat you fairly because you are a good person is a little like expecting the bull not to attack you because you are a vegetarian.—Dennis Wholey, television host, producer and author

Find out just what people will submit to, and you have found out the exact amount of injustice and wrong which will be imposed upon them; and these will continue until they are resisted with either words or blows, or both. The limits of tyrants are prescribed by the endurance of those whom they oppress.—Frederick Douglass, abolitionist, author, statesman and reformer (1818-1895)

Unwind

Isaiah 57:2—He will enter into peace—they will rest on their beds—everyone who lives uprightly.

Not long ago, I spoke to about 400 men on the topic of unwinding. I could not find the word *unwind* in Scripture, but its synonyms *relax* and *rest* are plentiful throughout God's word. There is a strong theological foundation for rest. Did you know that God modeled unwinding? Genesis 2:2 reads, *"God blessed the seventh day and declared it holy, for on it He rested from His work of creation."*

Now, why would an all-powerful God need to rest? I suggest that the answer to this question is because He ties His glory to the enjoyment of His effort. Work without reflection or enjoyment is meaningless. I suspect God wanted people to rest, so they could enjoy His effort. He established an Unwind Day and called it the Sabbath. He attached so much importance to His action that He blessed the day and declared it holy. He made a binding promise with His creation. The concept of rest is so important to us spiritually, mentally, physically and emotionally, that God made honoring the Sabbath the fourth command of the Ten Commandments! We unwind for His glory and the honoring of His work!

What happens when we do not unwind? We are making a statement to God that we do not need Him. All work and no rest will kill us. When we live as if we don't need God, we live without God. Furthermore, when we don't unwind we lose perspective. We are like greyhounds chasing mechanical rabbits. We put our eyes on our work, activities, problems and relationships and take our eyes off God. Our work becomes our idol and our identity.

So, how do you unwind according to God's agenda? *First, you need faith!* If you do not trust God, it is impossible to attain rest. King David wrote in the Psalms, *"I am at rest in God alone; my salvation comes from Him . . . Rest in God alone, my soul, for my hope comes from Him"* (Psa. 62:1,5). Without God's help it is impossible to truly relax because we have an infection called sin. Slowly it eats away our human fiber and leads to death.

Second, you need to pray! Jesus said in Mat.11:28-30:
Come to Me, all of you who are weary and burdened, and I will give you rest. All of you, take up My yoke and learn from Me, because I am gentle and humble in heart, and you will find rest for yourselves. For My yoke is easy and My burden is light."

Peter, one of Jesus' most dynamic disciples, late in his life wrote, *"Humble yourselves therefore under the mighty hand of God, so that He may exalt you in due time, casting all your care upon Him, because He cares about you"* (1 Pe. 5:6,7). How do you come to Jesus and shed your problems? Communicate with Him! Humbly enlist His help by sharing your struggles.

Third, you need a ranger buddy. A ranger buddy is a trusted friend who knows close hand how your life is going and has the courage to tell you when you need to slow down. We do not always see the signs that we are going too fast and need to slow down.

Fourth, you need to laugh. Doctors have found that laughing helps to protect the heart. As we learned earlier (See Apr 7), laughter increases pain tolerance and boosts the body's production of infection-fighting antibodies, which can help prevent hardening of the arteries and subsequent conditions like angina, heart attacks, or strokes. If we cannot laugh, we certainly are unlikely to relax.

Fifth, you need to rest! Benjamin Franklin taught, "He that can take rest is greater than he that can take cities." When I attended West Point, every cadet was issued a green comforter we called our *green girls*. Napping was an art. We did not get to nap much as plebes but when we became upperclassmen, we perfected the practice. Napping was therapeutic. We lived under high stress circumstances and expended tons of energy. King David wrote, *"I keep the LORD in mind always. Because He is at my right hand, I will not be shaken. Therefore my heart is glad, and my spirit rejoices; my body also rests securely"* (Psa. 16:8,9). If you want to unwind, then make time for quality rest.

Finally, you need to get away! When God created the earth, He did so for His and our pleasure. So move your nose around the rosemary. Bask in a sunset. Reflecting is not meant to be practical, it is meant to stir worship. The ability to unwind is enhanced by the wind's texture, the babbling creek, the songs of birds and the fragrant aroma of majestic firs. In Mark 6:31, Jesus said to His disciples, *"Come away by yourselves to a remote place and rest a while."* So many people were coming and going, demanding their time and sapping their energy, so much so, that they did not even have time to eat. Jesus took His men on retreats. If the King of kings made time to get away to remote places to unwind, so should we! So let go of that tightly wrapped tether pole and unwind!

Inspiration ✝ ✝ ✝

Who remembers when we used to rest on Sunday instead of Monday?—Kin Hubbard, cartoonist, humorist and journalist, (1868-1930)

Put off thy cares with thy clothes; so shall thy rest strengthen thy labor, and so thy labor sweeten thy rest.—Francis Quarles, English poet, (1592-1644)

Losing My Agenda

Prayer can be one of the most disingenuous exercises we undertake as Christians. When I go to the Lord in conversation am I intent on discerning His will or am I out to gain my own agenda? If I pray thinking I know what is best for me, immediately I have gone astray.

My life is *not* my own. It belongs to God. Therefore, I cannot know what is best for me other than the fact that I should be utterly dependent upon my Father in heaven. What I want to happen could be disastrous, and counter to what God intends. The highway of humanism carved with pavestones of independence leads me across ground my Lord never intended I traverse. Instead of perfecting holiness, I cultivate confusion.

Jeremiah 10:23—I know, LORD, that a man's way of life is not his own; no one who walks determines his own steps.

Effective prayer begins and ends with a commitment to agree with God's purpose. We see this throughout Scripture. This is precisely why the first three statements Jesus taught His disciples to pray were God-centered: *"Your name be honored as holy. Your kingdom come. Your will be done on earth as it is in heaven"* (Mat. 6:9,10). *"Your"* always trumps *"my,"* and the sooner we understand this, the more rapidly we will begin to see our life perspective transformed.

Since my life belongs to God, I approach Him with the heart of a servant. *"Lord, what would you have me do and be today?"* Now, I find that adversarial people or pernicious (deadly) problems, cannot rob me of my joy, for I know that God's will sovereignly guides me. Hallelujah! The best way to help both others and myself is to meet my Maker's specs. I approach Him in prayer intent on discerning His plan. Then I proceed in the confidence that He is able!

Inspiration   † † †

But this year I have started out to live all my waking moments in conscious listening to the inner voice, asking without ceasing, "What, Father, do you desire said? What, Father, do you desire this minute?"—Brother Lawrence & Frank Laubach in *Practicing His Presence*

Coram Deo

Friday evening I watered the young trees and shrubbery in my front yard. I noticed a plastic soft drink container wrapped in gray tape. It looked suspicious enough, so not wanting my children to pick it up, I chucked it across our road. (Don't ever do this!) The next morning while Bryan, Stephen, and I shot hoops in our driveway, a police car pulled alongside the curb across the street. Someone evidently reported the object and a bomb squad arrived. Sure enough, a poorly made bomb failed to explode. Perhaps you can imagine some of the thoughts that ran through our heads as we pondered the incident.

Later that morning, my wife called me. The minivan was acting up. So, she drove into Les Schwab for an inspection. The mechanic informed her the front brakes were metal-to-metal and the front tires were too worn for her to be driving safely. Money we set aside for taxes we now spent on our vehicle.

As I drove down to Eugene to conduct a wedding, I could not help thinking "as bizarre as this day has gone, I bet the interstate will be blocked with some accident." Sure enough! I had not gone fifty miles before I hit total gridlock. Cars lined up for miles because of a wreck. Fortunately, an exit was available and I was able to find an alternate route and arrive in time to officiate John and Kristi's wedding.

It was a great day. God gave me the opportunity to share from His Word with the wedding participants. By their comments afterwards, I could see their hunger for spiritual truth. I suspected as much. When adversity strikes, often holy opportunities are close at hand. Yet an even greater realization helped me through a challenging period.

Jeremiah 17:16—But I have not run away from being Your shepherd, and I have not longed for the fatal day. You know my words were spoken in Your presence.

The prophet Jeremiah seemed to have a clear understanding that he lived his life before the ever-watching eyes of God. Profoundly, he operated as a wise prophet. Most of us live as if God were as distant as some undiscovered galaxy. When our irritation is as thick as contaminated oil, when our eyes are on the wrong things, if we are not conscious of our all-seeing Father, we behave poorly! The Lord is, as Os Guinness notes, our Audience of One. He is the One we live to please!

We ought to cringe at the thoughts and actions we mindlessly commit before Him whose gaze fixes us with concern extended from a heavy heart. His love should inspire us to walk nobly and to do what honors Him. To live in the presence of God "coram deo" is our challenge, our privilege and our gift! Now go and be what pleases Him.

The Veneer of Tyranny May 9

Jeremiah 30:21—Jacob's leader will be one of them; his ruler will issue from him. I will invite him to Me, and he will approach Me, for who would otherwise risk his life to approach Me? This is the LORD's declaration.

A uniform can be a source of great inspiration or it can be the veneer of tyranny—it all depends on the heart of the one clothed. There is a man who cannot advance in his job. His ability to move up in his organization is stifled by the hands of a Napoleon-pretender, one with an insecurity complex too radioactive to handle. Perhaps you know the type?

Few things are more frustrating in life than serving a boss who derives his or her authority solely on position. "I outrank you," is this pseudo-leader's mantra, therefore "you must do whatever I tell you." "I resent you," is the follower's unspoken feeling; therefore, "I will only do what I have to do and nothing more." In this miserable environment, it is very hard to accept, let alone understand, the sovereignty of God.

If you work for a prima donna, here are some helpful suggestions. *First, understand that you are dealing with an insecure and unhappy person.* Very few people really want to be jerks. Instead of focusing on what this person does to annoy you, consider asking God to reveal to you the source of the problem. If the Holy Spirit gives you insight, you will have a powerful means to pray for the grief-giver. *Second, respond whenever possible, with kindness.* Jesus taught His followers that God "*. . . is gracious to the ungrateful and evil*" (Luke 6:35). His kindness to the undeserving should inspire us! *Third, recognize that God may be working on your character by the character for whom you're working.* Often we learn what not to do by observing firsthand what others are improperly doing. And in the belly of adversity, we learn much about our own ability to trust God through trying times and circumstances.

If you are in a position of leadership, I hope your employees or any who work for you find you to be inspirational. If you are guilty of hurting them via the position you hold, consider asking God to identify the insecurity, which causes you to rely on your rank or title instead of on Him. Do not justify your behavior by an "I know what's best for these wimps" attitude. Such thinking reveals pride and brings no glory to the Father you represent. Confess your failure to trust Him! Renounce your need to control by coercion. Win the hearts of those around you by practicing servant-leadership! Be devoted to God not to your authority!

Inspiration † † †

Leaders who are unable to love their people and who are unwilling to consider their needs, are insecure in their own identity.—Henry & Richard Blackaby in *Spiritual Leadership*

Worried About . . .

Jeremiah 38:17-20—Jeremiah therefore said to Zedekiah, "This is what the LORD, the God of Hosts, the God of Israel, says: 'If indeed you surrender to the officials of the king of Babylon, then you will live, this city will not be burned down, and you and your household will survive. But if you do not surrender to the officials of the king of Babylon, then this city will be handed over to the Chaldeans. They will burn it down, and you yourself will not escape from them.'" But King Zedekiah said to Jeremiah, "I am worried about the Judeans who have deserted to the Chaldeans. They may hand me over to them to abuse me." They will not hand you over," Jeremiah replied. "Obey the voice of the LORD in what I am telling you, so it may go well for you and you can live.

What happened? King Zedekiah sent for Jeremiah, the prophet and man of God to get specific instruction from God. He was facing imminent destruction from King Nebuchadnezzar and his Babylonian army. Jeremiah gave him the Lord's firm instruction. All he had to do was listen. But he didn't. When the invading army breached the walls, he tried to flee and was promptly captured.

What should have happened? If Zedekiah followed God's plan and simply surrendered, the Chaldeans would not have burned down Jerusalem and His temple. They would not have killed his sons and his commanders right before his eyes. They would not have put his eyes out leaving him blind and chained for the rest of what would be a miserable life. Had he obeyed it would have gone well for him.

How does this happen? Well, for starters, Zedekiah's priorities were cockeyed. He was more worried about his own countrymen, the Judeans, who deserted to the Chaldeans and what they might do to him than he was willing to believe God. Ironically, if he were going to worry, the man he should have feared most was King Nebuchadnezzar! Zedekiah had a poor relationship with God—so faith and obedience were not on his list of attributes. He relied on his own brain cells. Worry is man's postcard to heaven—"I can't trust You!"

Indigestion is to uncontrolled acid what worry is to uncontrolled thinking. If God speaks, we have a choice. Either we can listen to Him or we can ignore Him and suffer the consequences. What we are worried about reveals our condition. Worry is never the child of trust—it is the illegitimate offspring of Satan who long ago planted the first seeds of doubt in the minds of a man and a woman about what God *really* said. If you are anxious about . . . it is time again to listen to Jesus, who calmly stated, *"Don't worry about your life . . . Can any of you add a single cubit to his height by worrying?"* (Mat. 6:25,27)

Inspiration   † † †

Hot water does not burn a house.—Kenyan Proverb

911 Calls

It was 1:00 a.m. and the doorbell rang. I got out of bed, walked down the stairs, looked through the peephole and opened the door for a young police officer. "Sir, we received a 911 call from your home."

"Officer, was the call from 620-4081?"

"Yes, the dispatcher said all she could hear was static. She called back and left a message."

"I'm so sorry. This is the second time this week (midnight or later), this has happened. My computer is turned off and I don't know how you are getting called." I took him into my office and showed him the offending phone.

"Okay, you might want to call your phone company and have them check this out."

"Yes, I will. I'm sorry you had to come out here."

"No problem. Hope you can get back to sleep."

Lamentations 3:40—Let us search out and examine our ways, and turn back to the LORD.
2 Corinthians 13:5—Test yourselves to see if you are in the faith. Examine yourselves. Or do you not recognize for yourselves that Jesus Christ is in you?— unless you fail the test.

I called our phone company and explained my predicament. One customer service representative suggested my cordless phone battery might be low and therefore was initiating the call. She said I should run some tests over the next several days. However, I did not relish the prospect of the police getting another midnight false alarm. Finally, the company ran a diagnostic test on the phone line and noticing problems, dispatched a technician. Steve came out and looked at the equipment. He talked to me in our driveway.

"Sir, the problem is not with your phone it is in our external line. It is programmed for some strange reason to call 911 when it malfunctions."

"O great! At this rate I should throw a party for the Tigard police's midnight shift—they're all getting to know me!"

"I am going to fix this and change your line so this won't happen again." Thankfully, we had no further problems!

In meditating over these adventures, two thoughts challenge my mind. Unless I thoroughly examine what is wrong I may apply the incorrect solution. But there are some troubles I cannot solve no matter how hard I try. I need to call for an expert who can identify and fix the problem. David prayed, *"Test me, LORD, and try me; examine my heart and mind"* (Psa. 26:2). That is a great prayer! Periodically, I need God to show me sin that I may not see or weaknesses that require His hand to fix. He made me and if I will listen to Him, I will always have His solution.

Heartless

I've never had a ministry to the poor. Few of my friends are financially needy and those I work and live around are middle or upper class families. While my finances have often been sparse, compared to most in the world I am incredibly well off. Therefore, I wondered what it would be like to spend so many hours each week helping people with ever-converging problems from which escape seems bleak and overwhelming. I found joy. It is richly rewarding to share Christ with people so destitute they have nothing to hide and therefore are brutally honest. I made new friends with those grateful for prayer, a listening ear and the chance to vent frustrations. I am humbled by how good I really have it. I am confronted by the challenge of loving those who reek and those who know what is right to do but will make the wrong choices anyway. I am amazed by daily miracles, reduced to tears by unimaginable cruelties and confounded by an increasing sense of frustration. I cannot believe how many people need assistance that have attended churches for years and have no idea how they will get into heaven let alone get help on earth.

Can you imagine Jesus telling a poor single mother, *"You can only come to Me once a year for food."*! I once pastored a church where we set rules regarding how much help we would give people. I am embarrassed when I think of that now. *We* made rules to keep the needy from overwhelming our organization. Maybe that's the problem—we need to be overwhelmed! There is something amazingly healthy about coming destitute to God to help the destitute. Our faith blossoms when we let go of what we cling to and let God set the agenda. Our generosity grows when our trust is in Him and not in our policy and resources.

In Acts 4, we read of believers selling land and houses and giving the proceeds to the apostles to help anyone in need. I do not know anyone who would sell his or her land or a second house for me if I were in desperate need. The reason is that today we fix the responsibility for direness on the individual hurting to excuse taking responsibility corporately to alleviate the problem. We have lost the sense of adventure and utter excitement the early church had in embracing new believers into their midst with a mindset to help any and all who joined them. Now we view with suspicion anyone who comes through the door looking or acting needy. We have become so concerned about "protecting ourselves" that to the hurting we are heartless.

Lamentations 4:3,4—Even jackals offer their breasts to nurse their young, but my dear people have become cruel like ostriches in the wilderness. The nursing infant's tongue clings to the roof of his mouth from thirst. Little children beg for bread, but no one gives them any.

I'm not saying we must help everyone. We need the Lord's discernment and leading. However, the Bible *is* clear that we have an obligation to help those who are of the household of faith. Once years ago, I tried to get my sister minimal financial help from the large church she attended. I knew the pastor on the phone from whom I was seeking assistance. Sadly, he treated me like some annoying stranger. The staff of that church made my sister feel like a second-class citizen. I think of that experience often now. The world is not stupid. How will it find the gospel attractive if we repel the unattractive? The One who became poor to make us rich should never find us heartless. Let it be said of us, *"Through the proof of this service, they will glorify God for your obedience to the confession of the gospel of Christ, and for your generosity in sharing with them and with others"* (2 Co. 9:13).

Inspiration   † † †

God continually introduces us to people in whom we have no interest, and unless we are worshiping God the natural tendency is to be heartless toward them. We give them a quick verse of Scripture, like jabbing them with a spear, or leave them with a hurried, uncaring word of counsel before we go. A heartless Christian must be a terrible grief to our Lord.—Oswald Chambers in *My Utmost For His Highest*

Awakening

I read a story in the newspaper only to find out that it was far more relevant than I realized. The Oregonian reported a bad car accident after which a woman had to have an emergency cesarean to save the life of her baby. Incredibly, the husband and father, was one of my drill sergeants. He suffered two broken knees, a broken arm and head injuries. The driver of the other car happened to be a diabetic who blacked out. His car crossed the median forever altering two families' lives. By God's grace, no one perished.

Daniel 2:1—In the second year of his reign, Nebuchadnezzar had dreams that troubled him, and sleep deserted him.

The Babylonian king, Nebuchadnezzar was the most powerful ruler of his time. His empire was vast and his authority fearsome. God spoke to him in a dream that troubled his mind but which he could not recall. He gathered all the wise men, sorcerers and magicians and demanded they reveal his vision and interpret its meaning. Of course, it was an impossible request, which they were powerless to solve. Therefore, the king, evidently short on patience, ordered their deaths. Fortunately for them, the Hebrew prophet, Daniel, went before Nebuchadnezzar and with God's help, was able to not only tell the king his dream but also explain its meaning. The dream was the precursor to a second dream and a spiritual awakening, which would take place in the king's life over a year later. To read a most incredible story open your Bible to Daniel chapter four.

When I visited my sergeant, he was in remarkable spirits for someone immensely suffering. After talking with him, I placed my hand on his shoulder and asked if I could pray for him. With his consent, I went before God's throne. Afterwards, he tapped his hand on his heart and said, "Oooh, that really gets me here." Then as the reality of God's grace in sparing his life and the lives of his wife and children settled across his mind, he began weeping. He experienced an awakening that was profoundly touching.

Life is not a fixed formula. God's providential hand determines the length of your life. Only He knows when you will stop breathing on this orbiting planet. If you are reading this and do not yet have a personal relationship with the Lord, I hope that you will experience a spiritual awakening that will draw your heart to trust in Jesus before it is too late. It would be an eternal tragedy to miss His loving call because you refused to awaken from your spiritual slumber.

Inspiration   † † †

It is not enough to stand and appreciate the gate—one must enter.— John F. MacArthur, Jr. in *The Gospel According to Jesus*

Verdict

I had not been home long before my cell phone rang. Jay called and asked if I would come down to his place and pray. I could feel the heaviness in his voice. Driving home, I had just taken a call from a man whose wife was penniless and unable to provide food for herself and her two children. Complicating his situation, she was in the Philippines still recovering from a serious surgery. After sharing possible organizations that could help him, I was about to hang up when he asked if he could come in and meet with me. I understood that this was a spiritual request from an unchurched soldier and silently thanked God for the opportunity to be light to a man trapped in the shadows. Two phone calls, plenty of pain and the big heat tab in the sky was still descending.

Sassy opened the door and gave me her trademark, farmer's daughter hug (no frailty in her arms)! Then Jay asked her if we could be alone. As we sat at his small kitchen table he said, "Pastor, please open your Bible and read with me." Then he read from Acts 12:1-17. As he finished reading, he noted that the key to this passage was the earnest prayer of the saints for Peter. "Pastor, Sassy has Alzheimer's. We received the news today. Will you pray with me?"

Daniel 4:17—This word is by decree of the observers; the matter is a command from the holy ones. This is so the living will know that the Most High is ruler over the kingdom of men. He gives it to anyone He wants and sets over it the lowliest of men.

Every moment someone, somewhere on the globe, faces the reality that he or she is not in control. Those that do not know Jesus face the vicious grasp of an empty fate, bereft of joy, hope, or the song of salvation. Those who love Jesus possess the priceless knowledge that no verdict is final, except what passes from His lips. Doctors may name our disease, only God can name our eternity. We will all die but only those with the grace verdict will enjoy life with the Heavenly Father. Therefore, in our brokenness on earth, we who know the Savior can gather and talk to Him. No situation or affliction can steal us from His refuge. In the humility of honest prayer, we find a Lord who hears us and races to hold us! He loves us. His favor is not capricious. His blessings run deep and His verdict over our broken, *sinfested* lives is MERCY.

Inspiration † † †

It is impossible for human beings to save themselves.—Max Lucado in *The Applause of Heaven*

The verdict of the world is conclusive.—Saint Aurelius Augustine, Algerian philosopher and theologian, (354-430)

A Man to Emulate

Do you remember the story of Daniel in the lion's den? This godly man invoked jealousy in the hearts of the administrators and princes in Babylon. They did not like it that he was a better leader, or the fact that the king was planning to put Daniel in charge of the entire empire. So, they tried to destroy him by appealing to the ego of King Darius. They convinced the king to sign a law—a law that stated that people could only pray to the king for thirty days, or they would be thrown to the lions.

Daniel 6:10—But when Daniel learned that the law had been signed, he went home and knelt down as usual in his upstairs room, with its windows open toward Jerusalem. He prayed three times a day, just as he had always done, giving thanks to his God. (NLT)

Daniel knew his enemies were after him. He certainly understood their spiteful ambition. What amazes me about him though, is what he did not do.

- He did not go to King Darius and appeal for his life; citing past accomplishments.
- He did not hire a team of lawyers to find a legal loophole.
- He did not pray in hiding so that his accusers could not catch him.
- He did not dream up a law to punish his enemies and convince the king to sign it.
- He did not flee for his life.

Instead, he quietly went home and prayed—in keeping with his habit and conviction. Before open windows, he thanked God and calmly sought His help.

I am glad my parents named me Daniel. This prophet is such an amazing man to emulate. He is one of the few men recorded in Scripture that is completely above reproach. He challenges our need to defend ourselves. He gives us a powerful lesson in faith. He demonstrates humility, wisdom, and devotion in the teeth of hatred and before the impending jaws of hungry lions. I want to be like him.

Maybe you are experiencing life-threatening challenges. Perhaps you are under unfair attack by conniving people. *Okay*, God still loves you deeply—certainly more deeply than you love Him. You do not need to be afraid; you don't have to worry. You are not alone. So, instead of getting worked into a tizzy, why not get down on your knees and pray! Thank the Lord for His sovereign power. Praise the name of Jesus! Ask for His help. Then get up on your feet and trust that no matter what happens, He will see you through. Sure, you can be thrown to the lions. But no one can make the lions eat you, because the Lion King is the One you worship! The Lion of Judah is your Lord and Savior. And that's something to think about . . . in reveration!

Precious

Daniel and Joseph are two of my greatest Biblical heroes. I admire their impeccable character, inspiring faith, strong understanding of God's sovereignty and consistent obedience to God's will. Both of them excelled as leaders. Daniel was so highly esteemed by God, that when he asked Him questions, the Lord dispatched Gabriel (one of the most powerful angelic beings), to answer his concerns. Imagine praying and then having an angel walk in your room with God's response!

Daniel 9:23—The moment you began praying, a command was given. And now I am here to tell you what it was, for you are very precious to God. Listen carefully so that you can understand the meaning of your vision. (NLT)

To be precious in God's eyes, God must be precious in our eyes. Three times in the *New Living Translation*, an angel informed Daniel that he was *"very precious to God"* (see also 10:11,18). What made this man from Judah so special? I believe it was because Daniel lived to bring glory to God. He was far more concerned with God's reputation than his own condition. We saw how previously Daniel maintained the practice of praying before an open window even when his life was threatened. For him to change his habit and pray in private would have made God subservient to King Darius in the eyes of the Medes and Persians! If he rationalized that he was important to the King as his number one administrator and postponed praying for thirty days, in essence, he would have set himself above God. Daniel reckoned it was better to be man-meat for hungry lions than dishonor his Maker.

Friend, whatever your circumstance, *come hades or elevated H2O*, do you hold your heavenly Father as precious? If there is no time in your life for prayer, isn't it ludicrous to wonder why God seems distant? If He is not your best Friend, then what is He? Anything precious holds value, demands time and carves heart space. God is exceedingly awesome! Make Him precious and you will know just how much He loves you! Join with Peter who wrote, *"Now to you who believe, this stone is precious. But to those who do not believe, 'The stone the builders rejected has become the capstone'"* (1 Pe. 2:7).

Inspiration   † † †

That we must love one God only is a thing so evident that it does not require miracles to prove it.—Blaise Pascal

Any love that terminates on man is eventually destructive. It does not lead people to the only lasting joy, namely, God. Love must be God-centered, or it is not true love; it leaves people without their final hope of joy.—John Piper

Rafting the Deschutes

The Deschutes River in Oregon is 173.4 miles long. It runs through rugged forest and forlorn desert sometimes cascading with terrific roar, sometimes ambling like some peaceful toddler. It is a great river to fish for steelhead and salmon. On the lower Deschutes, people often come to whitewater raft. And for that experience, my son, Stephen and I, joined 17 folks from Southwest Hills Baptist Church.

Seven of us climbed into a large raft and excitedly took our assigned positions. As we looked down the river, Dan, our guide, gave us instructions. He told us how we should paddle, what commands he would give, and what we must do to be safe and successfully negotiate the rapids. I must confess I had my misgivings. Four of the boys on our raft were 14 years old and at least two of them were more interested in water fights than listening to Dan's wise words. I could just see us capsizing amidst rocks and someone getting hurt or drowning because we did not listen properly to Dan's commands. Not long before our trip, two people had died further upstream from accidents. I was glad Jim, Jack and Loren led us in praying for God's protection.

Hosea 2:18—On that day I will make a covenant for them with the wild animals, the birds of the sky, and the creatures that crawl on the ground. I will shatter bow, sword, and weapons of war in the land and will enable the people to rest securely.

God is interested in our safety. When He created the world, He made it to be a safe place. Unfortunately, man's sin turned the Garden of Eden into the globe of evil. How spectacular it will be when God restores the planet to its pristine state of safety!

Paddling down the Deschutes, Stephen and I learned several safety lessons:

●   *When we obeyed Dan's vocal commands,* our raft easily glided through turbulent waters. When we obey God, it is much easier to negotiate life. Doing what He asks brings peace that surpasses understanding.

●   *Disunity equals struggles.* If we did not paddle at the same time or if someone was distracted and not paddling, it threw off our rhythm and made us more vulnerable to the current below us. Danger was mitigated by teamwork. How often we fall victim to our enemy Satan, or people opposed to God, by our own independence or lack of cooperation!

●   The Deschutes is full of eddies—circular movements of water counter to the main current. Often in these broad whirlpools, we found calmness. *I wonder if God has not called us to be eddies.*

●   Rocks and/or the channeling of water by the ground form rapids. We could see the dangers ahead by observing the water and by listening to the sound of the river. Our objective was to bypass the rocks. *The Bible teaches us to avoid evil.* Sin is usually not hard to spot. When we observe or engage in bad behavior or hear wicked speech, we must take the appropriate action. Away from the rocks, we could swim safely.

● The Deschutes is cold! We shivered if we were wet and in the shade. However, in the sun we were warm. *Life with God's Son is warm!*

Safety is not something to take for granted. In the hands of our Father, we are always safe—hallelujah!

BRYAN D. YORK PHOTOGRAPHY
2008

Inspiration † † †

Safety doesn't happen by accident.—Author Unknown

Sowing

Hosea 10:12—Sow righteousness for yourselves and reap faithful love; break up your untilled ground. It is time to seek the LORD until He comes and sends righteousness on you like the rain.

Ella Wheeler Wilcox, author and poet wrote, "With every deed you are sowing a seed, though the harvest you may not see." Have you ever considered the notion that what you and I say is a form of planting? For example, if I whine constantly I create an environment of dissatisfaction and I reveal discontent with life. If I have a critical spirit and am harsh in the way I feel towards others, I create an atmosphere of distrust and rob my surroundings of joy. If I talk only of myself, I establish a place of pride and self-centeredness that leaves others with no desire to linger. If I speak negatively of others, I produce gossip or slander and hurt their reputation. I have created the perception in the listener "I wonder if he talks about me like this when I'm not around."

Conversation makes a statement as surely as the clothes we wear. When was the last time someone came to you and said, "I've just got to share with you something profound and cool that I read in the Bible" or, "please let me tell you about the rich time I had with the Lord this morning in prayer?" When was the last time *you* spoke words of eternal worth to the betterment of your hearers?

Most of us are good at talking about sports, food, weather, work, travel, family relationships, etc. But if there is a notable absence of God in our conversation, are we revealing that He has minor importance in our life?

We have the opportunity daily to share words that massage hearts. We have the incredible privilege to live and model godliness so that those around us are blessed. Our Father in heaven does not share trite and trivial words because He has no desire to reap dandelion children. He gives us words of hope and substance, love and power, because He wants us to be like Him. What are you sowing? I pray to God that this day and tomorrow you will make a difference in the lives of those around you because God is making a difference in you!

Inspiration   † † †

If we don't include the kingdom, repentance, and growth in kingdom living in the good news we preach today, we reduce and alter the message of Jesus and are guilty of devising a different gospel.—Jan David Hettinga in *Follow Me*

Most of us spend the first six days of each week sowing wild oats; then we go to church on Sunday and pray for a crop failure.—Fred A. Allen, comedian, (1894-1956)

Unrecognized

She sits on the sofa biting down on the flesh of her left index finger. It is an old habit and the sure indicator of mounting frustration. The pattern started near the end of college and extends through five jobs, a mediocre marriage and raising four children. Allisson hardly feels His presence anymore. She's surrounded by friends, and truth be told, spends hours each week instant messaging them or talking on the phone. She carts her kids to sports events. She has seen every elementary play and never missed a parent-teacher meeting. Pastor Mike calls her first if the nursery helper calls in sick. She is the model of dependability. So why does Allisson feel dry like some sponge left in the sun? Why does she cry when her husband asks her what is wrong?

Allisson doesn't know that last year her guardian angel protected her from a drunken driver. She doesn't understand that God put it on the hearts of a Christian board to give her a scholarship, sparing her enormous college debt. She missed God's comforting hand while her baby nearly died of pneumonia. Nor did she comprehend His leading in matching her with a man who needs her strengths as she needs his. She doesn't realize God's presence in her life because she is too focused on pleasing what's in the mirror.

Hosea 11:3,4—It was I who taught Ephraim to walk, taking them in My arms, but they never knew that I healed them. I led them with human cords, with ropes of kindness. To them I was like one who eases the yoke from their jaws; I bent down to give them food.

God taught Ephraim to walk but Ephraim ran away. He healed them of disease but they sacrificed to the Baals and burned incense to images. He led Ephraim with cords of kindness. They saw only ropes of restraint and broke loose to chase pleasure. God bent down and fed them when they starved but they longed for Egyptian food. We judge Ephraim for stupidity in failing to recognize and follow God but are we so different today?

Intimacy is never the fruit of neglect. Proper recognition requires appreciation. To be unrecognized one must be either unworthy, irrelevant, or unappreciated. God is unrecognized because the Bible is unconsumed. Meaningful worship dissolves beneath repetitious jingles that salute marketing at the expense of meditation. If God is unrealized, it is because Allisson embraced religion and misplaced relationship. She used to talk to Him regularly and listen for His guidance, but then other things grabbed her attention. She rarely has time now to pray. If her mother so infrequently communicated with her, she would call her dysfunctional and think she was mad at her! It is a terrible thing when Amazing Love goes unrecognized.

Dreams

Joel 2:28,32a—After this I will pour out My Spirit on all humanity; then your sons and your daughters will prophesy, your old men will have dreams, and your young men will see visions . . . Then everyone who calls on the name of Yahweh will be saved.

The Holy Spirit descended upon the believers at Pentecost and they spoke in other languages as the Spirit enabled them. This fiery event began a new phase of God working on earth through the lives of people transformed by the power of Jesus Christ. There is profound meaning in the word God impressed upon Joel and reimpressed upon Peter.

It is rare when old men dream dreams. Dreams die for many reasons. Some give up on life. Many resist the promptings of the Holy Spirit until His whispered visions are completely stifled. They feed the monster Skepticism and glorify the gods of cannot. Others cower beneath the controlling authority of dream-killers; those with manageable plans who cannot tolerate anyone else dreaming. You know who I mean, men intimidated by ideas, power and confidence that is not their own. Women too afraid to let the Holy Spirit have His way for fear He might wreck their neatly arranged plans. Others frustrated by a society that disdains its elderly, venerate the past. Speeches tell stories of what God did yesterday and reruns punctuate slumber. .

Dreams thrive for three reasons; the Holy Spirit is trusted, obeyed and honored. The Apostle John, exiled to the island of Patmos and near the end of his life, *"was in the Spirit"* and through his writing, we have Revelation (Rev. 1:9,10). God waited until Abraham was an old man to do His most spectacular work through him. It is not age that determines or precludes ministry, it is walking in the Spirit! The old men and women I know that dream, have no concept of retirement. They see each approaching day as a new opportunity for God to work through them! They embrace adversity as a robe to wear with dignity. They accept suffering as the cost of sin and the price for following Jesus. They grasp the folly of blaming heaven. They understand Satan's accusing strategy, his vicious lies, and persistent attacks, and repel him with God's Word. They whistle while others whine. They follow the call of God joyfully. They are pioneers like my parents, whose dreams are still fresh because they walk in obedience and worship a Father who delights to bless them.

I praise God for the dreams He gives! How about you, are you fresh with heaven's agenda? Does your life pulsate with holy meaning that glorifies God, or is it a tired billboard ready for dismantling? Do you understand what happens when the Holy Spirit is free to inspire—people call on the name of the Lord and He saves them! Kingdom builders are dreamers! Ask God to give you a fresh word and dare to dream!

Marriage—Conflict Resolution

Julie* smiled at me but her radiant ivories could not hide eyes that hurt. In five years with Curt, he had yet to give her flowers. She would drop hints. Once, she shared why her dad gave her mother special plants. But practical Curt, mentally pictured shriveled bouquets and concluded why waste money on something that will not last. Curt did not understand that flowers were not the real issue.

Someone once said, "Some marriages are made in heaven, but they ALL have to be maintained on earth." How do we improve our relationship with the one we love when we view things so differently? How do we resolve ever-present conflict?

Amos 3:3—Do two walk together unless they have agreed to do so? (NIV)

Steps to Conflict Resolution

● *Accurately identify the problem(s).* Often what causes us to inadequately resolve conflict is our preoccupation with symptoms at the expense of grasping the true issue. Consequently, we apply impotent solutions. Curt thought Julie was irritated with him for not buying flowers and consistently getting home from work late. He would apologize and tell her he loved her. However, her need went beyond hearing words. She needed to know she was *truly* valued, that she was more important to him than his job.

● *Identify and understand the values that underlie the problem.* Julie yearns for tangible demonstrations of love and spending time together. Curt holds to wisely spending money and being a great provider. Both of their values are important and need to be shared and understood. When we understand each other's values, we have a better appreciation for why we do the things we do.

● *Die to self!* Love trumps frugality. Isn't it more important that Curt effectively learn Julie's love language than save a few dollars? Since she is the one who is hurt, he needs to quit rationalizing his behavior and take the necessary action to honor her. Julie needs to be willing to share her true feelings even though it makes her vulnerable. Dying to self requires putting the needs of others above my own.

● *Be of one mind and live in peace.* Without unity, peace is hollow and unfulfilling.

○ Ask God for His help in resolving problems, remembering that He is with you.

○ Identify and agree upon steps needed to bring resolution. Julie does not expect Curt to bring her flowers every week—that would get expensive! After talking, she agrees to be honest in expressing why she is irritated. He commits to finding creative ways (beyond words), to demonstrate love. He pledges to spend more time with her.

    o   Give each other honest feedback and persevere at solving conflict.

Aim for perfection! Do not settle for a divided oneness. Resist giving up when troubles thrash peace. In addition, go out and purchase, *Two Fleas and No Dog* by Craig Hill. This is an absolute must read for any couple who cares about preserving their marriage.

Inspiration   † † †

There is a story about a man and wife who were celebrating their golden wedding anniversary—fifty years of married life. Having spent most of the day with relatives and friends at a big party given in their honor, they were back home again. They decided, before retiring, to have a little snack of tea with bread and butter. They went into the kitchen, where the husband opened up a new loaf of bread and handed the end piece (the heel) to his wife. Whereupon she exploded! She said, "For fifty years you have been dumping the heel of the bread on me. I will not take it anymore; this lack of concern for me and what I like." On and on she went in the bitterest of terms, for offering her the heel of the bread. The husband was absolutely astonished at her tirade. When she had finished he said to her quietly, "But it's my favorite piece."—James S. Hewett, *Illustrations Unlimited*

*Fictitious characters

Misunderstanding God

Obadiah 15—For the Day of the Lord is near, against all the nations. As you have done, so it will be done to you; what you deserve will return on your own head.

How many of us are uncomfortable with God's Old Testament track record? The fact that He commanded Israel to completely annihilate those who lived in the Promised Land disturbs our sense of decency and contorts our view of His love and mercy. So we glob on to Jesus as the remake of God's image and in so doing miss His message that He did not come to bring peace but a sword. God did not change, His method changed. The grace-bestowing Son, fulfilled the law man could not keep.

For God to be a God of grace, He must be a God of destruction. The sin beginning with Adam and Eve resides in our entire DNA. Before we go on, why did God order Israel to wipe out the Canaanites et al.? Was it their insistence in worshiping idols? Just as they resisted the Jews, so they persisted in rejecting God. When the Jews failed to dislodge them, they became the thorn and snare the angel describes in Jud. 2:3: *"Therefore, I now say: I will not drive out these people before you. They will be thorns in your sides, and their gods will be a trap to you."* The people Israel refused to destroy seduced her into worshiping hand-carved images, sacrificing children on the altar, and blaspheming the Almighty until she was more corrupt than her teachers were.

A sliver of wood penetrated my hand. It was stuck and I gave up trying to get it out. But it became infected. When we allow evil residency should we be surprised when it infects us? God deals ruthlessly with sin because it is rebellion towards Him. To expect Him to be gracious and loving and yet turn His back to sin would be as absurd as failing to practice good hygiene because we want to be fair to the bugs!

We do God a great injustice to judge Him wrong for destroying. *First, we cannot see into the hearts of man as He can.* Our sin-distorted view prevents us from being wisely objective. *Second, the very fact that we question the motives and actions of the One who created us and label them wrong, begs our condition!* *Third, we are quick to destroy that which offends us.* Thus, we become hypocritical when we deny God the right we practice ourselves. *Fourth, we are uncomfortable with God's holy hammer when it strikes our ability to please our flesh.* The real reason we would rather not see God pound on sin is because there are some sins *we* like. Besides a lack of faith that she was capable of destroying the Canaanites, the reason Israel did not displace them was her fascination with their evil.

While I may not understand God's methods, I must believe that He knows best and trust that when He asks me to have nothing to do with evil it is for my benefit. If I don't, then in truth I want to be god. As surely as Israel was corrupted, I will be corrupted. We take our cue from Jesus to love the sinner but not the sin. If we are serious about loving God, we ask Him to cut out whatever is cancerous inside us.

Oh Lord, don't let me excuse the place of sin in my life. Destroy it! Like the welder, put Your torch to that which is broken so that I will be strong and faithful.

Inspiration   † † †

We often give our enemies the means for our own destruction.—Aesop, author of Aesop's Fables, (mid 6th century B.C.)

Don't Run Away

Jonah 3:1,2—Then the word of the LORD came to Jonah a second time: "Get up! Go to the great city of Nineveh and preach the message that I tell you."

One could hardly blame him for disobeying God's instruction. The Assyrians were Israel's hated northern enemy. When God called Jonah to go to their capital city and warn them of His impending judgment, naturally his prejudice and nationalist pride stood in the way. The book of Jonah is one fascinating story of a man who placed his rights over God's and by so doing, failed to discern His higher will. Are we any different? Are you avoiding doing what God would have you do because your sense of personal rights stands in the way? Read on!

Don't Run Away

"Lord about this assignment and the warning I should bring
I think I'll go to Tarshish, so I'm headed out to sea.
Lord, I'm not a mercy man, I really couldn't care
Don't want to go to Nineveh, I don't wanna share."

Think I'll just go down below and take a little nap
Little sleep should cure my guilt and keep my conscience back
"Hey Captain quit shaking me can't ya see I'm tired?
What's that? A storm you say—you want me to call my God!"

The sailors rolled the dice to find out where to put the blame
Of course I was the guilty one so they asked me to explain.
I told them I'm an Israelite running from the Lord
The same One who made the sea—so cast me overboard.

Well the sea got worse and the sailors shook they tried to row for land.
But the more they stroked the worse it got until they finally prayed.
"Lord please don't let us die for killing an innocent man."
Then they threw me off the ship and the raging sea went bland.

The Lord He sent a giant fish it swallowed me complete.
With seaweed wrapped around my head it sank into the deep.
"Three days Lord that's pretty bad you know my hair is bleached!
I'm calling for help, hear me Lord I'll make Your will complete."

Well that big fish spit me out right up on the beach
And off I went to Nineveh it took three days to preach.
Those Ninevites believed the Lord and they began to fast
Even the king took off his robes and sat down in the dust.

"Lord, I'm not a mercy man and I'm really getting ticked
I don't like the Ninevites and Your love for them is sick.
So Lord just let me die I pray, just get it over with!
That's why I ran away—I knew it'd come to this!"

"Lord why'd You let the vine grow and kill it with a worm?
Why'd you go and give me shade then yank it so I'd burn?"
"Why Jonah if you care so much for a single vine
Don't you think that I should bring my love to all these lives?"

Jonah was not a mercy man—he should have been a vulture
But God is full of love and grace for each and every culture.
So when He tells you to go out and share about His Son
Don't run away, or find excuses, go and get it done!

Inspiration † † †

To put it bluntly, your flesh is a weasel, a poser, and a selfish pig. And your flesh is not you. Did you know that?—John Eldredge in *Wild at Heart*

Concerns about Earnestness

Jonah 3:8—Furthermore, both man and beast must be covered with sackcloth, and everyone must call out earnestly to God. Each must turn from his evil ways and from the violence he is doing.

Along with scores of other pastors, I received an email from Rick. Rick was riled because of the poor representation in Salem, Oregon's capital, by spiritual leaders against impending legislation that granted civil liberties and benefits to homosexuals. He felt we were failing in our duties as shepherds to speak out against sin.

I am deeply concerned that our nation is moving in a direction that violates our freedom of speech and religion guaranteed in our Bill of Rights. I am equally concerned about the breakdown of the family unit and threat to it by those who seek to legitimize perversion. The day will come when Christians who speak out against homosexuality will be subject to imprisonment, property seizure, or fines, for not accepting, hiring, or tolerating those whose behavior is clearly identified in Scripture as immoral. In essence, the sexual "rights" of one percent of the population will trump the moral rights of the majority of citizens against such behavior. When this happens, we will truly be living in the days when evil is called good and good is called evil.

Yet, there are many more concerns than just fighting horrible legislation.

● *There is a danger in being earnest of also being woefully inconsistent.* We feel good speaking out for certain rights while we often ignore obvious wrongs. Solomon wrote in Pro. 6:16-19:

Six things the LORD hates; in fact, seven are detestable to Him: arrogant eyes a lying tongue, hands that shed innocent blood, a heart that plots wicked schemes, feet eager to run to evil, a lying witness who gives false testimony, and one who stirs up trouble among brothers.

How is it that we feel so piously stirred up against homosexuality, yet, we look past those who are proud, liars, violent, schemers and producers of dissension? Clearly, these are things God hates. Pornography and gambling break apart families—are we zealous for safeguards against such behavior? What makes us think we can take on one sin while ignoring other sins? Could it be that we are mute about things for which we are often guilty? We look very hypocritical in the eyes of the world when we selectively champion certain issues while ignoring others.

● *There is a danger in equating earnestness with calling.* Unless God calls us to take a stand against a certain injustice, (such as William Wilburfor against slavery), we must be careful to ensure our time and energy are focused on what the Holy Spirit would have us do. I think that for many it is easier to speak up for their rights than it is to speak up for their Lord. We are universally and daily called to be salt and light, to share our faith. We are selectively and periodically called to focus our efforts on certain causes.

⬤   *There is a danger in misunderstanding God's agenda and subsequently, our responsibility.* Jesus vigorously denounced the religious leaders for their blatant hypocrisy, spoke about caring for the needy and angrily cleared out the moneychangers who were polluting the Temple. Yet, primarily He came to save people from their sins not denounce them for their sins (Mat. 1:21).   His ministry was primarily threefold: teaching, preaching the good news of the kingdom of God and healing (Mat. 4:23).

Romans 1:28-32 reveals that people reject God even though they know He exists. This rejection comes from a flesh-pleasing obsession. Therefore, when we confront evil in people, we must be careful to avoid focusing on the symptoms, while missing the real problem, which is the suppression of truth about God. God calls us to share truth by living out the truth! The essence of His truth is love. Without love, we revert to legalism, judgmental spirits and incessant faultfinding. Do you like it when people constantly point out your failings? What wins people's hearts is the unmistakable love God has for them. Christ did not come to set better laws; He came to fulfill the law. Laws do not spiritually save people.

A careful reading of the New Testament makes it abundantly clear that the world gets worse before Jesus returns. Consequently, our earnestness must first be in our Savior not in our safeguards. Our paramount concern should always be to share the Savior knowing we may suffer dire consequences. Should we speak out against evil—certainly! Should we advance righteousness—of course, but always in the context of humility, consistency and love. If we would see those around us enmeshed in evil as headed for hell, maybe we would understand that it is our hope in Jesus that they critically need. If the Holy Spirit leads me to drive to Salem I will go, otherwise, I will continue to love those stuck in perversion by sharing Jesus!

Inspiration   † † †

Let a man set his heart only on doing the will of God and he is instantly free. If we understand our first and sole duty to consist of loving God supremely and loving everyone, even our enemies, for God's dear sake, then we can enjoy spiritual tranquility under every circumstance.—A.W. Tozer

Earnestness is not by any means everything; it is very often a subtle form of pious self-idolatry, because it is obsessed with the method and not with the Master.—Oswald Chambers in *Christian Discipline*

Pop Can Tabs

Years ago, the Vietnam Traveling Wall arrived in Portland, Oregon. Etched in somber stone is the name of every veteran killed in Indochina. During the opening ceremony, I represented the 104th Division. Afterwards, the special people from the cemetery that planned the event invited me to dinner.

Laurie, one of the women who work at the Lincoln Memorial Center, gave me a tour of the grounds. She showed me a display put together by Milwaukee High School. Ken, the history teacher, had the teens collect tabs used to open soda pop cans. Each tab represented an American killed from the Revolutionary War to the current conflict in Iraq. Rows upon rows of tabs strung over wire represented each war. More Americans died in our Civil War than any other conflict (over 620,000) and this was graphically illustrated by panels that stretched out of sight in comparison to most conflicts depicted by a panel or less.

It took twelve years for the school to assemble this static presentation and every three days they add new tabs as Soldiers continue to die around the world. As I continued to think about what I witnessed, Laurie led me back inside for a salmon supper. At our table, a woman shared how her coworkers did not want to hear her talk about her Marine son and the war in Iraq. Another woman, whose son was shot down and killed in Mosul, shared how her 20-something female supervisor asked her to stop talking to coworkers about his death and the war. She quit her job in disgust. I was amazed at the irony of a high school that yearly honors America's veterans inside a city that in many ways has no stomach for protracted suffering and little tolerance for the notion that freedom comes at a cost.

Jeremiah 15:15—You know, LORD; remember me and take note of me. Avenge me against my persecutors. In Your patience, don't take me away. Know that I suffer disgrace for Your honor.

How fortunate we are that God responds to our failings with unlimited grace. As we approach another Memorial Day, let us remember those who lost their lives to preserve our liberties and let us praise and worship our God who never gets tired of us. As you remember those who died, please take time to pray for those alive but spiritually dead.

Inspiration   † † †

To give real service you must add something which cannot be bought or measured with money, and that is sincerity and integrity.—Douglas Adams, English author, (1952-2001)

Guarding the reputation of others is a deep and lasting service.—Richard J. Foster in *Celebration of Discipline*

The Ultimate Business Card

Nahum 1:7—The LORD is good, a stronghold in a day of distress; He cares for those who take refuge in Him.

In our culture, it is common for people to exchange business cards. Those tree-descended pieces tell others what we do, who we are and how we can be contacted. The information had better be good if we hope to gain anything.

Now imagine when you place your trust and allegiance in Jesus Christ, that He hands you His business card. The card's first line simply reads, *I AM*—the name by which God introduced Himself to Moses. The name Jesus applied to Himself—His deity, messiah-invoking calling card that nearly resulted in His stoning (John 8:58). The NIV study notes for Exo. 3:14 say of "*I AM who I AM*": The name by which God wished to be known and worshiped in Israel—the name that expressed His character as the dependable and faithful God who desires the full trust of His people.

The next line on Jesus' card is His title, the most profound label known to mankind: Everlasting Savior, Lamb of God, Living Water, Prince of Peace, King of kings, Lion of Judah, Son of Man . . . By His title we have hope. By His supernatural grace, our perfect Lord takes any who will follow Him and makes them good.

The dictionary gives twenty definitions for the word "good." When good comes from God, perhaps the most appropriate rending of the word is "worthy of respect, honorable, genuine." It is a great thing to be good—to wake up in the morning clean, morally upright; to have at the heart of our action honest concern for others; to feel the flow of worthy thoughts that lift the spirit up; to act in such a manner that we encourage those around us. O yes, it is good to be good.

So why not carry a God-card in your wallet or purse! His name is the name in which we hope, for His name is good! His name is the reminder that though life may be full of trials and challenge, our future is secure! By His blood, we are *good to go*!

Inspiration   † † †

And sometimes as I think of how precious the name of Jesus Christ is to God, how He delights to honor the name of His Son, I grow very bold and ask God for great things.—R.A. Torrey, evangelist, pastor, educator and author, (1856-1928), in *The Power of Prayer*

God has never, in the history of mankind, allowed his name to go long offended.—David Wilkerson, evangelist and pastor, (1931-2011)

Idolatry

Sam and I ate lunch with my Aunt B.J. in a Chinese restaurant. Prominently displayed on a counter was a large brass Buddha. That obese figure reminded me of the hundreds of millions of people who still worship inanimate man-made objects and live constantly in fear of offending evil spirits. Imagine how God must feel! He created us to fellowship with Him. He made us with a spectacular relationship in mind and what happens—people reject Him for their own creations.

Habakkuk 2:18-19—What use is a carved idol after its craftsman carves it? It is only a cast image, a teacher of lies. For the one who crafts its shape trusts in it and makes idols that cannot speak. Woe to him who says to wood: Wake up! or to mute stone: Come alive! Can it teach? Look! It may be plated with gold and silver, yet there is no breath in it at all.

An idol is a false god; an image adored. Idolatry constitutes excessive dedication to, or dependence upon, anything that replaces God. View idols as material objects and it is logical to bemoan anyone foolish enough to bow before them. Perhaps that is why Satan so easily seduces wealthy nations. We cannot see or admit to our idolatry.

Can work or self-dependence become idolatry? It can if we believe our fate is dependent upon our work and that it is more important than anything else we do. *"For it is by grace you have been saved, through faith—and this not from yourselves, it is the gift of God—not by works, so that no one can boast. For we are God's workmanship . . ."* (Eph. 2:8-10a NIV).

Can money become idolatry? It can if it steals our heart. *"You cannot serve both God and Money" (Luke 16:13b NIV). "For the love of money is a root of all kinds of evil, and by craving it, some have wandered away from the faith and pierced themselves with many pains"* (1 Ti. 6:10).

Can possessions become idolatry? Yes, when they consume our attention. *"Do not store up for yourselves treasures on earth . . . For where your treasure is, there your heart will be also"* (Mat. 6:19a,21 NIV).

Can another person cause idolatry? *"This is what the LORD says: 'Cursed is the man who trusts in mankind, who makes human flesh his strength and turns his heart from the LORD'"* (Jer. 17:5).

Let nothing steal our heart from God or devalue His throne! He is jealous for our love. After all He has done for us, how do we dare not make Him first? Our cause is not to emplace what will burn, or embrace what cannot save, or replace our preeminent Lord. *"Therefore, put to death whatever in you is worldly: sexual immorality, impurity, lust, evil desire, and greed, which is idolatry. Because of these, God's wrath comes on the disobedient"* (Col. 3:5,6). Our first cause is to love God! King David sang it well, *"How happy is the man who has put his trust in the LORD and has not turned to the proud or to those who run after lies!"* (Psa. 40:4).

Silence

Silence is golden. It is a paradoxical potion to a stressed spirit. I say paradoxical because often in our busyness, we cry out for God and we cannot hear Him. He may seem absent from the roar of everyday life. Indeed, I wonder if we crowd Him out by out incessant action. No wonder He impressed upon the sons of Korah *"Be still, and know that I am God; I will be exalted among the nations, I will be exalted in the earth"* (Psa. 46:10 NIV).

In the deafening silence of the Alaskan muskeg, the quiet becomes a soothing sonnet. Nature rises up and proclaims the majesty of God. The brilliant hues of a fading sun, the shimmering surface of a placid lake, the outstretched limbs of gnarled spruce, and the purple berries of a faithful bush do not whisper praise for some quixotic bang—they glorify their heavenly Maker.

Zephaniah 3:17—The LORD your God is among you, a warrior who saves. He will rejoice over you with gladness. He will bring you quietness with His love. He will delight in you with shouts of joy.
Mark 4:39—He got up, rebuked the wind, and said to the sea, "Silence! Be still!" The wind ceased, and there was a great calm.

May I encourage you to get off your proverbial freeway the next time you see a rest area! Find a place of stillness and wait for your loving Lord— the One to whom all creation sings. Let the chills of joy that come from an affirming heart encourage you. Let silence speak her peace. If you cannot find a place of quietness, ask the Lord who stilled the storm to bring you calm. Come away stronger, wiser, blessed, after lingering in your season of listening. God has not vanished. May He quiet you with His love! May you hear Him when He is ready to speak.

Inspiration † † †

Silence is one of the hardest arguments to refute.—Josh Billings, pen name of Henry Wheeler Shaw, humorist, (1818-1885)

Silence is the mother of truth.—Benjamin Disraeli

Silence is the element in which great things fashion themselves together.—Thomas Carlyle, Scottish essayist, satirist, and historian, (1795-1881)

Gentleness

We must have looked funny to the children and women watching us. Here we were, six men—each of us incapable of separating two plastic buckets. We tried twisting and pulling to no avail. One man used his pocketknife. I tried dropping the buckets on the floor. It was as if someone had super glued each set of buckets together. It felt like our manhood was on the line—this was getting embarrassing!

I happened to be holding two of the buckets and just used my thumbs to push when one of the boys watching us noticed movement. Sure enough, the buckets came apart. We discovered that by gentle coaxing we could easily separate the buckets. *Hmmm.*

Zechariah 9:9—Rejoice greatly, Daughter Zion! Shout in triumph, Daughter Jerusalem! See, your King is coming to you; He is righteous and victorious, humble and riding on a donkey, on a colt, the foal of a donkey.
Ephesians 4:2—Be completely humble and gentle; be patient, bearing with one another in love. (NIV)

God picked a donkey over a chariot for the grand entrance of His Son! So often, we resort to force to accomplish our will. Isn't it interesting that Jesus, the possessor of infinite power, sparingly picked up a whip? Jesus never slammed truth into the brains of His hearers. Neither does the Holy Spirit yell at us. His gentle whisper is quite capable of convicting our mischievous hearts. The Apostle Paul wrote, *"By the meekness and gentleness of Christ, I appeal to you . . .* (2 Co. 10:1 NIV).

Harsh words and overbearing authority beget resentment and foment bitterness. Gentleness engenders trust. So be gentle. Let people know your confidence (strength) is in the Lord. It's amazing what you can accomplish with the right application!

Inspiration † † †

In our rough-and-rugged individualism, we think of gentleness as weakness, being soft, and virtually spineless. Not so! . . . Gentleness includes such enviable qualities as having strength under control, being calm and peaceful when surrounded by a heated atmosphere, emitting a soothing effect on those who may be angry or otherwise beside themselves, and possessing tact and gracious courtesy that causes others to retain their self-esteem and dignity . . . Instead of losing, the gentle gain. Instead of being ripped off and taken advantage of, they come out ahead!—Charles R. Swindoll, pastor, author, radio program host

Power can do by gentleness what violence fails to accomplish.—Latin Proverb

Nepes

Have you ever wondered much about your soul, what it is, its purpose, etc.? There are four common theories as to the soul's origin. They are:

1. *Traducianism*—our soul and body come from our parents (Lutheran and Eastern Orthodox Churches).

2. *Preexistence of all souls* (Origen and Mormons)

3. *Reincarnation* (Hinduism)

4. Creationism—God creates a fresh soul for each body (Roman Catholics and most reformed theologians)

Zechariah 12:1—The word of the LORD concerning Israel. A declaration of the LORD, who stretched out the heavens, laid the foundation of the earth, and formed the spirit of man within him.

Scripture teaches that God breathed life into Adam (Genesis 2:7) and then rested after creation. Furthermore, we know from Rom. 5 that sin enters the world through Adam. These facts strongly led Tertullian, Martin Luther and others to argue for traducianism. Creationists counter by citing Isa. 42:5; Zec. 12:1; and Heb. 12:9, as evidence that God directly creates each human soul. Jerome, Calvin and Thomas Aquinas believed and taught this.[21]

A common understanding among Christians is that the soul is the eternal essence of a human, "the seat or locus of human will, understanding, and personality." Dichotomists believe that there is only a body and soul but trichotomists use 1 Th. 5:23 to refute this: *". . . And may your spirit, soul, and body be kept sound and blameless for the coming of our Lord Jesus Christ."* Saint Augustine described the soul as "a special substance, endowed with reason, adapted to rule the body."[22] He refused to choose sides between Traducian or Creation proponents. While he favored the former, he reflected honestly a great uncertainty.

Soul in the NT normally means an individual spiritual entity with a material body so that a person is thought of as a body-soul, spirit is the special gift of God which places one in relationship to him . . . it can be said that soul in Scripture is conceived to be an immaterial principle created by God, which is usually united to a body and gives it life; however, the soul continues to exist after death in human beings (Matt. 10:28; James 5:20; Rev. 6:9; 20:4), a condition which is ended at the close of this age (1 Co. 15:35-55).[23]

The Hebrew word, *nepes*, occurs 757 times in Scripture and primarily refers to life or soul, but in rare occasions, it synonymously refers to body and spirit. The most frequent reference to soul (23x), is in the form of exhortation to engage all of our heart and soul in seeking the Lord, or doing our best. I would call this "soul'd out for Jesus! The Greek word *psyche* means life or soul; *pneuma* means spirit and *soma* means body. Never are they used interchangeably. Genesis 35:18 depicts Rachel's *nephesh* as departing. Elijah prayed in 1 Ki. 17:21 that that widow's dead son would receive back his *nephesh*. Clearly in Scripture, the soul (life) separates from the body at death.

The soul is frequently mentioned in Scripture as capable of experiencing emotions ranging from sorrow (18x), bitterness, hate, to love, joy, etc. The soul yearns or waits for God (10x), finds refuge in Him, praises Him, and suffers during times of persecution or difficulty.

Ezekiel 18:4 says, "*. . . The soul who sins is the one who will die*" (NIV). Jesus taught that the soul and the body were both subject to punishment in hell. Matthew 10:28 reads, "*Don't fear those who kill the body but are not able to kill the soul; rather, fear Him who is able to destroy both soul and body in hell.*"

"Throughout the history of the Christian church, there has been no clearly defined and universally accepted metaphysical conception of the soul."[24] If this is so, then why is all this important to you and me? We know that we are destined to die and to be judged (Heb. 9:27). Whether it is our soul, or our spirit, or both which survive for eternity, God knows. In Mat. 11:28,29, Jesus said, "*Come to Me, all you who are weary and burdened, and I will give you rest. Take my yoke upon you and learn from Me, for I am gentle and humble in heart, and you will find rest for your souls*" (NIV). His words are a promise for all to whom He reveals His Father (see vs. 27). Clearly, the key truth with respect to the soul is knowledge of God. Is your soul at rest?

Inspiration †††

You don't have a soul. You are a Soul. You have a body.—C. S. Lewis

Who can map out the various forces at play in one soul? Man is a great depth, O Lord. The hairs of his head are easier by far to count than his feeling, the movements of his heart.—Saint Augustine

Just as the soul fills the body, so God fills the world. Just as the soul bears the body, so God endures the world. Just as the soul sees but is not seen, so God sees but is not seen. Just as the soul feeds the body, so God gives food to the world.—Marcus Tullius Cicero, Roman philosopher, politician, lawyer, orator (106-43 B.C.)

Stagnation

Stinking water is a sign of death. A putrid pond occurs because there is no intake of fresh water, no stream or bubbling spring that pours in to replenish and invigorate. Algae proliferate and choke out the oxygen necessary to sustain life. Brown slime wins the day.

God is not a fan of stagnation.

I know your works, that you are neither cold nor hot. I wish that you were cold or hot. So, because you are lukewarm, and neither hot nor cold, I am going to vomit you out of My mouth. Because you say, "I'm rich; I have become wealthy, and need nothing," and you don't know that you are wretched, pitiful, poor, blind, and naked . . . (Revelation 3:15-17).

Stagnation begins when we think we are without need, or we think only of our needs. We forget our utter dependence on God. Often our self-reliance is a subtle process of languishing. Truly, a sinful will cannot flourish. As we overlook the signs of our decay, we become calloused and insensate (witless and unfeeling).

The scary fact is that stagnation often occurs in the midst of religiousness. We become so content in form that we miss the *Former*. We feast on rote and rot. We read God's Word *to check the completion block* and stroll into His throne with our memorized shtick occasionally wondering why heaven seems remarkably indifferent! We choose that which makes us comfortable and miss the very prodding God wants to deepen us. We abandon commitments to our brothers and sisters to appease our own interests. *God help us!*

Malachi 1:10—"I wish one of you would shut the temple doors, so you would no longer kindle a useless fire on My altar! I am not pleased with you," says the LORD of Hosts, "and I will accept no offering from your hands."

It is not a good thing when God wishes we would shut our temple doors, when He finds our living sacrifice detestable. These are not days to stagnate. The end approaches and there will be an accounting for our condition. Without repentance and a strong fear of God, there can be no revival or blessed nourishment from His living water. King David in stagnation's abyss, cried out, *"God, create a clean heart for me and renew a steadfast spirit within me . . . Restore the joy of Your salvation to me, and give me a willing spirit"* (Psa. 51:10,12). Are you lethargic? Then cry out for God's merciful hand to discipline you. Ask His Holy Spirit to breathe upon your embers until they sustain that fiery joy that knows and relishes the privilege of walking in His presence. After all, God made you for rich river fellowship, not *pond*erous living.

Loving the Wrong Thing

Malachi 2:1-2—"Therefore, this decree is for you priests: If you don't listen, and if you don't take it to heart to honor My name," says the LORD of Hosts, "I will send a curse among you, and I will curse your blessings. In fact, I have already begun to curse them because you are not taking it to heart."

The calling of the priest is fraught with danger. And who are the priests?—all of God's children (1 Pe. 2:5). In this case, I refer to those who serve in any Christian organization in a position of authority. We ought to be in constant prayer for them. Most begin their spiritual service in eager anticipation for their desire is to please their Savior. So long as they hunger to hear His voice and avoid a complacent, quotidian (ordinary) love, they will do fine.

We must hold those who lead accountable for their walk with God. For as surely as that union wavers trouble will follow. What happens is not hard to understand. The subtle day arrives when God's servant falls more in love with what he or she does than with the One served. The office or organization becomes the source and place of fulfillment. The leader is seduced by the admiration of people, the power, and the constant high of standing in front. This euphoria crushes the need to spend time in prayer and spoils the appetite for holy, private communion with God.

One cannot live for the organization and remain true to the Vine. The former will suck the very lifeblood of its beholder. God may actually curse the blessings because they no longer have anything to do with Him. Satan offered Jesus all the kingdoms of the world and their splendor if He would worship him. Jesus said, *"Go away, Satan! For it is written: Worship the Lord your God, and serve only Him"* (Mat. 4:10).

Some of the bitterest people I know are those who sacrificially gave their all to being chairman of the board, leading worship, pastoring, or administrating. How can this be? If their heart found value in the organization, they were certain to disappoint for organizations are made of fallible people. In contrast, there is no trace of bitterness in those who suffer repeated defeat in battle whose hearts are set fully on knowing Jesus. Those who make Him Lord rise with joy and go to bed content in the assurance that what matters most is not the organization, not the position held, not the progress attained or the status achieved but rather a vibrant relationship with Almighty God.

Inspiration †††

Priesthood is not a convenient, historically conditioned form of Church organisation, but is rooted in the Incarnation, in the priesthood and mission of Christ himself.—Arthur Middleton, politician and signer of the Declaration of Independence, (1742-1787)

Ten Principles for Effective Training

Many people have studied the life and ministry of Jesus. There is much written about His three-fold ministry of teaching, preaching and healing revealed in the gospels. However, it seems to me that Jesus' most important work was His fourth ministry of training! Where would the world be today had He not invested His life in the lives of His followers? John Maxwell, a superb trainer of leaders says, "A leader is one who knows the way, goes the way and shows the way."

Both leaders and followers understand the importance of effective training. One of the reasons why I love the Bible is that it provides principles applicable to our lives at work and at home. Jesus was the world's greatest trainer! A careful study of His methods reveals an intentional approach to coaching that if applied by us yields life-changing results. May I share with you at least ten principles He demonstrated?

Effective training consists of:

● *Preparation*—Luke 6:12. Before Jesus embarked down the path of leading anyone, He spent a night in prayer. He sought His Father's direction in who He should train.

● *Obedience to God's Plan*—John 6:38. Jesus followed God's training strategy and plan.

● *Calling* and *Selection*—Luke 6:13. Many people followed Christ before He intentionally called twelve men to be His closely trained disciples.

● *Modeling*—Mat. 9:35. J. Oswald Sanders wrote in his book *Spiritual Leadership*, "It is a general principle that we can influence and lead others only so far as we ourselves have gone."

● *Vision-casting*—Mat. 9:37—"*The harvest is plentiful but the workers are few.*" Men and women rise to the challenge if they truly understand the need and the task before them!

● *Instructing*—Mat. 11:1. Effective training involves the careful application of truth. After Jesus left earth, His apostles amazed the world by their works, wisdom and heart because they learned from an awesome Teacher. They had many questions. He had perfect answers.

● *Simplicity*! Jesus modeled a simple, uncomplicated ministry.

● *Empowering*—Luke 9:1. God's Son gave His apprentices power and authority to minister. A bird has to leave the nest to fly!

● *Application* (hands-on)—Luke 9:2. The mark of an effective trainer is reproduction. Jesus sent His team out to do what He did. They came back successful and there was great celebration in heaven!

● *Commissioning*—Mat. 28:19,20. Go! The time comes when the trainer must let go and send out the trainees. The hand of the invisible leader lives on in the lives of the visibly affected.

Matthew 4:19—"Come, follow Me," Jesus said, "and I will make you fishers of men."

Inspiration † † †

We teach what we know, we reproduce what we are.—Richard Schmidgall

Affinity is not Easy

Matthew 5:43,44—You have heard that it was said, Love your neighbor and hate your enemy. But I tell you, love your enemies and pray for those who persecute you.

Last night was the second round of soccer playoffs for my coed team. During the game, one of our players chose not to follow the game plan I had laid out before we started play. Because she did not cover defensively her assigned competitor, the other team was able to score. When I called to her attention the fact that her failure to follow the plan cost our team she became argumentative and stomped off the field and went home.

Without Christ, I'd have been furious. I do not care for this woman and her whining, her arrogance and selfish spirit. I don't like the way she tries to bully others to get her own way. No one on our team cares for her. Without Jesus, I could think of lots of things to tell her. However, because of Jesus, I realize her attitude is the symptom of a deeper problem. She is unhappy. She needs the Savior.

I do not need to dislike her; I need to pray for her. I can have an affinity for this person because Jesus in me makes me able to love what my own flesh would detest. Affinity is not easy. If I love Jesus, I must learn to see people as He does. In doing so, my heart is changed.

How incredible that the God of the universe chose to have affinity with me, a sinful wretched creature. Mind boggling? Awesome! Humbling . . .

Inspiration   † † †

Want to see a miracle? Plant a word of love heart-deep in a person's life. Nurture it with a smile and a prayer, and watch what happens.—Max Lucado in *The Applause of Heaven*

Love is the affinity which links and draws together the elements of the world . . . Love, in fact, is the agent of universal synthesis.—Pierre Teilhard de Chardin, French philosopher, (1881-1955)

God does not regard the greatness of the work but the love with which it is performed.—Brother Lawrence & Frank Laubach in *Practicing His Presence*

Rock or Sand?

Matthew 7:21—Not everyone who says to Me, "Lord, Lord!" will enter the kingdom of heaven, but only the one who does the will of My Father in heaven.

Jesus tells the story of the wise and foolish builders. The wise person hears God's Word, applies it, and is likened to someone carving a foundation into solid rock to build a kingdom home. The foolish person hears God's Word but forsakes application. This person is like a builder who constructs a house on sand. The day arises when a storm of dynamic fury hits. Rock rules. Those in the subdivision of sand are ruined.

Why would anyone build on sand? Could it be that there are many people who honestly believe they are following God? They can quote from the Bible. They regularly attend church. They carry Jesus' business cards. They make their homepage *religion.com*. They recite a thousand rosaries and play the songs of KLOVE. But is He Lord if they build from the plans of their own blueprints? Is He Lord when His will is ignored by their whim? Is He Lord if His guidance is set aside for personal agendas? How simple it is to fly the flag of a rugged cross over earthly castles. But the proof of ownership is not sealed by flapping cloth. A house may look wonderful externally but sit on shifting ground. A limicolous (mud dwelling) existence awaits those who disregard observing God's Word.

A floor of sand is the mark of selfishness. A granular base warms the feet of fools, beckons whole communities to build in ease only for eventual erasure by the waves of a Father whose clear guidance was spurned. A basement in rock is the place of selflessness. The proof of ownership is inside the heart of those morally changed because they listened. When the lightning jigs, the thunder bellows and the high-pitched wail of a violent wind foretells disaster, people of the Rock snuggle in the arms of a heavenly Daddy safe because they put His words into practice. If it were not so His Kingdom would be a hollow place for those with clever mantras. Are you building on rock or on sand? The storm will tell.

Inspiration † † †

The "kingdom of Heaven" is a condition of the heart—not something that comes "upon the earth" or "after death."—Friedrich Nietzsche, German philosopher, (1844-1900)

There is no place in the Kingdom for a slacker, for such an attitude not only precludes any growth in grace and knowledge, but also destroys any usefulness on the world battlefield of evangelism.—Robert E. Coleman in *The Master Plan of Evangelism*

Be Made Clean

Matthew 8:2,3—Right away a man with a serious skin disease came up and knelt before Him, saying, "Lord, if You are willing, You can make me clean." Reaching out His hand He touched him, saying, "I am willing; be made clean." Immediately his disease was healed.

I recently engaged in a study of Jesus healing in the gospels as part of preaching through the book of Matthew. Healing was a huge part of Jesus' ministry. Jesus healed people because He loved them and out of obedience to the mission God gave Him. His miracles brought glory to God from those who witnessed or heard about His actions with the exception of most of the religious leaders, who resented Him for healing on the Sabbath.

Every time the sick or demon-possessed are mentioned in the New Testament in the presence of Jesus, He healed them. Jesus touched all kinds of needy people: Jews, Gentiles, old, young, those born with afflictions, those stricken with illness later in life, the demon-possessed etc. (Mat.4:23,24; 9:35,12:15, 14:35,36; 18:1,2)

Whenever healing did not take place in the gospels it was caused either by a lack of faith (Mat. 17:14-18; Mark 6:5,6) or a lack of prayer (Mark 9:25-29). Scripture further reveals that God's will was not always to bring healing—(2 Ch. 16:12,13; 2 Sa. 12:14-18; 2 Co. 12:7-10).

Jesus commanded His followers to heal those they encountered who were sick or demon-possessed in the towns they entered (Mat.10:1,8). After He ascended to heaven, healing continued to be a significant aspect of the Apostles' ministry. They were effective because He gave them His authority. *Healing always takes place under the context of God's authority.* Nowhere does Scripture say God removed His clout from us so that we cannot experience His healing power today!

One of the most potent ways we can witness to people in our community is to minister to those who are sick in the powerful name of Jesus. Is it possible that we do not pray for others to be healed because we are afraid God might not respond? Praying with someone for healing is a tremendous expression of love. If the Holy Spirit gives us the freedom to pray for someone afflicted we should do so. Whether or not the healing takes place, is not up to us but to God. I prayed God would heal my mother and she died. I prayed God would heal my son and He miraculously preserved his life. While I may not always understand God's plan or purpose, I can confidently rest assured that He knows what is best.

There are compelling reasons why Jesus healed *all* who came to Him. We need to follow His example. It is easy to criticize the political correctness (PC) movement. Yet, are we guilty of emphasizing spiritual correctness (SC)? *"Lord if you are willing"* is the pious prayer of the saint for the stricken. Often I wonder if that prayer could really be translated, "*Lord,*

I don't want to look bad, I don't want to let this person down and I certainly don't want You to look weak, so if this person isn't healed, obviously You were not willing."

This is hardly the stuff of faith! Are you willing to trust God to work through you to bring healing in the lives of those hurting around you? Then boldly go before the throne and ask! God may use you to reach a town, a city, a nation—whose real sickness is the need to know Jesus!

Inspiration † † †

Here bring your wounded hearts, here tell your anguish; Earth has no sorrow that Heaven cannot heal.—Thomas More, English author, (1478-1535)

We have every right to plead God's promises in holy persistence until God checks us or suggests that healing is not His will. Undoubtedly it would please God if our faith for healing were much stronger.—Wesley L. Duewel in *Touch the World through Prayer*

Partnership and the Trinity

In the fourth century AD, a bishop by the name of Athanasius gained fame for defending the Christian faith against a heresy spreading under the teaching of Arius, a bishop in Alexandria. Arius contended that God created Jesus and that He was not eternal or omnipotent like His Father. *The Athanasian Creed* was probably not composed until several decades after Athanasius' death in AD 373. It was never recognized by an ecumenical council as an official creed of the Church yet it remains an excellent summation of the doctrine of the Trinity. Here is part of what Athanasius taught:

> We worship one God in Trinity, and Trinity in Unity, neither confounding the persons, nor dividing the substance. For there is one Person of the Father, another of the Son, and another of the Holy Spirit. But the godhead of the Father, of the Son, and of the Holy Spirit, is all one, the glory equal, the majesty co-eternal. Such as the Father is, such is the Son, and such is the Holy Spirit. The Father uncreated, the Son uncreated, and the Holy Spirit uncreated. The Father incomprehensible, the Son incomprehensible, and the Holy Spirit incomprehensible. The Father eternal, the Son eternal, and the Holy Spirit eternal. And yet they are not three eternals, but one Eternal. As also there are not three incomprehensibles, nor three uncreated, but one Uncreated, and one Incomprehensible. So likewise the Father is Almighty, the Son Almighty, and the Holy Spirit Almighty. And yet they are not three almighties, but one Almighty. So the Father is God, the Son is God, and the Holy Spirit is God. And yet they are not three gods, but one God . . .

The Trinity is an essential component of what we believe about our God. Just as we cannot explain or understand Him because of His awesomeness, so we cannot articulate easily to anyone His three-in-oneness. It should not surprise us that monotheistic Muslims wrestle against our belief as we explain to them what surely seems polytheistic. This calls for humility in articulating a doctrinal tenet best seen at work and in purpose in God's holy Word.

What the Trinity teaches us that is so profoundly moving is divine partnership. If one purpose of leadership is to provide direction, surely another is to provide solution. God looked at the human race He made which clearly required both. There are unimaginable and imaginable ways He could have led us. As our Supreme Leader, He chose to relate and rescue us through Jesus and to redeem and raise us through His Spirit (Rom. 8:11).

What the Trinity calls us to is breathtakingly deep, extended partnership. In the passage below, we see just one of numerous examples of statements that Jesus made that reveal God's desire that we work with Him to accomplish His purpose.

Matthew 9:37,38—Then He said to His disciples, "The harvest is abundant, but the workers are few. Therefore, pray to the Lord of the harvest to send out workers into His harvest."

Can you meditate and move forward in the exhilarating truth that God wants to work with you? We are not some zoo creature He invented for celestial amusement. He made us to participate, to cooperate and find meaning in His eternal work for His eternal glory. As He works with Himself, so He wants to include us in unity. Are you living like a partner or did you stop believing at some point that God might truly want you teamed up with Him? Let us collaborate with God in prayer and in work in the humble realization that He wants us!

Inspiration † † †

The Doctrine of the Trinity teaches that within the unity of the one Godhead there are three separate persons who are coequal in power, nature, and eternity.—Walter Martin, pastor, Christian apologist, (1928-1989)

Accessible

Matthew 11:28—Come to Me, all of you who are weary and burdened, and I will give you rest.

I attended a conference and was surprised to discover a banquet fee of which I was unaware. I did not have enough cash. I did not bring my checkbook and the conference administrators could not take a credit card. This could have been a somewhat embarrassing dilemma. Fortunately, around the corner from the Ramada Inn was a 7-11 convenience store with an ATM. From it, I was able to access cash and pay my dues.

Do you ever have times where you feel trapped by discouragement? Your emotional wallet is empty. Your ability to call upon friends is stymied by their busyness. Your family is enmeshed with their own needs. Perhaps even the advice you receive is not enough to matter. The debris of insufficiency chokes all roads to relief.

God is far more valuable than a conveniently placed ATM machine. No matter where we are, He is accessible. He does not put your prayer on hold until He can get to them. He timelessly cares for you and me with unlimited resources. His love is perfect.

So how come when I pray nothing happens? Why are there times I feel God isn't there for me? If you have ever asked these questions, you are in good company with a multitude of other followers of the Almighty.

Perhaps the answer to accessibility is integrity. When we go to God the issue is not whether He is there, the issue is whether we are honest with Him. If we have preconceived notions as to how He must respond, we may completely miss what He is trying to tell us. If we are less than honest with our burdens, then God may withhold His aid from us. For example, what if I ask God to take away my discouragement and yet my real problem is overeating? I sense God is not there for me because I remain discouraged. However, the real cause of my discouragement is my unwillingness to ask God to address my inability to say no to food.

Notice Jesus said, *"All of you, take up My yoke and learn from Me, because I am gentle and humble in heart, and you will find rest for yourselves"* (11:29). If we come to God, we must be teachable. God is most accessible when we are most willing to learn from Him. Share truthfully what you are going through and need and you will encounter a loving Shepherd in whom you find rest and help in accordance with His timing and will. Sometimes our agenda precludes us from understanding that God's timing may be deliberately fashioned for our training and betterment. We may undergo suffering because our character is in need of refining. We may face unresponsiveness because He is testing our faith. The key is not to give up, but to persevere—asking for help and believing He cares!

Parables

Once there was a man who talked incessantly on the cell phone wherever he drove. Once in the phone zone he was oblivious to his surroundings. So on June 7 he missed his wife waving at him from her red car with a flat tire. Nor did he realize the bump on the road was a Siamese cat he ran over, the favorite pet of an autistic child. He nodded *yes* to the words of his backseat son who told him he thought he should turn right at the light. Not listening he continued straight ahead. Later he broke his boy's heart when he yelled at him for letting him get lost. He won a coveted contract but missed the ballgame.

Matthew 13:34,35—Jesus told the crowds all these things in parables, and He would not speak anything to them without a parable, so that what was spoken through the prophet might be fulfilled: I will open My mouth in parables; I will declare things kept secret from the foundation of the world.

Did you know that the preferred method of teaching for Jesus was telling parables? He taught this way for multiple reasons. *First, He knew that people would remember a story.* Even nonChristians can often recite a Bible lesson they learned as a child. *Second, Jesus was more concerned about reaching the heart than penetrating the mind.* The advantage of a story is that we can both remember and discover the meaning the Holy Spirit reveals. Jesus' listeners were sometimes clueless to what His stories meant (see Luke 8:10). Often He had to explain them to His closest followers. If a person's heart is not open, clarity of teaching is not the point is it? *Third, stories are popular in every culture and language and therefore invite replication. Fourth, parables provide an indirect means to deliver a strong exhortation. Fifth, parables deliver lessons from everyday life so that people can relate to the message.*

If you want to help people, remember that your life is a story and parables surround you. Instead of lecturing (boring) people with facts and information, consider sharing what God is teaching you in your day-to-day living! Yes, I know God's Word will not return void and it is noble to teach it. But Jesus did not expound verse by verse through Deuteronomy. Passing information in the form of facts or points is a weak mechanism for ensuring memory recall and a poor means for reaching hearts.

Your life is a treasure-trove of truth. Why settle for methods that research already shows is weak when God blessed you with experiences that will touch your hearers? Be vulnerable. Be real. Be fresh! (What God did in your life ten years ago is past history. What is He doing in your life today?) Do not poison children into hating spiritual principles! While you are excited about some Greek prepositional phrase, your listeners are negotiating the storms of life. They desperately need truth they can remember. Your sensitivity will mean much more to them than your smartness. So communicate effectively and if you are tired, have the courage to let someone else share until you are refreshed!

If you are a pastor or teacher, do not measure your effectiveness by those exiting who say, "That was a great message!" What do you think they are going to say, "Pastor X, you have a gift for making 30 minutes seem like two hours!" Ask them a week later what they remember or valued—that is a better test. I do not remember any sermon a pastor preached and I think I am a decent listener. What I remember are stories and real-life lessons shared by leaders willing to be vulnerable or creative under the leading of the Holy Spirit. You will know God is using you when your listeners share with others what you shared with them. Tie Scripture into practical examples of how it works out in your life and watch as God blesses your work in the lives of people!

Inspiration † † †

What people hear in a parable is determined by the kingdom sensitivity of their heart.—Jan David Hettinga in *Follow Me*

Life Saver

Fralsarkrans is the Swedish word for life preserver, the kind one throws from the side of a pool or a boat to rescue someone. The literal meaning of the word is "ring of salvation."

Have you ever considered that we all swim in the Sea of Mortality? Some people seem to readily understand this and aggressively seek help. Others stroke nonchalantly as if the dark water was nothing but a placid fluid to ignore. Still others debate while they swim what will enable them to escape drowning. They champion their individual gods, or hope by the quality and efficiency of their effort they will somehow survive.

Matthew 14:29,30—"Come!" He said. And climbing out of the boat, Peter started walking on the water and came toward Jesus. But when he saw the strength of the wind, he was afraid. And beginning to sink he cried out, "Lord, save me!"

Jin and Sui grew up in a rural town in mainland China. Though raised without knowing God, when others would make fun of Him they both felt discomfort. Jin shared how early on a fear of God resided in his heart. His wife, Sui, echoed his feeling.

Both of them moved to England to obtain degrees—Jin as a scientist and Sui in education and media. Later they moved to Sweden. Meanwhile, God began placing people in their path that faithfully expressed His love for them. Jin described it as if they were on a trajectory, a divine course that God placed them on to find Him. For example, while in England, Sui suffered incredible crippling pain after her son Michael was born. In desperation, she cried out to the God she did not know, for help. He responded by sending *Granny* an elderly English woman who had identical problems as a young mother. Granny prescribed the remedy to cure Sui's pain. She also radiated Christ's love!

Later when Sui faced the possibility of cancer, the couple again turned to God. However, this was not an easy decision. Both of them were skeptics. While in China, they saw the deficiencies of Chairman Mao's teachings. Still, how could they trust Jesus? How could they objectively measure and authenticate an unseen Savior? Mathematical equations could not heal pain. No amount of reasoning could dissipate their inner need to fill the void in their hearts with meaning.

On a cold New Year's Eve in Gothenburg, David, Melissa, my dad and I had the awesome privilege of sharing the last leg of a long trajectory Jin and Sui followed to Jesus. They humbly in faith recognized the Ring of Salvation (Jesus), God so lovingly offered them. Though far removed from the disciple Peter, who took his eyes off Christ and began sinking, they voiced similar words, "Lord, save me!" In a sea filled with sin, pain and uncertainty, they listened to God's voice in their hearts. They reached out and prayerfully took hold of His eternal hands.

Do you know someone without Christ? Are you willing to share the Ring of Salvation? I watched a soldier die, felled by a fatal blood clot in his brain. His death was sudden and unexpected and he left two young sons behind. I wonder if anyone ever took the time to share Jesus with him. We never know when our last breath will come. So let us have a sense of urgency about sharing Jesus with those who would never choose to spend an eternity apart from God.

Inspiration   † † †
Thou art the way, the truth and the life.
Without the way, there is no going.
Without the truth, there is no knowing.
Without the life, there is no living.—Thomas a Kempis, Catholic monk, author of *The Imitation of Christ*, one of the best known Christian books on devotion, (ca.1380-1471)

The Value Pipe

Recently I sat on a plane next to a man named John. Several months ago, John's wife of 15 years left him for another man. She was his second wife. His first wife left him after ten years of marriage for similar reasons. When I looked in his eyes, I saw a kind, confused man. I shared with John that the reasons his wives left him were not really about or because of him, they were about the emptiness in their hearts that marriage was not filling. Still interacting with his ex-wives, John knows that neither of them is happy. As he described his current journey to see his newest girlfriend, it was obvious that he also is unfulfilled.

Matthew 16:26—What will it benefit a man if he gains the whole world yet loses his life? Or what will a man give in exchange for his life?

Values shape both our decisions and our destiny. You and I can learn and know much about each other by studying what we pursue. Every one of us has values. We may not be conscious of them but they are there. Norman Douglas said, "You can tell the ideals of a nation by its advertisements." We are all walking advertisements! When Adam and Eve chose to disobey God's instruction in the Garden of Eden, it was a decision made over values. They chose to take what Satan enticed them to have over keeping God's dictum. They opted for knowledge of good and evil and in so doing died.

The problem of misplaced values is that we choose:

● *Good over best.* Saint Augustine taught:

Sin arises when things that are a minor good are pursued as though they were goals in life. If money or affection or power are sought in disproportionate, obsessive ways, then sin occurs. And that sin is magnified when, for these lesser goals, we fail to pursue the highest good and the finest goals . . . we ask ourselves why, in a given situation, we committed a sin, the answer is usually one of two things. Either we wanted to obtain something we didn't have, or we feared losing something we had.[25]

● *What is temporal over what is eternal.* Thomas a Kempis once said, "For a little reward men make a long journey; for eternal life many will scarce lift a foot once from the ground."[26] Ted Koppel, the famous journalist wrote:

> What is largely missing in American life today is a sense of context, of saying or doing anything that is intended or even expected to live beyond the moment. There is no culture in the world that is so obsessed as ours with immediacy. In our journalism, the trivial displaces the momentous because we tend to measure the importance of events by how recently they happened. We have become so obsessed with facts that we have lost all touch with truth.[27]

So how as God's children do we determine what constitute great values? Below is an illustration that might be of help as you answer this question.

The Value Pipe
"Put this in your pipe and live it!"

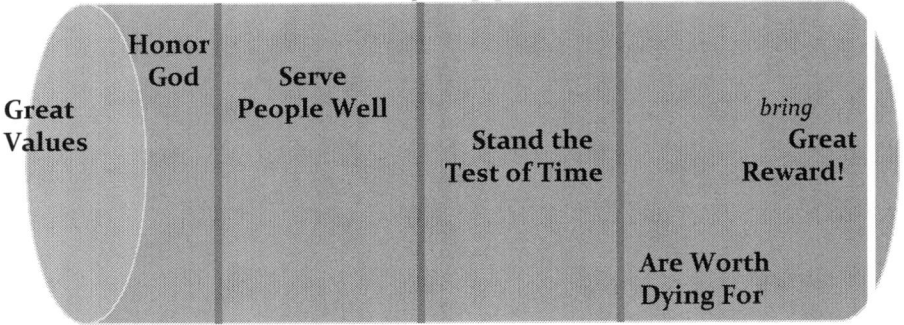

Great Values

Honor God

Serve People Well

Stand the Test of Time

bring Great Reward!

Are Worth Dying For

Inspiration ✝✝✝

No man knows what he is living for until he knows what he'll die for.— Peter Pertocci

Personal Values

There are certain books that essentially bypass the head and go directly to the heart. For example, *Organic Church* by Neil Cole is necessary read if you want challenge and inspiration in how to do ministry to reach people and remain Christ-centered. A nonfiction book that I highly recommend is *Hard Faith*. You can buy it off Amazon.com or purchase it directly from First Cause. I value *Hard Faith* because I know the author Dan Berg and I have seen firsthand how he successfully overcame incredible pain and adversity with his wife. The only reason Dan is walking well today aside from the ever-present grace of God, is that he stuck to his values. He wore the robe of faith when the world suggested other attire.

1 Timothy 4:7,8—But have nothing to do with irreverent and silly myths. Rather, train yourself in godliness, for, the training of the body has a limited benefit, but godliness is beneficial in every way, since it holds promise for the present life and also for the life to come.

Using the value pipe (honors God, serves people well, stands the test of time and is worth dying for) what values do you value? After careful reflection and the admission that this list is in no way exhaustive, here are values I love to champion. I value:

● <u>God</u> *above all* because He made me to love Him and my love brings Him glory! Jonathan Edwards said, "God is the highest good of the reasonable creature, and the enjoyment of Him is the only happiness with which our souls can be satisfied. To go to heaven fully to enjoy God, is infinitely better than the most pleasant accommodations here."

● <u>Faith</u> in God. Without faith it is impossible to please Him! (Heb. 11:6)

● The <u>Bible</u> as God's inspired Word and <u>truth</u> as revealed through the Holy Spirit. Haddon Robinson said, "In every generation the Bible will challenge the values of the age and its definition of success."

● <u>Prayer</u> as a vital discipline for communicating with God. Without prayer, I am self-dependent and headed for disaster. Through prayer, I experience divine blessings. Perhaps this is why Paul taught us to devote ourselves to prayer—Col. 4:2.

● <u>People</u>! I show this through *active <u>fellowship</u>* characterized by a sincere love for others. C.S. Lewis wrote, "Christians are like coals of fire. Together they glow; apart they grow cold."[28] Eph. 4:16 nicely illustrates this.

● The <u>Gospel</u>! Our responsibility is not to build our kingdom but rather to proclaim the Kingdom of God. The gospel should permeate our entire being—Col. 3:16,17.

● <u>Discipleship</u> in the spirit of 2 Timothy 2:2! Discipleship should training our children.

● *Holiness* as demonstrated by _obedience_ to Jesus who said, *"Be holy because I am holy"* (1 Pe. 1:16). Without holiness, we make a mockery of Christ's death on the cross.

● *Fruit of the Spirit* characterized in Gal. 5:22,23 and Eph. 4:1-3. If I do not experience the fruit of the Spirit, I exude a cold, lifeless legalism that is as attractive as burnt toast.

● *Stewardship*! Second Corinthians 9:6-15 nicely shows how stewardship ties directly into love for God, faith, the gospel, prayer and people!

Former U.S. President Dwight David Eisenhower said, "A people that values its privileges above its principles soon loses both." What we are concerned with should be what God is concerned with, for He, as the Creator, manufactured in our being a purpose that is eternal and when lived, glorious! Something to think about . . . in reveration!

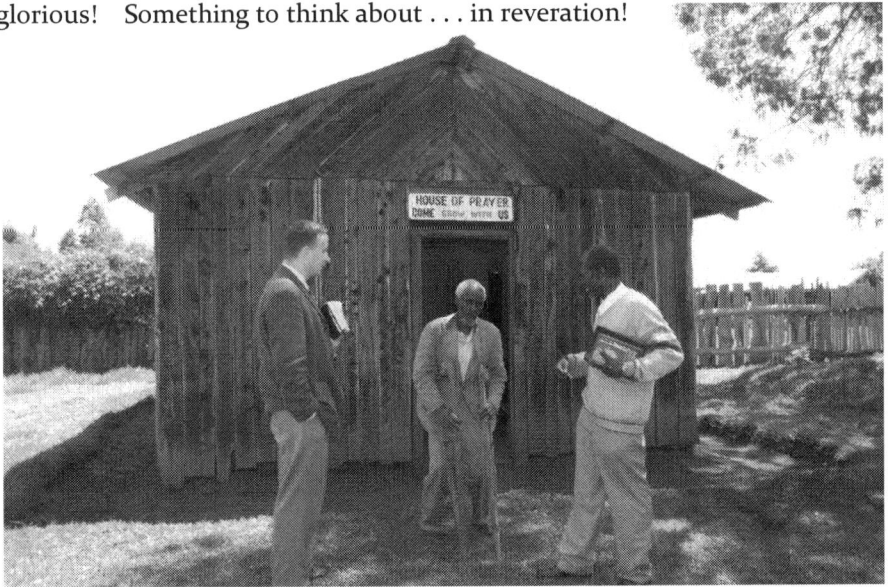

Inspiration † † †

If we are to go forward, we must go back and rediscover those precious values—that all reality hinges on moral foundations and that all reality has spiritual control.—Martin Luther King, Jr., clergyman, activist and leader (1929-1968)

The Power of Agreement

Why did God scatter people across the globe and confuse their languages? The Scriptural interpretation for an offended God is often tied to a literal reading of Gen. 11:4, *"Come, let us build ourselves a city, with a tower that reaches to the heavens."* But why would God be angry with people for plotting to fabricate some skyscraping tower? I do not know any stupid architects. No one can build anything that reaches heaven. Therefore, there had to be something about the purpose of the tower that drew God's wrath. Marvin Rosenthal provides us analysis from his careful research.

> The purpose of the tower of Babel was not to literally reach heaven— the ancients knew better than that—but to build a platform from which to better observe the heavenly bodies and practice astrology and worship of the sun. It was also intended to unify mankind into one kingdom, in direct defiance of God.

Pastor Chuck Swindoll, noted, "In Shinar a Ziggurat taller than all the others was uncovered with signs of the Zodiac etched into the stonework up towards its peak—a religious shrine."

Matthew 18:19—Again, I assure you: If two of you on earth agree about any matter that you pray for, it will be done for you by My Father in heaven.

Agreement is a power spiritual principle. Mat. 18:19 looks like a prayer formula. We must understand that the context by which agreement is consummated is made clear by the succeeding verse, *"For where two or three are gathered together in My name, I am there among them."* When we come together in prayer *in Jesus' name*, we must be in obedience to His will. We learn this studying the concept of agreement in Scripture. Jesus prayed in John 17:11, *"I am no longer in the world, but they are in the world, and I am coming to You. Holy Father, protect them by Your name that You have given Me, so that they may be one as We are one."*

Whenever Jesus speaks of unity in John 17, it is always defined by agreement and obedience to God's plan and will. Similarly, when Jesus speaks of name, He speaks of authority and power that is objectively harmonious.

Is bringing Jesus into our requests without a careful understanding of His will sacrilegious? Spiritual agreement is prayer that asks what God already wants. We learn this by closely studying Scripture and carefully following the leading of His Holy Spirit. The Babel account aptly shows us that agreement is exceedingly important. When mankind sinfully came together in accord, God was profoundly offended by the potential for unbridled evil and took decisive action. Conversely, whenever believers gather for prayer and correctly agree in Jesus' name, heaven comes down and glory fills our souls!

Our Cause or His Cause

Matthew 19:13,14—Then children were brought to Him so He might put His hands on them and pray. But the disciples rebuked them. Then Jesus said, "Leave the children alone, and don't try to keep them from coming to Me, because the kingdom of heaven is made up of people like this."

How could Jesus' disciples stand in the way of parents bringing their children to Him? The disciples were not as interested in Jesus as they were in their idea of what He should be. They were devoted to a cause. Their cause was to see Jesus be the Messiah who would sit as rescuer and ruler of Israel. Their work was to ensure that He succeed. Children therefore represented an interruption to their busy King. Little tykes were hardly the worthy audience of a Teacher in demand and were most certainly a distraction to the disciples' quest to further Jesus' ministry.

We criticize the disciples for being so insensitive. Yet we do the same thing they did. We block people from seeing Jesus if we are more devoted to our own causes than we are to Him. Whenever a holy task consumes a person yet no kindness or an appropriate love for those in close proximity exists, one can rightly conclude that this person is more devoted to his or her work than to Jesus. God is not in any way dependent upon us after all, He is omnipotent! He can easily accomplish His will. What He seeks is our devotion to Him. The sooner we understand this, the more relaxed and encouraged we will become about the purpose and meaning of life! When our eyes are on Jesus we see people as He sees them and that is a good thing!

Inspiration † † †

An explanation of cause is not a justification by reason.—C. S. Lewis

What we have to watch today is the competition of causes against devotion to Jesus Christ. One life, yielded to God at all costs, is worth thousands only touched by God.—Oswald Chambers in *The Servant as His Lord*

The world is now aware that the most unavoidable and most dangerous weapon that exists is the blind decisiveness of a man ready to sacrifice his life for an obscure cause.—Omar Bongo, President of Gabon

Cheap Thrills

Turn on the television these days and you are likely to see a "reality" program. Spawned by the show *Survivor*, Hollywood churns out *Fear Factor*, *The Amazing Race*, etc., in ever-increasing bizarreness to titillate our senses. However, these shows have little to do with reality; they are about the pursuit of thrills. A bored nation craves standing on the edge of immoral precipices. It is not enough to know someone is inebriated, now viewers must see vomiting—as if such disgusting behavior will in some way attract more people to the box of shame.

Thrill seeking is the drug of choice for the unfulfilled. However, like every other drug, the high does not last without increasing the dosage over time to find the ever-elusive buzz. The problem with perpetually seeking electrifying moments is essentially this—most of life is not thrilling. Generally living on a diseased planet challenges us in ways that seldom include being thrilled. Is this sad? Not at all—this *is* reality!

Matthew 21:8,9—A very large crowd spread their robes on the road; others were cutting branches from the trees and spreading them on the road. Then the crowds who went ahead of Him and those who followed kept shouting: Hosanna to the Son of David! Blessed is He who comes in the name of the Lord! Hosanna in the highest heaven!

Do not be easily impressed by emotionally charged crowds. Jesus did not experience euphoria when the throngs chanted His praise and dropped their cloaks before His donkey as it clopped towards Jerusalem. Luke wrote that He wept over the uncomprehending city. He saw the evil to come while they pumped their palms to the beat of liberation. Obsessing to make Him their political king, they missed His true mission. (Luke 19:41-44).

If you want thrills ask God to give you joy throughout the journey and stop lusting over magic mountains. Real thrill comes in the redeeming faith that knowing God means setting aside the quest for amusement to heed the call to be His servant. You can find thrill in the dreary rain if your heart is in love with Jesus. *Trust me, I live in Oregon!* When the commotion dies down (as it always does), the still small Voice is the true source of chills. So please, do not fixate on unreal programming. In addition, if you want to spend your money finding adventure—invest in God's kingdom. In the end, you will receive thrills that are eternal and fashioned by the Creator whose tastes exceed our wildest imaginations!

Inspiration †††

Superficiality is the curse of our age. The doctrine of instant satisfaction is a primary spiritual problem.—Richard J. Foster in *Celebration of Discipline*

Beware of Posing

Mattel used to make Barbie and Ken dolls. I do not know if they still do but I had a boss who all the employees referred to as "Ken" because he looked like an adult version of a Ken doll. He drove a fancy sports car and seemed never to have a hair out of place. Unfortunately, the likeness and label did not make him popular. Truly, he seemed to be all about himself and this cost many of us who worked for him because he did not look after our welfare. He berated us when it suited his ego and looked after his own concerns.

The need for recognition often orients us down a path perforated with traps. For example, if my primary motivation is to look good in front of others, I will be tempted to exaggerate facts in my favor. I may withhold information that colors me in an unfavorable light. I may spend more time posturing and posing when I should occupy myself with important matters like attending to the needs of others.

Matthew 23:1-6,12—Then Jesus spoke to the crowds and to His disciples: "The scribes and the Pharisees are seated in the chair of Moses. Therefore do whatever they tell you and observe it. But don't do what they do, because they don't practice what they teach. They tie up heavy loads that are hard to carry and put them on people's shoulders, but they themselves aren't willing to lift a finger to move them. They do everything to be observed by others: They enlarge their phylacteries and lengthen their tassels. They love the place of honor at banquets, the front seats in the synagogues, greetings in the marketplaces, and to be called ' Rabbi' by people . . . Whoever exalts himself will be humbled, and whoever humbles himself will be exalted.

Jesus taught about pride after observing religious leaders. He noted that the pursuit to look spiritual had become a greater priority than serving God. He said:

> *Woe to you, scribes and Pharisees, hypocrites! You are like whitewashed tombs, which appear beautiful on the outside, but inside are full of dead men's bones and every impurity. In the same way, on the outside you seem righteous to people, but inside you are full of hypocrisy and lawlessness.* (Mat. 23:27,28)

Ouch! That had to hurt men who prided themselves as the elite of society.

There is no reward in heaven for contrived applause on earth or phony appearances. Take the courageous step of setting aside ego and instead serve God and people. True reward will follow!

Inspiration † † †

Beware of posing as a profound person; God became a baby.—Oswald Chambers in *Not Knowing Where*

Rule-Obsessed

Matthew 23:13—But woe to you, scribes and Pharisees, hypocrites! You lock up the kingdom of heaven from people. For you don't go in, and you don't allow those entering to go in.

I know a man who sees everything black or white. Maybe you know him too. He is zealous for the truth. He is a defender of justice who confidently speaks for God. His critical eye is the first to spot error in others. He is meticulous in his theology, mastered in the school of answers, mindful of all the rules.

This same man breaks fellowship with those who are inconsistent in their behavior. He is quick to list and condemn others' faults. He inhales rules while exhaling legalism. He fathoms justice but cannot swallow mercy. He eloquently recites chapter and verse but knows not the melody of God's sweet grace.

How can this man be so right and yet so full of error? Easy—cease focusing on God and insist on protecting His laws and see what happens. Jesus blasted an entire religious group called the Pharisees for their religious hypocrisy. They built and designed Law subdivisions with well-articulated zoning instructions but were clueless towards the Law-Designer's intent. Ah but let's not bash the Pharisees—we are all just as easily culpable. Anyone who values *being right* above knowing God is set up to fail. How can I ever reach those who have no relationship with Him if I am too *holy* to associate with them? Note: Jesus never set up an office in the Temple; He spent His time outside with the sick, lame and searching.

One can proclaim God's Word and yet turn away God. Occasionally I receive letters from someone bent on proving that the only Biblical translation people should be using is the Authorized or King James Version (KJV). This person is consumed with being right but at what cost? Somehow, I do not believe the angels are sitting in heaven moaning because people left the KJV to use Holman CSB or the New International Version.

"Right" living is not the key to God's truth. God's truth is the key to right living.

Inspiration † † †

Many Christians think stoicism is a good antidote to sensuality. It isn't. It is hopelessly weak and ineffective. Willpower religion usually fails, and even when it succeeds, it gets glory for the will, not for God. It produces legalists, not lovers.—John Piper in *In Our Joy*

Broken Neck

June 17, 2001, Father's Day—a day I will not forget. Barbie left a message on our answering machine. Dad fell off a cliff. He broke his neck, knocked his two front teeth out and was listed in serious condition in Providence Hospital, Anchorage.

June 20, 2001, Dad's birthday—he was still alive at the age of 69. I can tell you just hearing his weak voice was a blessing. On the phone, he shared what happened. While putting on his waders to fish he lost his balance and toppled down a 35-foot escarpment onto the rocks and shallow water of Peter's Creek. The fall knocked him unconscious but the cold Alaskan water revived him. He had the presence of mind to hold his breath while the stream carried him toward the silt-laden Kahiltna River.

One of the men he brought to fish watched from above as Dad floated spread eagle and face down towards certain death. Below, five fishermen were casting for salmon. They could not see his body in the murky creek nor could Dad move his arms or legs. From above the observer screamed instructions to them where to position themselves to catch him. He went past the first three fishermen and the fourth man barely missed him. By God's grace, Dad floated into the chest of the 6'7" last man who was up to his chest waders in water. Gaining assistance from the closest angler, they pulled him to safety. Miraculously, because they did not have to do CPR or mouth-to-mouth breathing, Dad's neck did not snap. Slowly on the shore, he regained feeling in all his limbs. With a satellite phone, 911 was contacted and a helicopter life-flighted Dad to the hospital.

2 Corinthians 4:7,16,17—Now we have this treasure in clay jars, so that this extraordinary power may be from God and not from us . . . Therefore we do not give up; even though our outer person is being destroyed, our inner person is being renewed day by day. For our momentary light affliction is producing for us an absolutely incomparable eternal weight of glory.

Dad underwent surgery to fuse fractured bones. Today, he shares an analogy that came to him lying broken in the hospital. Jesus is the One who stands in the river to save us. The person helplessly floating towards death and an appointment with a holy God is the sinner. The man yelling from the cliff is the Christian calling out instructions on how to get to Christ. That accident was a decisive point in Dad's life. He recognized that God gave him a second life on earth. Seven years later, he is still sharing the good news that Jesus saves with anyone willing to listen.

Helplessness is the birthright of humanity. Adam and Eve's disobedience infected us all with a sin-condition. Thank God, He loves us! No matter how high the fall, how deep, fast moving, or cold the river, Jesus is there waiting to pull us out—if we will let Him!

Ironman

On the plane from Atlanta to Portland, I sat between a salesman and a lawyer. We had a great time sharing stories, food and funny video clips during our five-hour flight. Matt shared with us that he was headed to Coeur d' Alene, Idaho to compete in an Ironman competition. His goal was to swim 2.4 miles, bike 112 miles and run 26.2 miles in 12 hours! We pumped him with questions and he shared his training regimen, thrills and spills in past competitions. Then he told us the secret to his perseverance.

Years ago, Matt's best friend since elementary school, was diagnosed with cancer. Matt explained that when he competed for himself, his ability to endure languished, but when he ran for his suffering friend, it was much easier. Once, near the end of one run, his friend joined him and they crossed the finish line together. He showed us a picture of a heart and on the protruding valves the written names of friends and family who either have died of cancer or are battling the disease. They fuel his training drive. He runs for them. Andrew and I took inspiration from the commitment of this amazing 43 year-old athlete.

Matthew 26:67-68—Then they spit in His face and beat Him; others slapped Him and said, "Prophesy to us, Messiah! Who hit You?"
27:26— . . . But after having Jesus flogged, he handed Him over to be crucified.
27:29-30—They twisted together a crown of thorns, put it on His head and placed a reed in His right hand. And they knelt down before Him and mocked Him: "Hail, King of Jews!" Then they spit at Him, took the reed, and kept hitting Him on the head.
27:35—After crucifying Him they divided His clothes by casting lots.

As I think of the incredible perseverance it takes to complete an Ironman contest, my thoughts turn to the greatest Ironman of all. His name is Jesus. Remember He endured the physical beating and torture that eventually claimed His life. He withstood the mental mocking and harassment of His countrymen who despised Him. He weathered betrayal and abandonment by the men He personally trained for three years. At the most brutal moment, His own Coach turned His back on Him.

Jesus did not get a medal, a picture, or a shirt. He did not summon the power He possessed to fix a rigged competition. He simply bled for you and me. He carried our cross until He collapsed unable to drag the wood of shame to the top of that hill of hate. He did this without complaining, without replenishing fluids along that brutal course, before jeering crowds and most incredibly, full of love for the very people killing Him. It is one thing to swim, bike and run great distances. Imagine this Hero, who overcame a defeated team, sin and death to become the Savior of the world. Something to think about . . . in reveration!

Let's Take Our Shoes Off

Growing up I hated to be wrong and I was effective at arguing. As I get older and follow Jesus, I am learning that it does not matter who wins the debate. If I am falsely accused, I do not have to defend myself. I can give unfavorable circumstances to the Lord and trust Him to be my defense. Though I may disagree with others' opinions, I do not have to disagree with them. It is much better to pray and ask God to bring clarity.

I once planned an exercise for a military unit I led. We had a new boss. After I briefed the plan to him and his staff, he publicly berated it and asked the team if they thought it was any good. Only one officer came to my defense. I was furious. All I could do was stick up for the plan. Perhaps my boss was testing me to see what kind of leader I was. Ultimately, the training went off without a hitch and to his credit, the boss apologized for being wrong. But before he apologized, I complained to those around me about the way I was treated.

Matthew 27:12-14—And while He was being accused by the chief priests and elders, He didn't answer. Then Pilate said to Him, "Don't You hear how much they are testifying against You?" But He didn't answer him on even one charge, so that the governor was greatly amazed.

There are two kinds of Christians—those who dig in their heels and those who take their shoes off. When confronted with criticism of any sort, most of us become defensive. We say it is imperative to protect truth from battering, but in reality, it is our own pride we often defend. We love ourselves and cannot bear the thought of others thinking less of us for any reason. We erect walls and zealously defend our actions, words, or motives—even attacking our accusers to expose their errors.

When challenged by religious leaders who trumpeted false accusations against Him, Jesus remained silent. He took his shoes off. The One who was truth, rather than destroy His accusers, relied upon His Father. Watchman Nee wrote in *Spiritual Authority*:

No one on earth could ever be more authoritative than Christ, yet He never defended Himself. Authority and self-defense are incompatible. The one against whom you defend yourself becomes your judge. He rises higher than you when you begin to answer his criticism. [29]

Friends, if our battle is always to be right, we are fighting the wrong war. Our charge is to be right*eous*. We need not fear what people say; we need to fear God. He is our Defender! Nothing can overcome His authority. Our charge to follow Jesus comes through humility. It does not matter if we die—truth always rises from the tomb. What matters is that we honor God by giving Him our heart knowing the world considers us fools.

Fatherhood

I only saw him cry once and that was by accident. I came into the room to say "goodnight" and there beside the bed he and mom were shedding tears knowing his trip to Japan might cause him to miss the birth of my younger brother. Like many of his generation, he is not comfortable sharing emotion yet his volume knob for caring still turns. He has always been my hero—imperfect yet dynamic. His love for God flows unabated. He stands faithful and noble today like the snow-covered Mt. Hood.

He won the Silver Star and Purple Heart as a young marine fighting communism in Korea. However, his medals mean nothing compared to his thirst to see men know God's Son before the real war of sin takes them out. To this end, he relentlessly labors.

His physical strength still amazes me—four of us kids could never take him down. But his true strength comes from his faithful habit of rising each day to meet with his Father.

1 Thessalonians 2:11,12—As you know, like a father with his own children, we encouraged, comforted, and implored each one of you to walk worthy of God, who calls you into His own kingdom and glory.

I don't understand the mindset of idiotic producers of countless television shows and movies that mock and demean fathers. I guess they grew up without ever knowing what it means to be in the presence of a real man. Do we live in a society of deadbeat dads, self-centered males, ego-driven competitive rascals who have shirked the family? Sure we do. So let's just bash the whole lot of fathers and see what happens!

Alternatively, maybe it is time for those of us who know what it means to have God-fearing fathers to stand up and passionately say, *Thanks Dad! I love you. Your contribution to my growth is immeasurable. I will never forget your hard work to keep us kids clothed, fed and schooled. I'm a better man because you took the time to discipline me, give counsel, to listen, to watch me race, to cheer me on, to lift me up in victory and to hold me close in defeat. I am a better dad because you pass on wisdom. You keep your wedding vows. You refuse to compromise your integrity. You are not ashamed to give all glory to the One who gave you meaning. I am grateful Dad. I only hope I can do as great a job with the precious gifts God entrusted to me as you did with us.*

The Apostle Paul wrote, "Honor your father and mother—which is the first commandment with a promise—that it may go well with you and that you may have a long life in the land" (Eph. 6:2,3).

Inspiration † † †

A child is not likely to find a father in God unless he finds something of God in his father.—Austin L. Sorensen

Rising Ire

The more I looked at the bill the madder I got. It was ridiculous, outrageous, sheer robbery! So I called the phone company. I asked the customer service representative how Pluto (not their real name) could justify charging me $14.47 for a three minute collect call. He said I was not a Pluto client and therefore I had to pay the connection fee and the high rate charged. Attempting to control my ire, I explained that this was a great way to ensure I would never be one of their customers. He was unsympathetic, and suggested that is what I got for making a collect call.

Feeling my head warm, I called my local phone provider. Hoping to get some relief instead, I was lectured. The woman could care less that my bill was high, shared that she had known for 15 years not to make collect calls and that Pluto could charge me whatever they wanted. When I suggested I would not pay such a fee, she said she would note on my account our conversation and assured me I would be assessed a fine if the bill was unpaid. Cato once said, "An angry man opens his mouth and shuts up his eyes." Well, my eyes stayed open, but it was all I could do to keep the hinges of my mouth shut! A Hebrew proverb says, "The best way to know a man is to watch him when he is angry."

Mark 3:4,5—Then He said to them, "Is it lawful on the Sabbath to do good or to do evil, to save life or to kill?" But they were silent. After looking around at them with anger and sorrow at the hardness of their hearts, He told the man, "Stretch out your hand." So he stretched it out, and his hand was restored.

Anger as an emotion is not necessarily wrong. It is what we do with anger that determines its value. Jesus illustrates in the above passage, that there are times when anger is justified. When we encounter evil, we have a right to feel righteous anger, but that anger must be controlled such that God is honored. The moment we lose the ability to manage our mouths or emotions, we potentially stray into sin.

Solomon wrote, *"Don't let your spirit rush to be angry, for anger abides in the heart of fools"* (Ecc. 7:9). A French proverb notes, "Anger is a bad counselor." The Apostle Paul warned the Ephesians, *"Be angry and do not sin. Don't let the sun go down on your anger, and don't give the Devil an opportunity"* (Eph. 4:26,27). James, the brother of Jesus, taught—". . . *everyone must be quick to hear, slow to speak, and slow to anger, for man's anger does not accomplish God's righteousness"* (Jam. 1:19,20).

I did not say anything unkind to the phone representatives I spoke with as I struggled to remain polite. However, for the remainder of the day, I carried a lingering resentment towards a man and a woman I felt were rude. Instead of praying for them I smoldered. Instead of thanking God for a phone that works and the ability to make calls, I festered. My emotions ran feral. In short, I blew it.

Don't You Ever . . . !

Sam walked from the studio into the sanctuary. The amplifier levels were set incorrectly and the sound in the room from the instruments was unbalanced. So he adjusted the levels on the soundboard and moved the amp volumes up to full power. He removed the old paper arrows taped to the board assigning each channel a specific level. Now the system sounded great. Sam was pleased he had helped the church.

Two days later a small elderly woman asked him why he changed the settings. She ran the sound for the worship team and she was not happy. She backed Sam into a corner and singed his ears. She told him Fred had set the levels and he should have left them alone. An elder came over and completed the tongue lashing. "Don't you ever tamper with these controls again!" By now, Sam was feeling low. "Who is Fred?" he asked. To his amazement he found out Fred had not attended the church for four years. They were still working off levels he had set!

Mark 10:42-45—Jesus called them over and said to them, "You know that those who are regarded as rulers of the Gentiles dominate them, and their men of high positions exercise power over them. But it must not be like that among you. On the contrary, whoever wants to become great among you must be your servant, and whoever wants to be first among you must be a slave to all. For even the Son of Man did not come to be served, but to serve, and to give His life—a ransom for many."

If you have ever encountered a controller, you can relate to Sam's frustration. Controllers operate from a need to have everything work according to their plan and definition. They do not care how others do things because they know what is best. Underneath a bold exterior of confident leadership simmers insecurity. Controllers flourish by insulating themselves with "yes" men and by establishing rules and regulations that protect their philosophy. Often controllers are successful because they stay on task and provide stability to those who dislike change. They can be extremely effective in accomplishing their goals. Look closely, however, and you will discover mavericks, independent thinkers, and those creative individuals who bring freshness and breathe new life into stale organizations are not welcome and do not stay long.

Someone once said, "Authority does not make you a leader; it gives you the opportunity to be one." As we mature in Christ, we learn to let go of the need to control others. We recognize that such behavior reveals distrust in God because we rely more on our need for power than in His right to work His will. It is healthy to be surrounded by people who think differently than we do. God's plan often involves using those we would never pick in ways we would never imagine. What we need is a vibrant prayer life as opposed to calculating sound bites.

Excellent leaders are Spirit-led and grounded in humility—not like the officer James S. Hewett shares with us in *Illustrations Unlimited*:

A young second lieutenant at Fort Bragg discovered that he had no change when he was about to buy a soft drink from a vending machine. He flagged down a passing private and asked him, "Do you have change for a dollar?" The private said cheerfully, "I think so, let me take a look." The lieutenant drew himself up stiffly and said, "Soldier, that's no way to address an officer. We'll start all over again. Do you have change for a dollar?" The private came to attention, saluted smartly, and said, "No, sir!"[30]

Do you have a need to control? How much are you willing to give up so that others can grow? What are you afraid of—that people will be critical of you; that mistakes will happen; or, that you will not get your way? God loves you and He wants you to bear fruit—His succulent, soul-refreshing, life-energizing, joy-producing fruit. So trust Him. Let Him lead. Quit acting like Napoleon! Those who truly care about you will stand up and cheer!

Inspiration † † †

Most often, controllers are insecure in themselves and do not know the first principle of being free, so naturally they are uneasy with your or my being free.—Charles R. Swindoll in *The Grace Awakening*

Our scientific power has outrun our spiritual power. We have guided missiles and misguided men.—Martin Luther King Jr.

Growing true disciples is not about maintaining tight control.—George Barna in *Growing True Disciples*

His Name is John

The angel, Gabriel, told Zechariah that his wife Elizabeth would have a child and they were to call him *"John"* (1:13). Nine months later, elderly Elizabeth miraculously conceived this special baby and the neighbors and relatives gathered to celebrate his circumcision and to give him his name. According to well-established custom, they assumed he would take the name of his priestly father.

Luke 1:59-63—When they came to circumcise the child on the eighth day, they were going to name him Zechariah, after his father. But his mother responded, "No! He will be called John." Then they said to her, "None of your relatives has that name." So they motioned to his father to find out what he wanted him to be called. He asked for a writing tablet and wrote: HIS NAME IS JOHN. And they were all amazed.

There will come times in your life when God through the Holy Spirit will give you a clear word. He may ask you to make a move, a career change, to marry someone, to go in a direction counter to what you planned, to share your faith with a stranger, or to help someone in trouble. How He instructs you may vary. It is unlikely you will hear from Gabriel, but even that is possible!

Oswald Chamber wrote in *Notes On Ezekiel*, "There is no room for debate when God speaks." Once God gives you a word, go with it! However, be ready for opposition from unexpected places. Some will suggest that you misunderstood His word. Wise folks will question your judgment. This is simply because humans are prone to make assumptions and to be fallible in their brilliance. If God spoke to you, your responsibility is to be steadfast. Your reply is simple, *"His name is John!"*

Some will not like your decision. They will tell you, "But we've never done it that way before." Beware of the spiritually coated words that determine what God can or cannot do according to the dictates of human tradition. *"His name is John."*

When you remain firm against opinions and tradition, some people will resort to manipulation. They will go to someone close to you to seek agreement and change your mind. This is simply manipulation. Do not fall for it. *"His name is John."*

Jan David Hettinga wrote in *Follow Me*, "God's love language is obedience. God feels loved when He is obeyed. To profess love and refuse to obey is to communicate opposites to Him." The reason many of us fail in our obedience is we make room for discussion what God has already decided. God never asks us to rationalize, He expects us to reconcile. Stand firm in your walk and do what God tells you. The results will be glorious because His plan is perfect. *"His name is John."*

Otherworldly

Luke 2:13,14—Suddenly there was a multitude of the heavenly host with the angel, praising God and saying: Glory to God in the highest heaven, and peace on earth to people He favors!

You are lying down and it is dark outside. The air is warm as summer begins. Under the sheets you are ready to fall asleep after another long day. Outside your window, a star catches your attention. But is it a star? Strangely, it appears to be getting brighter, closer, with a cosmic twinkle you've not seen before. This is no plane or satellite in motion. The flight is too fast, the light too brilliant. You think of *The Night Before Christmas*, that jolly story of Santa. But this is real. Suddenly you see angels bursting into triumphant formations and the most gorgeous music you have ever heard radiates through your wide-awake body. They are proclaiming the birth of Jesus.

"Wait!" you cry. This event already happened. Shepherds told their friends, family and even strangers all the things they had heard and seen that blessed night outside Bethlehem. They glorified and praised God just like His celestial choir. So what gives? Why would God send His faithful to inspire what already transpired? And what are they doing here in June!

Just as quickly as they came, they vanish. You rub your eyes and pinch your arm to make sure you are not dreaming. You dash from window to window looking for angels. However, they are gone. Now sleep will not come. *"God am I hallucinating?"*

Then a voice firmly speaks across your heart chamber. "Go!" Again, it reverberates, only louder, "Go!" As if a gentle breeze parted the thick fog, you understand. God sent the angels to announce His Son. They were otherworldly. Jesus was born and raised the Son of Man—He was otherworldly. I placed my trust in Him and His Holy Spirit lives within me. I am otherworldly!

There won't be angelic singing above Bethlehem. Jesus will not walk the streets of my town. He doesn't need to—He has me. I am the one commissioned to share the joyful news. My lungs should expel the divine words with every other believer, "Joy to the world, the Lord has come; Let earth receive her King."

So are you singing? A weary world wants to rejoice—go be God's messenger! Tell the most incredible story with renewed enthusiasm to those who thought Santa was the point. After all, the star that led the way shining—that star is you!

Inspiration ✝✝✝

If one-tenth of what you believe is true, you ought to be ten times as excited as you are.—Sir Walter Moberly, British academic (1881-1974)

Be quiet and come out of him!

Luke 4:36—They were all struck with amazement and kept saying to one another, "What is this message? For He commands the unclean spirits with authority and power, and they come out!"

Jesus walked into a synagogue in the town of Capernaum one Sabbath day and began teaching. Who invited Him? What Rabbi did He follow or replace? What was it He said? We don't know. But what Luke records is that *"They were astonished at His teaching because His message had authority"* (4:32). What intrigues me in Luke's writing is what he didn't say. The fact that the people were astounded at Jesus' teaching implies that the typical lessons they received from the religious leaders were impotent—they were speaking words of little value.

As Jesus ministered, a man shouted at Him at the top of his lungs! Jesus, recognizing the presence of an agitated demon, silenced him and sternly cast him out. How long had the possessed-man attended that synagogue unbothered by the presence of men speaking words devoid of authority? Did they even know a troubled man was in their midst?

So how does Luke 4:31-37 apply to us? How we answer this says much about how we live our lives! Authority is synonymous with solution. For example, if my car is breaking down, I go to Richard, a talented friend who is a skilled mechanic. He diagnoses the symptoms and applies the correct work to make my Ford run. I can sit and listen to people talk about what is wrong with my car and hear all kinds of ideas but it will not get fixed until someone who knows what he is doing treats it.

God is our genuine life Authority! He made us therefore, He fully understands us. If we want to live life to its fullest, we must follow His manual and operate under the leading (authority) of His Spirit. Then we can weather adversity, failure and pain knowing He *is* in control. Then we can stop relying on people or *karma* for our success. What governs us in turn defines us. How long will we sit in the synagogue numbed by our own self-reliance or the influence of flesh-leaders and die accordingly!

God's authority is ours to relish and nourish. Walk with Him and do not be surprised if you hear yelling! Demons cannot abide the Lord's presence. Embrace His power and awe is renewed! Sit under the teaching of those ruled by Him and blessing ensues. When God is your leader, you reflect His solution and the world cannot help but be astounded.

Authenticate

Luke 5:18-19—Just then some men came, carrying on a stretcher a man who was paralyzed. They tried to bring him in and set him down before Him. Since they could not find a way to bring him in because of the crowd, they went up on the roof and lowered him on the stretcher through the roof tiles into the middle of the crowd before Jesus.

As a young officer in the Army, my unit often deployed to the field for training. To communicate with everyone else in the Battalion, we used radios. Before we could talk on the same channel, the commo officer, in charge of running the net, tested us to ensure we were genuinely part of the unit and not the *enemy*. He did this by giving us a code that we then had to apply to our own code matrix to find the correct response. Once the proper reply came, we could enter the net with everyone else already authenticated.

In Luke 5:17-26, Jesus is teaching in Capernaum, the town where Peter was from and a center of His operations. Jewish leaders from all over Israel came to hear Him speak. They were checking Him out. While Jesus spoke to an overflow crowd in someone's house, four men cleverly found a way to lower their paralyzed friend before Jesus. He complimented them for their faith. Instead of healing the man, He said, *"Friend, your sins are forgiven you."* Jesus had a much bigger agenda in mind than just healing the helpless man before Him.

Instantly the Pharisees thought Jesus was guilty of blasphemy, for only God had the authority to forgive sins. However, knowing their thoughts, He used this opportunity to authenticate His divinity by telling the paralyzed man to *"get up, pick up your stretcher, and go home"* (vs. 24). A phenomenal miracle validated God's Son!

In 2 Co. 4:6, Paul wrote, *"For God, who said, 'Light shall shine out of darkness'—He has shone in our hearts to give the light of the knowledge of God's glory in the face of Jesus Christ."* Just as both admiring and skeptical crowds repeatedly examined Jesus, so we as His followers also come under serious scrutiny. In order to authenticate the gospel message as genuine, our lives *must* change. If we claim to follow Jesus but live like the world, the gospel looks phony. God's light instead of shining in our hearts, flickers like some traumatized candle whose feeble shimmer makes the darkness sneer.

When the paralyzed man rose, the crowd experienced awe. When you rise what is the crowd filled with—do they see the glory of God cascading through you, or are they left with the mistaken impression that Christianity is a mere religious choice of little consequence? Those exposed to Jesus' power said, *"We have seen incredible things today"* (vs. 26b). Literally that phrase translates, "We have seen things which are contrary to opinion or belief." Quite simply they were mesmerized! It should be no different today. When you and I walk in the power of the Holy Spirit, His light shines through us and people cannot help but notice. Would to God they would say, "We have seen things which are contrary to opinion or belief."

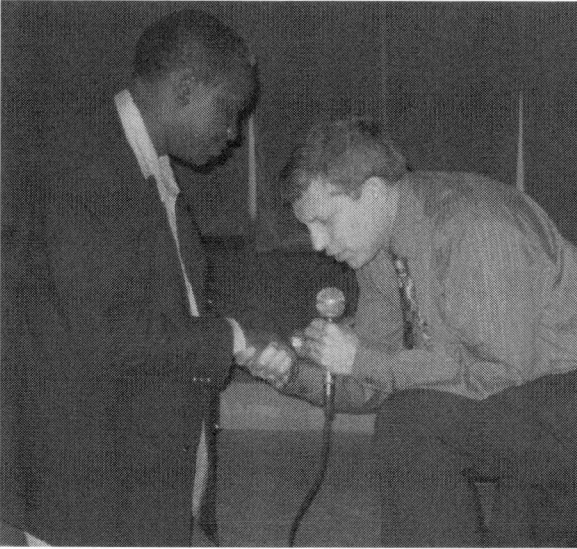

Inspiration †††

For the watching world, we ourselves serve proof that God is alive. We form the visible shape of what He is like.—Philip Yancey, author

Choosing Your Team

Luke 6:13—When daylight came, He summoned His disciples, and He chose 12 of them—He also named them apostles.

The fate of every business hangs upon the quality of the employees hired. The outcome of ministry rests upon the quality and performance of Jesus' disciples. Therefore, selection is an extremely important concept in the formation of teams and in accomplishing God's will! I would like to share with you seven principles of selection that my father, Ron York, utilizes as a result of over fifty years of ministry experience.

1.   *Intercede*: Jesus spent an entire night praying about those He should select among His followers to specifically train. The ministry of selecting begins, continues and completes in prayer for the simple reason that we need God's help to choose wisely.

2.   *Identify*: Robert Coleman, in his book *The Master Plan of Evangelism*, wrote, "Make a list of those you would like to see join you. Pray over the list. Ask God for guidance in selecting the right people for the right roles."[31]

3.   *Initiate*: Make an appointment with the people on your list, one at a time.

4.   *Involve*: Encourage them to be a part of something that you are doing or ask if you can be part of something they are doing. It might be a prayer walk, a Bible Study, a sports outreach or group activity. Sometimes being with a small group is better than meeting one-on-one.

5.   *Investigate*: Getting to know people and what God is doing in their lives is important if we are to have integrity in our inviting. What is on their heart? How is God leading them? What is it they need to learn? What fears do they have that keep them from following God's lead? Visit their home. Meet their family. The key is to ask questions and listen. Particularly we are looking to see if a person demonstrates qualities of *faithfulness*, *availability* and a *teachable spirit*. God will give you key insight.

6.   *Inspire*: Now we begin to sense a connection. Those we spend time with are beginning to get a picture of what God wants us to do. We now seek to cast vision for people in two ways. *First, we invite people to join the greatest enterprise in history—the Kingdom and purposes of the King of kings! Second, we inspire them with a foretaste of what God wants to do in their lives.* God is committed to seeing people transformed and developed. We invite people to adventure but also to personal growth and development. Ecclesiastes 10:10 says, *"If the ax is dull, and one does not sharpen its edge, then one must exert more strength; however, the advantage of wisdom is that it brings success."* God wants to sharpen us so we work with maximum effectiveness.

7.   *Invite*: Jesus said in Mark 1:17, *"Follow Me and I will make you fish for people!"* Had Jesus not selected disciples would we know God today?   Jesus asked and so should we. Caution! Beware of inviting people to fulfill your own agendas or agreeing to work with only people that are part of your church.   Selection is a process consecrated to building God's Kingdom, concentrated in prayer and confirmed by fruitfulness.

Inspiration † † †

Whatever the apparent gifts and abilities of people, we must look for those who want to move for Christ. Life is too short to expend excessive time and energy upon apathetic people.—Robert E. Coleman in *The Master Plan of Discipleship*

When it is Appropriate

Luke 6:36,37—Be merciful, just as your Father also is merciful. Do not judge, and you will not be judged. Do not condemn, and you will not be condemned. Forgive, and you will be forgiven.

The application of mercy often precludes the need to judge. James noted in Jam. 2:13, *"For judgment is without mercy to the one who hasn't shown mercy. Mercy triumphs over judgment."* But how can we go through life without judging? If that were the case, Scripture would seem to contradict Jesus. Let us see if we can apprehend what He wants us to understand. In studying the Bible, at least three instances appear when it is appropriate to judge:

1. *When the Holy Spirit prompts us to rebuke another's wrong behavior.* See 2 Sa. 12 where the prophet Nathan rebukes David for his adulterous affair with Bathsheba. Look at Acts 5 where Peter confronts Annanias and Sapphira for lying.

2. *When we are righteously upholding God's Word and its standards of behavior.* Paul rebuked Peter in Gal. 2:11 for his hypocrisy. In 1 Co. 5:9-11 he warned the Corinthians not to associate with other believers engaged in immoral behavior and he gave the Ephesians a list of sins to avoid in Eph. 5:3-7.

3. *When we are selecting leaders*—Titus 1:6-9. There is obviously a need to make judgment in determining whether a believer meets the qualifications necessary to be a deacon or elder.

So what does Jesus mean when He tells us not to judge others? May I suggest that there are at least five instances when we have no business judging others.

1. *We don't have the right to judge another person's motives unless there is a confession of guilt.* Only God can see into the heart and we must beware not to be junior Holy Spirits. While I can see what you do, I cannot see what you think.

2. *We do not have the right to judge another for behavior of which we ourselves are guilty.* This is what we call hypocrisy. Solomon wrote in Pro. 20:10, *"Differing weights and varying measures—both are detestable to the LORD."* Paul warned the Jews in Rom. 2:17-24 about blatant hypocrisy.

3. *We should not judge when our heart is not right with God.* The result is a bitter or critical disposition or false judgment. Judas objected to Mary washing Jesus' feet with expensive perfume. But the man was a thief. His heart was not right and his judgment was polluted (John 12:4-6).

4.   *We are not to have a disproportionate sense of justice.* Jesus said do not go after the speck in your brother's eye when your own eye contains a log. We also need to beware against selective judgment.   Too many Christians heavily denounce people engaged in homosexuality or those who have performed abortions while remaining mute regarding divorce and unmarried couples living together—rampant problems in our Christian community.   We look bad to the world and we hurt God's reputation when we pick up the bullhorn against selected sins while ignoring greed, anger, malice, slander, filthy language, lying, stealing and the rest of the sins that are consistently listed as abhorrent to God (Pro. 6:16-19 and Col. 3:5-10).   Holiness is never partially measured or determined.

5.   *We are not qualified to judge.*   In Luke 6:39, Jesus asks, *"Can the blind guide the blind?"* When we lack the information or maturity necessary to make a judgment call, prudence demands silence!

We should remember that when we set a standard we also are measured against that standard. If we give mercy, mercy gives to us. If we cut slack, slack is cut for us.   Conversely, harsh or legalistic behavior breeds reciprocity. Solomon noted in Pro. 21:13, *"The one who shuts his ears to the cry of the poor will himself also call out and not be answered."*

Inspiration   † † †

What keeps us from being qualified to judge?
1.   We do not know all the facts.
2.   We are unable to read motives.
3.   We find it impossible to be totally objective.
4.   We lack "the big picture."
5.   We live with blind spots.
6.   We are prejudiced and have blurred perspective.
7.   We, ourselves, are imperfect and inconsistent.—Chuck Swindoll in *The Grace Awakening*

Lordship

Haughty hears Wisdom reveal what is at stake
but he scorns being told what path he should take.
"Turn right," says the Son, but left the man goes.
"I like it my way, the way that I chose!"
Off the edge he plunges with a cry of dismay
For left without Wisdom there is no right way.

Luke 6:46—Why do you call Me "Lord, Lord," and don't do the things I say?

There is great danger in pressuring people to obey Christ. God did not call us to condemn or save souls, He called us to share the truth about His Son. The threats of hell will hardly deter a will set on self-determination. Only the Holy Spirit can reach inside the heart of a person and remove the blinders that cause one to falsely see God's authority as unjust and therefore worthy of resisting. The paradox of Christianity is that freedom comes through submission to the leadership of Jesus Christ. This profound mystery is revealed supernaturally and not by gimmick, eloquence or the profuse emotion of sincere saints.

Our privilege is to model and share the benefits of serving a Savior whose leadership if followed results in *"love, joy, peace, patience, kindness, goodness, faithfulness, gentleness, self-control"*—the fruit of His Spirit (Gal. 5:22).

Everyone on this planet bows to a lord. If I say I am free and bend to no one I perceive I am my own master. Yet by claiming independence, I fall under the jurisdiction of Satan (John 12:31), who chose to usurp God and in rebellion manipulated Adam and Eve into disobeying God's.

God blessed two adults with an awesome creation. They were to govern paradise! The only command they were given was to abstain from eating the fruit off the tree of the knowledge of good and evil. Adam and Eve determined their own will was master. A mankind focused on the tree of independence cannot see the forest of God's eternal power and divine nature.

If those who reject Christ to follow self or some other lord, experience the same enduring, unspoiled fruits described above, they deserve commendation. I have yet in life to find such a person with such fruit who has refused to kneel before the authority of Jesus. They may appear good, but when tested, the core is impure. The power of Jesus lordship accomplishes core transformation! No person with integrity will dismiss the value of godliness achieved by submitting to a worthy King. Those who desire His love will make Him Lord to His glory!

Inspiration † † †

Adam chose Eve over God.—John Eldredge in *Wild at Heart*

Centurion

Luke 7:1-10—When He had concluded all His sayings in the hearing of the people, He entered Capernaum. A centurion's slave, who was highly valued by him, was sick and about to die. When the centurion heard about Jesus, he sent some Jewish elders to Him, requesting Him to come and save the life of his slave. When they reached Jesus, they pleaded with Him earnestly, saying, "He is worthy for You to grant this, because he loves our nation and has built us a synagogue." Jesus went with them, and when He was not far from the house, the centurion sent friends to tell Him, "Lord, don't trouble Yourself, since I am not worthy to have You come under my roof. That is why I didn't even consider myself worthy to come to You. But say the word, and my servant will be cured. For I too am a man placed under authority, having soldiers under my command. I say to this one, 'Go!' and he goes; and to another, 'Come!' and he comes; and to my slave, 'Do this!' and he does it." Jesus heard this and was amazed at him, and turning to the crowd following Him, He said, "I tell you, I have not found so great a faith even in Israel!" When those who had been sent returned to the house, they found the slave in good health.

This is one of the most remarkable passages in the New Testament. A man deserving hate by the Jews as an unwelcome occupier, a leader of soldiers that held Israel subject to Rome, becomes the most celebrated example of faith Jesus encounters. There is so much we can learn from this man's profile that I would dare say that he gives us a pattern for how we ought to live our lives. Let us learn from what Luke tells us about this man.

- He was a Gentile (vs. 2)
- He loved people: his servant, the Jews and their nation (vs. 2,5)
- He put people above position (vs. 2,3)
- He was spiritually sensitive knowing that Jesus could help him (vs. 3)
- He was culturally sensitive; he worked through the Jewish elders to approach Jesus and recognized it would not be appropriate for Jesus as a Jew to come into his home (vs. 3,6)
- He knew how to cultivate friendships (vs. 3)
- He was highly respected; the Jewish elders plead with Jesus to help him (vs. 4)
- He loved God, helping the Jews to build a synagogue (vs. 5)
- He was unafraid of criticism for doing good for people Romans disdained (vs. 5)
- He was a man of humility. He did not feel worthy for Jesus to enter his home (vs. 6)
- He had incredible faith—*"just say the word!"* (vs. 7, 9)
- He was a leader, comfortable with the workings of authority (vs. 8)
- He was used to getting work accomplished (vs. 8) and the end result was that his faith was rewarded (vs. 10)

How many of us would like to be like the Centurion? May I share with you three principles which if we applied would help us to be like this incredible man?

1.   *Highly value people by truly loving God.*   The Centurion was a remarkable man first because he loved God. The foundation for achieving anything of significance always ties to loving God! Loving God means:

a.   *Understanding what God's thoughts are about people.*   Most Jews rejected Jesus because they did not have the love of God in their hearts—John 5:42—*"but I know you—that you have no love for God within you."* John 15:17—*"This is what I command you: love one another."*

b.   *Sensitivity to the needs of those around you.*   If we want to reach people with the gospel, we have to observe and care about their needs. 1 John 3:18—*"Little children, we must not love in word or speech, but in deed and truth."*

c.   *Becoming part of the solution when you have opportunity to see other's problems.*   Philippians 2:4—*"Everyone should look out not only for his own interests, but also for the interests of others."*

d.   *Putting people above position and security.*   There are consequences for taking a stand for Christ. Are you willing to pay the price for putting Jesus first, for sharing Him with others, knowing you could lose your job or be punished?   Ultimately, if we truly value people, we are compelled to share Christ! To do anything less is to consign them to hell as if it is not our problem.

e.   *Building valuable friendships.*   The Centurion did not associate only with Romans; he built friendships with the Jews. How can we expect to win anyone to Christ if all we know are Christians?

2.   *Cultivate a spiritually sensitive heart.*   So often we try to solve problems in our own strength and we are insensitive to what God may want us to do, or be able to do in us, if we will just trust Him!

a.   *Develop a spirit of humility*—Eph. 4:1-3.

b.   *Understand authority.*   We live in a society that questions authority, disrespects elected officials and slanders those who lead on a regular basis. You cannot walk according to the Spirit if you are skeptical according to the world.

3.   *Operate by faith.*   To operate by faith may mean to send Jesus home before you ever receive what you are after. We need to believe in the authority of God and put to death reliance on our flesh, our keen minds, our education, and our resources. God does not need these things to work His will. God simply desires that we would trust Him. Something to think about . . . in reveration!

Inspiration   † † †

Example is the best precept.—Aesop

She's a Sinner!

One man was a Pharisee, a religious leader zealous to maintain a sinless posture. The other woman was in all likelihood, a prostitute. The Pharisee invited Jesus into his home and whether by oversight, or by intent, failed to offer the common amenity of providing water for his guest to wash His feet. The woman, taking advantage of a custom that allowed the poor into a home for scraps, bathed Jesus' feet with grief-stricken tears, wiped them with her hair, kissed them in profound reverence and perfumed them—perhaps with the very oil she once used to lure men.

Luke 7:39—When the Pharisee who had invited Him saw this, he said to himself, "This man, if He were a prophet, would know who and what kind of woman this is who is touching Him—she's a sinner!"

The amazing thing about Luke's account in chapter 7:36-50, is not the love Jesus shows the woman, for Jesus came to seek and to save the lost (19:10). It is the callous hardness of the Pharisee that arrests my spirit. He focused on a sinful reputation and was oblivious to a broken heart. He failed to understand Isaiah's words, *"Yet He Himself bore our sicknesses, and He carried our pains . . ."* (Isa. 53:4a), and therefore doubted the legitimacy of the Prophet next to him. The smugness of personal piety quenched any awareness of need. The intrusion of a desperate doxy (religious view) upset his tidy dinner plans.

Forgive me, but I can't help but wonder—is this not an accurate caricature of the church? Do we congregate in our safe buildings, sing lovely songs and pontificate over Scripture all the while put off by the desperate affairs of ungodly people? Does the Savior we worship bear any semblance to the Savior who ministers? Why is it we can recite His parables and yet ignore their applications? While the Pharisee at least knew the reputation of the woman in his home, I find that most of us know little to nothing of our neighbors. He recited law; we recite security as an excuse to maintain fences. He found fault with the Master and we judge him for it, yet we do the same thing. We don't say it openly, but our unwillingness to share Christ with others reveals our discomfort with His commands. In the presence of God's Son, it is disturbing to think that we might be more concerned at maintaining order at the expense of delivering grace. The Pharisee worshiped at the altar of legalism. How many of us worship at the altar of protectionism? Is it possible our society is becoming more secular because we are so consumed with our holy clubs? God will surely judge us if we withhold love.

Jesus said to a woman's unspoken request, *"Your sins are forgiven . . . Your faith has saved you; go in peace"* (7:48,50). She received the gift of life, the host received a tutorial in love. What lesson will we learn from the Master?

"We're Going to Die!"

One day Jesus asked His disciples to go with Him across the lake. So they got in a boat and begin crossing the Sea of Galilee when a fierce storm without warning hit them.

Luke 8:24,25—They came and woke Him up, saying, "Master, Master, we're going to die!" Then He got up and rebuked the wind and the raging waves. So they ceased, and there was a calm. He said to them, "Where is your faith?" They were fearful and amazed, asking one another, "Who can this be? He commands even the winds and the waves, and they obey Him!"

Sometimes God wants us to go over to the other side of the lake. It would be easy for us to be safe and stay off the lake. But on the road home God often takes us places we would not choose, to teach us more about trusting Him and to build in us the character lessons we need. A major part of our learning comes from the journey itself and the unexpected storms that hit us and test our mettle.

How was it that Jesus was able to sleep through a life-threatening squall? Do you suppose it was because He had His Father's perspective? He knew that He was not going to die nor were His followers because that was not God's purpose. When we begin to understand God's purpose and will that is when we can truly sleep. It doesn't matter what we are experiencing now. It doesn't matter what we will face tomorrow. What matters is that *God's purpose always prevails.* This is the secret to victorious living. Panic attacks are mostly caused by circumstances that crush us. Peace is caused by God who upholds us. Isaiah 26:3—*"You will keep in perfect peace the mind that is dependent on You, for it is trusting in You."*

The disciples were both afraid and lacking in faith—the two are married. Whenever we are fearful, faith is lacking. They had gone through squalls before. But God manufactured a life-threatening storm and put them in a place where they had nowhere to escape. Why when it was so dangerous, would Jesus rebuke them for lacking faith and projecting fear? They did not have God's perspective in mind! Jesus turned their terror into a teaching point. "You don't have to fear storms when I'm with you, whether I'm sleeping or awake." The same truth holds for us..

In the midst of disaster we can calmly say, *"God, things are really bad right now but I know You are in charge!"* Most of us dislike situations where we are not in control. We try to set our environment so everything is manageable. The problem with this is that it sets us up to be fearful instead of faithful. On the road home, God wants us to trust Him. Are you willing to experience whatever He asks of you?

Plowing

Supervisor's 1st Work Week Evaluation of Prospective Employees:

●   Spends an inordinate amount of time talking but gets almost nothing done.

●   He is adept at doing anything but work.

●   Has great advice on how to improve the organization and loves to share past accomplishments but her work is sloppy and requires fixing.

●   Worked aggressively for a period but then burn out and quit.

●   Requires little supervision and gets the job done superbly.

Luke 9:61,62—Another also said, "I will follow You, Lord, but first let me go and say good-bye to those at my house. But Jesus said to him, "No one who puts his hand to the plow and looks back is fit for the kingdom of God."

Does it seem like Jesus was critically insensitive to the people who verbally committed to following Him in Luke 9:57-62? Why was He tough on them? For starters, He could see inside their hearts. He knew that verbal commitment was no guarantee of follow-through. Earlier He taught *"If anyone wants to come with Me, he must deny himself, take up his cross daily, and follow Me. For whoever wants to save his life will lose it, but whoever loses his life because of Me will save it"* (9:23,24). Self-denial and excuses cannot lie in the same bed together. When Jesus heard the word *but*, He knew *no* was not far behind.

How's your plowing? Are you committed to Jesus? To plow for Him means to cut dirt moving forward in Kingdom formation according to the will of the Father. Jesus knows fully well that our soil at times is harder than clay. Follow means when He gives instructions we do exactly what He says. It's easy to plow when the sun is pleasant, the birds sing and the earth moves with ease. But what about those times when the field is full of boulders? Are we ministering because Jesus leads us or because we cannot say no to the incessant bells of insistent people? Are we plowing in grace or stuck in furrows *by the tyranny of the urgent*? Do we stop plowing because we think we know better than Jesus does what we ought to be doing? If His words seem overbearing, it's probably because we've lost our bearing!

For three years Jesus perfectly trained 12 plowmen. On the night before His crucifixion, one betrayed Him and eleven fled! They left the field when hell seemed closer than heaven. And let's not criticize them and dare to pretend we would never have done such a disloyal thing. In truth, we leave the field all the time. So, again, I ask, how's your plowing? I'm not just asking you, I'm asking myself. Better to reach the end of the day knowing I did my best investing for eternal rewards than to rationalize why I didn't hook up the oxen so I could stay out of the rain.

Independence

Psalm 33:12,22—Happy is the nation whose God is the LORD—the people He has chosen to be His own possession! May Your faithful love rest on us, LORD, for we put our hope in You.
Proverbs 14:34—Righteousness exalts a nation, but sin is a disgrace to any people.

Independence is the state of freedom from the influence, design or control of someone or others. It is the ability to self-govern unfettered by foreign powers; the spitting loose of a tyrannical bit knotted to another's reins. A nation's independence when married to morality rings the joyful bell of liberty, stirs the anthem of patriotism and honors the preservation of justice. It models a people whose sum is greater than her parts. Independence is much more than fireworks, baseball and homemade apple pie. These are just the aroma of a greater truth—the right to assemble to worship as we please, the right to vote and own property, the right to free speech—all without fear of being hauled off to prison, of being tortured, or killed.

The threat to independence is greater perhaps today than any other time in our republic's history. I write this for three reasons. *First, an independence taken for granted by those who live free is one which is vulnerable to others seizing.* A complacent land is soon a conquered land. It may not be a foreign army attacking our shores we should fear most. Our complacency creates another more insidious threat—the disease of immorality. Our moral foundation daily crumbles beneath a growing virus of crime that festers in our cities and towns. What cherished freedom can we boast of if we cannot allow our children to play in their own neighborhoods alone without fear that they will become prey to some vulture of perversion? How do we diagnose illness if the television is the one doing the monitoring? How does a reputed $8,000,000,000+ pornography industry infect the minds of our citizens? What we are attracted to defines and redefines our constitution. If those who lead our nation abdicate the conviction that character matters, then what matters is that we are now led by characters.

Second, disdained independence eventually atrophies to meaninglessness. How is it disdained? By those who promote anarchy—rule-less independence fettered only to whim. We did not become a free land because our forefathers despised authority! We became a free land because they rejected tyranny and the unjust application of rule by those in power. They championed morality and the promotion of spiritual values taught by Scripture.

Third, the dark side of independence is selfishness which rips apart the fabric of decency clothing a nation. Do we not live in a land today which basically promotes pleasure over principle? People tired of facing their responsibilities escape reality through drugs and short-lived euphoria. Wanton consuming outweighs thoughtful conserving. Winning is more important than telling the truth. What happens to others is irrelevant unless it concerns ME!

One of the best ways to gauge selfishness is to listen carefully to a nation's speech. We are a country that coins euphemisms to de-emphasize problems and excuse intolerable behavior. Instead of labeling a person an alcoholic or drug-addict we address him as chemically-dependent and fault the genes. The logical extension of absolving personal and collective responsibility for immoral behavior or conduct is the promotion of malfeasance. It is no wonder that Dr. Laura is the Jewish prophetess radio listeners tune in to. Many people are so ill from the candy of rationalization that they hunger for the bread of absolutes she steadfastly dishes up.

Our independence ought not to be bartered away on the world's flea markets. We have a rich history; rights mortgaged by the blood of countless patriots. We still carry coins that define our independence as trust in our Sovereign Maker. If we go to a cashless economy even that reminder will be lost.

Never forget the priceless treasure of holding citizenship in a land that allows you yet to own a Bible, to bow your head and pray to God, to congregate in fellowship, to breathe words of faith and sing songs of worship. If we ever lose these inalienable rights it will be because we fell asleep when we should have watched and prayed.

May God bless you and give you a spirit of dependence on Him. May God bless America and give her yet another chance to repent and be restored to the greatness that brings Him glory from sea to shining sea.

Inspiration † † †

If society becomes corrupt like a dark night or stinking fish, there's no sense in blaming society. That's what happens when fallen human society is left to itself and human evil is unrestrained and unchecked. The question to ask is "Where is the church?"—John Stott British Anglican cleric, (1921-2011), in "Christians: Salt and Light," *Preaching Today*, Tape No. 109.

Valuable

Imagine if the world were a scale it would not be able to measure this treasure. If we took all the money minted and printed throughout history from the entire globe and made one gigantic deposit in an effort to buy this prize, it would be like licking the pyramids in order to dissolve them. If the earth's greatest musicians and singers composed the perfect melody, it could not touch the soul like this gift from heaven. *God's love cannot be weighed or purchased or matched.* It is eternal in life and measureless in amount.

I often drive down the freeway and tell the Lord I love Him. Immediately chills go down my spine as He responds. Nothing is as liberating and joy producing as God's awesome love.

Luke 12:24—Consider the ravens: they don't sow or reap; they don't have a storeroom or a barn; yet God feeds them. Aren't you worth much more than the birds?

What makes us valuable is the fact that our Creator loves us! Are you empty inside and wandering through life like a wilted kite? Do you realize your value? The Lord knew your name before you were born. He gave you a unique design and purpose not so He could assemble some gigantic human puzzle, but because His infinite capacity cries out for more fellowship with human beings. That is right. You are valuable. God wants your heart included in His forever family.

The next time you see the bumper sticker "Life Sucks" on the car in front of you, consider asking the Lord to reveal His incredible love to that pessimistic occupant. And if by chance the car is yours, remember this— God loved you enough to let His perfect Son be massacred by people who believed their value was in how pious they looked. They thought that obeying His will meant protecting their legal interpretations of His laws. Only a twisted sense of value could condemn a loving Savior to death!

Do not measure your value by those things that will burn or fade with time. Set your esteem in the snow-crested peaks of God's personal love for you. Follow Him and you will glow in the warmth of His acceptance. Something to rejoice over . . . in reveration!

Inspiration † † †

Grace means there is nothing we can do to make God love us more. . .
—Philip Yancey in *What's So Amazing About Grace?*

Paganism

There is a tendency among those who call themselves Christians to belittle or make light of the convictions of people devoted to animate and inanimate objects. It is as if those who consecrate themselves to Mother Earth or who view themselves as gods are less genuine somehow in their convictions. It is in devaluing their convictions that we lose any right to be heard.

Luke 12:29-31—Don't keep striving for what you should eat and what you should drink, and don't be anxious. For the Gentile world eagerly seeks all these things, and your Father knows that you need them. But seek His kingdom, and these things will be provided for you.

What makes the Christian unique from the pagan is not validity of conviction. We have no right to say we are more sincere than another is. The issue is not how passionate one runs, but rather, who or what one is running after. What makes Christianity unique is that God reached down to us and through His awesome Son saved us! We do not impress Him or make the God-team by our efforts. We become His children by recognizing our inadequacy (sin), our need for forgiveness, and the justifying grace that can only come through a perfect Mediator. We let go of this kingdom in which we exist for His kingdom we pray will come. It is this journey of letting go and trusting God, which makes us distinct from pagans.

What man-made religion or hedonistic constitution produces salvation from sin? The pagan may seek escape from a painful reality. He may worship life and believe in cyclic renewal or regression but he cannot escape dirt. Only the Maker of dirt can redeem and wash whiter than snow, the sin-tainted, pride-mangled, deteriorating matter wrapped around an eternal soul. To fight over whose convictions are genuine is like grabbing smoke. Let pagans have their say and honor their right to clasp whatever they value. Then walk with integrity after the Lover of humanity. Because you love Him and live to know Him, God may use you to help another see the Light. The most effective witness is not the one who uses the loudest megaphone but rather the one who holds and obeys the still small voice.

Inspiration † † †

But if I know what is imperfect, I must have knowledge of the perfect; otherwise I would not know it is not-perfect . . . All non-Christian world views are ultimately self-contradictory. For example, skepticism refutes itself because it is internally self-contradictory. If skepticism is true, it is false.——Norman Geisler in *Christian Apologetics*

Surrender

Luke 14:33—In the same way, therefore, every one of you who does not say good-bye to all his possessions cannot be My disciple.

Come and meet a most peculiar of people. They embrace relinquishing their right to themselves to serve the will of some invisible Deity. They bow their heads respectfully in what they call prayer to send their words through a blank sky to some cosmic location called heaven believing their Creator-Father hears them.

They say God has a Son called Jesus. This Man-God is their hero. What is so bizarre is that this Jesus fellow, though a reputed miracle worker and profound teacher, willingly allowed Himself to be crucified on a cross at the behest of religious leaders who hated Him. He was utterly first-class in His ability to give up. This crucified Teacher, according to His enthusiastic disciples, rose from the dead! They say He lived a sinless life and then He took upon Himself the sins of the whole world. He laid down His life sacrificially to save all that would place their trust in Him.

These people are part of a global trust. What civilization on earth is untouched by teachings of Jesus and God as taught from a book they venerate as holy and call the Bible? Never mind that clever men wrote from ancient times, these people *actually believe* divine inspiration was behind the pen of each writer.

They abide by archaic commandments established by God on stone for a rebellious populace. Most annoyingly, they feel compelled to share their faith with others. Throughout this planet, they willingly relinquish their lives rather than renounce their loyalty to their Savior. In a world of relativism they remain fixed on an absolute notion that only one way exists to overcome sin and death and that is through faith in Jesus. This Lord makes claims no other religion matches. These followers testify Jesus has changed their lives and given them hope, peace, and meaning in life.

Any fool knows that to run up the white flag means defeat. Unconditional surrender is the fate of the vanquished—a scary proposition. Yet these fools throw down their right to do as they please to obey their God. They embrace submission as if it were nobler than independence. They yield where most defy. They are imperfect ambassadors for their holy Lord yet their notion of love, life and God provoke the heart. One cannot help but wonder if the lock confining emptiness is opened by a key called surrender.

Inspiration † † †

Conversion is a complete surrender to Jesus. It's a willingness to do what he wants you to do.—Billy Sunday, athlete, evangelist, (1862-1935)

Blind Spots

I was driving home yesterday when the woman in front of me pulled into my lane. Evidently, I was in her blind spot. I slammed on the brakes while at the same time maneuvering as quickly as possible to get around her car. Somehow, we avoided colliding and both continued on our way. It would have been easy to get angry (it happened too fast to honk!), and to mutter about incompetent drivers, but why? I know what it is like not to see someone in the other lane and just miss kissing metal! The antidote to that simple driving mistake is to add an extra mirror, or take the time to turn my head and look for another vehicle.

Luke 18:41—"What do you want Me to do for you?"
"Lord," he said, "I want to see!"

Did you ever stop to consider that we all drive through life with blind spots? Several things can cause us not to see or pay attention to potential danger around us. Often we cannot see spiritual issues clearly because of pride. Suppose someone flatters you with intent to gain some advantage. If your need is to have your ego stroked you may miss the coming trap or not see the hidden agenda of the one manipulating you. Or, because of our personality, we easily note what appeals to us and gloss over those things which seldom concern us.

If you are wired practically, you may zero in on fixing inefficiency yet clearly miss that someone is emotionally hurting. If mercy is not your strength, your need to be efficient may appear to others as cold and hardhearted.

It may be that we are lazy and do not take the time to pay attention to our surroundings. Accidents often occur because someone was not paying attention. If we do not make the effort to observe and discern what is going on in the lives of people or circumstances around us, we are set up to experience trouble.

Holding ourselves accountable to a trusted friend to see what we miss is valuable. Prayer is a fantastic aid to curing our lapsed vision. We ask the Holy Spirit to help us be discerning so that we do not stumble or fail to see danger. The more we trust Him to guide us, the more aware we are of what previously we could not see—let alone understand. While we may not be completely blind like the man who approached Jesus, his words might still be our inspiration. *Lord, I want to see!*

Inspiration † † †

The only thing worse than being blind is having sight but no vision.—Helen Keller

Interest makes some people blind, and others quick-sighted.—Francis Beaumont, English playwright, (1584-1616)

Nirvana

You have no doubt heard someone say, "All roads lead to God." While the statement may be sincere and reflect a desire to be nonjudgmental, it reveals a great lack of judgment. To understand this one needs only to visit India where the prevailing religions of Hinduism and Islam reside together in a dance of pain. A country gifted with incredibly smart people remains mired in poverty, disease, and a resigned acceptance of chaos as normative.

The contrast between Hinduism, Islam and Christianity is as stark as light to the absence of light. While most Indians maintain a fatalistic outlook, those who follow Jesus reveal a joy in the journey and a great hope in the great finale. Those who love God's Son and choose to make Him their Lord truly shine like lights in the darkness. They are not cowed by death or frustrated by the belief of endless reincarnations. They are unwilling to let people suffer because it is their *karma*. Rather they choose to share a transforming love as refreshing as cold water to parched lips.

While visiting India, repeatedly I met Christians who believed in the power of God because they experienced physical, emotional, and spiritual healing. I saw the effects of grace on faces acquainted with suffering. I prayed with Hindus eager to embrace a Jesus who offers mercy and hope not found in their hundreds of thousands of deities. I watched men and women, young and old, worship with contagious zeal the Almighty God.

It makes more sense to be an atheist than to propose that any belief regarding God or gods is valid. You cannot have it all ways without committing intellectual suicide. Jesus made the claim that no one can come to God except through Him (John 14:6). The validity of His words is profoundly visible in the lives of His Indian disciples. Jesus gives life meaning! In contrast, those who seek nirvana find emptiness. By rejecting Jesus' offer of salvation, Hinduism renders life miserable and Muslims live without the love of a grace-giving Savior.

John 1:4,5—Life was in Him, and that life was the light of men. That light shines in the darkness, yet the darkness did not overcome it.

Perhaps you have never experienced the joy of living a liberated life. If you would like to know God He makes it simple to find Him—simply admit that you are a sinner, place your trust in Jesus, and ask Him to forgive your sins and to be your Savior and Lord. *"Now the Scripture says, No one who believes on Him will be put to shame . . . For everyone who calls on the name of the Lord will be saved"* (Rom. 10:11,13). It is not too late! You are not beyond hope! God loves you and offers you the opportunity to live with Him in glory forever! If you take this step for the first time, will you write me at: dan@firstcause.org so I can rejoice and pray with you! You have done something to think about . . . in reveration!

Wilderness and Civilization

I wish everyone could take a seven-day hiatus into the wilderness. There are no phones to ring. Trees do not hold ticking clocks. The ground may be uncomfortable and the weather may be cold but the air is clean and perspectives change. Sitting around a campfire for hours, the mind begins to clear. Beads of stress from a culture of busyness evaporate under stars undulled by neon lights. The sound of a rushing river soothes the soul. The cries of a vigilant falcon pierce the thin air and send chills down the spine.

Scents become stronger—reddish flowers atop a carpet of tundra make Nordstrom perfume seem artificial. Taste comes alive to stomachs famished from hard work, eager to receive food slowly, without rush, in a place free of frenzy. One can listen here. Conversation is sane and appealing. Attire is simple but thoughtful for one must prepare for whatever surprises may come across the horizon. Here survival has meaning and life becomes simple again.

Civilization can advance intellectually, culturally, materially, artistically, and scientifically but without Jesus it always implodes. Eventually people turn on each other in ways more brutal than any animal could imagine. Civilization is coated with sin. It is diseased and without cure. Even in its most enlightened, advanced state, it slays its unborn to maintain its convenience.

John 1:11—He came to His own, and His own people did not receive Him.

Jesus spent 40 days in the wilderness on a camping trip His Father prepared for Him. Then He returned to a civilization He allowed to crush Him. But not before He sang God's heavenly love song or before He taught in parables too marvelous to understand. Not before He healed the diseases and cast out demons of countrymen desperate and defeated. Not before He eluded the traps of plotting religious leaders with godly wisdom or calmed the storm and changed water into wine. Certainly not before He trained a band of followers who would change the world forever because of what they learned from the Son of Man.

Go out into the wilderness and listen to what God has to say. Then go back into the city and let the love of the One who loves you extend to people desperate to find hope and meaning.

Inspiration † † †

Civilization is the lamb's skin in which barbarism masquerades.—Thomas Bailey Aldrich, poet, (1836-1907)

Truth

John 1:14—The Word became flesh and took up residence among us. We observed His glory, the glory as the One and Only Son from the Father, full of grace and truth.

Ten top reasons why people tell me they resist following Jesus.

1. Religion is a personal thing. Mind your own business.
2. They have never seen a clear presentation as to who Jesus is.
3. They would have to change how they live in order to obey him.
4. Their family would be upset.
5. Jesus was just a prophet like Mohammed, Buddha, Moses etc.
6. They do not believe Jesus is God or the only way to him. (In other words what is important is not path-selection but path-sincerity.—See Matthew 7:13,14)
7. At a critical point(s) in life, Jesus/God did not meet their needs.
8. What they see of Christians is unimpressive and they have no desire to be affiliated.
9. Christianity did not work for them.
10. They like Jesus as Savior but do not want him as Lord.

It's easy to fall into the trap of responding to those who resist following Christ with unwise zeal. Before you fire your spiritual shotgun with blasts of Scripture pellets, perform amazing pen and ink drawings of a bridge, or whip out a yellow booklet of four spiritual laws listen to Peter: *"simply concentrate on being completely devoted to Christ in your hearts. Be ready at any time to give a quiet and reverent answer to any man who wants a reason for the hope that you have within you."* (1 Pe. 3:15 PT).

Holy truth—this is good advice! Who is the Savior—you or Christ? What does God ask us to set apart—our illustrations and debate skills, or Jesus as Lord? The truth that we are responsible for is the *hope* that we have in Christ. We are not responsible for providing the hope someone else does not have. Beware of reducing Christianity to mental assent, to a formula, when Scripture clearly teaches the evidence of faith is a changed life! If Jesus is the truth, He will prove Himself as true to anyone who is honestly searching. Very few people reject Jesus because they conclude He is not the truth. Just the opposite, they stumble over His exclusive claims. They reject Him because of pride.

Jesus never said, "You will know the truth now go set others free." He said, *"You will know the truth and the truth will set you free"* (John 8:32). My testimony concerns what the Truth has done in my life. Yes, I'm more than excited to share anytime about that awesome, knee bending, heart mending, peace sending, sin ending, Truth! And you should be too! Praise God, that is effulgence (brilliant radiance)!

More Truth

2 John 1-4—The Elder: To the elect lady and her children, whom I love in truth— and not only I, but also all who have come to know the truth because of the truth that remains in us and will be with us forever. Grace, mercy, and peace will be with us from God the Father and from Jesus Christ, the Son of the Father, in truth and love. I was very glad to find some of your children walking in truth, in keeping with a command we have received from the Father.

Five times the Apostle John mentions truth in the introduction of his letter. What we learn through him about truth should enrich us. *First, the basis for his love for the elect lady and her children comes from a position of truth.* Some writers have translated verse 1 as *"truly love."* However, the Greek context makes it clear that John is not defining his love *as* true (using truth as an adverb), but rather that his love is based in truth (a noun)—a key distinction. We see this unfold in verses 10 and 11, where John commands believers *"If anyone comes to you and does not bring this teaching, do not receive him into your home, and don't say "Welcome," to him; for the one who says, "Welcome," to him shares in his evil works."* Love extends because of rightness.

Second, truth is something that God's children come to understand. In the process of this, love is corporately shared. The proof that we are God's children is obedience to His command: *"the one who loves God must also love his brother"* (1 Jn. 4:21b).

Third, truth is not some passing fad or possession that can be lost. It remains in us and will be with us for eternity. John states this as a promising assurance. The reason for this is God is eternal and He is truth! *"Now to the King eternal, immortal, invisible, the only God, be honor and glory forever and ever. Amen"* (1 Ti. 1:17). Jesus proclaimed, *"I am the way, the truth, and the life . . . When the Spirit of truth comes, He will guide you into all the truth"* (John 14:6, 16:13). Knowing this should greatly encourage us!

Fourth, the grace, mercy and peace that God through Jesus bequeaths us, remains with us substantiated through truth and love. Truth without love could not tolerate extending us the privilege of adoption. Love without truth would make grace, mercy and peace capricious—as dependable as a cat responding to voice commands.

Fifth, John is very happy when he sees young believers doing what is right. As a parent, few things encourage me as much as seeing my children make wise decisions and live honorably because they value obeying God's instruction. I know experientially that when they prize truth, they will be blessed and experience the fullness of God's activity in their lives. Genuine gladness is truth-encased. So live in truth and have complete joy!

New Birth

I love to watch newborns. They are so helpless and dependent upon their parents. And as they grow there is an absolute trust in the one providing care. A baby does not say, "Put me down! You might drop me you blubbering giant!" Babies do not enter the realm of doubt. They may exercise stubbornness or wail like fire trucks but always from a position of need or will and never doubt.

John 3:3,4—Jesus replied, "I assure you: Unless someone is born again, he cannot see the kingdom of God."
"But how can anyone be born when he is old?" Nicodemus asked Him. "Can he enter his mother's womb a second time and be born?"

Jesus challenged Nicodemus, a devout Pharisee, to be born again. He was not insulting this learned scholar who didn't get it. Nor was He being clever in a game of wits. Jesus' point was simple. If you want to get into God's kingdom, you must let go of everything you so dearly hold on to and put your trust in Me! To be born again is not a surgical operation. It is like my youngest son, Stephen, who used to leap off the stairs into my arms. It means listening to the Holy Spirit who whispers to our hearts "It is all about humility and trust, dying to selfish adultery to follow Christ, who died on the cross for you." Jesus said, *"For God loved the world in this way: He gave His One and Only Son, so that everyone who believes in Him will not perish but have eternal life"* (John 3:16).

Max Lucado in his book *3:16* shares a marvelous truth about the word "again" in John 3:3. There are two Greek words that mean "again"—*palin* and *anothen*. Jesus chose the word *anothen*, which denotes a repeated action but requires the original source to repeat it. *Anothen* means "from above, from a higher place, things which come from heaven or God."[32] Conversely, *palin* just means to redo an action committed before. Even in the simple choice of the word "again," Jesus illustrates the power of God at work in birth! Something to think about . . . in reveration!

Inspiration †††

Human salvation demands the divine disclosure of truths surpassing reason.—Saint Thomas Aquinas, Italian Catholic priest (Dominican Order), philosopher and theologian, (1225-1274)

Misplaced Principles

John 3:17—For God did not send His Son into the world that He might condemn the world, but that the world might be saved through Him.

I enjoy spending time with people who are searching for meaning in life. I find that often many of them grapple with tough questions. They sincerely yearn to know God. Repeatedly I find that most of these folks will not go to church. They have tried. They have attended different fellowships but left in frustration. Three themes regarding their disappointment emerge.

1. *Church is irrelevant to their needs.*
2. *They see little difference between the people going to church and themselves.*
3. *They do not measure up to the principles Christians tout and feel judged for their shortcomings.*

When we become Christians, the Holy Spirit makes us conscious of sins that as nonbelievers mattered little to us. But always He does this in the context of drawing us closer to our Holy Father. Language is a good example of this. Before a person knew Jesus, swearing may have been no big deal. When Jesus becomes Lord, the individual, under godly conviction, cleans up her language. Now she exports her personal experience as a standard to uphold by admonishing anyone around her who swears. Co-workers feel uncomfortable and stop socializing with the new *fanatic*. They do not see Jesus as a Savior but rather as a rule-promoter. Yet, believers stroke the rookie for taking a stand. Therefore, she takes her cue from them! Forgetting that it was God's grace that reached her, she draws attention to people's shortcomings instead of to Christ. Now we have a problem.

When principles become more important than Jesus, we lose our heart for those without Christ. We judge the unmarried couple living together and instead of seeing their need for Jesus we focus on their immorality. The neighbor who prefers wine coolers will not invite us over because we preach against drinking. While our list of principles grows, our tolerance and heart for the hurting shrinks. While our motives may be right, the message we broadcast stinks.

We should take our cue from Jesus. He spent much time with sinners. Why was it that the lost flocked to Him? Could it be that He focused on their hearts and not on their habits? Principles are not the problem, our priorities are the problem. It is the job of the Holy Spirit to convict. It is the job of Christians to be lights. When we reverse the order, we become junior holy spirits and we actually help, rather than hinder, Satan.

Assimilation

John 4:34—"My food is to do the will of Him who sent Me and to finish His work," Jesus told them.

We must make a conscious effort to move beyond what we know to what we do. There is a subtle contempt among many believers for Biblical truth. This contempt lives in the phrase—"You can't tell me anything I haven't already heard." What is meant is—"I know what I'm supposed to do; whether I choose to do anything is not your concern!" This is nothing less than pride. God resists the proud—Jam. 4:6. Do not let this happen to you! How can we avoid becoming smugsters (self-righteous know-it-alls), and be the truth-assimilators God desires?

● *Recognize that without humility truth is framed in a black and white sketch called dogma.* Intellect does not advance the Kingdom of Heaven. What advances the Kingdom is what we do with what we know.

● *Ask God to enable us to assimilate the truth His Holy Spirit reveals in our daily living.* Assimilation is "the conversion of nutriments into living tissue." Our Lord came so that we could become living tissue—holy, God pleasing, gospel-revealing saints.

Is there anything God would have you do that you might be resisting? Is there a message those who love you wish you would hear and apply that you defy? To assimilate truth on the road home is to make the journey more joyful.

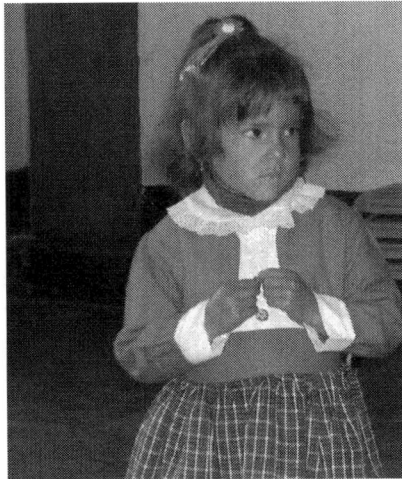

"You Give Them Something to Eat"

There are times in my life where God gives me opportunity to minister but because of inconvenience or poor priorities, I chose to do my own thing. In meditating on Luke 9:10-17, I am convicted by many thoughts. The disciples, earlier sent out by Jesus, returned from ministering in teams of two and reported to Him all that happened. They were tired and hungry and Jesus recognizing this took them away to care for their needs. However, the crowds were of a different opinion and situation. They raced around the Sea of Galilee to intercept the Son of God and His men at their remote landing.

Instead of escaping 5,000 men and the uncounted women and children, Jesus welcomed them, taught them and healed the sick. He set aside the needs of His team and perhaps His own wants to minister to the crowd God brought to Him. I wonder what thoughts ran through the minds of His men!

John 6:5-7—Therefore, when Jesus looked up and noticed a huge crowd coming toward Him, He asked Philip, "Where will we buy bread so these people can eat?" He asked this to test him, for He Himself knew what He was going to do. Philip answered, "Two hundred denarii worth of bread wouldn't be enough for each of them to have a little."

In Luke's account, the disciples appealed to Christ to send away the crowd to surrounding villages to find food and lodging. But Jesus said, *"You give them something to eat"* (Luke 9:13). In John's account, Jesus tests Philip. After Philip's response, Andrew informs Jesus (verse 9) of a small boy's five barley loaves and two tiny fish and comments, *"but what are they for so many?"*

If God brings people to us that He wants us to minister to, will He not also provide us the resources and strength we need to accomplish the ministry? The disciples looked at their surroundings and discounted the opportunity to get involved meeting needs. There were too many hungry people in a remote location with insufficient food. In addition, they were tired and hungry. Too often, I am like the band of twelve. It is easier to find reasons not to minister than to apply faith.

God does not call us to be reporters or independent operators. He calls us to be responsible and exercise faith. He does not see problems but rather opportunities. When we understand this and get involved doing His will, we experience the extra twelve baskets of food the satisfied crowd could not eat!

Inspiration † † †

You are not only responsible for what you say, but also for what you do not say.—Martin Luther

If God Chooses

John 6:37,44—Everyone the Father gives Me will come to Me, and the one who comes to Me I will never cast out . . . No one can come to Me unless the Father who sent Me draws him, and I will raise him up on the last day.

Does the idea of choosing seem controversial? The doctrine of election (God sovereignly selecting people for salvation), may seem unfair. We conjure up memories of playground decisions where the best athletes are picked first, while the weaker members are divvyed up reluctantly, or sent away by those possessing the power to decide. Yet, the concept of election (a theme that runs throughout Scripture), is evident in Jesus' statements in John 6. While it is not possible to cover this subject fully in a devotional, we can glean some helpful truths from God's Word.

Election is about the accomplishing of God's purpose according to His pleasure and will (Eph. 1:4,5). Romans 9:11 notes, *"for though they had not been born yet or done anything good or bad, so that God's purpose according to election might stand."* Later we read, *"So receiving God's promise is not up to us. We can't get it by choosing it or working hard for it. God will show mercy to anyone He chooses"* (Rom.9:16 NLT).

God's purpose is vast, beyond comprehension. He sees unfettered by time, unlimited in scope, and with no weakness. He is perfectly powerful, administering mercy and grace based on just reasoning. *"What should we say then? Is there injustice with God? Not! For He tells Moses: I will show mercy to whom I show mercy, and I will have compassion on whom I have compassion"* (Rom.9:14,15). Conversely, while made in God's image, we nevertheless make determinations based on thinking and emotions tainted by our sin-condition. We do not expect a doctor to treat according to the sentiments of a patient, whose reasoning is clouded by illness. Nor should we superimpose our notions of fairness on God from our depraved status.

If God elects people for salvation, then how can He blame those who do not listen to Him? Romans 9:19b (NLT) says, *"Haven't they simply done what He makes them do?"* Paul counters such logic by writing, *"But who are you, O man, to talk back to God?"* He then quotes the prophet Isaiah, *"Shall what is formed say to him who formed it, 'why did you make me like this?'"* (Rom.9:20 NIV). God as the Author of life writes mercy or punishment for each life as He deems. Only He knows the outcome for each person. Yet, His sovereign working is never an excuse for our resignation. Contrary to those who insist that evangelism is unnecessary, (since God preordained who should be saved), Jesus commanded His disciples (and us by logical extension), to preach His gospel (Mat. 28:19,20).

Paul obeyed Jesus. He wrote for the Roman church to teach:
If you confess with your mouth, 'Jesus is Lord,' and believe in your heart that God raised Him from the dead, you will be saved. With the heart

one believes, resulting in righteousness, and with the mouth one confesses, resulting in salvation" (Rom.10:9,10).

If the words above were powerless because salvation was "fixed," the gospel would be a limited message and a cruel hoax. Therefore, we conclude that election is marvelous because it is administered by the perfectly capable hands of our loving Father who knows what we do not know, to accomplish what we will later know.

Inspiration † † †

An ocean liner leaves New York bound for Liverpool. Its destination has been determined by proper authorities. Nothing can change it. This is at least a faint picture of sovereignty. On board the liner are scores of passengers. These are not in chains, neither are their activities determined for them by decree. They are completely free to move as they will. They eat, sleep, play, lounge about on the deck, read, talk, altogether as they please; but all the while the great liner is carrying them steadily onward toward a predetermined port. Both freedom and sovereignty are present here, and they do not contradict. So it is, I believe, with man's freedom and the sovereignty of God. The mighty liner of God's sovereign design keeps its steady course over the sea of history.—A.W. Tozer in *Knowledge of the Holy*

Emancipated

John 8:36—Therefore if the Son sets you free, you really will be free.

Once upon a time, a loving Creator created fireworks. But alas, the Designer's enemy deceived the first two fireworks made into believing they could perform as equals to their Maker. Their rebelliousness tainted every succeeding generation of firework with a competitive "My pop's better than your pop!" mentality.

In language: some boomed; some banged like gunfire; some shrieked in irritating shrill; some whined while others *whooshed* and *pshewwwed*; some roared in bass while others whistled in octaves every dog deplores.

In motion: they zipped and zapped in streaks; they tottered and bounced recklessly; they spun like tops costumed in green and then purple; they rocketed as if nothing could stop them or they were content to sit and flare; they arched high into the sky to dance frenetically in brilliant colors; and they floated like parachutes casting circles of light.

In size: some were tiny and easily missed against those that were huge; some were elongated rockets; some were box-like while others were round; some were fat and some were sleek; some were particularly beautiful with their exquisite design.

In talent: many had a single purpose to make noise, give light, move or smoke; a few were superstars—overwhelming in their ability to create sight, sound and motion; some had short fuses while others were completely lacking; and then there were bombs that never amounted to anything— refusing to ignite.

For the Designer, every firework was special each having an intended purpose. Unfortunately, the vast majority refused to believe Him. They were more content to sit miserably in their containers, ignoring Him while pretending they were a splendid extension of the big bang, or worshiping inferior duds of their own making. Finally, their patient Maker fashioned His Son to live among them and be like them. He was the most splendid of all firecrackers only to be extinguished (by jealous pyrotechnics), and come back to life!

He brought emancipation to all that trusted and loved Him. No longer would the greatest thrill be that of going out with a bang only to be judged as deficient by the Creator. Indeed, He taught and trained His followers to burn so that others would see and smell His aroma. He offered the promise of forgiveness for every wayward firecracker willing to be lit and guided by Him. He would one day transform each convert into a perfect light to shine spectacularly forever with the Father of lights. He brought hope, joy and peace to a chaotic world of competing missiles. Who will respond to His guarantee?

Offended

CPT Bob climbed the tower. His soldiers were there to rappel off the tall wooden platform. Atop the platform, he inspected the training and noticed a simple granny knot improperly anchored the rope. Therefore, he pointed out to the Lieutenant, Officer in Charge (OIC), the problem. The LT disagreed, said the knot was fine and ordered Bob off the tower. He was in charge and he resented the intrusion of this reserve officer. Bob reminded him that safety was everyone's responsibility and that he would not allow his soldiers to go down the tower under such unsafe conditions. Again, the LT told him to leave. After more heated words, Bob descended the stairs and walked over to the nearest phone to report an unsafe condition. While he was on the phone, one of his soldiers leaning over the edge shrieked as his rope came loose. He fell straight to the ground and broke his spine.

Why—why did such a needless tragedy take place? Perhaps one active duty lieutenant thought to himself, "What does this reservist Captain know!" Maybe he was insecure. Regardless of the thought process that wound through his brain, the result was a horrendous accident for which he would spend the rest of his life regretting.

John 9:32-34—"Throughout history no one has ever heard of someone opening the eyes of a person born blind. If this man were not from God, He wouldn't be able to do anything."
"You were born entirely in sin," they replied, "and are you trying to teach us?" Then they threw him out.

The Apostle John gives his eyewitness account of Jesus healing a man born blind. Rather than celebrate a colossal miracle, the Pharisees were offended. They did not like this upstart Galilean breaking their Sabbath laws to do good deeds. Despite repeatedly interrogating the seeing man to find fault with Jesus, he mocked them, provoking an outburst of insults. Even when he shared poignant truth in the meditation above, they could not stand the possibility of being wrong and reacted in anger (John 9).

Why does Jesus offend people? I best understand this question when I honestly admit what offends me. *I do not like being wrong.* It is embarrassing to be exposed. I am older than you are. I am more educated. I have experience that qualifies me—who are you? These are pride lines. Self-importance that refuses to admit God's truth constitutes a medical condition called spiritual blindness and it is forever fatal. Were it not for God's grace grabbing me by the throat and exposing me to my own sin and need for redemption, I would die with this disease.

Are you offended by the Son of God who says He is the only way to salvation? What are you hiding? What are you clinging to that outweighs eternal life with a loving Savior? Are you willing to bet eternity on the knot you've tied?

Do you know someone offended? Have you forgotten your own healing? Do you take for granted vision at the cost of praying for those stumbling in the dark? How many shrieks must you hear of those falling before you earnestly share the truth?

Oh God wake us up!

Inspiration † † †

It is a serious thing to be offended with Jesus; it means stagnation of character. Jesus Christ can never save offended people, because people who are offended with Jesus shut up their natures against Him; they will not see in Him—the Son of God—their Savior; they will not hear His words of life.—Oswald Chambers in *God's Workmanship*

When you are offended at any man's fault, turn to yourself and study your own failings. Then you will forget your anger.—Epictetus, Greek sage and stoic philosopher (55-135)

Labels

Charles and I were having a discussion when I asked him what would happen if a truck came around the bend at a high speed and accidentally struck and killed him? What would he say to God when the Lord asked him why He should let him into heaven? Charles said, "Well the operative answer would be that I believe in Jesus Christ and am sorry for my sins."

Indeed, when most people give me that answer I assume they are Christians. In Charles case, he had lived a dangerous lifestyle as a gang member in Los Angeles. At a point when he was despairing of life, he heard loud music in a church and went inside. There he heard the gospel message and at the age of 22 prayed to receive Christ. Most people would label Charles a Christian because of that action.

But hold the bus. Now seventeen years later, Charles is still struggling to make sense of life. When I asked him about Jesus, he had no idea that God's Son was sinless. Nor did he understand why He came to earth or what role He played in providing salvation. Charles knew the name Jesus but had no intimate relationship or understanding of the Lord. The extent of his spiritual knowledge was a one-time event. He heard of the Shepherd, called His name and then left to continue wandering in other fields with other herds. Therefore, it was a great joy to fill him in on who Jesus really is, why He matters and what He wants to do in Charles' life. Charles left Main Street with a challenge to start following the Lord Jesus Christ.

John 10:4,14—When he has brought all his own outside, he goes ahead of them. The sheep follow him because they recognize his voice . . . "I am the good shepherd. I know My own sheep, and they know Me."

The danger with labels is that we make an assumption about people that may be wholly absent of fact. *Just because a person has prayed to receive Christ does not mean that person knows Christ.* Perhaps one of the deepest flaws in Christianity is we have multitudes of people wandering the planet who classify themselves as Christians but who have no spiritual education, training, or understanding of what it means to be a follower of Jesus. Labels invite laziness. They spur prejudice and affix meaning that in fact may constitute identity theft.

Charles and I had a splendid time talking about the church and why it is important to be in fellowship with those who *know* Jesus, whose belief is founded in daily living with the One whose unfailing love changes our lives, gives us hope and meaning in our journey on the road home. Hallelujah! God in His faithfulness brought to us a lost man to reveal the true nature and purpose of His Son. So, the next time I hear someone say he or she is a Christian, I may just ask, "Oh really, and what exactly does that mean!"

Branches of the Vine

John 15:5—I am the vine; you are the branches. The one who remains in Me and I in him produces much fruit, because you can do nothing without Me.

I look back on my high school years (10-12) in the Philippines as some of the most meaningful, formative years of my life. Faith Academy is located on a hill in a township outside of Manila. In the class of '77 there were 61 of us. Because we were somewhat isolated, it was a fantastic place to build relationships.

In 2008, about thirty of us from the classes of '76 and '77 met in Nashville, Tennessee, for a reunion over the 4th of July weekend. Many of us had not seen each other for over 32 years yet it took no time to rekindle friendships and to reminisce laughingly over memories forged in our teens.

Saturday night, Bruce shared with the group that the thing, which most bonded us and what mattered for our remaining years, is the gospel. It was a heartfelt affirmation of the truth that our rich heritage is tied to Jesus. The gospel is our hope. The gospel is our compass pointing heavenward on the road home. It is our constant reminder that life no matter how difficult is worth living, because Jesus found us worth saving. Some in our midst were going through very difficult times, yet because of the One inside us, we were able to provide love and understanding.

We are branches of the Vine. Branches do not always grow straight. Some twist and turn—tangled by years of pain and moving in unintended directions. Some are full of fruit—testimony to the rich blessings which come from deep abiding. Some are thin and barren—in need of pruning. Some are strong and wrap around others with a grip that gives the word encouragement such amplitude that all want to burst into song. Some point in their own unique direction yet carry the same texture and conviction that attest to Vine-living.

We are branches of the Vine. Branches do not always understand what the Vine is doing. However, we have the freedom to ask for His help and to share our challenges. The Vine promises that so long as we abide in Him, He will provide and we will bring glory to the Father.

We are branches of the Vine. The fellowship that comes from a body, which grows from Him, defies explanation. Personalities that would normally clash find unity in expression. Temperaments made for competition lovingly serve each other. Small embraces large, tall bends to meet short, gregarious affirms shy, insecure melts beside understanding and heaven claps as worship ascends from the vineyard.

I look forward to my heritage with brothers and sisters on eternal ground fashioned by the Vine for fruitful living. The Vine is beyond amazing. To be His branch is beyond blessing.

Tundra

John 18:1—After Jesus had said these things, He went out with His disciples across the Kidron Valley, where there was a garden, and He and His disciples went into it.

Five men camped along the Tulik River in the remote tundra of the Arctic Circle near the Brooks Range. Our intent was to hunt caribou and ptarmigan, and fish for grayling. For many men, few things exceed the thrill of hunting. It is a great test of wit, skill, perseverance, and careful planning which, if executed properly, results in the successful acquisition of food. For us it was a time of camaraderie and challenge.

The tundra of Alaska is very difficult to walk. The ground in August is uneven, wet and full of plant life which when stepped on, often gives way, causing the foot and ankle to slide either left or right. Most of our time we spent either looking for game or ponderously packing out meat.

Life can be like walking through tundra. The hunter tenses in excitement at that climactic moment when the target is in sight. For this moment, he dreams and plans. However, in reality, most of his life is in the valley where each step can be challenging and tedious. We prefer chills down the spine to sweat down our backs. But if we make exhilaration our goal, we are destined to despise what is ordinary and necessary. In fact, the valley is important. While there, God teaches us much about our character and purpose. It is on the tundra where the Lord of the heavens wants to mold us to be like Him.

Perhaps you have grown tired of your environment, occupation, or place in life. Are you fatigued beneath the weight of a boring pack? Are you frustrated by an endless plain where God's voice seems absent? Well, take heart! Give the extraordinary, heavenly Father your ordinary trials! Imagine the blessing you can be to those around you if daily you exude peace and joy through what most would consider mundane or discouraging! Our Savior is not merely interested in us when we reach the ridge. He is with us through the valley! He will teach us in the tundra!

Inspiration † † †

Your valley may be a darkness where you have nothing but your duty to guide you, no voice, no thrill, but just steady, plodding duty; or it may be a deep agonizing dejection at the realization of your unfitness and uncleanness and insufficiency. Let God put you on His wheel and whirl you as He likes, and as sure as God is God and you are you, you will turn out exactly in accordance with the vision He gave you. Don't lose heart in the process.—Oswald Chambers in *So Send I You*

How to Share Your Testimony

John 19:35—He who saw this has testified so that you also may believe. His testimony is true, and he knows he is telling the truth.

At least twelve times seventeen-year old Bryan shared his testimony in India. His story of God miraculously healing his inoperable, incurable brain tumor was a mighty testament to God's power. His dedication to serve God was an encouragement to all who heard him. Bryan reinforced what I have always believed—the most effective means of evangelism is often sharing our story.

If you know Jesus as your Savior and your Lord, you have a unique story—a testimony to God's authenticity. While people may refuse to accept a gospel tract and scoff at you for trying to explain Christianity, very few people will be so rude as to reject your life story. The most credible way to share Jesus is to share what He means to you, what He has done and is doing to change your life.

It is amazing isn't it! We will gladly tell a stranger, or all our friends, about a health product if it makes us feel better. We will eagerly share a great recipe or tell folks about a great product that is on sale. However, when it comes time to share about the One who gives us hope we become strangely mute, afraid to speak for fear we might offend someone. Many in the world are dying without truth for what we should be willing to die to tell them. The Apostle Paul wrote, *"For I am not ashamed of the gospel, because it is God's power for salvation to everyone who believes, first to the Jew, and also to the Greek"* (Rom. 1:16). Brothers and sisters, you also have experienced that power Paul proclaimed, for God also saved and equipped you!

1 John 5:10—*("The one who believes in the Son of God has the testimony in himself. The one who does not believe God has made Him a liar, because he has not believed in the testimony that God has given about His Son.")*

Here is a simple guide that that will help you prepare your testimony:

1. *Pray and ask the Lord for wisdom and guidance as you write out your story* (Jam. 1:5,6).

2. *Use a simple outline*:
   - What your life was like before you personally knew Christ.
   - How you came to know and have a personal relationship with Jesus—be specific!
   - What your life became like after you received Christ. What changes has He made in you?

   How do you relate to Him now?

3. *Be sincere and honest in looking for an opportunity to share.* Have a strong interest-grabbing introduction. Example: *"Can I tell you about the greatest thing that has ever happened to me?"*

4.   *Write your testimony in a manner that will allow you to speak so that others feel like they can associate with your past and present experiences.* Focus on *how* you became a Christian and not just why it is great to be a Christian.

5.   *Emphasize how good God's grace and mercy is.* The intent of the testimony is to point a person to Christ. God's objective truth is more important than our subjective experience. It is important that a person understand that faith is based on historical facts and the authenticity of Christ and our lives reflect this truth.   While our feelings may be important enough to share, be sure to emphasize Scripture that defines how we are lost and why we need salvation. (John 3:16; Rom. 3:23, 6:23, 10:9,10).

6.   *Practice presenting your testimony to someone who can constructively listen and give you feedback as to clarity, style and content.*   Memorize and practice it until it becomes natural.

7.   *Share with enthusiasm in the power of the Holy Spirit*—1 Co. 2:4,5.   When you share, be sure to end with a strong conclusion.   A good testimony is like an appetizer, it stimulates hunger for more!   If your listener asks to hear more that is a great sign.   But even if they do not you should be encouraged that you were faithful to share.

Things to Avoid:

1.   *Forcing your testimony on someone, or setting him or her up.*   Do not argue or use high-pressure methods of getting a *decision* for Christ.   The Holy Spirit is the One who draws people to God so we do not need to preach at people or try to make them feel guilty.

2.   *Christianese or glittering generalities in your speech.*   Words like *saved, born-again, convicted, converted, redeemed,* and *sanctified* do not make sense to the average non-Christian.

3.   *Mannerisms.*   Watch out for distracting mannerisms when you speak— such as rubbing your nose, jingling coins in your pocket, swaying, clearing your throat, or repetitively saying *um, like* or *you know.*

4.   *Overemphasizing past sins in your life* lest you turn a person away from seeing the need for Christ, since the person listening, may not feel like such a bad person.

5.   *Emphasizing church denominations or religious organizations—especially in a derogatory way.*   Do not speak critically or negatively about other individuals or groups.   Keep the focus on Jesus!   Salvation is through Him not some denomination, order or fellowship.

6.   *Giving the impression that the Christian life is easy or without struggles.*

Empowered

Acts 1:8—But you will receive power when the Holy Spirit has come upon you, and you will be My witnesses in Jerusalem, in all Judea and Samaria, and to the ends of the earth.

After Jesus communicated the words above to His apostles, He ascended into heaven! He knew they were ready to get after God's will. Luke, the writer of Acts, establishes for us in this verse the theme of his book to Theophilus. Therefore, it is extremely important that we understand its application to us for it provides our missiological foundation and strategy.

I.   *Foundation*—Once we become followers of Jesus Christ we receive the Holy Spirit and the direct result of this is that we are empowered. Without the Holy Spirit, the church cannot advance. We know from the Word of God that the Holy Spirit is essential to us for:

1.   Eternal Life—The Spirit alone gives eternal life—John 6:63, Rom. 8:6,11

2.   Truth—The Spirit is our Counselor who guides us in what is right and in what we can expect in the future. He convicts the world of its sin, of God's righteousness and His impending judgment —John 14:16,17, 16:8,13.

3.   Teaching—The Spirit teaches us all things and reminds us of Jesus' words and importance—John 14:26, 15:26, 16:14; Acts 1:2

4.   Strength—The Spirit helps us in our weakness leading us to righteousness, peace and joy; furthering the gospel by working miracles in and through us—Rom. 8:26, 14:17, 15:19

II.   *Strategy*—Jesus next communicated the essential role for His followers. They were to be worldwide witnesses! Beginning in Jerusalem (where they were gathered), the gospel would extend across their nation, into the adjoining country of Samaria and out into the whole world. Today, across the globe, we are the generational fruit of obedient apostles!

Therefore, here is the key question. How are we contributing to the furtherance of the gospel? The foundation and strategy are just concepts unless you and I are obedient to the Lord's leading. He has empowered us! We have life, truth, teaching and strength. But unless we are obedient to His call, we are like unplugged Christmas lights. Are you shining for Jesus? Have you asked the Lord how He wants to empower you for the expansion of His mighty kingdom?

Inspiration   † † †

Whenever God acts in power to accomplish His purposes, the divine Paraclete does the work.—Robert E. Coleman in *The Master Plan of Discipleship*

Obscurity

They are mentioned in one paragraph in the Bible and then (with the possible exception of Acts 15:22) never again. They walked near Jesus from the time John baptized Him to His ascension to heaven but we know next to nothing about them. What kind of personality and gifting did each man have? How frequently did they gain access to the Master?

Jesus promised His disciples in Mat.19:28: *"I assure you: In the Messianic Age, when the Son of Man sits on His glorious throne, you who have followed Me will also sit on 12 thrones, judging the 12 tribes of Israel."*

Peter and his fellow apostles felt the need to replace Judas, after he turned traitor and betrayer before ending his life. Judas was not going to sit on a throne judging anyone after his wretched behavior. After much prayer and deliberating, the apostles selected two candidates—Joseph (called Barsabbas or Justus) and Matthias.

Acts 1:26—Then they cast lots for them, and the lot fell to Matthias. So he was numbered with the 11 apostles.

No doubt, Matthias was thrilled to become one of the twelve. But I wonder what emotions and thoughts went through Joseph's mind. He missed the closest election to a heavenly throne anyone has ever had! He was a lot throw away from getting his name written on one of the twelve foundations for God's heavenly city (see Rev. 21:14)! Somehow, I do not think that mattered. These two men were special. They were godly and God-fearing. They were loyal and commanded the respect of eleven powerhouses—trained by the greatest disciplemaker the world has ever known. I suspect they faithfully served God to their dying day. We will not know the rest of the story until we get to heaven because the New Testament leaves them heroes in obscurity.

Hmmm. Imagine following the King of kings faithfully for years behind the scenes, out of the crowd's sight, all the while making it easier for someone more gifted and popular to be a blessing. Imagine, sweeping floors while praying for hurting people; making meals for the sick and quietly delivering them when no one sees; singing songs of worship out of tune to the Father who hears your heart; reading God's Word when every muscle in your body aches with no relief; walking lonely without your smiling mate—martyred by evil.

Perhaps you march to the unglamorous beat of obscurity. If you love Jesus and faithfully follow Him, don't despair. Your hard work may never find mention in any paper; the pastor in your church of thousands may never know your name. You may never even win so much as a red ribbon. It's okay friend. Your name is in the Book of Life. You have no idea how awesome the rewards are that you will reap eternally for humility, grace, integrity and love. God sees all.

The Greatest Gift

Acts 2:38—"Repent," Peter said to them, "and be baptized, each of you, in the name of Jesus the Messiah for the forgiveness of your sins, and you will receive the gift of the Holy Spirit."

It is the nature of man to exalt the experience as opposed to experience what is exalted. How rich it is to be shaken! Yet the glory is not in the emotional surge. The Apostles did not start The First Church of the Shakees. They did not fall victim to exalting their experiences, they witnessed with fervor about Jesus.

The glory is in knowing God! The glory exists in obeying His Word. The glory is in experiencing the fruit of the Spirit. The glory is in the boldness in sharing Christ under the leading of the Holy Spirit. Beware of racking up frequent flyer miles rushing from one reported sighting of God's Spirit at work to another. If we chase after tongues of fire, we have missed the whole point of filling! If we must travel to find where God's Spirit is at work, then our entire relationship with Him is suspect. God is here alive and well, looking for glory in those willing to prove faithful.

Peter told his listeners that they would receive the gift of the Holy Spirit after repentance and baptism. The baptism symbolized their faith in Jesus. Beware of those who would make you jump through their hoops or meet extra Biblical criteria before you can receive the Holy Spirit. The New Testament is clear that God gives His Spirit to us when we repent of our sin and place our faith in Jesus as Savior and Lord. Ephesians 1:13-15 teaches us:

In Him you also, when you heard the word of truth, the gospel of your salvation—in Him when you believed—were sealed with the promised Holy Spirit. He is the down payment of our inheritance, for the redemption of the possession, to the praise of His glory."

I prefer the NIV word choice of "*deposit*" rather than "*down payment.*" Essentially, what we learn is that the baptism of the Holy Spirit is a fruit of salvation that is sustaining. We are sealed! Do not confuse baptism of the Holy Spirit with filling of the Holy Spirit. The former comes at salvation and is permanent. The latter constitutes those special times God anoints us for works of service or to enable us in ministry to do that which we could not do on our own.

One final thought: this gift from God is a special endowment do not take it lightly. When God gives of Himself to us, we have no right to then "live like hell." To do so is to demean the Gift and takes us right into the realm where Paul admonishes the church, "*And don't grieve God's Holy Spirit, who sealed you for the day of redemption*" (Eph. 4:30). The baptism of the Holy Spirit is the greatest gift we will ever receive and that is most certainly something to think about . . . in reveration!

Lillian

Until she passed away, I loved to meet with Lillian for prayer. She lived in a retirement community called King City. Brick walls separated each house and the only way to enter a home was through the garage or a gate in the front. Whoever designed her neighborhood obviously valued privacy and security. There was little sense of community. No wonder lonely Lillian loved to meet for fellowship.

Acts 2:46,47—And every day they devoted themselves to meeting together in the temple complex, and broke bread from house to house. They ate their food with gladness and simplicity of heart, praising God and having favor with all the people. And every day the Lord added to them those who were being saved.

Is technology sucking the lifeblood out of fellowship? Nowadays, people can spend time alone just listening to music on their I Pods, watching DVDs on their laptops, playing computer games or surfing the net. Even normal phone conversations are falling victim to text messaging. A pastor recently noted sad statistics for his church. In the past year, hospitality decreased 50% among church members.

Camaraderie is a critical component of spiritual growth! It:

1. *Centers our focus on our shared interest and relationship with God.* We honor Him by coming together to partake of communion, worship, studying the Word and sharing. *"Happy are the people with such blessings. Happy are the people whose God is the LORD"* (Psa. 144:15b).

2. *Creates accountability and helps us encourage one another.* The writer of Hebrews stated, *"And let us be concerned about one another in order to promote love and good works, not staying away from our meetings, as some habitually do, but encouraging each other, and all the more as you see the day drawing near"* (Heb. 10:24,25).

3. *Empowers us "because your strength comes from rejoicing in the Lord"* (Neh. 8:10b); *"A cord of three strands is not easily broken"* (Ecc. 4:12b). When firs grow in close proximity, their overlapping root system gains them enormous power to resist the wind. The solitary tree falls!

4. *Improves our ability to reach the world with the gospel.* First, people draw near to Jesus when they see the genuine love we have for Him and each other as we see in Acts 2:47. Second, God gifts us each with talents and spiritual gifts for furthering His kingdom. If we neglect coming together for fellowship the corporate body suffers and we deprive people from observing dynamic ministry.

Do not be a solitary tree without the support of others. Do know that you matter and the more you mingle with a heart set on honoring God, the more you will experience the profound solidarity heaven favors! *Lillian, I can't wait to see you again in heaven!*

Christianity

Acts 3:6—But Peter said, "I have neither silver nor gold, but what I have, I give to you: In the name of Jesus Christ the Nazarene, get up and walk!"

You have undoubtedly heard someone say, "Oh I believe Christianity is just another path towards heaven. I'm glad it works for you but I've got my own path." Intellectually, it is quite rational to lump Christianity as another religion in a cosmos filled with man-made roads to meaning. After all, if someone has never come into a personal and meaningful relationship with Jesus Christ, then why shouldn't he or she see Christians as no different from Buddhists, Muslims, Mormons, Jehovah Witnesses, Baha'i, Hindus etc.?

The next time someone so easily dismisses what you consider invaluable, ask that person what she really knows about Jesus? Inquire if she has heard that Jesus offers something no one else has—eternal life. Find out if she knows the cost Jesus paid for her and the historicity of His resurrection from the dead. Ask if she has compared the truth claims of each major (minor for that matter), religion to see what contradictions exist and what each offers.

If a person is truly searching for answers and meaning to life, then she or he will take the time and make the effort to conduct meaningful research to find the answers. If a person is *unwilling* to do this, then that person is most likely closed or offended in some way by the absolute claims of Jesus. There is nothing we can do by wit or argument. Our responsibility is to model Christ-likeness and pray!

The proof that Christianity is for real, to a person in the hunt for truth, in many ways begins with the lifestyle of those who call themselves believers. If our lives do not demonstrate the power of heaven to change sin natures, and if our faith and obedience indicate no difference from any other person, then should we expect a passionate interest in Jesus? If the Christian is irrelevant than all that is left is "ity."

Inspiration ✝✝✝

The Buddhist eight-fold path, the Hindu doctrine of *karma*, the Jewish covenant, and Muslim code of law—each of these offers a way to earn approval. Only Christianity dares to make God's love unconditional.—Philip Yancey in *What's So Amazing About Grace*

If your Christianity is not contagious it may be contaminated.—Chester H. Johnson, quoted in www.geocities.com/jpchapel/quotes.html

Uneducated Men

Acts 4:13—When they observed the boldness of Peter and John and realized that they were uneducated and untrained men, they were amazed and knew that they had been with Jesus.

Imagine turning on your television for the evening news just in time to hear the anchor report, "Today nothing special happened so why don't you turn off the TV and enjoy whatever it was you were doing." *That day will never happen!* Stations compete for viewers even if it comes to sensationalizing two snails laboring across a dirt trail to keep our interest.

Throughout history in virtually every society, people gravitate towards excitement like moths to light. Life on the clay is never as pulse pounding as shooting rapids. Today's cage fighting mimics yesterday's gladiators wrestling lions, or knights jousting for the hand of some gorgeous princess. From century to century, people seek fame and fortune, value and meaning. Newspapers and radios tell us who hits the most home runs, who make the most money, who drives the fastest cars, who stars in the most acclaimed movie, who looks the most glamorous, etc. To an ego-centered world, to be ordinary is boring, dull and unacceptable.

Had Jesus not performed miracles and taught with wisdom to astound the most learned religious leaders, He would have been ignored as a carpenter. He dazzled the Jews with miracles not even the revered Moses performed. However, Jesus' intent was never to attract attention to Himself. His mission was spiritual—to seek and to save mankind from sin (Luke 19:10). He did not leave heaven for earth to capture the glory of a hero-starved nation clamoring for a king and an end to Roman rule.

> *He grew up before Him like a young plant and like a root out of dry ground. He had no form or splendor that we should look at Him, no appearance that we should desire Him. He was despised and rejected by men, a man of suffering who knew what sickness was. He was like one people turned away from; He was despised, and we didn't value Him.* (Isa. 53:2,3)

Jesus came to serve not to be served. He modeled holiness with perfect humility. He suppressed the on-call power befitting the Son of God to die a crucified Son of Man—suspended between two common criminals.

Have you ever asked the question, "Why would God want to use me?" You would not be alone if you had. However, your worth to God is not determined by what spectacular things you pull off. No diplomas, trophies or Nobel prizes are *FedExed* to heaven. God is far more impressed with children who are faithful in the little than those whose lives are like fancy fireworks. His desire is that we would be content with what we have—not miserable for what we have not. Perhaps this is why He reminds us in His Word to *"Stop your fighting—and know that I am God"* (Psa. 46:10).

Are you still feeling mundane? Consider this! God sent His Holy Spirit to dwell in the lives of those who placed their faith in His Son. If this is you, you are a temple of the Almighty. You have access to the throne room of the Ancient of Days. You hold a place in the Book of Life that guarantees you the privilege of worshiping God forever with a new body that will never know decay, pain or sorrow! For now, your Creator placed you in a unique body. Hair loss, glasses, braces, love handles or crippling diseases do not faze him. He is interested in your love. That is right, the no-word-can-adequately-describe Holy Father seeks the fellowship of ordinary you! If you will worship the Lord so that others see Jesus at work in your life, you have no idea what God may do through you. Just look what God did through an unschooled fisherman named Peter. Whoa! Goodbye mediocre. Hello GLORY!

Inspiration   † † †

It is inbred in us that we have to do exceptional things for God; but we have not. We have to be exceptional in the ordinary things, to be holy in mean streets, among mean people, and this is not learned in five minutes.— Oswald Chambers in *My Utmost For His Highest*

We Need a Lift!

Moving is a major endeavor that saps our energy probably more than we do even realize. Fortunately, I have only had to move three times in the past seventeen years. Moving is a painful adventure. The pleasure in meeting new people and making new friends is offset by the sadness of leaving old friends and familiar haunts. The excitement of moving is tempered by the reality of transporting stuff, cleaning, repairing, putting the home on the market and trying to figure out how to use furniture not designed to fit in the new place.

When we moved from Tigard to Newberg, Oregon, my friend Brian, lent me a large truck. The beautiful thing about that truck was that it had a lift. So instead of having to figure out how to maneuver heavy furniture and boxes up into the back of the truck, all we had to do was push the metal switch which made the hydraulic steel plate go up or down depending on what we were trying to do—what a back-saver!

Acts 4:31—After this prayer, the meeting place shook, and they were all filled with the Holy Spirit. Then they preached the word of God with boldness. (NLT)

When God gets involved in our lives amazing things happen. In Acts 4:29, the believers prayed *"And now, Lord, consider their threats, and grant that Your slaves may speak Your message with complete boldness."* He responded and the Holy Spirit filled them. The result was that they went out and preached the gospel with boldness. God gave them a *lift*!

The danger of moving in our own strength is that it is not hard to be injured. The same holds true in ministry. If we try to minister out of our own wisdom, power and strength, we are set up for mediocrity and the possibility of being hammered by Satan. We need a lift! Infinitely greater than a steel plate that raises and lowers to help us carry loads, is the Holy Spirit, who brings God's power to bear when and where we need it as we serve Him! The Holy Spirit lifts us beyond our human frailty into that spiritual dimension where we are transformed to do and be what He wants for His glory. Need a lift? Ask God for His help and you will be amazed at what follows.

Inspiration ✝✝✝

Personal revival occurs whenever the Holy Spirit is allowed to expand His supervision in our lives.—Jan David Hettinga in *Follow Me*

When leaders neglect the Holy Spirit's role in their lives they never reach their full potential as spiritual leaders.—Henry & Richard Blackaby in *Spiritual Leadership*

Two Types of Martyrs

When I wake up each morning, my first task is to let Bear out and retrieve the newspaper. Before I read the headlines, I wonder what new tragedy has rocked people from their illusive peace. In Iraq, yet another person has blown himself up and taken the lives of bystanders. What propels these martyrs to so willingly die?

Of course, the answer is their cause. The more noble the cause, the greater people see themselves as heroic in laying down their lives. There are two kinds of martyrs: those who die for their cause and those who die for their *Cause*. The former focus on an agenda and see no conflict in destroying the lives of those who disagree with them. The latter see Jesus and amplify their faith in Him. Their objective is not to impose their views but to be faithful to God and to let the Holy Spirit lead them.

Acts 7:55,56—But Stephen, filled by the Holy Spirit, gazed into heaven. He saw God's glory, with Jesus standing at the right hand of God, and he said, "Look! I see the heavens opened and the Son of Man standing at the right hand of God!"

While stones smashed his body, Stephen felt no hate for the hurlers. He remembered the life of His Savior who, while suspended in agony, prayed *"Father, forgive these people, because they don't know what they are doing"* (Luke 23:34 NLT). Stephen died a martyr for his first Cause. Centuries later, if those in power had learned from his example, they would never have enflamed soldiers with religious propaganda launching them across Europe and the Middle East as crusaders. They died for a secondary cause—to Christianize heathen civilizations. Men motivated by greed and power sent them out. Zealous potentates called Christ Lord, but ignored His lordship. They disdained what Jesus taught, *"Love your enemies and pray for those who persecute you"* (Mat. 5:44). Stephen's death draws our eyes to Jesus and brings glory to God. Those who perished as crusading martyrs discredited God and have caused countless lives to see Him as a tyrant, no different from the gods of any other people. Sad isn't it?

Sabina Wurmbrand, a Romanian woman familiar with suffering for Christ taught, "A martyr does not make the truth. The truth makes a martyr." What truth makes you?

Inspiration † † †

The blood of the martyrs is the seed of the church.—Tertullian, Roman author, (160-225)

Voice of the Martyrs estimates that more than 150,000 people die for Christ each year, an average of more than four hundred per day.—Randy Alcorn in *Heaven*

Baptism

How many people who profess to follow Jesus Christ have never been baptized? What time normally elapses between a person putting their faith in Jesus and getting baptized? In asking these questions, I must admit that I am increasingly amazed at the disparity of what we live out versus what the Bible teaches.

Baptism is important to God (and therefore should be to us), or it would not have received the emphasis we find in the New Testament. Before Jesus left His followers to return to heaven, He specifically commanded them to make disciples and as part of the process, baptize them in the name of the Father, Son and Holy Spirit (Mat. 28:19,20).

I remember training to be a counselor for a Billy Graham Crusade. We trained in how to share the gospel but I do not recall any mention of baptism. I cannot remember watching any crusade or attending any church where the decision to follow Christ immediately led to baptism. Yet, this was the standard practice of the early church!

The Greek word for baptize is *baptizo*. The root of this word in the first century meant immersing a garment into bleach and then into dye, both cleansing and changing the color of the cloth. In the Bible, baptism meant immersing people under water—typically in a river or lake. Both infant baptism and sprinkling as a form of baptism occurred after Saint Augustine's (354-430 A.D.) clear formulation of the doctrine of original sin. People baptized their babies to ensure their salvation should they die. Because many people believed immersing a baby under water was unsafe, the technique of sprinkling became normative. This practice was not Biblical yet still became part of Catholic and many Protestant churches' tradition.[33]

Acts 8:36—As they were traveling down the road, they came to some water. The eunuch said, "Look, there's water! What would keep me from being baptized?"

In every case of conversion described in detail in the book of Acts, baptism also occurs. Clearly, it was a major practice of the Apostles and the natural conclusion to preaching Christ. Baptism alone does not save a person. Nor should anyone preach that without baptism, a person *cannot* be saved, or we are adding a condition for which passages like Rom. 10:9,10 make no mention. Obviously, the thief on the cross Jesus promised salvation to, did not come off his cross to be baptized. We do not expect those who confess Christ on their deathbed, or who die accidentally shortly after believing in Him to go to hell because they missed the water!

In studying New Testament passages consider some helpful facts:

● John baptized with water whereas Jesus baptized with the Holy Spirit and with fire—Mat. 3:11.

● Repentance precedes baptism—Acts 2:38, 19:4.

● Baptism included both sexes—Acts 8:12.

- Water is the substance used for baptism—Acts 8:36-38.
- Baptism is done in God's Name to those who have become believers—Mat. 28:19, Acts 10:47,48.
- Whole households were often baptized meaning both adults and children could be baptized—Acts 16:15.
- Baptism symbolized a washing away of sins—Acts 22:16.
- Baptism saves us (not the removal of the filth of the flesh, but the pledge of a good conscience toward God) through the resurrection of Jesus Christ—1 Pe. 3:21.
- Our baptism is symbolic of Jesus' death and resurrection and symbolizes our future resurrection—Rom. 6:3,4; Col. 2:12.
- Evidently, in the early church, there were people who were baptized on behalf of those who had died but were unbaptized—1 Co. 15:29.
- We are baptized into Christ—Gal. 3:26,27.
- There is only one baptism necessary—Eph. 4:4-6.

If you have never been baptized but you have placed your faith in Jesus, why wait, get baptized! We impoverish ourselves and weaken the church when we neglect this practice. *Baptism is an outer expression of faith for the inner change that has taken place when Jesus became our Lord.* It shows our sorrow over sin and demonstrates commitment to following after God! As such, it is a powerful testimony to all who witness it. If you have not been baptized and have the ability, I highly recommend immersion over sprinkling. (This does not imply that those who were sprinkled at an age they understood the sacrament must be immersed!) It is deeply meaningful and symbolic and obeys what the Scripture teaches. As a sacrament, baptism holds tremendous meaning and value and honors God, which as we know, is something to think about . . . in reveration!

Noticed

Bryan and I watched an exciting high school football semi-final game at PGE Stadium in Portland. We were excited to root for the Southridge Skyhawks, the team he once helped manage. They competed superbly, won their game and ended up playing for the state championship. I imagine it must be a heady feeling to win big and feel the love and adulation of adoring fans. Unfortunately, fame and fortune are all too fleeting. The need for notice and to be important lasts for a while until some new hero or star emerges.

Have you ever wondered who God notices?

Acts 10:4—Looking intently at him, he became afraid and said, "What is it, Lord?" And he told him, "Your prayers and your acts of charity have come up as a memorial offering before God."

Cornelius was a Roman centurion who served with the Italian Regiment in the town of Caesarea (about 70 miles NW of Jerusalem). Besides being a good leader, the Bible tells us he was a devout and God-fearing man. The Jews who knew him respected him, (an amazing fact in that Jews despised the Roman occupiers of their land). Evidently, he was not a man of prejudice. He worshiped the God of Abraham and may have adhered to many of the Jewish laws and practices. The Caesarean Jews noticed him and liked what they saw.

What captures my attention is what Luke tells us about Cornelius in the passage above. An angel relayed to him in person that he had God's attention! God enjoyed his prayer life and his generosity to the poor, so much that he literally made him the conduit by which the gospel leaped from the Jews to the Gentiles. Acts 10 is a pivotal chapter in the book. God leads the Apostle Peter to violate Jewish law and enter the home of Cornelius where he, his family and close friends have assembled in obedience to God's instructions. They embrace the good news Peter proclaims about Jesus and the Holy Spirit falls upon them confirming that God intended salvation for Gentiles as well as Jews.

Heavenly notice for right living is profoundly important. When we know what pleases God and obey His will, we are investing in what is eternal. Therefore, the next time you think about how nice it would be if someone would just take notice of you consider this. Pray for the fulfillment of God's will here on earth. Pray for others. Give to the poor. We already know God is pleased with these actions.

Inspiration † † †

If the life of a Christian is to be pleasing to God it must be properly adjusted to Him in all things.—Watchman Nee in *Sit Walk Stand*

Listening

The husky man stopped gathering firewood to check on his son. He scanned the surroundings with no lad in sight. *"Nicholas!"* Repeatedly he yelled his son's name. Only silence replied. I could see by his face and body language his rising fear. Nicholas was happily peddling his tricycle around the track the last time I saw him. He waved at me as I went running by him. But where had he gone. Fowler Middle School's track is adjacent to Fanno Creek and woods. A young boy could easily get lost or hurt. So I stopped running to join the father's search. I found Nicholas dragging his wheels on the far side of the creek seemingly oblivious to his father's cries. Days later, I can still hear *"Nicholas!"* ringing in my ears. I remember the look of gratitude in a father's eyes. I am compelled to think about listening.

Acts 10:33—Therefore I immediately sent for you, and you did the right thing in coming. So we are all present before God, to hear everything you have been commanded by the Lord.

Young Nicholas was either distracted or lost in daydreams, too absorbed to hear his dad. Listening is an art that seems greatly endangered. I wonder how many times God calls my name and I don't hear Him! How often do I miss His instructions? Better yet, what causes spiritual deafness or selective hearing?

Nine Reasons Why People do not Listen
1. Hard, hostile hearts—Exo. 8:19
2. Stubborn, rebellious pride—Neh. 9:29; Psa. 81:11
3. Foolishness—Pro. 12:15, 18:13; Ecc. 5:1
4. Complacency—Isa. 32:9
5. Idolatry—Isa. 65:11,12; Jer. 11:10
6. Dissatisfaction with the message or messenger—Jer. 6:10; John 9:27
7. False security—Jer. 22:21
8. Evil is preferred—Zec. 1:4
9. Distractions—Luke 10:40

If we want to know and follow God, we must listen to His voice. Although He rarely audibly speaks, His Holy Spirit directly communicates to us through the Bible, through others, through circumstances and by directly speaking to our hearts. Listening literally saves our lives! Therefore, we ought to know what will help us pay attention to our Father.

May I share with you:
Nine Principles That Will Make Us Better Listeners
1. We submit to God by *carefully* paying attention to His words—Exo. 15:26, 23:21,22; Psa. 85:8
2. We are quick to listen, slow to speak—Jam. 1:19

3. We understand that silence promotes listening—Deu. 27:9,10

4. We recognize our need for help—Exo. 18:19 (Moses listens to his father-in-law)

5. We love and fear God—Deu. 30:20; Psa.66:16

6. We are eager to gain wisdom—Pro. 1:5, 8:33; Acts 10:33

7. We trust the one speaking—John 10:3

8. We concentrate (free ourselves of distractions) so as to hear the Lord—Luke 10:39

9. We value truth—John 18:37

"So we are all present before God, to hear . . .

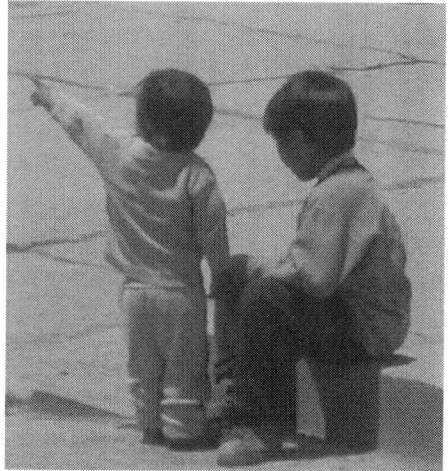

Inspiration † † †

Good listeners, like precious gems, are to be treasured.—Walter Anderson, German writer, (1885-1962)

Faith Is

The cliff broke away like the sloped nose of a roman gladiator. As I walked closer to the edge, his feet stopped moving. Stephen would go no closer. He pulled at my sweater intentionally as if to say, "Forget it, I'm not taking another step!" When I picked him up his arms circled me in pythonic grip. "It's okay," I told him. "I'm not going to let you get hurt." With his gap-toothed grin and an audible sigh, he relaxed in my arms. So long as I held him, we could follow the ridge and marvel together at the roar of the surf and the whine of the wind. In addition, the little girl who watched him decided that she too could walk the trail beside the clouds.

Acts 11:21—The Lord's hand was with them, and a large number who believed turned to the Lord.

If we could hear the stories eyes tell, the questions they ask, how wise we would become. For every day, eyes follow our movement, evaluate our behavior and reflect thoughts only God knows. What seems inconsequential in its ordinary state becomes over time a powerful treatise to whether faith is any good. How do you act in lines, when deadlines pile up, around a rude co-worker or a screaming child, when your head aches, when the bully throws you down and spits on all you treasure? Do you bite your lips and become ill? Do you hang your head like some victory-deficient person? Are you as stable as nitroglycerine? Do you smile and reflect a peace that is surreal? Is your confidence unshakable?

When we reach the maturity to say, "*Lord, my life is in Your hands to do with as You will.*" an amazing transformation occurs. We no longer look at the cliff and fear falling. We rest in the security that He who made us, knows what He is doing.

If we live believing God loves us, then our faith goes beyond personal blessing—it is as good as seed in another person's heart. *Faith is.* Therefore, circumstances are secondary. Trials and triumphs are not what matter. Our goal is not to win over the opinions of people. At stake is not being right. We do not have to pretend. There is no reason to quit; no need to doubt. What matters is that we have a simple child-modeled trust in our Father; a trust that blesses all who behold it.

Faith is. And in that *is*, every eye upon us draws closer to the One who is truly awesome. "*Now faith is the reality of what is hoped for, the proof of what is not seen*" (Heb. 11:1). Our faith enables others to become sure that the unseen hands we trust are genuine. So live as you believe, if you say you believe.

Inspiration † † †

I love the recklessness of faith. First you leap, and then you grow wings.—William Sloane Coffin

Commissioned

Jenny and Joe are back. Do not talk to them about ministry or what happened after six months in Kuala Lumpur. They are hurting right now and it will take time for them to heal. They left with a banquet and profound expectations but returned bankrupt and badly shaken

Acts 13:2,3—As they were ministering to the Lord and fasting, the Holy Spirit said, "Set apart for Me Barnabas and Saul for the work that I have called them to." Then, after they had fasted, prayed, and laid hands on them, they sent them off.

Growing up I often remember hearing Christian leaders implore their listeners to leave their homes and go out as missionaries. The proof text used was Mat. 28:19, *"Go, therefore, and make disciples of all nations, baptizing them in the name of the Father and of the Son and of the Holy Spirit."* To be a missionary was the ultimate mark of commitment to Jesus. However, is it really? Jesus' strategy to reach the world is hinges on a commandment in which the emphasis is on making disciples. His words were not a blanket endorsement to every future follower to hop a donkey to Delhi. Only those commissioned should go.

The early church did not jump to the conclusion that they were to be missionaries to the world. It took persecution and direct leading by the Holy Spirit to get them going. There was no automatic assumption, "O I'm supposed to take the gospel and travel." Instead, there was a humble (and perhaps fearful) sense of waiting on God for instruction as to how to proceed in ministry. It was in the context of worshiping God that Paul and Barnabas were set apart by the Holy Spirit to be missionaries.

If our Lord has not called us to missions, to embark is presumptuous and dangerous. If we go because our emotions are aroused for the plight of the poor, our focus is not on God but rather the needy and we soon are overwhelmed. If we go because an organization asks, but we have no such leading from the Lord, our trust is in the wisdom of the group and we should not be surprised if the assignment is a misfit and fiasco. If we go out of guilt that someone has to do it, when times get rough we are set up to resent God. If we go because we feel qualified and have the right credentials, we are predisposed to pride and an unsightly fall.

The Holy Spirit is the One who commissions. A discerning body of believers recognizes the call and carefully supports the one going. If opposition arises or hardships occur, the one sent has the faith and peace that ministry arises from God's mercy and there is no need to lose heart (2 Co. 4:1). Are you called? Respond in obedience. Are you confused? Wait until the Lord speaks. Are your priorities straight? Love the Lord your God with all your heart mind and soul! It is not the call but the Caller we worship!

Fatwood

Acts 13:48—When the Gentiles heard this, they rejoiced and glorified the message of the Lord, and all who had been appointed to eternal life believed.

Behold the *Fatwood*—"Nature's Greatest Fire starter!" From the stump of the pine tree comes wood rich with resin that burns with intensity and is excellent for making fires in the ol' fireplace. We can learn a lot from fatwood.

When we try to win people to Christ on hype or with emotion, we are like those attempting to ignite logs with lots of twigs. The little sticks look good at first in their high burn. But they die creating worthless smoke—far before the logs are truly lit.

Evangelism is not about creating gimmicks to lure souls to Jesus. Seven stanzas of *Just As I Am* may seem like the best song to coax a sinner forward, but if that's what we're relying on and not the Holy Spirit, we're guilty of manipulation at worst, poor judgment at best. What happens when people so consumed with creating the perfect match forget how to build a fire?

The gospel is the *simple* message:

If you confess with your mouth, 'Jesus is Lord,' and believe in your heart that God raised Him from the dead, you will be saved. With the heart one believes, resulting in righteousness, and with the mouth one confesses, resulting in salvation. Now the Scripture says, No one who believes on Him will be put to shame. (Rom. 10:9-11).

It's not lyrically pleasant but I'd change the words in Kurt Kaiser's song *Pass It On*, from "It only takes a spark to get a fire going," to "It only takes the fatwood to get the fire going!" Ask the Holy Spirit to use you to kindle hearts to seek the Lord. Evangelism must *resinate* (sorry I could not resist that play on words) with the right stuff. Be that fat piece of resin-filled wood ready for God to use to ignite those around you!

Inspiration † † †

So long as he remains in this world, every Christian has two responsibilities. The first is to put on the mind of Christ; the second is to carry that mind into the post-Christian public square—into whatever is public, whether that should mean media, marketplace, or profession, or include university, association, or Congress.—J. Budziszewski in *The Revenge of Conscience*

My business is to preach the gospel, I repair shoes to pay the expenses.—William Carey, English missionary to India known as "the father of modern missions" (1761-1834)

The Labor of Thinking

Acts 17:2,3—As usual, Paul went to them, and on three Sabbath days reasoned with them from the Scriptures, explaining and showing that the Messiah had to suffer and rise from the dead, and saying: "This is the Messiah, Jesus, whom I am proclaiming to you."

It is my goal to read 24 books each year. Part of this discipline involves choosing books that cover a wide range of subjects. There is no end to the number of good books one can read. Scientists tell us we use so little of our brain. I discovered how little my brain was when I journeyed into the realm of Probability and her cousins Electrical Engineering and Thermal Dynamics. Nevertheless, I also learned how much greater my mind could be stretched than I would have dared imagine. It is better to be challenged in what is difficult than to be difficult about being challenged.

Discerning people withhold their wallets from fanatics. A fanatic typically is a person who embraces a cause with lots of heart and little brain. Paul was not a fanatic. He was completely zealous in his efforts to proclaim and assert the authenticity of the gospel message. *"It is right for me to feel this way about all of you, since I have you in my heart; for whether I am in chains or defending and confirming the gospel, all of you share in God's grace with me"* (Php. 1:7). How can we give the reason for our hope if we cannot think? How can we share the reality of Christ if we do not understand the reality of those who live around us?

Fear in presenting Christ to a questioning world suggests we are unprepared to think or lack the knowledge we ought to have. The test is not whether we have all the answers (we don't), but whether we are willing to convey with sound reasoning the hope we have in Jesus. A sure faith is never an excuse to stop thinking. Jesus is relevant to the issues people are grappling with today! Let us be mentally sharp so He can work through us!

Inspiration † † †

There is no expedient to which a man will not go to avoid the labor of thinking.—Thomas A. Edison, inventor, (1847-1931)

If I Grow My Hair Long

Relevance according to *The American Heritage Dictionary* means "Pertinence to the matter at hand." It is the buzzword of evangelicals who fear that many Christians are so isolated within their own social creeks that they have lost their connection to mainstream society and their ability to share Christ. It is a noble concept when properly applied for it requires that one observe, listen and relate to what is important to another.

Christian contemporary music is one example of applying relevance. Rock and roll performed by Elvis, the Beatles and the Rolling Stones radically shifted musical boundaries. As secular rockers became followers of Jesus they naturally wrote songs for the Lord formatted within the fast-moving style they were accustomed to playing. Soon many churches recognized that by incorporating contemporary music into their services they were able to broaden their worship style and attract people into church who would have been alienated by music they were unaccustomed to hearing. Those who objected to this change missed the reality that many of their venerated hymns were themselves tunes adapted from popular tavern songs.

Acts 17:23—For as I was passing through and observing the objects of your worship, I even found an altar on which was inscribed: TO AN UNKNOWN GOD Therefore, what you worship in ignorance, this I proclaim to you.

While walking among the Athenians and their many gods, Paul chose to be relevant. He used their altar *"TO AN UNKNOWN GOD"* to proclaim the Creator. Those that accepted Paul's message understood that they must abandon their polytheism to worship the one true Deity. Relevance to be an effective method always points people away from their idolatry to God. When it ceases to do this secularization trounces the gospel.

Many Christian radio stations market young *hip* artists playing songs the industry deems as *hits*. Part of the intent is to be relevant and attract young nonbelievers to listen. However, the songs seekers are exposed to frequently contain poor theology. They come from young men and women who have had little time to mature in the faith and whose message too often reduces worship and discipleship to trite jingles. If I grow my hair long and dye it purple, pierce my tongue and listen to the same music as my neighbor to reach him for Jesus my behavior begs the question *"who is the one being influenced?"*

Those who misdefine relevance and justify it by winning first-time converts seem to miss the reality of sterility. To accept and follow Christ is to become a *"new creation"* (2 Co. 5:17). If conversion is but a slightly altered state of perversion, there is little distinction between a follower of Jesus and a worldly person. This according to Scripture cannot be so! Relevance carried too far becomes irrelevance. Our faith loses its redemptive value if we compromise truth in order to sell. Relevance is not fashioned by a fear of offending people. It is prayerfully crafted that our light (a distinct contrast to darkness), might be understood!

God-honoring relevance pertinaciously (stubbornly) proclaims Him and His Word. We do not dilute His truth to make it palatable to others. We do not act like the devil to share about Christ. When the Bible commands us to abstain from immorality, filthy speech and anything that would replace Jesus as Lord, we obey! In doing so, we offer those who are hopeless the opportunity to find hope. The gospel by itself is always relevant! While our techniques and methods may vary, the message remains the same. Jesus Christ died and rose from the dead to save us from our sin; something to think about . . . in reveration!

Inspiration † † †

Never question the relevance of truth, but always question the truth of relevance.—Dr. Craig S. Bruce, Canadian software developer

17 Months of Double House Payments August 9

Our house sat on the Oregon market for seventeen months. Finally, my wife and I decided to pull the listing. We faced several hard decisions. Do we rent? Do we try to sell with a different realtor? Are there other options in this morass of uncertainty?

Acts 18:9-11—Then the Lord said to Paul in a night vision, "Don't be afraid, but keep on speaking and don't be silent. For I am with you, and no one will lay a hand on you to hurt you, because I have many people in this city." And he stayed there a year and six months, teaching the word of God among them.

Many Bible scholars believe Paul was discouraged and unclear whether to remain in Corinth after facing hostile resistance from the Jews. This pattern of persecution in city after city, no doubt began to wear on God's ambassador. His insecurity is something most of us can identify with as we ask the timeworn question, "How do we determine God's will when we live in the valley of uncertainty?" I believe the book of Acts is the best book in the New Testament to answer this question.

Acts provides us repetitive examples of what the early disciples experienced in overcoming uncertainty. In the first 18 chapters, there are at least seven ways we can discern God's will each characterized by a definitive trait—faith. Without faith, it is not just impossible to please God it is also difficult to discern His will.

How do we determine God's will and overcome uncertainty? By faith walking:

● With *prayer, fasting, worship* and *active listening to the Holy Spirit.*—1:24-26; 10:9,19,30,31; 11:5,12; 13:2,3; 9:10,15; 10:3-7,10-16; 16:9,10

● And *observing God's activity.* Dr. Henry Blackaby wrote in his book *Experiencing God,* "Find out what God is doing and get involved!"—2:4; 8:39; 15:7-9; 16:6,7

● And *knowing God's Word*—1:15,16,20; 2:17-21,25-28,31,34,35; 3:22-24; 4:11; Stephen's address in chapter 7; 8:32,33; Paul's address in 13:16-41; 15:15-18; 17:2,3

● And *receiving godly counsel and teaching.*—2:42; 15:23-29

● *Willing* to *obey godly leaders* (to include *angels*) and *His Spirit*—2:22; 5:19,20,29,32; 6:2-6; 8:26,27,29,30; 9:3-6,17; 10:7,8,33; 11:28; 14:3

● *Cognizant of circumstances, opportunities and opposition.*— 8:1,4; 11:19-22; 13:42,44, 50,51; 14:5-7; 15:2,37-40; 16:14-25; 17:10-13;18:6

● *Taking action* that *furthers God's kingdom.* Unless God directs us to do nothing, we should be actively engaged doing that which we already know He has commanded/called us to do.—3:2-6; 9:27; 14:8-10,21-23; 16:3; 17:16-31

Digging Deeper

Have you ever noticed how bookstores bulge with books on how to be a successful leader? Many aspire to be the quintessential person in charge. Did you know that the most authoritative book in the world on leadership is the Bible? Not only does the Bible give us the inspiring example of the perfect leader—Jesus Christ, it also is packed with descriptive accounts of other men and women who were fantastic leaders.

The key to discovering the qualities that make worthy leaders requires that we spend in-depth time not just looking at the stated words in a descriptive passage, but also meditating on what is implied. For example, there are obvious qualities underlined for a gifted leader in the passage below. Carefully study the five verses Luke uses to describe Apollos and see if you can spot further implied qualities that reveal him as a model leader.

Acts 18:24-28—A Jew named Apollos, a native Alexandrian, an eloquent man who was powerful in the Scriptures, arrived in Ephesus. This man had been instructed in the way of the Lord; and being fervent in spirit, he spoke and taught the things about Jesus accurately, although he knew only John's baptism. He began to speak boldly in the synagogue. After Priscilla and Aquila heard him, they took him home and explained the way of God to him more accurately. When he wanted to cross over to Achaia, the brothers wrote to the disciples urging them to welcome him. After he arrived, he greatly helped those who had believed through grace. For he vigorously refuted the Jews in public, demonstrating through the Scriptures that Jesus is the Messiah.

Stated Qualities:
- Eloquent
- Fervent in spirit
- Teacher
- Accurate
- Bold spokesman
- Apologist

Implied Qualities:
- Effective learner with a brilliant mind—Apollos was from Alexandria, which during his lifetime was one of the three great centers of learning in the world. By Luke's account, we can tell Apollos had a sharp mind and that he was very educated.
- God-centered—he focused on the Scriptures as opposed to pleasing his flesh
- Teachable—he listened to what Priscilla and Aquila taught him
- Greatly respected—Priscilla and Aquila valued him enough to take him into their home and invest time in him; the brothers believed in his leadership enough to write a letter to those in Achaia to welcome him

● Effective trainer—he helped those who already believed in their faith (see 1 Co. 3:6 for further proof)

Just as we can learn much about leaders by meditating in Scripture, so we can learn much about life burrowing further into God's Word. This is why I think all of us need to invest daily time in Bible Study—there is so much wisdom we need! Hmm, it is time to do some more digging!

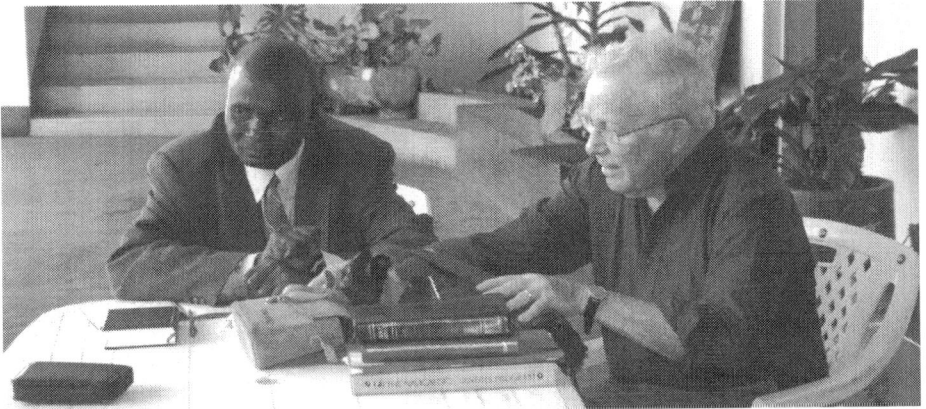

Inspiration † † †

Those who do not study are only cattle dressed up in men's clothes.—Chinese Proverb

The more we study, the more we discover our ignorance.—Percy Bysshe Shelley, English Poet, (1792-1822)

Pastors

Acts 20:28—Be on guard for yourselves and for all the flock, among whom the Holy Spirit has appointed you as overseers, to shepherd the church of God, which He purchased with His own blood.

What is a pastor? When we study the New Testament we discover many interesting answers to this question.

- The Greek word for pastors found in Eph. 4:11, is the same word for shepherds. Three times in the New Testament we find this word used to describe Christians caring for other Christians (Eph. 4:11; Acts 20:28; 1 Pe. 5:2).
- The words overseer, bishop and elder are interchanged with shepherd.
- Acts 20:17, 28-31 teaches pastors to:
  - keep watch over themselves
  - keep watch over the flock of which the Holy Spirit made them overseers
  - shepherd the church of the Lord
  - be on guard against false teachers and those who distort God's truth to gain a following
- 1 Timothy 5:17-19 establishes that elders:
  - who effectively lead should be well paid especially those whose work is preaching and teaching
  - are to be protected against accusation unless there are two or three witnesses
  - who sin are to be rebuked publicly so that others will be fearful of wrongdoing
- Titus 1:5-9 describes the qualifications pastors must possess.
- Peter taught in 1 Pe. 5:2,3 that pastors:
  - should serve from a willing spirit according to God's will
  - are not to be greedy for money but eager to serve
  - are not to lord over those they serve but rather be good examples

The fulfilled-pastor will readily share that the key to his ministry is that he does not have to do everything! He is not the most important person in the church. He is one of a God-loving, people serving, faith-breathing, word-devouring, gospel-proclaiming team of joyful disciples. He knows that God never intended for one person to carry a hundred people.

The effective pastor requires protected time to meet with his Father for spiritual nourishment. He needs respected time for him to invest in his family. You can tell much about his ministry from his marriage. He cherishes friends who love him for who he is—not because of his position; friends who discern and apply balm when he is the target of those who throw stones; and, friends who recognize and compensate for his imperfections.

The God-fearing pastor views his ministry with humility because he knows his own weaknesses and the grace that allows him to minister. He asks for an abundance of prayer for strength, wisdom and protection. His security is not in his profession but rather in his relationship with Jesus Christ. He lives not for applause or popularity, for his hero is the Lion, who left heaven to lay down His life as a Lamb.

Inspiration † † †

Percentage of pastors who report a major clash with a church member at least once a month: 40

Who feel ill suited to face the rigors of the pastorate: 50

Who have a lower self-image than when they began ministry: 70

Who say the ministry has influenced their family negatively: 80

Who feel inadequately trained for ministry: 90—Fuller Institute of Church Growth, "To Verify," *Leadership*

Playing the One Stringed Violin

Nicolo Paganini, (1782-1840), ranks as one of the greatest violinists of all time. One night while playing a difficult piece of music a string on his violin snapped and hung down from his violin. Surrounded by the orchestra he continued to play. Then a second string broke. Still, this clever musician improvised and continued playing. A third string snapped—forever worthless. Undaunted, Paganini played magnificently on the one remaining string before a stunned crowd. When he finished they jumped to their feet screaming and cheering *"Bravo! Bravo!"* Paganini waited until the noise abated; then as everyone sat back down, he raised his violin high for everyone to see. The violinist nodded to the conductor to begin the encore. He placed the single-stringed Stradivarius beneath his chin and played one final piece. Can you imagine the buzz of that crowd as they returned home from that concert?!

Acts 27:34—Therefore I urge you to take some food. For this has to do with your survival, since not a hair will be lost from the head of any of you.

Paul expressed the words above on a ship so storm-tossed, that he and all aboard went without food for 14 days while fighting to survive. Instead of giving up in exhaustion, he took bread, thanked God in front of them all, ate and encouraged them to do the same. In the middle of the terrifying tempest, he modeled confidence and thanksgiving. The next day the centurion spared Paul and the other prisoners from a soldier's plot to kill them. Their ship ran aground forcing everyone to swim for shore. As if all this was not enough, a viper bit the shivering hand of Paul as he picked up brushwood for a fire. The islanders concluded his luck was so bad that he must be a murderer! Yet, when nothing happened to him, they said he was a god. Quitting was not part of Paul's vocabulary.

When the strings on your violin snap do you quit playing? The easy choice is to stop and blame the string-makers for a weak product or walk away in frustration before sympathetic onlookers. It is far easier to bemoan challenge than to make the most of the least. The rare person presses on courageous in the face of deprivation and adversity.   But wait a minute, Jesus calls us to be rare!

When circumstances do not go as you hoped, do you die inside? Quitting is the natural outcome of fear, fatigue and insecurity. So do not go there! You worship the Winner. It is not too late to climb up the rigging with your one-stringed violin and shout above the thunder, "I am a conqueror through Jesus who loves me! Death or life, angels or demons, present or future, mountain crag or bog and anything else created—nothing can stand between God's love and me thanks to my Lord Jesus Christ!" (Rom. 8:37-39 paraphrased). Do not be a quitter! Live for God's glory with faith and joy!

Potholes

Standing in line in Dubai ready to get our tickets, my brother, Nate, talked to the Emirates ticket representative. She was from Nairobi and was impressed to hear Nate was doing humanitarian work with an orphanage in Kisumu. So she upgraded all our tickets to business class! We arrived in Nairobi, refreshed and encouraged at God's blessing. As we prepared to fly to our next destination, Kisumu, it became clear that we would be heavily taxed for our excess baggage. Nate suggested we drive instead and save expenses. Because this would give us a better opportunity to see the countryside and save money, we all agreed.

The road to Kisumu starts out on a new highway. We passed over an 8,000-foot shelf that overlooked the famous Great Rift Valley and not much later a herd of wild zebras. Soon the sun set and the road changed. Suddenly, the road was a maze of never-ending ruts and holes. Nicholas, our driver, lurched from side to side dodging as many craters as he could. Buses, cars and trucks came past us, often barely missing us! Their blinding high beams screamed at us as if to say, "Get out of my way!" The smell of exhaust fumes and plumes of dust filled the van in conspiracy with bottom-jarring bumps and twists that made sleep impossible. Hour after hour slowly churned and the "five" hour drive was now over seven. In all my years of travel, the road to Kisumu assumed first place as the mother of potholes. Somehow, after midnight, we pulled into YGC Orphanage, with our axels still intact and our spirits still motivated.

Acts 28:19,20—Because the Jews objected, I was compelled to appeal to Caesar; it was not as though I had any accusation against my nation. So for this reason I've asked to see you and speak to you. In fact, it is for the hope of Israel that I'm wearing this chain.

The Apostle Paul could have escaped a sentence that left him under house arrest in Rome. Instead of taking the easy road of acquittal at the hands of a sympathetic court, he appealed to Caesar. He chose the road of *potholes* to reach Italy, a nation in which he knew God wanted him to minister...

By taking the rutted road to Kisumu and not the plane, we experienced a great joy. The money we saved in great part allowed us to purchase a welding machine and a generator for YGC Orphanage. The generator allows the school to operate on days when there are power outages (a frequent occurrence). It also keeps their internet café open so that they have a steady source of revenue.

Praise God for potholes! Sometimes the road home takes twists we did not expect. Sometimes the road is rough for a reason. However, on the journey, if our hearts are right to serve God, He can turn even the worst bumps into opportunities.

Finely Evolved Creatures?

Romans 1:20—From the creation of the world His invisible attributes, that is, His eternal power and divine nature, have been clearly seen, being understood through what He has made. As a result, people are without excuse.

Author of *Origins of Life*, theoretical physicist Freeman J. Dyson says, "As we look out into the universe and identify the many accidents of physics and astronomy that have worked to our benefit, it almost seems as if the universe must in some sense have known that we were coming." *Hmm.* It is not the universe that knew we were coming!

Naturalism described in *The American Heritage Dictionary* is, "The system of thought holding that all phenomena can be explained in terms of natural causes and laws without attributing moral, spiritual, or supernatural significance to them." Naturalists believe that the world evolved on its own and reject the notion that a designing God is responsible for life. By holding to this view, they set aside powerful evidence that begs a Designer. To exalt chance over an omnipotent Creator gives the naturalist the right to independence.

For anyone embracing the notion that we are just finely evolved creatures bereft of a Creator, sin is essentially a non-issue. The proliferation of naturalistic thought undermines the importance of absolutes for life is devoid of supernatural meaning. Live as you please for when you die, you die! However, in Genesis we discover the Lord formed us from the dust of the ground with no intention that we would end up dust in the wind. He calls us to live holy lives in accordance with His divine will. If we need evidence that He exists, we need only examine what is around us. If the beauty of nature does not impress us, mathematics and science certainly provide compelling proof for design and therefore, a Designer.

Dr. Walter Bradley in "*The Designed 'Just So' Universe*" writes:
There are certain universal constants that are an essential part of our mathematical description of the universe. A partial list is found in Table 2 and includes Planck's constant "h", the speed of light "c", the gravity force constant "G", the mass of the proton, electron, and neutron, the unit charge for the electron or proton, and the weak force, strong nuclear force and electromagnetic coupling constants, and Boltzmann's constant, k . . . This is only an illustrative but not exhaustive list of examples of cosmic coincidences that clearly demonstrate that the four forces in nature have been very carefully scaled to give a universe that provides long-term sources of energy and a variety of atomic building blocks which are necessary for life.[34]

Dr. Bradley's article goes on to share how finely tuned and delicately established each force of nature is shaped to allow for life. He offers faith-affirming evidence for design. I encourage you to read his article and the writings of other scientists shared at www.origins.org. There is great evidence that God designed life. The more we understand the intricacy and beauty of what He made, the better we will be able to share the intimacy and hope that come from knowing our unseen Father.

Inspiration † † †

The laws of nature are written by the hand of God in the language of mathematics.—Galileo Galilei, Italian physicist, mathematician, astroner and philosopher (1564-1642)

The equations of physics have in them incredible simplicity, elegance and beauty. That in itself is sufficient to prove to me that there must be a God who is responsible for these laws and responsible for the universe.—Paul Davies, Australian astrophysicist

Astronomy leads us to a unique event, a universe created out of nothing and delicately balanced to provide exactly the conditions required to support life. In the absence of an absurdly-improbable accident, the observations of modern science seem to suggest an underlying, one might say, supernatural plan.—Nobel laureate Arno Penzias

No Plaque or Ceremony

He walked into work and people were crying—not a good sign. The warehouse manger, not his boss, called him into his office and read him a form letter announcing that he would be let go. "Dan, your job has been eliminated." Dan put his hand on the manager's hand and said, "Dave, don't make this any harder on yourself than you need to. You're my friend." Dave started crying. "Somebody's going to have to escort you out of the building."

Thirty-one years, the prime years of his life, Dan faithfully served Wickes, a furniture company. His spotless record, written commendations and superb service to thousands of customers in the end mattered to the corporate headquarters as much as a crumpled, empty soda can. His boss did not even have the guts to break the news to him, nor did Wickes offer him any prior notice that his job would end. No plaque or ceremony was given to honor his loyal, faithful service. No retirement benefits would ease the sting of his release. The only thing waiting for him was a taxicab to take him home. To a corporation fixated on making money, he had become a financial liability. It is not surprising that a company so callous and ungrateful went out of business— it is what we call *poetic justice*.

Romans 1:21-22—For though they knew God, they did not glorify Him as God or show gratitude. Instead, their thinking became nonsense, and their senseless minds were darkened. Claiming to be wise, they became fools.

Ingratitude is the symptom of a corrupted heart. Businesses that treat their employees shabbily do so because they worship the dollar and workers are merely a means to an end. The irony is that those companies that take care of their employees and show gratitude, gain far more loyal and hardworking people than does any company fixated on profit. Studies show that employees will leave a higher paying job with thankless supervisors to take a lower paying job where they are appreciated. It makes sense doesn't it! We all want to be valued. It hurts when we are spit like some piece of gristle.

People who ignore God have already muted their praise button. If they cannot show gratitude to the Father who sent them a Savior, is it surprising that they will not see the hard work you have done? Thanksgiving represents one day a year when we give gratitude to God for all He has done for us. *Thanksliving* should be our habit. The Apostle Paul wrote the Thessalonians, *"Give thanks in everything, for this is God's will for you in Christ Jesus"* (1 Th. 5:18). We live thankfully knowing in the end the Lord rewards us. *"My reward is with Me to repay each person according to what he has done"* (Rev. 22:12).

Justification

I want to be good and I suspect the same is true for you. Yet, despite my best intentions, I do not live a perfect life. The deeper I get to know my Lord the more aware I am of my shortcomings. For this reason, I find the concept of justification to be somewhat overwhelming. God in His profound holiness did not have to go to any length to rescue me from sin. He does not need me and most certainly, I have offended Him repeatedly. Yet, inexplicably through His vast love, He chose a horrific path to blaze a terrific salvation.

Romans 3:21-24—But now, apart from the law, God's righteousness has been revealed—attested by the Law and the Prophets—that is, God's righteousness through faith in Jesus Christ, to all who believe, since there is no distinction. For all have sinned and fall short of the glory of God. They are justified freely by His grace through the redemption that is in Christ Jesus.

Justification is a critical starting component of our salvation. *Theologically, to be justified means we are free of the guilt and penalty attached to our sin.* Justification calls us good. Only God is capable of doing this because of His sovereignty and perfect nature. By His judicial act of pardoning us through the atoning sacrifice of Jesus on the cross, God bridges our estranged relationship with Him. By taking our sins upon Himself and defeating death, God's perfect Son sacrificed His life to gain us the opportunity for salvation!

We cannot earn justification. We inherit a sin nature and we fulfill that nature by sinning. No matter how hard we try, we break God's laws. To simply say we love God, to be baptized, to attend a church, to keep the sacraments, or to be born into a Christian family, is not enough—these do not make us righteous before our holy Magistrate. Just as a diseased person cannot dispel cancer by doing good deeds, so our noble efforts cannot earn God's pardon for our sin-condition. So how do we become justified?

The Holy Spirit inspired the Apostle Paul primarily in the book of Romans to teach us that justification originates with God's grace. We appropriate it by our faith in Jesus. Justification contains within it forgiveness. It precedes our moral transformation and sanctification (which is the process of our becoming holy). The result of justification is peace with God, adoption into His family, and the promise that we inherit eternal life with Him.

Like me, you may not feel worthy of justification. Yet, the great love that compelled God to pursue us ought to inspire us to pursue Him! True and certain faith in Jesus does not end with acceptance in what He did (while we go on with our own pursuits), but rather a lifelong yearning to follow Him and in so doing to become like Him.

Craig is Blind

Craig is blind. I stare in utter amazement as he works the controls on his soundboard. How does he do it? How can this man be a recording engineer without the ability to read dials? Soon he ushers me into a recording chamber but trips momentarily on my guitar case placed inconveniently in his pathway. Sheepishly I realize that the biggest hazard to Craig is me!

The more time I spend with Craig, the more I am reminded of what a difference it makes to follow Jesus Christ. This musician extraordinaire and his partially-blind, artistic wife literally know what it means to walk in darkness. Yet they live with the rarified dignity that comes from spiritual hope and the invisible vision it produces.

Romans 5:1,2—Therefore, since we have been declared righteous by faith, we have peace with God through our Lord Jesus Christ. Also through Him, we have obtained access by faith into this grace in which we stand, and we rejoice in the hope of the glory of God.

Imagine if God lived visibly among us. Suppose He refused to allow Satan the opportunity to reign on earth, so he could wreak no havoc. Furthermore, He made us impervious to sin and its destructive results. Under such conditions, faith would be an unnecessary attribute. What lends us dignity is the ability to trust our Maker while negotiating the constantly changing water above the stove of hell.

Dignity is not fashioned by an easy life; after all, no one earns esteem by lounging on the couch. It is defined, illustrated and confirmed by our willingness to rise above the evil that besets us and to believe that He who promised eternal life is able to deliver.

We don't achieve our worth because we have superior coping skills. God grants us hope through the holiness of His Son, who died to give us honor. Therefore, by faith in Christ we become heirs to the eternal glory He reserves for His children. A blind recording engineer can walk with his head held high not just because he knows the layout of the room, but also because the King of kings loves him.

Inspiration   † † †

Faith makes a Christian, Life proves a Christian, Trials confirms a Christian, Death crowns a Christian.—Charles H. Spurgeon

Dignity does not consist in possessing honors, but in deserving them.—Aristotle

Fruit Trees

In my backyard are several fruit trees. Each one is shielded to some degree from the traversing sun by fir, cedar and maple that are older and tower above them. What is fascinating is how the apple, cherry, plum and apricot contort their branches in the best direction possible to capture maximum sunlight.

Romans 5:3-5—And not only that, but we also rejoice in our afflictions, because we know that affliction produces endurance, endurance produces proven character, and proven character produces hope. This hope does not disappoint, because God's love has been poured out in our hearts through the Holy Spirit who was given to us.

Without the sun no fruit will come. To survive and be strong, tree limbs stretch in whatever direction that yields maximum exposure to sunlight. Suffering, (being shaded from the sun), causes perseverance. Spring and summer each tree races to be the best ray catcher. Any trunk that gives up growing soon will have no fruit for showing. Perseverance produces character. Each woody plant is unique in configuration as it strains towards the light. Its shape, health and the quality of fruit identify its character. Character produces hope. Each woody plant finds reward for its uncompromising quest for light by receiving the energy it needs to remain healthy.

Without the Son no fruit will come. To survive and be strong, we must stretch our hearts in whatever direction that yields maximum obedience to His will. Suffering, (whatever opposes His will), causes perseverance. Daily we must die to fleshly cravings, lustful eyes and worldly pride (1 John 2:16), so as to become like Him. If we quit trying to follow Jesus, we will cease to bear fruit—*"for the fruit of the light results in all goodness, righteousness, and truth"* (Eph. 5:9). Perseverance produces character. We are unique as we strain to become like Christ. Our attitude, behavior and the way God is able to work through us measures our character. Character produces hope. As we seek to live as children of light, our Father, who pours out His immeasurable love into our hearts through His Holy Spirit, rewards us. No one who faithfully reaches for the Son will come away disappointed!

Inspiration † † †

Other men see only a hopeless end, but the Christian rejoices in an endless hope.—Gilbert Beenken

In a world of injustice, God once and for all tipped the scales in the favor of hope. And he did it by sitting on his hands so that we could know the kingdom of God.—Max Lucado in *The Applause of Heaven*

Messy Desk

My office is the scene of constant battle. On the front line of my desk, two forces are engaged—the Pile Army led by General Intentions versus the Orderly Army led by General Tidy. The Pile Army constantly bombs the white-painted plain where I work with papers, books, writing instruments, mail, business cards, pictures and occasionally food and drink. Tidy is outgunned, outmaneuvered and so seldom wins victories that his army is often prone to quit fighting. Bills, deadlines and voting ballots are sporadically missed—all casualties beneath the deadly aim of Intention's battle captain—Procrastination. On occasion, when I take trips, my wife visits the frontlines and brilliantly supports the Orderly forces with such pragmatic movements that I can actually see my desktop when I return.

Romans 7:15,18—For I do not understand what I am doing, because I do not practice what I want to do, but I do what I hate . . . For I know that nothing good lives in me, that is, in my flesh. For the desire to do what is good is with me, but there is no ability to do it.

Let us condense Paul's confession to the Romans into one word—*intentions*. While messy desks are somewhat humorous, a life of missed opportunities and incorrect actions is sorrowful. Intentions are like a journey that goes nowhere. We feel the prompting of the Holy Spirit to share Jesus with a hurting friend but we are afraid of rejection so we say nothing. We know that we should stop eating food that makes us fat but we indulge anyway with an eye for tomorrow. Family devotions disappear before urgent deadlines. Thank-you notes die the death of neglect. We want to join a home group but myriad activities block the way. *Should have* turns into guilt, then morphs into rationalization.

Forget that intentions may be splendid, so are candles. Until the wick is lit, it is unfulfilled light. If Jesus lived by intentions, could the wood that made the cross instead have built a throne? (Mark 14:36b) Fortunately, Jesus knew His Father rewarded obedience, not the thought of obeying. And He knows how weak our flesh is. His grace handles the sins of what we knew but failed to do, as well as what we knew not to do but did anyway. Therefore, the next time you sense the Spirit prompting you to act, do not wait—do it! Seize the moment through the power of Christ, who yielded to the cross thereby conquering sin, death and good intentions!

Inspiration † † †

Good intentions are not enough. They've never put an onion in the soup yet.—Sonya Levien, Russian screenwriter, (1888-1960)

The Deity of Jesus

Romans 8:9—You, however, are not in the flesh, but in the Spirit, since the Spirit of God lives in you. But if anyone does not have the Spirit of Christ, he does not belong to Him.

I once spoke with a woman who was interested in moving to our city and getting involved in our church. She asked me many questions regarding our doctrine. Then the conversation narrowed to a discussion of Jesus Christ.

In the third century AD, a heresy broke out in the church known as *Dynamic Monarchianism.* Adherents of this belief denied that Jesus was God. They believed He was a created being, infused with power at the time of His birth—a Savior to be worshiped but not God. I was quite stunned and dismayed to hear that this woman believed such things. Her honest reasoning was that if one studied Scripture to know God one should conclude that there is but one Lord and that Jesus is not Him.

Now, I would be the first to admit that the whole concept of the Trinity is hard to understand and a cause of stumbling for more than just Muslims. However, the complexity of a subject does not render it false. Scripture soundly proves the deity of both Christ and the Holy Spirit.

Gnostics and those who deny that Jesus is God often cite Colossians 1:15 as a convenient proof text. *"He is the image of the invisible God, the firstborn over all creation."* This passage supposedly shows Jesus was created. What this argument fails to consider is that in Psalm 89:27 David is also called God's *"firstborn, greatest of the kings of the earth."* The Greek word for *firstborn* does not mean, *first created* which is an entirely different word. Rather, it means, that Jesus holds the place of supremacy over all creation. Furthermore, if Mary's boy-child was created in Bethlehem, why would Paul, a well-trained religious leader, say He was the firstborn over all creation? He was not an idiot!

Isaiah 45:12 is one of many Old Testament verses stating that God is the creator of mankind and the earth. Yet, Col. 1:16-19 says Jesus was the Creator and that the fullness of God dwells in Him. The God the Old Testament describes as our Creator the New Testament reveals to be Christ!

God commanded the Israelites to worship no other gods (Exo. 20:3-5). To worship Jesus but claim He is not God then would make one guilty of idolatry. To be consistent, if Jesus is not God then it is entirely inappropriate to worship Him. Yet in Rev. 7:9-17, Jesus-worship takes center stage before God's throne. He receives honor as the Lamb of God!

If Jesus is not God, then God could not bless those who are Trinitarians. To do so would be to make a mockery of Himself. Yet, we see a world of believers who worship and attest to the deity of the Holy Spirit and Christ who are dynamically empowered by God. Therefore, the burden of explanation falls on those who deny the trinity to explain why God so richly works in the lives of those who give His Son and Spirit the same honor accorded Him.

In John 10:30,31 Jesus said, *"The Father and I are one."* Hearing Him the Jews picked up stones to stone Him." Why? By their own words in verse 33, they sought to kill Him because He claimed to be God. Now if He was making false claims He was a liar, but if He was a liar then the fullness of God could not have been His for God cannot lie. And if His claim was one in purpose only, the Jews would not have been so infuriated. They hated Him because as in John 8:58, He attributed to Himself what only God could claim.

These are but a few reasons why we can with confidence worship God the Father, God the Son and God the Holy Spirit. Something to think about . . . in reveration!

Inspiration † † †

We propose that undeniability is the test for the truth of a world view and unaffirmability is the test for the falsity of a world view.—Norman Geisler in *Christian Apologetics*

Compare Scripture with Scripture. False doctrines, like false witnesses, agree not among themselves.—William Gurnall, English author, (1617-1679)

Predestination

Predestination according to *The American Heritage Dictionary* means, "The doctrine that God has foreordained all things, especially that God has elected certain souls to eternal salvation." It occurs six times in the New Testament and comes from the Greek word, "προοριζω" (proorizo). In Ephesians, Paul reveals that love is the motivation behind predestination and that it is an accolade to God's grace freely distributed through Christ. To the church in Rome he wrote that God's foreknowledge "προγινωσκω" *proginosko*—from which we get the word *prognosis*), is included in predestination. Furthermore, those He predestined were also called, justified and glorified (Rom. 4:29,30)!

Luke depicts the negative side of predestination in Acts 4:28. God's power and will worked in the lives of Herod, Pontius Pilate, Gentiles and Jews in Jerusalem to conspire against Jesus before they were ever born! Honestly, it seems very unfair that God would choose some for evil and others for adoption. In truth, we cannot know why or how His pleasure and will were determined until we someday have the privilege of coming before His throne to ask Him. Paul taught the Corinthian believers that God's secret wisdom was destined for our glory before time began (1 Co. 2:7). I look forward to the timeless day when what God has hidden is revealed.

Romans 8:29-30—For those He foreknew He also predestined to be conformed to the image of His Son, so that He would be the firstborn among many brothers. And those He predestined, He also called; and those He called, He also justified; and those He justified, He also glorified.

The danger with predestination is when we make a minor doctrine into a philosophical dogma. Too many of God's children have determined that they are absolved of the need to share the gospel since God already chose who would receive salvation. This is absurd! Why did Jesus command His disciples to *"Go into all the world and preach the gospel to the whole creation"* (Mark 16:15)? Their responsibility to make disciples extends to us the same Christ-given mandate. Our job is not to use God's knowledge of who will reject and who will receive Him as a respite from obedience but rather to agree with Paul in Rom. 10:14: *"But how can they call on Him in whom they have not believed? And how can they believe without hearing about Him? And how can they hear without a preacher?"* May we be the voice that proclaims truth! May we pray souls into the Kingdom of God in accordance with His will that everyone would come to repentance (2 Peter 3:9).

Inspiration †††

He who believes his doctrine to be perfectly right and true has only to lift his hands and touch his ears and discover they are the long furry ears of a donkey.—Martin Luther

When Pain Seems Intolerable

There will come a time in your life when sorrow surrounds your heart and the light of life seems remote, flickering against the howling wind of affliction. In times of tenebrific anguish, it is important to realize that you are emotionally at a much deeper level than most that are around you. This heightens the possibility that they will not understand what you are experiencing. If you are in a prolonged state of anguish, many will tire of your depressed condition and suggest you need to quit feeling sorry and move on with life. Misery may love company but not for long.

There is hardly ever an easy solution to anguish. However, there is always a course of action that proves right. It is the spiritual heart-cry. When life is a mess and pain seems intolerable, cry out to God. Tell Him what you are facing. Let Him hear the full measure of your pain. The psalmist wrote in Psalm 118:5, *"In my anguish I cried out to the Lord, and He answered by setting me free."*

Romans 9:1-2—I speak the truth in Christ—I am not lying; my conscience is testifying to me with the Holy Spirit—that I have intense sorrow and continual anguish in my heart.
Luke 22:44—Being in anguish, He prayed more fervently, and His sweat became like drops of blood falling to the ground.

If your child came to you in distress, would you stand indifferent like an Arizona cactus? God, our heavenly Father, delights in responding to His children. He will give you the strength you need to go through your time of anguish. He will set you free! He knows something about anguish. He was in both gardens.

Inspiration †††

Most do not fully see this truth that life is difficult. Instead, they moan more or less incessantly, noisily or subtly, about the enormity of their problems, their burdens, and their difficulties as if life were generally easy, as if life should be easy. They voice their belief, noisily or subtly, that their difficulties represent a unique kind of affliction that should not be and that has somehow been especially visited upon them, or else upon their families, their tribe, their class, their nation, their race or even their species, and not upon others. I know about this moaning because I have done my share.—M. Scott Peck, psychiatrist, (1936-2005) in *The Road Less Traveled*

The Antidote to Busyness

Kathy's birthday was last Sunday. I am sure she resigned herself to a lonely day, after all, her husband was in Minnesota and none of her children live close. Cissy, Charlie, Brian, Chad, Roger, Sharil and Paula surprised her in her apartment by bringing a cake, writing her a poem and giving her a plaque. She cried so hard they cried!

John and Denise had to leave their home and find a place to store their stuff until they could get into another rental. Six folks sacrificed their time to help make the move happen.

Romans 12:1—Therefore, brothers, by the mercies of God, I urge you to present your bodies as a living sacrifice, holy and pleasing to God; this is your spiritual worship.

One of the things I love about fellowship is observing the lives of the people who frequently make themselves available to serve. My wife is the champion of serving. Many a late night she is up working on food or crafts to help others. Don, Beth, Pat, and Paula are friends that regularly open their homes for fellowship. Whether it's hospitality, sharing Scripture, lifting loads or just interacting, association is made sweet on the journey to Jesus by availability.

Do you think Jesus keeps attendance records in heaven on who showed up for church? I believe He is far more interested in who arrives when problems or opportunities sprout. Because that is what He did—He identified needs and met them. *"For even the Son of Man did not come to be served, but to serve, and to give His life—a ransom for many"* (Mark 10:45).

God made His Son available 24/7. But He didn't just make time for the children or to train the faithful. He also came for mocking, beatings, cursing, and the full range of hatred finally manifested in crucifixion. If His resume says nothing about vacation time, possessions accumulated, or winning *Rabbi of the Year* awards, we ought to take notice. Jesus never copped the *I'm too busy to be the Messiah today* attitude. He gave His all for His Father!

Availability is the antidote to busyness and the aroma of worship. It starts by a willingness to suppress fleshly wishes in order to help others. It is correctly fashioned by sensitively listening to the Holy Spirit for His directions. It is voluntary, cheerful obedience. Instead of building *My Space*, it builds His will. It is not about carving time once a week for church and checking off *God-time* as good. It is about hourly willingness to serve, however the Master leads—in small ways and big ways, whether inconvenienced or uncompensated. What matters is that we are willing to be instruments in the hands of God to further His kingdom.

God calls us to be living sacrifices. To fulfill this calling we must be available! One cannot die on an altar by abstention or please the Father with excuses. We are to make use of ourselves while we have the opportunity. If the royal law is to love the Lord our God *wholeheartedly, wholesouledly* and *wholemindedly* we have to be *wholly* available for Him. If the royal law is to love our neighbors as ourselves, neighbor service is mandatory. If we *do not have time* for the people who do not have Jesus maybe we should ask ourselves if Jesus has us. If we *do not have time* for the people who have Jesus maybe we should ask ourselves who we are worshiping. If we *do not have time* for Jesus, maybe we should ask if He will have eternity for us.

God, by Your mercy, help us be available to serve so the world will see more of Your Son!

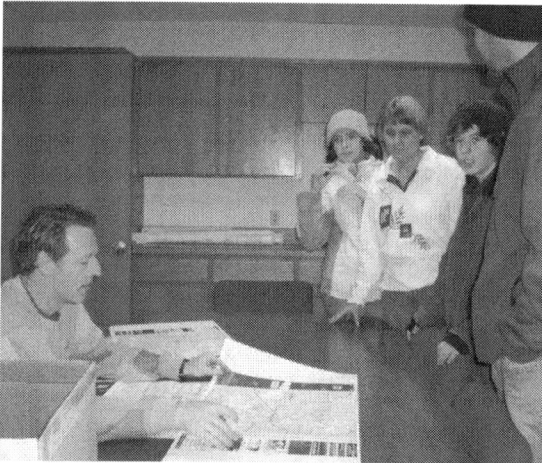

Inspiration †††

In a world where people are ruled by their calendars and the rule of the calendar is "No more—all full," is it reasonable to expect people to make spiritual growth a top priority?—George Barna in *Growing True Disciples*

We Have Different Gifts

Romans 12:6—According to the grace given to us, we have different gifts . . .

I have always thought it amazing how our society glorifies the quarterback but completely misses the water boy. The hero has no heroics without a supporting cast. If a team achieves victory, it is the result of teamwork. In this context, we should understand the value, function and place of spiritual gifts.

First, none of us has any right to feel special because of giftedness. Gifts are not a reflection of a superior brain, talented genes or advanced motor skills. Spiritual gifts are from the Holy Spirit and they represent the grace He bestows (Rom. 12:6, 1 Co. 12:4-11, Eph. 4:7). Therefore, the operative attitude that should accompany the exercise of any gift is humility, for grace is a blessing we do not deserve.

Second, Paul wrote, "we have different gifts." Different means not the same and that is clue (Rom. 12:6, 1 Co.12:4, 28-30) into God's thinking. Those who constantly advocate the importance or supremacy of one gift are not only unbalanced but also guilty of distorting context. For example, to insist that believers must speak in tongues in order to be saved or to prove they have the Holy Spirit is not only bad hermeneutics (the science and methodology of interpreting Biblical texts), but also cultish. We may desire certain gifts but our focus should be on the Giver and not on the gifts. The former produces peace, humility and contentment. The latter invites judging, sparks dissension and fosters a have, have-not mentality.

Third, the exercising of our gifts is never one-dimensional. Attitude and attributes accompany gifts and determine their efficacy. For example, prophesying requires faith, mercy necessitates cheerfulness, and without diligence, leadership is as effective as a microwave oven with only 30 seconds of electricity (Rom. 12:6-8).

Fourth, gifts are operative under the authority and strategy of the Holy Spirit. "A manifestation of the Spirit is given to each person . . . one and the same Spirit is active in all these, distributing to each one as He wills" (1 Co. 12:7,11). We do not need to be tangled up in fights over whether gifting is permanent for a person or changes. What matters is that the Holy Spirit is in charge and He will do what He deems best for the body.

Fifth, the purpose of gifts is to "produce what is beneficial . . . for the training of the saints in the work of ministry, to build up of the body of Christ, until we all reach unity in the faith and in the knowledge of God's Son," for the accomplishment of God's will (1 Co.12:7; Eph. 4:12,13). Spiritual gifts are not to cause division, pride or the mistaken notion that we are indispensable. When we employ our spiritual gifts in obedience to the Holy Spirit, the world sees grace at work and the results make fantastic seem like a lame adjective!

They Stood Up

I took great privilege in attending a gathering in San Antonio, Texas, of World War II veterans from the 104th Timberwolf Division. These venerable survivors gather each year to reminisce of war memories, catch up in recent events and celebrate each other along with any accompanying children affectionately known as "pups."

Major General T.K. Moffett shared with the gathered assembly a video production of the current 104th Division. At one point in the CD, the 104th band played the Star Spangled Banner for a group of Soldiers headed to Iraq. Immediately upon hearing the national anthem, 30-40% of the gathered audience rose to their feet and stood at attention until the song finished playing. Chills ran down my spine as I witnessed this incredible patriotism. We had already stood that morning for a live rendition of the national anthem. Yet, many of these men and women would not think of sitting while the national anthem played—even if it were part of a video.

Romans 13:7—Pay your obligations to everyone: taxes to those you owe taxes, tolls to those you owe tolls, respect to those you owe respect, and honor to those you owe honor.

Kathleen and I want our three children to understand and value the concept of respect. When elders walk into the room, we expect them to stand up, give eye contact and respond appropriately. We hope that they will hold the Bible as sacred Scripture and not take their Lord for granted but revere Him. They are to treat people kindly and not speak poorly of others or take revenge when mistreated. I get angry and discipline them if I hear them use sarcasm or speak disrespectfully to their mom. Why? Because Lev. 19:3 says, *"Each of you is to respect his mother and father. You are to keep My Sabbaths; I am the LORD your God."* If we are honorable and they do not respect us, they will not respect God. One cannot dishonor the created and honor the Creator.

In the Bible, God held people accountable for respecting: their leaders (Exo. 22:28), their parents, the Sabbath, holy offerings (Lev. 22:2), the elderly (Deu. 28:50), commands (Pro. 13:13), husbands (Eph. 5:33), wives (1 Ti. 3:11), masters (1 Ti. 6:1), and marriage (Heb. 13:4). Is there any reason why God would not want these same things respected today?

In observing those WWII vets and their spouses, I noted superlative behavior. First, most of them were respectful towards God. He held the preeminent place in their ceremonies as evidenced by prayer and message. Second, they were respectful of their nation and the values they fought to defend—liberty, justice and the right to pursue happiness. Third, they were polite and respectful not just to each other but to all of us attending their meetings. Most were kind, gentle and exceedingly loving. It was inspiring to be in their presence. Elderly friends like Art and Betty Sorensen and Mel Morasch welcome me as part of their extended family.

Loss of respect is a sure sign of a nation's decay. When God is disdained, hell is attained. If people are slighted a nation is blighted. Wherever there is devaluation of customs, traditions, authority or objects, there will quickly arise a proliferation of self-centeredness, lawlessness, relativism and pollution. No nation on earth has ever escaped the downward decline of respect. This by itself proves the existence and power of sin. To think we can achieve utopia by human effort is as laughable as trying to stop graffiti. We can erase markings but we cannot mute the cry of the restless, meaning-seeking heart in a world whose back is towards God.

I suspect that respect for God grows in the sincere heart of one whose life is nearly over. *Oh Lord, may we fall on our knees before You and give You the glory due Your name. May we live like You are in the room beside us and may You grant us the mercy we have too often ignored in our prideful condition.*

Inspiration † † †

A child who is allowed to be disrespectful to his parents will not have true respect for anyone.—Billy Graham

Bimbo

The most amazing thing happened while I was away on a trip to Japan. A small group of Americans taught a few Japanese, slang expressions we use in the U.S. I joined in the brainstorming to supply words like "rad," "holy cow," "get a grip" etc. About ten minutes later, I left to return to my own workstation. My two Japanese coworkers were reading the latest copy of the newspaper *Stars and Stripes*. They wanted me to explain what the word "bimbo" meant in the title line of a front-page article about a woman involved with a key American leader. *The American Heritage Dictionary* uses the following definition of the word *bimbo*: bim·bo *n*. 1. *Offensive. Slang.* A woman, especially one who is perceived as vacuous or as having an exaggerated interest in sexuality.

It was rather embarrassing to explain a slang term used to inculpate (incriminate) the leader of my own nation, but it triggered a flurry of thoughts. Our repute is solidified by our conduct and character. Infidelity rapidly trashes one's status.

Romans 13:13,14—Let us walk with decency, as in the daylight: not in carousing and drunkenness; not in sexual impurity and promiscuity; not in quarreling and jealousy. But put on the Lord Jesus Christ, and make no plans to satisfy the fleshly desires.
1 Thessalonians 4:3-5,7—For this is God's will, your sanctification: that you abstain from sexual immorality, so that each of you knows how to possess his own vessel in sanctification and honor, not with lustful desires, like the Gentiles who don't know God . . . For God has not called us to impurity, but to sanctification.

The Apostle Paul challenged the Roman believers to walk morally. If you want to be clean, live and act as Jesus did. Whenever we take our focus off of Him we are subject to our own sin nature and its plotting thoughts. To delve into the realm of immorality, to be bimboish does not just hurt us, it also hurts the reputation of the One we represent. God's will that we be set apart and live holy lives predicates on the fact that He is a perfect Father with the highest of standards. Let us make sure that what we model is not the chasing of skirts or the feeding of lusts but rather the decency that makes our Lord proud.

Inspiration ✝✝✝

Infidelity does not consist in believing, or in disbelieving, it consists in professing to believe what he does not believe.—Thomas Paine, English author, (1737-1809)

A Ship Called *Me*

Romans 14:8—If we live, we live to the Lord; and if we die, we die to the Lord. Therefore, whether we live or die, we belong to the Lord.

There is much agreement in the world as to the wisdom of having a mentor. However, there is little talk of anyone having a master. Is this because the prevailing dogma has always been *I am the Captain of my own ship*? If I adhere to the notion that I know what is best for me, my compass is set to the course of my vision. Unfortunately, this vision is sorely limited in at least two major ways. First, I do not know what tomorrow holds. Therefore, the best plans I make may be thoroughly dashed by what happens in the future. Second, I am influenced by a competing team of advisors—both internally and externally.

- Petty Officer Greed contentiously opposes Petty Officer Generous.
- Admiral Pride thinks Admiral Humble is a weenie.
- Boatswain Mercy finds Boatswain Insensitive overly critical.
- Ensign Justice chafes at Ensign Lenient's unwillingness to obey the rules.

Even in the safest of harbors, barnacles accumulate. I cannot achieve peace in a vessel always at war.

> A ship called *Me* set out to sea launched from a pier of dreams.
> For water deep and vast unknowns to test her wooden beams.
> With Captain Self perched at the wheel the rudder gives to waves
> That only One who sent His Son, can ever hope to brave.
> Will this ship forever sink torn by great disaster?
> It all depends on who's in charge—the mortal or the Master.

Heaven witnesses the chaos of billions of skippers all trying to guide their crafts through turbulent waters. Those who insist on trusting manmade solutions, find themselves wrecked on reefs of sin. Some realize their hopelessness. They send out a desperate *Save Our Ship*! (SOS Morse code). They receive an answer from the Lord of the Universe—*Sent My Son* (SMS). Jesus knows the way home! The prudent course of action is to schedule a permanent change of command. Every Captain Self must step aside for the One who went where no others could go.

Immediately an amazing change takes place. When I give up my right to be in charge and agree to let the Lord lead I gain a Master:

- Who is my protector—He safely guides me through every storm.
- Who is discerning—He sees the hidden reefs of sin I am oblivious to with their jagged rocks of harmful motives and false agendas.
- Who is all-powerful—no winds of adversity or ancient enemy can sink my ship when He commands.

- Who is accessible—He has an open-door policy. I can always go to Him for advice or help.
- Who is perfectly fair and just—when I make mistakes and bring them to His attention He does not make me walk the plank. He forgives me, disciplines me according to His wise judgment and sets me back on course.
- Who trains me—He harnesses His winds of providence to take me to places I would not choose to go that I might learn lessons He knows I will need for later journeys.
- Who is generous and kind—He gives me exactly what I need for life, lavishes His love upon me making the voyage full of purpose and meaning.

Who is your Master?

Strength As One

My college class motto is *"Strength As One."* I believe it is more profound than we realized when we selected it. What makes our class special is a collective sense that our ability exponentially increases through our unity. Implied in our unity is an understanding that we are accountable to one another.

Romans 14:11,12—For it is written: As I live, says the Lord, every knee will bow to Me, and every tongue will give praise to God. So then, each of us will give an account of himself to God.

From the onset of the creation of humanity, God established accountability:

> *The LORD God took the man and placed him in the garden of Eden to work it and watch over it. And the LORD God commanded the man, "You are free to eat from any tree of the garden, but you must not eat from the tree of the knowledge of good and evil, for on the day you eat from it, you will certainly die."* (Gen. 2:15-17)

Throughout the Bible, God holds people accountable to obey Him (John 14:15) in their speech (Mat. 12:36) and for what they produce (John 15:2,5).

Jesus modeled for us what accountability looks like. In John 6:38,39 He said, *"For I have come down from heaven, not to do My will, but the will of Him who sent Me. This is the will of Him who sent Me . . . that I should lose none of those He has given Me but should raise them up on the last day."* God held Jesus responsible to do His will and He in turn accounted for the people God gave Him. After Jesus departed, God sent the Holy Spirit to maintain that accountability. *"But the Counselor, the Holy Spirit—the Father will send Him in My name—will teach you all things and remind you of everything I have told you"* (John 14:26).

Just as God holds us accountable, so we are answerable to each other as His family members. Perhaps the greatest Biblical example of this is Paul's analogy in his letter to the Corinthians.

> *So the body is not one part but many. If the foot should say, "Because I'm not a hand, I don't belong to the body," in spite of this it still belongs to the body. And if the ear should say, "Because I'm not an eye, I don't belong to the body," in spite of this it still belongs to the body . . . So the eye cannot say to the hand, "I don't need you!" nor again the head to the feet, "I don't need you!" . . . so that there would be no division in the body, but that the members would have the same concern for each other. So if one member suffers, all the members suffer with it; if one member is honored, all the members rejoice with it.* (1 Co. 12:14-16,21,25,26)

The best way we can relate and care for one another is through accountability.

When we are not accountable, three things happen:

1.   *We set ourselves up for sin.* I remember as a teenager, an American soldier who was part of the team my father led in Seoul, Korea. Johnny got involved with another woman in an illicit relationship. Instead of being responsible to the team, he left and quit walking with God.

2.   *The body suffers.* Without encouragement and love, people shrivel up like plants without water. Likewise, when one member of the body falls into sin, becomes discouraged or physically ill, it affects us all.

3.   *We lose the Lord's blessing.* God never intended for us to go through life alone, apart from each other. To go solo or to disdain being answerable is to veer from His plan and inevitably, we suffer.

So how can we keep unity through accountability? *First, remember that unity with Christ involves strict accountability to God. Second, we need true friends I call ranger buddies. Third, real friendship calls a willingness to be vulnerable, available and honest.* Without these qualities, accountability is like a car without gas.

Do not try to paddle across the ocean by yourself! Be blessed with strength as one!

Inspiration † † †

If we want unity, we must all be unifiers. If we want accountability, each of us must be accountable for all we do.—Christine Gregoire, Washington State governor

We must reject the idea that every time a law's broken, society is guilty rather than the lawbreaker. It is time to restore the American precept that each individual is accountable for his actions.—President Ronald Reagan

Nemesis

Before I go to bed, I let the dogs out to do their thing. A most amusing pattern has developed. Dusty, our Labrador retriever runs around the perimeter of the back yard and grunts—a well refined canine message! He knows if he barks I will get mad at him for waking our great neighbors. So he's modified his approach to accomplish his objective—scare the whiskers off the cats next door, forewarn the raccoons and occasional skunks that it's a good time to vacate. It doesn't matter if an active heartbeat is anywhere near, every night he's going to run down the fence line with his hair at attention while his lungs expel a guttural warning. I happen to know it's all show—but to the surrounding creatures he is their nemesis. If it were not for the fence, they would be in trouble.

Romans 16:20—The God of peace will soon crush Satan under your feet. The grace of our Lord Jesus be with you.

In Greek mythology, Nemesis was the goddess of retributive justice or vengeance. *The American Heritage Dictionary* defines a nemesis as an unbeatable opponent. Those of us who love God have a nemesis. He lurks ever ready to take us down. His name is Satan. But the real god of vengeance is not invincible. Once he operated with virtual impunity against all people. However, God in His creative grace gave us something far better than a fence—His holy Son. When we place our trust in Jesus, we receive protection the devil cannot defeat. He can roar, intimidate, tempt, cause suffering and grief but he cannot destroy us. The God of peace rules. The Son of God saves. So the next time you feel the heat from the world's biggest bully, call on the name of Jesus and watch who goes running!

Inspiration † † †

Everything Satan says against you is an argument why Christ should love you the more.—F.B. Meyer British pastor, (1847-1929), in *Meet For The Master's Use*

Signs and Wisdom

My son, Bryan and I were driving down a steep road when we encountered a peculiar sign. It said, "Caution—Hill Obscures View." *Well duh!* We laughed at the great wisdom displayed! Maybe it is the way my brain works, but that set me to thinking about signs and miracles. Does it seem like people are unimpressed with the obvious and bore easily in an age where technology renders the sufficient obsolete?

1 Corinthians 1:22,23—For the Jews ask for signs and the Greeks seek wisdom, but we preach Christ crucified, a stumbling block to the Jews and foolishness to the Gentiles.

Throughout Jesus' ministry, religious leaders insisted that He produce signs proving that He was the Messiah. However, Jesus did not comply. He exercised supernatural power only when it was in keeping with God's will. When the gospel spread to the Gentile world, signs retained their popularity but to cerebral Greeks it was the wonder of wisdom that mattered. Not much has changed twenty centuries later.

Countless people gravitate towards ministries where signs find continual emphasis. Now I am not one who believes that miracles were limited to the time of Christ and the Apostles. I personally saw God miraculously heal my son Bryan from an incurable brain tumor. Around the world, there are verifiably accurate reports of God raising people from the dead and healing incurable diseases. In India, I visited a retreat center where AIDS patients were supernaturally healed. As a result, many placed their faith in Jesus. There is nothing inherently wrong with admiring signs or wonders.

There are also those who are skeptical of anything that defies natural laws. They venerate rational thought. They refuse to believe what is supernatural and confine God to only what is acceptable according to rationalism. Some yearn to amass knowledge but miss Solomon's observation: *"The wise man has eyes in his head, but the fool walks in darkness. Yet I also knew that one fate comes to them both"* (Ecc. 2:14).

Our central focus should never be on miracles or philosophical acuity. If we worship the One crucified for our sin and resurrected for our salvation, we will experience His power and grow wiser. Jesus did not multiply five loaves to impress 5000 men. He wanted them to understand that He was the Bread of Life. *"So Jesus said to them, 'I assure you: Unless you eat the flesh of the Son of Man and drink His blood, you do not have life in yourselves'"* (John 6:53). After this teaching, many no longer followed Him. The *wise* tripped over what sounded like a cannibalistic statement while the unschooled fisherman recognized the *"Holy One of God"* (John 6:66,69).

Take Off the Training Wheels

1 Corinthians 2:1,2—When I came to you, brothers, announcing the testimony of God to you, I did not come with brilliance of speech or wisdom. For I determined to know nothing among you except Jesus Christ and Him crucified.
2:4,5—My speech and my proclamation were not with persuasive words of wisdom, but with a demonstration of the Spirit and power, so that your faith might not be based on men's wisdom but on God's power.

Caution! Beware of turning your own experiences into principles for others to follow. Experiences are wonderful when kept in the proper context. However, when our experiences take center stage instead of Jesus Himself, we are in danger of becoming junior holy spirits. The Bible tells us God imprisoned Paul and allowed him to suffer greatly in ministry. Spiritual giant that he was, Paul did not preach to others that they must suffer as he did to grow. He did not superimpose his experiences or his well-honed ministry skills on the Corinthians when he visited them. He came with a fresh determination to worship Christ with them on a daily, visible basis. Are you living a Christian life that is rich because you are feeding each day from new times with the Lord? Or, are you surviving on the dwindling fat of what God did for you in the past?

"Wow, may I share what I am learning from my time with God!" surpasses *"Let me tell you what God did in my life twelve years ago."* The example we export to those around us is determined by what we import from our Heavenly Father.

Do you remember when you first learned how to ride a bike? The hardest step was removing the training wheels. It seemed a whole lot easier to ride with four wheels than two—didn't it? I cannot teach my children how to ride a bicycle until they let me take off the training wheels. It is an issue of trusting their balance over the two side wheels—Security and Familiarity. Amazingly, once they let those wheels go and agree that falling down is not the end of the world, they realize those side-attachments slowed them down and prevented them from leaving the paved road.

How is your bicycle configured?

● Do people see Jesus in you or the rites and rules of organized religion?

● Do you trust the Holy Spirit to lead you in relating to people such that you do not depend on the timeworn tools others gave you?

● Do you become anxious without security and exasperated with unfamiliarity or have you discovered the thrill of going off the ramp?

I pray that you will experience the awesome pleasure of riding with God today. Let Him have the handlebars, get off the brakes. Slide back on the ol' banana seat and trust the steering of the One who has never had an accident and who needs no collision insurance. He will not fail you. He is the greatest!

Labor Day

1 Corinthians 3:12-15—If anyone builds on the foundation with gold, silver, costly stones, wood, hay, or straw, each one's work will become obvious, for the day will disclose it, because it will be revealed by fire; the fire will test the quality of each one's work. If anyone's work that he has built survives, he will receive a reward. If anyone's work is burned up, it will be lost, but he will be saved; yet it will be like an escape through fire.

Labor Day is a holiday celebrated in America the first Monday in September. It is unclear who first conceived of this day but for over 100 years, it has served as a tribute and dedication to the social and economic achievements of American workers. Regardless of what country we live in, work is an important facet of our everyday lives.

As I reflect on work in Scripture, here are some thoughts to consider:

I. Our work comes from God.

A. *He is the work originator—Gen. 2:2. "By the seventh day God had finished the work He had been doing; so on the seventh day He rested from all His work."*

B. *He has a universal work plan—John 4:34. "'My food is to do the will of Him who sent Me and to finish His work,' Jesus told them."* Jesus worked the plan God had for Him. We ought to do the same.

C. *We need to understand what He would have us do—Eph. 5:15-17. "Pay careful attention, then, to how you walk—not as unwise people but as wise—making the most of the time, because the days are evil. So don't be foolish, but understand what the Lord's will is."* Our work should fit God's plan. Our plan should fit God's work. Four principles will help us in determining and following God's will:

1. *Worship leads to direction—Acts 13:2.* The key to finding His will is found in worshiping Him. Plenty of people are happy to tell you what they think you should or should not do. Never settle for opinions that come minus prayerful seeking and humble worship. When God sets you apart or calls you to a work, whether it be sweeping floors or leading a corporation, do not second-guess Him, and do not sell Him short, get after it. God can take what we think is mundane and make it marvelous.

2. *Empowerment comes through Christ—Php. 4:13.*

3. *Beware of substituting activity for abiding.* Watchman Nee wrote, "To have God do His own work through us, even once, is better than a lifetime of human striving." Someone once said, "Activity itself proves nothing: the ant is praised, the mosquito swatted." Andrew Murray noted, "Do not confound work and fruit. There may be a good deal of work for Christ that is not the fruit of the heavenly Vine."

4. *Our will is subordinate to God's will.* Many people are spiritually unproductive because they refuse what God would have them do to pursue what they would rather do.

II. Our work should be God pleasing.

A. *It should be honorable*—Tit.3:1. *"Remind them to be submissive to rulers and authorities, to obey, to be ready for every good work."*

B. *We should be wholehearted*—Col. 3:23,24. *"Whatever you do, do it enthusiastically, as something done for the Lord and not for men, knowing that you will receive the reward of an inheritance from the Lord—you serve the Lord Christ."*

"Every job is a self-portrait of the person who does it. Autograph your work with excellence."—Unknown

C. *He will test what we have done*—See Meditation passage on the previous page.

May I ask you a question? Are you writing in the sand? Will you work be washed away by the tide because it is from the flesh? Or are you writing on the Rock? Will your work be a testimony to the One who loves you and called you according to His purpose? Something to think about . . . in reveration!

Inspiration † † †

Idleness is a constant sin, and labor is a duty. Idleness is the devil's home for temptation and for unprofitable, distracting musings; while labor profit others and ourselves.—Anne Baxter, actress, (1923-1985)

There is no excellence without labor. One cannot dream oneself into either usefulness or happiness.—Liberty Hyde Bailey, scientist, (1858-1954)

All labor that uplifts humanity has dignity and importance and should be undertaken with painstaking excellence.—Martin Luther King, Jr.

Preoccupation

- God was in the room when he showered, shaved and grabbed a quick breakfast and read the headlines and entire sports section.
- God was in the car when she drove to school. He saw the traffic jam and her fluster. He listened to the DJ jabbering. He heard her singing.
- God was in the office while he labored on his sales presentation. He felt the worry on his face. He read his thoughts about his coworkers.
- God was in the hospital as she obsessed on the receptionist and rationalized that flirting was not the same thing as cheating.
- God was in the family room each night when they gathered to watch their favorite television programs.
- God listened as they sang at church how much they loved Him. He observed their tepid interest in the message and eagerness to depart.

1 Corinthians 3:16,17—Don't you know that you are God's sanctuary and that the Spirit of God lives in you? If anyone ruins God's sanctuary, God will ruin him; for God's sanctuary is holy and that is what you are.
6:19,20—Do you not know that your body is a sanctuary of the Holy Spirit who is in you, whom you have from God? You are not your own, for you were bought at a price; therefore glorify God in your body.

In both work and in issues of purity we must consider the Holy Spirit's residence in our lives. When and if we remember who lives in us, how and why we live should be wonderfully effected.

I am appalled to think what God thinks of my thoughts on those days when I'm infatuated with my flesh and not with Him. I am embarrassed that the majority of my time is fixated on what I would like as opposed to what He deserves. The hitch is not that I do not love my Father. The challenge is that I don't see Him. Therefore, I go about my day mostly forgetting that He is right inside me every step on the road home.

Wherever I walk, God walks with me. Wherever I stay, He abides. When people see me, they are supposed to see Him. I am a moving temple. Do you know that sanctuaries never get secular holidays? The Savior bought our temples. We do not own them! Therefore, when I sin I mess up the abode of my Owner. When I live for that which will burn horrendously, I miss the warmth of Him who burns *holifically*. The problem with preoccupation is that most of the time it is concentrated on things of such little consequence and value.

If each of us who are God's children would remember *who* occupies us and live accordingly, we might dramatically reverse the growing sin movement! As my friend Jan Arensmeier notes, "That which is the preoccupation of our mind is the object of our devotion."

None of These Rights

Welcome to the age of authoritarianism. Can you pick up a newspaper without finding some new intrusion by politicians or activists who would attempt to further regulate what you can and cannot do? I fear that many of us are caught in the adrenaline rush to be right, to be treated in a certain manner, and to be left alone by an overbearing big brother. Are we becoming increasingly preoccupied with the fear of living in a society ever more hostile to our faith?

There is a growing outrage among many believers today that our religious rights are being threatened. We have never recovered from losing the right to pray out loud in public schools. We are appalled at the treatment Christians receive in what should be a Judeo-Christian nation. We are finding it more attractive to congregate with those of like-mind thereby making us an even more distinct sub-culture.

Have no fear! It is not the authority of government, or the laws of a nation that determine our status. We may lose our freedoms. We may find like most people in other lands, that to be a Christian takes not just faith but also courage. Regardless of the views or dictates of others, God's authority reigns supreme.

1 Corinthians 9:15—But I have used none of these rights, and I have not written this to make it happen that way for me. For it would be better for me to die than for anyone to deprive me of my boast!

Our responsibility is to be obedient to our fantastic Father in heaven. If His Spirit so leads us we may fight to preserve our constitutional rights. However, let us never forget that the constitution of the land is not our primary concern. Our prime motive should be to march to the beckon and beat of God's voice. If we die at the hands of men, we live forever by the grace of Christ. If we bow before God's authority, our joy will be complete in Him despite our earthly circumstances. "What He says I will do. Where He sends I will go!" He is Lord and that is what matters most.

Inspiration † † †

The great *dominant note is* not the needs of men, but the command of Jesus.—Oswald Chambers in *My Utmost For His Highest.*

Watch Out for Sneaker Waves!

Along the Oregon coast are posted signs warning people to beware of sneaker waves. Children playing on logs in the sand have died because a large wave came in and rolled the huge timber over them as if twirling matchsticks. Others were knocked down and pulled out to deeper water only to drown.

We warned our children about these waves before letting them join their grandparents for two days of adventure on the coast. Nevertheless, while they were having fun on the sand a sneaker wave caught them by surprise. Two escaped. One fell down. His coat instantly filled with water and he could not get up. He thought he was going to die. Grandpa saw his plight and pulled him out of the water. Three children learned a valuable lesson about the power of the ocean.

1 Corinthians 10:6-12—Now these things became examples for us, so that we will not desire evil as they did. Don't become idolaters as some of them were; as it is written, The people sat down to eat and drink, and got up to play. Let us not commit sexual immorality as some of them did, and in a single day 23,000 people fell dead. Let us not tempt Christ as some of them did, and were destroyed by snakes. Nor should we complain as some of them did, and were killed by the destroyer. Now these things happened to them as examples, and they were written as a warning to us, on whom the ends of the ages have come. Therefore, whoever thinks he stands must be careful not to fall!

Did you know that the Bible is loaded with warnings? God understands the danger of sin. He informs us through Scripture of the consequences of evil because He loves us and wants to protect us. Yet many of us would rather play in the sand and pretend no wave could ever take us under. We rationalize immoral behavior because we do not like warnings. We mute our conscience button. We suggest that God's Word is open to a variety of interpretations as opposed to submitting to its irrefragable (indisputable) admonitions. In short, self-serving moral relativism is favored over reverent obedience. Do you resist God's cautionary guidance to please your flesh?

If the Holy Spirit brings conviction to your heart, take heed of His prompting! *"The one who trusts in himself is a fool, but one who walks in wisdom will be safe"* (Pro. 28:26).

Inspiration † † †

He is not a honest man who has burned his tongue and does not tell the company that the soup is hot.—Yugoslav proverb

Example is Leadership

1 Corinthians 11:1—Follow my example, as I follow the example of Christ. (NIV)

In the journey of life, everyone parades past glass windows. Eyes will watch your actions today. Ears will hear your words and attempt to define your heart. Hearts will measure your character. The manner in which you walk, the nonverbals you express, how you listen, each of these are the brush strokes shaping your caricature on the canvas others paint.

Countless times, I have been in a room and had someone apologize for crude, vulgar language—not because I said something, but because of what they had not heard me say. Many of you have experienced similar occurrences. The best sermon a person may ever glean is how you and I live our lives. King David wrote in Psa. 16:8, *"I keep the LORD in mind always. Because He is at my right hand, I will not be shaken."* He understood a potent truth—keep God in front. By doing so, one's life is not defined by circumstance but by faithful-stance.

Do not despair if you are not behind a microphone, if you labor behind the scenes, if your life seems as riveting as a tired rerun. Get up this morning armed with the knowledge that what you do does matter! How you live is important! You have no idea how much God can use you to be an encourager to others. Perhaps it will be a child, a co-worker, a spouse, employees, or a neighbor, who will learn a valuable lesson by what you model. Ask God right now to give you the blessing of being a blessing to someone else—before the sun rolls past the horizon!

Do you suppose God celebrates when you and I measure our thoughts and actions and patiently resolve to be like His Son? Aspire to be an example for the glory of the One who loves you. *"For God is not unjust; He will not forget your work and the love you showed for His name when you served the saints—and you continue to serve them"* (Heb. 6:10).

Inspiration † † †

Example is not the main thing in influencing others, it's the only thing . . . Example is leadership.—Albert Schweitzer, French theologian, (1876-1965)

The leader is both the messenger and the message.—Henry & Richard Blackaby in *Spiritual Leadership*

Each of You are a Part

Fran* came in the ministry center for food. She is a tall woman with a firm handshake and eyes that tell me she is weathering brutal storms. She sits across from me and shares her story. Her husband is 6' 3" and once weighed 240 lbs. Now he weighs 140 lbs and is barely clinging to life. For years he sprayed Crossbow, a chemical treatment that kills weeds, on poison oak and blackberries. Often when the summer heat bore down he took off his protective gloves. Eventually, the amount of chemicals that penetrated his skin produced a condition that is now killing him.

Fran's two misbehaving sons are in high school. She deals herself with severe epileptic seizures. As life tears her apart, it is all she can do to cope. She was raised a Catholic and from her childhood always attended the same church. Her husband is a Methodist and sometimes they frequent a local Methodist church. I ask her if either church knows of their situation and suffering. She nods yes. I ask her what they are doing to help her and she says "Not much."

1 Corinthians 12:25-27—This makes for harmony among the members, so that all the members care for each other. If one part suffers, all the parts suffer with it, and if one part is honored. All the parts are glad. All of you together are Christ's body, and each of you is a part of it. (NLT)

Paul makes it gemstone clear in the verses above that when one person in the church suffers, the *whole* church should suffer. There is no slick means of evading this teaching in the letter to the Corinthian church. I do not think the Lord's intent was that we always suffer. I think His intent was that we be compassionate, long-suffering and sensitive to those with whom we fellowship. Before she left, I asked Fran to read 1 Co. 12 to her priest and share her sense of isolation.

Friends, please understand if I vent with you for a moment. If the church does not take up its God-given mandate to care for its members, then it is *not* an organism that God intended for protection and growth it has become an organization, a gathering that may be valuable, but certainly is not in compliance with God's will. Organisms cannot help but suffer when a member is in pain whereas organizations grow callous and practice surgery. It is much easier to cut off *the leprous* as unclean.

Revival comes when we persevere with the hurting and seriously trust God in prayer for their healing! Yes, He still heals people today! If we do not believe this then we seriously limit His working by our own unbelief and we set ourselves up not to care. God will not awaken organizations. He works with organisms! We are to be the body of Christ not the club of Christ. We are to care not just congregate.

*Not her real name

Orderly

Why is it that the one year you get a flu shot you get the flu? Why does your dog shake off muddy water when you have just changed into good clothes? Why does your husband get sick on the day you are supposed to go on a family vacation? Why is it that the day you are ready to complete your project the power goes out? Why do microphones work fine in rehearsal but then screech during the play? Why do people get mad at other drivers right after leaving church? Why do camera batteries go dead just when your son takes his first steps? Why does some stranger's toddler pitch a fit at the climax of your daughter's recital?

1 Corinthians 14:40—But everything must be done decently and in order.

I am glad Paul taught the Corinthians to exercise orderliness in worship and sharing but you have to wonder what disruptions he experienced that elicited his instruction. When is life ever truly orderly! With groups of people (or by ourselves) how often does anything go exactly as we plan? How do we have fitting worship amidst hidden agendas? It is easy to have a good attitude and know how to respond when equipment works correctly, people behave and the pitcher throws a fastball when you're looking for a fastball.

Ahhh but wait! Perhaps it is possible to be orderly even in the center of chaos. If our hearts are set on obeying God *everything* we do or say should be *fitting*! The orderly way means:

● We take our instruction from the Holy Spirit and wait for His leading

● We do not contradict God's Word

● We set our eyes on Jesus—not the pain, disappointments, adversity, fear, failures, or expectations and opinions of other people.

● Programs never take priority over the Savior

● We want God to be glorified

● Life's surprises, challenges and problems don't control our attitude, character and behavior

An orderly way comes from settled spirits at peace because our trust is steadfastly in God (Isa. 26:3). When the Holy Spirit inspired Paul to write the word *"everything,"* He showed us that nothing excuses us individually or corporately from exercising our gifts and living our lives such that walk and worship are pleasing and magnify God's greatness!

Inspiration † † †

Good order is the foundation of all things.—Edmund Burke, Irish statesman, author, orator, philosopher (1729-1797)

Broken Fellowship

Winston Churchill said, "We make a living by what we get, but we make a life by what we give." Last week, the head of our food ministry terminated our operations. Nine people lost their jobs and The Road Home lost its office and meeting place. In one swift move, life took an unexpected detour! Why shut down a ministry that last year resulted in over 78 people putting their faith for the first time in Jesus, hundreds of families receiving food and free dental assistance plus prayer and encouragement? Better yet, why treat a ministry like a business and let the fear of lawsuits trump eternal investments? I felt like telling the owner, "When you die, you won't stand before lawyers, you'll stand before God, so lead accordingly!" But he was acting according to what he felt was right. He generously gave to help us move on. Rather than protest, it was nobler to pray and seek God's leading.

I feel badly for the folks who lost their jobs—especially my son, Bryan. But I learned something valuable. I got to see firsthand how people handled disappointment and who rose up to encourage. Somehow, a chapter closing brought to the forefront something else that has bothered me for a long, long time.

Someone should write a paper on the honorable way to leave a fellowship. It is sad how many disciples do not know how to leave the company of believers they have interacted with for a protracted time, in a God-honoring way. Rather than talk to the leader(s) and share their concerns, or seek the blessing of the body, they just stop coming. Fellowship is broken with words unspoken. Too often, the reasons for leaving are rationally pious but bereft in kindness; judgmental and graceless; self-oriented and not self-sacrificing. Church deficiencies, problems in the body or better-services-elsewhere logic somehow warrants the notion that fellowship can be severed. Do you know of any Scripture that extols fellowship hopping?

I think the unexpected termination of jobs is easier to absorb than the unannounced ending of shared worship. I do understand why so many ministers leave the ministry in droves. The severed cords of interaction without explanation become too painful. The cost to the spouse and children of watching *friends* just leave creates hurt and fear in them of ever trusting, or making the effort to be close to those who say they are committed.

2 Corinthians 1:3-5—Blessed be the God and Father of our Lord Jesus Christ, the Father of mercies and the God of all comfort. He comforts us in all our affliction so that we may be able to comfort those who are in any kind of affliction, through the comfort we ourselves receive from God. For as the sufferings of Christ overflow to us, so our comfort overflows through Christ.

Consider two ministry-saving, morale-boosting, joy-producing truths. *First, God supremely loves us.* If we will follow Him and rest in the assurance that He is in control, knows our troubles, and truly cares about us we *will* experience His phenomenal comforting. He is the blessed Comforter.

Second, God raises up people who are faithful fellowship builders. "Now I hope in the Lord Jesus to send Timothy to you soon so that I also may be encouraged when I hear news about you. For I have no one else like-minded who will genuinely care about your interests; all seek their own interests, not those of Jesus Christ" (Php. 2:19-21). True comforters have three qualities. First, their primary focus is in meeting the interests of Jesus Christ. Second, they have an ongoing concern for the welfare of their fellow saints. Third, by virtue of humility, their own interests are secondary to Jesus and others (2:3,4). *God help us to be like Timothy!*

Comforters are an awesome reflection of the Father of consolation. How deeply blessed I am when brothers and sisters care. Listen! *What's best for me Christianity* never impresses the world. The way we will reach those who do not know Christ is by building strong, committed relationships with those God places around us—maintaining accountability, forgiving, edifying and modeling loyalty for the expansion of His kingdom and the advancement of His glory! If you have left fellowship with no explanation or blessing, you've hurt people. Trust me on this. Make it right and honor God; heal the wound and regain favor. Do not make excuses or put off reconciling as the leader's responsibility—that's selfish and unfair. By repairing fellowship, you become a comforter. In the process, you gain peace.

Inspiration   † † †

I will forever be grateful to the people who knew there wasn't much they could do, who felt no pressure to explain it all to us, who if they felt inadequate didn't focus on it, but decided instead to simply, quietly, share the burden with us.—Carol A. and William J. Rowley in *On Wings Of Mourning*

In poverty and other misfortunes of life, true friends are a sure refuge. The young they keep out of mischief; to the old they are a comfort and aid in their weakness, and those in the prime of life they incite to noble deeds.—Aristotle

A System of Moral Principles

A home improvement con artist swindled a 100-year-old blind woman. He rang the woman's bell, unsolicited, to offer to do any repair work needed. The woman told him that for years she had struggled with a door that was difficult to open because it rubbed against the rug. To fix the problem, she agreed to pay the man $8,000, to jack up her house.[35]

2 Corinthians 1:12—For our boast is this: the testimony of our conscience that we have conducted ourselves in the world, and especially toward you, with God-given sincerity and purity, not by fleshly wisdom but by God's grace.

Ethics is a system of moral principles essential in guiding a person to do the correct thing that includes trustworthiness, respect, dependability, fairness, caring, and honesty. God built in each of us a moral compass that allows us to determine right from wrong. However, knowing that our conscience was not enough, He also gave us His Word that spells out what is acceptable and unacceptable behavior and conduct in His sight. Ethics encompasses those moral principles meant to steer us in how we should live.

Increasingly we live in a world content and perhaps even focused on blurring the line between right and wrong. A reporter for India Times notes most qualified doctors do not teach medical ethics to medical students in college. As institutions in the U.S. and other nations disdain the need to teach ethics is it any surprise that there are moral scandals among leaders and employees who should know better?

So what do we do? Those of us who are older must teach our children the meaning and importance of ethics. Our example is to reflect the moral principles God expects. When we live out those principles, we offer the world a direct example of Jesus and the value of holiness. Without a godly emphasis on truth, the world quickly descends into bottomless quicksand.

David refused to kill King Saul even though the evil king meant to destroy him. *"Afterwards, David's conscience bothered him because he had cut off the corner of Saul's robe"* (1 Sa. 24:5). David later wrote, *"I will praise the LORD who counsels me-even at night my conscience instructs me"* (Psa. 16:7). Paul proclaimed, *"I always do my best to have a clear conscience toward God and men"* (Acts 24:16). *"Instead, we have renounced shameful secret things, not walking in deceit or distorting God's message, but in God's sight we commend ourselves to every person's conscience by an open display of the truth"* (2 Co. 4:2).

Ethics matter. Jesus came to live out holiness so we would see how Adam should have lived and be freed from his curse.

Mashach

A·noint *tr.v.* a·noint·ed, a·noint·ing, a·noints. 1. To apply oil, ointment, or a similar substance to. 2. To put oil on during a religious ceremony as a sign of sanctification or consecration. 3. To choose by or as if by divine intervention—*The American Heritage Dictionary.*

2 Corinthians 1:21, 22—Now the One who confirms us with you in Christ, and has anointed us, is God; He has also sealed us and given us the Spirit as a down payment in our hearts.

The Hebrew word, *mashach* means to anoint, smear or consecrate. Thousands of years ago, there were three types of people God consecrated or specially set apart for service—priests, kings and prophets. Priests were anointed because they served before the presence of a holy God. *"You must not go outside the entrance to the tent of meeting or you will die, for the LORD's anointing oil is on you . . ."* (Lev. 10:7). Kings were anointed for their office of leadership. *"Samuel told Saul, 'The LORD sent me to anoint you as king over His people Israel. Now, listen to the words of the LORD'"* (1 Sa. 15:1). Prophets were anointed because they served as God's mouthpieces to proclaim His word. *"You are to anoint Jehu son of Nimshi as king over Israel and Elisha son of Shaphat from Abel-meholah as prophet in your place"* (1 Ki. 19:16).

The Hebrew word, *Mashiach* or Messiah, means "anointed one." Christ means "anointed." In Acts 10:38 Luke reveals that God anointed Jesus with the Holy Spirit and with power and that He did amazing things because God was with Him. Jesus' divinity permeated His humanity. As the perfect Son of Man, His death upon the cross paid for our sins thereby making it possible for all who put their trust in Him to receive the Holy Spirit. We have His anointing and purified hearts when He has our faith and obedience (Acts 5:32, 15:9).

It is essential that we understand the distinction between anointing and infilling. In Scripture, the word anoint works in two ways: to pour oil over someone for healing or consecration, and to describe God's consecration of Jesus or us. God may specially fill us at certain times for His service through the heightened extension of the Holy Spirit's power but do not confuse this with our anointing. The former comes at the time of salvation and is a permanent deposit. The latter is a special gift provided at God's discretion to supernaturally accomplish His will. For example in Acts we read the statement *"filled with the Holy Spirit"* (See Acts 4:8,31, 7:55). Peter, Stephen and the other believers mentioned, already possessed the Holy Spirit, He just took on a more active role.

Beware of those who tell the Holy Spirit what to do. The Bible clearly reveals that whenever people are in God's presence they are overwhelmed. The same holds true today. When the Spirit is in our midst, we are awestruck. Our fear of Him precludes any notion that we order Him to meet our spiritual bidding. Our anointing is not accomplished by the orders of men or because we give a certain amount of money. Furthermore, God's anointing is untied to an office or religious function.

But you have an anointing from the Holy One, and you all have knowledge . . . The anointing you received from Him remains in you, and you don't need anyone to teach you. Instead, His anointing teaches you about all things, and is true and is not a lie; just as it has taught you, remain in Him" (1 Jn. 2:20, 27).

Walk with Jesus. Your anointing is secure in Him and you are on His team. He will not exclude you nor does He want you to follow those who would suggest that your anointing is up to them. The only anointing we do is the pouring of oil accomplished with prayer under the leadership of the Holy Spirit.

Inspiration † † †

God doesn't call the prepared; He prepares the called.—Linda Seaman

Getting the Boot

My daughter Sarah once prepared to go on a missions trip to Cameroon, Africa for two months. Through the generosity of a company that sells footwear, she received a pair of Danner boots made of leather and gore-tex. Gore-Tex is a durable substance that allows the skin to breathe yet is waterproof. Unfortunately, the directions from the mission organization were explicit that only all-leather boots were acceptable.

My wife called to make sure Sarah's boots would be acceptable. The woman on the phone at the mission headquarters said "Absolutely not." She claimed that gore-tex would break down for anyone working with cement. I knew this would not be a problem as Sarah would not be living in wet cement and was quite capable of cleaning her boots. So I called the organization. I spoke to a young man and stated that I would prefer my daughter wear these boots, as they would serve her well. He cited problems they had with non-leather boots coming apart. I agreed that poorly made boots can unravel but asserted that her boots were high-quality Danners! He didn't care and as the conversation progressed, became increasingly rude. I stated that if this was the way the organization treated people who had legitimate questions then I was not sure I wanted my daughter to go with them. The temperature of my blood surely rose four degrees! The young man asked if I would like to speak to his director.

I reasoned with the man in charge to no avail. For twenty years this organization used leather-only boots and they were not about to change their policy. I gave up. Boiling blood usually results in sinful words; at least leather tongues do not start fires.

2 Corinthians 2:15,16—For to God we are the fragrance of Christ among those who are being saved and among those who are perishing. To some we are a scent of death leading to death, but to others, a scent of life leading to life. And who is competent for this?

Paul asks an amazing question in the verse above: *"who is competent for this?"* Six verses later in chapter three he gives the answer to his query.

Not that we are competent in ourselves to consider anything as coming from ourselves, but our competence is from God. He has made us competent to be ministers of a new covenant, not of the letter, but of the Spirit; for the letter kills, but the Spirit produces life" (3:5,6).

The Danner defeat was an enlightening prelude to Paul's message. Do not measure competence by legalism. By our own efforts, we cannot keep God's Law! Nor can we keep from sin which results in our death. Furthermore, when competency is based on following rules, two side effects often emerge—a prideful attitude (rudeness or condescension), and inflexibility (unwillingness to accept what is different).

Our competency must come from God. Through His strength, we can live holy lives. Through Christ's blood, we gain forgiveness from sin and eternal life. Through the Holy Spirit, we become able ministers of His new covenant. Moreover, if our competency runs in His leading, our perspective and understanding of rules will form with an attitude of humility and a willingness to act even when it takes us out of our comfort zone. So the next time you give someone the boot, make sure you are following the Spirit and not the leather.

Inspiration † † †

A stone is not aimed at a hen with chicks.   Meaning: Avoid attacks or confrontations in front of kids—Kenyan proverb

A cage is a cage, even if its bars are gold.—Malayalam proverb

On the Day After

⚫ The day after my mother died, her absence was deeply felt; I missed her, but I knew that I would see her again in a better place. I understood and shared her faith.

⚫ The day after Gander, I wept for the loss of my best friend and the memories of 248 101st Airborne soldiers killed mysteriously in a plane crash. I struggled before God with their erasure.

⚫ The day after my son, Bryan's brain-stem tumor was discovered, a doctor's foreboding prognosis echoed through my numb mind. I breathed the air of helplessness, and choked over dead dreams.

⚫ The day after September 11, I could not return to Oregon from Georgia. There were no commercial flights in our land—an unprecedented grounding. I wondered if vulnerability and the pain of so many murdered would bring our land back to the God it increasingly ignored. The pain of loss reawakened.

Romans 8:35—Who can separate us from the love of Christ? Can affliction or anguish or persecution or famine or nakedness or danger or sword?

Every person will experience *the day after*. There is no place on earth immune to trouble. This day is a time for introspection. If we choose not to examine what we do not understand, or fail to assess what we have felt and experienced, then we are hardly better than robots. Introspection is not afraid to challenge the obvious or embrace the illusive. If done honestly, it leads us through our vulnerability to value questions.

Disasters swirl our emotions and may often leave us bewildered. On *the day after*, tragic memories rock our views toward God. The proliferation of suffering eats at the notion there might be a caring Creator. But if God is only the creation of an insecure humanity, or exists but is uncaring, then what purpose is there in life? Why settle for a purposeless life and refuse to give a purposeful God a chance just because the sin caused by our rebellion exists? Would a just and holy Creator condone evil, or would He instead provide the grace to overcome it? Why would He give us the freedom of choice knowing we would repeatedly break His heart, unless He truly sought our heartfelt love? Is it possible that pain results in deeper questions?

Peter was a devoted follower of Jesus. The Messiah radically changed his life. So great was his devotion, history records he died for his faith on an upside down cross. Peter understood and proclaimed God's simple and wise plan for saving humanity. *"'Repent,' Peter said to them, 'and be baptized, each of you, in the name of Jesus the Messiah for the forgiveness of your sins, and you will receive the gift of the Holy Spirit'"* (Acts 2:38).

Saul, a Jesus-hater, after personally encountering God's Son completely jettisoned his former dogma to walk after Christ. He wrote, *"if you confess with your mouth, 'Jesus is Lord,' and believe in your heart that God raised Him from the dead, you will be saved"* (Rom. 10:9). He noted that salvation is a forever gift (Rom. 6:23). In the face of unbelievable catastrophes and personal suffering, he discovered the credible power of an incredible Savior. Like Peter, he died for his faith.

On *the day after* can we afford not to ask the most important questions? Dare we ignore our mortality? Do we believe the unique and required plan of God for achieving His grace? When suffering comes how will we cope? We have the opportunity to evaluate our own condition and the gift of life God offers. Right now, we have the privilege to decide. *The day after* may be too late!

Inspiration †††

Introspection is right because it is the only way we shall discover that we need God. Introspection without God leads to insanity.—Oswald Chambers in *The Servant As His Lord*

Mud, Mud, Mud

Bark Blowers sells bark, dirt, sand, and stones to people who have landscaping needs. I drive past their company virtually every day I am in town. Currently their parking lot is a disaster. Even their large trucks are in danger of getting stuck in a mud-rutted, quagmire. Twenty-four days of rain will do that.

Several years ago, the owners laid a foundation of gravel to keep their lot firm and drivable. However, what was on top could not overcome what was below. Their company is located on marshy ground. After prolonged rain, the water table rises such that mud literally swallows rocks to become mush.

2 Corinthians 4:16,17—Therefore we do not give up; even though our outer person is being destroyed, our inner person is being renewed day by day. For our momentary light affliction is producing for us an absolutely incomparable eternal weight of glory.

Sometimes no matter what I do or think, I cannot escape mud! I want my life to be orderly and sane yet circumstances conspire such that I encounter chaos and stress. For example, I picked up a schedule for soccer fields for my adult coed league. It should have been ready months ago. Instead, it was not only late but we had seven weeks of playing time taken off our season with a weak explanation from the presiding city official. I had to scramble for an entire day to find alternate fields. On top of this huge snafu, I could not access labels I needed from a website to print a major mailer and my hard drive threatened to crash. We were supposed to go to the coast with our children for the weekend but two family members were sick. Mud, mud, mud, everywhere I turned.

I aim to rejoice in convoluted weeks. Spiritual development does not occur because everything goes right. There are those days when I seek a word from God and all I hear is a deafening silence. Perhaps the rocks cry, "persevere." Opposition and conflict, disappointment and pain all work together. They remind me that I am not to base my faith and disposition on circumstances or the actions and attitudes of people, but rather on the Lord who gives me breath.

Sometimes we have to spin in order for God to teach us new lessons. On occasion we have to sit, stifled and unable to move forward, to be reminded that we are not in control. And yes, God may even allow us to undergo intense suffering, life-threatening trauma. What is important is that we not lose heart. If you are struggling right now, do not lose perspective. God has not stopped loving you! What He allows in your life ultimately leads to His glory and your spiritual betterment if you will trust Him. Something to think about . . . in reveration!

Kooley's Awakening

It started with watching mediocre movies with his friends and descended into pornography. Kooley felt miserable and tried to rationalize his actions. He felt trapped until one night he listened to his father, Genghis, preach a message he'd heard countless times. On this evening late into 1994, God's Word pierced Kooley's heart. He felt the potent pull of the Holy Spirit. Tears filled his eyes and plunged downward washing away built-up shame. Later that night he repented of his sin and honestly asked Jesus to become His Lord and Savior. Lingering guilt gave way to enduring peace. Love came and filled a 14-year-old boy in Trivandrum, India.

2 Corinthians 5:17—Therefore if anyone is in Christ, there is a new creation; old things have passed away, and look, new things have come.

Spiritual newness does not come via church attendance or affiliation. It is not deserved by birthright, inherited by papal pronouncement or earned by good deeds. We can make fresh resolutions but declarations and improved performance will not induce the Holy Spirit to take up residency in us. Even the best-intentioned sinner is still just that! Spiritual transformation comes through God's application of mercy. Jesus said, *"This is why I told you that no one can come to Me unless it is granted to him by the Father"* (John 6:65). The reason so many people miss Jesus' grace is that they are determined to earn God's favor through their own effort and on their own terms—an impossibility. Human effort merely calcifies the very nature God abhors.

To be new one must first be repentant. The paradox of spiritual life is dying to self. For Kooley it meant dying to illicit movies and the termination of time with unprincipled teens. His remorse was insufficient for killing his old nature. Remorse drops tears for getting caught. It may even cry while the rest of the body engages in wrongdoing. Repentance cannot condone compromise. It requires change and necessitates divine power to overcome a nature bound by dirt.

If we remain committed to obeying Jesus, our new nature is preeminent, glorifies God and emits a luster the Father uses to draw others to Himself. Today, Kooley radiates newness. His passion for God warms the hearts of those around him who sense the Spirit and see the changes taking place in his life.

Inspiration † † †

Before a sinful man can think a right thought of God, there must have been a work of enlightenment done within him.—A.W. Tozer in *The Pursuit of God*

The Ministry of Reconciliation

2 Corinthians 5:18—Now everything is from God, who reconciled us to Himself through Christ and gave us the ministry of reconciliation.

Dick played in my soccer league years ago. I had not seen him in at least five years. So I was surprised twice on Sunday morning when I received a call from Young's Funeral Home informing me that he died and that he had listed me as his minister.

Five days later, I began his service by sharing Psalm 139 and the fact that God knew Dick and lovingly created him and desired to have a relationship with him. I could give no words of hope regarding his location or allay the unspoken fears of those wondering his fate. Instead, I shared the gospel and the powerful need for each person to know Jesus Christ, the only One capable of forgiving us for our sins and providing us eternal life. My remarks were in stark contrast to the rest of the service.

For well over an hour friends and family paid tribute to Dick's humor, his giftedness as an artist and his love for life. There was no mention of anything spiritual. Instead, coarse humor became the hymn of choice in a vain attempt to ease grief amidst a sea of suffering. I left that place saddened by a crowd looking for solace in all the wrong places.

A week later, on the same day as the National Day of Prayer, I stood at Dick's gravesite and prayed for the family and few friends that gathered at the cemetery. I felt the Holy Spirit's nudging to do something I have never before done at a gravesite. I invited anyone present who was hurting to come and sit in one of the nine empty chairs by the silver encased casket, so I could pray for them. Every chair quickly filled. I then invited those still standing to come, place their hands on those seated, and join in agreement with me as I prayed. It was a deeply moving time. The sense of inadequacy that gnawed on my heart a week earlier gave way to gratitude that God gave me another opportunity to share His love.

I am afraid Dick lies in ground that smells more like the soil of Sodom than the dirt our ancestors turned long ago when God was actually feared. How profound the need is right now for our nation to be reconciled with God. My own prayerlessness and need for a greater sense of urgency for the salvation of my unbelieving friends convicts me. These are great days to ask God to use us to help reconcile people to Him.

Inspiration † † †

Reconciliation restitches the unraveled, reverses the rebellion, rekindles the cold passion. Reconciliation touches the shoulder of the wayward and woos him homeward.—Max Lucado in *3:16*

We Are Ambassadors

The hero stands and surveys the majestic scene. His ears catch the music anthems as the London Philharmonic Orchestra plays in honor of each represented nation. His eyes scan the dignitaries of 140 different countries as they mingle—Zambians, Koreans, Brazilians, Turks, Ukranians, Indians, Filipinos, Costa Ricans, French, Nigerians, Chinese. . .

Spectacular and exotic gifts from all over the planet fill a tent the size of a football field. Countless friends have traveled the globe to be here. Bulbs incessantly flash. Microphones and wires seem as numerous as the branches of the stately olive tree centered in the pavilion. At the sound of triumphant trumpets all heads turn to the Man. Jesus walks down the red carpet to receive the newly minted World-Medallion of Honor. Heaven's 2000 year-old ambassador to earth walks to the center of the platform, and before the hanging microphones says . . .

NO!!! God did not plan it this way. Jesus did not establish residency on earth for a 2000-year stint as heaven's ambassador. His Father brought His death and sin conquering, cross-carrying Son home to heaven.

2 Corinthians 5:20—Therefore, we are ambassadors for Christ; certain that God is appealing through us, we plead on Christ's behalf, "Be reconciled to God."

You, that's right—you, received the royal nod from God to be His ambassador. God intentionally made you and equipped you with special gifting to serve His throne. There is no one else like you. You are made with a mission—commissioned to proclaim the greatest news that can ever circle the planet.

Now if the Holy Spirit is nudging you, get into action! There is a world out there waiting to hear God's appeal. You, along with all of Jesus' disciples, represent God. What greater honor could one have than to be His spokesperson!

Inspiration † † †

The primary responsibility of the ambassador is to carry out the president's foreign policy. When ambassadors become more concerned with how they are treated by those they live among than in carrying out the president's policy whose authority is promulgated?—Oswald Chambers in *My Utmost For His Highest*

The Battle Of Antietam

While attending the Army War College, I had the opportunity with my classmates to spend a day walking the ground of the infamous Battle of Antietam. Antietam was the bloodiest single day in the history of the United States. On September 17, 1862, 23,110 casualties littered the ground fought over by Confederate and Union Armies. Antietam is a small river in the state of Maryland close to West Virginia and Pennsylvania. As I read the many plaques and battle literature, I could not help but think of all of the lives lost and the folly of a leader who could have ended the Civil War, but instead prolonged it.

Private Barton Mitchell put down his gear, rolled over on the grass to relax and spotted a piece of paper wrapped around three cigars. He discovered a copy of General Robert E. Lee's battle plan for the Confederate campaign into Maryland. Amazingly, the document revealed the positions of the Rebel army. This incredible find reached General George McClellan, then in charge of the Union forces. McClellan possessed all the information he needed to crush Lee's army and thereby end the war, instead, true to his nature, he acted cautiously. He failed to attack immediately at the perfect opportunity. When he attacked, he did not press his advantage decisively. Antietam ended in a draw and the Confederate Army escaped back into Virginia.

Haggai 1:7—The LORD of hosts says this: "Think carefully about your ways."
Proverbs 26:12—Do you see a man wise in his own eyes? There is more hope for a fool than for him.

General McClellan was a proud and cautious man. He was sure that he could defeat his enemies by careful maneuvering. He was so convinced of his own greatness that he repeatedly refused to listen to the advice of President Abraham Lincoln, who implored him to take the initiative and attack. We can learn many lessons from this leader with enormous potential, who failed to bring victory to a nation weary of war.

In Proverbs, we read of the folly of acting in haste (21:5). We *should* be careful before we speak and act. It is wise to be wary provided our trust is in God and not in ourselves. However, we must also ensure that our caution is not indecisiveness. If we are proud of slowly making decisions, and consistently avoid taking action, our focus may not be on obeying God but rather on protecting our own reputation. Immediately, we are in danger of missing opportunities in which God wants us to act. We lose the victory of what He has for us today by plotting for tomorrow. If we fear making mistakes or suffering criticism when God wants to stretch our faith, whose kingdom are we truly serving? Jesus said that in order to follow Him we must deny ourselves. Perhaps that denial means letting go of our unwillingness to act.

Convent Tunnels

In 1725, Franciscan monks established the Convent of Ocopa to evangelize and civilize the tribes of the Peruvian jungle. Located about 45 minutes from the city of Huancayo in the central Andes, this monastery contains a library with over 25,000 volumes of antique literature. Adorning many of the walls of the splendid building are paintings that date 200-300 years in age. It is a most impressive place where the walls literally seem to breathe with stories.

Another convent built for nuns once stood less than 1/8th of a mile away. That building no longer exists. Pastor Enrique Nickel shared with us that some of the monks tunneled from their building to the one housing the nuns. Many of the women became pregnant and had abortions. Eventually, the embarrassment and inability to stop the misbehavior led to the destruction of the sister's convent.

2 Corinthians 6:3—We give no opportunity for stumbling to anyone, so that the ministry will not be blamed.

Today is not so much different from times past. Until Jesus returns, men and women will wrestle with sin natures. Sadly, so often people want nothing to do with following Christ because they cannot get past the venal actions of those who profess loyalty to Him. Clergy commit adultery. Treasurers skim money from church bank accounts. Hypocrisy is not limited to race, color, creed or geographical boundaries.

There is always an explanation for what causes us to fall into immorality. The moment we refuse to let Christ rule our hearts we are vulnerable to sin. Periodically we ought to ask ourselves two questions:
1. *What do I truly crave?*
2. *Am I willing to deny what I want to obey what God says?*

When we as Jesus' disciples fail, the result is exponentially harmful. Those who see followers flop rationalize their own inability to be holy. This was precisely why the Apostle Paul strove zealously not to sin. He could not bear the thought of a discredited ministry lest the name of Christ be slandered. We must, at all costs, remember that Jesus comes first. If we are unwilling to live holy lives, then what matters most is not God, or the service He entrusted to us. The world is dying to see what living is really all about. What kind of ministry are you living? I pray you and I set as our first cause to be faithful followers of Jesus.

Inspiration † † †

I know my own soul, how feeble and puny it is: I know the magnitude of this ministry, and the great difficulty of the work; for more stormy billows vex the soul of the priest than the gales which disturb the sea.—John Chrysostom, Turkish pastor, (347-407)

Unequal

The telephone rang and it was Effron. He and I played soccer together for over 10 years but we had not seen each other in quite awhile. Effron asked if I would be willing to officiate his impending marriage to Ramona*. I shared with him that I would be honored but first I would need to meet with them three times to do premarital counseling. He sounded a little surprised but agreed and so we set a night to meet.

I arrived at Effron's house and immediately learned that he and Ramona had lived together for the past two years. Both of them were divorced and this would be their second marriage. My assumption was that neither of them were believers.

I asked them questions about their background while we relaxed in their warm living room. Slowly, I turned the discussion toward spiritual issues. Ramona openly stated that she believed in God and had asked Jesus Christ to be her Savior. She also went on to share that she had been angry with God and had not been in church for five years. Effron, contended that spiritual issues were not that important to him. He did believe in God and that God would someday judge all people. So now, unbeknownst to them, they were in a predicament.

2 Corinthians 6:14-17b—Do not be mismatched with unbelievers. For what partnership is there between righteousness and lawlessness? Or what fellowship does light have with darkness. What agreement does Christ have with Belial? Or what does a believer have in common with an unbeliever? . . . For we are the sanctuary of the living God, as God said: I will dwell among them and walk among them, and I will be their God, and they will be My people. Therefore, come out from among them and be separate, says the Lord.

Ramona said she had never read 2 Co.6:14. I shared with them that I will marry two unbelievers or two believers, but I will never conduct a marriage between a Christian and a nonChristian. Based on their spiritual mismatch, I could not conduct their marriage. Effron grew agitated and stated that he would not put his trust in Jesus and then gave his reasons.

What they wanted was a pastor to put a moral stamp of approval on their illicit joining. But there can be no union called *lirk* or *daght*, we are either light or dark and in God's eyes, it definitely matters . . .

Several days later, the telephone rang and it was Effron. He called to cancel what should have been our second meeting. I hoped to discuss his hang-ups concerning Jesus but he stated that he did not want me to be disappointed and that at this point in his life he really was not concerned with examining who Jesus is. "Effron, when you are ready to tackle tough issues, please call me." "I will," he said and parted with a final comment, "I love you." That took me by surprise.

When it comes to unequal, many people believe the God of the Old Testament is not the same as the God of the New Testament. The biggest reason I hear for this assertion is the stern anger, judgment and wrath He dispenses before sending Jesus. Many reject the B.C. God as unfair and cannot understand why He commanded and approved *wholesale* slaughter of pagan nations. However, remember that God did not call for Israel to wipe out every Gentile nation on the planet. He called them to destroy the seven nations localized in the Promised Land He led them to occupy. His instruction in Deut. 7:1-4 to the Israelites is powerful proof why the Holy Spirit led Paul to instruct believers not to join with unbelievers.

- *"Make no treaty with them, and show them no mercy."*
- *"Do not intermarry with them."*
- *"Do not give your daughters to their sons or take their daughters for your sons, for they will turn your sons away from following Me to serve other gods, and the LORD's anger will burn against you and will quickly destroy you."*

Why did God sanction the killing of women and children? This is a hard thing to understand and accept, but God mandated destruction for these seven nations for rebelliously aligning against Him. If Israel failed to destroy them, they would one day turn her to idolatry. *History records that this is exactly what happened.* Eventually, God's wrath burned against Israel because they made Him jealous by spurning Him for other gods and because they lived even more wickedly than the Canaanites, thus discrediting His holy name.

We make ourselves "better" than God or try to make God better when we suggest His character improved as evidenced after Jesus came. Yet, this conflicts with Scripture that demonstrates God's immutable nature. The Psalmist wrote, *"In the beginning You laid the foundations of the earth, and the heavens are the work of Your hand. They will perish, but You remain . . . But You remain the same, and Your years will never end"* (Psalm 102:25-27). Remember, Jesus is not a created Being. He is God's Son who created the earth (Col. 1:16), and worked with His Father throughout history. His character does not change but His grace unfolds. Those who choose to dance with Him must not marry those who choose to dance without Him. His actions are consistent with what He will do in the final judgment.

I suspect that many people think that by making a case that God is inconsistent they can then rationalize breaking His dictates. "Oh it doesn't matter that I sin, He will forgive me." This is frightening logic that fails to account that God *will* judge us for our actions. Unless you are yoked with an unbeliever, do not rebel against God's teaching. If you are already married to someone without Christ, then faithfully pray for his or her salvation and ask the Father to help you be holy as Jesus is holy.

*Not their real names

Heartmissing

Part of me is lost and I don't like it. If I could skip this day in time or have never lived it I know I would be the worse for it but at least I would not sense this absence that came too fast! Heartrending is too strong in meaning for what I am feeling. Perhaps in this poignant period a more apt description is *heartmissing*. The good news is she is only three and a half hours away. The bad news is there are 206 miles between us.

Sarah and I drove from Newberg to Seattle. I gave her the speech I have pondered giving and she wrote each point down. What do you tell your daughter as she leaves home to start college? In life reflecting, two areas prominently emerge—my relationship with my heavenly Father and my relationship with people. If my precious girl can learn from my mistakes and pursue what I know to be gold, I know God will bless her.

One essential for me in knowing God is feeding daily in His Word. Scripture breaths wisdom, His view on life, and the essence and substance of faith—without which, existence would be meaningless. The other key is communication. Most of my life when I have prayed God seemed distant and the whole act mechanical. As I have learned to praise and tell Him how much I love Him, I feel His presence far more often.

People are complex and every relationship unique. However, there are principles that clearly assist forming friendships and working with others. *First, humility is the key to earning trust. Second, serving is the water that truly replenishes thirst.* Jesus washed the feet of His followers so they would understand the central importance of looking at the needs of others before their own needs were covered. *Third, listening is the medicine that solves many ailments.*

2 Corinthians 7:6-7—But God, who comforts the humble, comforted us by the coming of Titus, and not only by his coming, but also by the comfort he received from you. He announced to us your deep longing, your sorrow, your zeal for me, so that I rejoiced even more.

On this cloudy, chilly day, Sarah received my safety message and other personal requests. The CD played Randy Stonehill's song, *"Song for Sarah."* All too quickly, the drive ended at her Seattle Pacific dorm. We carried in her things and I met one of her roommates. Finally, in the Subaru, I told her how much I love her, how proud I am of her and fought back cascading tears. As she walked away, I understood from the other end how my parents felt when I left home.

Heartmissing is the heaviness of absence in the presence of the unknown. In this turn on the road home, I experience more than just the letting go of my daughter. *Heartmissing is the longing to be with God in the relationship He intended from the very beginning to be perfect and have no end.* Something to think about . . . in reveration!

He Made Me Hit Him

When crocodiles cry their tears are not like our tears at all. A crocodile's glandular excretions act to expel excess salt from its eyes. When a man is remorseful but not repentant, he acts like a crocodile. He sheds tears but they are not from a true sense of shame over wrongdoing, but rather to put off the one aware of the sin. Remorse is that sensation we experience for getting caught. Repentance is the revulsion we taste for the evil in our lives.

We would have as much need for God as a crocodile has for friends if our sin or misfortune did not destroy us. At least that seems to be the prevailing thought of an affluent people. Yet in truth, didn't God create us for fellowship with Himself? Isn't His goal that we might experience His love while we worship Him? Yet too often, our fallen nature erupts like some thrashing behemoth. Unless we are truly sorry, we will not come to God on His terms.

As a child, I had a knack for getting into trouble by clouding the truth! I was remorseful when caught but not enough to stop my quibbling ways. It was not until I understood the pain my lying caused others that I truly repented. My father brought this truth to bear when after catching me in yet another lie, he took off his shirt, got down on his knees and grabbing a wooden paddle, made me hit him—an act I could only do once before melting in tears. He took my punishment! When I realized Jesus hung on a cross for me, I begin to apprehend the depth of God's kindness extended to me to rescue me from my own sin!

2 Corinthians 7:10—For godly grief produces a repentance not to be regretted and leading to salvation, but worldly grief produces death.

The true mark of repentance according to Jesus is that our actions produce fruit (Mat. 3:8). Our conduct and character edify those we touch in the process of everyday living. *If we find that we cannot stop sinning it is sure sign that we have not truly repented.* Genuine repentance breathes humility, honesty and a renewed sense of purpose to do only that which will please and honor God. Never fear repenting! The tears that flow from true repentance before God bring the most wonderful cleansing one can experience. For it is out of repentance that we first learn who God really is. True joy comes when those chains we have sought to hide finally come clanging free—released by the Lord who by grace breaks the grip of sin.

Inspiration † † †

I don't think many of us Christians take confession seriously enough. If we did, our lives would be radically different. When you're totally honest about your sins, something happens.—Bill Hybels in *Too Busy Not to Pray*

Don't Put Ashes in Cardboard Boxes

It was early in the morning and Doris was cold. She asked Dan if he would warm up the house. So he got up and only barely awake, emptied the ashes from the wood stove into the cardboard box and set it behind the stove. Then he built a new fire and went back to bed. It was not long before he awoke to the screams of Doris yelling his name. Their home was rapidly filling with smoke. Dan ran into the family room just in time to see flames darting up the corner wall. Quickly he found the fire extinguisher but instead of attacking the flames he sprayed directly into the box below and the blaze was contained.

It took a whole day, but Dan, with the help of Tom and Nicole, completely restored the damage. In the process of cleaning up, a neighbor came over to see what had happened. Near disaster turned into an opportunity to share about the Lord. Out of what could have been a life-ending tragedy, seeds took root.

2 Corinthians 10:4b-5—We demolish arguments and every high-minded thing that is raised up against the knowledge of God, taking every thought captive to the obedience of Christ.

Ashes should be stored in metal containers. Sometimes the cause of battle is rooted in our own carelessness. Compounding the problem is our tendency to assail what we think is the obvious enemy. Had Dan sprayed the flames on his wall, he might have lost his home. The problem was not the flames but rather what fueled them—embers missed when he shoveled out ashes.

God asks us to do something. We are only half-prepared to hear Him and so we respond incompletely. Then when troubles surface we blame Satan, others, or our circumstances as the gist of our inability to obey. Not every predicament is caused by obvious enemies. We may skirmish against the perceived threat and miss the possibility that we ourselves fuel the fire. Unless we have died to self and signed up to follow Christ wholeheartedly, we are in danger of fighting in the wrong manner the wrong matter. When we go into battle let us be sure we are attacking the real problem.

A metal bucket replaced a cardboard box. A bitter neighbor saw in action what faith in God accomplishes. God graciously spared a wonderful family. Life is all about learning lessons and one of those lessons involves learning how and what to battle.

Inspiration † † †

A gem is not polished without rubbing, nor a man perfected without trials.—Paul Vithayathil's collection of *Proverbs and Wise Sayings*

Unashamed Tears

There was a period in the early '90s when just hearing certain Christian songs on the radio station would bring me to tears. I was never a crying kind of person. From what I learned growing up, and after serving for years as a tough, Infantry officer, I thought that guys were not supposed to cry. However, losing my best friend and 247 other soldiers to the Gander crash, followed by almost losing my son, Bryan, to a brain-stem tumor really softened me up. I changed from being a man used to telling people to trust God and to get over their problems to a man who better understood what it meant to suffer. Suffering people do not appreciate *pat* answers. Suffering people have an astute understanding of what really matters. Trials have a profound way of reshaping us and the stain of tears is no shame.

2 Corinthians 11:26-30—On frequent journeys, I faced dangers from rivers, dangers from robbers, dangers from my own people, dangers from the Gentiles, dangers in the city, dangers in the open country, dangers on the sea, and dangers among false brothers; labor and hardship, many sleepless nights, hunger and thirst often without food, cold, and lacking clothing. Not to mention other things, there is the daily pressure on me: my care for all the churches. Who is weak, and I am not weak? Who is made to stumble, and I do not burn with indignation? If boasting is necessary, I will boast about my weaknesses.

Spiritual growth does not proceed well along the level path of landscaped sidewalks. Nor can we manufacture growth by choosing to walk only the pot-holed roads of life. Spiritual growth comes when we get serious about Jesus—not ministry, not finances, not friendships or sermons—just Jesus. He will lead us where we would not choose, to make us what we ourselves could never become.

Brokenness is the badge of discipleship. It is the sign that we are willing to relinquish the quest for our own glory because the spotless Lamb of God dazzles us. It is the recognition that unconditional surrender to God's will accomplishes the freedom we so desperately desire. It is the final cry of one fully stripped of any sense of personal accomplishment. All that seemed to matter smashed against the reef of Myway. It is amidst our recognition that all that we held as dear floats away splintered and useless when God reaches down and begins the work through us He intended.

Inspiration † † †

My own will and desires were now very much broken, and my heart was with much earnestness turned to the Lord, to whom alone I looked for help in the dangers before me.—John Woolman, pastor, (1720-1772)

Bryan the Lion

I will never forget the day I was driving three year-old Bryan home from yet another radiation treatment. I was discouraged in the front seat and somehow my son must have sensed it. From the back seat, he spoke nine incredible words. "Don't worry Dad; God will take care of it."

There is probably not a week that goes by where I do not learn from my oldest son. Bryan's right leg is one inch shorter than his left. He is vulnerable to bouts of dizziness. He cannot take Stephen down wrestling despite being five years older. His brother has all the speed and power he was never given. He might be the last one picked on a team but that does not stop him from eagerly participating. Radiation may have taken its toll on him and robbed him of natural growth but it cannot dampen his contagious spirit. For seventeen years, his brain-stem tumor remained dormant. That which the doctors pronounced incurable, God healed.

Bryan the lion views life from a wide-angle lens. He has had to learn patience, overcome physical disorders, deflect the withered arrows of doubt that assault his self-esteem and wrestle with questions many of us do not have to ask. Yet he does not linger in the valley of *Whaticannotdo*. He does not let the fear of death paralyze his living. He walks with Jesus.

2 Corinthians 12:9,10—But He said to me, "My grace is sufficient for you, for power is perfected in weakness." Therefore, I will most gladly boast all the more about my weaknesses, so that Christ's power may reside in me. So because of Christ, I am pleased in weaknesses, in insults, in catastrophes, in persecutions, and in pressures. For when I am weak, then I am strong.

God is not just a Father we learn about from the Bible and those special times of prayer. God is the very real, loving Lord we see at work in the lives of people. His grace is sufficient for us. His power is made perfect by our weaknesses. I see His might at work in my son whom I love dearly. I watch him fall, laugh and get back up. I see his tender heart. I admire his gentle affection and the natural gift he has for putting people at ease. He is a great listener with a gift for making everyone feel important. Bryan did not choose to complain about his lot in life or take issue with God for his tumor. He locked his faith as a child in One he has never seen yet continuously trusted. A Savior unintimidated by limitation continues to bless his character. He uses Bryan's testimony to bring people to Himself all around the world (India, Peru, Kenya . . .)—people who hear his story and want the Savior he has.

Inspiration † † †

Christ accepts us as we are, but when he accepts us, we cannot remain as we are.—Walter Trobisch, pastor, author (1923-1979)

Pretermit

Occasionally that day will come when she does not feel well. Yet instead of focusing on herself, she labors to provide for her family. She home schools three growing kids without complaining. She faithfully manages a household whose routine is weekly interrupted by the unknown flow of people that come with the territory called ministry. Her efficiency is amazing. Her refusal to complain is inspiring.

The verb *pretermit* means to intentionally disregard or permit to pass unnoticed or unmentioned. It is a mental act that characterizes my wife. She does not dwell on what we do not have or trip over the broken pathway of adversity. She will not focus on herself because her eyes are too set on serving those she loves. She is the closest example I know to selfless abandonment.

2 Corinthians 12:15—I will most gladly spend and be spent for you. If I love you more, am I to be loved less?

Describe a football game and most men will quickly capture the concept of abandonment—throwing oneself with reckless, physical joy at an opponent in order to win. Abandonment for us men is about letting it all go to celebrate victory. However, life is rarely lived on the gridiron. The truer sense of abandonment is the daily sacrifice that so typifies many men and women who work tirelessly to serve their families. As many will attest, serving is often a thankless, taken-for-granted ritual.

Spiritual abandonment means to give up our right to ourselves moment-by-moment in order to follow God (Rom. 12:1). It is the essence of worship. When God's children abandon themselves to serve Him heaven celebrates, hell shudders.

The key to letting go in order to obey God is to find out what we are clutching. An honest examination often reveals that what most gets in the way of my serving God is my preoccupation with what I perceive to be my "rights." I want to do, rest, think and feel on my terms. Gradually, as I learn to relinquish myself to His authority I discover how much more awesome it is to entrust myself to my Heavenly Father who guides, cares and provides perfectly!

Inspiration † † †

It is one thing to *act* like a servant; it is quite another to *be* a servant.— Richard J. Foster in *Celebration of Discipline*

You make a living by what you get, but you make a life by what you give.— Unknown

By God's Power

Beria Emulous paces the floor. He is angry with Crassus Arrogate, a man who controls information to protect his dominion. The two consistently spar. On the surface, they remain civil but underneath these two gray veterans are cauldrons.

Mr. Emulous knows the Lord. One would think that he would pray for Arrogate and not let the man irritate him. If only it was that easy. He resents the fact that his authority is constantly ignored. He is tired of the bullying mannerisms of Crassus and the pack of loyal dogs he's trained who serve him. Under the old leadership, he could not touch him. Now a new regime is in place, leaders with whom he has a shared background, and so he seizes his opportunity. Emulous convinces his new boss that Arrogate is trouble. He shares information that puts his adversary in a bad light. Through careful manipulation, he uses his power to emasculate the team downstairs. Everyone knows now who is in charge. But at what cost has Emulous succeeded?

2 Corinthians 13:4—In fact, He was crucified in weakness, but He lives by God's power. For we also are weak in Him, yet toward you we will live with Him by God's power.

When abused at the office, ridiculed in the neighborhood, and made weak by those who misuse their strength, we should rejoice in our weakness. Our calling is not to grapple for control. The world is not impressed with our faith when they see us take down bullies by our cunning. They want Jesus when they see unflappable love. They see heaven at work when hell's screams fall on deaf ears. If Jesus could turn plain water into wine, do you suppose He could have turned murderous rabbis into rabbits? Maybe we should learn from what He did not do!

Are you tired of people pushing you around? I imagine Jesus was weary of the constant schemes of His enemies. Still, He remained perfect because His Father's mission was more important than His own reputation. He said it should be so for us as well. *"Then He said to them all, 'If anyone wants to come with Me, he must deny himself, take up his cross daily, and follow Me'"* (Luke 9:23). This is a hard lesson for us to learn. Control is not an easy thing to relinquish. Take courage—your strength is in the Lord. Live for Him and not for yourself and you will experience true freedom and *wonder-working power!*

Inspiration   † † †

Every believer who wants to make a difference for Christ can count on living in the crosshairs of the enemy.—Stu Weber in *Spirit Warriors*

349

Jerry Shares on Restoration

I am continuously amazed at how effectively Satan derails relationships among Christians through bad reports and conflict. Ministry teams that functioned well suddenly divide over petty issues. Churches split. Friendships end often without either party working hard to find the source of the problem. How quickly we believe bad information about fellow believers without bothering to investigate the facts or appreciate the potential for misunderstanding. I realize why bad news sells newspapers—trouble is as attractive as a bug-zapper. But how sad it is that Christians so easily judge and condemn each other at the expense of God's kingdom when we should be champions of forbearance.

Beware of those who trumpet the protection of their reputation as justification for hurting others and not resolving conflict. What they really shield is their pride. Beware of those who are unable to forget and forgive offenses committed long ago. Failure to forgive reveals a begrudging attitude. Be aware that it is easy to disagree, find fault and feel self-righteous. It is much more difficult to trust God with our *rights* and work to bring peace where trouble has nested.

2 Corinthians 13:11—Finally, brothers, rejoice. Be restored, be encouraged, be of the same mind, be at peace, and the God of love and peace will be with you.

Recently our African brethren experienced assaults on their unity through some miscommunication. Relationships were strained and it became apparent that competing agendas existed which threatened their cohesiveness. Jerry Anze, our Nigerian pathfinder, in reflecting on what happened, wrote a wonderful paper on restoring relationships. We can all benefit from the wisdom he shares.

The Bible says God has given us the *ministry of restoring relationships* (2 Co. 5:18-6:1). If we want God's blessings in our lives, we must learn to be peacemakers. Jesus said, *"Blessed are the peacemakers, because they will be called sons of God"* (Mat. 5:9). Peacemaking is not avoiding conflict. Running away from a problem, pretending it does not exist, or being afraid to talk about it is actually cowardice. Peacemakers are rare because peacemaking is hard work!

To Restore a Relationship:

● *Talk to God before talking to the person.* If you talk to God first instead of gossiping to a friend, you will discover that either God changes your heart or the other person without your help.

● *Take the initiative.* It does not matter whether you are the offender or the offended, God expects you to make the first move. When fellowship is strained or broken, plan a peace conference immediately. Do not procrastinate or make excuses. Acting quickly reduces the spiritual damage in you. The Bible says sin, including unresolved conflict, blocks our fellowship with God and keeps Him from answering our prayers. It also makes us feel miserable.

● *Listen.* Before attempting to solve any disagreement, you must listen to people's feelings and opinions. Pay close attention and let them unload emotionally without being defensive. The Bible says look out for one another's interest, not just for your own (Php. 2:4).

● *Confess your part of the conflict.* If you are serious about restoring a relationship, you should begin with admitting your own mistakes or sin. Jesus said it's the way to see things more clearly; first, get rid of the log from your own eye, then perhaps you will see well enough to deal with the speck in your friend's eye (Mat. 7:5). Confession is a powerful tool for reconciliation!

● *Attack the problem not the person.*

● *Cooperate as much as possible.* Do everything on your part to live at peace with everybody (Rom. 12:18).

● *Emphasize reconciliation not just resolution.* Reconciliation focuses on the relationship while resolution focuses on the problem. Christians often have legitimate, honest disagreements and differing opinions, but we can disagree without being offensive. We can walk arm-by-arm without seeing eye-to-eye on every issue. Jesus was never afraid of conflict. There were times that He provoked it for the good of everyone. Sometimes we need to avoid conflict, sometimes we need to create it, and sometimes we need to resolve it.

Thanks Jerry! Let us make it our ambition to be restorers! Let us build up, edify, fortify and protect each other because we operate out of LOVE!

Inspiration † † †

Reconciliation should be accompanied by justice, otherwise it will not last. While we all hope for peace it shouldn't be peace at any cost but peace based on principle, on justice.—Corazon Aquino, Filipina president

Understanding Truth

The doorbell rang and I answered it to find two young men well dressed and eager to speak with me. I invited them in and Kathleen provided them something to drink. After initial pleasantries, I asked them if Jesus was created. They said He was and so I let them know we had a major theological disagreement. I showed them from Scripture how it is impossible for Jesus to be created. They then said they misspoke and that we are all eternal. I replied that now we had another impasse. They pointed me to verses in Scripture where God revealed His knowledge of us before we were born. I countered that just because God foreknew us did not mean our souls preexisted. Furthermore, if we were eternal and godlike we would not need Jesus to give us eternal life.

One of the young men asked if I had ever prayed and asked God to reveal to my heart if their nonbiblical writings were true. I said I had not and would not. I said, "If you really believe your literature is true would you ask God to show you if Confucius' writings were true? Furthermore, why would I ask God an unnecessary question? I already have revealed, sufficient truth in the Bible. How can you follow a belief system that is based on the writings of a man convicted of breaking the law, a man with a shady reputation . . . a religion that changes its policies to fit its time (polygamy, which heaven blacks may enter, etc.)?"

My two guests were not happy with me. They became visibly upset when I shared that "If you are right and I am wrong it does not matter because by your standards I will still get to heaven. But if I am right and you are wrong, then the Bible states you will be eternally separated from God under horrific punishment." At this point they shared that they did not come to debate with me. Again, I had to disagree. "Actually, you did come to debate with me. Your intent was that I would agree with you and want to become a believer in your teachings. But if in fact we were to have a fair debate then you must listen to me share with you what is required to become a real Christian." They could take no more and left stating that even if their founder had a bad reputation they still knew they were right and were proud that they were . . .

I pray for those two young men and the countless people around the world in many ways like them. They were taught well. They had done a nice job memorizing Scripture. They were sincere and polite. Unfortunately, the god of this age who misrepresents Jesus blinds them. They could not see the futility of their logic nor admit that their doctrine was actually counter to what the Bible teaches. They did not understand that the Apostle Paul warned the Galatians about false gospels long before their founder claimed to receive revelation from an angel.

Galatians 1:8,9—But even if we or an angel from heaven should preach to you a gospel other than what we have preached to you, a curse be on him! As we have said before, I now say again: if anyone preaches to you a gospel contrary to what you received, a curse be on him!

Friends, either we believe the Bible and the fact that it is complete or we do not. Do not embrace a religion or set of teachings because it looks good, is family-friendly or *feels right* or you compromise truth to lesser standards. The gospel message is clear—just read John 3:16. *"For God loved the world in this way: He gave His One and Only Son, so that everyone who believes in Him will not perish but have eternal life."* Romans 10:9,10 reinforces how we obtain salvation:

> *If you confess with your mouth, 'Jesus is Lord,' and believe in your heart that God raised Him from the dead, you will be saved. With the heart one believes, resulting in righteousness, and with the mouth one confesses, resulting in salvation.*

Whenever someone advocates books that *correct* or contradict Scripture; teach the need to practice secret handshakes or other rituals to get into celestial heaven; follow a teacher other than Jesus, immediately beware! The Bible stands on its own merit as truth. It is genuine. There is no need for another prophet to enlighten us about salvation, and to claim there is, actually makes Jesus to be a liar—contradicting the Bible. Remember, only Jesus lived a perfect life, claimed to offer salvation and backed it up by rising from the dead! Every other teacher who claimed or claims to have new revelation or truth lived imperfect lives, could not make salvation claims and died. So why would you ever want to *improve* on what a perfect Savior taught with what a tainted sinner adds! There is only one way to obtain joy and experience the fruit of the Spirit and that is to know the authentic Lord. Anything else is deception.

Inspiration   † † †

There are different kinds of fire; there is false fire. No one knows this better than we do, but we are not such fools as to refuse good bank notes because there are false ones in circulation; and although we see here and there manifestations of what appears to us to be nothing more than mere earthly fire, we none the less prize and value, and seek for the genuine fire which comes from the altar of the Lord.—William Booth, British Methodist preacher, founder of The Salvation Army, (1829-1912)

I No Longer Live

Galatians 2:19,20—For through the law I have died to the law that I might live to God. I have been crucified with Christ; and I no longer live, but Christ lives in me. The life I now live in the flesh, I live by faith in the Son of God, who loved me and gave Himself for me.

The Apostle Paul makes a revolutionary statement in the preceding verse. He states, *"I no longer live."* What a preposterous statement—of course he still lived or he would not have been alive to write. However, you correctly note, *Paul is not talking about existence but rather identification.* Paul is telling us that he no longer lives for himself—his self-centered desires, his education, his citizenship in Rome, or his standing among the religious elite. Instead, he affirms the truth that his old way of thinking was put to death on the cross with Jesus. He lives for Christ. He places his life in the hands of the Lord who loved him and gave Himself for him.

Do you know what it means to hang with Christ? It means to stop excusing what you are not doing on the basis of your temperament or gifting. It means to cease forming arguments against Christian service because it does not agree with your personality or dreams. It does not allow you to define ministry by your style and your fellowship by those for whom you have a natural affinity. If you cannot be a missionary, you cannot be crucified with Christ. If you cannot serve in the nursery, you cannot be crucified with Christ. If you cannot share your faith, you cannot be crucified with Christ. Crucifixion puts to death your *cannots!* In Christ, you can do anything He calls you to do because you no longer live for yourself but for Him. This does not mean God will send you to the remotest part of China as a missionary. It means you are willing to go wherever He sends you whenever!

This is not a message we hear preached often but if we will take the time to examine Scripture, we will see the truth that our design and equipping does not limit God's ability to use us. This is why Jesus taught His disciples to pray, *"Your kingdom come. Your will be done on earth as it is in heaven"* (Mat. 6:10).

The fact that God gave us a temperament is helpful for us to understand. It is also useful to know how He equips people. However, the key to Christianity is not defining my walk by my temperament but rather being willing to say, *"I live by faith in the Son of God."*

Inspiration   † † †

The trouble with us today is that we think crucifixion with Christ is an experience we have somehow to attain. It is not. It is something God has done, and we have only to receive it.—Watchman Nee in *Changed into His Likeness*

God's Promises

Galatians 3:14—The purpose was that the blessing of Abraham would come to the Gentiles in Christ Jesus, so that we could receive the promise of the Spirit through faith.

Imagine living in a village as a fisherman and trusting the sea as your friend and provider. One beautiful day without warning, it destroys your home and boat and drowns your family with one horrifying wave. Suddenly life no longer offers any hope or meaning. Join the world many found themselves along the coasts of the three nations hardest hit by the great tsunami—Indonesia, Sri Lanka and India. I had the opportunity to travel to an Indian coastal town and give money and medical supplies to a church ministering directly to people whose lives were ruined. Yet the greatest thing we gave was not money or rebuilding broken infrastructures rather, it was the message of hope about the God we worship. Our God is a covenant maker and a promise keeper.

Our God tells us what He is going to do. You can study the passages listed below to see fascinating accounts of God's promises throughout history to people.

Major Covenants in the Old Testament

Promise Made to:	Bible Passage	Sign of the Covenant
Noah	Gen. 9:8-17	Rainbow
Abraham	Gen.12:2,3;15:13-16	Abraham's descendents inherit Canaan
	Gen. 17:1-22	Circumcision of males
Israel	Exo.3:17,20; Deu.29:2-6	Israel's deliverance from Egypt
	Exo. 19:5; Deu.5:2-22; 26:16-19	Ten Commandments
	Exo.32:13,14; Num. 14:13-24	Moses' reminds God of His promise
	Deu.11:12, 22-25; 12:10	God's care and protection
	Deu.15:6	Israel's ability to rule and prosper
	Deu.28	Blessing of Israel tied to obedience
	Isa.7:14, 9:1,2,6,7; 11; 42:1-4; 53; Mic. 5:2; Hos.11:1; Zec.9:9; Jer. 31:31-34	Messiah foretold and new covenant
Phinehas	Num. 25:10-13	Lasting priesthood

David	2 Sa.7:5-16; Psa.133:11,12	Great name and eternal throne
Solomon	2 Ch.7:14-22	Throne established if obedient

Major Covenants in the New Testament

Promise Made to:	Bible Passage	Sign of the Covenant
Mankind	John 3:16-18,36; 4:14; 6:35-58; 8:12;14:1-3; Acts 2:21; Rom.6:23; 8:1,11;10:9,10,13;11:29; 2 Co.4:14; Eph.1:7; Heb.9:15, 13:20	Salvation in Christ and eternal life
	Mat.25:31-46; Rom.2:16; 2Co.5:10	Final judgment
	Mat.24:27; 26:64; Acts 1:11 1 Th.4:16-18; Rev.1:7	Second coming
Believers	14:26; 15:26; 16:13; Rom.8:26; Eph.1:13,14	Holy Spirit given
	Mat.5-7; 16:27	Reward for conduct
	John 14:13,14; 16:24; 1 John 5:14	Answered prayer
	2 Th.3:3; 1 Pe.5:10; 2 Pe.1:3	Protection and provision

Our God fulfills His Word. The following passages bear truth to this fact: Deu. 7:8,9; Jos. 23:14; Psa. 111:5; 119:140; Psa. 145:13; Acts 13:32,33; Heb. 6:17,18; 10:23; 2 Pe. 3:9.

God links His promise to Abraham to us! A reading of Gal. 3:14-25 makes this point clear. Our responsibility and joy is to share with people the reality that by making Abraham's God their God, they make his blessing their blessing.

I encourage you to study the passages listed because they testify to the power of our promise keeping Father. Understanding His promises builds our faith and gives us a reason for the hope we have. Can you imagine living without a promise? Can you fathom the emptiness of going through life with the thought that there is nothing but a future as dust?

Inspiration ✝✝✝

As the gospels present it to us, the mission of Jesus of Nazareth is about the way in which the community of God's people—historically, the Jewish people who had first received the law and the covenant—is being re-created in relation to Jesus himself.—Rowan D. Williams, British, Archbishop of Canterbury

How Can I Know For Sure?

Perhaps one of our most unstated worries is that we might not get into heaven. Does this thought trouble you? I suspect the reason many Christians hesitate to talk about this is they do not want to be labeled unspiritual or identified as a *doubting Thomas*. Yet, people's apprehension towards the afterlife was a real and meaningful dread. Read what Paul wrote to the Galatians in the verses below:

Galatians 5:4,5—You who are trying to be justified by the law are alienated from Christ; you have fallen from grace! For by the Spirit we eagerly wait for the hope of righteousness from faith.

Notice that any hope we have of gaining entrance into heaven through law keeping is spurious and actually alienates us from Christ! Why? Because *we cannot keep* the law. Law abiding does not gain eternal assurance. Jesus said to His law-conscious countrymen in John 7:19, *"Didn't Moses give you the law? Yet none of you keeps the law!"* In Galatians 2:16 Paul taught:

> yet we know that no one is justified by the works of the law but by faith in Jesus Christ. And we have believed in Christ Jesus, so that we might be justified by faith in Christ and not by the works of the law, because by the works of the law no human being will be justified.

If we think we can earn God's favor and enter heaven through our effort to be morally good or through our good works, again we are mistaken. Observe what happens in Mat. 19:16,17:

> Just then someone came up and asked Him, "Teacher, what good must I do to have eternal life?" "Why do you ask Me about what is good?" He said to him. "There is only One who is good. If you want to enter into life, keep the commandments."

If the man could not be good enough, why did Jesus tell him to keep the commandments knowing that also was impossible? Could it be He was trying to point the ruler to Himself?

Paul reinforced Jesus' teaching on goodness when he penned in Rom. 3:12, *"All have turned away, together they have become useless; there is no one who does good, there is not even one."* To the Ephesians he wrote in Eph. 2:8,9, *"For by grace you are saved through faith, and this is not from yourselves; it is God's gift—not from works, so that no one can boast."*

So how in the world do we ever gain confidence that we will live forever with God? First, we have to believe Jesus' declaration. *"No one comes to the Father except through Me"* (John 14:6b) and place our faith in Him. *"Everyone who believes in Him (Jesus) will not perish but have eternal life"* (John 3:16b). Paul testifies in Rom. 1:16—*"For I am not ashamed of the gospel, because it is God's power for salvation to everyone who believes . . ."* God's grace pours upon us as a direct response to our faith in Jesus.

Second, we glean from the meditation passage above, that our hope for salvation cannot come from ourselves—it must come *"by the Spirit."* *The reason we can know with certainty that we have eternal life is the presence of the Holy Spirit in us!* Ephesians 1:13,14 (NIV) says,

> And you also were included in Christ when you heard the word of truth, the gospel of your salvation. Having believed, you were marked in him with a seal, the promised Holy Spirit, who is a deposit guaranteeing our inheritance until the redemption of those who are God's possession—to the praise of his glory.

Third, *"Therefore, since we have been declared righteous by faith, we have peace with God through our Lord Jesus Christ"* (Rom. 5:1). Our faith in Christ allows God to declare us "good." His declaration is not fickle! God never breaks His word! So our faith should result in our having peace! If we do not have peace in our salvation, then our problem is a lack of faith—quite simply, we do not really trust God.

Fourth, Peter wrote in 1 Peter 1:3-5:

> Blessed be the God and Father of our Lord Jesus Christ. According to His great mercy, He has given us a new birth into a living hope through the resurrection of Jesus Christ from the dead, and into an inheritance that is imperishable, uncorrupted, and unfading, kept in heaven for you, who are being protected by God's power through faith for a salvation that is ready to be revealed in the last time.

Peter declares our inheritance of eternal life to be *imperishable, uncorrupted and unfading*—kept in heaven for us! God's power secures our faith!

If I offered you a one-dollar coin there is only one way you can have it and that is to believe my offer is sincere and take it. Once you take that coin, it belongs to you. So remember that God offered you salvation. The only way you could take it was by faith. Now it is yours. So believe it. Don't let sin make you doubt. Until we are with God in heaven, we are still infected with a sin nature. If you sin, confess it, turn from evil and move on with Jesus, who is faithful to forgive (1 John 1:9). Do you need to obey God's law? Yes—His law makes us better. Do you need to perform good works? Absolutely. Our conduct and character prove faith true. We would make a mockery of the cross if we claimed to believe in Jesus and then lived like the Devil's minions. So, love God. Believe in His Son and *rest assured* you will live with Him forever. Something to think about . . . in reveration!

Noticed or Unnoticed?

On this morning, a woman climbed into her car. She stopped by a Starbucks to get her caffeine jolt for the morning. Later she pulled into the parking lot at work and said "hi" to a few other employees who also just arrived. During the course of her day, she will lead or serve many different people. She may talk on the phone, send and pick up email messages, and converse with her boss, those who work for her, and others nearby. After work, she will drive home, have dinner, call a couple friends, and watch television or read a book before going to bed.

Each day the routine is similar. This woman we all know will go through life with lots of questions and far fewer answers. She will ponder who to date and who to avoid. If she marries, she will learn how to relate to a spouse and the extended family to which he is connected. If she has children, she will wrestle with how to teach them values and provide them a moral compass. This may lead her to find a religion that offers relevant answers and meaning to life. Whatever spiritual decisions she makes depend largely upon what she has experienced and observed in life.

Galatians 6:7-10—Don't be deceived: God is not mocked. For whatever a man sows he will also reap, because the one who sows to his flesh will reap corruption from the flesh, but the one who sows to the Spirit will reap eternal life from the Spirit. So we must not get tired of doing good, for we will reap at the proper time if we don't give up. Therefore, as we have opportunity, we must work for the good of all, especially for those who belong to the household of faith.
1 Peter 2:12—Live such good lives among the pagans that, though they accuse you of doing wrong, they may see your good deeds and glorify God on the day He visits us.

If you know Jesus and sell coffee, what kind of service do you render? If you radiate the love of Christ, every morning grouch you serve will notice. Some day someone will decide to put off work to find out your secret of joy.

When you go to work, do you look for opportunities to model love? If you do, then you understand when people approach you and say:
- Why are you so happy?
  - Why don't you swear like the others?
    - Why don't you gossip?
      - What is it about you that makes you different?

They are really giving you an opportunity to share about Jesus and the change He has made in your life. Or, perhaps Jesus is the Savior you have never shared because you concluded:

- I would not know what to say if someone came to me for answers.
    - That is the pastor's job.
        - No one notices me, what I do is not important.
            - I do not have anything to offer, I am just ordinary.

Reject such nonsense.

Virtually every day you and I are with people we have the chance to model what we believe by our conduct, character and communication. It is our responsibility and privilege to reach them. The Holy Spirit will give us the words to say to the wounded seeker. He will provide us opportunities to minister if we will just listen to His quiet urging and have the faith to believe He can use us.

The Christian life is not about a relentless thirst for precious mountain top experiences with God. Those are exceptional gifts God occasionally gives for our benefit. It is in the every day living of life in ordinary places surrounded by ordinary faces that we have the extraordinary opportunity to model Jesus. Take joy in the reality that God reached inside your heart and made an eternal difference. He could have designed a talking rainbow or conducted a live telecast from the heavens with His thundering invitation. Instead, He chose to entrust His work to us! *"How can people have faith in the Lord and ask Him to save them, if they have never heard about Him?   And how can they hear, unless someone tells them?"* (Rom. 10:14 CEV)

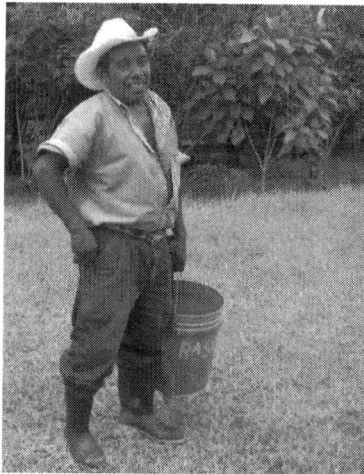

She Carries Julie

Little Julie is ragged and dirty. Two buttons are missing from her soiled dress. Her hair is matted and she owns no brush. One shoe is missing. What were once light blue sleeves are now gray. The frail fabric is torn in many places. She can only wink with one eye, and her mouth long ago lost its vibrant expression. She was dragged by a dog, punched by teasing boys, and twice left outside in bone-chilling rainstorms. For any casual passerby, she is all but useless—but not to Amy. She carries Julie wherever she goes. She tells her stories, puts her to bed, and kisses her hard plastic cheeks. Amy does not see a worn-out doll. Julie is her beautiful treasure and she loves her.

Ephesians 1:4,5—Long ago, even before He made the world, God loved us and chose us in Christ to be holy and without fault in His eyes. His unchanging plan has always been to adopt us into His own family by bringing us to Himself through Jesus Christ. And this gave Him great pleasure. (NLT)

Consider how amazing God is. He looks down from heaven at creatures that are all sick with the disease of sin. He watches us choose repeatedly to ignore Him. He sees us suffer. He hears our cries and feels our grief as we stumble along. He knows our good thoughts as well as our bad intentions. He gives us the freedom to do as we please and sees us fill up our time with countless activities that seldom involve Him. Yet, He does not turn His back on us, or deposit us in some subterranean dumpster.

Consider how amazing God is. Before He made us, He loved us! Despite our shortcomings, He is so enamored with us that He went to the nth extreme to preserve His relationship with you and me.

Consider how amazing God is. He wants to adopt *us* into *His* family! Rather than dispatch a few asteroids to pulverize this rebellious planet, He offers us incredible terms—trust in His Son; follow His leadership and He will forget our transgressions and forever remove our guilt. Then, as if that grace was not enough, He sent His Holy Spirit to help us through our earthly journey. Meanwhile, Jesus is preparing awesome homes for us and we get new, perfect bodies that will never breakdown. He loves us. Just imagine how much Amy loves her worn and ratty doll and magnify that a trillion times, and you will have a taste of how much God loves you and me. Something to think about . . . in reveration!

Inspiration † † †

My eternal soul is under Heavenly coverage, and Jesus isn't known for dismissing clients.—Max Lucado in *Let the Journey Begin: God's Roadmap for New Beginnings*

Fulfillment

Ephesians 1:9,10—He made known to us the mystery of His will, according to His good pleasure that He planned in Him for the administration of the days of fulfillment—to bring everything together in the Messiah, both things in heaven and things on earth in Him.

Fulfillment brings closure to initiation. It also means measuring up or satisfying. How we define fulfillment dictates what kind of life we will lead. Say I determine that I am my own captain, then I determine my fulfillment by what I can and cannot do. If I concede control of my life to others then my fulfillment yields to the will of those in power. If I believe that God is the One leading me then my fulfillment rests in gripping firmly the rope of His will.

Henry Blackaby, wrote in his book *Experiencing God*:

What is God's will for my life?—is *not* the right question. I think the right question is, What is God's will? Once I know God's will, then I can adjust my life to Him. In other words, what is it that God is purposing where I am. Once I know what God is doing, then I know what I need to do. The focus needs to be on *God*, not *my life!*[36]

Are you feeling unfulfilled? Does your fruit basket seem empty? Don't drink from the pity pail or frustration glass your enemy loves to fill and keep you drinking. Do not give up! God has never yet lost His will! He knows what is best for you and me and that best is always the accomplishment of His mission. Do not be afraid to stop what you are doing and wait upon the Lord for His guidance. Set aside preoccupation with what you do not know and discover what He is doing around you. Listen to His Word and the leading of the Holy Spirit. If you will take your eyes off yourself and look for Him He promises to lead you and never forsake you.

The secret to fulfillment is Jesus Christ, the Savior of the lost. We know it inside just as we know to floss our teeth! When will we have the strength to go after His will and trust His voice? Can you camp on the beach of Desolation, eat from the can of Hardship and sleep on the sand of Uncertainty yet experience joy because your security is in your relationship to your heavenly Father? Can you live in the hamlet of Prosperity with all its trappings, work a great job and yet measure fulfillment not by what you own, or do, but by obeying the voice of your King? May God free us from the quicksand of self-fulfillment, give us an unquenchable thirst to know His will and the courage to live as He leads, for His glory, that we might know the thrill of fulfill!

Inspiration † † †

The Son OF GOD became a man to enable men to become sons of God.—C.S. Lewis in *The Joyful Christian*

God's Power

Ephesians 1:18-21—I pray that the eyes of your heart may be enlightened so you may know what is the hope of His calling, what are the glorious riches of His inheritance among the saints, and what is the immeasurable greatness of His power to us who believe, according to the working of His vast strength. He demonstrated this power in the Messiah by raising Him from the dead and seating Him at His right hand in the heavens far above every ruler and authority, power and dominion, and every title given, not only in this age but also in the one to come.

Power is the ability or capacity to deliver. Many people believe that all religious roads have the means with which to bring us to God as long as a person is sincere in what he or she believes. Such thinking directly contradicts the Bible's teaching that it is not our sincerity of mind or effort that broker our salvation but only God's redemptive power extended to us through His Son, Jesus Christ.

If the eternal fate of our souls is our concern, we need assurance that whoever or whatever we place our faith in has the power to provide eternal life. God said in Isa. 45:22, *"Turn to me and be saved, all the ends of the earth. For I am God, and there is no other."*

It is sobering to consider the hundreds of millions of people who entrust their well-being to the teaching of teachers opposed to God and His Word. *"This is what the Lord says: Cursed is the man who trusts in mankind, who makes human flesh his strength and turns his heart from the Lord"* (Jer. 17:5). The Apostle Paul reminds us in 1 Co. 1:25, *"God's foolishness is wiser than human wisdom, and God's weakness is stronger than human strength."*

Consider those who worship idols, fabricated objects a sledgehammer could crush. What idol-represented spirit has ever demonstrated purity and brought men back to life? God will not count as justified those who deny His existence or substitute worshiping Him to follow idols or men claiming to be gods. Paul noted in Rom. 1:20, *"From the creation of the world His invisible attributes, that is, His eternal power and divine nature, have been clearly seen, being understood through what He has made. As a result, people are without excuse."*

Only one Man claimed the ability to provide salvation to His followers and supported His claim by sinless living and resurrection from the dead. His power was real not imaginary. Jesus was a visible demonstration of God's power at work on earth specifically for our salvation. *"For the Son of Man has come to seek and to save the lost"* (Luke 19:10). If you know Jesus, you know what it means to have a changed life. You know the power of assurance that no matter what happens to you on earth, you have a place with God in heaven. *"For to those who are perishing the message of the cross* is foolishness, but to us who are being saved it is God's power" (1 Co. 1:18). "God raised up the Lord and will also raise us up by His power" (1 Co. 6:14).

What makes Christianity unique is not simply its message of hope. What religion doesn't offer hope in some shape or form? The distinctive quality of Christianity is what God has powerfully done for us! Every other belief system depends upon what we have done for God or more commonly, ourselves. Only God could extend grace as credit to a morally bankrupt humanity. Only He exerts might from a heart of immeasurable love! Only He has the authority to condemn or save our souls. The Bible makes a compelling case for His incomparable supremacy. "Yours, LORD, is the greatness and the power and the glory and the splendor and the majesty, for everything in the heavens and on earth belongs to You. Yours, LORD, is the kingdom, and You are exalted as head over all" (1 Ch. 29:11).

Are you feeling weak? Then consider "For His divine power has given us everything required for life and godliness, through the knowledge of Him who called us by His own glory and goodness" (2 Pe. 1:3).

Do you know someone who is afraid? Share "Indeed, God is my salvation. I will trust Him and not be afraid. Because Yah, the LORD, is my strength and my song, He has become my salvation" (Isa. 12: 2).

Need a power surge? "God—He clothes me with strength and makes my way perfect" (Psa. 18:32).

Inspiration † † †

God doesn't give us power over other people through the development of godliness. He gives us power over ourselves; power over our old self-in-control nature; power to stop practicing sinful behavior and to start practicing godly behavior.—Jan David Hettinga in Follow Me

Identity Crisis

Ephesians 1:22,23—And God has put all things under the authority of Christ, and He gave Him this authority for the benefit of the church. And the church is His body; it is filled by Christ, who fills everything everywhere with His presence. (NLT)

It seems to me that we live in a time when the church in our nation is suffering a significant identity crisis. Oswald Chambers wrote in *Approved Unto God,* "The Church does not lead the world nor echo it; she confronts it. Her note is a supernatural note." It is this supernatural note of grace that transforms sinful lives into righteous ones that I believe we must regain if we are to effectively serve as Christ's ambassadors.

There is a wide scale movement among many Christians to shape the politics of our land. Jesus was not a politician. He came to seek and to save the lost (see Luke 19:10). His disciple making strategy did not consist in training His followers to reshape Rome or Jerusalem's policies. He challenged them to go out into the world and proclaim the gospel. Whenever the church wraps itself around political issues, it must ensure that the Holy Spirit is the promoter of such action and she must understand for how long the season should last! Otherwise, she may find her heart more moved by legislation than by love for her Heavenly Father. How many people reject the gospel because their perception of Christians stems from what we fight for instead of who we live for?

A second common movement among believers is to identify with the pagan so as to be able to share Christ. Again, the Holy Spirit must be the promoter of what we do or do not do. Relevancy is fine so long as the truth is not compromised for the technique. Satan is no idiot. When we adopt the behavior, dress, or style of those around us, it is a fair question to ask, "Who is really the influencer?" Furthermore, relevancy taken too far leaves the nonbeliever asking, "Why should I become a Christian if Christians are so eager to act like me?"

Buildings or possessions cannot define the confronting church. Nor should organization or denomination define her. Heaven is not configured by Baptist, Catholic, Methodist, or Pentecostal regions. Letters of membership do not forwarded through pearly gates. Her foundation is not tradition, laws, vision or creed. Nor is Sunday morning attendance what distinguishes her identity. The church is God's people, the priesthood of believers, gathered to love Him and to serve His will. She builds upon Jesus and her worth comes in knowing and obediently following Him. When this occurs, the world has to take notice because God's message is dynamic, absolute and invaluable. Therefore, the church's main concern is not whether the lost like or dislike her. *Her member's mission is threefold: self-denial, daily cross bearing and vigilant following* (Luke 9:23).

As she does this, God will enable her to love her neighbors, to suffer for Him under the hands of those who reject His call, and to shine in a sin-darkened planet. This is what the church is to be.

God help us to set aside what divides us and to be humble that we might come together in sincerity of heart to worship Him! We have brothers and sisters around the world who risk their lives just to own a Bible, just to meet in fellowship, just to share their faith. What hurt they would feel if they ever saw how spoiled and weak and self-preoccupied we have become. More than ever, they need us to pray for them. They need us to listen to whatever the Holy Spirit prompts us to sacrifice for the furtherance of His kingdom. Will you start today?

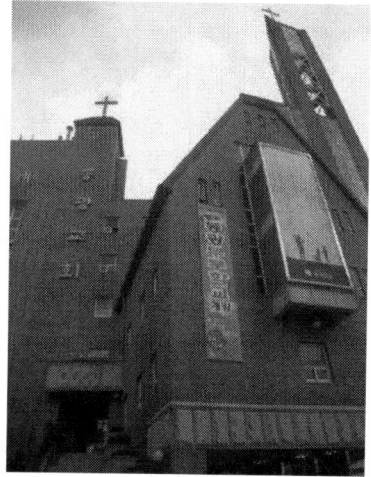

Inspiration †††

I think if the church did what they were supposed to do we wouldn't have anyone sleeping on the streets.—Michael W. Smith

The church must be the critic and guide of the state, and never its tool.—Lynn Lavner, comedian

Christians who have influence in political life must feel as individuals responsibility in front of their own faith. And the duty of encouraging laws that are not in contradiction with the Commandments comes within the mission of the Church.—Karl Lehmann, German pastor

Children Under Wrath

This is another one of those topics most of us ignore—to our own peril. We want God to be just and fair but we often fail to understand that His fairness is effectual in part because of His wrath. How can anger have anything to do with fairness? Well, let someone try to grab your daughter and abuse her and you will have a good idea. Watch someone blatantly run a red light and see if your blood begins to boil. The Bible teaches us *"God is a righteous Judge, a God Who expresses His wrath every day"* (Psa. 7:11 NIV).

We should not think that wrath is an unusual quirk in God's personality. It is an emotion consistently triggered by His rebellious children. There are at least fifteen Hebrew words and four Greek words used in the Bible to depict God's wrath. Four hundred and ninety-three times the Bible refers to His wrath, anger or fury. Considering that there are 629 total usages of these words a full 78% of the time the Bible mentions them it is referring to God. While we look forward to hearing about His love and His mercy, when was the last time you heard mention of His wrath?

Ephesians 2:3—We too all previously lived among them in our fleshly desires, carrying out the inclinations of our flesh and thoughts, and by nature we were children under wrath, as the others were also.

With a sin nature and a world oversaturated with evil, it is easy to become numb to the fact that God hates sin. Why doesn't He just relax and cut us slack knowing we are imperfect? Why does God need to get angry? Maybe it's because:

● *If He compromises by giving in to our sin then He compromises His holiness and therefore forfeits justice.* The reason God cannot let a good person into heaven is that there is no way to determine *good.* Either we are perfect or we are imperfect. Pollution warrants wrath! Only through the sacrificial death of a pure Savior could grace enter the picture and could God's anger disappear for those willing to believe in Jesus. *"For God did not appoint us to wrath, but to obtain salvation through our Lord Jesus Christ"* (1 Th. 5:9).

● *Our sin nature literally pulls us away from God hampering our ability to fellowship with Him—the very reason for which He created us.*

● *Wrongdoing hurts us, hurts others and ultimately hurts the Lord who made us and wants what is best for us.*

● *If God didn't get angry about sin He couldn't really love us and that would be an eternally frightful proposition.*

Inspiration † † †

The most violent expression of God's wrath and justice is seen in the cross. —RC Sproul in *The Holiness of God*

Circulation

Evu* lost his wife twelve years ago to breast cancer. He is angry with God because He did not answer his prayer to take his life and spare Lori's. Yet, Evu readily shared that God had often answered his prayers. He clearly saw the hand of His Maker at work keeping him from death. Several years ago when a construction project at Portland airport collapsed killing three men, Evu's life was spared because of a cell phone call from a friend that lasted so long he was not on site when it rained cement. When Evu later asked his friend why he called him, the friend responded that he felt led to do so! Clearly, God has a plan for this man with a special heritage. Amazingly, his dad worked with Martin Luther King Jr. during the civil rights movement.

Evu is a black man in a white farming community. None of his family lives in Oregon. It makes little sense why he should live where he is, alone with his dog, isolated and depressed. He is articulate, free to share his sense of humor and full of good ideas. However, his zest for life is about as fresh as a six-day-old doughnut.

Ephesians 2:19-21—So then you are no longer foreigners and strangers, but fellow citizens with the saints, and members of God's household, built on the foundation of the apostles and prophets, with Christ Jesus Himself as the cornerstone. The whole building is being fitted together in Him and is growing into a holy sanctuary in the Lord.

What do you say to a person who lost the love of his life and can't find his way? How do you cope when getting up in the morning is drudgery because life no longer seems worth living? May I suggest that a major contributor to the reason people stay smothered by negative thinking relates to a major faulty premise? We think life is about us! But stop, it is not about us at all, it is about God. Our lives are to be lived for His glory not our gains and grins. Our lives should be sacrifices of worship not monuments to self. The reason so many people wear hopelessness as everyday clothing is because God is not first.

Unlike so many people I counsel, Evu has a rich foundation. His godly parents instilled in him a fear and love for God. Therefore, he listened when I shared, "Evu, you have to get back in circulation. You need to be worshiping with other believers. They need you as much as you need them. God meant for us to be members of a family. Together we are His house. And guess what, staying home alone feeling mad at your Father is no way to spend your life! So get back in circulation man."

Thrice Evu mentioned that he would come out for fellowship. Unfortunately, he never came. He's the kind of person I'd love to have in my circle of friends. Will you intercede for all the Evus out there (you probably know one), that God would remind each one how much he or she is loved?

*Not his real name

Capacity

Ephesians 3:20-21—Now to Him who is able to do above and beyond all that we ask or think—according to the power that works in you—to Him be glory in the church and in Christ Jesus to all generations, forever and ever. Amen.

When we look at a glass to fill it we stop pouring before the water reaches the top of the cylinder. When we stand on the staircase and contemplate jumping (for those of us who have not yet attained full maturity), we only leap as far as we think we can without getting hurt. When we drive an automobile, we know what speeds to go to operate the vehicle safely. When given a task by God, we measure what we will do by what we determine is our capacity. And immediately we superimpose our notion of our capability upon our Creator.

Once we become children of God, we must rearrange what we view is possible to allow for God to do what He wills. We determine capacity when we say "no" to God. The Bible nowhere tells us only to do what we think we can. Rather, it reminds us repeatedly of God's power and then illustrates what His power is capable of accomplishing. Many of us store up treasures so that life will be luxurious when we are old because we don't really believe God will see us through. Consequently, He cannot use us to reach our needy neighbors. Our ability to minister depends on how we define capacity.

Am I suggesting you forgo food because Jesus is the only nourishment you need? No—unless God specifically calls you to go hungry for a season. Nor should you boycott doctors for a sick daughter thinking that you must only trust God to heal her. Remember, God gives us physicians and many love Him! Don't underestimate His ability. Whose strength are you living on? Do not define your capacity by common sense—to do so deifies the mind. Define it by faith in the One for whom awesome is an inadequate descriptor. *"But we have this treasure in jars of clay to show that this all-surpassing power is from God and not from us"* (2 Co. 4:7).

Inspiration   † † †

Most people want to serve God, but only in an advisory capacity.—Unknown

The more we serve Christ now, the greater our capacity will be to serve Him in Heaven.—Randy Alcorn in *Heaven*

Call of God

Providentially, Jerry Anze discovered *Reveration* years ago and signed up many African pastors to receive this weekly devotional. Over time, he began to correspond with me and to invite me to come to Nigeria to minister. Because I had never met him, I resisted his requests. But in January 2007, I invited him to join us in Kenya so I could get to know him, he could see our work firsthand and then together we could seek God's will regarding future ministry. I am so glad God brought Jerry into my life . . .

Brother Jerry shared with the Kenyans about his life years ago. He was an alcoholic who turned to marijuana and harder drugs. His friends were immoral and in order to party with them, he stole money from his father. While he was engaged in evil, Jerry's mother, concerned for his soul, fasted for three days and prayed for his salvation.

One day in front of a cave with two pagan friends, Jerry happened to stare at some beautiful trees when he heard a voice say, *"This is the beauty of the Lord."* Feeling very parched he heard the same voice say, *"This is a little taste of what hell is like."* Jerry noticed that a rock was pressing against his back. The voice said, *"This is the weight of your sins."* All of this sobered Jerry to the point that he left his friends and returned to his home on the last day of his mother's fast. The next day a pastor named Manasseh Wakawa came to his home and led him to understand his need to put his faith in Jesus Christ. Manasseh taught Jerry how to be a Jesus-follower.

Ephesians 4:1-3—I, therefore, the prisoner in the Lord, urge you to walk worthy of the calling you have received, with all humility and gentleness, with patience, accepting one another in love, diligently keeping the unity of the Spirit with the peace that binds us.

Can you imagine how blessed we were as Jerry shared with us the call of God on his life to be an evangelist. Likewise, Jerry grew as our Leadership team trained him. God so interlaced our hearts that by the end of our trip Jerry agreed to join our First Cause Pathfinder Team. This team actively shares Christ and creatively looks for ways to expose people to their need for spiritual training and replication.

Recently Jerry sent me this message from Nigeria:
> The past 13 days caught me training about 1,300 people on Soul Winning One-to-One across 5 States. 600 plus of the people trained were pastors. After the training, we went out of the streets and saw the Lord move in a MIGHTY way! It is evident that the Lord has created a hunger in the hearts of people and they need only to be approached with the life-changing and high-powered Gospel of Jesus Christ! This is evident as we witnessed across the 5 States with tremendous results! We spoke to 4,794 people in 13

days 3,103 got saved! Including 334 Muslims, 1,535 were already born again and 156 rejected our message. The Gospel is the power of God unto salvation...PLEASE PRAY: that the Lord will sustain and integrate these new converts into different churches where they will be nurtured.

God's purpose for us is that we would make disciples of all nations! Jerry strongly feels the call of God burning in his heart. The Lord is using him to make a huge difference across Africa. Will you ask God to give him wisdom and strength and to provide for his needs as he serves with us in training people to share their faith while pointing them to the critical task of making disciples?

What about you? Do you understand the call of God on your life? Are you following His plan? We hold the very Key in our hearts so how can we not be compelled to share with the world the Lord who unlocks the door to heaven!

Inspiration † † †

The call of God is like the call of the sea, no one hears it but the one who has the nature of the sea in him.—Oswald Chambers in *My Utmost For His Highest*

The Lost Art of Training

Ephesians 4:11-13—And He personally gave some to be apostles, some prophets, some evangelists, some pastors and teachers, for the training of the saints in the work of ministry, to build up the body of Christ, until we all reach unity in the faith and in the knowledge of God's Son, growing into a mature man with a stature measured by Christ's fullness.

What causes a nation to move from a God-fearing heritage to a position where millions of preborn infants are murdered, drugs are actively destroying healthy lives, the god of materialism owns the biggest temples, and convenience and evil daily mug truth? Why is it that Christians today seem more anemic and helpless than at any other time in our nation's brief history?

Could one answer be that we have substituted teaching for training? Consider the fact that we have plenty of Bible schools, seminaries, churches of every size and persuasion, informative radio, television and internet broadcasting, and more spiritual programs than anyone could count. But passing information is not the same thing as training and the proof is the spiritual condition of the nation. Soldiers don't become proficient in their profession by sitting in classrooms or reading books, they go through basic and continuous training that prepares them for combat. The harder and more disciplined the exercise the more we respect the final product. Marine recruiters seldom have trouble filling their quotas because they have created an attractive warrior ethos. The reason *semper fi* lasts for life, is quality transcends commonplace.

Why is it the military understands what God's children seem to have lost? In the absence of a tight regimen, our busyness steals away time that should be spent fellowshipping with God and spiritual mentors. We prefer spiritual video games and junk food to working out and eating right. Our needs bypass God's plan. Spiritual *consultants* coach pastors not to promote any kind of program or series for more than six weeks because that is the extent of most people's willingness to commit. Trainers are becoming an endangered type. In my town, I can only think of one man who I know is actively engaged in training. We have become so good at finding fault in believers, that we justify the weaknesses of trainers as an excuse to ignore their prophetic voices.

We need teachers and yes, teaching is important! If you loved your daughter, you would not instruct her how to drive your car without training. God sent Jesus to earth to select and train twelve men. Training was a critical component to propagating the gospel. He knew that Torah-teaching rabbis weren't changing the nation—let alone the world.

Effective training requires a heavy investment of time between two or more people. Accountability is established. Principles are modeled, taught, demonstrated, tested and validated when the learner is able to personally apply and then pass on to others for their successful application what was trained. If you are a gifted trainer, for God's sake, keep at it and don't let the Devil discourage you. If you need training, for God's sake get engaged! Find a trainer and make yourself accountable. Quit making excuses. We are in a war and the spiritual survival of our nation is at stake.

Inspiration †††

Each of the twelve disciples abandoned his profession. Each lived a minimalist lifestyle, carrying few possessions and having no enduring sense of residential stability . . . In short, they had no life apart from what they were being trained to do.—George Barna in *Growing True Disciples*

Mote Doesn't Care

Mote (not his real name) worked in the building for years. As I got to know him I was amazed at his disdain for women—particularly his own wife. He would ridicule her at every chance and belittle her publicly. He made her seem stupid. He complained of her shortcomings yet seemed clueless to his own failings. The more I got to know him the more I could appreciate the pain his wife must have endured. Perhaps most grievous, was knowing that he was unfaithful to her and completely uncaring.

I tried for years to befriend Mote and basically got nowhere. I prayed for him and served him when reality suggested I should have fired or at least reprimanded him. For a man with potential to do well it was ironic how much stress he caused. I often wondered, what made him so prickly, so insecure as to be mean-spirited and cynical?

Ephesians 4:17-19—Therefore, I say this and testify in the Lord: You should no longer walk as the Gentiles walk, in the futility of their thoughts. They are darkened in their understanding, excluded from the life of God, because of the ignorance that is in them and because of the hardness of their hearts. They became callous and gave themselves over to promiscuity for the practice of every kind of impurity with a desire for more and more.

I'm sure you know someone who is difficult to get along with, a proverbial *pain in the saddle*. Callous people are unconcerned if others are hurt because in truth they don't care. But there are sure clues to the cause of this coldhearted state, this pitiless, thick-skinned behavior. Paul gives us a clear answer in his letter to the Ephesians.

The layering of evil desires causes callousness. For example, a man gravitates towards what the Bible forbids. He feeds his eyes with pornography or lust for other women. This habit if left unchecked, devalues women. When impure desires increase in appetite an immediate conflict emerges. The conscience decries the flesh. A man hates to be conflicted so he squashes the voice that condemns the carnal. Now the heart finds its own arteries stiffening. Hard hearts resist the life and Word of God. When His light is quenched, dark thoughts are free to roam and immorality increases in scope and magnitude. Evil belittles kindness and mocks love. Futile thinking comes from knowledge bereft of God; callousness comes from running the road to destruction.

You and I know what it is like to build calluses. Isaiah says we have all strayed and left God's path. But praise God, He loves us so much that instead of destroying us like we deserve, He punished His perfect Son in our place (Isa. 53:6). Tenderness comes with the absence of flesh and only a tender Father would tender His Son to settle our debt.

Cynics

It's a dazzling day in Dallas. As you walk to your car, you spot another woman who attends the same aquatics class. "Hi! That's a nice outfit Shrena." She looks at you surprised but then mutters, "Yeah, sure" (like you really care)! Surprised, at her response you innocently ask, "Shrena, are you alright?" But it's too late. She walks away, ducks in her Audi and drives out of the parking lot.

Later at work, Hank, a deacon in your church, sits next to you in a budgetary meeting. You mention to him how it seems like the new CFO is making significant improvements in the accounting arena. He looks over and with a sarcastic smirk, replies, "You think he's doing a good job? He's just manipulating the numbers. If he looks good, the bonuses are great and then he's out of here!"

Ephesians 4:20-24—But that is not how you learned about the Messiah, assuming you heard Him and were taught by Him, because the truth is in Jesus: you took off your former way of life, the old man that is corrupted by deceitful desires; you are being renewed in the spirit of your minds; you put on the new man, the one created according to God's likeness in righteousness and purity of the truth.

It's hard to keep a good attitude when a cynic enters the scene. The word *cynic* comes from the Greek word *kunikos*, an adjective meaning *doglike*. The word most likely applied to the Cynic philosophers because of the nickname given to Diogenes of Sinope, the prototypical Cynic who often impersonated a dog in disgusting fashions. In 1596, the word was first used to mean *faultfinder*, a precursor for how we use the term today. *The American Heritage Dictionary* points out:

> The meaning "faultfinder" came naturally from the behavior of countless Cynics who in their pursuit of virtue pointed out the flaws in others. Such faultfinding could lead quite naturally to the belief associated with cynics of today that selfishness determines human behavior.

What was good for Greek philosophers is not acceptable for God's children. Jesus, never froze on the flaws of those around Him, He pursued His Father's will. So should we. While the pursuit of virtue is commendable, the art of painting defects robs us of joy and harmfully blemishes those disdained.

If you are a cynic then at some point in time, you have been hurt and refused to let God bring healing. Instead of forgiveness, you spin resentful thoughts. Sadly, that attitude of sarcasm and biting wit chains you to the ground. You can never advance and minister as God would have you. Let go! Stop rationalizing your judgmental spirit and caustic words with the errors of your brothers and sisters. Put on a Jesus-attitude! In a world of darkness, start shining! Get out there and be a blessing! It's easy to be negative—Satan didn't tell Eve of God's greatness. He coaxed her with what she didn't have.

Build Them Up

Jenny stopped by to get food. I felt bad because I couldn't remember her name. But she graciously dismissed my forgetfulness and explained that she was still without a job. I reassured her that we were glad to help her and her five children. I'd invited Jenny to our fellowship many times so we could spiritually encourage her but for multiple reasons she had not come. This time I shared with her that she was a remarkable woman and that many people had come to get food from us as a result of her seeing their need and encouraging them to come. I told her that she was highly regarded in the neighborhood and that I was disappointed she had not come to our Saturday evening gatherings, not because she was missing us but rather we were missing her.

Jenny's face radiated with joy. She declared that she would come on Saturday. That's when the inspiration hit me, one of those ideas I think angels on special assignment plant in our brains. I shared with her that I had a large sack of cookie dough that we had not put to use. Would she be willing to make cookies we could give out to people coming in for food? Oh man, she loved that idea (as did her 12-year-old daughter). Just a few hours later, she came back with a plate of scrumptious cookies and a request for eggs. This is the kind of supply and demand I love!

Ephesians 4:29—No rotten talk should come from your mouth, but only what is good for the building up of someone in need, in order to give grace to those who hear.

Paul teaches us not to rip people with our speech. Then he manifests affirmation. Our Lord wants us to speak so that people are encouraged. This process of building people up should be according to *their* needs. I think sometimes we encourage or discourage people according to *our* needs. We have a self-seeking agenda.

There are plenty of ways to tear a person down. How much better it is to build up! Jesus constantly does this for us. Though I deserve punishment for sin, He forgives me and loves me. There are days when I do not even try to stop good tears from flowing because of the vastness of God's affirmations. How can I not work to affirm others who just need reminding that they are special, like the single mom across the street who is doing her best to take care of her kids, with no work and many challenges?

Friend, Jesus left heaven to affirm you. He suffered unjustly to resolve your condition. He died to give you life and reanimated so your faith ignites with hope. Now if you believe this good news, trust Him with your needs and make the time this week to affirm those around you. Praise God for what will happen!

Imitation

Ephesians 5:1,2—Therefore, be imitators of God, as dearly loved children. And walk in love, as the Messiah also loved us and gave Himself for us, a sacrificial and fragrant offering to God.

Imitation conveys a sense of inferiority in most people's minds. Can copies ever be as good as the original? The Bible teaches us that our mission is to be like God. How at odds this is when our society screams that we are to be independent! Ephesians calls us to live a life of love for God and others. But it would seem that each succeeding generation further refines a "me-first" philosophy. Why should I be like God?

● *To be like God means there are many things we cannot do—5:3-7,11,18*

● *To be like God results in good fruit—goodness, righteousness, and truth—5:8,9*

● *To be like God we should understand His will and what pleases Him—5:10,17*

● *To be like God we are properly filled—5:18* The Greek present tense indicates that the filling of the Spirit is not a once-for-all experience. Repeatedly, as the occasion requires, the Spirit empowers for worship, service and testimony. [37]

● *To be like God we need wisdom to live carefully, maximizing every opportunity because we live in evil times—5:15,16*

● *To be like God we submit to one another out of reverence for Christ—5:21-33*

Based on love, God asks us to be like Him. We know that He will not make anyone follow Him. But He clearly warns us of the great cost for defying His will—eternal separation from His presence. Unless we are committed to imitation, we remain vulnerable to independence. Over time, the fruit of each becomes obvious—light vs. darkness. Why should I be like me when I love who God IS!

Inspiration † † †

Who is so wise as to have a perfect knowledge of all things? Therefore trust not too much to thine own opinion, but be ready also to hear the opinion of others. Thought thine own opinion be good, yet if for the love of God thou foregoest it, and followest that of another, thou shalt the more profit thereby.—Thomas à Kempis

Light

Ephesians 5:8-10—For you were once darkness, but now you are light in the Lord. Walk as children of light—for the fruit of the light results in all goodness, righteousness, and truth—discerning what is pleasing to the Lord.

Forget about finding the switch—it is not on your forehead! You won't find replacement bulbs in church. If you know and follow Jesus, if He's your Lord, you are a light. And if you didn't know it already, you are a special light! But unless you are deeply in love with God and obeying Him, you won't understand how brilliant God intends you to be!

I believe the body of Christ is a symphony orchestra of light. We are uniquely made, gifted, and called to serve our Heavenly Father. The Holy Spirit is our Conductor. The Word of God is our sheet music. And if you're not playing, the song is not sounding the way it should.

Darkness battles light. The songs that originate in man's heart, or hold the fury of Satan's rebellious script, pulsate like some unending heavy metal song. In the end, despair is the final score. But darkness needs light. How many sit yearning for the chance to play in God's concert hall unsoothed by the songs of a dark world, unclear what the purpose of life is and unsure how to proceed?

"Everything exposed by the light is made clear" (Eph. 5:13). When you play what God writes you sound incredible! You reveal what others without Jesus are missing. You inspire those in need of Jesus—the Light of the world! If your light is strong, people will respond in ways you never dreamed! The Lord will use you to draw others to Himself. Conversely, if your light is dim, the song of hope comes across flat or sharp and no one around you is likely to seek the Composer.

Whether the Spirit leads you to play in harmony, to take the melody, to be unnoticed in the string section, or to crash powerful cymbals, is not important. God is not preoccupied with what instrument we play, or what section we sit in, or who notices us. His desire is that you and I would know Him. The deeper we love Him the more intense our light will glow to His glory! Have you ever used a Coleman lantern? When you pump it, the light becomes exceedingly brighter! Hmmm. *Let your light shine that people may see . . .*

Inspiration † † †

Darkness cannot drive out darkness; only light can do that. Hate cannot drive out hate; only love can do that.—Martin Luther King, Jr.

Making Music to the Lord

There are mornings when I wake up when I don't want to read my Bible. I don't want to pray. Surprised? No, you are not because you have the same feelings. Admit it. There are days we get out of bed and put on our selfish clothes, brush our selfish teeth, eat our selfish breakfast, drive our selfish car so we can sit at our selfish desk consumed with all those selfish thoughts of what we feel like doing the completely selfish day. We actually feel justified in skipping the time we ought to spend with our Lord. Why? Because we are busy! And if you'd care to go deeper, because at the center of our gnarly bodies is a heart that pumps: thump, thump, rebel, thump, thump, rebel! It is usually easier to be self-absorbed than it is to meet with an invisible Friend.

Maybe we need a reminder as to why God made us. My wife knows I love her when I set aside time to strengthen our relationship by listening to her, sharing with her what's on my heart and protecting our time from outside distractions. If God created us in His image, is it possible that the inner need we have to be in a healthy relationship with those we love is a reflection of what God is looking for with us?

The evidence that one truly knows God is not proved in the effort expended for His name. The 11th-13th century Crusaders proved this quite effectively. They slaughtered people in God's name while out to gain power and fortune for themselves. We sometimes make service a badge of honor when the real value is our relationship with our Maker. Think about it— what can we *really* do for God that He cannot already do Himself? We can love Him! He cannot love Himself like we can love Him.

Ephesians 5:19—speaking to one another in psalms, hymns, and spiritual songs, singing and making music to the Lord in your heart,

I have never seen a flower put out breath-taking petals that didn't have its roots embedded in good soil. Nor have I seen a father who didn't thrill to the voice of the little child who climbed in his lap to say, "Daddy, I love you." Friend, when's the last time you told your Father in heaven that you love Him? Relationships do not get strong by happenstance; they require conscious, disciplined exertion. Let's make the effort to make our relationship with God special, after all, He set aside eternity to fellowship with us!

> . . . I pray that you, being rooted and firmly established in love, may be able to comprehend with all the saints what is the breadth and width, height and depth, and to know the Messiah's love that surpasses knowledge, so you may be filled with all the fullness of God" (Ephesians 3:17-19).

Full Canteens

Imagine you were in a desert stranded for a week eventually exhausting all supplies. Around the wadi comes a camel-striding stranger who sees your plight and says, "Here, let me help you." He then pulls out a canteen and hands it to you. Grateful, you place the container on your lips and wait for life-renewing water. But the canteen is empty. "What kind of cruel joke is this!" you ask. The stranger smiles and says, "Ah, it is not the liquid but the thought of liquid that is sufficient."

Philippians 1:9-11—And I pray this: that your love will keep on growing in knowledge and every kind of discernment, so that you can determine what really matters and can be pure and blameless in the day of Christ, filled with the fruit of righteousness that comes through Jesus Christ, to the glory and praise of God.

The word *Christian* has become like the empty canteen. I often meet people who call themselves *Christians* but when queried really cannot explain what the word means. To some it is their spiritual heritage—"my parents are Catholics." To others it is a national/cultural affinity. Still others see it as a religious selection. Ask the common Muslim in the Middle East, and he may define a Christian by what he sees streaming from the western media. America the *Christian nation* is relentlessly addicted to sex and materialism. To the European, *Christian* may conjure thoughts of legalism, stilted and archaic reasoning.

Rather than describe myself as a Christian, I tell people I am a follower of Christ. In essence, that is what Christian means. But whether the concept has merit relates to what kind of canteen I am—empty or filled. A true Christian is a wise lover of Jesus and people, approves of excellence and strives to be holy. Wise lovers see people as God sees them and act appropriately. Approvers of excellence choose attitudinally and in conduct what brings glory to God. Holy people obey God's laws. To be like Jesus is to make an eternal difference in a transient world.

The world is thirsty! Let's give them full canteens! If we give them Jesus and they hate us, that is a desert of a different order.

Inspiration † † †

A human life, filled with the presence and power of God, is one of God's choicest gifts to His church and to the world.—Arthur Pierson in *George Muller of Bristol*

The most eloquent prayer is the prayer through hands that heal and bless. The highest form of worship is the worship of unselfish Christian service. The greatest form of praise is the sound of consecrated feet seeking out the lost and helpless.—Billy Graham

Persecuted Saints

Philippians 1:29-2:4—For it has been given to you on Christ's behalf not only to believe in Him, but also to suffer for Him, having the same struggle that you saw I had and now hear about me. If then there is any encouragement in Christ, if any consolation of love, if any fellowship with the Spirit, if any affection and mercy, fulfill my joy by thinking the same way, having the same love, sharing the same feelings, focusing on one goal. Do nothing out of rivalry or conceit, but in humility consider others as more important than yourselves. Everyone should look out not only for his own interests, but also for the interests of others.

Through the dark tunnel of ivy and rock one by one they came.
They huddle together around the stone table sharing the water and bread.
Hands that are gnarled hold hands of a child, every heart scripted in bold,
Seventy quietly singing the words of a hymn no paper can hold.

He moves from the shadows and holds up the book,
the only one this village owns.
He reads holy words and then softly prays
before he explains what he's learned.
He fills them with courage this cobbler by trade
but really a pastor-at-large,
One-step ahead of those who would seize him and lock him inside of a jail.
They worship and praise the Name that's rejected,
ridiculed, slandered and scorned.
They'll die full of joy despite brutal suffering
to be with the One they adore.
Across the same planet their brothers are living
too many too spoiled to care.
Basking in wealth and the *right* to be happy
with no clue what crosses they bear.

Who will fall on their knees to pray for the suffering—
bend for the church underground?
Who will give from their heart to provide them with Bibles—
food for spiritual souls?
No soldiers, no demons, no army can stop them,
for God is the keeper of hearts.
The song of His bride will never stop singing
for Jesus the Lamb overcomes!

Perspective

Philippians 3:8,9—More than that, I also consider everything to be a loss in view of the surpassing value of knowing Christ Jesus my Lord. Because of Him I have suffered the loss of all things and consider them filth, so that I may gain Christ and be found in Him, not having a righteousness of my own from the law, but one that is through faith in Christ—the righteousness from God based on faith.

Drafting is such an amazing art. I find it fascinating how engineers depict buildings and objects through the skillful drawing of lines and shading of areas. *The American Heritage Dictionary* defines *perspective* as: "The technique of representing three-dimensional objects and depth relationships on a two-dimensional surface."

Could it be that spiritual perspective is the technique of representing an invisible God and the depth relationship of His attributes on the sin-flattened plain of mortal earth? When we love our enemies, we reveal God! When we demonstrate patience through adversity, our lives portray a supernatural dimension. The linear two-dimensioned relationship between humans becomes a three-dimensional triangle when God is involved.

Perspective also means "A mental view or outlook." When adversity comes, I want to know Jesus who weathered hostility and was murdered. When temptation raises its stormy head I want to know Christ who Himself suffered through temptation (Heb. 2:18). When times are good, I want to know my Father and thank Him for what I have. When I am confused, I want to know the omniscient One. When I am weak, I want to be close to the Almighty. When I am joyful, I want to worship my Savior! When I am honored, I want to glorify the Lord who made me. Whether busy or inactive, tired or energetic, thoughtful or amused, balanced or dizzy, sick or healthy, fulfilled or discouraged, driven or grounded, criticized or praised, popular or opposed, filled or empty—I want to know God. How I view life is proportional to how well I know life's Creator.

O God, stoke the passion to know You! Replace the selfish lens that see only me and cover them with Songlasses, those glorious lens that reveal You, the epitome of AWESOME!

Inspiration † † †

Faith gives you an inner strength and a sense of balance and perspective in life.—Gregory Peck, actor, (1916-2003)

Memories

Philippians 3:12-14—Not that I have already reached the goal or am already fully mature, but I make every effort to take hold of it because I also have been taken hold of by Christ Jesus. Brothers, I do not consider myself to have taken hold of it. But one thing I do: forgetting what is behind and reaching forward to what is ahead, I pursue as my goal the prize promised by God's heavenly call in Christ Jesus.

There is a phrase that I am weary of hearing among Christians. Three short words that convey a very sad truth—"I used to . . ."

I ate breakfast with a man who has little time today to serve God. The gist of most of our conversation centered on his past. He wistfully recalled his days in college when he was radically on fire for God. He laced memories with events. In vain I tried to steer the conversation to the present—to ask the question, "Yes, but what is God doing in your life *now*! What is He calling you to be and do?" But the clinging vines of "I used to . . ." overgrow his way.

Do you find that when you talk about your relationship with God it is the past that comes to mind? Do you relate your value to Christ by what you once did? Perhaps I am asking in a kind way, "are you living on spiritual vapors?" We readily would admit we should forget those bad things in our past that only weigh us down. However, even what is good can weigh us down! We let what we did in the past excuse us for what we do no do in the present. Don't let this happen! You and I serve a dynamic incredible Father. Don't let the want ads of this world catch your eyes and steal your zeal to serve Him. Press on toward the goal of becoming Christ-like!

People don't hunger for a past-tense God they want a Lord who is active today. If your means of relating to Him relates to what happened long ago, get on your knees and seek His presence now.

Inspiration †††

Memories are the key not to the past, but to the future.—Corrie Ten Boom, Dutch Christian Holocaust survivor, (1892-1983)

If you read history you will find that the Christians who did the most for the present world were just those who thought most of the next—C.S. Lewis

Heaven

Stephen wanted to talk and pray with me. Normally, he wants to pray with his mom before he goes to sleep. So I had a pretty good idea his biggest theological fear was gnawing again on his seven-year old mind. You see he's afraid he's not going to heaven. Compounding that anxiety is an inability to conceptualize heaven (sound human?), combined with the concern that eternity could be profoundly boring—after all, forever is a long time!

So, we had a good discussion again about the fact that he's placed his faith in Jesus and that God deeply loves him. I probably should have read to him what Jesus said to His disciples. *"Let the little children come to me, and do not hinder them, for the kingdom of heaven belongs to such as these"* (Mat. 19:14). We talked about how wonderful heaven is going to be. What a blast it will be to have special bodies, to worship God in the presence of mighty angels, to not have to be afraid of anything including nightmares!

Philippians 3:20,21—but our citizenship is in heaven, from which we also eagerly wait for a Savior, the Lord Jesus Christ. He will transform the body of our humble condition into the likeness of His glorious body, by the power that enables Him to subject everything to Himself.

I know a place where there will be no more sickness or need to comfort those burdened with heavy loss. No gnawing guilt will exist for sins of the past. There won't be headlines announcing moral failure at the highest levels or disasters that have claimed the lives of thousands. People won't say mean things. Work will be divinely rewarding. Traffic jams will not exist. There won't be any cavities and the crowns sure won't go on teeth!

It will not matter if the streets are paved in gold—my knees will never hurt again on any surface. My lowly body will know transformation! And I can't wait! How about you—are you pumped that life on earth is just a nanobeep! It won't be long before spectacular will *really* be awesome. What makes heaven so great? Emmanuel—*God with us,* forever! Truly something to think about . . . in reveration.

Inspiration † † †

To go to heaven fully to enjoy God, is infinitely better than the most pleasant accommodations here.—Jonathan Edwards

One of the greatest things about Heaven is that we'll no longer have to battle our desires. They'll always be pure, attending to their proper objects . . . Thinking of Heaven leads inevitably to pursing holiness . . . —Randy Alcorn in *Heaven*

The Message of Hope

Tim graduated from High School with no sense of purpose or ambition so he joined the Army. While at the reception station where new soldiers are in-processed, a chaplain handed out Bibles. Tim remembered the New Testament his dad kept from World War II and decided to take one he could keep as his own memento.

The Army sent Tim to Germany, where unfortunately, he got involved with the wrong crowd using drugs and drinking alcohol to pass the time. His assignment was to sit for six hours at night in a tower guarding a nuclear weapons site. With nothing to do for long periods of time, he began to ask questions like, "Who am I? . . . What's my purpose in life?" One day he grabbed his Bible, took it up into the tower and began reading it. Many nights as he read he said it was like the Bible spoke directly to him. Finally, on Christmas day in 1971, Tim read the plan of salvation written on the back page of his Bible and made a decision to follow Jesus Christ as his Lord and Savior.

Tim got involved in a local chapel and a chaplain nurtured him in his faith. After leaving the military and attending college, he felt a strong call to serve God. He attended seminary and came back into the military to be an Army chaplain. Years later during a field exercise, he sat down with another soldier on a night so dark they could not see each other. The young soldier said he had never talked to a preacher before and listened intently as Tim shared how God changed his life. A year later, he received a letter from that same soldier telling him how he placed his faith in Jesus because of what Tim shared that night.

Colossians 1:5b-6—You have already heard about this hope in the message of truth, the gospel that has come to you. It is bearing fruit and growing all over the world, just as it has among you since the day you heard it and recognized God's grace in the truth.

Tim and fourteen other senior Army officers gather for several hours each day as a small group working toward the completion of a Masters Degree in International Strategic Studies. One of our classmates opened up his heart to me at a restaurant during one of our gatherings. Essentially, he believes all religions are the same and he cannot understand why people do not just get along. I thought of Tim and how wonderfully God transformed his life through the power of the gospel. What God did in Tim, in you and in me, He wants to do across the planet. We pray that this officer with lots of questions will one day meet *the* Answer and discover the gospel is life transforming. The message of hope should always grace our lips; the word of truth that gives our heart an eternal beat! Without it we have nothing, with it we have everything!

The Cross

Colossians 1:19,20—For God was pleased to have all His fullness dwell in Him, and through Him to reconcile everything to Himself by making peace through the blood of His cross—whether things on earth or things in heaven.

Folly! The word in this case means madness and it describes the reactive opinion of those offended by the gospel message. As Justin wrote in Apology I, "They say that our madness consists in the fact that we put a crucified man in second place after the unchangeable and eternal God, the Creator of the world." That anyone could place trust in a crucified "criminal" proclaimed as a Savior was absurdity.

Disgrace! Why would God let Jesus suffer a humiliating end on a cross in a manner reserved for slaves, criminals and those of the lowest class? Moses taught the Jews that anyone who hung on a tree as punishment for a capital offense fell under God's curse (Deu. 21:23). Hanging victims were a stigma not associated with grace.

Cruel! Many believe the Persians initiated the practice of crucifixion. Regardless, historical evidence shows widespread practice of this horrible means of execution among barbaric peoples. They flogged, spit on, mocked and forced Jesus to wear a thorny crown crammed on his head. They spiked his four limbs to wooden beams causing Him to asphyxiate. On His beaten shoulders sat the sins of a caustic world His broken-hearted Father sent Him to save.

Symbolic! Martin Justin wrote in his book *Crucifixion*, "This form of execution, more than any other, had associations with the idea of human sacrifice, which was never completely suppressed in antiquity."[38] God allowed His Son to take on the most wretched state humanity could muster. He smothered depravity with love. The bleating of lambs slaughtered to atone for those who could not keep the law ended with the silenced heartbeat of God's Lamb.

Salvation! If our convictions, conduct and character die with Christ then we no longer live but Christ lives in us! He went to unthinkable lengths to rescue us from our own rebelliousness. If we stray from the cross and what it means we mire in self-centeredness. We lose our bearings. We miss our Hero and forget why He came. He embraced the cross to become the Bridge—our only way home.

Reflection! When was the last time you pondered the pain and suffering Jesus endured for you? If our hearts are complacent toward the One who bled for us, what passion will fill our lungs with the liberating message of truth for those still stumbling?

Inspiration † † †

The cross is the focal point of all history.—Tom Julien in *the Three Princes*

Spiritual Filters

"Maximize the god within you!" Welcome to the arena of self-help teaching spun from the mouths of success gurus. The gist of their message runs something like:

   ● Do your best and overcome your fears for the key to success lies within you!

   ● Go after your dreams. Listen to your inner voice it will never fail you.

   ● Be sincere. Persevere and believe in yourself. You can be whatever you want to be!

Colossians 1:28,29—So, naturally, we proclaim Christ! We warn everyone we meet, and we teach everyone we can, all that we know about Him, so that, if possible, we may bring every man up to his full maturity in Christ. This is what I am working at all the time, with all the strength that God gives me. (J B Phillips)

Positive humanism does much for the spirit initially but where does it eventually lead us? Perhaps the answer lies in how we define success. The Bible teaches us that no matter how well we keep the law, work, or treat others we will still fall short of God's standard because of our sins. Supremacy of effort may make us rich, famous and powerful but when we die, we will stand naked and accountable before a perfect God.

Should we do our best? Absolutely! The Apostle Paul wrote in Col. 3:23, *"Whatever you do, do it enthusiastically, as something done for the Lord and not for men."* But does the key to my success lie in my effort, or in my reliance upon God to accomplish in me what I cannot do myself? When I stand before God for judgment, the issue is not how many toys I accumulated on earth, or how happy I was, but whether or not I put Christ first in my life. If I can do all things *through* Christ, it is logical that I cannot do all things without Him! Those who teach self-fulfillment propagate a gospel counter to what Scripture teaches and this is nothing short of idolatry.

Jeremiah wrote in Jer.17:9, *"The heart is more deceitful than anything else and desperately sick—who can understand it?"* These words stand in stark contrast to the message that abounds today exalting the heart. To pursue our dreams and go after the voice we hear from within may seem honorable but to whom are we listening? Is it God leading me or is it my own will to do what suits me? Ask Judas. He didn't betray Jesus because he was a jerk. He turned Him over to the authorities because he believed Jesus was not doing what the Messiah should do.

If we espouse to be Jesus' disciples, we must run any success or motivational teaching we hear through spiritual filters:

- *Does this teaching replace Jesus Christ with me at the center?*
- *Is the teaching consistent with what Scripture reveals I should do?*
- *If I follow this teaching what is the logical end result?*
- *Who leads the one teaching? Is he or she a teacher who follows God and is above reproach?*

Before we over hype in motivational messages, let us make sure the content glorifies God and leads us where His Holy Spirit wants us to go—for His glory!

Inspiration † † †

I've heard a lot of sermons in the past 10 years or so that make me want to get up and walk out. They're secular, psychological, self-help sermons. Friendly, but of no use. They didn't make you straighten up. They didn't give you anything hard . . . At some point and in some way, a sermon has to direct people toward the death of Christ and the campaign that God has waged over the centuries to get our attention.—Garrison Keillor

Christianity begins not with a big DO, but with a big DONE.—Watchman Nee, Chinese church leader, teacher in *Sit Walk Stand*

Continue to Live in Him

Lacrosse is a rapidly growing sport in our community. Stephen got involved as a player and I enjoyed helping coach his team. I am quite amazed at how quickly the boys advanced in their skills. And I've made a not-so-surprising observation. Those players who carry their sticks around constantly and work on throwing the ball and catching it against any available wall or with other teammates, are far more proficient than those who only pick up their sticks when required.

Colossians 2:6,7—So then, just as you received Christ Jesus as Lord, continue to live in Him, rooted and built up in Him, strengthened in the faith as you were taught, and overflowing with thankfulness. (NIV)

Jesus implores us to *"continue to live in Him."* As I contemplate the concept of continuance the question arises, "How do I remain faithful?"

● *Jesus must have my heart.* If He is not first in my love, foremost in my priorities, then other passions will squeeze Him out and I will set down my cross to carry other treasures.

● *Jesus must have my eyes.* God's Son calls out, *"Follow Me!"* I will bear fruit when my purpose, goals, objectives and vision center on obeying the Lord on the road to heaven because my faith remains in Him.

● *Jesus must have my mind and spirit.* Two things root and build up my mind, character, attitude and emotions. *First, I need faithful time mastering Scripture* (hearing, reading, studying, memorizing and meditating). God's Word builds in my life the wisdom I need to persevere, resist the enemy, say "no" to my unruly flesh and "yes" to the leading of the Spirit. *Second, I need regular fellowship with other believers who also are intent on continuing in Him.* The Holy Spirit empowers and gifts God's children so we edify each other.

● *Jesus must have my ears and mouth.* As I learn to listen to Him, to seek His will, worship Him and to share what is on my heart, He deepens my faith, guides me in how I should live, reassures my spirit and meets my needs in accordance with His plan.

Every sinner understands the value of continuing when it comes to power, prestige, winning and gaining wealth. Some people will forsake everything to accomplish on earth what cannot be maintained. The wise saint understands the value of continuous abiding in Christ because He is omnipotent, the Name above all names, the Wearer of the Victor's Crown and the Creator of life and matter, who promises eternal reward and fellowship to all who follow Him!

Succulents

The 301 complex overlooks a valley framed by gently rolling California hills. When the round red ball of heat sinks, the view is amazing. Several nights ago after the sun had vanished, I stopped walking and stood transfixed by the beauty of a mature oak tree in front of an expansive sky wearing a bluish hue I don't ever remember seeing. I wished the moment would last as I thanked God for His painting.

Someone told me that when the rains come the entire landscape will turn pale gray-green. Now it is brown and arid. To liven up my window ledge I bought six small plants. David, a landscaper by hobby, carefully arranged them in containers full of sand, a round stone and gnarled branch. Succulents are plants with fleshy, water-storing leaves. In my collection are aloes and cactus that delight the eye by their unique shapes and colors. In a sea of sand succulents stand green and survive. For them fullness is the key to survival. They hold precious water and live where most plants would wither and die.

Colossians 2:9,10—For in Him the entire fullness of God's nature dwells bodily, and you have been filled by Him, who is the head over every ruler and authority.

The One who paints the sky, who creatively called into existence trees and flowers, loves His followers so magnificently that He fills them with His Spirit. Did you know that if you believe in Jesus you are a succulent? Jesus said, *"If anyone is thirsty, he should come to Me and drink! The one who believes in Me, as the Scripture has said, will have streams of living water flow from deep within him"* (John 7:37b, 38).

The Holy Spirit is our fullness in a world stuck on empty. He is the Living Water that flows inside us and makes us vibrantly green, alive in His love. Fullness comes because of faith and rewards hope with God's eternal presence. By divine grace, fullness transforms us uniquely for the glory of the Father. We will bear fruit if our emerald lives are internally nourished by drinking His Word. Christ fulfills us and we ought to be thankful!

The plants on my window ledge whisper a parable. Succulents are not afraid to take heat, testify of their source of life and hold out their arms in expectation for Christ's return. Fullness . . . streams of living water flowing within us . . . something to think about . . . in reveration!

Inspiration † † †

To be filled with God is a great thing, to be filled with the fullness of God is still greater; to be filled with all the fullness of God is greatest of all.—Adam Clarke, British theologian (1760-1832)

Distractions

The radiant bride stood beside the groom. Sitting next to me, Dan wondered what chemical process takes place that allows a woman to practically glow! There was a spiritual vibrancy as well. It was obvious that Jason and Shelby were committed as much to glorifying God as they were to consummating their marriage. But I found it difficult to concentrate.

The flower girl stood in front of the bridesmaids. She walked to her position in splendid fashion correctly dropping petals from her basket. However, it was too much for her to stand still through the ceremony. She scratched herself pulling at her dress. She made faces. She bent over to pick up petals and smiled at the audience. She definitely enjoyed her prominent position. Her mother, from several rows back, discretely motioned for her to stop moving. No matter how hard I tried to focus on the bride and groom I constantly found my eyes running to that little girl.

Colossians 3:1,2—So if you have been raised with the Messiah, seek what is above, where the Messiah is, seated at the right hand of God. Set your minds on what is above, not on what is on the earth.

"Seek what is above," the verb *seek* calls for a continual and habitual action. The idea is that we relentlessly pursue heaven (as Jesus prayed, *"Your kingdom come"*). Our affections and focus are on Christ with the result that we live to be like Him. We pursue holiness infused with a spirit opposed to sinful, earthly lusts. We refuse to be preoccupied with those things that will burn one day.

Paul goes on to write, *"set your minds on what is above,"* but this verb *set*, has a different meaning.[39] Paul is referring more to our inner disposition. Combining verses one and two, we discover that God is looking for both action and attitude that reveal we are loyal to heaven's agenda.

Many things tug at me and pull my eyes from my beloved Jesus. Distractions are as common in life as dandelions are to yards. How about you? Are you easily sidetracked from godly living by a multitude of insignificant diversions? Let's resolve to keep our eyes on Jesus! Let's renew our commitment to Him! Watch what happens to your actions when heaven fills your thoughts.

Inspiration †††

To be fully engaged, we must be physically energized, emotionally connected, mentally focused and spiritually aligned with a purpose beyond our immediate self-interest.—Jim Loehr and Tony Schwartz in *The Power of Full Engagement*

Fundamentals

Colossians 3:17—And whatever you do, in word or in deed, do everything in the name of the Lord Jesus, giving thanks to God the Father through Him.

Major General T.K. Moffett walked back and forth in front of the assembled soldiers. The new boss from Mississippi had just finished his first day commanding the 104th Division and he elected to share with his soldiers his leadership philosophy:

1. *Do the right thing.*
2. *Treat others the way you would like to be treated.*
3. *Do your best.*

In the shower the next morning, I realized that I was able to recall each of his adages.   (Normally I'm fortunate if I can remember one point within minutes after any speaker's message!)   Further reflection revealed profound wisdom in Moffett's precepts.

"Do the right thing"—these four words demand moral integrity and upright conduct. They remind me of Jesus' departing words to the woman brought before Him for committing adultery: *"From now on sin no more"* (John 8:11b, NASB). They imply proper risk assessment and that I operate in a safe manner. If I am hesitant about something, or some course of action, I probably shouldn't do it.

"Treat others the way you would like to be treated" is a restatement of Jesus' teaching: *"Therefore, whatever you want others to do for you, do also the same for them—this is the Law and the Prophets"* (Mat. 7:12). These words challenge me to care for people and create a positive work environment. I know what hurts me. I am very good about taking care of myself. Therefore, there is no excuse for mishandling others.

"Do your best," address motivation and attitude. They allow for mistakes but insist on progress and a commitment to quality that comes from the heart. Paul wrote the Ephesians, *"Render service with a good attitude, as to the Lord and not to men"* (Eph. 6:7).

Confusion is the child of complexity. So often, I think we go astray because we forget to keep things simple. We forget the essentials. We lose sight of obeying God and striving to be like His Son in our frenzy to please ourselves. Consequently, we sacrifice tenets and acquire trouble. If godly rules form the foundation of our conduct and nourish our character, then God and those around us receive honor.

Inspiration † † †

The Disciplines are God's way of getting us into the ground; they put us where He can work within us and transform us. By themselves the Spiritual Disciplines can do nothing; they can only get us to the place where something can be done. They are God's means of grace.—Richard J. Foster in *Celebration of Discipline*

Devoted to Prayer

Colossians 4:2—Devote yourselves to prayer; stay alert in it with thanksgiving.

I have *never* encountered a godly Christian who is not devoted to prayer. Certainly, I know talented believers. There is a great abundance of disciples who are full of knowledge of the Bible and equipped with great people skills. I know many Christians who possess a solid business savvy and a knack for administrating. There is no shortage of believers raised in Christian homes who faithfully attended church all their lives. But I have *never* encountered a godly Christian who is not devoted to prayer.

I would rather hang my coat with one genuine intercessor and strong prayer warrior than a thousand who consider prayer a precursor to eating and a transition to meeting. Why? Because the man or woman who is devoted to God as evidenced by an effective prayer life, *discerns the mind of Christ.* To know the mind of Christ is to recognize God's will. It is the practice of prayer that teaches us about the character of God. It is the exercise of prayer that builds up our flabby spiritual muscles. It is the conduct of prayer that ushers us into the presence of the Lord who loves to fellowship with us. Without prayer, we are in danger of presumption. We mistakenly teach others that it is our own hard work or intelligence that accomplishes ministry.

I remember a preaching professor in seminary who drilled into us the importance of putting long hours into sermon preparation. His teaching was sound but it was devoid of any passion for God. His goal was to move the audience by the beauty of his sermons. Our class was notable for its absence in prayer. While he was critiquing our messages and pretending to walk righteously, he was cheating on his wife. It was not long before he left his spouse for another woman. Today, his life is a spiritual shipwreck.

O God, teach us how to pray! Deepen our longing to be with You!

Do you feel spiritually burnt-out? Have you lost your way? Are you going through the motions impressing people yet knowing your walk with God is flat? Friend, get on your knees now! Resolve to establish daily time to meet with your Father in heaven. Be devoted to prayer. Don't talk about it—do it! If you need help, find someone who prays and become a prayer partner. Be cautious about praying to see God work—that is a weaker reason for going to Him. Pray to know Him. Pray to discover His character and will for your life. If you and I will be faithful to pray, God will revitalize us. He will take us to a deeper understanding of Himself. Then He can use us for the work of His ministry. Then we can say 'Glory!' and know what it means!

Teaming Up in Cameroon

Seventeen teenagers endured the grueling heat, humidity and bugs of their Florida boot camp. They came from all across the country and Canada. Most of them had never met before yet they all had a common bond. The rules were strict and the discipline tough.

They traveled by plane and bus until reaching Nsongwa and Ngie, Cameroon. In the heart of Africa they came—willing servants of an incredible Father, to share the good news of Jesus Christ. Some of them contracted Malaria; all of them tolerated worms and parasites. When many were sick, the rest pitched in to serve them and maintain their responsibilities. They backpacked over many miles to take the gospel to remote villages. They shared their burdens, took turns encouraging each other, prayed, sang, worked and ministered to strangers with uncommon zeal and inspiring passion. In the end, over 600 people made decisions to follow Jesus. Friendships were forged— some that will last for a lifetime. How do I know this? My daughter, Sarah, and her friends Becky and Naomi sacrificed their summer to go with **Teen Missions** to Africa. All three of them sensed God leading them to be missionaries and God in His wisdom, taught them one summer in 2005 the value of teamwork.

Colossians 4:7-14—Tychicus . . . will tell you all the news about me . . . He is with Onesimus . . . They will tell you about everything here. Aristarchus, my fellow prisoner, greets you, as does Mark, Barnabas' cousin . . . and so does Jesus who is called Justus. These alone of the circumcision are my co-workers for the kingdom of God, and they have been a comfort to me. Epaphras . . . greets you . . . Luke, the loved physician, and Demas greet you.

In the Bible, the only reference to the word team refers to horses tied to a chariot. The word teamwork is never used. Yet the concept is pregnant throughout Scripture. Jesus trained a team and their collective work of evangelism and discipleship turned the world upside down. We see Paul's teammates in the passage above. Collectively they labored through persecution, in sickness and health with joy and sorrow. They traveled as messengers from church to church. Solomon noted, *"if somebody overpowers one person, two can resist him. A cord of three strands is not easily broken"* (Ecc. 4:12).

If the team is focused on Jesus, the work will be Christ-centered and the collective efforts of many yields amazing results. It is so easy to focus on our individual journey and solitary needs that we forget the importance of working together with our fellow brothers and sisters. Perhaps this is why Heb. 10:24, 25 says, *"And let us be concerned about one another in order to promote love and good works, not staying away from our meetings, as some habitually do, but encouraging each other, and all the more as you see the day drawing near."*

Gentle Among You

Three children walked down the aisle to their rehearsed places. The wee lassies stood four steps up on one side with the little lad on the other. While the two prim girls faithfully stood still, the boy inched towards the edge of the step, cheerfully smiled, leaned his body backward and slid down a step as only a limber child could. Twice more the process repeated until he was now on the main floor. Jonathan, the Best Man, saw what was happening, turned toward the boy and motioned him to move back to his place. Embarrassed, he went up two stairs, laid down with his face in his hands and quietly shook. Soon, the tears fell in torrents and he stood up wailing, quickly fleeing to his mother's arms. He sobbed for what seemed like minutes, upstaging the wedding so that his father had to carry him out. While Josh and Katie went on to become man and wife, I thought of the tender spirit of that boy and the loving manner in which his parents embraced him. If they were concerned about the crowd, they didn't show it. Instead, they ministered to their little boy.

1 Thessalonians 2:6,7,11—Nor did we seek glory from men, either from you or from others, even though as apostles of Christ we might have asserted our authority. But we proved to be gentle among you, as a nursing mother tenderly cares for her own children . . . Just as you know how we were exhorting and encouraging and imploring each one of you as a father would his own children. (NASB)

The Greek word, *τροφοσ (trophos)*, can mean a nursing mother or a wet nurse. In the ancient world, a wet nurse "not only had strict contractual stipulations, but often came to be a very trusted person whose influence lasted a lifetime."[40] Paul metaphorically emphasizes the care with which his team labored to nurture the Thessalonians. It is a word picture from which God intends for us to learn.

I wonder how many children grow up wanting nothing to do with Jesus because their parents invoked God's name to beat them. I wonder how many grapple with low self-images because all they ever heard was how they never measured up. I wonder how many become mean and legalistic because the Bible of justice shook before their eyes while the Bible of mercy missed their hearts. I wonder . . .

St. Francis DeSales taught, "Nothing is as strong as gentleness; nothing is as gentle as real strength." Nurturing is God's invention, an indispensable formula for growth. Nine times the Bible reminds us of our refuge under His caring wings! Ninety times may we remember what the Psalmist wrote, *"If I say, 'My foot is slipping,' Your faithful love will support me, LORD"* (Psa. 94:18).

Two Miles Just to Get Water

Mahesh and Seetha Gopal* were raised in Hindu families. They married and operated a successful business but their lives were unfulfilled until they met Christ. When they chose to follow Jesus, they encountered persecution from their relatives and countrymen. Eventually, they moved away to Wayanad, a city in the hill country of northern Kerala. They bought a piece of land and built a house. Seetha asked her new neighbors if she could draw water until they could afford to dig their own well. But they refused to share with her because she and her husband were Christians. So, everyday, the Gopals walked two miles to get their water.

The time finally came when they could afford to dig their own well. Amazingly, they did not have to tunnel deep before striking a spring; their water literally gushed forth! But shortly after they obtained water, Wayanad went through a long drought and the neighbors wells dried up. The only water to be found in their village now belonged to them. Mahesh and Seetha graciously shared with all of their neighbors the water God provided. They ministered kindness to the very people who mistreated them. Today, their well continuously springs up giving ample testimony to the Living Water who saw their predicament and graciously responded.

1 Thessalonians 3:4—In fact, when we were with you, we told you previously that we were going to suffer persecution, and as you know, it happened.

The reason we fear persecution is we set our eyes on what we desire instead of what God desires. We embrace power because vulnerability entails sacrifice. We love praise because it puffs what insults pummel—our pride. We opt for the easy way because a hard ship means a stormy passage. But how can God work through us when we are strong and scarcely think we need Him? It was in the training camp of persecution that Paul and his companions grew mightily. He realized that weakness forced him to rely on God and therefore made him strong. May it be so with us.

Our Father knows how much we can take but how much of our Father will we take? Often what makes our testimony relevant to a skeptical world is our willingness to endure persecution for the sake of the gospel. It is through trials that people best observe the genuineness of our faith. And it is through trials that God deepens our dependence upon Him! So don't be afraid of the plight. The same One who bubbles the water in Wayanad through the well of His persecuted children, wants to bubble His love through you!

*Not their true names, the story however is real.

1 Thessalonians 4:3,7—For this is God's will, your sanctification: that you abstain from sexual immorality . . . For God has not called us to impurity, but to sanctification.

Hank Acephalous graduated near the top of his West Point class. As a newly commissioned second lieutenant, he continued to excel by earning the coveted ranger tab. He was set to join the elite Ranger battalion at his new post. Life was good.

On the first day of duty in Bravo Company, his commander Captain Sovereign, spent an hour with him explaining the conduct, attitude, commitment and example expected of him. The main point of the message was simple. "Acephalous, just because you wear a tab doesn't make you a ranger. If you want to be one of us you must look, act and think like a ranger. Our mission and methods are purposely distinct from other units. Affirm and espouse the ranger creed. I'll help you grow. Follow me and do as I do."

But what if Acephalous believed he was already top notch? He wore the rank of an officer and the badges that showed what he could do. He would follow Sovereign's word only when it appealed to him. He would have sex with the wife of one of his squad leaders because she found him attractive. He would do whatever brought him pleasure. How long do you think this leader would last before his unit and the Army found him unfit and threw him out of the Army?

Sanctification means to be set apart. But set apart from what? If the purpose of Jesus coming to earth was to save us from our sin, then at its core, sanctification implies holiness. Jesus' liberation effort fulfilled God's intent that we should become holy, as He is holy. Therefore, sanctification is a process that involves shedding our independence from God as characterized by feeding our selfish desires. It is the Holy Spirit washing us as we bathe in the tub of obedience. This washing renders us distinct from the sin-caked population that pridefully rejects the notion of submitting to Christ. The English philosopher William Ames noted, "Sanctification is the real change in man from the sordidness of sin to the purity of God's image."

Sadly, countless people identify themselves as Christians with no intention of surrendering their own will to comply with God's will. They assume they are Christians because of the country or family they were born in, the church they attend, the works they accomplish, the company they keep or the stadium in which they walked forward to receive Christ. *It is impossible for sanctification to take place in a person unwilling to obey Christ's leadership.* In such a person, Jesus is not Lord but rather a Savior-icon to be run up the flagpole of a camp intent on accomplishing its own agenda. This very day, people are being slaughtered, or forced to leave their homes, brutally traumatized by fellow humans who claim to be Christians. It is God's intent that when people hear our claims to be Christians they see godliness. When they don't, is it hard to understand why they would want nothing to do with Jesus?

To be sanctified is to be thrilled by the invisible touch of a loving Lord who knows how to wean us from the fruitless deeds of darkness to become children of light. Do you feel like a flashlight dimmed by a dying battery? Perhaps it is time to ask the question, "Am I willing to let God do His work in me that I might be holy?" Have I falsely assumed that I could live the rest of my life on my own terms? To choose the latter is not to be sanctified but rather *wrecktified*. May the grace of God give you the courage to run the race for Christ—set apart for His glory!

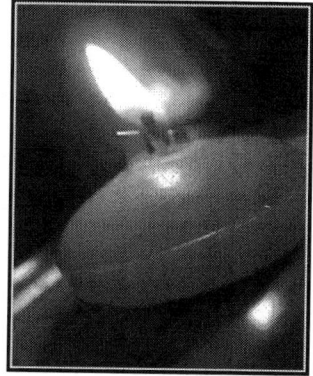

Inspiration † † †

Sanctification is an immediate work of the Spirit of God in the soul of the believer, purifying and cleansing his nature from the pollution and uncleanness of sin, renewing him in the image of God, and thereby enabling him from a spiritual and habitual principle of grace, to yield obedience to God according to the tenor and terms of the New Covenant, by virtue of the life and death of Christ.—John Owen, English church leader and theologian, (1616-1683)

We need only try to escape the world by running away from it to discover how much we love it, and how much it loves us.—Watchman Nee in *Love Not The World*

Bettis Hates God

Bettis hates God. He thinks the whole concept of yielding one's heart to a Divine Creator is bunk. It's heavenly tyranny foisted on earth. He didn't choose to be born so where's the fairness in damnation if he opts not to play by God's rules? He resists the notion of truth being defined for him. He'd rather rebel.

We may think Bettis is crazy to scorn a loving God, to literally play with fire. But he holds the God-given right of refusal. The beauty of free will is that we *can* rebel. What value would there be in creating creatures devoid of the ability *to choose to love*?

2 Thessalonians 2:10b—They perish because they did not accept the love of the truth in order to be saved.

God was extremely gracious to give us free will. Anyone who is a parent can understand to some degree God's purpose. My heart is blessed when my children freely express their love for me. It would not be the same if they came and mouthed affection under the spirit of coercion, or were programmed to obey me.

Two things we ought to understand about our will. *First, we either open or harden our hearts toward God during our time on earth. Second, God is the One who initiates drawing us to Himself.* Our will is exercised in response to His call. *"No one can come to Me unless the Father who sent Me draws him, and I will raise him up on the last day"* (John 6:44). The danger for Bettis is that by rebelling he places his hope in the fact that once he dies, he still has the capacity to determine his fate, despite the fact that the Bible warns we will all face God's judgment (Heb. 9:27).

Do people reject God because they don't believe He is Lord, or because they do not want to do what He asks? Satan would have us believe that the essence of life is our right to choose. God wants us to understand that our purpose in life is to know Him. Adam and Eve preferred Satan's line and we have suffered ever since. However, the very fact that God gave us free will should be a reminder to us that we ought to respect the rights of those who resist the gospel message.

If living in opposition to God leads one to enduring peace, genuine fulfillment and joy then by all means oppose God and hope the Bible is wrong. Truth stands upon its own merit. May we who love Jesus faithfully pray for a world of Bettises shackled by sin, in need of the Savior, yet free to select eternal isolation from a God who will not make men love Him. His awesome love sent Jesus to bridge the great divide—we decide whether to go aCROSS.

Down the Mountain

2 Thessalonians 2:13—But we must always thank God for you, brothers loved by the Lord, because from the beginning God has chosen you for salvation through sanctification by the Spirit and through belief in the truth.

The Sergeant Major looked over the railing as soldiers from his unit went over the edge. He had over twenty-five years in the Army but he had never rappelled before. As we stood in line, I saw no trace of fear in his eyes. He sought no excuse to leave the tower and climb back down the wooden steps. Instead he placed his trust in: the instructors who taught him how to tie a rope seat around his waist; the rappel master who sent him off the platform over the wall; the belay man 45 feet below, poised to pull his rope taut and break a possible fall; and the all important rope and metal D-ring safely holding his weight.

We each stand on our own mountain and look over the Ledge of Decision. Far below is a jagged surface called Death—the end of our known journey. Countless signs offer a way to avoid the overhang and go down the mountain. Man's paths that lead down are broad and well traveled in contrast to the narrow, winding descent God fashioned.

On the ledge, a single golden rope wraps around a metal anchor engraved with the word GRACE. Beside it is a book whose contents reveal the only way to negotiate the overhang and find God is to attach oneself to the rope and climb down. The rope was placed here by God's Son who although perfect, allowed Himself to be cast off the ledge by His enemies in order to make a way beyond Death to Life.

Belief always involves choice. The most important decision we make is to whom or what we entrust ourselves to for negotiating life. If we know how important it is to check our equipment before we go off the side of a tower, we ought to examine carefully what we believe before we launch ourselves down the cliffs of life.

To rappel on God's rope is to secure our soul in humility to the way of salvation anchored in *grace* by a perfect Savior. It is bounding off the edge of what is known, believing that nothing can separate us from the love of Christ. The only rope-burn from this rappel is the burning away of sin as one swoops with the ecstatic joy only a divine Rappel master could create.

Inspiration † † †

One life is all we have and we live it as we believe in living it. But to sacrifice what you are and to live without belief, that is a fate more terrible than dying.—Joan of Arc, French heroine, (1412-1431)

Tell a Man He is Brave

Thomas Carlyle (1795-1881), a British historian and essayist, once said, "Tell a man he is brave, and you help him to become so." His words amplify the word *encourage* which means to impart courage, to fill with hope, and instill confidence. George Adams wrote, "Encouragement is oxygen to the soul." I remember coming around the track in the mile relay and hearing the cheers of the crowd. Their voices and the steady clapping of their hands inspired me to run my fastest to win. It is no secret why the home team has the advantage. Fans yelling support provide motivational energy athletes harness to succeed.

God is the author of encouragement. He saw us stumble in the garden. He listened as we grumbled in the desert. He felt the sting of our unfaithfulness in every promised land He gave us. Every hour He watches us across the globe fully aware of our sin and yet patiently He waits for us to respond to His bottomless love. For this reason, Paul could write to the Thessalonians the words written below.

2 Thessalonians 2:16,17—May our Lord Jesus Christ Himself and God our Father, who has loved us and given us eternal encouragement and good hope by grace, encourage your hearts and strengthen you in every good work and word.

Jesus' love is bigger than our failures. His patience exceeds our shortcomings. His desire to be with us should thrill our souls and generate unceasing hope. Encouragement is like tasting sherbet for the first time, like jumping into a cold pool on a hot day, like receiving a long hug from an old friend, or absorbing a standing ovation for faithful service. The fact that we need encouragement is the proof that we need God. Inside we yearn for more and Jesus is the One capable of delivering that life we crave.

If God is in you and you are paying attention to His words, you will be encouraged! Do you feel like giving up? God loves you! Are you in pain? God loves you! Are you backsliding? God loves you! Are you rebellious? Go with the world and you will find the holy peace eaten out of you by every maggot of deception, doubt and fear. But God still loves you! Are you complacent and tired of serving your Lord? God loves you! Are you self-absorbed? His love beckons! What you pay attention too determines your direction. Follow God and you cannot help but soar—He lifts you up! And for His sake and glory find someone today and encourage them to be strong in Him! Encouragement was never meant to sit alone. Something to think about . . . in reveration!

Inspiration ✝✝✝

Love, by definition, seeks to enjoy its object.—C.S. Lewis in *The Joyful Christian*

Understanding God's Love

If someone were to ask you what the secret for living a fulfilled life is, what would you say? John recorded Jesus' prayer for Himself, His disciples, and all believers in John 17. Jesus asked God to make it clear to the world that He loved them even as He is loved. Of all the things Jesus could have asked how profound that He focused on His Father's love (vs. 23-26). Then I discovered that all 27 books of the New Testament share vital truths about love! *Hmmm.*

2 Thessalonians 3:5—May the Lord direct your hearts to God's love and Christ's endurance.

The key to living a fulfilled life comes through a commitment on our part to embrace that God is love and loving to us. Love is patient, kind, humble, others-focused, truth affirming, protecting, trusting, hopeful, long-suffering and *never fails* (1 Co. 13:4-8). When we grasp that this is God's desire for us, our lives cannot help but be profoundly changed.

It may seem obvious that God's love is important. But knowing this is not the same thing as understanding it. The former speaks to a mental awareness while the latter reveals a Christ-centeredness. A man can know God loves him and end his life because of depression. However, what man who understands his significance, by appreciating God's love, can commit suicide—no matter how depressed he is—because his life is not his own! It belongs to the Lord. A woman aware God loves her can operate independently from Him. But no woman who fathoms the depths of her Father's love can stand a day separated from Him!

To understand God's love requires effort on our part. His love is not capricious. It is extended to those obedient to His will. It is magnified by purity. We must believe that He knows what is best for us and accept His plan even when it counters what we would choose. His love is jealous. He rewards those who place Him first before all else in priority and principle.

Understanding God's love liberates us from legalism, the need to have all the answers, and the mindset that we must do significant things to be significant. It gives us the ability to rest in the midst of tempests. Animated joy replaces mechanical, by the numbers living. Hope is the speech of choice. Peace transcends physical suffering. Confidence bounces above persecution. Value is attained regardless of our upbringing, circumstances, or the voices of demon-accusers.

Understanding His love enables us to persevere! Our nail-spiked Savior willingly hung on the cross confident of His Father's love; deeply determined in His own love for mankind. When divine love is misunderstood, ignored, rejected, and rebelled against, people wilt beneath the suns of strain and moons of melancholy. Test your own heart. Are you living a meaningful life or is life just mean?

Deep Inside I Knew

1 Timothy 1:5—The goal of this command is love, which comes from a pure heart and a good conscience and a sincere faith.

I was spending time with the Lord not long ago when the thought came to my mind; do not watch the Odyssey tonight. Instantly a battle commenced. Where did that thought come? Why shouldn't I watch the Odyssey? There is nothing wrong . . . All day long I rationalized against that *random* thought. Deep inside I knew the gentle unmistakable voice of the Holy Spirit was at work.

I watched the Odyssey. There was nothing wrong with what I saw. But a friend called to say a relative had died. She was getting ready to go on a trip and wanted to let me know and see what work needed to be completed before she left. I did not give her the attention she deserved because the Odyssey was about to begin. Had I listened to the small message I would have been ready for the hurting voice. God knew. The test of conscience is not always measured by whether what I do is right or wrong but rather by my willingness to obey.

Inspiration † † †

A bad conscience is a snake in one's heart.—Paul Vithayathil's collection of *Proverbs and Wise Sayings*

My conscience is held captive by the Word of God and to act against conscience is neither right nor safe.—Martin Luther

God's Godness

God's qualities are indescribable, incomprehensible and thereby awe-inspiring. If you are beset with problems stop for a period and begin to reflect on God. We are a curious people so wrapped in ourselves and easily prone to discouragement. What we desperately need is to get our eyes off our humanity and gaze where it is impossible to see—God's *Godness*.   Robert Russell shares in his book *Releasing Resentment* that Martin Luther once was depressed over a prolonged period. One day his wife came downstairs wearing all black. Martin Luther asked her, "Who died?" She said, "God has." He answered, "God hasn't died." She replied, "Well, live like it and act like it."

1 Timothy 1:17—Now to the King eternal, immortal, invisible, the only God, be honor and glory forever and ever. Amen.

Now to the King—stop racing around, drop to your knees and pay homage to the King! In our modern day, we have lost what it means to come into the presence of royalty! Every day we serve The KING!

Eternal, Immortal—Charles Haddon Spurgeon said, "As well might a gnat seek to drink in the ocean, as a finite creature to comprehend the Eternal God." André Gide noted, "I cannot tell where God begins, still less where he ends. But my belief is better expressed if I say that there is no end to God's beginning."

Invisible—A. W. Tozer preached, "Do not try to imagine God, or you will have an imaginary God." He is unseen but we need not rely on our imagination. *"From the creation of the world His invisible attributes, that is, His eternal power and divine nature, have been clearly seen, being understood through what He has made. As a result, people are without excuse"* (Rom. 1:20).

The only God—An early Hasidic song from *The Oxford Book of Prayer* states, "Wherever I go—only Thou! Wherever I stand—only Thou! Just Thou; again Thou! Always Thou! Thou, Thou, Thou! When things are good, Thou! When things are bad—Thou! Thou, Thou, Thou!"

Be honor and glory for ever and ever—When we look beyond ourselves to God we find hope that confounds logic, peace that transcends disorder and love that brings meaning to life. He is due the entire honor. He deserves all the glory. *Amen!*

Inspiration   † † †

All of God's acts are consistent with all of His attributes. No attribute contradicts any other, but all harmonize and blend into each other in the infinite abyss of the Godhead. All that God does agrees with all that God is, and being and doing are one in Him.—A. W. Tozer

Discharged in Disgrace

Across the table sat a man of large girth and hostile demeanor—one who formerly served as a platoon sergeant. This noncommissioned officer faced legal charges that if proved, would eject him from the army dishonorably. He was caught stealing equipment from his own soldiers, lying and shirking his duties.

The defense attorney praised the many years of service this Sergeant First Class had given his nation. He cited his past achievements as if reading an updated military version of Who's Who. Then he looked at the lieutenant and said mockingly, "Have you ever served in Viet Nam?" The lieutenant shook his head no. "Do you see the ribbons on this man's uniform? He has been awarded for bravery in combat. He served his country with distinction. What gives you the right to cast judgment on this man . . . to jeopardize his career? You have but a fraction of the time in service he has."

Tension filled the room like a rocket teetering on the edge of booster failure. All eyes fastened on the young lieutenant. He thought for a long moment. He chose not to answer the attorney's question but rather to ask his own. "Did this man reenlist in the Army so he could continue to serve in the military?" The defense attorney nodded in agreement. "When he reenlisted did he raise his right hand and swear an oath beside the American flag and before God, that he would faithfully discharge his duties?" Again, the defense attorney moved his head in affirmation.

"Then the issue before us is not what this man did in Viet Nam, or what medals adorn his chest. What matters is that he violated the very standards of the Uniform Code of Military Justice he swore to obey. He violated his word. He shirked his responsibility to lead as a senior NCO. He broke the law and caused dissension among the very troops he was given the privilege to lead."

The defense was silent. No worthless remarks would spoil the freshened breeze of truth. But one could not help but feel sadness for a soldier forced to leave with eighteen years of military experience. He forfeited his retirement to embrace disgrace. Why? Because somewhere along the way, he jettisoned doing what was right. He twisted the meaning of duty. He determined that his reputation and years of sacrifice justified breaking the law.

1 Timothy 3:13, 4:12—For those who have served well as deacons acquire a good standing for themselves, and great boldness in the faith that is in Christ Jesus . . . No one should despise your youth; instead, you should be an example to the believers in speech, in conduct, in love, in faith, in purity.

May God give us the humility to understand that our reputation is only as sacred as what we do today. One fall can erase years of hard, honorable climbing. If we choose to swim in the pond of pride we will surely drink the poisoned water of arrogance until eventually what drowns is our good name.

You may be tired of walking with integrity as you watch many around you bend the rules, flaunt immorality and seemingly get ahead. Don't give in or give up! Your reputation matters to God and it has a far greater effect on those around you than you might ever realize.

When a saint falls, God's perfect name is abused, the scorn of those who seek reason to disobey is enflamed and we collectively suffer a damaged reputation. Consider then, what is achieved by modeling a life of faithfulness to God and His Word. You become an inspiration to others. When they need meaningful answers, guess whom they will seek out? Keep shining for Jesus, He's worth betting your reputation on!

Inspiration †††

Reputation is what men and women think of us; character is what God and angels know of us.—Thomas Paine

It takes many good deeds to build a good reputation, and only one bad one to lose it.—Benjamin Franklin

Character is like a tree and reputation like a shadow. The shadow is what we think of it; the tree is the real thing.—Abraham Lincoln

Reaching the Next Generation

George Barna is a seasoned pollster and director of the Barna Group. His group's survey results in 2006 reveal some disturbing trends. Listed below are three of the twelve most significant findings for that year.

- Only 15% of those who regularly attend a Christian church ranked their relationship with God as the top priority in their life.
- 61% of young adults (churched at one point during their teen years) were spiritually disengaged (i.e., not actively attending church, reading the Bible, or praying). Only 1/5th of twenty-somethings (20%) maintained a level of spiritual activity consistent with their high school experience.
- 75% of teenagers engaged in at least one type of psychic or witchcraft-related activity . . . fewer than 30% received any teaching from their church about elements of the supernatural.[41]

What disturbs me about these statistics is that they are a harbinger of disaster for our future if you believe as I do, that what happens with and to our youth is critical for the world's future. Here are some thoughts to ponder:

- If 85% of those who regularly attend church do not place God as the top priority in their life, then guess what message young people are observing first-hand—God is not that important.
- I contend that the 61% of those in their 20's who are spiritually disengaged had weak habits to begin with in the area of Bible reading, prayer and regular fellowship. Most churches philosophically tap the youth pastor and the youth group as the key to the spiritual development of their children. The problem with this philosophy is:

1. It subtly encourages parents to relinquish or shirk their responsibility and privilege to disciple their children at home and in any other venue possible—Deu. 6:5-7.

2. It unfairly burdens one youth pastor with the expectation of training all the youth which means this person must have significant skills in the area of delegation, training, teaching, planning, resourcing, etc.

3. Most youth pastors are not trained to be disciple makers. Few seminaries and Bible Colleges offer strong leadership training which means we are churning out leaders strong in knowing how to promote activities with media/technology-savvy, but are impoverished when it comes to providing in-depth leadership training.

4. Most youth groups promote activities that favor recruiting those who are unchurched or entertaining those who are churched at once-a-week programs or events. Instead of challenging our youth, we are molly coddling them and then we wonder why they have no depth in Christ! Children who understand that faith costs, and yet, is highly rewarding because God is real

and awesome, are much better prepared for life-long service than are those who participate in activities which often mirror the world and do not speak to the inner needs and hunger of the soul. The church in China is numerically exploding under persecution while the church in America is imploding under amusement.

5.   Youth groups tend to be age-segregated which means young men and women are missing the input and wisdom of seniors, working adults, and others at different yet meaningful stages of life.

●   The number of Americans now engaged in witchcraft or psychic activity is skyrocketing yet the church is strangely mute about the mystic darkness Satan perpetuates. If we don't wake up and warn our children to the dangers that proliferate in an increasingly Jesus-hostile land, we are basically sending them out into a field of land mines while we close our eyes and hope they don't misstep! So what is the solution?

1 Timothy 4:12—No one should despise your youth; instead, you should be an example to the believers in speech, in conduct, in love, in faith, in purity.

Most Bible scholars think Timothy was about 17 years old when Paul recruited him to his team. Paul saw in him a heart for God. Notice the high standards Paul expected of him in the verse above. He called on Timothy to set the example in five key areas—speech, behavior, love, faith and purity. What he expected of Timothy, he practiced in his own life.

One of the most tragic occurrences in life is a shrinking heart. The fresh love a person has at a tender age for God should not become twisted, disdained or set aside for some take-your-pick worldly obsession. Like Paul, we must determine to love God. We must model and believe passionately in reproducing the spiritual essentials which bring about spiritual growth. Effective modeling teaches our young people why following Christ matters, shows them how, gets them started in what we are doing to grow, keeps them going and sees that they pass what they learned on to others!

Our youth are our future! To those of you who are young, do not be discouraged! Keep your eyes on Jesus and ask Him to help you fall deeper in love with Him each day so that you can serve Him for God's glory! And if you are part of a youth group that is spiritually unchallenged, respectfully share with the leader that you would like to have more meat and less cotton candy!

Inspiration †††

I am afraid that the schools will prove the very gates of hell, unless they diligently labor in explaining the Holy Scriptures and engraving them in the heart of the youth.—Martin Luther

Progress

Day one: Piles of dirt, stacks of tree limbs and lots of pickup trucks, cars and tractors. Men are standing around drinking coffee and talking. Day two: see day one. Day three: see day one. Day twelve? For the first time I see trenches dug and fresh gravel heaps. For all the men and equipment, it does not seem like much has happened on this city project.

I suppose if I were to go away on an extended trip and return, the differences on that lot I prayer walk past would be significant. I know (by faith) that by the end of summer a beautifully constructed park will occupy what now looks like mere mound shifting.

1 Timothy 4:14,15—Do not neglect the gift that is in you; it was given to you through prophecy, with the laying on of hands by the council of elders. Practice these things; be committed to them, so that your progress may be evident to all.

Spiritual growth is like watching a snail cross the Grand Canyon. If I were to daily measure improvement in my maturity and in my relationship with God even as an optimist, I would be hard-pressed to show progress. But when I view over time His incredible workings and value in my heart, I am astounded at the difference time spent in the Bible and with Him makes in building my life and our relationship.

I think we Christians embrace secular society's fascination with McQuick solutions (with apologies to McDonalds). We hear of *life changing* seminars or the newest and greatest method for instant growth.   If it seems like Bible reading is drudgery, prayer is hard and God is distant, don't give up! The field becomes a park but never overnight. I'm sure the neighbors are sick of the dust and noise construction brings. But they'll soon forget the inconvenience when their kids have swings and a great place to play.

By setting aside time for God you *are* moving forward.   Your advancement is not just earthly but eternal. Progress may not come by what is fun, easily measurable, or popular. Development may be forged in the mundane oven of faithfulness. It may contort in the process of obedience. It is made brilliant by dull labor and wise through perseverance. If progress were easy, Judas might have kissed Jesus differently, Moses could have sold his desert time-share and Peter would have walked across the entire lake.

Billy Graham's reputation as a paragon of godliness comes through decades of faithful living. He sticks with his calling focused on his Savior one day at a time.   He and (insert your favorite saint here), prove that progress is not fantasy or encrypted mystery. It is finding and following what God wants—as Scripture and His Spirit reveal. As my dad likes to say, "inch by inch it's a cinch; yard by yard, it's too hard!"

Wine

1 Timothy 5:23—Don't continue drinking only water, but use a little wine because of your stomach and your frequent illnesses.

I once read an article that the sale of red wine in Japan had skyrocketed. A television show in that country extolled the benefits of drinking a little red wine each day in order to fight heart disease and cancer. The Japanese are very health conscious and boast the highest life expectancy in the world. Naturally, they responded to this report with the result that red wine sales quadrupled.

In our own country, the array of health products consumers are challenged to purchase is more than just a little mind-boggling. Welcome to the world of vitamins, anti-oxidants, herbs, etc. Melatonin is supposed to help people get to sleep or recover faster from jet lag. If I get a cold, I am upset that Echinacea is not doing its job! Television commercials annoyingly cater to the ever-growing health challenges of the aging baby boomers.

Not many people want to die. Consequently, there will always be a strong demand for remedies to improve and prolong life. The next time someone offers you a new health tip or asks for your advice; why not share the greatest cure known to man! God gave us guaranteed victory over sin and death through His precious Son—if we would just confess our sin, place our trust in Him by making Him our Savior and Lord. By faith, we carry in our hearts the key to eternal live—a forever life free of every pain or affliction known to man. A life in the presence of the Almighty filled with indescribable joy.

We, who know and love Jesus Christ, have a ceremony we celebrate called communion. We take a small piece of wafer or bread and eat it in remembrance of Jesus who allowed His body to be hung, pierced and destroyed to save our souls. We drink a small cup of wine or juice to commemorate the blood that He shed on the cross for the remission of sins. It is a sacred ceremony—one that the Apostle Paul wrote, *"For as often as you eat this bread and drink the cup, you proclaim the Lord's death until He comes"* (1 Co. 11:26).

Some drink wine to forget and escape their problems. Some drink hoping to avoid disease. But the greatest drink is the cup lifted to honor in gratitude our champion—Jesus. He is the permanent cure to disease. Something to think about . . . in reveration!

Inspiration †††

Men are like wine—some turn to vinegar, but the best improve with age.— Pope John XXIII, Italian clergyman, (1881-1963)

Apprenticeship

1 Timothy 6:11,12—Now you, man of God, run from these things; but pursue righteousness, godliness, faith, love, endurance, and gentleness. Fight the good fight for the faith; take hold of eternal life, to which you were called and have made a good confession before many witnesses.

As we saw earlier, Paul had a father-son type relationship with Timothy. When we read 1 and 2 Timothy, we are reading letters of a mentor to his spiritual apprentice. Both letters contain warm fatherly advice and spiritual instruction that if followed would ensure Timothy success. Paul invested time in Tim because he realized that what he passed on to this reliable man would be invested in other faithful believers who in turn would be qualified to train others (2 Ti. 2:2).

Is it noteworthy that God did not send Jesus to earth to establish religious training institutes? Jesus came and poured His life into twelve followers, eleven of whom left everything to follow the world's greatest Teacher. His strategy was hands-on training. The master Mentor's results were world changing. The apostles used the same approach.

Someone will say, "How can I do this when I have no one to train?" Do you have children? Raise them in the fear of the Lord. Pour your life into their spiritual development and expect lasting fruit. Do you have friends? Set up regular appointments to study Scripture and pray.

Others will reply, "I'm too weak to help anyone else. I don't know enough about God yet." Seek out a true God-follower and request that person's help. Become an apprentice that you might someday lead others. And don't short sell yourself. As you learn, teach someone spiritually younger. A brand new believer already has great truth to pass on to those not yet enamored with Christ!

Still others will state, "I'm too busy and besides my life isn't worth emulating . . ." Well, whose kingdom are you living for? God never said it would be easy to follow Him. It takes hard work and sacrifice *because* we live in a fallen world. Yet, the sacrifices we make to grow in our love for God and help others grow are invaluable. I would rather struggle to make time to spend with my Father and put forth the extra effort to train apprentices than have all the riches and comforts this world can offer. What greater joy can we have than in seeing those we have taught walking with God . . . training others!!!

Inspiration †††

What would happen if we were to focus on the four out of every ten adults and one out of every three teenagers who have already asked Jesus Christ to be their Savior—and do everything we can to help them grow into inspired, unmistakable disciples of Jesus?—George Barna in *Growing True Disciples*

Build Me a Son!

2 Timothy 1:3—I thank God, whom I serve with a clear conscience as my forefathers did, when I constantly remember you in my prayers night and day.

Constant prayers can simply mean that someone is perseverant in praying for others as Paul did for Timothy. But a constant prayer can be a solitary composition that endures on the strength of love, honesty and sheer poetic beauty.

I do not remember much about my mother—she died of cancer when I was nine. But in my late twenties, a family friend, Georgia, gave me a prayer she had in her possession. My mother wrote it for me. I hang this prayer on the wall in my office as a constant reminder to live a life that is worthy of my Father in heaven. Her words amaze, humble and inspire me. I hope they will be a blessing to you as they are to me.

Build Me A Son
by Elizabeth Helen York

Build me a son, Heavenly Father, who loves You more than himself or others.
Build me a son who receives his orders for the day from You before he meets a man.
Build me a son who has in him the attributes You possess:
- Love: that sent Christ to die for us
- Gentleness: that leads us like a shepherd
- Joy: that fills our hearts to overflowing
- Long-suffering: that never tires under stress
- Goodness: that showers others with blessing upon blessing
- Faith: that he may always know Your perfect will for him
- Meekness: that he may see himself as Your humble servant
- Honesty: that he may be known as a man of truth
- Chastity: that his heart may be pure toward women and men
- Giving: that spirit that gives to others continually
- Comfort: that he may know how to weep with the sorrowful
- Wisdom: that makes him not worldly wise, but a godly man
- Submissive: that he will possess a servant's spirit toward You and others.

Build me a son who when he is old enough, will let You, his Heavenly Father, choose a helpmate for him that will draw him closer to You through the years, and will always be a godly and submissive wife."

Inspiration † † †

Prayer is never answered due to the position of the person who prays but on the promise of the provision of God.—Judson Cornwell, author

This Morning

2 Timothy 1:8-10—So don't be ashamed of the testimony about our Lord, or of me His prisoner. Instead, share in suffering for the gospel, relying on the power of God, who has saved us and called us with a holy calling, not according to our works, but according to His own purpose and grace, which was given to us in Christ Jesus before time began. This has now been made evident through the appearing of our Savior Christ Jesus, who has abolished death and has brought life and immortality to light through the gospel.

This morning as I was enjoying my time with God I was thrilled by the realization that God extended His grace to me before the beginning of time. There was that wonderful moment of electricity down my spine. I find in my heart a bubbling up of love for our Lord.

Consider that the God of the universe calls and saves us irrespective of our efforts. The more I grow in knowing God the less impressed I am with humanity and myself. I do not mean this in a disparaging way. I simply mean God's love completely overwhelms my feeble notion of love. He calls to us not because we can give something back! He calls to us to fulfill His own purpose—to make us holy and bring us into a relationship with Himself.

In a society that measures everything by time isn't it mind-boggling that God before the beginning of time extended His grace to us?!!!

In a world that defines life from dust to dust how remarkable that Jesus ushers in eternal life—real immortal life, the stuff scientists cannot fathom or measure! And He, this great Lover and Giver, thought it all up for us before He launched time. Words are not needed to express the kind of gratefulness such grace invokes.

Inspiration † † †

Grace teaches us that God loves because of who God is, not because of who we are.—Philip Yancey in *What's So Amazing About Grace*

From faith, hope, and love, the virtues of religion referring to God, there arises a double act which bears on the spiritual communion exercised between God and us; the hearing of the word and prayer.—William Ames

Preserving Context

2 Timothy 2:15—Be diligent to present yourself approved to God, a worker who doesn't need to be ashamed, correctly teaching the word of truth.

There is a major ingredient of truth that is often trashed today. It seems to have been discarded by our hurry up society as an unnecessary encumbrance. It is what we know as *context*. "The whole truth and nothing but the truth" has fallen victim to the sound bite. The tree has become more important than the forest.

Truth without context is like a tire without rubber. It will roll temporarily on rims but not very far and with significant damage. Context is vitally important for two basic reasons:

1. *Context helps us determine accurate meaning.* To ignore context is to amplify distortion. Our society is increasingly skeptical of those whose occupations specialize in posturing information for image at the expense of veracity. Valuing truth demands taking the time to understand what the author meant in the setting in which he or she communicated.

2. *Context helps us make sound decisions.* Whoever coined the phrase "there are two sides to every story" was very wise. Many of us have bemoaned rushing to judgment on the sole basis of one person's version of events.

It is precisely because we do not protect context that we are subject today to the eroding of basic freedoms. For example, our judicial system defends the notion that it is compelled by the Constitution to enforce a separation of church and state. Consequently, a public school teacher cannot keep a Bible on his or her desk in many states. Yet nowhere does the First Amendment include the phrase "separation of church and state." It reads:

> Congress shall make no law respecting an establishment of religion, or prohibiting the free exercise thereof; or abridging the freedom of speech, or of the press; or the right of the people peaceably to assemble, and to petition the Government for a redress of grievances. [42]

A close examination of the setting in which the Constitution was written reveals that the first act of the United States Congress was to authorize the printing of 20,000 Bibles for the Indians. President George Washington, with the request of both Houses of Congress issued a "National Thanksgiving Proclamation" to God!

Yet, it is not our eroding spiritual freedoms we should fear most, it is becoming irrelevant because we danced with the quibble instead of embracing the Light. If our cry is to discern God's truth then we must honor His Word even when it hurts our senses, even when it is unpopular.

> *For the time will come when they will not tolerate sound doctrine, but according to their own desires, will accumulate teachers for themselves because they have an itch to hear something new. They will turn away from hearing the truth and will turn aside to myths"* (2 Ti. 4:3,4).

If for God 's sake, we will value the truth, for God's glory we will live in His light!

Inspiration † † †

The Bible was written in several languages, embraces many literary forms, and reflects cultures very different from our own. These are important considerations for properly understanding the Bible in its context.—Troy Perry, pastor

Truth always must be seen in the context of the time and place where people live.—Robert E. Coleman in *The Master Plan of Discipleship*

Robbed of Gold

Boos descended upon the row of stern-faced officials. The crowd was more than displeased. They were incredulous. Jamie Sale and David Pelletier sat stunned themselves. They skated their best routine on ice. Everyone expected marks that would award the Canadian figure skaters a gold medal. Instead, they were mulcted (fined) by dubious deductions. The Russian dynasty of gold continued. But the snow-capped mountains around Salt Lake City could not contain the growing allegations of conspiracy among several judges.

2 Timothy 4:8—In the future, there is reserved for me the crown of righteousness, which the Lord, the righteous Judge, will give me on that day, and not only to me, but to all those who have loved His appearing.

Isn't it reassuring to know that when our final Olympic event (life on earth) is over, we will stand before a perfect Judge! We will not have to tremble wondering if subjective impression gives us heaven or hurtles us hell-ward. There will be no need to fear conspiracy among a triune God. The standards are clear and the judging will be perfect.

Jesus did not say, "If I like you, I'll let you in." God's Son never taught, "If you work hard enough you can earn my favor." Instead, He lived a flawless life on earth—something no one else has accomplished! By His holiness, He took our failing scores upon His own shoulders and hung for them on a cross. By His blood, He offered us a chance to stand and be acquitted if we would admit our sins and trust in Him. No one has the talent or skill to skate by Jesus and earn perfect marks. But He knows that. That is why when He judges there will be grace. His score bears the permanent mark of informed mercy.

Jamie and David felt the profound disappointment of second place. But unlike so many athletes today, they did not whine or bitterly denounce their judges. They took their marks and moved on knowing there are more important things in life than a weighted medallion. I was reminded of Jesus. Better than Jamie and David, He never sinned. Yet His judges condemned Him to die. They yelled, "crucify"! They burned their own Savior with blistering false charges. He did not complain. He did not call fire from heaven on those blithering fools. He died. He arose. He sits at the right hand of God and when the time comes for us all to be judged He will perform as always—perfectly.

Inspiration † † †

The highest reward for a person's toil is not what they get for it, but what they become by it.—John Ruskin

They Deny Him

It must be difficult to be a professional basketball coach. It seems with each passing year that an increasing number of players are disrespectful to their coaches, referees, other players and the fans. What should be a poetic team exercise of unselfish sportsmanship is more like a circus of *I-isms* where a player's attitude and action state, "It's all about me."

It must be difficult to be God. Daily He observes unruly, disrespectful children who seem more than willing to grieve His Spirit, ignore the commands of His Son and disdain His appointed leaders. What should be a marvelous demonstration of unity and fruit bearing instead is a proclamation that many are worshiping at either the First Church of Me or its sister across the street, the *I-Church*.

Titus 1:16—They profess to know God, but they deny Him by their works. They are detestable, disobedient, and disqualified for any good work.

One reason we struggle with self-denial is that we have failed to understand belonging. The moment we choose to follow after Christ we belong to Him! But even if we rejected Jesus, we still belong to God. The fact that He allows us to exercise free will doesn't negate the reality that He owns us. Our eternal future is determined by Him. If we snub Him on earth, He promises the consequence will be eternal suffering. If we worship Him, He promises, the consequences will be forever rewarding.

What makes self-denial difficult boils down to our failure to understand ownership. *"Summoning the crowd along with His disciples, He said to them, 'If anyone wants to be My follower, he must deny himself, take up his cross, and follow Me'"* (Mark 8:34). The mistake many Christians make is to focus on the cross Jesus asks them to carry. The cross represents suffering and God's plan and we instinctively withdraw from pain or an agenda that is not our own. The setting aside of our ambition, plans and rights to carry out Christ's agenda seems unfair. However, God is not concerned with our concept of fairness; He is concerned with His will being accomplished. The former is self-centered, self-gratifying and eventually ends up opposing God. Lucifer is a great example of this.

When we put our focus on Christ and following after Him, we begin to understand ownership and self-denial is no longer a pressing issue. The cross becomes a welcome part of a sanctified pilgrimage. We discover that true freedom is the pursuit of meeting the Creator's intent. Joy is born in the realization of God's purpose and blessing is bathed in hearing His voice say, "Well done!"

Avoiding Frostbite

Titus 2:11-13—For the grace of God has appeared, with salvation for all people, instructing us to deny godlessness and worldly lusts and to live in a sensible, righteous, and godly way in the present age, while we wait for the blessed hope and the appearing of the glory of our great God and Savior, Jesus Christ.

During winter Ranger school, a technique my father taught me came in handy for protecting my feet. Dad is a marine, (you discover in life there is no such thing as *was* a marine), who fought in the Korean war. He made a vow that he would never complain about the heat for the rest of his life because of the brutal winters on the Korean peninsula. Even living in the tropical Philippines, I never heard him utter the slightest comment regarding heat.

Dad's technique for avoiding frostbite was to keep a pair of wool socks against his stomach. Whenever his feet were numb or wet with perspiration, he would change into a fresh dry pair. That faithful habit saved his hammertoes from getting nailed by the breath of a merciless cold. Many men wouldn't take the time to carry an extra pair of socks and keep them dry. Their lack of discipline cost them dearly.

Discipline is fundamental to our survival. If we don't make the effort to drink, eat and sleep right, our bodies will shut down. Discipline is vital for growth. If we want our minds to expand, we must study. If we want our bodies to be healthy, we must work out!

Spiritual gain also requires discipline. God knows how prone we are to forsake "the harder right for the easier wrong"—to disobey laws He established for our welfare. We can work hard trying to "be spiritual" and fail miserably. Discipline apart from God's grace is as effective as trying to keep a car running forever with only original parts.

Jesus modeled discipline by showing us how to turn away from ungodliness and worldly passions. After a 40 day fast in the desert, He blew apart Satan's temptations with the thundering power of Scripture (Matthew 4:4). Every trap the religious establishment set to embarrass or discredit Him failed. They could find no fault in the Son of Man. Jesus met temptation but refused to succumb. No son or daughter of Adam ever mounted the platform to receive the gold medal for Perfection. Only Jesus lived a holy, sinless life.

Satan cheered His crucifixion and thought His discipline a pathetic waste of time. Heaven roared when He rose up from the grave. He took "just say no" to the limits, loaded the sins of the world on His back and by one perfect sacrifice rocked the gates of hell—permanently. By His example, we learn how to live self-controlled, upright and godly lives. The Apostle Paul wrote:

> I have been crucified with Christ; and I no longer live, but Christ lives in me. The life I now live in the flesh, I live by faith in the Son of God, who loved me and gave Himself for me. I do not set aside the grace of God; for if righteousness comes through the law, then Christ died for nothing (Gal. 2:19b-21).

Paul recognized that discipline through grace cannot fail for grace makes a way where none existed. Therefore, the key to spiritual discipline is to make Jesus' core values our core values, His behavior our standard, His instruction our tenets. He is perfect that we can be made perfect.

Saying no to temptation is not easy! Don't expect to run a spiritual race and not get side cramps. The Bible says we can expect to suffer when we seek to be like Jesus. So we need to be prepared! It's little habits like taking the time to carry extra socks that make a big difference over time. Here are some spiritual disciplines I work hard to perpetuate to prevent becoming a casualty to sin:

● *Daily nourishment in God's Word.* The Bible gives me my marching orders, reveals dangers, provides instruction in how to grow, and lets me know how God expects me to live. Trying to follow Jesus without the Bible would be like hang gliding blindfolded.

● *Consistent time in prayer*—listening to the Holy Spirit, sharing from the heart, confessing where I've blown it.

● *Weekly fellowship* with followers focused on worshiping God.

● *Weekly accountability* to a ranger buddy—we keep close tabs on our weak areas and encourage each other to be faithful.

Unfortunately, discipline is not a popular word today. It is much easier to give in to the flesh so we repeatedly break God's commandments because: someone abused us growing up; "the majority can't be wrong"; living holy costs us popularity, power, position or prominence; we were born different from others; God understands and will forgive me; "only the good die young"; it is easier to disobey.

Don't lose heart in your desire to live above the swamp of sin. *"In struggling against sin, you have not yet resisted to the point of shedding your blood"* (Heb. 12:4). Spiritual discipline is much more than identifying what we ought to do, it is having the courage to walk step-by-step in accordance with God's will! Take the grace God extends in Christ and be strong in the Lord!

Inspiration †††

The surest test of discipline is its absence.—Clara Barton, teacher, nurse and humanitarian who organized the American Red Cross, (1821-1912)

Discipline is the soul of an army. It makes small numbers formidable; procures success to the weak, and esteem to all.—George Washington

Consider God

Philemon 8-10—For this reason, although I have great boldness in Christ to command you to do what is right, I appeal, instead, on the basis of love. I, Paul, as an elderly man and now also as a prisoner of Christ Jesus, appeal to you for my child, whom I fathered while in chains—Onesimus.

Typically, we view leadership as a trait comprised of courage, strong will and that rare ability to see what must be done and inspire people to action. Too often though, we see those who occupy positions of leadership harness power or vested authority to coerce others into giving in. But how often do we hear about leadership from the vantage of love?

Consider God, the ultimate Leader of all leaders. In order to free us from the deadly effect of sin so that we could have a viable relationship with Him, He appealed to us on the basis of love. He sacrificed His Son instead of smoking Satan. He made Himself like us to reach us instead of throwing us away and starting all over.

Consider Jesus. If we knew we were spending our last night with our dedicated team before certain death, most of us would summon our most inspirational thoughts and issue directives we consider critical to mission accomplishment. Jesus washed His follower's feet. He appealed to them on the basis of love.

Consider the Holy Spirit. He speaks with a still small voice when He could so easily split the atoms. He assumes control if we will listen, interceding for us *"with unspoken groanings"* (Rom. 8:26b) based on love.

If I want my children to obey me, I do not raise my voice I raise my heart. If they are to embrace what is true and noble they must know what it means to be truly and nobly embraced. I learn this from my Father who moves me to tears by His excellent patience, kindness, and gentleness. So often, I fall short of His will yet I find His authority sewn with mercy. He inspires me to do what is right from the basis of love.

St. Augustine wrote, "Do you wish to rise? Begin by descending. You plan a tower that will pierce the clouds? Lay first the foundation of humility." Do you wish to lead? Start with love. Do you hope for success in the lives of those you serve? Model Christ-likeness. The world's concept of leadership is based on gain. Heaven's concept of leadership is based on love. The former sees you for what you will do the latter for who you are.

Inspiration † † †

You do not lead by hitting people over the head—that's assault, not leadership.—President Dwight D. Eisenhower, 5 star general, (1890-1969)

Drifting

When we navigate with a compass, we must stay on the precise azimuth or we get off course. Just walking across uneven land, over hills and through brush will change our direction and can easily cause us to get lost. I remember as a child in Japan, descending from the top of Mt. Fuji with two other boys. We left the sure circular path to take a short cut. But coming down the steep slope, we walked at an angle and ended up far away from our intended destination, lost and separated from the rest of our group. One of my two friends had already been lost in Red Square. Getting lost on Mt. Fuji and ending up in a police station *really* traumatized him! Fortunately, our parents found us and we each gained a great story to tell people.

Hebrews 2:1—We must therefore pay even more attention to what we have heard, so that we will not drift away.

I received a letter from Barb with an update on her children. She shared about her little grandson. He has such a fierce temper that he will hold his breath and pass out! She observed that even little children demonstrate the sin nature so prevalent in all of us. Morality is not something we easily attain and maintain on perfect course. The author of Hebrews communicates this to his readers. We have a responsibility to pay attention to the truth God reveals to us otherwise we will drift away.

Drifting objects in water are easy to spot. A piece of wood is caught in the strongest current and floats with it. In some ways, this illustrates what happens with followers of Jesus. There are at least five currents, often subtle, which pull us away from God's course. Many of us float with *distractions*. Instead of making time to be with the Lord, we fill our lives with other activities. We set aside what is best or right for what is alluring or convenient.

Some of us are misled by *deception*. We put greater stock in science, education, tradition or what is popularly deemed correct at the expense of faith, steadfastness and the willingness to listen intently to the leading of the Holy Spirit. The voice of the world holds more weight than the whispers of heaven or the words of Scripture.

Others of us drift because of *demands*. Jobs and relationships can suck the spiritual life out of us if we let them. We become so busy needing to meet expectations or please people that we neglect to make time for spiritual nourishment. We stop looking to God and live by our calendars and the never-ending parade of events and projects. We forget how to rest with minds racing to the next . . .

Difficulties cause drifting. Sickness or sadness weighs us down. We become so absorbed in our pain that we doubt our Healer. Persecution and adversity cause us to fear standing with Jesus. We run confused like Elijah, far into the desert only to be burned in the process.

Certainly, *disobedience* creates drift. Whenever we tell God "No!" and go our way should we be surprised when we can no longer feel His presence or experience His blessing?

So, let's reset our azimuths. Let's keep *"our eyes on Jesus, the source and perfecter of our faith"* (Heb. 12:2). Let's paddle out of those foolish, twirling eddies and get back on track with our Lord. There is no fulfillment in deviating from truth on the road home!

Inspiration † † †

I find the great thing in this world is not so much where we stand, as in what direction we are moving: To reach the port of heaven, we must sail sometimes with the wind and sometimes against it, but we must sail, and not drift, nor lie at anchor.—Marjorie Holmes, author

Too many of us are caught acting as Christians. The life of many Christians to-day is largely a pretence. They live a 'spiritual' life, talk a 'spiritual' language, adopt 'spiritual' attitudes, but they are doing the whole thing themselves. It is the effort involved that should reveal to them that something is wrong.—Watchman Nee in *Sit Walk Stand*

Miracles

Hebrews 2:4—At the same time, God also testified by signs and wonders, various miracles, and distributions of gifts from the Holy Spirit according to His will.

There are those in Christendom who honestly believe that God no longer works miracles—His supernatural workings ended after the time of Christ and the early Apostles. Without meaning to be disrespectful, I have always believed such notions to be hogwash for two reasons. First, I see nothing in Scripture that restricts God from defying the laws of physics in the lives of people today. Second, I have witnessed firsthand, His awesome handiwork.

When I was a boy, I, along with a great number of people, prayed that my mother would be healed of cancer. She died. When the doctors informed my wife and me that our son Bryan had little to no chance of surviving a brain-stem tumor a large number of us prayed that our son would be healed of cancer. He was miraculously cured during a time of worship and prayer for his healing. He remains alive on earth and serves as a great inspiration to the many who know him. Why does the Holy Spirit intervene and miraculously touch some people while at other times remain seemingly aloof and silent?

There will always be those who refuse to believe God does anything on earth anymore. Life membership in the Skeptics Club is free for the taking. For many it is difficult to trust in a miracle-working Father when the most familiar music one hears is the sound of a kicked bucket. Yet, across the globe right now, God is at work—in a remote Indian village, a teeming Korean metropolis, a dilapidated Malawi shack, a packed Brazilian stadium. If we could stop for a moment and don supernatural headphones, we would hear His voice instructing His angels, directing His servants, proclaiming His will! How and why we may not understand, but make no mistake, He is at work—there are too many accounts across the earth by followers of Jesus to deny this truth.

Jesus taught His disciples to pray, *"Our Father in heaven, Your name be honored as holy. Your kingdom come. Your will be done on earth as it is in heaven"* (Mat. 6:9,10). Jesus' teaching on prayer was not a one-time teaching for a one-time generation. This was a divine directive to be taught to a chain of disciples each willing to arise, place their faith in God, and repeatedly request *"Do your will on earth,"* here—this planet, today—this hour! Much of that work will be leading naturally those who are obedient. But some of that work will be supernatural intervening on behalf of those who call upon His name. There is the miraculous and the mira*clueless*. We miss the former and live in the latter if we slap on God human fetters of disbelief.

Inspiration †††

Miracles are a retelling in small letters of the very same story which is written across the whole world in letters too large for some of us to see.—C. S. Lewis

If God wants to perform a small miracle; he places us in difficult circumstances; If he wants to perform a mighty miracle, he places us in absolutely impossible circumstances—Watchman Nee

Like Her Mother

Vanadium stared at the brawny sweat-laden arms of Dowson as he slammed the pick repeatedly into the soil. All she wanted was a nice hole. But he was getting nowhere. Finally, frustrated and tired, he motioned for her to come outside. "It's no use! This hill is made of granite. Are you sure we can't put this feeder somewhere else?"

"No! I want it right here" she stubbornly insisted. She threw down her glass that shattered, splattering Martini across a thirsty ground. She was about to say something snide when he threw up his hands and turned away and in so doing awakened an old memory. It was thirty years ago on this same day, her father quietly closed the door and led two frightened children away from a screaming mother. He gave up living with a contentious wife who refused to stop drinking and badly abused them. The last memory Vanadium had of her mother was a glass smashing against a closed door.

Tears formed and began a downward journey. The sweet little girl who sang to Jesus, the studious teen who inspired others by her faithful love for God, the young bride praised by a church full of friends had somehow become like her mother!

Hebrews 3:7,8a, 12—Therefore, as the Holy Spirit says: Today, if you hear His voice, do not harden your hearts as in the rebellion, on the day of testing in the desert . . . Watch out, brothers, so that there won't be in any of you an evil, unbelieving heart that departs from the living God.

(Two years later) Vanadium Denison* speaks to a class of young married couples. Her eyes sparkle, her voice is gentle and they can only marvel at the transformation. They listen closely to words born from lessons learned. Hardness cannot possess a heart by storming it. It wins by subtle steps. It misleads thoughts and then pampers pride so that it cannot admit to being wrong. It establishes habits that feed an eager flesh. It disdains as stale and irrelevant—truth. Soon a diet of soap operas replaces the hour of prayer. The office gossip becomes tastier than God's Word. Hardness welcomes compromise like some long-lost brother. Social drinks expand to stashing bottles. Sharing about the Lord becomes taboo for He might offend her liberated friends. Going to church is not fulfilling for hardness finds the faults of others and twists them. Like parched ground that will not give, hardness gains strength by drought. My friends, if you want to be like Jesus you can't live like Judas.

Inspiration † † †

I think there is only one quality worse than hardness of heart and that is softness of head.—Theodore Roosevelt

*Fictitious person

The Right Food

The Thanksgiving holiday is supposed to be about remembering how blessed we are by our Almighty Father in heaven. If gratitude is the point, food is the reminder. In truth, a hearty feast is a wonderful custom for celebrating our blessings. Not a Thanksgiving goes by for me that I don't think back to traveling to Newburgh, NY with my roommate and best friend, Dave Mead. We would totally stuff ourselves at his grandmother's house—eating was a competitive sport for two young cadets.

Hebrews 5:13,14—Now everyone who lives on milk is inexperienced with the message about righteousness, because he is an infant. But solid food is for the mature—for those whose senses have been trained to distinguish between good and evil.

Without food, we could not survive. However, it's not just eating that is important, it is what kind of food we eat that determines our health. If all we ever drank was milk, our bodies would be nutrient-deficient and we would fall increasingly susceptible to germs and disease. You say, "Well duh!" But, increasingly I am finding miserable Christians (which should be an oxymoron). The common denominator is that they are content to drink milk. They will occasionally attend church, infrequently talk to God and that pretty well sums up their spiritual diet. The consequences of this anemic habit are poor decision-making, nonexistent spiritual fruit, a propensity to sin, a high-guilt load and a weak relationship (friendship) with God.

Spiritual maturity is a direct byproduct of disciplined eating! If we want to know God, we *must* chew on His Word. Those who consistently require teaching on the *"elementary truths"* of Scripture (vs. 12) will not progress to teaching about living righteously. Generally, a dust covered Bible reveals a stagnant believer.

God never intended for us to sit down to a banquet of milk. Praise Him! He gives us an assortment of fruit, vegetables, meat and grains we are to digest for His glory and our gain! If you want to know the difference between good and evil look at what you are eating!

Inspiration † † †

Put your nose into the Bible everyday. It is your spiritual food. And then share it. Make a vow not to be a lukewarm Christian.—Kirk Cameron, actor

Vigilant

Outside my study window, a squirrel sits in our tire swing. He bends his head beneath the black rubber but only for a moment. Quickly he pops back up and surveys the yard. This process repeats for several minutes until a small Voice reminds me of a vital truth. The squirrel knows he has natural enemies he must avoid to survive; whether it is Bear, our good-natured Rottweiler, Mel, our stalking cat, or some dive-bombing hawk. There are no old, careless squirrels in our neighborhood.

Amos 6:1—Woe to those who are at ease in Zion and to those who feel secure on the hill of Samaria—the notable people in this first of the nations, those the house of Israel comes to.

God does not like complacency, the cousin of laziness and the indifferent spirit that gives the enemy ample opportunity to destroy us. Peter warned us, *"Be self-controlled and vigilant always, for your enemy the devil is always about, prowling like a lion roaring for its prey"* (1 Pe. 5:8 PT). But how heeded is his solemn advice?

After consuming a large meal on Thanksgiving, my proclivity is towards sleep. Holidays hardly inspire alertness. In the midst of mirth are the pawprints of Satan. To be vigilant requires three conditions. *First, we must know what we value.* When we lose sight of what is most important and take for granted what is sacred, we slide into complacency and stop protecting what matters. *Second, we must know our enemies.* There will always be those who would destroy what we value, to impose what they deem important. Jesus warned Peter that Satan does not have *"in mind the things of God, but the things of men"* (Mat. 16:23b NIV). The things of men are cravings, lustful eyes and pride (see 1 John 2:16). There is an ever-growing cast of those who hate what God loves. Therefore, if we think we have no enemies, then somewhere along the way we stopped identifying with Jesus. *Third, we must decide to what extent we are willing to go to protect what we value.* Unless we are willing to die for Christ, we have frail motive to be alert. Jesus told Peter in John 21:18, *"I assure you: When you were young, you would tie your belt and walk wherever you wanted. But when you grow old, you will stretch out your hands and someone else will tie you and carry you where you don't want to go."*

The storm clouds are gathering; the days grow short. In the midst of Thanksgiving, don't be caught unprepared. Be alert! Be vigilant!

Inspiration †††

We are not weak if we make a proper use of those means which the God of Nature has placed in our power... the battle, sir, is not to the strong alone it is to the vigilant, the active, the brave.—Patrick Henry, Virginian Governor, statesman, (1736-1799)

After Waiting Patiently

"I don't get it," she says. Her eyes finish a sentence bereft of words. She cannot understand why her morale seems as withered as the orchid that drops its petals before a gray sky. She thinks the mark of spiritual authenticity is the ability to call on God and experience His resolving touch to her whatever problem. But when He does not come or meet her expectations, her patience slips another notch. It's as if He does not care. Slowly she slips into a state of spiritual lethargy marked by three words, "I don't care!"

If prayer seems as useful as removing weeds by hand, patience seems as valid as turtles trying to fly. The driver to our right cuts us off and we fume. The boss treats us unjustly and to God we cry "FOUL!" We wait for recognition that never comes. We sing our hearts out before a microphone turned off. What good is it to serve when things do not turn out right? So we blare to the beat of the temper tantrum.

Hebrews 6:11-12,15—Now we want each of you to demonstrate the same diligence for the final realization of your hope, so that you won't become lazy, but imitators of those who inherit the promises through faith and perseverance . . . And so, after waiting patiently, Abraham obtained the promise.

If there were no promises from God, patience would be pointless. Life would be best lived by seizing pleasure by the throat. Isn't impatience in truth lack of faith? We hardly believe that God understands our circumstances and is truly sovereign. The proof of our unbelief is our perpetual lapse into frustration. Conversely, patience confirmed is our ability to stand unfazed by a chain of events whose links seem unending.

If it is patience that you want, then it is faith you must have—a faith welded securely to God's promises. When Patience holds hands with Faith, they are always headed to Joy's house to feed on God's promises. They will not be lassoed to the stake of selfishness. Their freedom to walk and wait comes in the secure belief that *Lord* means possessor of ultimate authority. What God says He is able to do, He will do for our betterment, when He is ready. Hallelujah!

Inspiration † † †

Have patience with all things, But, first of all with yourself.—Saint Francis de Sales, Swiss pastor, (1567-1622)

Patience is the companion of wisdom.—Saint Augustine

Stuck on the Tarmac

Saturday night I was supposed to be at a banquet in Beaverton. Instead, I found myself sitting on a broken plane in Denver. The United pilot informed us that a navigational piece of equipment on our jet was not operable. We waited for mechanics to fix the broken system and watched as the little red ball in the sky fell out of view. Finally, our good-humored pilot confessed that the job was more complicated than expected. While he could fly the plane to Oregon without the instrument's help, he elected not to as a matter of safety. He needed the assurance that if anything should go wrong that system would work and warn us should the aircraft be too close to the ground. Because we knew we would be winging over large mountains, we clapped our hands in agreement. Finally, almost four hours later, we took off on a different plane United provided.

What was the focus of everyone on that aircraft? It was to reach our intended destination! When confronted with adversity coupled with being stuck in an airport for an extended period, it was amazing how heightened the urge was to get home. But I heard no complaints about our pilot's decision. We needed assurance that our metal-skinned bird could safely perform.

I am so glad that my Pilot is perfectly able to bring me home. He is not dependent upon equipment. He has no industry-imposed sleep requirements. He is unfazed by the needs of His passengers. While I don't know when I will arrive at my final destination, there is no doubt that I will reach it. My Lord who leads me has never failed. His love, leadership and wisdom are legendary. He has a perfect safety record. His only crash was deliberate and His enemies were stunned to learn He survived!

Hebrews 10:21-23—and since we have a great high priest over the house of God, let us draw near with a true heart in full assurance of faith, our hearts sprinkled clean from an evil conscience and our bodies washed in pure water. Let us hold on to the confession of our hope without wavering, for He who promised is faithful.

Brother Lawrence & Frank Laubach wrote in *Practicing His Presence,* "Men amuse themselves with trivial devotions which change daily instead of making faith in God the rule of their conduct." The measure of true assurance comes through testing. The ability to look past death with confidence comes through faithfully entrusting our lives to Jesus. He claims to be the only One capable of bringing us to heaven (John 14:6). Do you believe Him?

Tenacity

Hebrews 10:34,35—For you sympathized with the prisoners and accepted with joy the confiscation of your possessions, knowing that you yourselves have a better and enduring possession. So don't throw away your confidence, which has a great reward.

Have you ever observed young children competing in sports? I think one of the most hilarious, heartwarming sights is watching boys and girls on a soccer field. Usually one or two kids understand the game and are competitive. They typically score the goals or perform heroically on defense. Meanwhile, the rest of the players sort of meander around as a herd not sure what to do, not overly motivated but having fun.

Years ago, I played basketball with my seven-year old nephew, Joshua Ennis. We teamed up against my two boys. I thought it would be a fun time of hoops before we headed home. Instead, I got to see what tenacity looks like. Josh was all over the court. He made swarming bees look slow. There was not a rebound, or dribble, or shot he did not contest. He unselfishly passed the ball and essentially ran rings around the three of us. Even Stephen, our resident speedster was impressed. I don't believe there was ever one moment when Josh didn't think he would win. It didn't matter if the score was against us. He gave his all. He reminded me of his competitive mother, (my sister) Barbie, another good athlete.

I've been around quitters before. You probably have too. In fact, I remember times in my life when I have given up and have had to address character issues. I can think of people I've let down. I also know it's pretty hard to keep a good attitude working with people, who when the going gets tough, have a 101 ways to exit the arena. Conversely, it is exhilarating to be teamed up with those who are focused on serving God well and come Hades or high water are not giving up.

Do you know Jesus as your Lord and Savior? If so, you are privy to a dynamic truth.

For this is what love for God is: to keep His commands. Now His commands are not a burden, because whatever has been born of God conquers the world. This is the victory that has conquered the world: our faith. And who is the one who conquers the world but the one who believes that Jesus is the Son of God? (1 Jn. 5:3-5).

God gave you the victory through Jesus Christ! So if you are sitting on the sidelines pouting, feeling defeated, looking like a spare tire with a spike through the center, knock it off! Get up and believe! Jesus will give you the strength you need if you will only trust Him and persevere! The world will never fall in love with a Savior whose followers live as if they have lost! Would you? Tenacity is a must!

Living with PTSD

Felix and Brenda* came into our center for food. She wore the look of a bruised, defeated woman. Felix walked hunched and tired. Somberly he described how gang members in Boise, Idaho robbed them, beating them nearly to death. He subsequently suffered grand mal seizures and Brenda several mini-strokes. They were able to identify only one of their attackers. He was imprisoned for attempted murder and robbery but refused to reveal his accomplices so Felix and Brenda were relocated to protect them from further attack.

Imagine not being able to sleep at night fearing another assault. Picture the smashing of peace by emotional breakdowns and you get an idea why doctors diagnosed Felix as suffering *Post Traumatic Stress Disorder* (PTSD) and elected to sedate him with medicine.

Felix shared that the drugs were not alleviating his anxiety. But I had something far better than medicine to give him. "Felix, what is the worse thing that can happen to you?" He paused and thought before speaking, "I die." "That's right, and if you die that is a bonus because you will be with Jesus." He thought about that and smiled. Felix and Brenda both love the Lord, but their relationship flounders on a reef smashed by waves of evil.

David lived for years constantly on the run from a king and an army bent on destroying him. He continually endured hardships. Yet, he wrote, *"Even when I go through the darkest valley, I fear no danger, for You are with me; Your rod and Your staff—they comfort me"* (Psa. 23:4). Paul was beaten, stoned and left for dead, shipwrecked, imprisoned multiple times and constantly harassed for his beliefs. Yet knowing he would be killed he confidently stated, *"For me, living is Christ and dying is gain"* (Php. 1:21). How did these Biblical heroes live without fearing evil?

Hebrews 11:37-40—They were stoned, they were sawed in two, they died by the sword, they wandered about in sheepskins, in goatskins, destitute, afflicted, and mistreated. The world was not worthy of them. They wandered in deserts, mountains, caves, and holes in the ground. All these were approved through their faith, but they did not receive what was promised, since God had provided something better for us, so that they would not be made perfect without us.

We can live with PTSD and be in bondage to fear. Or we can live with *Present Tranquillity Following Jesus* (PTFJ) bonded by faith. It comes down to choice. I know people who suffer the ravages of war, who experienced unmentionable horrors yet walk serenely because they believe in their Shepherd! His rod and staff are sufficient. Faith <u>cannot</u> be defeated by sin, disease or suffering. We choose to either trust God or suffer the consequences that come when we let our problems replace Him.

Felix and Brenda go to bed and rest with Jesus. If you are murdered, the same God who allowed you to die will eternally bathe you in His glowing love. Faith is not intimidated by stress! Faith *is* nourished by appropriating favor! In the midst of pain, God loves us. In the trials we endure, His mercy is sufficient. His promises are real, eternal and distinctly fashioned for our joy. Either we live confidently believing or we fearfully live dying.

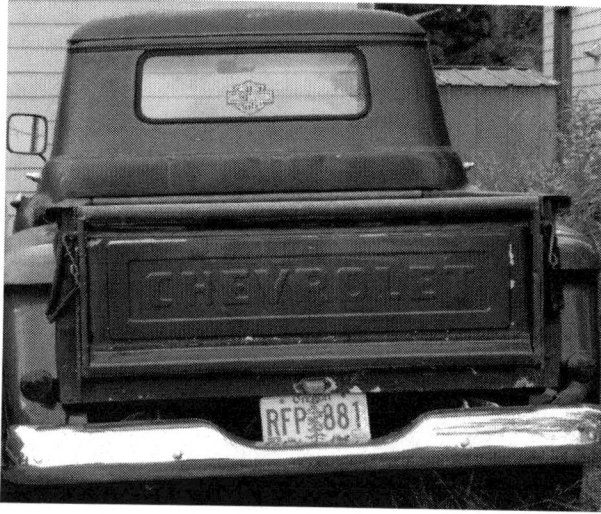

Inspiration † † †

Faith is not belief without proof, but trust without reservation.—D. Elton Trueblood, author, theologian, (1900-1994)

God is not looking for nibblers of the possible but for grabbers of the impossible—Charles Thomas Studd (known as C.T.) English cricketer and missionary to China, India and Central Africa, founded the Worldwide Evangelisation Crusade (now WEC International), (1860-1931)

Faith is not a product but a process. It is a pilgrimage, a long journey in which we need refreshment and rest along the way. And prayer provides that needed refreshment—Robert V. Thompson, pastor

*Not their real names

Instead He Went Out

Hebrews 12:25—See that you do not reject the One who speaks; for if they did not escape when they rejected Him who warned them on earth, even less will we if we turn away from Him who warns us from heaven.

A man with leprosy came to Jesus and begged Him on his knees, *"If you are willing, you can make me clean"* (Mark 1:40 NIV). Jesus was filled with compassion and touched the leper—healing him. Then He did a curious thing. He strongly warned the man not to tell anyone but to go and show himself to a priest and offer the sacrifices that Moses commanded regarding cleansing. Jesus told him this would be a testimony to them (the priests and fellow Jews).

Mark goes on to write, *"Instead he went out and began to talk freely spreading the news"* (1:45 NIV). The word *"instead"* ought to get our attention. It is the precursor of disobedience and a signal that God's instruction is about to be waylaid. This man undoubtedly thought, "Whooooowee! I'm not a leper anymore. Jesus is awesome! I'll tell people about Him since He just helped me!" We sympathetically agree and understand why he would trumpet the great news—"I'm healed!"

I've read the passage in Mark countless times and I have to admit, I've always glossed over his action as both understandable and *no big deal.* It is not as if he was rejecting Jesus as the author of Hebrews mentions in the passage of meditation. But wait a second, while disobedience may not be total rejection it is certainly partial rejection. Selective disobedience to God's instruction is still refusal to follow His will. In truth, I'm like the healed leper—I can think of times when God has brought His word to mind and I liked my idea better.

That *harmless* broadcasting severely crimped Jesus' ministry. As a result of all the commotion, Jesus could not enter a town openly. He had to stay outside in lonely places (1:45). *Hmmm.* I wonder how many times I've left the Savior lonely because I chose celebration when He wanted silence. I wonder how many times I've pushed my agenda because it seemed *right—* resisting the Holy Spirit's leading. I wonder how many victories I might have experienced if I had just listened and obeyed. If Jesus possesses the power to make me clean, what gives me the right ever to ignore His guidance? The bath of grace is so luxurious it's easy to spurn the soap of discipline. I am reminded again, of how important obedience is. What God says I need to do.

Inspiration †††

The magnitude of an offence is determined, not alone by the nature of the offence, but by the dignity of the one against whom it is committed.—J. Oswald Sanders in *The Holy Spirit And His Gifts*

Angels as Guests

Benjamin Franklin is quoted as saying, "Fish and visitors smell in three days." He must have had some trying guests underfoot! Pastor Erwin W. Lutzer of the Moody Church in Chicago taught:

Hospitality is a test for godliness because those who are selfish do not like strangers (especially needy ones) to intrude upon their private lives. They prefer their own friends who share their life-style. Only the humble have the necessary resources to give of themselves to those who could never give of themselves in return.

Hebrews 13:2—Don't neglect to show hospitality, for by doing this some have welcomed angels as guests without knowing it.

Imagine encountering someone you don't know, a person in need. In kindness, you reach out and minister whether by word, providing food, giving shelter or lending monetary assistance. You give with no concern for repayment. What if you were being tested by God? I'd hate to find out I was with an angel and behaved like a devil.

Hospitality is the ability to serve strangers or friends by welcoming acts of kindness. By doing this we honor God. It can be as much a one-time action as a long-extended practice. Professor Joe Aldrich faithfully taught his students, "People don't care how much you know until they know how much you care." In a land that deifies selfishness, hospitality gives its last glass of water to a hot, weary traveler. In a society that perfects privatization, hospitality has the faith to be vulnerable by opening up our hands to serve anyone for Jesus.

If your church is not growing, run a hospitality diagnostics check. Are you welcoming visitors? I don't mean the official handshake from an assigned greeter. Who is making the time to find out as much as possible about the newcomers and then works to welcome them to the fellowship?

I grew up in a family where people constantly lived in our home. It wasn't always convenient. Sacrifices were involved, personalities did not always mesh. But I learned by watching my parents that investing in the lives of people is profoundly rewarding.

It's not easy to be hospitable. Perhaps you're tired. Take heart friend! Your caring spirit blesses in ways you'll never know. Refresh yourself in the Master. Keep your eyes on Him. The Jesus who washed His disciples' feet wants to work through our hands to bless those hungry to know His love.

Inspiration † † †

Hospitality is one form of worship.—Jewish Proverb

A New Altar

Hebrews 13:10-14—We have an altar from which those who serve the tabernacle do not have a right to eat. For the bodies of those animals whose blood is brought into the holy of holies by the high priest as a sin offering are burned outside the camp. Therefore Jesus also suffered outside the gate, so that He might sanctify the people by His own blood. Let us then go to Him outside the camp, bearing His disgrace. For here we do not have an enduring city; instead, we seek the one to come.

Can you see the early Christians trembling? What could they offer to counter the religious leaders of their day whose Mosaic laws centered on the altar? The author of Hebrews wastes no time in dealing with this crisis. Under the inspiration of the Holy Spirit he reminds his fellow believers that they had the final perfect altar—the cross! Jesus Christ made the ultimate sacrifice for mankind while crucified. Once for all, sin was dealt with forever. But it is not the cross that is to be worshiped. It is the risen Savior we follow. This must challenge us deeply!

Whom do I serve? Is my citizenship in the Nation of Pride? Is my home in the State of Carnality? Which county holds my life certificate: Pleasure, Power, Prestige, or Possession? Where exactly is home—98765 Fleshly Dr.? If so, I serve myself. The city of Sin is never easy to leave but I must walk away from it if I am to follow the Lord.

Whom do I serve? The people around me are not stupid. It is not my business card that reveals who I work for but rather my character/action card. They know who rules the city and the cost it takes to leave. The same Lord I follow has often called them to depart.

Whom do I serve? I'd rather be foolish in the eyes of the world for believing there is only one road home than compromise my faith on the altar of manmade religion. Call me a fool for seeking an unknown heaven managed by an unseen God. Just let me be a worthy idiot in His eyes. If mocking is the price, what a pittance compared to the eternal glory of worshiping Jesus. *"For consider Him who endured such hostility from sinners against Himself, so that you won't grow weary and lose heart"* (Heb. 12:3).

Inspiration † † †

Word-centeredness and Spirit-fullness are joined at the altar of songful worship, and this balance confronts anyone's temptation to sacrifice either since both are made interdependent.—Jack Hayford in *Worship His Majesty*

The Road Home Rally

So this is not exactly what you would expect in a devotional, but let's do something different today—something that will require you to set aside some extended time, invite over friends and take a test. Yep—a test! You probably are too engaged to pull this off today, and if so, don't worry about it, just schedule a time in the not too distant future, and do what I suggest. I am not trying to be bossy; I just have the advantage of experience. I did with a group what I am about to ask you to do and it was quite productive (and revealing)!

Invite up to 12 people (no more than that and they all must be Jesus-followers) over to your home or a central place to meet.   You are going to examine how much you and your friends really know about key spiritual areas. Our spiritual comprehension is critical to our witness, our growth and our understanding of God. The directions are simple and straightforward. Have fun and please let me know how the event turns out—or how it can be improved! You can email me at dan@firstcause.org.

The Road Home Rally

● Fellowship: Write down one spiritual lesson you learned this past week and why it was important for you. {Each person who remembers a lesson should get to share.}

● Witnessing: Drama Sketch: (5 minutes) Depending on how many are gathered, divide into groups of three and have each group pick and act out one of the scenarios below:

1. Create a drama sketch that illustrates sharing the gospel with a classmate at school, a co-worker, a neighbor or a family member

2. Create a drama sketch that shares the gospel with someone who just lost a close relative.

3. Have one person share a three-minute testimony that explains: life before knowing Jesus, how they came to know Christ and what it is like now that they follow Him.

● Worship: Choose a worship song to sing together, and then after singing it analyze why that song is important. Ask each person: "Is worship in my life currently stale or vibrant?"

● Bible: Memorize Psalm 25:4,5 then take the Scripture Quiz. {Divide questions up among the members or have everyone find all the answers depending on how much time you have together.}

1. Find two musical instruments mentioned in Psalms

2. List three of the ten commandments and cite where they are found in the Bible.

3. Why was God angry with King Manasseh of Judah? (Hint: Look in 2 Kings)

4.   What was Nehemiah's brother's name, what city did Nehemiah put him in charge of and why did he choose him to be in charge as well as Hananiah?

5.   What promise did Job make in chapter 31 of Job and what can we learn from his example?

6.   List three passages in Isaiah that foretell the coming of Jesus

7.   What King was so angry that he threw 3 men in a furnace and what were the names of the 3 victims? (See the book of Daniel)

8.   What is amazing about the book of Hosea? {Hint: What did God ask Hosea to do?}

9.   Which gospel account tells the story of a man who was an invalid for 38 years and Jesus found lying beside a pool?   (Cite the chapter and verses)

10.   Name at least five men who accompanied Paul on his missionary journeys.

● Prayer:

1.   List five things for which you would like to praise God

2.   List and pray for the names of five people that do not know Jesus

3.   Each person share one personal prayer request

● Hospitality: Have each person share the last time he or she served someone and what was the outcome? Come up with a group idea of how you all could collectively serve a needy nonChristian family/person and model the love of Christ.   Go do it on the agreed upon date.

● Apologetics:

1.   How would you answer someone biblically who says there are many ways to get to heaven?

2.   How would you defend your faith against someone who says there are no absolutes?

3.   What verse in the New Testament tells us to be prepared to give an answer for the reason for what we believe?

James 1:4—Perseverance must finish its work so that you may be mature and complete, not lacking anything.

Inspiration † † †

Would that so-called Christian people would more earnestly and searchingly ask themselves why it is that, with such possibilities offered to them their actual attainments should be so small.—Alexander Maclaren, Scottish Baptist pastor, (1826-1910)

Kalimina

In Chimpembelle Village, Zambia, Onedy Kalimina's uncle died. When the Head Man dies, one of his relatives on the mother's side is chosen to replace him. As it happened, the 22 year-old Kalimina was chosen. He was taken to the village witch doctor who prepared a charm called *Chitumya*. Then he was asked to kneel down and pray *"Chitumya come into me and I come into you."* After praying this, Kalimina took a ceremonial bath and put on an armband for protection that no one else was ever to see. This occurred in 1990.

While taking a college course, a friend shared with Kalimina about Jesus Christ. The Holy Spirit convicted him and on February 20, 1991, he knelt down and confessed his need for Christ. At 6:00 a.m. the next morning, he heard a voice calling "Kalimina, the child of God does not put on that band." Twice more the voice repeated the same message. So Kalimina responded, *"What do I do?"* In response, he heard the voice say, "Take that band off your arm, put it in a plastic bag and go to the mountain." He obeyed. On the mountain the voice said, "Pray *'Satan I now renounce with your works and word. I am now for Jesus.'"* After doing this, he threw away the band and immediately felt unburdened.

Kalimina for the first time went to church. While there he heard a voice speaking, "Kalimina, look at where the pastor is standing. That is where you will stand." He heard this message three times. Emboldened, Kalimina shared his faith in Jesus with his two wives. They both put their trust in the Lord and began attending church with him. Yet again, the voice spoke telling him that he must share Jesus with people but having two wives was a conflict. So he went to prayer.

While praying, Kalimina had a vision. His second wife was about to board a train for a journey. When the train came, he got his bag and jumped aboard. But his wife was still not on so he jumped off to be with her. After this vision, the voice said, "The train is ministry and you cannot go on it with the second wife." Three days later, he dreamed he was on a journey with his first wife and they were taking a car. Kalimina jumped into the car but the wife was not there so he got out and then woke up. He cried out, *"God I'm confused. This is my first wife. I can't leave the wife of my youth!"* But God was quiet.

One year later, Kalimina's second wife came to him and said, "I am not your wife, I must go back to my parents." Now he was left with his first wife. A year later she died. So he went looking for his second wife only to find she had married another man. So the single father with five children cried out, *"Lord, why has my first wife died?"* God spoke to him and said, "I want you to go into ministry with a different wife." So he asked God for a wife who loved Jesus, loved children and loved farming.

James 1:18—By His own choice, He gave us a new birth by the message of truth so that we would be the firstfruits of His creatures.

In 1999, the Lord gave Kalimina a widow with four of her own children. Hephziba told him she wanted to work for God, keep orphans and farm. They soon added two more children for a total of eleven kids. Today, the oldest is nineteen and the youngest is eleven. With his family, he walks the seven kilometers to the church he pastors, a trek that takes an hour and a half. In 2005, Kalimina led a Head Man, Ezlon, in a nearby village to Christ and helped him escape his charms.

Recently, our disciple making leaders at a pastors' conference in Kabwe, Zambia trained Kalimina. This wonderful man committed his life to be an equipping leader for disciple making. They were able to spend time training him in his own home where he holds godly influence over the 400 villagers. Two Head Men hope to spread what they have learned to other villages. Will you pray for God's strength and blessing to be upon Kalimina and Ezlon as they bring hope with training to those who are famished for truth? Whether you are in an African village or a metropolitan city, it doesn't matter who you are or where you are, God wants to use you to serve Him and share the gospel. He chose to give us new birth by His incomparable truth so that we might bear fruit!

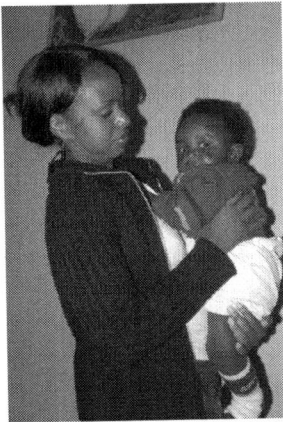

Inspiration † † †

Discipleship is not a program. It is not a ministry. It is a lifelong commitment to a lifestyle.—George Barna in *Growing True Disciples*

Don't Assume, Interact

I am convinced that I have found one of the causes of cancer—it's a small mass of cells that when left on its own rapidly grows into a destructive monster. The cells are called assumptions.

The head of an organization was badly floundering. Her managers were avoiding her because her leadership style was making their lives miserable. Her employees were looking for jobs with other companies. Her corporate headquarters debated if she would have to be replaced. It all seemed off kilter because this woman has a great personality, is bright and should be effective in leading her folks. What went wrong?

I spent time with Kim and her top manager, Rob.* He was so upset with her that he could not sit and face her in the room. It was obvious that he was hurt and angry. In asking a series of questions, we were able to make some important discoveries. First, Kim was given a mandate before taking over the organization that she needed to "clean house" because her group was the poorest performer in the corporation with the wrong people making leadership decisions. So she came down and immediately took charge and in doing so, alienated almost everyone. Instead of getting to know the people and assessing what actions she should take, she jumped in as a micromanaging dictator.

As a people-person, Kim often took the time to get out of her office and meet with her employees. Unfortunately, she also often tasked them with work bypassing their bosses. Her intentions were good. She knew her managers were busy and wanted to save time. But her actions alienated them because they felt distrusted. She also had a penchant for changing her mind when decision-making. This caused uncertainty among her team leaders and doubt regarding her competency.

Rob, in listening to Kim, began to see why she behaved the way she did. Kim, likewise, noticed his hurt and realized the consequences of her actions. Painfully they worked through a series of assumptions each had created towards how Kim should lead. As they interacted, healing began to take place. By the time we were done meeting, both were able to face each other and affirm that they valued each other and wanted very much to work as a team. This same process then was duplicated with Nancy, another manager greatly at odds with Kim. It was a fascinating example of what happens when leaders fail to interact properly and resort instead to blaming.

James 1:19,20—My dearly loved brothers, understand this: everyone must be quick to hear, slow to speak, and slow to anger, for man's anger does not accomplish God's righteousness.

The prefix "inter" according to the *Encarta World English Dictionary* means "*between, among, mutual, reciprocal.*" When combined with action we get the word interaction, which is defined as "*communication between or joint activity involving two or more people.*" James, the brother of Jesus, gives us rich wisdom on the topic of interaction. We must be great listeners, choose our words carefully and not have quick tempers. Without effective interaction, people are constantly negotiating the quagmire of misunderstanding.

The keys to good interaction require:

- Constant communication: active listening with wise speaking
- Trust
- Empathy
- Honesty

God, realizing how corrupted we are by our sin nature, solved our curse by sending Jesus to live among us. He defined interaction by becoming like us so as to empathize with our situation. He moved beyond our confined intellect to reach our unrefined hearts. For those who recognized their ineptitude and responded in faith to His love overtures, He indwelt Himself! Just think, God values us and wants to interact with us so much that He placed His Holy Spirit inside us to testify with our spirit that we are His children! His Spirit intercedes for us with unspoken groanings (Romans 8:16,26). That is interaction at its best. Something to think about . . . in reveration!

Inspiration †††

The components of a belief, then, are three: first, it is something of which we are aware. Second, it satisfies the irritation caused by doubt. And finally, it involves the establishment in our nature of a rule of action or a *habit.*—Norman Geisler in *Christian Apologetics*

Don't Make Assumptions. Find the courage to ask questions and to express what you really want. Communicate with others as clearly as you can to avoid misunderstandings, sadness and drama. With just this one agreement, you can completely transform your life.—Miguel Angel Ruiz, Mexican author

Assumptions are the termites of relationships.—Henry Winkler, actor

*All names are fictitious to protect identities.

True Religion

Religion: 1.a. Belief in and reverence for a supernatural power or powers regarded as creator and governor of the universe.   b. A personal or institutionalized system grounded in such belief and worship.   2. The life or condition of a person in a religious order. 3. A set of beliefs, values, and practices based on the teachings of a spiritual leader. 4. A cause, a principle, or an activity pursued with zeal or conscientious devotion.—*The American Heritage Dictionary*

When I typed in the word *religion* on Yahoo's search engine, it gave 1,010,000,000 listings.   Assuming we could subtract 15% of those as repeat entries, if I were to spend just five seconds visiting each site with no break, it would take 49,682 days (over 2,070 years) just to visit them all! Sometimes I wonder if people have the same sense when they approach this subject. Everyone has an opinion about religion—but who is right?

The word *religion* occurs five times in the New Testament drawing from three different Greek words. The first two occurrences have to do with the teachings of Judaism. The third usage pertains to practical application by widows who follow Jesus Christ. Then we have the final two instances in the book of James.

James 1:26, 27—If anyone thinks he is religious, without controlling his tongue but deceiving his heart, his religion is useless. Pure and undefiled religion before our God and Father is this: to look after orphans and widows in their distress and to keep oneself unstained by the world.

In this passage, striking truths about religion emerge which lead to profound implications.

● Unpolluted—God expects us not to let the world stain us by its penchant for sin!

● God expects us to care for those who are needy and hurting.

● Religion that does not produce godly speech is rubbish!

Who do you know that is untainted by sin? James wrote, "Adulteresses! *Do you not know that friendship with the world is hostility toward God? So whoever wants to be the world's friend becomes God's enemy*" (4:4). Who do you know that is impartial? "*If you really carry out the royal law prescribed in Scripture, You shall love your neighbor as yourself, you are doing well. But if you show favoritism, you commit sin and are convicted by the law as transgressors*" (2:8,9). Who do you know that utters flawless speech? "*. . . no man can tame the tongue. It is a restless evil, full of deadly poison*" (3:8).   No human-manufactured religion is capable of meeting God's standard.

Good without God is like seeds without water. Any definition of religion that calls for our achievement in order to accomplish success is fatally flawed *if* there is a God and the Bible is accurate in stating His standards. This is what makes Christianity distinct from every other religion. Only Jesus is able to deliver what God accepts. He reaches to save us but based on our relationship to Him and not on our merit. *"For His divine power has given us everything required for life and godliness, through the knowledge of Him who called us by His own glory and goodness"* (2 Pe. 1:3). When we revere and love Him obeying the leading of His Holy Spirit, our lives reveal the seal of eternal life that springs from a temporal existence adorned with meaning. We have hope that stands above pain and suffering. We have joy that is unquenchable and vibrantly inspiring. How we define religion reveals what we know of Christ.

Inspiration †††

Religion is the possibility of the removal of every ground of confidence except confidence in God alone.—Karl Barth

Show a man his failures without Jesus and the result will be found in the roadside gutter. Give a man religion without reminding him of his filth, and the result will be arrogance in a three-piece suit.—Max Lucado in *The Applause of Heaven*

443

What Good Is It?

Do you know how to tell the difference between a real Rolex watch and a fake one? A fake Rolex can be purchased inexpensively in Bangkok, Thailand and several other Southeast Asian countries. Those who don't know much about watches may think they are getting the real thing. Others buy them for the image they project. But it's easy to spot a phony watch. On a real Rolex, the second hand rotates in a smooth steady fashion—the workmanship of master craftsmen. The second hand of a fake Rolex jumps from position to position.

James 2:14,19,26—What good is it, my brothers, if someone says he has faith, but does not have works? Can his faith save him . . . You believe that God is one; you do well. The demons also believe—and they shudder . . . For just as the body without the spirit is dead, so also faith without works is dead.

Billy Sunday was credited as saying, "Going to church doesn't make you a Christian any more than going to a garage makes you an automobile." I can say I have faith and claim to be a Christian. But if my life does not show the signature handiwork of Christ changing me to be like Him, you may rightfully question my claim. The proof of authentic faith is evidenced by our obedience to God. This does not mean we are 100% holy as we negotiate life. There are times our nature, despite our best efforts, is not conformed to the will of the Master. But a man or woman who follows after Jesus does not make sin lord and champion.

The Bible is clear in stating that faith without action is dead. In other words, the test of a true Christian is faith that produces action! If we think we are Christians just because we believe in Jesus we need to stop and consider the fact that even Satan believes in Jesus. I don't think we will see him in heaven!

Inspiration † † †

The Christian is not one who has gone all the way with Christ. None of us has. The Christian is one who has found the right road.—Charles L. Allen, pastor, (1913-2005)

Being a Christian is more than just an instantaneous conversion; it is like a daily process whereby you grow to be more and more like Christ.—Billy Graham

Adulteresses!

James 4:4—Adulteresses! Do you not know that friendship with the world is hostility toward God? So whoever wants to be the world's friend becomes God's enemy.

James' readers must have been mildly offended by his strong words in the verse above. My jaw would definitely tighten if someone called me an adulterous person. So what is it that James wants us to understand?

First, we should know that when Scripture speaks of the world in this context, it is not referring to the earth but rather human society and its evil influences (see 1:27). James admonishes his readers for being unfaithful to God by embracing the practices of a corrupt civilization.

Second, remember that the Bible teaches that God is a jealous God. Moses wrote, *"You are to never bow down to another god because the LORD, being jealous by nature, is a jealous God"* (Exo. 34:14). Jealously indicates the true depth of one's love! What if God didn't' care about our values or friendship? He would ignore us for being irrelevant and our damnation would be of little consequence to Him. But if He condoned our rebellious natures and our corrupt systems, *His holiness* would be irrelevant and *His love* would never have suffered the sacrifice of Jesus.

In the book *Gold Fears No Fire*, Ralph Toliver writes about a Christian Chinese family that suffered much persecution in communist China. The authorities determined to prove that their wisdom negated the need for anyone to follow some ancient outmoded Deity. The more the government attempted to stamp out Christianity the more the church flourished. A Chinese believer understands that friendship with the world is hatred towards God. But what about those Christians who live where only subtle opposition to God exists?[43]

Here's what happens to Christians who like what the world has to offer. We are slowly anesthetized to evil because life is *good*. Materialism fills our hearts until we disdain becoming living sacrifices. We become more concerned about how people view us than in what God tells us to do. How we look replaces who we are. We accept busyness over worship and justify intention to excuse negligence. We search for happiness unaware of why our joy is robbed. We find fault with others and make use of labels to avoid our own responsibility. Can you see why James was concerned? The sooner we recognize this and repent, the sooner we shall find again our longing for God and reap the blessings He bestows on a faithful people. There is no peace where love is betrayed.

Inspiration † † †

The world is a net; the more we stir in it, the more we are entangled.—Proverb

Continuous Glowing

1 Peter 1:3-5—Blessed be the God and Father of our Lord Jesus Christ. According to His great mercy, He has given us a new birth into a living hope through the resurrection of Jesus Christ from the dead, and into an inheritance that is imperishable, uncorrupted, and unfading, kept in heaven for you, who are being protected by God's power through faith for a salvation that is ready to be revealed in the last time.

Recalescence is the sudden glowing which takes place in metal that is cooling. It is caused by the liberation of the latent heat of transformation. It is a hot word picture that imperfectly depicts what happens to us who are spiritually born in Christ. The truth is the Holy Spirit is constantly at work in our lives as we determine to worship God. Accordingly, there will be not one sudden glowing, but continuous times when the brilliant light of God bursts from our lives as the dazzling display of divine transformation. This is what we call regeneration!

Our bodies are decaying. My knees and joints are proof enough for me! Yet in the midst of physical cooling down are we spiritually heating up? That's right! The more we know, worship and obey God, the more we are regenerated. This is why Paul wrote in 2 Co. 5:17—*"Therefore if anyone is in Christ, there is a new creation; old things have passed away, and look, new things have come."* The key is to be *"in Christ."*

Today, you and I have the opportunity to be *IN CHRIST*. Think of the song "Shine Jesus Shine!" Shine Buddha shine offers no salvation. Shine Mohammed shine gives no grace. There's no name but the name of Jesus to take the frail, flesh-encased human and set off an eternal glow. Jesus brings the warmth that takes off the sin-chill. He regenerates us for God's glory. Are you a lamp to a world that feels the darkness?

Inspiration † † †

Truth cannot be denied unless some truth is being affirmed.—Norman Geisler in *Christian Apologetics*

Choosing Christ brings mystery, rejecting Him brings despair.—Brother Lawrence & Frank Laubach in *Practicing His Presence*

Proof

Dan and Doris once led a Bible Study for a Hispanic family. One evening, after logging 340 miles on the road with his job, Dan borrowed Tom's pick-up truck to help the family move to another location in Hillsboro. One of the nephews, Jacob, about twenty-one years of age, accompanied Dan as they transported furniture. Jacob shared with him his desire to get away from a hazardous lifestyle that involved gangs and all that goes with spending time with bad company. While Dan listened, he spoke of his need for God—something he had not told anyone else.

About 11:00 p.m., the truck they were driving broke down on the freeway. Already exhausted, and now stranded, this was a trial for which Dan did not volunteer. But, he put his head on the steering wheel and prayed, "*Lord, you know our situation, please help us fix this truck so we can move this furniture.*" About five minutes later, a man in a rig towing a trailer stopped behind them. He asked what was wrong and if he could help. As it turned out, he was a mechanic. After looking at the engine, he discovered that the fuel line for one of the gas tanks was shut off. He connected the line and the truck roared to life! After the man was done, the subject of heaven came up. Dan was able to share with the mechanic that God's love was sufficient to save him if he would trust in Christ.

Dan said, "*Jacob's jaw dropped and his eyes were wide open.*" He could only shake his head in amazement. Rarely will anyone stop alongside a freeway late at night to help two men. It was apparent that God directly answered Dan's prayer. When the two men rejoined the rest of the family, Jacob told his wife, "*We are definitely going to Dan's church on Sunday!*"

1 Peter 1:6,7—You rejoice in this, though now for a short time you have had to be distressed by various trials so that the genuineness of your faith—more valuable than gold, which perishes though refined by fire—may result in praise, glory, and honor at the revelation of Jesus Christ.

Sometimes we Christians get so caught up in defending our values and searching for the right way to communicate the gospel message that we forget that what people desperately need is to experience God! When we pray in faith to the Lord and expect Him to intervene, we nourish His life in us and give evidence of His reality. Jacob saw God ratify Dan's prayer and it profoundly moved him. It is proof far more than platitudes that beckons hearts to trust in an open-handed Father. Our neighbors, co-workers and unsaved family members are attracted to Jesus by what they see Him doing in our every day living, as opposed to our Sunday morning excursions to what most view as a quick *God-fix*. Do you need confirmation that God is real? Then put Him to the test. Don't talk about what He did in your life twenty years ago; rely on Him to work through you right now! All right—let's get going . . . *on the road again!*

447

Tulo

In an Indonesian restaurant in Sweden, Jonathan, a Swede who grew up in the Congo, shared with us Tulo's* story. Tulo and 44 of his friends and relatives (to include a two-week old baby), fled Bukavu, Congo, to escape an enemy intent on taking their lives. For one month, they walked approximately 700 km (434 miles) and lived off monkey meat, fruit and anything else they could scrounge until they reached the city of Kisangani. It took a week in a hospital for Tulo to recover—others remained longer. Miraculously, none of these Jesus-followers died!

In a Catholic Church in the same country, a priest celebrated mass. While the people worshiped, rebels attacked by throwing grenades in the building killing everyone inside, over 1000 people perished! Anup Shah reports in *Conflicts in Africa*, "At the end of April, 2001, the International Rescue Committee estimated that there have been around 2.5 million deaths since the outbreak of the fighting in August 1998, with the majority dying of malnutrition and disease that has resulted from the war."[44] Warring tribal factions and soldiers from Rwanda and Uganda are using the unrest to profit from Congo's vast natural resources. In 2008, Congo is still at unrest and tribal violence is again on the rise.

1 Peter 4:12-14—Dear friends, when the fiery ordeal arises among you to test you, don't be surprised by it, as if something unusual were happening to you. Instead, as you share in the sufferings of the Messiah rejoice, so that you may also rejoice with great joy at the revelation of His glory. If you are ridiculed for the name of Christ, you are blessed, because the Spirit of glory and of God rests on you.

It was hard to sit across from Tulo and imagine the horrors this quiet, young man experienced. By God's grace, through the help of missionaries, he was able to escape to Nairobi, Kenya. I could not help asking myself soul-searching questions. Why are we so ignorant of a human disaster that dwarfs so many other tragedies? Are we ignorant to the suffering that goes on around us by intention? Are we ignorant to the suffering that goes on around us by intention?

For years, the top selling books in Christian bookstores were the *Left Behind* series. It is very popular to believe in the rapture and firmly look forward to bypassing tribulation. But we must not lose sight of what of our brothers and sisters around the world are enduring. How many die or flee every day because they choose to follow Jesus—in Sudan, Somalia, China, North Korea, Laos, Pakistan, etc.? Someday in heaven we will sit at the feet of those, who on earth, we would have crossed the road to avoid. In our haste to shun suffering we dishonor our Lord who bled for our sins. *God help us!*

*Not his real name for protection purposes.

Cerro de Pasco

Cerro de Pasco sits over 14,000 feet in elevation in the central Andes of Peru. It is a bleak place. Besides the lack of trees and barren terrain, the atmosphere around this mining town is oppressive. In the community where the engineers reside, a blue signboard welcomes the spirit recognized as *lord of the mines*. Pastor Marco, Felipe and two other young men of the church we visited, walked us around the central plaza one evening. They pointed out the many bars and discussed the rampant problems of alcoholism, adultery, prostitution, incest, animal sacrifices and demon-worship. They discussed the pride among the inhabitants—a *machoism* that scorns outsiders and keeps the many different churches from coming together as a united body.

1 Peter 5:8,9—Be sober! Be on the alert! Your adversary the Devil is prowling around like a roaring lion, looking for anyone he can devour. Resist him, firm in the faith, knowing that the same sufferings are being experienced by your brothers in the world.

In a dilapidated neighborhood, we stopped to eat with Jose and his family. This humble man made a decision to follow Jesus. Yet when he started attending church a strange malady caused such great pain in his feet that he could not walk. We sensed the work of Satan. So after anointing his head with oil our team prayed for healing. Then we learned that one of Jose's daughters was struggling in her relationship with Jesus. She no longer helped lead worship. When we spoke with her, she wept. She shared how a menacing voice told her, *"You are mine!"* We explained to her the power of Christ and that He would protect her if she would obey Him. We then prayed for her.

The pain in Jose's feet left him. His daughter was restored to fellowship. Many people scoff at the notion that there is a devil. They belittle and scorn as primitive any suggestion that he is alive and capable of inflicting harm. But the same Bible that proclaims the reality of God teaches the existence of Satan. To dismiss him as myth is to deny the truth of Scripture. To ignore the unmistakable trail of destruction he sows in lives around the world is the height of human foolishness.

Our God is supreme! Our responsibility is to trust in His might. We need not fear a demon behind every bush, but we ought to be vigilant. By following Christ, we attract the attention of a fallen-angel devoted to opposing God's will. If we fail to respect his ability, we may find our own feet afflicted by his schemes. Jesus taught His disciples to pray, *"deliver us from the evil one"* (Matthew 6:13). I hope you are praying and I ask that you remember before God, your brothers and sisters striving to serve Jesus on the battleground of Cerro de Pasco.

Promises

David Wilkerson, author of *The Cross and the Switchblade*, and pastor of Times Square Church in New York City, (until he passed away), every year sent out a calendar to his newsletter recipients with a daily promise from God's Word. It was an inspired habit meant to encourage his readership with the reality that God gives us promises we can rely upon to help us through life.

Dwight L. Moody once said, "God never made a promise that was too good to be true." The fearless fighter and leader of Israel, Joshua, reminded the Israelites, *"None of the good promises the LORD had made to the house of Israel failed. Everything was fulfilled"* (Jos. 21:45). King David would echo Joshua's words hundreds of years later when he proclaimed in praise, *"Your kingdom is an everlasting kingdom; Your rule is for all generations. The LORD is faithful in all His words and gracious in all His actions"* (Psa. 145:13).

2 Peter 1:3,4—For His divine power has given us everything required for life and godliness, through the knowledge of Him who called us by His own glory and goodness. By these He has given us very great and precious promises, so that through them you may share in the divine nature, escaping the corruption that is in the world because of evil desires.

Behold the sea with all its boats! Some row to the song *Que Sera, Que Sera* and stroke with the peace of resignation. Some glide on the finest of craft with the best equipment. With a determined heart and a set mind, they move by their own compass to conquer, and they fail according to the power of the flesh. Some steam under the flag of nature, or a prophet, or sovereign nation, intent on finding meaning according to the dictates of the banner they serve. Some set their sail to the wind of the Holy Spirit. They travel with their hope on the heavenly covenants God extended through His Son—Jesus.

Every boat encounters storms. Each endures hardships and enjoys celebrations until all eventually submerge before the unceasing waves of an ocean of death. Only one captain has ever gone down and come up victorious. This famous Pilot gives us the mother of all promises, the covenant of eternal redeemed life with God Himself. Through His glory and goodness, He pledges His power to see us through our earthly voyage. Therefore, we have the opportunity to live with the certain joy that God's promises are relevant and effective. Is life getting you down? Who's your Promise Keeper?

Inspiration † † †

Let God's promises shine on your problems.—Corrie Ten Boom

What's a Minute Worth?

Vainly I searched my desk for my pocket calendar. I needed it to determine which days to submit for pay for working at my reserve center. If I don't look at my calendar on a daily basis there is a good chance I will miss an appointment. I'm somewhat bound by a schedule and dependent upon the information I write down on little squares.

Calendars are helpful but they also are problematic. Because I measure my time in units, it is easy to expect God to do the same, to intervene or act according to my needs or plans. Such expectations can easily set me up for disappointment. Can't He see my frustration? Why won't He act when I need Him to act! If I am impatient, I may proceed prematurely and therefore be out of step or miss His will. My clock-ticking existence misunderstands His transcendent timelessness.

2 Peter 3:8—Dear friends, don't let this one thing escape you: with the Lord one day is like 1,000 years, and 1,000 years like one day.
Psalm 39:5—You, indeed, have made my days short in length, and my life span as nothing in Your sight. Yes, every mortal man is only a vapor. Selah

If a day is like a thousand years what is a minute worth? We have limited faculties and therefore flawed perception. Our omnipotent God sees everything with no misunderstanding. He is not a Master of whim or One who rambles or digresses. So here is the challenge. Will I trust that He will perfectly intervene in my life and circumstances, as well as the lives of others, when the time is appropriate? If the answer is "yes," I find agreement with Solomon's words, *"To man belong the plans of the heart, but from the Lord comes the reply of the tongue . . . In his heart a man plans his course, but the Lord determines his steps"* (Pro. 16:1,9 NIV). God *will* speak when the timeless moment is right. If the answer is "no," then I obviously think I know better than God does when He should act. *Hmmm!* That's rather presumptuous and foolish. Isn't it better that I rely on His sovereign love, knowing that He cares about my days? Hallelujah!

Inspiration † † †

The biblical God is not governed by time because He is the Lord of time. God is in time in the sense that He is sovereignly present in all the events of time, confronting His people with His warnings and His promises. However, this is not the same as saying that God is caught up in time or governed by it. Humankind cannot bind Him to special sacred time; rather, He encounters humankind in each moment of their temporal existence, offering each new day as an opportunity for judgment in the event of their willful stubbornness or for redemption in the event of their repentance.—*Holman Bible Dictionary*

Propitiator

He takes from the right hand of God the scroll, uniquely worthy to open its seals. Twenty-four elders fall down in reverence before Him while heaven's halls reverberate with a new song sung in His honor. He was slaughtered yet He lives. Not only does He accomplish something no other person or god could, He extends the reality of God's love to a world desperately intent on going its own way. This Hero is Christ Jesus and He is our Propitiator.

1 John 2:1,2—My little children, I am writing you these things so that you may not sin. But if anyone does sin, we have an advocate with the Father—Jesus Christ the righteous One. He Himself is the propitiation for our sins, and not only for ours, but also for those of the whole world.

Propitiation is not a word you will use often or find common to the English language. Yet without this word applied by the Word, we would be eternally dead. As Pastor Tim Arensmeier pointed out during our *'81 Advance*, this theological term is extremely important to us—especially in the arena of forgiveness. Essentially propitiate means to satisfy, atone for, or appease. Jesus' thirty-three years of life on earth were without sin. His enemies crucified Him, yet unwittingly followed God's set plan to make His Son the solution to our problem.

As the Propitiator, Jesus accomplished three critical things. *First, He* atoned for *our transgression, thereby, making us pious.* Our sin is removed by His sacrifice. *Second, He makes us favorable before God whose emotional and moral wrath towards our evil is satisfied.* He stood in our condemned place and satisfied the justice God demanded for us to enter His presence. *Third, He fulfills the love of God who created us to have an eternal relationship with Him!* John Stott rightly clarifies in his book, *The Cross of Christ*, that propitiation "does not make God gracious . . . God does not love us because Christ died for us, Christ died for us because God loves us."

The question left hanging is what will we do about this great divine intervention? God's action through Jesus, though universal in scope, is selective in application. According to Scripture, only those who rightly confess their sin and apply genuine faith in Jesus can hope for Him to propitiate. The Judge will not force anyone to call upon His Son for help—faith must come freely. But "*without faith it is impossible to please God*" (Heb. 11:6). Nor will He let Jesus be the Advocate for those who scorn, dismiss Him or put their trust in self-effort or some other savior. Salvation is found in no other system of belief, no other religious icon or figure. There is only One Savior worthy whereby we can find access to heaven . . . something to think about . . . in reveration!

"As Good As What He Loves"

1 John 3:5,6—You know that He was revealed so that He might take away sins, and there is no sin in Him. Everyone who remains in Him does not sin; everyone who sins has not seen Him or known Him.

Dan kicked the ball away from the goalie and was trying to break free when the enraged keeper threw him to the ground injuring his shoulder and neck. Dan said it was all he could do to keep from jumping to his feet and punching the guy. Sports have a way of revealing a nature inside of us we don't like to admit exists. Jesus wrestled against sin and pinned it to the mat in triumph. How? He completely trusted and obeyed His Father. He did not succumb to the world (a place and system associated with sin and ruled by Satan). If we want to be righteous, we have to be like Jesus.

Righteousness is accomplished by two things: faith and obedience. Jesus modeled this by trusting His Father and fulfilling His will. Even though He was righteous, Jesus died the death of a criminal. There is a great lesson in this. Often, we expect because of our good behavior that others will treat us properly. When we are treated poorly, our sense of justice is violated. But if we become bitter we reveal that our righteousness lacks faith and we may be acting out of our own strength. True righteousness is right doing and right being. These come about by setting our hearts and minds on . . . *"whatever is true, whatever is honorable, whatever is just, whatever is pure, whatever is lovely, whatever is commendable—if there is any moral excellence and if there is any praise—dwell on these things"* (Php. 4:8). Saul Bellow, winner of the Nobel Prize for literature, wrote, "A man is only as good as what he loves."

If I read secular literature, listen to secular music, watch secular programs, interact with secular people and neglect meditating on God's truth and communicating with Him throughout the day then I should not be surprised to find myself often discouraged, full of critical thoughts, and unfruitful in serving God. What I think and dwell upon influences how I feel and act.

There was a time when to wind down at night I would play online backgammon. However, because of my competitive nature I found myself playing for hours. I had to set time boundaries for myself. Finally, I reached the point of realizing that all the time spent playing backgammon was really a nonproductive way to end my day. How much better to use the time to pray for others or read. So much of righteousness is dependent upon marrying faith and obedience. When I realize my time is not my own but belongs to God, I am far more apt to invest wisely, sensitive to His leading. In the end, what we make of Jesus determines what the world makes of us.

Vodou

Andre flew from Benin to join our First Cause team in Kenya. He is a wonderful man who served for many years as a pastor before obeying God's call to venture out in evangelism and a more open-ended ministry. Andre serves as the spiritual advisor to his nation's president, a God-fearing leader. As such, God is using him to influence many important officials in his country. We were very blessed by Andre's humility, contagious love for God, and the enthusiasm with which he embraced our disciple maker training.

One morning as we finished our team devotions Andre looked very troubled and asked if he could share. Through great tears he communicated to us that his parents were Vodou priests and that he felt particularly responsible that his mother had left Christ to return to Vodou (he had the privilege of leading her to the Lord during a period when she was very ill). We deeply felt Andre's pain and agreed to fast and pray with him for his parent's deliverance.

1 John 4:1-3a—Dear friends, do not believe every spirit, but test the spirits to determine if they are from God, because many false prophets have gone out into the world. This is how you know the Spirit of God: Every spirit who confesses that Jesus Christ has come in the flesh is from God. But every spirit who dos not confess Jesus is not from God.

Vodoun became the official religion of Benin in 1996. This ancient religion began in this French-speaking nation. Today over 30 million people follow it in West Africa to include about 80% of Benin's population. Slaves exported this religion to Haiti and other Caribbean islands and variations of it are practiced in southeastern United States.

West African Vodou is steeped with spirit worship. Each family of spirits has priest and priestess hood that are often hereditary. In many African clans, deities might include *Mami Wata*, who are gods and goddesses of the waters; *Legba*, who in some clans is virile and young . . . *Gu*, ruling iron and smith craft; *Sakpata*, who rules diseases; and many other spirits distinct in their own way to West Africa. Vodou deities are linked to each African clan-group. Its clergy is central to maintaining the moral, social, and political order and ancestral foundation of its villagers. Therefore, it has a fierce hold upon the population.[45]

Andre shared with us the powerful demonic hold Vodou has on his parents. People who practice this religion live in fear of offending spirits and are under the rule of witch doctors that wield tremendous power. Satan oppresses people for soul control but God extends His grace for soul redemption. Will you join us in praying for the salvation of Lekobinou and Ayedoun Allomadin Tinkpon (Andre's parents). We pray that they will renounce Vodou and place their trust in Jesus and in doing so be used mightily by God to bring those they influence to Christ! *"Now this is the confidence we have before Him: whenever we ask anything according to His will, He hears us.*

And if we know that He hears whatever we ask, we know that we have what we have asked Him for." (1 John 5:14,15)

Inspiration † † †

Do not let us think for a moment that Satan opposes God only by means of sin and carnality in men's hearts; he opposes God by means of every worldly thing.—Watchman Nee in *Love Not The World*

Loving People

1 John 4:7,21—Dear friends, let us love one another, because love is from God, and everyone who loves has been born of God and knows God . . . And we have this command from Him: the one who loves God must also love his brother.

1 John 4:7-21 provides us a wonderful foundation for understanding the importance of loving one another. Four principles stand out in this passage:

Principle #1: Our love for one another is to be an ongoing action—vs. 7. Thirty-five times in the Psalms, God's love is described as enduring forever! When John tells us to love one another, he is not talking about a one-time-if-I-feel-like-it kind of love. Love is not to be like a light switch. It should not be based on feelings or on how we are treated.

Principle #2: Love comes from God and God is love—vs. 7,8,10,16,19. Can you imagine what life would be like if God chose not to love us? It would be like hell. We cannot manufacture love on our own. We have to ask God to help us to love others—our nature is to love ourselves first. If you want to learn how to love, ask God to give you a loving heart.

● Everyone who loves has been born from God and knows God—vs. 7,16.

● The evidence of godliness is that we are continuously able to love people!

● The person who does not love does not know God—vs. 8.

● Love looks like Jesus, who sacrificed His own life on our behalf—vs. 9,10.

Principle #3: The way God loves us is the way we are to love one another— vs. 11. Philippians 2:1-11 is a terrific picture of the sacrificial, others-centered, edifying, God-glorifying love, Jesus brought to earth!

● If we love one another, God lives in us and His love is perfected in us—vs. 12,16.

● You cannot love God and hate your brother—vs.20, the two are mutually exclusive. You cannot disfellowship another believer because you don't like him or because he has wrongly treated you in the past. Unless he is willfully defiant in rebellious sin, denying fellowship defies 1 Co. 13:5 and Psa. 130:3 which communicate that love keeps no record of wrongs. Thank God!

● Loving one another is not optional—vs. 21.

Principle #4: There is no fear where love exists—vs. 18. We don't need to be afraid of what people will think of us or how they will treat us. We just need to love! The world desperately wants something in which to believe. The world is not impressed by hype, it is hungry for hope. Both faith and hope run eternal. But God *is* love and that is why *"the greatest of these is love!"* (1 Co. 13:13)

She Doesn't Belong Here!

Romans 8:5,8—For those whose lives are according to the flesh think about the things of the flesh, but those whose lives are according to the Spirit, about the things of the Spirit . . . Those whose lives are in the flesh are unable to please God.
Romans 13:14—But put on the Lord Jesus Christ, and make no plans to satisfy the fleshly desires.

It's amazing what an angel will do. She sat on the low wooden bench and watched as the people passed by her. Her faded, yellow dress did not match the orange socks pulled just below her knees. Tangled hair and a face unmarked by soap whispered her motherless fate. She held in one hand a beanie baby—a three-legged dog, while in the other she clutched a mystery bag of who knows what treasure. Her feet lightly swung as if to some hidden melody. One shoe revealed a severed heel that if she walked would have flapped to its own rap. The other shoe no longer had lace long enough to tie a bow.

On this day in the mall, we will learn much about human nature . . .

- Some pass her by oblivious to her existence, brains locked on checklists
- Some glimpse her appearance and turn in disgust
- Some point her out and smirk the sneer of the unkind
- Some engage her eyes and quickly look away
- Some never see her because of who they are
- Some never see her because of who they aren't

Not far away from her silent perch, Santa sits by a brightly lit, 16-foot noble, while a quartet band belts out their brass rendition of Jingle Bells. A line of children stand impatiently, waiting to sit on the hefty lap of their bearded hero—to fill his ears with their plotted dreams. None of them see the child with moistened eyes or acknowledge her presence. After all, she is a flat note in a chorus of celebration.

What thoughts go through her tender mind—this child who sits in frozen time? Across the way, an old woman stops and takes in the surrounding scene. Her hair is gray and brushed into neat waves that have lapped a million shores. She walks slowly but with calm assurance. She approaches the child, bends down and lovingly looks inside her widened eyes. No words pass between them as she extends her curled fingers to join warm hands. Then she leads her to the front of the line.

"Hey, you can't cut! Go back to the end of the line."

"What are you doing lady? That girl can't see Santa! She doesn't belong here."

The voices rise in sirens of protests. And then abruptly stop before the voice of a ten-year old who finds compassion a higher form of valor than selfishness. "Come on. You can take my place." Surprised by this unforeseen action, the crowd grows silent and stares. The old woman with her hands the back of the girl guides her forward and helps her climb into the large, red lap of this year's Santa. He bends down after gently brushing her hair and asks her what she would like for Christmas. She looks up and smiles. He asks her again aware of an impatient throng, but she only stares in his hazel eyes.

And then he understands. This yellow butterfly cannot speak.

Napoleon Bonaparte once said, "Where flowers degenerate man cannot live." What once was a celebration of God's greatest gift to mankind has become a commercial hunting season. Jesus said, *"a tree is known by its fruit"* (Mat. 12:33). Perhaps those are the words we should ponder.

May we be the aroma of God's grace to a lonely world—not the pungent smell that emanates from a sinful nature. *"Let brotherly love continue. Don't neglect to show hospitality, for by doing this some have welcomed angels as guests without knowing it"* (Heb. 13:1,2).

Inspiration † † †

The test of a nature is the atmosphere it produces.—Oswald Chambers in *Shade of His Hand*

Scorn

A small crowd of perhaps a hundred gathered for the tree lighting. Four strands of multicolored lights ran up the 40-foot fir. The air was festive and the mood light. Christmas songs were sung off-key while boys and girls eyes roved frantically for Santa. One after another, dignitaries walked forward and gave their remarks. Then the emcee asked the Chaplain to give the blessing.

If they expected a short, generic prayer before the lights were lit, they were disappointed. Frank reminded them why God sent His Son, Jesus to earth. He spoke of love and the real reason Christmas is celebrated. He tied the season to the Savior while skillfully untying the commercial knot that strangles the Babe in a manger. Then Frank bowed his head and prayed. He asked God to bless each person with His grace and ended his prayer with the name of Christ Jesus.

Psalm 22:6-8—But I am a worm and not a man, scorned by men and despised by people. Everyone who sees me mocks me; they sneer and shake their heads: "He relies on the LORD; let Him rescue him; let the LORD deliver him, since He takes pleasure in him."

If looks could obliterate life, Frank was slain repeatedly. He strayed from the politically correct "Happy Holidays," to invoking a "Merry Christmas." Instead of praying to a generic god all could enjoy he invoked Jesus' name. He dared to shift the focus from an overweight man in red with his popular large bag to a controversial Messiah. The horror! Did twisted smiles and rigid body language reveal thoughts like, "Oh, this man is a fool. Does he really think anyone believes this religious nonsense!"

If you think scorn is dead, try taking a public stand for Jesus. Increasingly, people do not want to hear that Name above all names. In some ways, it is easier to be shot than to be scorned. Scorn infers dislike or contempt. Most of us want to be liked, so to put ourselves in a place where we may face derision is too tough. Who wants to be contemptible?

Jesus regularly endured condescending mockery from influential religious leaders to proclaim His Deity and purpose. They hated Him! In their fury, they honed scorn to cries for His crucifixion. They reveled in His pain as twisted thorns were thrust down His brow. He took it all because His mission to save us outweighed His need to preserve His divine dignity. His example transcends power.

Scorn is a sure revealer of sinful pride. When we refuse to stand for Jesus because we fear the cost of being maligned, we unwittingly reveal disdain for the very One who died for us. Thus to avoid scorn is to scorn. May God help us boldly say, *"For I am not ashamed of the gospel, because it is God's power for salvation to everyone who believes, first to the Jew, and also to the Greek"* (Rom. 1:16).

He Often Withdrew

What manner of love for those of His image—yet deeply flawed, possessed God to send His Son to be conceived a baby? What marvelous humility flowed from our omnipotent Lord that His Son should bypass the greatest of human protocols to be born in a smelly stable? Like the wise men that followed the star, we trace the life and ministry of Jesus, joyful that His holy journey liberated us from the dungeon of sin. But there is so much more to His story, so much more to who He is.

Who speaks of the loneliness that must have gripped Mary's Son? Sure His mission was to seek and to save the lost (Luke 19:10). Nevertheless, His deity was confined to our skin and bones. When He withdrew to lonely places was it because He was lonely? Imagine the daily press of overwhelming crowds crying out to be healed, to be rid of terrifying demons, to be recognized first, to matter. What town or village existed without pain for Him to heal?

Yet even after the most pressing of days, Jesus did not cry "Enough! I quit! You don't understand! You don't get it, do you?" The Son of Man would not flee to heaven. No—no matter what His day entailed, He established a divine habit—He withdrew to solitary places to fellowship with His Father through prayer.

Luke 5:15,16—But the news about Him spread even more, and large crowds would come together to hear Him and to be healed of their sicknesses. Yet He often withdrew to deserted places and prayed.

Do you walk in the middle of this congested season that bears little resemblance to dignified worship and feel alone? Do you dread this time of year because: you are estranged from family; you have suffered the crippling loss of a loved one; life brings little meaning; you feel soiled by sin before an innocent Savior? In a world of continents, do you feel like an island? If so, I'd like to offer an encouraging word.

Loneliness is an indicator of dejection. When introspective it can lead to the darkest of depressions. The challenge of the lonely person is to overcome the lie that no one cares. Jesus knows all about loneliness. The Lord forsaken in the garden understands exactly what it's like to be isolated. There is no hidden hurt in your heart He fails to notice. Yet, He will not shower you with pat answers. He won't place on your shoulders a "get-over-it" blanket or suggest that you should be joyful like those around you. Instead, He will wait for you to come to Him.

He will listen as you speak. He is not put off by the broken tears of an anguished spirit. When you are ready, and trust Him enough, then He will gently remind you that He loves you. There is no alone found in worship. In the presence of the Savior—loneliness meets comfort. Let our Father in heaven be your Father on earth.

A Decree Went Out

Luke 2:1—In those days a decree went out from Caesar Augustus that the whole empire should be registered.

"*Please*! This is ridiculous! Those confounded Romans have conspired to make our lives miserable. Mary, I don't know what to say. Why would God send us from Nazareth to Bethlehem when you are almost ready to have a baby?!"

"Joseph, I don't know why. But we must go. Surely God has His reasons for letting this happen."

Can you hear their conversation? Joseph and Mary know they are to become the parents of God's own Son. Near the culmination of what should be a joyous time they are rudely uprooted by a bothersome census. Joseph must somehow transport his expectant wife 70 miles of unpaved road on a trip ending at Bethlehem's 2460 foot elevation. They had no bus, car, or train to transport them—only their feet and perhaps a donkey—talk about demands!

God providentially sent His servants on a difficult journey. In the military, leaders make risk assessments before they conduct missions. Their goal is to maximize safety and minimize risk. No wise commander would send a woman about to conceive on such a treacherous journey. Yet heaven's Commander worked through Caesar Augustus to fulfill His word. Sometime between 750 and 686 B.C., Micah prophesied that Jesus would be born in Bethlehem. That was where the angels and shepherds would celebrate the arrival of mankind's Savior.

We sing with raised candles the story of a silent night and conveniently forget about the stormy days . . .

You will face demands upon your life this next year that will not be easy. You will be asked to do what seems ridiculous. The temptation will come to question God, to doubt His leadership. The urge to complain may bubble up like acid reflux. When these demands come, I hope you will remember the story of Joseph and Mary—it is not just for Christmas. It's a daily reminder that God works in mysterious ways through multiple means to accomplish His grand will for His own glory. To share in that glory we must believe in His power. That is what faith is all about and that is truly something to think about . . . in reveration.

Inspiration ✝✝✝

I do not pray for success, I ask for faithfulness.—Mother Theresa, Albanian sister and founder of Missionaries of Charity (1910-1997)

$10 For Fishing

William did an amazing thing this past Christmas. The eleven-year old son of Cindy and David carefully selected each Christmas gift for his parents and his older brother Walt. The dynamics of this family are not unusual. The oldest son has close ties to his dad while the youngest is close to his mother. That is why William's gift was so special. He desired to have a better relationship with his father. So he wrote David a touching letter that pointed out his own understanding of why their relationship was weak. Then he mentioned his desire to be close to his father. Inside the letter was $10 William gave to his dad to purchase a fishing pole so they could go spend time together as father and son—fishing.

Philemon 20,21—Yes, brother, may I have joy from you in the Lord; refresh my heart in Christ. I am confident of your obedience, I am writing to you, knowing that you will do even more than I say.

Paul evidently led a runaway slave named Onesimus to Jesus. Through Paul's mentorship, Onesimus grew to become a wonderful disciple and close *son* to the elderly saint. But Paul knew that Onesimus belonged to Philemon, a slave owner who had also become a Christian. Sensitive toward doing the right thing, Paul sent the young slave back to his master with a personal letter. In the meditation above, the context of the request is that Philemon would do the right thing by granting Onesimus freedom and sending him back to Paul who earnestly desired his help in furthering the gospel.

The hallmark of followers of Jesus is sensitivity. The Holy Spirit works within our conscience through His quiet but firm voice leading us in how we should treat people. Cindy was my high school classmate in the Philippines. She shared with me how William's letter and the ten-dollar bill are framed on a wall in their home as a reminder to his dad of his son's love.

William, like Paul, demonstrated amazing discernment—careful not to offend others and to build up those around him. Brothers and sisters, we must be careful that we do not become so focused on our reputation, rights and needs that we become insensitive to those around us. Look for opportunities to bless people, especially those with whom you struggle. Be sensitive. By doing so, you reveal love—the kind that originates in heaven. As this year draws to a close, is there anyone with whom you need to mend the relationship?

Inspiration †††

It seems that the further maturing believers go in their walk with the Spirit of God, the more sensitive they must become to the subtleties of stronghold pockets of resistance.—Jan David Hettinga in *Follow Me*

Christmas

Micah 5:2—Bethlehem Ephrathah, you are small among the clans of Judah; One will come from you to be ruler over Israel for Me. His origin is from antiquity, from eternity.

December 25 was first celebrated as a pagan party. The pagans knew that at this point in their calendar the shortest day and longest night had passed, that slowly the sun would rise higher and remain longer in the sky, bringing with it the promise of spring. The Emperor Aurelian (A.D. 270-275) capitalized upon the heathen worship of the sun and in the year A.D. 274, officially declared Dec. 25th as the birthday of the Unconquered Sun (dies natalis solis invicti). [*These Times.* December, 1981. p. 22]

Historians did not begin to date history from Christ's birth until the sixth century when a monk of Rome, Dionysius Exiguus, introduced the method. We know now that Dionysius erred in his computations and dated Christ's birth some four or five years too late in history. Rather than adjusting the dates for all historical events, books simply list Christ's birth at about 4 B.C. Regardless of the year, we can be reasonably sure that Jesus was not born during the month of December. In the Middle East, December is not a month when shepherds or sheep remain in the open fields at night. Winters in the mountain regions of Judea are not a time for flocks to be long exposed to the elements of nature. Because of the cold weather and the chilling rains, it is most unlikely that they would be outdoors. More likely, Jesus was born sometime after the rains of April and before those of November—the season sheep would be found in the open fields at night.

The early church did not celebrate Christ's birth. How then did Dec. 25 inherit Christian emphasis? Evidently, sometime during the early fourth century, Christians began searching for the proper day to celebrate the birth of Jesus. Some churches celebrated it on January 6, others April 20, May 20, March 29, and September 29. So much confusion existed that Saint Cyril, bishop of Jerusalem, about the middle of the fourth century, inquired of the Roman bishop, Julius, regarding the correct date. Julius wrote Cyril that he personally favored Dec. 25. Refusing to accept this date as valid, Cyril and the Jerusalem church continued celebrating the event for many years on January 6. In A.D. 354, two years following the end of Saint Julius' reign, the new Roman bishop, Liberius, ordered all his people to celebrate Dec. 25 as the correct day of Christ's birth. Over time, this date won consensus and was adopted by most of Christendom.

Where did the name Christmas originate? In the medieval ages, the celebration of Christmas took the form of a special mass said at midnight on the eve of Christ's birth. Since this was the only time in the Catholic church year when a midnight mass was allowed, it soon became known in the Old English as *Christes Masse* (Christ's Mass), from which is derived the word *Christmas*.

So we Christians come together to celebrate. The joy of Christmas is not founded in the tree or ornaments, lights or gifts, food or music, vacation or company but in the realization that our Heavenly Father sent His Son to save us. Let us remember that our great purpose is worship. If Dec. 25 reminds us anew of our precious Lord, then let us celebrate with vigor. If Dec. 25 is an opportunity for us to share the good news the angels brought, let nothing hold us back! May we be reminded every day that God loved us so vastly that He became like us to win us. May our hearts be filled with a love for Him that exceeds containment. For in truth, the word Christmas, if we adopt a Spanish suffix, means *"more Christ!"*

Inspiration †††

All we could ever imagine, could ever hope for, He is . . . All this, and infinitely more, alive in an impoverished baby in a barn. That is what Christmas means—to find in a place where you would least expect to find anything you want, everything you could ever want.—Michael Card in *The Promise*

We consider Christmas as the encounter, the great encounter, the historical encounter, the decisive encounter, between God and mankind. He who has faith knows this truly; let him rejoice.—Pope Paul VI, Italian clergyman, (1897-1978)

Not Sure He's There

According to *The American Heritage Dictionary*, an agnostic is "One who believes that there can be no proof of the existence of God but does not deny the possibility that God exists." There are two kinds of agnostics—those who have no interest in God and see no compelling evidence to change their minds, and those who have not found Him and consequently have no reason to suggest He exists.

The mistake we make with agnostics is to become defensive. The hair on our neck stands at attention and every brain cell goes on alert to fight. We don't want to be wrong. We want the skeptic to see the light. But what agnostic sees evidence of God in the arena of argument? If the focus is conversion, will the doubter see Christ or our need to win?

The Bible commands us to be prepared when questioned about our faith (1Pe. 3:15). It compels us to pray for the lost (Acts 26:29). It contends that our primary motivation towards people must be love (Mat. 22:37-39). But underneath everything we do is the fundamental truth that God reveals Himself to people through His Holy Spirit (1Co. 2:12-14). Without the Holy Spirit, we cannot understand God, let alone believe He exists. Therefore, the challenge for us is not to loudly condemn the faithless, but rather to live so that His impact on our behavior is unmistakable evidence of His invisible presence.

1 John 5:10—The one who believes in the Son of God has the testimony in himself. The one who does not believe God has made Him a liar, because he has not believed in the testimony that God has given about His Son.

Our message is not to be predicated upon wise and persuasive words but rather on God's power (1 Co. 2:4,5)! Conduct is an awesome orator. Our obedience before God is what the agnostic needs modeled! If a picture is worth a thousand words, godliness is worth a million movies. Perhaps a sadder phrase than "I cannot accept" is the phrase, "I've not seen . . ." Every society has its agnostics. If only every society had disciples of Jesus inflamed with love for the Lord who *is* alive and makes every breath worth taking!

Inspiration † † †

Complete agnosticism is self-defeating; it reduces to the self-destructing assertion that "one knows enough about reality in order to affirm that nothing can be known about reality."—Norman Geisler in *Christian Apologetics*

Agnosticism has nothing to impart. Its sermons are the exhortations of one who convinces you he stands on nothing and urges you to stand there too.—Anna Julia Cooper, teacher (1858-1964)

I Pray You May Prosper

3 John 2—Dear friend, I pray that you may prosper in every way and be in good health, just as your soul prospers.

In the early second century, life among believers was far from perfect. An aging Apostle John mentions Diotrephes, a Gnostic church leader who caused problems in teaching and the way he treated believers in the church. This culminates in John's warning to his readers not to imitate those who are evil (vs.9-11). From the time of John until now, in every century, truth was threatened, bashed, mistreated, and horribly violated by those inspired by the prince of darkness.

There is a sense, in talking to people around the country, that America continues an unabated moral slide characterized by a materialistic obsession, addictions of every variety, and a rapid abandonment of God. There are plenty of statistics I could cite from researchers such as George Barna or Gallup, which reveal that while our country may abound in wealth, it is decaying spiritually. Increasingly what Christians and nonChristians clutch as prospering is diametrically opposed to what Scripture states. But I submit that this should not surprise us. The Bible tells us that as time approaches Jesus' return, the love for God that should burn like a blowtorch will dwindle to a candle's flicker (see Mat. 24:12).

The danger in spotting increasing evil is sporting increasing pessimism. This is why I find John's third letter to be a great encouragement. In the midst of addressing the serious problem of Gnosticism, Jesus' favorite disciple recognizes the primacy of truth and then encourages and wraps his readers in a blessing to prosper—the right way!

So, let's learn from this tiny book of Scripture and make application. *I pray God's blessing upon you in the spirit of His love that transforms my life and gives me infinite hope.* I have taken John's blessing and passed it to you with the expectation that you will prosper according to God's desire. Will you do the same towards those fellow believers you love? On this day, let's initiate a movement to prosper spiritually! Let's claim a holy revival around a weary planet and reenergize the saints that call Jesus "Lord" for His glory.

Inspiration †††

Prospering just doesn't have to do with money.—Joel Osteen, pastor and author

Some people are always TELEGRAPHING TO HEAVEN for God to send a cargo of blessing to them, but they are not at the wharf-side to unload the vessel when it comes.—F.B. Meyer in *Meet For The Master's Use*

Standing in Glory

Jude 24,25—Now to Him who is able to protect you from stumbling and to make you stand in the presence of His glory, blameless and with great joy, to the only God our Savior, through Jesus Christ our Lord, be glory, majesty, power, and authority before all time, now, and forever. Amen.

Some of the most gifted athletes in the world compete for the right to be world champions, to receive around their neck the coveted gold medal. Some of the brightest human beings bask in the glory of winning a Nobel Prize. Male and female leaders who spent the best years of their lives serving their country, yearn to be promoted to the rank of general or admiral. Great business minds turn work into currency and reach incredible pinnacles of wealth. Those who achieve their desires or more than they hoped for, often at the height of achievement, feel a nagging realization, "There's got to be more to life than this!"

Some never gain their dreams. Daily living presents them with an unending series of disappointments and pains. No matter how hard they exert effort, the results are never enough. Life seems hollow.

I don't know which camp typifies your experience, or, perhaps you've lived a combination of both. But you met Jesus and made Him your Lord and Savior and now on the road home you hold fast to your faith in Him. Regardless of whether you've stood on the platform of victory or floundered in the mud of mishap, your greatest day is yet to come, the day you will be *standing in glory*.

Imagine how awesome that moment in timelessness will be—the Lord will call you from your procumbent position of reverence, to stand! Your Creator will walk you before heaven's hallowed crowd, that cheering throng of fame. You will stand in His glory—blameless. Your heart will feel joy so exponentially powerful as to make those chills that ran down your spine on earth seem trivial.

Never again will you stumble! No more will you know the taste of sourness, the reflection of pain, the embarrassment of wrongdoing. Standing in glory before God, He is exalted and you are examined and found clean. Your faith is His credit. Your redemption is His majesty. Your victory over death is His power. Your admittance before His throne is His authority before all time, now, and forever.

This is a magnificent moment to praise God. Victory is ours—hallelujah! Emancipation is our heritage and it is a safe one, no one can take from us. So let us renew our commitment today to walk as victors, appropriating now what God promises. Let's be radiant lights. Let's sing at the top of our lungs to our Redeemer, the gratitude that fills our soul as we look forward to *standing in His glory*!

By Your Blood

Revelation 5:9—And they sang a new song: You are worthy to take the scroll and to open its seals; because You were slaughtered, and You redeemed people for God by Your blood from every tribe and language and people and nation.

A young woman walks into church for the first time. She sits down in a pew filled by strangers. In the course of a service unlike anything she has experienced, a hymn is sung. She sees the title, *"There is a Fountain Filled with Blood"* and inwardly recoils. Later she listens as around her people sing, *"My hope is built on nothing less than Jesus' blood and righteousness."* Why, she wonders, would anyone venerate the blood of someone else! To her worldly mind, the notion of singing about any kind of blood is grotesque and backward—the primitive custom of a weird people. If such blood is left unexplained, can we blame her if she never sets foot in a church again?

The author of Hebrews wrote:

According to the law almost everything is purified with blood, and without the shedding of blood there is no forgiveness . . . But now He has appeared one time, at the end of the ages, for the removal of sin by the sacrifice of Himself (Heb. 9:22,26b).

A holy God could not fellowship with a sinful people. Therefore, He established laws requiring that blood of certain animals be shed as an appeasement for sins committed. Unfortunately, His laws were disobeyed. It was impossible for the blood of bulls and goats to take away sins (Heb. 10:4). So God, based on His love for humanity, took drastic measures. He sent His own Son Jesus to earth and allowed Him to be killed as a once-for-all perfect and final sacrifice. Unlike any other offering, Jesus rose from the dead. His sinless life and victory over death established a means by which we could be saved. *"What could wash away my sins, nothing but the blood of Jesus!"*

If we take for granted the blood Jesus shed for us, we devalue the most awesome gift history has ever recorded. If we fail to explain to those who have never heard of Christ, the power and beauty of His blood, we miss the gospel message. Not creed, recited formula, church affiliation, works or knowledge save us. It is the blood of Jesus that purchased us for God. This is why communion is so significant. We deliberately remember that Jesus was pierced for us. Blood represents life—the most precious thing we own. For our Lord to lose His life for us on a cross is incredible. His blood is not gruesome or gory it is the essence of glory. We owe it to all the world to give a full and accurate confession of this marvelous gift packaged in holy grace. As Martin Luther stated, "Blood alone moves the wheels of history."

Tribulum

Revelation 7:14—I said to him, "Sir, you know." Then he told me: These are the ones coming out of the great tribulation. They washed their robes and made them white in the blood of the Lamb.

Most American Christians are familiar with the term *rapture*. The belief that Christians will avoid living through the tribulation is largely attributed to 1 Th. 4:17—*"Then we who are still alive will be caught up together with them in the clouds to meet the Lord in the air; and so we will always be with the Lord."* The fictional series *Left Behind* glamorizes this view and reinforces the notion that the church will escape the tribulation.

I am not an expert in eschatology (the branch of theology concerned with the end of the world), but I am concerned with the implications of what we profess to believe. I also believe we are nearing the time of the end. Right now as you are reading this, someone on this planet is tortured for his or her faith in Jesus Christ. In the last 100 years, more Christians were martyred for their faith than the total of every century dating back to Christ's crucifixion. Try explaining to Christians in China, Somalia, Sudan, North Korea, Egypt, Nigeria, Cambodia, Laos, Saudi Arabia, Iran, Cuba, Yemen, Libya, Indonesia . . . that they will not have to go through the tribulation because they will be raptured! I am sure they will be comforted as they show you pictures of mutilated loved ones, as they reveal scars from brutal beatings and relate with joy, stories of repeated persecution all because they refuse to renounce their allegiance to Christ.

Oswald Chambers noted in *The Servant As His Lord:*

The word *tribulation* has its root in the Latin *tribulum*—a sledge for rubbing out corn, literally, a thing with teeth that tears . . . God allows tribulation and anguish to come right to the threshold of our lives in order to prove to us that His life in us is more than a match for all that is against us.

Around the world, there is a steady onslaught of litigation, imprisonment and torture for those who dare share about Christ or hold to Biblical teachings. Does the hope of rapture color our reality and lead to ambivalence towards those who are suffering? How we view the tribulation determines what we do in preparation.

When the day comes when you are told you cannot share your faith if it offends others, will you be ready and willing to suffer by choosing God's laws over man's laws? Most of our brothers and sisters already answer that question everyday in places where Jesus is not welcome. Dr. Tom White, the Director of The Voice of the Martyrs (VOM), reminds us that the real meaning of passion is not about intense desire or feeling. Rather it stems from the Latin word "pati" which means to suffer. To be passionate about God means to be willing to suffer in following Him.

If we cannot feel the pain of our afflicted Christian family in other lands and are disinclined to help them or at least pray for them, then we do not understand tribulation or what it means to be the body of Christ. It seems shallow and selfish to suggest God will liberate us in days ahead while ignoring the plight of His children everywhere else. Tribulation is here. The great tribulation will come. God help us to be faithful today so that our hope is not in what we miss but rather in what we have.

Inspiration † † †

Tolerance implies no lack of commitment to one's own beliefs. Rather it condemns the oppression or persecution of others.—John F. Kennedy, 35th President of the United States, (1917-1963)

It requires more courage to suffer than to die.—Napoleon Bonaparte, French military and political leader (1769-1821)

To endure the cross is not tragedy; it is the suffering which is the fruit of an exclusive allegiance to Jesus Christ.—Dietrich Bonhoeffer

Revelation 20:14,15—Death and Hades were thrown into the lake of fire. This is the second death, the lake of fire. And anyone not found written in the book of life was thrown into the lake of fire.

To this day, I remember a painting that hung in our home when we lived in South Korea. It was a graphic depiction of a lake of fire filled with people grotesquely suffering. It was an attention-getter which brought curious people into a conversation with my dad that for some led to salvation. I wish I had that painting today. I'd hang it in my office. Sure, it would offend people. But I would rather upset someone with the reality of God's upcoming judgment than withhold information that could result in their eternal suffering.

Ancient Jews referred to a place that followed death as the pit (*shachath*). David wrote in Psa. 55:23, *"You, God, will bring them down to the pit of destruction; men of bloodshed and treachery will not live out half their days. But I will trust in You."* According to *Parson's Bible Dictionary* the word *sheol* occurs 65 times in the Old Testament and signifies the underworld: a designation for the dead from which there is no return; a place without praise of God; a place where the wicked were sent to be punished; and a place from which the righteous were rescued. Job 26:6 state, *"Sheol is naked before God, and Abaddon (destruction) has no covering."* Abaddon was the name of the angel of destruction who guarded the bottomless pit, the abyss, a place mentioned nine times in Scripture.

Easton's Bible Dictionary describes three words used in the New Testament to signify hell: *Hades, Gehenna* and *Tartarus*.[46] *Hades* is synonymous with *sheol*. It is the name of the Greek god of the underworld and the underworld itself. It is described as a prison, with gates and bars and locks located below. (See Mat. 11:23, 16:18; 1 Pe. 3:19, Rev. 1:18). *Tartarus*, (used only in 2 Pe. 2:4), describes where God sent angels that sinned. It is a dark, miserable, subterranean region the ancient Greeks regarded as a place where the most wicked spirits were sent to be punished. *Gehenna* is a valley outside Jerusalem where human sacrifice to the Ammonite god Molech was conducted. It was associated with evil and became a common word to connote future punishment. Jesus said, *". . . And whoever says to his brother, 'Fool!' will be subject to the Sanhedrin. But whoever says, 'You moron!' will be subject to hellfire"* (Mat. 5:22).

The Bible is clear that all people will one day be judged. *"And just as it is appointed for people to die once—and after this, judgment"*—Heb. 9:27. Isaiah quoted God's warning against those who rebelled against Him—*"As they leave, they will see the dead bodies of the men who have rebelled against Me; for their maggots will never die, their fire will never go out, and they will be a horror to all mankind"* (Isa. 66:24). Revelation 20:11-15 teaches that a day will come when God will sit on His great white throne and cast judgment on all mankind. People ask how a loving God could sentence anyone to such a horrible fate. Billy Graham wrote, "God will never send anybody to hell. If man goes to hell, he goes by his own free choice. Hell was created for the devil and his angels, not for man. God never meant that man should go there." Dante Alighieri wrote in the thirteenth century, "If you insist on having your own way, you will get it. Hell is the enjoyment of your own way forever."

Why does God permit anyone to experience eternal torment in bubbling liquid? Only God the Creator can speak for God the Judge. We cannot be God's defender, we are always His advocate. Jesus commands us to share the gospel and the value of the good news is heightened by the reality of the bad news! Our perfect Savior didn't just talk about nice things. He warned people that the consequence of their evil was impending judgment. To fail to point out the cost of sin and rejecting Jesus Christ reveals a blatant lack of concern. Hell is hell! If we cannot see it for its consuming fury, then perhaps, we miss the gospel for its overriding love. Therefore, not to speak of hell is a hellacious way to treat people.

Inspiration † † †

We don't like to think about death; yet, worldwide, 3 people die every second, 180 every minute, and nearly 11,000 every hour. If the Bible is right about what happens to us after death, it means that more than 250,000 people every day go either to Heaven or Hell.—Randy Alcorn in *Heaven*

There is no redemption from hell.—Pope Paul III, Italian clergyman, (1468-1549)

Jesus spoke of hell often. Thirteen percent of His teachings refer to eternal judgment and hell. Two-thirds of his parables relate to resurrection and judgment.—Max Lucado in *3:16*

Notes

WHY FIRST CAUSE?

God put a new song in our mouths, a hymn of praise to Him so that people would see and revere Him and put their trust in Him (Psalm 40:3). This is what First Cause is all about. Our goal is to share the inspired songs (not just music but also a metaphor for written and spoken words) to all who God will bring us in contact with so that they too might have the deep love and trust for Him that makes life rich with meaning and joyful. He is our First Cause and we love sharing His message.

WHAT WE DO

We emphasize three ministries: prayer, coaching and providing resources designed to help people grow spiritually. Our goal is to help those who are hungry for purpose and meaning in life to be successful spiritually, physically, emotionally and socially.

To learn more about First Cause, to access or sign up for free weekly devotionals, or to order our products, visit http://www.firstcause.org.

About the Author

Daniel York grew up as a missionary kid, the son of Ron and Betty York. He lived in Okinawa, Korea, Japan, the Philippines, and throughout the United States. In 1977, after graduating from Faith Academy in the Philippines, he spent four years as a cadet at West Point. Following his graduation from West Point in 1981, he served with the 101st Airborne (Air Assault) Division before joining the Army Reserves in 1986. Dan served on staff with The Navigators for ten years, during which time he received a Master of Divinity from Bethel Seminary (West) in San Diego, CA, before moving with his family to Oregon in 1991 to plant and pastor Horizon Community Church. In 2000, he started the nonprofit First Cause, an organization committed to worship and leadership training. He has authored five books and recorded seven albums of original music.

Dan was promoted to Major General in 2012. As of 2013, he serves as the Division Commander of the 76th Operational Response Command headquartered at Fort Douglas, UT. He is married to Kathleen over 30 years and is the father of three children: Bryan, Sarah and Stephen. Sarah is married to Mark Tegtmeier and gave Dan and Kathleen their first grandson Jadon.

Dan's life verse is Psalm 40:3—*"He put a new song in my mouth, a hymn of praise to our God. Many will see and fear and put their trust in the Lord."*

Daniel York—FC Director

Bible Marking Code   36+Themes

Colors & Symbols

Gray = Prophecy   **Orange** =Healing   **Pink** = Fasting

Teal = Humility   **Yellow** = Prayer and Light or words pertaining to it

Brown = Obedience, Compliance, Follow

π = Altar, offering   B = Book of Life

+ = Discipleship   S = Serve, servant, minister

Blue (Light) = Love   Blue (Dark) = Holiness, Holy Spirit, Pure

Verse Number Squared □ = Apologetics   ℔= Leadership   ^ = Truth

＿ = Underlined Verses Memorized   ⟶ = Key Thought

Green = Faith, hope, trust

Verse Number Circled = Christ's return

G = Grace; GB = Blessing; GF = Favor

🍎 = Fruit $ = Money, giving, generous

P = Promise; Pc-Conditional; Pf-Fulfilled; Pr-Remembered

Black = Notes

Ω = Idols, Idolatry   ✓= Salvation

★ = Key Verse;   ①= Verse of the Year

J = Judgment, punishment inflicted; Jc-Conditional; Jf-Fulfilled; Jp-Predicted;
Jv-Vengeance;   Ju = Just, Justice; Ju/ = injustice

＿ = Underlined key phrases or verses

Purple = Worship, Praise, Thanksgiving

! = Joy, Excitement   Δ = Trinity

♪= Music, singing, Instruments

＿Purple underlines = Word Name when referencing God

W= Wisdom: Knowledge, Learning, Understanding, Discerning, Insight,
Revelation

Red = Fear of God

♡ = Heart   ♥ = Wholehearted   # = Pride, Arrogance

⊗ = Power, Strength, Might, Stronghold

☹= Adversity, Suffering, Pain, Hardship

Other Books and Music by Daniel York

Lost on Mount Fuji

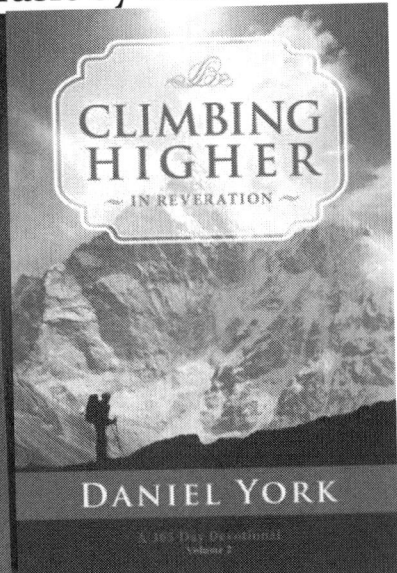

Climbing Higher in Reveration Vol 2

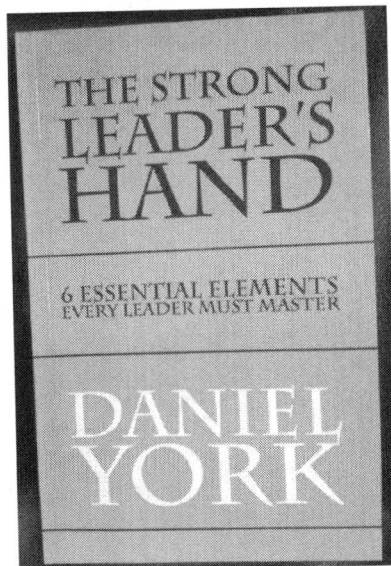

The Strong Leader's Hand

To order go to **www.firstcause.org** and click on products

All songs are original compositions

Where Were You?   **See His Star (Christmas)**

Evidence

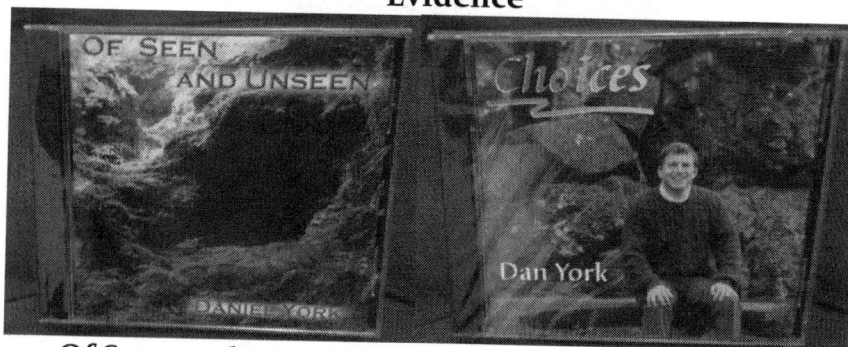

Of Seen and Unseen   **Choices**

To order go to **www.firstcause.org** and click on products

Endnotes

1 Oswald Chambers in *The Complete Works of Oswald Chambers. Studies in the Sermon on the Mount*. Oswald chambers Publications Association, Limited, 2000, Discovery House Publishers, Grand Rapids, Michigan. All Chambers quotes in this devotional came from this collection and are noted by their individual titles.

2 George Barna, *Growing True Disciples* (Colorado Springs, CO: Waterbrook Press, 2001)

3 Brother Lawrence & Frank Laubach, *Practicing His Presence*, ed. Gene Edwards (Texas: Sowers of the Seed, Incorporated, 1973)

4 Philip Yancey, *Where Is God When It Hurts*, (Grand Rapids: Zondervan, 1990)

5 John Powell, *The Christian Vision: the truth that sets us free* (Texas: Argus Communications, 1984) p. 121.

6 C.S. Lewis, *The Problem of Pain*, (New York: The MacMillan Company, 1967)

7 Robert Coleman, *The Master Plan of Discipleship*, (Michigan: Baker Publishing Group, 1998)

8 Jack Hayford, *Worship His Majesty*, (California: Regal, 2000)

9 Brandon Sanders, *Heroes to Remember*, (Lincoln: Writer's Press, 2000) p. 459.

10 Dietrich Bonhoeffer, *Letters and Papers From Prison*, (New York: Simon and Schuster, 1971)

11 Richard Bach, *Illusions The Adventures of a Reluctant Messiah* (New York: Random House, 1977)

12 James Terry White, *Character Lessons in American Biography for Public Schools and Home Instruction*, 1909

13 Dr. Vincent Muli Wa Kituku, *Overcoming Buffaloes At Work & In Life*, 2008

14 Henry T. Blackaby, Richard Blackaby, *Spiritual Leadership: Moving People on to God's Agenda, Revised and Expanded*, (Nashville: B&H Publishing Group, 2011)

15 http://people.howstuffworks.com/laughter.htm

16 Definitions taken from *The American Heritage Dictionary* Fourth edition. Pickett, Joseph P. et al. Boston: Houghton Mifflin Company, 2000. All references to this dictionary throughout the book are from this version.

17 Martyn Lloyd-Jones, *Seeking the Face of God: Nine Reflections on the Psalms*, (Great Britain: Crossway Books, 1991)

18 http://www.answering-islam.de/Main/Andy/Songs/commentary.html

19 Helen Keller, *The Open Door*, (New York: Doubleday, 1957) p. 52

20 Henry Drummond, *Addresses by Professor Henry Drummond*, (New York: Fleming H. Revell Company, 1891)

21 http://mb-soft.com/believe/txn/manot.htm#soul

22 http://en.wikipedia.org/wiki/Soul#Christian_beliefs

23 http://mb-soft.com/believe/txo/soul.htm

24 http://mb-soft.com/believe/txo/soul.htm

25 Saint Augustine , *The Confessions of St. Augustine*. (Chicago: Moody Publishers, 2007)

[26] Thomas a Kempis, *The Imitation of Christ*

[27] Ted Koppel in a speech to the International Radio and Television Society, quoted in Harper's (Jan. 1986). Christianity Today, Vol. 32, no. 8.

[28] C.S. Lewis, *Mere Christianity*, (New York: MacMillan Publishing Company, 1952)

[29] Watchman Nee, *Spiritual Authority*, (New York: Christian Fellowship Publishers, Inc., 1972)

[30] James S. Hewitt, *Illustrations Unlimited*, (Illinois: Tyndale House Publishers, 1988)

[31] Robert E. Coleman, *The Master Plan of Evangelism*, (New Jersey, Fleming H. Revell, 1964

[32] Max Lucado, *3:16 The Numbers of Hope.* (Thomas Nelson, 2007, Quote taken from *The New Testament Greek Lexicon*, "anothen."), p. 7

[33] Charles Swindoll, *Signposts Along Life's Journey.* (Insight for Living, 1997)

[34] http://www.leaderu.com/offices/bradley/docs/universe.html

[35] http://www.ethicsineducation.com/intro.htm

[36] Henry T. Blackaby & Claude V. King, *Experiencing God*, (Nashville: B&H Publishing Group (January 1998)

[37] *The NIV Study Bible.* (Grand Rapids, Michigan: Zondervan Corporation. 1985)

[38] Martin Hengel, *Crucifixion*, (Philadelphia: Fortress Press, 1988)

[39] Fritz Rienecker and Cleon Rogers, *Linguistic Key to the Greek New Testament.* (Grand Rapids, Michigan: Zondervan 1976)

[40] Ibid

[41] www.barna.org/

[42] United States Constitution, Bill of Rights, First Amendment

[43] Ralph Toliver, *Gold Fears No Fire*, (OMF Books, 1986)

[44] http://www.globalissues.org/article/84/conflicts-in-africa-introduction

[45] http://en.wikipedia.org/wiki/Voodoo#African_origins

[46] Matthew George Easton, *Easton's Bible Dictionary (Thomas Nelson*, 1897)